Coding
Interview
Questions

By
Narasimha Karumanchi

☀ **Concepts**   ☀ **Problems**   ☀ **Interview Questions**

Acknowledgements

Mother and *father*, it is impossible to thank you adequately for everything you have done, from loving me unconditionally to raising me in a stable household, where you persistent efforts traditional values and taught your children to celebrate and embrace life. I could not have asked for better parents or role-models. You showed me that anything is possible with faith, hard work and determination.

This book would not have been possible without the help of many people. I would like to thank them for their efforts in improving the end result. Before we do so, however, I should mention that I have done my best to correct the mistakes that the reviewers have pointed out and to accurately describe the protocols and mechanisms. I alone am responsible for any remaining errors.

First and foremost, I would like to express my gratitude to many people who saw me through this book, to all those who provided support, talked things over, read, wrote, offered comments, allowed me to quote their remarks and assisted in the editing, proofreading and design. In particular, I would like to thank the following individuals.

- *Mohan Mullapudi*, IIT Bombay, Architect, dataRPM Pvt. Ltd.
- *Navin Kumar Jaiswal*, Senior Consultant, Juniper Networks Inc.
- *A.Vamshi Krishna*, IIT Kanpur, Mentor Graphics Inc.
- *Hirak Chatterjee*, Yahoo Inc.
- *Kondrakunta Murali Krishna*, B-Tech., Technical Lead, HCL
- *Chaganti Siva Rama Krishna Prasad*, Founder, StockMonks Pvt. Ltd.
- *Naveen Valsakumar*, Co-Founder, NotionPress Pvt. Ltd.
- *Ramanaiah*, Lecturer, Nagarjuna Institute of Technology and Sciences, MLG

Last but not least, I would like to thank *Directors* of *Guntur Vikas College, Prof.Y.V.Gopala Krishna Murthy & Prof.Ayub Khan [ACE Engineering Academy], T.R.C.Bose [Ex. Director of APTransco], Ch.Venkateswara Rao VNR Vignanajyothi [Engineering College, Hyderabad], Ch.Venkata Narasaiah [IPS], Yarapathineni Lakshmaiah [Manchikallu, Gurazala]* and *all our well – wishers* for helping me and my family during our studies.

-*Narasimha Karumanchi*
M-Tech, *IIT Bombay*
Founder, *CareerMonk.com*

Preface

Dear Reader,

Please Hold on! I know many people do not read the preface. But I would strongly recommend that you go through the preface of this book at least. The reason for this is that this preface has *something different* to offer.

This book assumes you have some basic knowledge about computer science. The main objective of the book is not to give you the theorems and proofs about *Data Structures* and *Algorithms*. I have followed a pattern of improving the problem solutions with different complexities (for each problem, you will find multiple solutions with different, and reduced complexities). Basically, it's an enumeration of possible solutions. With this approach, even if you get a new question it will show you a way to think about all possible solutions. This book is very useful for interview preparation, competitive exams preparation, and campus interview preparations.

As a *job seeker* if you read the complete book with good understanding, I am sure you will challenge the interviewers and that is the objective of this book.

This book is very useful for the *students* of *Engineering Degree* and *Masters* during their academic preparations. In all the chapters you will see that more importance has been given to problems and their analysis instead of theory. For each chapter, first you will read about the basic required theory and this will be followed by a section on problem sets. There are approximately 700 algorithmic problems and all of them are with solutions.

In most the chapters you will see more importance given to *problems* and analyzing them instead of concentrating more on theory. For each chapter, first you will see the basic required theory and then followed by problems.

For many problems, *multiple* solutions are provided with different levels of complexities. We start with *brute force* solution and slowly move towards the *best solution* possible for that problem. For each problem we will try to understand how much time the algorithm is taking and how much memory the algorithm is taking.

It is *recommended* that the reader does at least one complete reading of this book to get full understanding of all the topics. In the subsequent readings, you can go directly to any chapter and refer. Even though, enough readings were given for correcting the errors, there could be some minor typos in the book. If any such typos are found, they will be updated at *www.CareerMonk.com*. I request you to constantly monitor this site for any corrections, new problems and solutions. Also, please provide your valuable suggestions at: *Info@CareerMonk.com*.

Wish you all the best. I am sure that you will find this book useful.

-*Narasimha Karumanchi*
M-Tech, *IIT Bombay*
Founder, *CareerMonk.com*

Table of Contents

Coding Interview Questions

Other Titles by *Narasimha Karumanchi*

- IT Interview Questions
- Elements of Computer Networking
- Data Structures and Algorithms Made Easy (C/C++)
- Data Structures and Algorithms Made Easy in Java
- Data Structure and Algorithmic Thinking with Python
- Data Structures and Algorithms for GATE
- Peeling Design Patterns

Chapter-1

PROGRAMMING BASICS

The objective of this chapter is to explain the basics of programming. In this chapter you will know about data types, pointers, scoping rules, memory layout of program, parameter passing techniques, types of languages and problems related to them.

1.1 Variables

Before getting in to the definition of variables, let us relate them to an old mathematical equation. Many of us would have solved many mathematical equations since childhood. As an example, consider the equation below:

$$x^2 + 2y - 2 = 1$$

We don't have to worry about the use of this equation. The important thing that we need to understand is, the equation has some names (x and y), which hold values (data). That means, the *names* (x and y) are placeholders for representing data. Similarly, in computer science we need something for holding data, and *variables* is the way to do that.

1.2 Data types

In the above-mentioned equation, the variables x and y can take any values such as integral numbers (10, 20.), real numbers (0.23, 5.5) or just 0 and 1. To solve the equation, we need to relate them to kind of values they can take and *data type* is the name used in computer science for this purpose. A *data type* in a programming language is a set of data with predefined values. Examples of data types are: integer, floating point unit number, character, string, etc.

Computer memory is all filled with zeros and ones. If we have a problem and wanted to code it, it's very difficult to provide the solution in terms of zeros and ones. To help users, programming languages and compilers provide us with data types. For example, *integer* takes 2 bytes (actual value depends on compiler), *float* takes 4 bytes, etc. This says that, in memory we are combining 2 bytes (16 bits) and calling it as *integer*. Similarly, combining 4 bytes (32 bits) and calling it as *float*. A data type reduces the coding effort. At the top level, there are two types of data types:

- System-defined data types (also called *Primitive* data types)
- User-defined data types

System-defined data types (Primitive data types): Data types that are defined by system are called *primitive* data types. The primitive data types provided by many programming languages are: int, float, char, double, bool, etc. The number of bits allocated for each primitive data type depends on the programming languages, compiler and operating system. For the same primitive data type, different languages may use different sizes. Depending on the size of the data types the total available values (domain) will also changes.

For example, *"int"* may take 2 bytes or 4 bytes. If it takes 2 bytes (16 bits) then the total possible values are -32,768 to +32,767 (-2^{15} to 2^{15}-1). If it takes, 4 bytes (32 bits), then the possible values are between $-2,147,483,648$ and $+2,147,483,647$ (-2^{31} to 2^{31}-1). Same is the case with remaining data types too.

User defined data types: If the system defined data types is not enough then most programming languages allow the users to define their own data types called as user defined data types. Good example of user defined data types are: structures in $C/C++$ and classes in *Java*.

For example, in the snippet below, we are combining many system-defined data types and call it as user-defined data type with name *"newType"*. This gives more flexibility and comfort in dealing with computer memory.

```
struct newType {
    int data1;
    float data 2;
    ...
    char data;
};
```

1.3 Data Structure

Based on the discussion above, once we have data in variables, we need some mechanism for manipulating that data to solve problems. *Data structure* is a particular way of storing and organizing data in a computer so that it can be used efficiently. A *data structure* is a special format for organizing and storing data. General data structure types include arrays, files, linked lists, stacks, queues, trees, graphs and so on.

Depending on the organization of the elements, data structures are classified into two types:

1) *Linear data structures*: Elements are accessed in a sequential order but it is not compulsory to store all elements sequentially (say, Linked Lists). *Examples*: Linked Lists, Stacks and Queues.
2) *Non − linear data structures*: Elements of this data structure are stored / accessed in a non-linear order. *Examples*: Trees and graphs.

1.4 Abstract Data Types (ADTs)

Before defining abstract data types, let us consider the different view of system-defined data types. We all know that, by default, all primitive data types (int, float, etc.) support basic operations such as addition and subtraction. The system provides the implementations for the primitive data types. For user-defined data types also we need to define operations. The implementation for these operations can be done when we want to actually use them. That means, in general user defined data types are defined along with their operations.

To simplify the process of solving the problems, we combine the data structures along with their operations and call it as *Abstract Data Types* (ADTs). An ADT consists of *two* parts:

1. Declaration of data
2. Declaration of operations

Commonly used ADTs *include*: Linked Lists, Stacks, Queues, Priority Queues, Binary Trees, Dictionaries, Disjoint Sets (Union and Find), Hash Tables, Graphs, and many other. For example, stack uses LIFO (Last-In-First-Out) mechanism while storing the data in data structures. The last element inserted into the stack is the first element that gets deleted. Common operations of it are: creating the stack, pushing an element onto the stack, popping an element from stack, finding the current top of the stack, finding number of elements in the stack, etc.

While defining the ADTs do not worry about the implementation details. They come into picture only when we want to use them. Different kinds of ADTs are suited to different kinds of applications, and some are highly specialized to specific tasks.

By the end of this book, we will go through many of them and you will be in a position to relate the data structures to the kind of problems they solve.

1.5 Memory and Variables

First let's understand the way memory is organized in a computer. We can treat the memory as an array of bytes. Each location is identified by an address (index to array). In general, the address 0 is not a valid memory location. It is important to understand that the address of any byte (location) in memory is an integer. In the diagram below n value depends on the main memory size of the system.

Address	Memory Value	
0		X
1		
2	...	
...	...	
2000	X	
...		
$2^n - 1$		

To read or write any location, CPU accesses it by sending its address to the memory controller. When we create a variable (for example, in *C: int X*), the compiler allocates a block of contiguous memory locations and its size depends on the size of the variable.

The compiler also keeps an internal tag that associates the variable name X with the address of the first byte allocated to it (sometimes called *symbol table*). So when we want to access that variable like this: $X = 10$, the compiler knows where that variable is located and it writes the value 10.

Size of a Variable: *Sizeof* operator is used to find size of the variable (how much memory a variable occupies). For example, on some computers, $sizeof(X)$ gives the value 4. This means an integer needs 4 contiguous bytes in memory. If the address of X is 2000, then the actual memory locations used by X are: 2001, 2002, 2003, and 2004.

Address of a Variable: In *C* language, we can get the address of a variable using *address − of* operator (&). The code below prints the address of X variable. In general, addresses are printed in hexadecimal as they are compact and also easy to understand if the addresses are big.

```
int X;
printf("The address is: %u\n", &X);
```

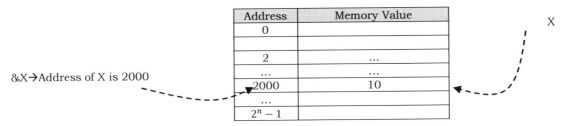

1.6 Pointers

Pointers are also variables which can hold the address of another variable.

1.6.1 Declaration of Pointers

To declare a pointer, we have to specify the type of the variable it will point to. That means we need to specify the type of the variable whose address it is going to hold. The declaration is very simple. Let us see some examples of pointer declarations below:

```
int *ptr1;
float *ptr2;
unsigned int *ptr3;
char *ptr4; void *ptr5;
```

Here *ptr1* is a pointer that can point to an *int* variable, *ptr2* can point to a *float*, *ptr3* to an *unsigned int*, and *ptr4* to a *char*. Finally *ptr5* is a pointer that can point to anything. These pointers are called *void* pointers, and there are some restrictions on what we can do with void pointers.

1.6.2 Pointers Usage

As we said, pointers hold addresses. That means we can assign the address of a variable to it. Let us consider the sample code below:

```
int X = 10;
int *ptr = &X;
```

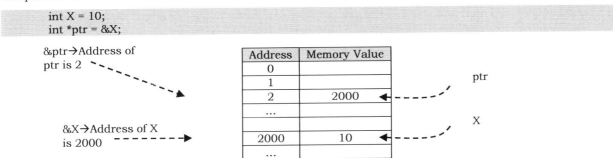

Here, we first declare an integer named *X* and initialize it to the value 10. Then we create a pointer to *int* named *ptr* and assign the address of *X* to it. This is called, *"making the pointer ptr point to X."* A common operation is done with a pointer and is called *indirection*. It is a way to access the contents of the memory that it points to. The indirection operator is represented by the asterisk symbol. Do not confuse this operator with the use of the same asterisk symbol in the declaration of pointers. They are not the same thing. If we would like to access the contents of the memory where *ptr* points to, we will do it like this: $*ptr$. Let's see a small code that shows pointer indirections.

```
int X = 10;
int *ptr = &X;
printf("X contains the value %d\n", X);
printf("ptr points to %p\n", ptr);
printf("there lies the value %d\n", *ptr);
*ptr = 25;
printf("now X contains the value %d\n", X);
```

Here we first declare *X* and *ptr* just like before. Then we print *X* (which is10), followed by *ptr*, i.e., the contents of the variable *ptr* which is an address; the address of *X*. And finally we print $*ptr$, which is the value of the memory location where *ptr* points to (again 10, since it points to the location occupied by the variable *X* in memory).

Finally we change the contents of the location where *ptr* points to by writing $*ptr = 25$. This means assign the value 25 to wherever *ptr* is pointing to. Note that when we do that, what is actually happening is that the value of *X* is being modified. This is because, *ptr* holds the address of *X*, and changing the contents of the memory at that address changes the value of *X*.

One limitation of *void* pointers, i.e. pointers that can point to any type, is that they cannot be *dereferenced*. This is because each variable type takes different amount of memory. On a 32-bit computer for example usually an int needs 4 bytes, while a *short* 2 bytes. So in order to read the actual value stored there, the compiler has to know how many consecutive memory locations to read in order to get the full value.

1.6.3 Pointer Manipulation

Pointers are useful as they allow us to perform arithmetic operations on them. This might be obvious to the careful reader, since we said that pointers are just integers. However, there are a few small differences on pointer arithmetic that make their use even more intuitive and easy. Try the following code:

```
char *cptr = (char*)2;
printf("cptr before: %p ", cptr);

cptr++;
printf("and after: %p\n", cptr);
```

We declare a pointer named *cptr* and assign the address 2 to it. We print the contents of the pointer (i.e. the address 2), increment it, and print again. Sure enough the first time it prints 2 and then 3, and that was exactly what we expected. However try this one as well:

```
int *iptr = (int*)2;
printf("iptr before: %p ", iptr);

iptr++;
printf("and after: %p\n", iptr);
```

Now the output, on my computer, is *iptr* before: 2 and after: 6! Why does this pointer point to the address 6 after it is incremented by one and not to 3 as the previous pointer? The answer lies with what we said about the *size of* variables. An int is 4 bytes on my computer. This means that if we have an int at address 2, then that int occupies the memory locations 2, 3, 4 and 5.

In order to access the next int we have to look at the address 6, 7, 8 and 9. Thus when we add one to a pointer, it is not the same as adding one to any integer; it means give me a pointer to the next variable which for variables of type int, in this case, is 4 bytes ahead. The reason that in the first example with the char pointer, the actual address after incrementing, was one more than the previous address is because the size of char is exactly 1. So the next char can indeed be found on the next address.

Another limitation of void pointers is that we cannot perform arithmetic on them, since the compiler cannot know how many bytes ahead the next variable is located. So void pointers can only be used to keep addresses that we have to convert later on to a specific pointer type, before using them.

1.6.4 Arrays and Pointers

There is a strong connection between arrays and pointers. So strong in fact, that most of the time we can treat them as one and the same. The name of an array can be considered just as a pointer to the beginning of a memory block as big as the array. So for example, making a pointer point to the beginning of an array is done in exactly the same way as assigning the contents of a pointer to another:

```
short *ptr;
short array[10];
ptr = array;
```

And then we can access the contents of the array through the pointer as if the pointer itself was that array. For example this: ptr[2] = 25 is perfectly legal. Furthermore, we can treat the array itself as a pointer, for example, $*array = 4$ is equivalent to $array[0] = 4$. In general $*(array + n)$ is equivalent to $array[n]$.

The only difference between an array, and a pointer to the beginning of an array, is that the compiler keeps some extra information for the arrays, to keep track of their storage requirements. For example if we get the size of both an array and a pointer using the *sizeof* operator, sizeof(ptr) will give us how much space does the pointer itself occupies (4 on my computer), while sizeof array will give us, the amount of space occupied by the whole array (on my computer 20, 10 elements of 2 bytes each).

1.6.5 Dynamic Memory Allocation

In the earlier sections, we have seen that pointers can hold addresses of other variables. There is another use of pointers: pointers can hold addresses of memory locations that do not have a specific compile-time variable name, but are allocated dynamically while the program runs (sometimes such memory is called *heap*).

To allocate memory during runtime, C language provides us the facility interms of *malloc* function. This function allocates the requested amount of memory, and returns a pointer to that memory. To deallocate that block of memory, C supports it by providing *free* function.

This function takes the pointer as an argument. For example, in the code below, an array of 5 integers is allocated dynamically, and then deleted.

```
int count = 5;
int *A = malloc(count * sizeof(int));
.........
free(arr);
```

In this example, the $count * sizeof(int)$ calculates the amount of bytes we need to allocate for the array, by multiplying the number of elements, to the size of each element (i.e. the size of one integer).

1.6.6 Function Pointers

Like data, executable code (including functions) is also stored in memory. We can get the address of a function. But the question is what type of pointers do we use for that purpose? In general, we use function pointers and they store the address of functions. Using function pointers we can call the function indirectly. But, function pointers manipulation has its limitation: it is limited to assignment and indirection and cannot do arithmetic on function pointers. Because for function pointers there is no ordering (functions can be stored anywhere in memory). The following example illustrates how to create and use function pointers.

```
int (*fptr)(int);
fptr = function1;
printf("function1of 0 is: %d\n", fptr(5));
fptr = function2;
printf("function2 of 0 is: %d\n", fptr(10));
```

First we create a pointer that can point to functions accepting an *int* as an argument and returning int, named *fptr*. Then we make *fptr* point to the *function1*, and proceed to call it through the *fptr* pointer, to print the *function1* of 5. Finally, we change *fptr* to point to *function2*, and call it again in exactly the same manner, to print the *function2* of 10.

1.7 Techniques of Parameter Passing

Before starting our discussion on parameter passing techniques, let us concentrate on the terminology we use.

1.7.1 Actual and Formal Parameters

Let us assume that a function $B()$ is called from another function $A()$. In this case, A is called the *caller function* and B is called the *called function* or *callee function*. Also, the arguments which A sends to B are called actual arguments and the parameters of B function are called formal arguments. In the example below, the *func* is called from *main* function. *main* is the caller function and *func* is the called function. Also, the *func* arguments *param1* and *param2* are formal arguments and i, j of *main* function are actual arguments.

```
int main() {
    long i = 1;
    double j = 2;
    func( i, j ); // Call func with actual arguments i and j.
}
// func with formal parameters param1 and param2.
void func( long param1, double param2 ){
}
```

1.7.2 Semantics of Parameter Passing

Logically, parameter passing uses the following semantics:

- IN: Passes info from caller to *callee*. Formal arguments can take values from actual arguments, but cannot send values to actual arguments.
- OUT: Callee writes values in the caller. Formal arguments can send values from actual arguments, but cannot take values from actual arguments.
- IN/OUT: Caller tells callee value of variable, which may be updated by callee. Formal arguments can send values from actual arguments, and can also take values from actual arguments.

1.7.3 Language Support for Parameter Passing Techniques

Passing Technique	Supported by Languages
Pass by value	*C, Pascal, Ada, Scheme, Algol*68
Pass by result	*Ada*
Pass by value-result	*Fortran*, sometimes *Ada*
Pass by reference	*C* (achieves through pointers), *Fortran, Pascal var params, Cobol*
Pass by name	*Algol*60

1.7.4 Pass by Value

This method uses in-mode semantics. A formal parameter is like a new local variable that exists within the scope of the procedure/function/subprogram. Value of actual parameter is used to initialize the formal parameter. Changes made to formal parameter *do not* get transmitted back to the caller.

If pass by value is used then the formal parameters will be allocated on stack like a normal local variable. This method is sometimes called *call by value*. Advantage of this method is that, it allows the actual arguments not to modify.

In general the pass by value technique is implemented by copy and it has the following disadvantages:

- Inefficiency in storage allocation
- Inefficiency in copying value
- Costly copy semantics for objects and arrays

Example: In the following example, main passes func two values: 5 and 7. The function func receives copies of these values and accesses them by the identifiers a and b. The function func changes the value of a. When control passes back to main, the actual values of *x* and *y* are not changed.

```
void func (int a, int b) {
    a += b;
    printf("In func, a = %d    b = %d\n", a, b);
}
int main(void) {
    int x = 5, y = 7;
    func(x, y);
    printf("In main, x = %d    y = %d\n", x, y);
    return 0;
}
```

The output of the program is: In func, a = 12 b = 7. In main, x = 5 y = 7

1.7.5 Pass by Result

This method uses out-mode semantics. A formal parameter is a new local variable that exists within the scope of the function. No value is transmitted from actual arguments to formal arguments. Just before control is transferred back to the caller, the value of the formal parameter is transmitted back to the actual parameter.

This method is sometimes called *call by result*. Actual parameter *must* be a variable. $foo(x)$ and $foo(a[1])$ are fine but not $foo(3)$ or $foo(x * y)$.

1.7.6 Parameter collisions can occur

Let us assume that there is a function $write(p1, p1)$. If the two formal parameters in write had different names, which value should go into $p1$? Order in which actual parameters are copied determines their value. In general the pass by result technique is implemented by copy and it has the following disadvantages:

- Inefficiency in storage allocation
- Inefficiency in copying value
- For objects and arrays, the copy semantics are costly
- We cannot use the value of actual argument for initializing the formal argument

Example: Since C does not support this technique, let us assume that the syntax below is not specific to any language.

In the following example, main uses two variables x and y. They both were passed to $func$. Since this is pass by result technique, the values of x and y will not be copied to formal arguments. As a result, the variables a and b of $func$ should be initialized. But in the function only b is initialized. For this reason, the value of a is unknown, whereas the value of b is 5. After the function execution, the values of a and b will be copied to x and y.

```
void func (int a, int b) {
    b = 5;
    a += b;
    printf("In func, a = %d    b = %d\n", a, b);
}
int main(void) {
    int x = 5, y = 7;
    func(x, y);
    printf("In main, x = %d    y = %d\n", x, y);
    return 0;
}
```

The output of the program is: In func, a = garbage value b = 5. In main, x = garbage value y = 5.

1.7.7 Pass by Value-Result

This method uses inout-mode semantics. It is a combination of Pass-by-Value and Pass-by-Result. Formal parameter is a new local variable that exists within the scope of the function. Value of actual parameter is used to initialize the formal parameter. Just before control is transferred back to the caller, the value of the formal parameter is transmitted back to the actual parameter. This method is sometimes called *call by value − result*.

Pass by Value − Result shares with *Pass − by − Value* and *Pass − by − Result*. The disadvantage is that it requires multiple storage parameters and time for copying values. Shares with Pass-by-Result the problem associated with the order in which actual parameters are assigned. So this technique has some advantages and some disadvantages.

Example: Since *C* does not support this technique, let us assume that the syntax below is not specific to any language.

In the following example, *main* uses two variable x and y. They both were passed to *func*. Since this is pass by value-result technique, the values of x and y will be copied to formal arguments. As a result, the variables a and b of *func* will get 5 and 7 respectively.

In the *func*, the values a and b are modified to 10 and 5 respectively. After the function execution, the values of a and b will be copied to x and y. The disadvantage of this method is that, for each argument a new allocation is created.

```
void func (int a, int b) {
    b = 5;
    a += b;
    printf("In func, a = %d    b = %d\n", a, b);
}
int main(void) {
    int x = 5, y = 7;
    func(x, y);
    printf("In main, x = %d    y = %d\n", x, y);
    return 0;
}
```

The output of the program is: In *func*, $a = 10\,b = 5$. In *main*, $x = 10\,y = 5$

1.7.8 Pass by Reference (aliasing)

This technique uses inout-mode semantics. Formal parameter is an alias for the actual parameter. Changes made to formal parameter *do* get transmitted back to the caller through parameter passing. This method is sometimes called *call by reference* or *aliasing*. This method is efficient in both time and space. Disadvantages of *aliasing* are:

- Many potential scenarios can occur
- Programs are not readable

Example: In *C*, the pointer parameters are initialized with pointer values when the function is called. When the function *swapnum()* is called, the actual values of the variables a and b are exchanged because they are passed by reference.

```
void swapnum(int *i, int *j) {
    int temp = i;
    i = j;
    j = temp;
}
int main(void) {
    int a = 10, b = 20;
    swapnum(&a, &b);
    printf("A is %d and B is %d\n", a, b);
    return 0;
}
```

The output is: A is 20 and B is 10

1.7.9 Pass by Name

Rather than using pass-by-reference for input/output parameters, *Algol* used the more powerful mechanism of *Pass − by − Name*. In essence, you can pass in the symbolic "*name*", of a variable, which allows it both to be accessed and updated. For example, to double the value of $C[j]$, you can pass its name (not its value) into the following procedure.

```
procedure double(x);
    real x;
begin
    x := x * 2
end;
```

In general, the effect of pass-by-name is to textually substitute the argument expressions in a procedure call for the corresponding parameters in the body of the procedure, e.g., double($C[j]$) is interpreted as $C[j] := C[j] * 2$. Technically, if any of the variables in the called procedure clash with the caller's variables, they must be renamed uniquely before substitution. Implications of the *Pass − by − Name* mechanism:

1. The argument expression is re-evaluated each time the formal parameter is accessed.
2. The procedure can change the values of variables used in the argument expression and hence change the expression's value.

1.8 Binding

In the earlier sections we have seen that every variable is associated with a memory location. At the top level, *binding* is the process of associating the *name* and the thing it contains. For example, association of variable names to values they contain. Binding Times: Based on the time at which association happens, binding times can be one of the following:

Static

* *Language design time*: Binding operators to operations (for example, " + " to addition of numbers).
* *Language implementation time*: Binding data types to possible values (for example, "*int*" to its range of values).
* *Program writing time*: Associating algorithms and data structures to problem.
* *Compile time*: Binding a variable to data type.
* *Link time*: Layout of whole program in memory (names of separate modules (libraries) are finalized.
* *Load time*: Choice of physical addresses (e.g. static variables in *C* are bound to memory cells at load time).

Dynamic • *Run time*: Binding variables to values in memory locations.

Basically there are *two* types of bindings: *static* binding and *dynamic* binding.

1.8.1 Static Binding (Early binding)

Static binding occurs before runtime and doesn't change during execution. This is sometimes called *early binding*.

Examples:
* Bindings of values to constants in *C*
* Bindings of function calls to function definitions in *C*

1.8.2 Dynamic Binding (Late binding)

Dynamic binding occurs or changes at runtime. This is sometimes called late binding.

Examples:
* Bindings of pointer variables to locations
* Bindings of member function calls to virtual member function definitions in *C + +*

1.9 Scope

A scope is a program section of maximal size in which no bindings change, or at least in which no redeclarations are permitted. The scope rules of a language determine how references to names are associated with variables. Basically there are *two* types of scoping techniques: *static* scoping and *dynamic* scoping.

1.9.1 Static Scope

Static scope is defined in terms of the physical structure of the program. The determination of scopes can be made by the compiler. That means, bindings are resolved by examining the program text. Enclosing static scopes (to a specific scope) are called its *static ancestors* and the nearest static ancestor is called a *static parent*. Variables can be hidden from a unit by having a "*closer*" variable with the same name. Ada and *C + +* allow access to these (e.g. class_name:: name). Most compiled languages, *C* and *Pascal* included, use static scope rules.

Example-1: Static scope rules: Most closest nested rule used in blocks

```
for (...){
        int i;
        { ...
                {
                        i = 5;
                }
        }
        ...
}
```

To resolve a reference, we examine the local scope and statically enclosing scopes until a binding is found.

Example-2: Static scope in nested function calls. In the code below, with static scoping, the *count* variable of *func2* takes the value of global variable value (10).

```
int count=10;
void func2() {
    printf("In func2=%d", count);
}
void func1(in) {
    int count = 20;
    func2();
}
int main(void) {
    funct1();
    return 0;
}
```

1.9.2 Dynamic Scope

Dynamic scope rules are usually encountered in interpreted languages. Such languages do not normally have type checking at compile time because type determination isn't always possible when dynamic scope rules are in effect.

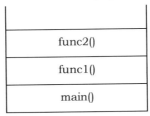

In dynamic scoping, binding depends on the flow of control at run time and the order in which functions are called, refers to the closest active binding. If we look at the second example of static scoping, the *count* variable of *func2* takes the value of *func1* variable value (20). This is because, during runtime the *func2* is called from *func1* which in turn called from main. That means *func2* looks at the stack and starts searching in the back ward direction.

Let us take another example. In the code below, the *count* variable of *func3* takes the *count* value of *funct1()*.

```
int count=10;
void func3() {
    printf("In func3=%d", count);
}
void func2() {
    func3();
}
void func1(in) {
    int count = 30;
    func2();
}
int main(void) {
    funct1();
    return 0;
}
```

func3 searches the stack in reverse direction and find the count in funct1().

Note: For the above example, if we use *static* scope then the *count* variable of *func3* takes the value of global *count* variable (10).

1.10 Storage Classes

Let us now consider the storage classes in *C*. The storage class determines the part of memory where storage is allocated for the variable or object and how long the storage allocation continues to exist. It also determines the scope which specifies the part of the program over which a variable name is visible, i.e. the variable is accessible by name. There are four storage classes in *C* are automatic, register, external, and static.

1.10.1 Auto Storage Class

This is the default storage class in *C*. Auto variables are declared inside a function in which they are to be utilized. Also, keyword *auto* (e.g. auto int number;) is used for declaring the auto variables. These are created when the function is called and destroyed automatically when the function is exited. This variable is therefore private(local) to the function in which it is declared. Variables declared inside a function without storage class specification is, by default, an automatic variable.

Any variable local to main will normally live throughout the whole program, although it is active only in main. During recursion, the nested variables are unique auto variables. Automatic variables can also be defined within blocks. In that case they are meaningful only inside the blocks where they are declared. If automatic variables are not initialized they will contain garbage.

Example:

```
int main() {
    int m=1000;
    function2();
    printf("%d\n",m);
}

void function1() {
    int m = 10;
    printf("%d\n",m);
}

void function2() {
    int m = 100;
    function1();
    printf("%d\n",m);
}
```

Output:
```
10
100
1000
```

1.10.2 Extern storage class

These variables are declared outside any function. These variables are active and alive throughout the entire program. Also known as global variables and default value is zero. Unlike local variables they are accessed by any function in the program. In case local variable and global variable have the same name, the local variable will have precedence over the global one.

Sometimes the keyword *extern* is used to declare this variable. It is visible only from the point of declaration to the end of the program.

Example-1: The variable *number* and *length* are available for use in all three functions

```
int number;
float length=7.5;
main() {
    . . .
}
funtion1() {
    . . .
}
funtion1() {
    . . .
}
```

Example-2: When the function references the variable *count*, it will be referencing only its local variable, not the global one.

```
int count;
main() {
    count=10;
    .....
}
funtion() {
    int count=0;
    .....
    count=count+1;
}
```

Example-3: On global variables: Once a variable has been declared global any function can use it and change its value. The subsequent functions can then reference only that new value.

```
int x;
int main() {
    x=10;
```

```
        printf("x=%d\n",x);
        printf("x=%d\n",fun1());
        printf("x=%d\n",fun2());
        printf("x=%d\n",fun3());
    }
    int fun1() {                        Output:
        x=x+10;                             x=10
        return(x);                          x=20
    }                                       x=1
    int fun2() {                            x=30
        int x;
        x=1;
        return(x);
    }
    int fun3() {
x=x+10;
return(x);
    }
```

Example-4: External declaration: As far as main is concerned, *y* is not defined. So compiler will issue an error message. There are two ways to solve this issue:

1   Define *y* before main.
2   Declare *y* with the storage class extern in main before using it.

```
    int main() {
        y=5;
        . . .
    }
    int y;
    func1() {
        y=y+1;
    }
```

Example-5: External declaration: Note that extern declaration does not allocate storage space for variables

```
    int main() {
        extern int y;
        . . .
    }
    func1() {
        extern int y;
        . . .
    }
    int y;
```

Example-6: If we declare any variable as extern variable then it searches that variable either it has been initialized or not. If it has been initialized which may be either extern or static* then it is ok otherwise compiler will show an error. For example:

```
    int main() {
        extern int i;   //It will search the initialization of variable i.
        printf("%d",i);
        return 0;
    }
    int i=2;          //Initialization of variable i
    Output: 2
```

Example-7: It will search any initialized variable *i* which may be static or extern.

```
    int main() {
        extern int i;
        printf("%d",i);
        return 0;
    }
    extern int i=2;              //Initialization of extern variable i.
    Output: 2
```

Example-8: It will search any initialized variable *i* which may be static or extern.

```
    int main() {
        extern int i;
```

```
        printf("%d",i);
        return 0;
}
static int i=2;              //Initialization of static variable i.
Output: 2
```

Example-9: Variable *i* has been declared but not initialized.

```
int main() {
        extern int i;
        printf("%d",i);
    return 0;
}
Output: Compilation error: Unknown symbol i.
```

Example-10: A particular extern variable can be declared many times but we can initialize at only one time. For example:

```
extern int i;              //Declaring the variable i.
int i=5;                   //Initializing the variable.
extern int i;              //Again declaring the variable i.
int main() {
  extern int i;      //Again declaring the variable i.
    printf("%d",i);
    return 0;
}
Output: 5
```

Example-11:

```
extern int i;              //Declaring the variable
int i=5;                   //Initializing the variable
int main() {
    printf("%d",i);
    return 0;
}
int i=2; //Initializing the variable
Output: Compilation error: Multiple initialization variable i.
```

Example-12: We cannot write any assignment statement globally.

```
extern int i;
int i=10;                  //Initialization statement
i=5;                       //Assignment statement
int main() {
    printf("%d",i);
    return 0;
}
Output: Compilation error
```

Note: Assigning any value to the variable at the time of declaration is known as *initialization* while assigning any value to variable not at the time of declaration is known as *assignment*.

Example-13:

```
extern int i;
int main() {
    i=5;       //Assignment statement
    printf("%d",i);
    return 0;
}
int i=10;   //Initialization statement
Output: 5
```

1.10.3 Register Storage Class

These variables are stored in one of the machine's registers and are declared using *register* keyword. e.g. register int count;

Since register access is much faster than a memory access, keeping frequently accessed variables in the register leads to faster execution of program. Since only few variables can be placed in the register, it is important to carefully select the variables for this purpose. However, *C* will automatically convert register variables into non-register variables once the limit is reached. Don't try to declare a global variable as register because the register will be occupied during the lifetime of the program.

1.10.4 Static Storage Class

The value of static variables persists until the end of the program. It is declared using the keyword static like:

```
static int x;
static float y;
```

It may be of external or internal type depending on the place of their declaration. Static variables are initialized only once, when the program is compiled.

1.10.4.1 Internal Static Variables

Are those which are declared inside a function? Scope of Internal static variables extends up to the end of the program in which they are defined. Internal static variables are almost same as auto variable except they remain in existence (alive) throughout the remainder of the program. Internal static variables can be used to retain values between function calls. *Example*: Internal static variable can be used to count the number of calls made to function.

```
int main() {
    for(int i=1; i<=3; i++)
        stat();
}

void stat() {
    static int x=0;
    x = x+1;
    printf("x= %d\n",x);
}
```

Output:
```
x = 1
x = 2
x = 3
```

1.10.4.2 External Static Variables

An external static variable is declared outside of all functions and is available to all the functions in the program. An external static variable is similar to simple external variable except that the former is available only within the file where it is defined whereas simple external variable can be accessed by other files.

1.10.4.3 Static Function

Static declaration can also be used to control the scope of a function. If you want a particular function to be accessible only to the functions in the file in which it is defined and not to any function in other files, declare the function to be static.

```
static int power(int x, int y) {
    . . .
}
```

1.11 Storage Organization

When we write a program and execute it, lot of things happen. Now, let us try to understand what happens internally. Any program we run has some memory associated with it. That memory is divided into 3 parts as shown below. Storage organization is the process of binding values to memory locations.

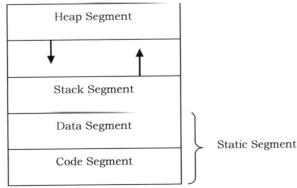

Static Segment: As shown above, the static storage is divided into two parts:
- *Code segment*: In this part, the programs code is stored. This will not change throughout the execution of the program. In general, this part is made read-only and protected. Constants may also be placed in the static area depending on their type.
- *Data segment*: In simple terms, this part holds the global data. In this part, the program's static data (except code) is stored. In general, this part is editable (like global variables and static variables come under this category). These includes the following:
  - o   Global variables

o   Numeric and string-valued constant literals
o   Local variables that retain value between calls (e.g., static variables)

Stack Segment: If a language supports recursion, then the number of instances of a variable that may exist at any time is unlimited (at least theoretically). In this case, static allocation is not useful.

As an example, let us assume that a function $B()$ is called from another function $A()$. In the code below, the $A()$ has a local variable *count*. After executing $B()$, if $A()$ tries to get *count,* then it should be able to get its old value. That means, it needs a mechanism for storing the current state of the function, so that once it comes back from calling function it restores that context and uses its variables.

```
A() {
    int count=10;
    function();
    count=20;
    . . . . . .
}
B() {
    int b=0;
    . . . . . .
}
```

To solve these kinds of issues, stack allocation is used. When we call a *function*, push a new activation record (also called a frame) onto the run-time stack, which is particular to the *function*.

Each frame can occupy many consecutive bytes in the stack and may not be of a fixed size. When the *callee* function returns to the *caller*, the activation record of the callee is popped out. In general the activation record stores the following information:

- Local variables
- Formal parameters
- Any additional information needed for activation
- Temporary variables
- Return address

Heap Segment: If we want to dynamically increase the temporary space (say, through pointers in *C*), then the *static* and *stack* allocation methods are not enough. We need a separate allocation method for dealing with these kinds of requests. *Heap allocation* strategy addresses this issue.

Heap allocation method is required for dynamically allocated pieces of linked data structures and for dynamically resized objects. Heap is an area of memory which is dynamically allocated. Like a stack, it may grow and shrinks during runtime.

But unlike a stack it is not a *LIFO* (Last In First Out) which is more complicated to manage. In general, all programming languages implementation we will have both heap-allocated and stack allocated memory.

1.11.1 How do we allocate Memory for both?

One simple approach is to divide the available memory at the start of the program into two areas: stack and heap

1.11.1.1 Heap Allocation Methods

Heap allocation is performed by searching the heap for available free space. Basically there are two types of heap allocations.

- *Implicit heap allocation*: Allocations are done automatically. For example, *Java/C#* class instances are placed on the heap. Scripting languages and functional languages make extensive use of the heap for storing objects.
- *Explicit heap allocation*: In this method, we need to explicitly tell the system to allocate the memory from heap. Examples include:
  o   statements and/or functions for allocation and deallocation
  o   malloc/free, new/delete

1.11.1.2 Fragmentations

Sometimes the small free blocks will get wasted without allocating to any process and we call this *fragmentation*. Basically there are two types of fragmentations:

- *Internal heap fragmentation*: If the block allocated is larger than required to hold a given object and the extra space is unused.
- *External heap fragmentation*: If the unused space is composed of multiple blocks. No one piece may be large enough to satisfy some future request. That means, multiple unused blocks, but not one is large enough to be used.

1.11.1.3 Heap Allocation Algorithms

In general, a linked list of free heap blocks is maintained and when a request is made for memory, then it uses one of the techniques below and allocates the memory.

- *First − fit*: select the first block in the list that is large enough to satisfy the given request
- *Best − fit*: search the entire list for the smallest free block that is large enough to hold the object

If an object is smaller than the block, the extra space can be added to the list of free blocks. When a block is freed, adjacent free blocks are merged.

1.12 Programming Techniques

1.12.1 Unstructured Programming

Generally, people start programming by writing small programs consisting only of one *main* program. This programming technique runs into problems once the program becomes large. For example, if the same statement sequence is needed at different locations within the program, the sequence must be copied.

1.12.2 Procedural Programming

n this method, we combine sequences of statements into one single place. A procedure call is used to invoke the procedure. After the sequence is processed, flow of control proceeds right after the position where the call was made. By introducing parameters as well as procedures of procedures (subprocedures) programs can now be written that are more structured and error free.

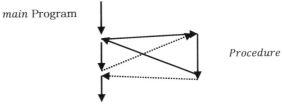

1.12.3 Modular Programming

With modular programming, procedures of a common functionality are grouped together into separate modules. It is now divided into several smaller parts which interact through procedure calls and which form the whole program. Each module can have its own data.

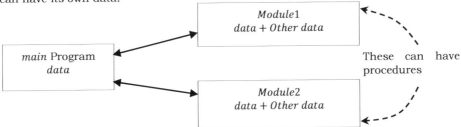

1.12.4 Object-oriented Programming

It is programming language model organized around *objects* instead of functions and *data* rather than logic. Object-oriented programming views the problem as objects we want to manipulate instead of logic required to manipulate them. The first step in OOP is to identify all the objects we want to manipulate and how they relate to each other (called *data modeling*). Once we have identified an object, we generalize it as a class of objects and define the kind of data it contains and any functions (also called *methods*) that can manipulate it.

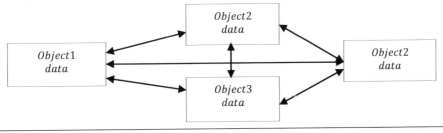

The idea behind object-oriented programming is that a computer program may be seen as a collection of objects that act on each other. In traditional view, a program can be seen as a collection of functions or simply as a list of instruction to the computer. Each object is capable of receiving messages, processing data and sending messages to other objects. Each object can be viewed as an independent little machine or actor with a distinct role or responsibility.

In order to act as an object-oriented programming language, a language must support three object-oriented features:

- Polymorphism
- Inheritance
- Encapsulation

1.13 Basic Concepts of OOPS

The following are the basic of object-oriented programming languages.

1. Class and object
2. Encapsulation
3. Abstraction
4. Data hiding
5. Polymorphism
6. Inheritance
7. Dynamic binding
8. Message passing

1.13.1 Class and Object

Object is the basic unit of object-oriented programming. Objects are identified by its unique name. An object represents a particular instance of a class. There can be more than one instance of an object. Each instance of an object can hold its own relevant data.

An Object is a collection of data members and associated member functions (also called *methods*). For example whenever a class name is created according to the class an object should be created without creating object can't able to use class.

A class is a basic unit of encapsulation. It is a collection of function code and data, which forms the basis of object-oriented programming. A class is an abstract data type (ADT), i.e., the class definition only provides the logical abstraction. The data and function defined within the class, spring to life only when a variable of type class is created.

The variable of type class is called an object which has a physical existence and also known as instance of class. From one class, several objects can be created. Each object has similar set of data defined in the class and it can use functions defined in the class for the manipulation of data. For example, the class of *Cat* defines all possible cats by listing the characteristics and behaviors they can have; the object *Abyssinian* is one particular cat, with particular versions of the characteristics. A *Cat* has hair; *Abyssinian* has *ruddy* hair.

All objects are instances of a class. Depending upon the type of class, an object may represent anything such as a person, mobile, chair, student, employee, book, lecturer, speaker, car, vehicle or anything which we see in our daily life. The state of an object is determined by the data values they are having at a particular instance.

Objects occupy space in memory, and all objects share same set of data items which are defined when class is created. Two objects may communicate with each other through functions by passing messages.

Examples:
1. Animal can be stated as a class and lion, tiger, elephant, wolf, cow , etc., are its objects.
2. Bird can be stated as class and sparrow, eagle, hawk, pigeon, etc., are its objects.
3. Musician can be stated as a class and Himesh Reshmia, Anu Malik, Jatin-Lalit are its objects.

1.13.2 Encapsulation

Encapsulation is the mechanism that binds together function and data in one compact form, called *class*.

The data and function may be private or public. Private data/function can be accessed only within the class. Public data/code can be accessed outside the class. The use of encapsulation hides complexity from the implementation. Linking of function code and data together gives rise to objects which are variables of type class.

1.13.3 Abstraction

Abstraction is a mechanism to represent only essential features which are of significance and hides the unimportant details. To make a good abstraction we require a sound knowledge of the problem domain, which we are going to implement using OOP principle. As an example of the abstraction consider a class *Vehicle* .

When we create the *Vehicle* class, we can decide what function code and data to put in the class such as vehicle name, number of wheels, fuel type, vehicle type, etc., and functions such as changing the gear, accelerating/decelerating the vehicle. At this time we are not interested in vehicle works such as how acceleration, changing gear takes place. We are also not interested in making other parts of the vehicle to be part of the class such as model number, vehicle color, etc.

1.13.4 Data Hiding

Data hiding hides the data from external access by the user. In OOP language, we have special keywords such as public, private, protected, etc., which hides the data. There are *three* types of access specifier. They are

- Within a class members can be declared as either *public protected* or *private* in order to explicitly enforce encapsulation.
- The elements placed after the *public* keyword is accessible to all the user of the class.
- The elements placed after the *protected* keyword is accessible only to the methods of the class.
- The elements placed after the *private* keyword are accessible only to the methods of the class.
- The data is hidden inside the class by declaring it as *private* inside the class. Thus private data cannot be directly accessed by the object.

1.13.5 Polymorphism

If we divide the word polymorphism we get *'poly'*, which means many and *'morphism'*, which means form. Thus, polymorphism means more than one form.

Polymorphism provides a way for an entity to behave in several forms. In simple terms an excellent example of polymorphism is *Lord Krishna* in *Hindu* mythology. From programmers' point of view polymorphism means one interface, many methods.'

It is an attribute that allows one interface to control access to a general class of actions. For example, we want to find out addition of three numbers; no matter what type of input we pass, i.e., integer, float, etc. Because of polymorphism we can define three versions of the same function with the name *addition3*. Each version of this function takes three parameters of the same time, i.e., one version of *addition3* takes three arguments of type integer, another takes three arguments of type double and so on. The compiler automatically selects the right version of the function depending upon the type of data passed to the function *addition3*. This is also called as *function polymorphism* or *function overloading*.

The two types of polymorphism are the following:

1. Compile time polymorphism
2. Run time polymorphism

1.13.6 Inheritance

Inheritance is the mechanism of deriving a new class from the earlier existing class. The inheritance provides the basic idea of reusability in object-oriented programming. The new class inherits the features of the old class. The old class and new class is called (given as pair) base-derived, parent-child, super-sub.

The inheritance supports the idea of classification. In classification we can form hierarchies of different classes each of which having some special characteristics besides some common properties. Through classification, a class needs only definition of those qualities that make it unique within its class.

Examples:
1. In the example given below, we have a vehicle class at the top in hierarchy. All the common features of a vehicle can be put in this class. From this, we can derive a new class, i.e., two wheeler, which contains features specific to two-wheeler vehicles only.
2. As another example we can take an engineering college as the top class and its various departments such as computer, electronics, electrical , etc., as the sub classes. The university to which the engineering college is affiliated may be its parent class.

1.13.7 Types of Inheritances

There are five different types inheritances.

- Single Inheritance
- Hierarchical Inheritance
- Multi-Level Inheritance
- Hybrid Inheritance
- Multiple Inheritance

1.13.7.1 Single Inheritance

Single inheritance is the simplest form of inheritance. When a class extends another one class only then we call it a single inheritance. The below flow diagram shows that class B extends only one class which is A. Here A is a parent class of B and B would be a child class of A.

When a single derived class is created from a single base class then the inheritance is called as single inheritance.

1.13.7.2 Hierarchical Inheritance

When more than one derived class are created from a single base class, then that inheritance is called as hierarchical inheritance. In such kind of inheritance one class is inherited by many sub classes. In the example, class B, C and D inherits the same class A. A is parent class (or base class) of B, C, and D.

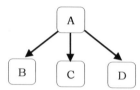

1.13.7.3 Multi-Level Inheritance

When a derived class is created from another derived class, then that inheritance is called as multi level inheritance.

Multilevel inheritance refers to a mechanism in object oriented technology where one can inherit from a derived class, thereby making this derived class the base class for the new class. As you can see in figure C is subclass or child class of B and B is a child class of A.

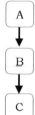

1.13.7.4 Hybrid Inheritance

Any combination of single, hierarchical and multi level inheritances is called as hybrid inheritance. In simple terms we can say that Hybrid inheritance is a combination of Single and Multiple inheritance. A hybrid inheritance can be achieved in the Java using interfaces.

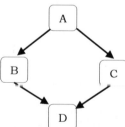

1.13.7.5 Multiple Inheritance

When a derived class is created from more than one base class then that inheritance is called as multiple inheritance. But multiple inheritance is not supported by Java using classes and can be done using interfaces.

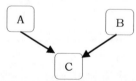

Handling the complexity that causes due to multiple inheritance is very complex. Hence it was not supported in Java with class and it can be done with interfaces.

Note: Refer *Problems* section for more details.

1.13.8 Dynamic Binding

Binding means *linking*. It involves linking of function definition to a function call.

- If linking of function call to function definition, i.e., a place where control has to be transferred is done at compile time, it is known as *static* binding.
- When linking is delayed till run time or done during the execution of the program then this type of linking is known as *dynamic* binding. Which function will be called in response to a function call is find out when program executes.

1.13.9 Message Passing

In C++ and Java, objects communicate each other by passing messages to each other. A message contains the name of the member function and arguments to pass. The message passing is shown below:

object. method (parameters);

Message passing here means object calling the method and passing parameters. Message passing is nothing but calling the method of the class and sending parameters. The method in turn executes in response to a message.

Problems and Questions with Answers

Question-1   What is the output of following code snippet?

```
#include<stdio.h>
int main(){
    printf("%d\t",sizeof(9.75));
    printf("%d\t",sizeof(60000));
    printf("%d",sizeof('D'));
    return 0;
}
```

Answer: 8   4   4 [assuming Linux GCC Compiler]. As you know size of data types is compiler dependent in c. On other compilers:

Compiler	Expected Output		
Turbo C++ 3.0	8	4	2
Turbo C ++4.5	8	4	2
Linux GCC	8	4	4
Visual C++	8	4	4

Question-2   What is the output of following code snippet?

```
#include<stdio.h>
int main(){
    double number=7.2;
    int  variable =7;
    printf("%d\t",sizeof(!number));
    printf("%d\t",sizeof(variable=25/2));
    printf("%d", variable);
    return 0;
}
```

Answer: 4   4   7 [assuming Linux GCC Compiler]. *sizeof (Expr)* operator always returns the an integer value which represents the size of the final value of the expression expr. Consider on the following expression:

!number = !7.2 = 0

0 is int type integer constant and it size is 4 by in Linux GCC compiler. Consider on the following expression:

variable = 25/2 => var = 12 => 12 and 12 is int type integer constant.

Any expression which is evaluated inside the *sizeof* operator its *scope* always will be within the sizeof operator. So value of variable var will remain 7 in the *printf* statement.

Question-3   What is name mangling?

Answer: C compiler links a function or symbol by *prepending* with under score. For example, *main*() function links to symbol name _main() and a variable *counter* (int *counter*;) will link to _count. For C + + compiler this will not work. C + + has function overloading mechanism. If C + + uses only under score before function name to link its symbol the purpose of overloading will not be resolved. For example, we have a function *test*() and overloaded as:

```
int test(int a, int b)
int test(int a, int b, int c)
```

Now if C + + uses _test() as symbol name then the two function body can never be linked. To solve this, C + + linker uses *me mangling*. Name mangling is the mechanism of C + + compiler to link functions and variables of same names to resolve them to some unique symbol names by altering the names with some extra information line index, argument size etc.. Function name mangling is done as

<function index><*function name*>@<*argument size*>

and variable name mangling is done as

?<*variable name*>@@<*UNIQUE ID*>.

For the above example,

int test(int a, int b) links to _1test@8
int test(int a, int b, int c) links to _2test@12

Question-4   Explain preprocessor directives and macros in C/C++.

Answer: When we write a C program, first we compile the program and then run the program. The compiler is a program that converts the source code into machine code. We can imagine the compiler as having two parts: the preprocessor and the rest of the compiler. To understand the preprocessor, let us take an example. Generally, we write an include statement in the beginning of a C program as:

#include<stdio.h>

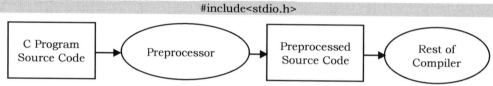

The preprocessor sees this statement and includes all function prototypes available in stdio.h file into the actual C program source code. The resultant source code is called 'preprocessed source code' which is given as input to the rest of the compiler. In the next step, the compiler converts this source code into machine code. This machine code is run during the time of running the program.

The preprocessor is a program inside the C compiler that does some activities like including the header files or macros before the actual compilation takes place.

The preprocessor provides the following facilities:

- Inclusion of header file code into our C program. For example, we write

#include<stdio.h>

In this case, all the function prototypes which are available in the header file <stdio.h> will be physically copied into the C program by the preprocessor.

- *Macro expansion*: We can define macros which represent some fixed set of statements. Whenever the macro is used in the program, it is replaced by the corresponding set of statements by the preprocessor. For example, we can write a macro, as:

#define MAX 100

Where ever we use MAX in the rest of the program, its value 100 is substituted in the place of MAX. This type of macro is called 'constant' since the value of PI is fixed.

- *Conditional compilation*: Using special preprocessing directives, we can include or exclude parts of the program according to various conditions. For example, we can write a statement which looks like if...else:

```
#ifdef AIX
    Code suitable for AIX
#else
    Code suitable for LINUX
#endif
    Code common to both the types
```

This is called conditional compilation because depending upon the type of the computer, certain code will be included. For example, before main() function, if we write

#define AIX

Then, the code suitable for AIX will be included into the program. If the #define statement is not included, then the code related to Linux will be included.

The preprocessor is also called 'macro processor' since it allows us to define macros and helps to resolve them. Let us understand that the preprocessor statements will start with a hash symbol (#). These preprocessor statements are also called 'directives' as they are instructions (directions) to the preprocessor.

Question-5   What is the output of following code snippet?

```
#include<stdio.h>
void main(){
    printf("%s",__DATE__);
}
```

Answer: Feb 17 2014.

1.13 Basic Concepts of OOPS

In C/C++, the following predefined macro names shall be defined by the implementation:

LINE	The line number of the current source line (a decimal constant).
FILE	The presumed name of the source file (a character string literal).
DATE	The date of translation of the source file.
TIME	The time of translation of the source file.

Question-6   What is the output of following code snippet?

```c
#include <stdio.h>
int main(){
    int a=43;
    printf("%d\n",printf("%d",printf("%d",a)));
    return 0;
}
```

Answer: 4321.

The *printf()* function will return the number of characters printed. For example, the code below prints 10005 (4 characters in 1000 plus \n character).

```c
int a=1000;
printf("%d",printf("\n%d",a));
```

Question-7   What is the output of following code snippet?

```c
#include<stdio.h>
#define ABC    30
#define XYZ    10
#define XXX    ABC - XYZ
void main(){
    int   a;
    a = XXX * 10;
    printf("%d ", a);
}
```

Answer: -70. Expression XXX * 10 would be converted to ABC – XYZ * 10 = 30 – 10 * 10 = -70.

Question-8   What is the output of following code snippet?

```c
#include<stdio.h>
#define  calculator(A, B)    (A * B) / (A - B)
void main(){
    int A = 20, B = 10;
    printf("%d ", calculator(A + 4, B -2));
}
```

Answer: 4. calculator(A + 4, B -2)) would be converted to (A + 4 * B - 2) / (A + 4 - B -2) = (20 + 4 * 10 - 2) / (20 + 4 - 10 -2) = 58 /12 = 4.

Question-9   What is the output of following code snippet?

```c
#include<stdio.h>
#define  calculator(A, B)    (A * B) / (A - B)
int main(){
    int k = 5;
    if (++k < 5 && k++/5 || ++k <= 8);
    printf("%d ", k);
    return 0;
}
```

Answer: 7. The first condition ++k < 5 is checked and it is false (Now k = 6). So, it checks the third condition (or condition ++k <= 8) and (now k = 7) it is true. At this point k value is incremented by twice, hence the value of k becomes 7.

Question-10   What is the output of following code snippet?

```c
#include<stdio.h>
void func(int, int);
main(){
    int   a = 5;
    printf("Main: %d %d ", a++, ++a);
    func(a, a++);
    void func(int a, int b){
```

```
        printf("\nFunc: a = %d  b = %d ", a, b);
    }
```

Answer: Main : 6 7   Func : a = 8 b = 7 [based on Linux GCC]

The solution depends on the implementation of stack. In some machines the arguments are passed from left to right to the stack. In this case the result will be

Main: 5 7   Func: a = 7 b = 7

Other machines the arguments may be passed from right to left to the stack. In that case the result will be

Main: 6 7   Func: a = 8 b = 7

Question-11   What is the output of following code snippet?

```
#include<stdio.h>
int main(){
    int *temp, *ptr, i;
    ptr = temp = (int *) malloc( 4 * sizeof(int));
    for (i=0; i<4; i++)
        *(temp+i) = i * 10;
    printf("%d\n", *ptr++);
    printf("%d\n", (*ptr)++);
    printf("%d\n", *ptr);
    printf("%d\n", *++ptr);
    printf("%d\n", ++*ptr);
    return 0;
}
```

Answer: 0   10   11   20   21

Based on operator precedence the expressions would be converted as shown below.

```
*ptr++    →  *(ptr++)
*++ptr    →  *(++ptr)
++*ptr    →  ++(*ptr)
```

Question-12   What is the output of following code snippet?

```
#include<stdio.h>
void func(int);
static int  value = 5;
int main(){
    while (value --) func(value);
    printf("%d\n", value);
    return 0;
}
void func(int val){
    static int value = 0;
    for (; value < 5; value ++)
        printf("%d\n", value);
}
```

Answer: 0   1   2   3   4   -1

Question-13   What is the output of following code snippet?

```
int main(){
    typedef struct {
        int    a;
        int    b;
        int    c;
        char   ch;
        int    d;
    }xyz;
    typedef union {
        xyz X;
        char y[100];
    }abc;
    printf("sizeof xyz = %d sizeof abc = %d\n",sizeof(xyz), sizeof(abc));
    return 0;
}
```

Answer: Size of xyz = 20 Size of abc = 100

This is the problem about Unions. Unions are similar to structures but it differs in some ways. Unions can be assigned only with one field at any time. In this case, unions x and y can be assigned with any of the one field a or b or c at one time. During initialisation of unions it takes the value (whatever assigned) only for the first field. So, The statement $y = \{100\}$ intialises the union y with field $a = 100$.

In this example, all fields of union x are assigned with some values. But at any time only one of the union field can be assigned. So, for the union x the field c is assigned as 21.50. Thus, The output will be

```
Union 2 : 22 22 21.50
Union Y : 100 22 22 ( 22 refers unpredictable results )
```

Question-14   What are the similarities and differences between $C++$ and *Java?*

Answer: There are many similarities and differences between $C++$ and *Java.*

- *Java* does not support *typedefs*, *defines*, or a *preprocessor*. *Java* supports *classes*, but does not support *structures* or *unions*.
- All $C++$ programs require a function named *main*.
- All classes in *Java* inherit from the *Object* class.
- All function or method definitions in *Java* are contained within the class definition.
- Both $C++$ and *Java* support *class* (*static*) methods or functions that can be called without the requirement to instantiate an object of the class.
- The *interface* keyword in *Java* is used to create the equivalence of an abstract base class containing only method declarations and constants. No variable data members or method definitions are allowed. (True abstract base classes can also be created in *Java*). The *interface* concept is not supported by $C++$.
- *Java* does not support *multiple inheritance*. To some extent, the *interface* feature provides the desirable features of multiple inheritance to a *Java* program without some of the underlying problems.
- *Java* does not support *automatic type conversions*.
- Unlike $C++$, *Java* has a *String* type, and objects of this type are immutable (cannot be modified). Quoted strings are automatically converted into *String* objects. *Java* also has a *StringBuffer* type. Objects of this type can be modified.
- Unlike $C++$, *Java* provides arrays as objects with *length* member, which tells how big the array is. An exception is thrown if you attempt to access an array out of bounds.
- *Java* does not support *pointers* (at least it does not allow you to modify the address contained in a pointer or to perform pointer arithmetic). Much of the need for pointers was eliminated by providing types for arrays and strings. For example, the oft-used $C++$ declaration *char * ptr* needed to point to the first character in a $C++$ null-terminated "string" is not required in *Java*, because a string is a true object in *Java*.
- The scope resolution operator (::) required in $C++$ is not used in *Java*. The dot is used to construct all fully-qualified references. Also, since there are no pointers, the pointer operator ($\rightarrow$) used in $C++$ is not required in *Java*.
- In $C++$, *static* data members and functions are called using the name of the class and the name of the static member connected by the scope resolution operator. In *Java*, the dot is used for this purpose.
- Like $C++$, *Java* has primitive types such as $int, float,$ etc. Unlike $C++$, the size of each primitive type is the same regardless of the platform. There is no unsigned integer type in *Java*. Type checking and type requirements are much tighter in *Java* than in $C++$.
- Unlike $C++$, *Java* provides a true *boolean* type.
- Conditional expressions in *Java* must evaluate to *boolean* rather than to integer, as is the case in $C++$. Statements such as $if(x + y)$... are not allowed in *Java* because the conditional expression doesn't evaluate to a *boolean*.
- The *char* type in $C++$ is an 8-bit type that maps to the ASCII (or extended ASCII) character set. The *char* type in *Java* is a 16-bit type.
- $C++$ allows the instantiation of variables or objects of all types either at compile time in static memory or at run time using dynamic memory. However, *Java* requires all variables of primitive types to be instantiated at compile time, and requires all objects to be instantiated in dynamic memory at runtime. Wrapper classes are provided for all primitive types except *byte* and *short* to allow them to be instantiated as objects in dynamic memory at runtime if needed.
- In $C++$, unless you specifically initialize variables of primitive types, they will contain garbage. Although local variables of primitive types can be initialized in the declaration, primitive data members of a class cannot be initialized in the class definition in $C++$.
- In *Java*, you can initialize primitive data members in the class definition. You can also initialize them in the constructor. If you fail to initialize them, they will be initialized to zero (or equivalent) automatically.
- Like $C++$, *Java* supports constructors that may be overloaded. As in $C++$, if you fail to provide a constructor, a default constructor will be provided for you. If you provide a constructor, the default constructor is not provided automatically.
- All objects in *Java* are passed by reference, eliminating the need for the *copy constructor* used in $C++$. (In reality, all parameters are passed by value in *Java*. However, passing a copy of a reference variable makes it possible for code in the receiving method to access the object referred to by the variable, and possibly to

modify the contents of that object. However, code in the receiving method cannot cause the original reference variable to refer to a different object.)

- There are no destructors in *Java*. Unused memory is returned to the operating system by way of a *garbage collector*, which runs in a different thread from the main program. This leads to a whole host of subtle and extremely important differences between *Java* and *C* + +.
- Like *C* + +, *Java* allows you to overload functions. However, default arguments are not supported by *Java*.
- Unlike *C* + +, *Java* does not support *templates*. Thus, there are no *generic* functions or classes.
- Unlike *C* + +, several *data structure* classes are contained in the "standard" version of *Java*.
- *Multithreading* is a standard feature of the *Java* language.
- Although *Java* uses the same keywords as *C* + + for access control: *private*, *public*, and *protected*, the interpretation of these keywords is significantly different between *Java* and *C* + +.
- There is no *virtual* keyword in *Java*. All non-static methods always use dynamic binding, so the *virtual* keyword isn't needed for the same purpose that it is used in *C* + +.
- *Java* provides the *final* keyword that can be used to specify that a method cannot be overridden and that it can be statically bound. (The compiler *may* elect to make it *inline* in this case.)
- The detailed implementation of the *exception handling* system in *Java* is significantly different from that in *C* + +.
- Unlike *C* + +, *Java* does not support *operator overloading*. However, the (+) and (+=) operators are automatically overloaded to concatenate strings, and to convert other types to *string* in the process.
- As in *C* + +, *Java* applications can call functions written in another language. This is commonly referred to as *native methods*. However, applets cannot call native methods.

Question-15   What is the difference between assignment and initialization in C++?

Answer: Consider the following code snippet:

```
MyTempClass one;
MyTempClass two = one;
```

Here, the variable two is initialized to one because it is created as a copy of another variable. When two is created, it will go from containing garbage data directly to holding a copy of the value of one with no intermediate step. However, if we rewrite the code as

```
MyTempClass one, two;
two = one;
```

Then two is assigned the value of one. Note that before we reach the line two = one, two already contains a value. This is the difference between assignment and initialization – when a variable is created to hold a specified value, it is being initialized, whereas when an existing variable is set to hold a new value, it is being assigned.

If you're ever confused about when variables are assigned and when they're initialized, you can check by sticking a const declaration in front of the variable. If the code still compiles, the object is being initialized. Otherwise, it's being assigned a new value.

Question-16   Explain overloading in C++.

Answer: C++ allows you to specify more than one definition for a function name or an operator in the same scope, which is called function overloading and operator overloading respectively. An overloaded declaration is a declaration that had been declared with the same name as a previously declared declaration in the same scope, except that both declarations have different arguments and obviously different definition (implementation).

When you call an overloaded function or operator, the compiler determines the most appropriate definition to use by comparing the argument types you used to call the function or operator with the parameter types specified in the definitions. The process of selecting the most appropriate overloaded function or operator is called overload resolution.

Function overloading in C++

You can have multiple definitions for the same function name in the same scope. The definition of the function must differ from each other by the types and/or the number of arguments in the argument list. You cannot overload function declarations that differ only by return type. Following is the example where same function print() is being used to print different data types:

```
#include <iostream>
using namespace std;
class printData {
  public:
    void print(int i) {
       cout << "Printing int: " << i << endl;
    }
    void print(double f) {
       cout << "Printing float: " << f << endl;
    }
```

```
    void print(char* c) {
        cout << "Printing character: " << c << endl;
    }
};
int main(void){
    printData pd;
    // Call print to print integer
    pd.print(5);
    // Call print to print float
    pd.print(500.263);
    // Call print to print character
    pd.print("Hello C++ Programmer");

    return 0;
}
```

When the above code is compiled and executed, it produces the following result:

```
Printing int: 5
Printing float: 500.263
Printing character: Hello C++
```

Operator overloading in C++

We can redefine or overload most of the built-in operators available in C++. Thus a programmer can use operators with user-defined types as well. Overloaded operators are functions with special names the keyword operator followed by the symbol for the operator being defined. Like any other function, an overloaded operator has a return type and a parameter list.

```
Box operator+(const Box&);
```

declares the addition operator that can be used to add two Box objects and returns final Box object. Most overloaded operators may be defined as ordinary non-member functions or as class member functions. In case we define above function as non-member function of a class then we would have to pass two arguments for each operand as follows:

```
Box operator+(const Box&, const Box&);
```

Following is the example to show the concept of operator over loading using a member function. Here an object is passed as an argument whose properties will be accessed using this object, the object which will call this operator can be accessed using this operator as explained below:

```
#include <iostream>
using namespace std;
class Box{
  public:
    double getVolume(void) {
        return length * breadth * height;
    }
    void setLength( double len ) {
        length = len;
    }
    void setBreadth( double bre ) {
        breadth = bre;
    }
    void setHeight( double hei ) {
        height = hei;
    }
    // Overload + operator to add two Box objects.
    Box operator+(const Box& b) {
        Box box;
        box.length = this->length + b.length;
        box.breadth = this->breadth + b.breadth;
        box.height = this->height + b.height;
        return box;
    }
    private:
        double length; // Length of a box
        double breadth; // Breadth of a box
        double height; // Height of a box
};
// Main function for the program
int main( ){
```

```
    Box Box1;      // Declare Box1 of type Box
    Box Box2;      // Declare Box2 of type Box
    Box Box3;      // Declare Box3 of type Box
    double volume = 0.0; // Store the volume of a box here

    // box 1 specification
    Box1.setLength(6.0);
    Box1.setBreadth(7.0);
    Box1.setHeight(5.0);
    // box 2 specification
    Box2.setLength(12.0);
    Box2.setBreadth(13.0);
    Box2.setHeight(10.0);

    // volume of box 1
    volume = Box1.getVolume();
    cout << "Volume of Box1 : " << volume <<endl;

    // volume of box 2
    volume = Box2.getVolume();
    cout << "Volume of Box2 : " << volume <<endl;
    // Add two object as follows:
    Box3 = Box1 + Box2;
    // volume of box 3
    volume = Box3.getVolume();
    cout << "Volume of Box3 : " << volume <<endl;
    return 0;
}
```

When the above code is compiled and executed, it produces the following result:

```
    Volume of Box1 : 210
    Volume of Box2 : 1560
    Volume of Box3 : 5400
```

Question-17   What is the difference between overloading and overriding?

Answer:

	Method Overloading	Method Overriding
Definition	Methods of the same class shares the same name but each method must have different number of parameters or parameters having different types and order.	Sub class have the same method with same name and exactly the same number and type of parameters and same return type as a super class.
Meaning	Method Overloading means more than one method shares the same name in the class but having different signature.	Method Overriding means method of base class is redefined in the derived class having same signature.
Behavior	Method Overloading is to "add" or "extend" more to method's behavior.	Method Overriding is to "Change" existing behavior of method.
	Overloading and Overriding is a kind of polymorphism. Polymorphism means "one name, many forms".	
Polymorphism	It is a compile time polymorphism.	It is a run time polymorphism.
Inheritance	It may or may not need inheritance in Method Overloading.	It always requires inheritance in Method Overriding.
Signature	Methods must have different signature.	Methods must have same signature.
Relationship of Methods	Relationship is there between methods of same class.	Relationship is there between methods of super class and sub class.
Criteria	In Method Overloading, methods have same name different signatures but in the same class.	In Method Overriding, methods have same name and same signature but in the different class.
Number of Classes	Method Overloading does not require more than one class for overloading.	Method Overriding requires at least two classes for overriding.

Example	Class Addition {
	    int add(int a, int b) {
	        return a + b;
	    }
	    int add(int a) {
	        return a + 20;
	    }
	}
		Class A { // Super Class
		    void display(int num) {
		        print num ;
		    }
		}
		//Class B inherits Class A
		Class B { //Sub Class
		    void display(int num) {
		        print num ;
		    }

```
                                                                    }
```

Question-18   Explain copy constructor in C++.

Answer: The copy constructor is a constructor which creates an object by initializing it with an object of the same class, which has been created previously. The copy constructor is used to:

1. Initialize one object from another of the same type.
2. Copy an object to pass it as an argument to a function.
3. Copy an object to return it from a function.

If a copy constructor is not defined in a class, the compiler itself defines one. If the class has pointer variables and has some dynamic memory allocations, then it is a must to have a copy constructor. The most common form of copy constructor is shown here:

```
classname (const classname &obj) {
    // body of constructor
}
```

Here, obj is a reference to an object that is being used to initialize another object.

```cpp
#include <iostream>
using namespace std;
class Line{
    public:
    int getLength( void );
    Line( int len );          // simple constructor
    Line( const Line &obj); // copy constructor
    ~Line();                  // destructor
    private:
    int *ptr;
};
// Member functions definitions including constructor
Line::Line(int len){
    cout << "Normal constructor allocating ptr" << endl;
    // allocate memory for the pointer;
    ptr = new int;
    *ptr = len;
}
Line::Line(const Line &obj){
    cout << "Copy constructor allocating ptr." << endl;
    ptr = new int;
    *ptr = *obj.ptr; // copy the value
}
Line::~Line(void){
    cout << "Releasing memory!" << endl;
    delete ptr;
}
int Line::getLength( void ){
    return *ptr;
}
void display(Line obj){
    cout << "Length of line : " << obj.getLength() <<endl;
}
// Main function for the program
int main( ){
    Line line(10);
    display(line);
    return 0;
}
```

When the above code is compiled and executed, it produces the following result:

```
Normal constructor allocating ptr
Copy constructor allocating ptr.
Length of line : 10
Releasing memory!
Releasing memory!
```

Let us see the same example but with a small change to create another object using existing object of the same type:

```cpp
#include <iostream>
using namespace std;
```

```
class Line{
    public:
    int getLength( void );
    Line( int len );           // simple constructor
    Line( const Line &obj); // copy constructor
    ~Line();                   // destructor
    private:
    int *ptr;
};
// Member functions definitions including constructor
Line::Line(int len){
    cout << "Normal constructor allocating ptr" << endl;
    // allocate memory for the pointer;
    ptr = new int;
    *ptr = len;
}
Line::Line(const Line &obj){
    cout << "Copy constructor allocating ptr." << endl;
    ptr = new int;
    *ptr = *obj.ptr; // copy the value
}
Line::~Line(void){
    cout << "Releasing memory!" << endl;
    delete ptr;
}
int Line::getLength( void ){
    return *ptr;
}
void display(Line obj){
    cout << "Length of line : " << obj.getLength() <<endl;
}
// Main function for the program
int main( ){
    Line line1(10);
    Line line2 = line1; // This also calls copy constructor
    display(line1);
    display(line2);
    return 0;
}
```

When the above code is compiled and executed, it produces the following result:

```
Normal constructor allocating ptr
Copy constructor allocating ptr.
Copy constructor allocating ptr.
Length of line : 10
Releasing memory!
Copy constructor allocating ptr.
Length of line : 10
Releasing memory!
Releasing memory!
Releasing memory!
```

Question-19   What is shallow and deep copy in $C++$?

Answer: A *shallow copy* of an object copies all of the member field values. This works well if the fields are values, but may not be what we want for fields that point to dynamically allocated memory (pointers). The pointer will be copied. But the memory it points to will not be copied. The field in both the original object and the copy will then point to the same dynamically allocated memory, which is not usually what we want. The default copy constructor and assignment operator make shallow copies.

Deep copy copies all fields, and makes copies of dynamically allocated memory pointed to by the fields. To make a deep copy, we need to write a copy constructor and overload the assignment operator, otherwise the copy will point to the original.

Question-20   What is object slicing in $C++$?

Answer: When a derived class object is assigned to base class, the base class contents in the derived object are copied to the base class leaving behind the derived class specific contents. This is referred as *object Slicing*. That is, the base class object can access only the base class members. This also implies that the separation of base class members from derived class members has happened.

```
class base{                          int main(){
    public:                              base b;
        int i, j;                        derived d;
};                                       b=d;
class derived : public base{             return 0;
    public:                          }
        int k;
};
```

Here *b* contains *i* and *j* whereas *d* contains *i*, *j* & *k*. On assignment only *i* and *j* of the *d* get copied into *i* and *j* of *b*, *k* does not get copied and on the effect object *d* gets sliced.

Question-21   Are there copy constructor and assignment constructor in java?

Answer: There is such a thing as a copy constructor in Java, but it does not play the special role that such constructors do in C++. A copy constructor in Java is just like any other constructor: we call it with new.

```
public class A {
    private int x;
    public A(int x) { this.x = v; }
    public A(A that) { this.x = that.x; }
}
...
A temp1 = new A(5);
A temp2;
temp2 = new A(temp1);
...
```

There are no assignment constructors, or anything much like them, in Java. That is because Java does *not* have operator overloading. The assignment operation (=) is always a shallow copy.

Java does have the notion of a *clone* (copy) method. Any object can support the clone() method; by convention the method implementation is supposed to perform a deep copy
of the object on which it is called, and return the copy.

Question-22   Explain templates concept in C++.

Answer: C++ templates are the foundation of generic programming, which involves writing code in a way that is *independent* of any particular *type*. A template is a formula for creating a generic class or a function. The library containers like iterators and algorithms are examples of generic programming and have been developed using template concept.

There is a single definition of each container, such as vector, but we can define many different kinds of vectors for example, *vector < int >* or *vector < string >*. You can use templates to define functions as well as classes, let us see how do they work:

Function Template

The general form of a template function definition is shown here:

```
template <class type> ret-type func-name(parameter list){
    // body of function
}
```

Here, type is a placeholder name for a data type used by the function. This name can be used within the function definition.

The following is the example of a function template that returns the maximum of two values:

```
#include <iostream>
#include <string>
using namespace std;
template <typename T>
inline T const& Max (T const& a, T const& b) {
    return a < b ? b:a;
}
int main (){
    int i = 49;
    int j = 10;
    cout << "Max(i, j): " << Max(i, j) << endl;

    double f1 = 23.5;
    double f2 = 10.7;
    cout << "Max(f1, f2): " << Max(f1, f2) << endl;
```

```
    string s1 = "Hello";
    string s2 = "World";
    cout << "Max(s1, s2): " << Max(s1, s2) << endl;
    return 0;
}
```

If we compile and run above code, this would produce the following result:

```
Max(i, j): 49
Max(f1, f2): 23.5
Max(s1, s2): World
```

Class Template

Just as we can define function templates, we can also define class templates. The general form of a generic class declaration is shown here:

```
template <class type> class class-name {
    .
    .
    .
}
```

Here, type is the placeholder type name, which will be specified when a class is instantiated. You can define more than one generic data type by using a comma-separated list.

Following is the example to define class Stack<> and implement generic methods to push and pop the elements from the stack:

```
#include <iostream>
#include <vector>
#include <cstdlib>
#include <string>
#include <stdexcept>
using namespace std;
template <class T>
class Stack {
  private:
    vector<T> elems;     // elements
  public:
    void push(T const&); // push element
    void pop();          // pop element
    T top() const;       // return top element
    bool empty() const{     // return true if empty.
        return elems.empty();
    }
};
template <class T>
void Stack<T>::push (T const& elem) {
    // append copy of passed element
    elems.push_back(elem);
}
template <class T>
void Stack<T>::pop () {
    if (elems.empty()) {
        throw out_of_range("Stack<>::pop(): empty stack");
    }
    // remove last element
    elems.pop_back();
}
template <class T>
T Stack<T>::top () const {
    if (elems.empty()) {
        throw out_of_range("Stack<>::top(): empty stack");
    }
    // return copy of last element
    return elems.back();
}
int main() {
    try {
        Stack<int>      intStack; // stack of ints
        Stack<string> stringStack;   // stack of strings
```

```
    // Update int stack
    intStack.push(7);
    cout << intStack.top() <<endl;

    // Update string stack
    stringStack.push("hello");
    cout << stringStack.top() << std::endl;
    stringStack.pop();
    stringStack.pop();
  }
  catch (exception const& ex) {
    cerr << "Exception: " << ex.what() <<endl;
    return -1;
  }
}
```

If we compile and run above code, this would produce the following result:

```
7
hello
Exception: Stack<>::pop(): empty stack
```

Question-23   Explain *vitual* functions in $C++$.

Answer: When a function call is made, $C++$ matches a function call with the correct function definition at compile time. This is called *static binding*. We can specify that the compiler match a function call with the correct function definition at run time and this is called *dynamic binding*. We declare a function with the keyword *virtual* if we want the compiler to use dynamic binding for that specific function. The following example demonstrates static binding:

```
class A {
   void f() {
      cout << "Base Class A" << endl;
   }
};

class B: A {
   void f() {
      cout << "Derived Class B" << endl;
   }
};
```

```
void g(A& arg) {
   arg.f();
}
int main() {
   B x;
   g(x);
}
Output of the example: Class A
```

When function $g()$ is called, function $A::f()$ is called, although the argument refers to an object of type B. At compile time, the compiler knows only that the argument of function $g()$ will be a reference to an object derived from A, it cannot determine whether the argument will be a reference to an object of type A or type B. However, this can be determined at run time. The following example is the same as the previous example, except that A::f() is declared with the *virtual* keyword:

```
class A {
   virtual void f() {
      cout << "Base Class A" << endl;
   }
};
class B: A {
   void f() {
      cout << "Derived Class B" << endl;
   }
};
```

```
void g(A& arg) {
   arg.f();
}

int main() {
   B x;
   g(x);
}
Output of the example: Class B
```

Question-24   What are *abstract* classes and *interfaces*? What is the difference between them?

Answer: An *abstract* class is a class that cannot be instantiated and is usually implemented as a class that has one or more *pure virtual* (abstract) functions.

A *pure virtual* function is one which must be overridden by any concrete (i.e., non-abstract) derived class. This is indicated in the declaration with the syntax "= 0" in the member function's declaration.

```
class AbstractClass {
public:
   //pure virtual function makes this class Abstract class
   virtual void AbstractMemberFunction() = 0;
   virtual void NonAbstractVirtualMemberFunction(); //virtual function
   void NonAbstractMemberFunction();
};
```

In general an abstract class is used to define an implementation and is intended to be inherited from concrete classes. If a class has *only* pure virtual functions then we call it *pure abstract* class or an *interface*. The concept of interface is mapped to pure abstract classes in *C + +*, as there is no keyword *interface* in *C + +* the same way that there is in *Java*. That means, in *Java* we can use an *interface* keyword to define pure abstract classes as shown below.

```
interface InterfaceClass {
    void function1(int value);
    void function2(int newValue);
    void function3(int someValue);
}
```

In object-oriented programming, a *virtual* function is a method whose behaviour can be overridden within an inheriting class by a function with the same signature to provide the polymorphic behavior. Therefore according to definition, every non-static method in *Java* is by *default* virtual method except *final* and *private* methods. The method which cannot be inherited for polymorphic behavior is not a virtual method.

In design, we want the base class to present only an interface for its derived classes. This means, we don't want anyone to actually instantiate an object of the base class. We only want to upcast it, so that its interface can be used. This is accomplished by making that class abstract using the *abstract* keyword. If anyone tries to make an object of an abstract class, the compiler prevents it. An abstract class can have executable methods and abstract methods can only subclass one abstract class.

The *interface* keyword takes this concept of an abstract class a step further by preventing any method or function implementation at all. We can only declare a method or function but not provide the implementation. The class, which is implementing the interface, should provide the actual implementation. In interface, all methods are abstract. A class can implement any number of interfaces.

Difference between *abstract* and *interface* classes in *Java*:
- Main difference in methods of a *Java interface* are implicitly abstract and cannot have implementations. A *Java* *abstract* class can have instance methods that implement a default behavior.
- Variables declared in *Java* interface are by default final. An abstract class may contain non-final variables.
- Members of *Java* interface are *public* by default. A *Java* abstract class can have the usual flavors of class members like private, protected, etc..
- *Java* interface should be implemented using keyword *implements* and a *Java* abstract class should be extended using keyword *extends*.
- An interface can extend another *Java* interface only, an abstract class can extend another *Java* class and implement multiple *Java* interfaces.
- A *Java* class can implement multiple interfaces but it can extend only one abstract class.
- Interface is absolutely abstract and cannot be instantiated, a *Java* abstract class also cannot be instantiated, but can be invoked if a main() exists.

Question-25   What's the difference between *memcpy* and *memmove*?

Answer: *memmove* gives guaranteed behavior if the memory regions pointed to by the source and destination arguments overlap. *memcpy* makes no such guarantee, and may therefore be more efficiently implementable. When in doubt, it's safer to use memmove. It seems simple enough to implement *memmove*; the overlap guarantee apparently requires only an additional test:

```
void *memmove(void *destination, void const *source, int size){
        register char *dptr = destination;
        register char const *sptr = source;
        if(dptr < sptr) {
                while(size-- > 0)
                        *dptr++ = *sptr++;
        } else {
                dptr += size;
                sptr += size;
                while(size-- > 0)
                        *--dptr = *--sptr;
        }
        return destination;
}
```

The problem with this code is in that additional test: the comparison (dptr < sptr) is not quite portable (it compares two pointers which do not necessarily point within the same object) and may not be as cheap as it looks.

With *memcpy*, the destination cannot overlap the source at all. With *memmove* copying takes place as if an intermediate buffer was used, allowing the destination and source to overlap. This means that *memmove* might be very slightly slower than *memcpy*, as it cannot make the same assumptions. In other words, *memcpy* copies source to destination without checking for overlapping of source and destination memory areas. *memmove* copies source to destination carefully by checking for overlapping of source and destination memory areas.

Question-26   What is the output of following code snippet?

```
#include <stdio.h>
int main(void){
   int a = 3;
   int b;
   b = sizeof(++a + ++a);
   printf("a=%d    b=%d\n", a, b);
   return 0;
}
```

Answer: a=3   b=4

sizeof gives the number of bytes allocated for an operand. Hence, the evaluation of ++a will get cancelled and *a*'s value remains unchanged.

Question-27   Compare C++ and Java performance.

Amswer: In addition to running a compiled Java program, computers running Java applications generally must also run the Java virtual machine (JVM), while compiled C++ programs can be run without external applications. Early versions of Java were significantly outperformed by statically compiled languages such as C++. This is because the program statements of these two closely related languages may compile to a few machine instructions with C++, while compiling into several byte codes involving several machine instructions each when interpreted by a JVM.

Since performance optimization is a very complex issue, it is very difficult to say in numbers the performance difference between C++ and Java in general terms. And given the very different natures of the languages, definitive qualitative differences are also difficult to draw. There are inherent inefficiencies as well as hard limitations on optimizations in Java given that it heavily relies on flexible high-level abstractions, however, the use of a powerful JIT compiler (as in modern JVM implementations) can resolve some issues.

Certain inefficiencies that are inherent to the Java language:

1. All objects are allocated on the heap. For functions using small objects this can result in performance degradation and heap fragmentation, while stack allocation, in contrast, costs essentially zero. However, modern JIT compilers mitigate this problem to some extent with escape analysis or escape detection to allocate objects on the stack.
2. Lack of access to low-level details prevents the developer from improving the program where the compiler is unable to do so.

Benefits of Java's design:

- Java garbage collection may have better cache coherence than the usual usage of malloc/new for memory allocation.
- In Java, thread synchronization is built into the language.

Also, some performance problems exist in C++ as well:

- Allowing pointers to point to any address can make optimization difficult due to the possibility of interference between pointers that alias each other. However, the introduction of strict-aliasing rules largely solves this problem.
- Because dynamic linking is performed after code generation and optimization in C++, function calls spanning different dynamic modules cannot be inlined.
- Because thread support is generally provided by libraries in C++, C++ compilers cannot perform thread-related optimizations.

Question-28   Explain *virtual tables* in *C + +*.

Answer: To implement virtual functions, *C + +* uses a special form of late binding known as *virtual table*. The virtual table is a lookup table of functions used to resolve function calls in a *dynamic/late* binding manner. The virtual table is also called *vtable*, *virtual function table* or *virtual method table*.

The virtual table is actually quite simple, though it's a little complex to describe in words. First, every class that uses virtual functions (or is derived from a class that uses virtual functions) is given its own virtual table. This table is simply a static array that the compiler sets up at compile time.

A virtual table contains one entry for each virtual function that can be called by objects of the class. Each entry in this table is simply a function pointer that points to the most-derived function accessible by that class.

Second, the compiler also adds a hidden pointer to the base class, which we will call *_vptr. *_vptr is set (automatically) when a class instance is created so that it points to the virtual table for that class. Unlike the *this pointer, which is actually a function parameter used by the compiler to resolve self-references, *_vptr is a real pointer.

That means, it makes each class object allocated bigger by the size of one pointer. It also means that *_vptr is inherited by derived classes. Let's take a look at a simple example:

```
class Base{                  class D1: public Base{         class D2: public Base{
public:                      public:                        public:
    virtual void                 virtual void                   virtual void
        function1() {};              function1() {};                          function2() {};
    virtual void                                      };                                      };
        function2() {};
};
```

Since there are 3 classes here, the compiler will set up 3 virtual tables: one for Base, one for D1, and one for D2. The compiler also adds a hidden pointer to the most base class that uses virtual functions. Although the compiler does this automatically, we'll put it in the next example just to show where it's added:

```
class Base{                       class D1: public Base {          class D2: public Base{
public:                           public:                          public:
    FunctionPointer *__vptr;          virtual void function1() {};     virtual void function2() {};
    virtual void function1() {};                             };                              };
    virtual void function2() {};
};
```

When a class object is created, *__vptr is set to point to the virtual table for that class. For example, when an object of type Base is created, *__vptr is set to point to the virtual table for Base. When objects of type D1 or D2 are constructed, *__vptr is set to point to the virtual table for D1 or D2 respectively.

Now, let's see how these virtual tables are filled out. Because there are only two virtual functions here, each virtual table will have two entries (one for function1(), and one for function2()). Remember that when these virtual tables are filled, each entry is filled out with the most-derived function an object of that class type can call.

Base's virtual table is simple. An object of type Base can only access the members of Base. Base has no access to D1 or D2 functions. Consequently, the entry for function1 points to Base::function1(), and the entry for function2 points to Base::function2().

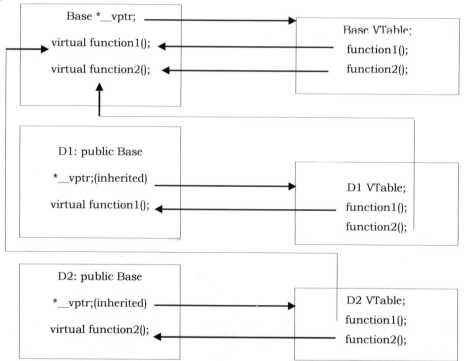

D1's virtual table is slightly more complex. An object of type D1 can access members of both D1 and Base. However, D1 has overridden function1(), making D1::function1() more derived than Base::function1(). Consequently, the entry for function1 points to D1::function1(). D1 hasn't overridden function2(), so the entry for function2 will point to Base::function2(). D2's virtual table is similar to D1, except the entry for function1 points to Base::function1(), and the entry for function2 points to D2::function2().

In the diagram: the *__vptr in each class points to the virtual table for that class. The entries in the virtual table point to the most-derived version of the function objects of that class are allowed to call. So consider what happens when we create an object of type D1:

```
int main(){
    D1 cClass;
}
```

Because cClass is a D1 object, cClass has it's *__vptr set to the D1 virtual table. Now, let's set a base pointer to D1:

```
int main() {
    D1 cClass;
    Base *pClass = &cClass;
}
```

Note that because pClass is a base pointer, it only points to the Base portion of cClass. However, also note that *__vptr is in the Base portion of the class, so pClass has access to this pointer. Finally, note that pClass→__vptr points to the D1 virtual table! Consequently, even though pClass is of type Base, it still has access to D1's virtual table. So what happens when we call pClass→function1()?

```
int main() {
    D1 cClass;
    Base *pClass = &cClass;
    pClass→function1();
}
```

First, the program recognizes that function1() is a virtual function. Second, uses pClass→__vptr to get to D1's virtual table. Third, it looks up which version of function1() to call in D1's virtual table. This has been set to D1::function1(). Therefore, pClass→function1() resolves to D1::function1()!

Now, you might be saying, "But what if Base really pointed to a Base object instead of a D1 object. Would it still be called D1::function1()?". The answer is no.

```
int main() {
    Base cClass;
    Base *pClass = &cClass;
    pClass→function1();
}
```

In this case, when cClass is created, __vptr points to Base's virtual table, not D1's virtual table. Consequently, pClass→__vptr will also point to Base's virtual table. Base's virtual table entry for function1() points to Base::function1(). Thus, pClass→function1() resolves to Base::function1(), which is the most-derived version of function1() that a Base object should be able to call.

By using these tables, the compiler and program are able to ensure function calls resolve to the appropriate virtual function, even if you're only using a pointer or reference to a base class!

Calling a virtual function is slower than calling a non-virtual function for a couple of reasons: First, we have to use the *__vptr to get to the appropriate virtual table. Second, we have to index the virtual table to find the correct function to call. Only then can we call the function. As a result, we have to do 3 operations to find the function to call, as opposed to 2 operations for a normal indirect function call, or one operation for a direct function call. However, with modern computers, this added time is insignificant.

Question-29   Write a function for swapping two integers without using third integer (ie. without using any temporary variable).

Answer: There are multiple solutions for this problem. The code snippet below exploits those.

```
#include<stdio.h>
int main(){
    int a=15,b=25;

    //Method one
    a=b+a;
    b=a-b;
    a=a-b;
    printf("a= %d  b= %d",a,b);

    //Method two
    a=a+b-(b=a);
    printf("\na= %d  b= %d",a,b);

    //Method three
    a=a^b;
    b=a^b;
    a=b^a;
    printf("\na= %d  b= %d",a,b);

    //Method four
    a=b-~a-1;
    b=a+~b+1;
    a=a+~b+1;
    printf("\na= %d  b= %d",a,b);
```

```
    //Method five
    a=b+a,b=a-b,a=a-b;
    printf("\na= %d  b= %d",a,b);
    return 0;
}
```

Question-30   What does 'public static void' mean in Java?

Answer: The *public* keyword is an access specifier, which allows the programmer to control the visibility of class members. When a class member is preceded by public, then that member may be accessed by code outside the class in which it is declared. (The opposite of public is private, which prevents a member from being used by code defined outside of its class.) In other words, public means that the method is visible and can be called from other objects of other types.

In this case, main( ) must be declared as *public*, since it must be called by code outside of its class when the program is started.

The keyword *static* allows main( ) to be called without having to instantiate a particular instance of the class. This is necessary since main( ) is called by the Java interpreter before any objects are made.

The keyword *void* simply tells the compiler that main( ) does not return a value. As you will see, methods may also return values.

Question-31   What if the *main* method is declared as *private*?

Answer: The program compiles properly but at runtime it will give "Main method not public." message.

Question-32   What if the *static* modifier is removed from the signature of the main method?

Answer: Program compiles. But at runtime throws an error "NoSuchMethodError".

Question-33   What if I write *static public void* instead of *public static void*?

Answer: Program compiles and runs properly.

Question-34   What if I do not provide the *String* array as the argument to the method?

Answer: Program compiles but throws a runtime error "NoSuchMethodError".

Question-35   What is the first argument of the *String* array in main method?

Answer: The String array is empty. It does not have any element. This is unlike C/C++ where the first element by default is the program name.

Question-36   If I do not provide any arguments on the command line, then the *String* array of Main method will be empty or null?

Answer: It is empty. But not null.

Question-37   What is the main difference between an *ArrayList* and a *Vector* in *Java*?

Answer: Java arrays are faster than an ArrayList/Vector and therefore it may be preferable if we know the size of the array upfront (because arrays cannot grow as Lists do).

ArrayList/Vector are specialized data structures that internally use an array with some convenient methods like add(..), remove(...), etc. so that they can grow and shrink from their initial size. ArrayList also supports index based searches with indexOf(Object obj) and lastIndexOf(Object obj) methods.

Question-38   Discuss about constructors, destructors and their order of execution in inheritance.

Answer: The process of creating and deleting objects in C++ is not a trivial task. Every time an instance of a class is created the constructor method is called. The constructor has the same name as the class and it doesn't return any type, while the destructor's name it's defined in the same way, but with a '~' in front:

```
class Base{
public:
Base ( ) {
  cout << "Base constructor" << endl;
}
~Base ( ){
  cout << "Base destructor" << endl;
}
};
```

Base class constructors are always called in the derived class constructors. Whenever you create derived class object, first the base class default constructor is executed and then the derived class's constructor finishes execution.

1. Important Notes

1.13 Basic Concepts of OOPS

- Whether derived class's default constructor is called or parameterized is called, base class's default constructor is always called inside them.
- To call base class's parameterized constructor inside derived class's parameterized constructor, we must mention it explicitly while declaring derived class's parameterized constructor.

2. Base class Default Constructor in Derived class Constructors

```
class Base{
      int a;
      public:
          Base() { cout << "Default base constructor"<<endl; }
};
class Derived : public Base{
      int b;
        public:
          Derived() { cout << "Default derived constructor"<<endl; }
          Derived(int i) { cout << "Parameterized derived constructor"<<endl; }
};
int main(){
    Base b;
    Derived d1;
    Derived d2(20);
}
```

Expected Output:

```
Default base constructor
Default base constructor
Default derived constructor
Default base constructor
Parameterized derived constructor
```

You will see in the above example that with both the object creation of the Derived class, Base class's default constructor is called.

3. Base class Parameterized Constructor in Derived class Constructor

We can explicitly mention to call the Base class's parameterized constructor when Derived class's parameterized constructor is called.

```
class Base {
      public: int x;
      public:
      Base(int i){
          x = i;
          cout << "Base Parameterized Constructor"<<endl;
      }
};
class Derived : public Base{
      public: int y;
      public:
      Derived(int j) : Base(j){
          y = j;
          cout << "Derived Parameterized Constructor"<<endl;
      }
};
int main(){
    Derived d(20) ;
    cout << d.x <<endl; // Output will be 20
    cout << d.y <<endl; // Output will be 20
}
```

Expected Output:

```
Base Parameterized Constructor
Derived Parameterized Constructor
20
20
```

4. Why is Base class Constructor called inside Derived class ?

Constructors have a special job of initializing the object properly. A Derived class constructor has access only to its own class members, but a Derived class object also have inherited property of Base class, and only base class constructor can properly initialize base class members. Hence all the constructors are called, else object wouldn't be constructed properly.

5. Constructor call in Multiple Inheritance

It's almost the same, all the Base class's constructors are called inside derived class's constructor, in the same order in which they are inherited.

```
class A : public B, public C ;
```

In this case, first class B constructor will be executed, then class C constructor and then class A constructor.

6. Upcasting in C++

Upcasting is using the Super class's reference or pointer to refer to a Sub class's object. Or we can say that, the act of converting a Sub class's reference or pointer into its Super class's reference or pointer is called Upcasting.

```
class Super{
    int x;
    public:
    void funBase() { cout << "Super function"; }
};
class Sub : public Super{
    int y;
};
int main(){
    Super* ptr; // Super class pointer
    Sub obj;
    ptr = &obj;

    Super &ref; // Super class's reference
    ref=obj;
}
```

The opposite of *Upcasting* is *Downcasting*, in which we convert Super class's reference or pointer into derived class's reference or pointer. We will study more about *Downcasting* later

7. Functions that are never Inherited

Constructors and Destructors are never inherited and hence never overrided. Also, assignment operator = is never inherited. It can be overloaded but can't be inherited by sub class.

8. Inheritance and Static Functions

- They are inherited into the derived class.
- If you redefine a static member function in derived class, all the other overloaded functions in base class are hidden.
- Static Member functions can never be virtual.

9. Hybrid Inheritance and Virtual Class

In Multiple Inheritance, the derived class inherits from more than one base class. Hence, in Multiple Inheritance there are a lot chances of ambiguity.

```
class A{
    void show();
};
class B:public A {};
class C:public A {};
class D:public B, public C {};
int main(){
    D obj;
    obj.show();
}
```

In this case both class B and C inherits function show() from class A. Hence class D has two inherited copies of function show(). In main() function when we call function show(), then ambiguity arises, because compiler doesn't know which show() function to call. Hence we use Virtual keyword while inheriting class.

```
class B : virtual public A {};
class C : virtual public A {};
class D : public B, public C {};
```

Now by adding virtual keyword, we tell compiler to call any one out of the two show() functions.

10. Hybrid Inheritance and Constructor call

As we all know that whenever a derived class object is instantiated, the base class constructor is always called. But in case of Hybrid Inheritance, as discussed in above example, if we create an instance of class D, then following constructors will be called : before class D's constructor, constructors of its super classes will be called, hence constructors of class B, class C and class A will be called.

When constructors of class B and class C are called, they will again make a call to their super class's constructor. This will result in multiple calls to the constructor of class A, which is undesirable. As there is a single instance of virtual base class which is shared by multiple classes that inherit from it, hence the constructor of the base class is only called once by the constructor of concrete class, which in our case is class D.

Question-39   Explain how HashMap works in *Java*.

Answer: HashMap works on principle of hashing, we have *put*() and *get*() methods for storing and retrieving data from HashMap. When we pass an object to *put*() method to store it on HashMap, HashMap implementation calls *hashcode*() method HashMap key object and by applying that hashcode on its own hashing funtion it identifies a bucket location for storing value object.

The important part here is HashMap stores both *key + value* in bucket, which is essential to understand the retrieving logic. If we fail to recognize this and assume it only stores value in the bucket they will fail to explain the retrieving logic of any object stored in HashMap.

What will happen if two different objects have same hashcode?

Now the confusion starts. The interviewer may say that since Hashcodes are equal, objects are equal and HashMap will throw exception or not store it again, etc. Then you might want to remind them about equals and hashCode() contract that two unequal objects in *Java* can have equal hashcode. Some will give up at this point and some will move ahead and say "since hashcode() is same, bucket location is the same and collision occurs in hashMap. Since HashMap uses a linked list to store in bucket, value object will be stored in next node of linked list.

How will you retrieve if two different objects have same hashcode?

After finding bucket location, we will call keys.equals() method to identify correct node in linked list and return associated value object for that key in *Java* HashMap.

What happens On HashMap in *Java* if the size of the Hashmap exceeds a given threshold defined by load factor?

Until we know how hashmap works we won't be able to answer this question. If the size of the map exceeds a given threshold defined by load-factor e.g. if load factor is .75 it will act to re-size the map once it fills 75%. *Java Hashmap* does that by creating another new bucket array twice the size of previous hashmap, and then starts putting every old element into that new bucket array. This process is called rehashing, because it also applies hash function to find new bucket location.

Question-40   What is the difference between *HashMap* and *HashTable* in *Java*?

Answer:
- The HashMap class is roughly equivalent to Hashtable, except that it is non-synchronized and permits nulls. (HashMap allows null values as key and value whereas Hashtable doesn't allow nulls).
- HashMap does not guarantee that the order of the map will remain constant over time.
- HashMap is non-synchronized whereas Hashtable is synchronized.
- Iterator in the HashMap is fail-fast while the enumerator for the Hashtable is not and throw ConcurrentModificationException if any other Thread modifies the map structurally by adding or removing any element except Iterator's own remove() method. But this is not a guaranteed behavior and will be done by JVM on best effort.

Question-41   Explain *Java* threads.

Answer: Java provides has support for multithreaded programming. A multithreaded program contains two or more parts that can run concurrently. Each part of such a program is called a thread, and each thread defines a separate path of execution.

As discussed earlier, a process consists of the memory space allocated by the operating system that can contain one or more threads. A thread cannot exist on its own; it must be a part of a process. A process remains running until all of the non-daemon threads are done executing. Multithreading enables us to write very efficient programs that make maximum use of the CPU, because idle time can be kept to a minimum.

Creating a Thread

In Java, we have two ways in which this can be accomplished:

- We can implement the Runnable interface.
- We can extend the Thread class itself.

Create Thread by Implementing Runnable

The simplest way to create a thread is to create a class that implements the *Runnable* interface. To implement Runnable, a class needs to only implement a single method called run( ), which is declared like this:

```
public void run( )
```

We will define the code that constitutes the new thread inside run() method. It is important to understand that run() can call other methods, use other classes, and declare variables, just like the main thread can.

After we create a class that implements *Runnable*, we will instantiate an object of type Thread from within that class. Thread defines several constructors. The one that we will use is shown here:

```
Thread(Runnable threadObject, String threadName);
```

Here, *threadObject* is an instance of a class that implements the *Runnable* interface and the name of the new thread is specified by threadName.

After the new thread is created, it will not start running until you call its start( ) method, which is declared within Thread. The start( ) method is shown here:

```
void start( );
```

Example

Here is an example that creates a new thread and starts it running:

```java
// create a new thread.
class NewThread implements Runnable {
  Thread t;
  NewThread() {
    // create a new, second thread
    t = new Thread(this, "Demo Thread");
    System.out.println("Child thread: " + t);
    t.start(); // Start the thread
  }
  // Entry point for the second thread.
  public void run() {
    try {
      for(int i = 5; i > 0; i--) {
        System.out.println("Child Thread: " + i);
        Thread.sleep(50);  // sleep for a while.
      }
    } catch (InterruptedException e) {
      System.out.println("Child interrupted.");
    }
    System.out.println("Terminating child thread.");
  }
}
public class ThreadDemo {
  public static void main(String args[]) {
    new NewThread(); // create a new thread
    try {
      for(int i = 5; i > 0; i--) {
        System.out.println("Main Thread: " + i);
        Thread.sleep(100);
      }
    } catch (InterruptedException e) {
      System.out.println("Main thread interrupted.");
    }
    System.out.println("Main thread terminating.");
  }
}
```

This would produce the following result:

```
Child thread: Thread[Demo Thread,5,main]
Main Thread: 5
Child Thread: 5
Child Thread: 4
```

```
Main Thread: 4
Child Thread: 3
Child Thread: 2
Main Thread: 3
Child Thread: 1
Terminating child thread.
Main Thread: 2
Main Thread: 1
Main thread terminating.
```

Create Thread by Extending Thread

The second way to create a thread is to create a new class that extends Thread, and then to create an instance of that class. The extending class must override the run( ) method, which is the entry point for the new thread. It must also call start( ) to begin execution of the new thread.

Example

Here is the preceding program rewritten to extend Thread:

```java
// Create a second thread by extending Thread
class NewThread extends Thread {
  NewThread() {
    // Create a new, second thread
    super("Demo Thread");
    System.out.println("Child thread: " + this);
    start(); // Start the thread
  }
  // This is the entry point for the second thread.
  public void run() {
    try {
      for(int i = 5; i > 0; i--) {
        System.out.println("Child Thread: " + i);
        // Let the thread sleep for a while.
        Thread.sleep(50);
      }
    } catch (InterruptedException e) {
      System.out.println("Child interrupted.");
    }
    System.out.println("Terminating child thread.");
  }
}
public class ExtendThread {
  public static void main(String args[]) {
    new NewThread(); // create a new thread
    try {
      for(int i = 5; i > 0; i--) {
        System.out.println("Main Thread: " + i);
        Thread.sleep(100);
      }
    } catch (InterruptedException e) {
      System.out.println("Main thread interrupted.");
    }
    System.out.println("Main thread terminating.");
  }
}
```

This would produce the following result:

```
Child thread: Thread[Demo Thread,5,main]
Main Thread: 5
Child Thread: 5
Child Thread: 4
Main Thread: 4
Child Thread: 3
Child Thread: 2
Main Thread: 3
Child Thread: 1
Terminating child thread.
Main Thread: 2
```

Main Thread: 1
Main thread terminating.
Thread Methods:

Following is the list of important methods available in the Thread class.

Function	Description
public void start()	Starts the thread in a separate path of execution, then invokes the run() method on this Thread object.
public void run()	If this Thread object was instantiated using a separate Runnable target, the run() method is invoked on that Runnable object.
public final void setName(String name)	Changes the name of the Thread object. There is also a getName() method for retrieving the name.
public final void setPriority(int priority)	Sets the priority of this Thread object. The possible values are between 1 and 10.
public final void setDaemon(boolean on)	A parameter of true denotes this Thread as a daemon thread.
public final void join(long millisec)	The current thread invokes this method on a second thread, causing the current thread to block until the second thread terminates or the specified number of milliseconds passes.
public void interrupt()	Interrupts this thread, causing it to continue execution if it was blocked for any reason.
public final boolean isAlive()	Returns true if the thread is alive, which is any time after the thread has been started but before it runs to completion.

The previous methods are invoked on a particular Thread object. The following methods in the Thread class are static. Invoking one of the static methods performs the operation on the currently running thread.

Function	Description
public static void yield()	Causes the currently running thread to yield to any other threads of the same priority that are waiting to be scheduled.
public static void sleep(long millisec)	Causes the currently running thread to block for at least the specified number of milliseconds.
public static boolean holdsLock(Object x)	Returns true if the current thread holds the lock on the given Object.
public static Thread currentThread()	Returns a reference to the currently running thread, which is the thread that invokes this method.
public static void dumpStack())	Prints the stack trace for the currently running thread, which is useful when debugging a multithreaded application.

Example

The following SampleThreadClassDemo program demonstrates some of these methods of the Thread class. Consider a class PrintMessage which implements Runnable:

```java
// File Name: PrintMessage.java
// create a thread by implementing Runnable
public class PrintMessage implements Runnable{
    private String message;
    public PrintMessage(String message){
        this.message = message;
    }
    public void run(){
        while(true){
            System.out.println(message);
        }
    }
}
```

Following is another class which extends Thread class:

```java
// File Name: GuessingANumber.java
// create a thread to extend Thread
public class GuessingANumber extends Thread{
    private int number;
    public GuessingANumber(int number){
        this.number = number;
    }
    public void run(){
        int counter = 0, guess = 0;
```

```
  do{
    guess = (int) (Math.random() * 100 + 1);
        System.out.println(this.getName() + " guesses " + guess);
      counter++;
    }while(guess != number);
    System.out.println("** Guess Correct! " + this.getName() + " in " + counter + " guesses.**");
  }
}
```

Following is the main program which makes use of above defined classes:

```
// File Name: SampleThreadClassDemo.java
public class SampleThreadClassDemo{
  public static void main(String [] args){
    Runnable hello = new PrintMessage("Hello");
    Thread th1 = new Thread(hello);
    th1.setDaemon(true);
    th1.setName("hello");
    System.out.println("Starting hello thread...");
    th1.start();
    Runnable bye = new PrintMessage("Bye Bye");
    Thread th2= new Thread(bye);
    th2.setPriority(Thread.MIN_PRIORITY);
    th2.setDaemon(true);
    System.out.println("Starting Bye thread...");
    th2.start();
    System.out.println("Starting thread3...");
    Thread th3= new GuessingANumber(27);
    th3.start();
    try{
      th3.join();
    }catch(InterruptedException e){
      System.out.println("Thread interrupted.");
    }
    System.out.println("Starting Thread 4...");
    Thread th4 = new GuessingANumber(75);
    th4.start();
    System.out.println("main() is ending...");
  }
}
```

This would produce the following result. You can try this example again and again and you would get different result every time.

```
Starting hello thread...
Starting Bye thread...
Hello
Hello
Hello
Hello
Hello
Hello
Bye Bye
Bye Bye
Bye Bye
Bye Bye
Bye Bye
.......
```

Question-42   Explain how synchronization works in *Java*.

Answer: Synchronization in *Java* is an important concept since *Java* is multi-threaded language where multiple threads run parallel to complete program execution. Synchronization in *Java* is possible by using java keyword "synchronized" and "volatile". In Summary *Java synchronized* keyword provides following functionality essential for concurrent programming:

- *synchronized* keyword in *Java* provides locking which ensures mutual exclusive access of shared resource and prevents data race.
- *synchronized* keyword also prevents reordering of code statement by compiler which can cause subtle concurrent issue if we don't use synchronized or volatile keyword.

1.13 Basic Concepts of OOPS

- *synchronized* keyword involves locking and unlocking. Before entering into synchronized method or block thread needs to acquire the lock at this point it reads data from main memory than cache and when it releases the lock it flushes write operation into main memory which eliminates memory inconsistency errors.

Synchronized keyword in *Java*: Any code written in synchronized block in *Java* will be mutually exclusive and can only be executed by one thread at a time. We can have both static synchronized method and non-static synchronized method and synchronized blocks in *Java* but we cannot have synchronized variable in *Java*. Using *synchronized* keyword with variable is illegal and will result in compilation error.

Instead of *Java* synchronized variable we can have *Java* volatile variable, which will instruct JVM threads to read value of volatile variable from main memory and don't cache it locally. Block synchronization in *Java* is preferred over method synchronization in *Java* because by using block synchronization we only need to lock the critical section of code instead of whole method. Since *Java* synchronization comes with cost of performance we need to synchronize only part of code, which absolutely needs to be synchronized.

Example of synchronized method in *Java*: Using synchronized keyword along with method is easy. It can be done by applying synchronized keyword in front of method. What we need to be vigilant about is that static synchronized method locks on class object lock and non-static synchronized method locks on current object (this).

So it's possible that both static and non-static *Java* synchronized methods run in parallel. This is the common mistake a naive developer does while writing *Java* synchronized code.

```
public class Counter{
    private static int count = 0;
    public static synchronized int getCount(){
      return count;
    }
    public synchoronized setCount(int count){
      this.count = count;
    }
}
```

In this example of *Java* synchronization code is not properly synchronized because both getCount() and setCount() are not locked on same object and can run in parallel. This results in incorrect count. Here getCount() will lock in Counter.class object while setCount() will lock on current object (this). To properly synchronize this code in *Java* you need to either make both methods static or non-static or use *Java* synchronized block instead of *Java* synchronized method.

Example of synchronized block in Java: Using synchronized block in *Java* is also similar to using synchronized keyword in methods. Only important thing to note here is that if object used to lock synchronized block of code, Singleton.class in the example below is null then *Java* synchronized block will throw a NullPointerException.

```
public class Singleton{
    private static volatile Singleton _instance;
    public static Singleton getInstance(){
      if(_instance == null){
        synchronized(Singleton.class){
          if(_instance == null)
            _instance = new Singleton();
        }
      }
      return _instance;
}
```

This is a classic example of double checked locking in Singleton [refer *Design Interview Questions* chapter for more details]. In this example of *Java* synchronized code we have synchronized only critical section (part of code which is creating instance of singleton) and saved some performance because if we synchronize the whole method every call of this method will be blocked while you only need to create instance on first call.

Important points of synchronized keyword in Java:

- Synchronized keyword in *Java* is used to provide mutual exclusive access of a shared resource with multiple threads in *Java*. Synchronization in *Java* guarantees that no two threads can execute a synchronized method which requires same lock simultaneously or concurrently.
- You can use *Java* synchronized keyword only on synchronized method or synchronized block.
- Whenever a thread enters a *Java* synchronized method or block it acquires a lock and whenever it leaves *Java* synchronized method or block it releases the lock. Lock is released even if thread leaves synchronized method after completion or due to any *Error* or *Exception*.
- *Java* Thread acquires an object level lock when it enters an instance synchronized java method and acquires a class level lock when it enters static synchronized *Java* method.

- *Java* synchronized keyword is re-entrant in nature. It means if a *Java* synchronized method calls another synchronized method, which requires same lock then current thread which is holding lock can enter that method without acquiring lock.
- *Java* Synchronization will throw NullPointerException if object used in *Java* synchronized block is null e.g. synchronized (myInstance) will throws NullPointerException if myInstance is null.
- One Major disadvantage of *Java* synchronized keyword is that it doesn't allow concurrent read which you can implement using

java.util.concurrent.locks.ReentrantLock.

- One limitation of *Java* synchronized keyword is that it can only be used to control access of shared object within the same JVM. If we have more than one JVM and need to synchronize access to a shared file system or database, the *Java* synchronized keyword is not adequate. We need to implement a kind of global lock for that.
- Java synchronized keyword incurs performance cost. Synchronized method in Java is very slow and can degrade performance. So use synchronization in java when it is absolutely required and consider using java synchronized block for synchronizing critical section only.
- Java synchronized block is better than java synchronized method in java because by using synchronized block you can only lock critical section of code and avoid locking whole method, which can possibly degrade performance. A good example of java synchronization around this concept is *getInstance()* method *Singleton* class.
  - It's possible that both static synchronized and non-static synchronized method can run simultaneously or concurrently because they lock on different object.
  - *Java synchronized* code could result in deadlock or starvation while accessing by multiple thread if synchronization is not implemented correctly. To know how to avoid deadlock in java see here.
  - According to the *Java* language specification you cannot use java synchronized keyword with constructor. It's illegal and results in compilation errors. So you cannot synchronize constructor in Java, which seems logical because other threads cannot see the object being created until the thread creating it has finished it.
  - You cannot apply java synchronized keyword with variables and cannot use Java volatile keyword with method.
  - Java.util.concurrent.locks extends capability provided by java synchronized keyword for writing more sophisticated programs since they offer more capabilities e.g. Reentrancy and interruptible locks.
  - *Java synchronized* keyword also synchronizes memory.
  - Important method related to synchronization in Java are wait(), notify() and notifyAll() which is defined in Object class.
  - Do not synchronize on non-final field on synchronized block in *Java* because reference of non-final field may change any time and then different threads might synchronize on different objects i.e. no synchronization at all. example of synchronizing on non-final fields:

```
private String lock = new String("lock");
synchronized(lock){
    System.out.println("locking on :" + lock);
}
```

If you write synchronized code like above in *Java* you may get a warning "Synchronization on non-final field" in IDE like Netbeans and InteliJ.
  - It's not recommended to use String object as lock in Java synchronized block because string is immutable object and literal string and interned string get stored in String pool. So by any chance if any other part of code or any third party library uses same String as it's lock then they both will be locked on same object despite being completely unrelated which could result in unexpected behavior and bad performance. Instead of String object it is advised to use new Object() for Synchronization in Java on synchronized block.

```
private static final String LOCK = "lock";   //not recommended
private static final Object OBJ_LOCK = new Object(); //better
public void process() {
    synchronized(LOCK) {
        ........
    }
}
```

  - From *Java* library Calendar and SimpleDateFormat classes are not thread-safe and requires external synchronization in Java to be used in multi-threaded environment.

Question-43   Solve producer/consumer problem using *Java* threads.

Answer: refer *Operating System Concepts* chapter.

Question-44   What is the size of empty class in $C + +$, *Java*?

Answer: Since each object needs to have a unique address (also defined in the standard) we can't really have zero sized objects. Imagine an array of zero sized objects. Because they have zero size they all line up on the same address location. So, it is easier to say that objects cannot have zero size. Even though an object has a non-zero size, if it actually takes up zero room it does not need to increase the size of derived class.

```
#include <iostream>
class A {};
class B {};
class C: public A, B {};
int main() {
    std::cout << sizeof(A) << "\n"; //Prints 1
    std::cout << sizeof(B) << "\n"; //Prints 1
    std::cout << sizeof(C) << "\n"; //Prints 1
}
```

Question-45   What's the value of i++ + i++ in C and C + +?

Answer: It's undefined. Basically, in C and C + +, if we read a variable twice in an expression where you also write it, the result is undefined. Don't do that. Another example is: v[i] = i++; Related example: func(v[i],i++);

Here, the result is undefined because the order of evaluation of function arguments is undefined. Having the order of evaluation *undefined* is claimed to yield better performing code.

Question-46   What is the difference between *int main*() and *int main(void)* in C and C++?

Answer: In C++, there is no difference. In C++ having a function func(void) and func() is the same thing. In C, in a prototype (not in C++ though) an empty argument list means that the function could take any number of arguments (in the definition of a function, it means no arguments). In C++, an empty parameter list means no arguments. In C, to get no arguments, you have to use void.

```
void foo(void);
```

That is the correct way to say *no parameters* in C, and it also works in C++. But:

```
void foo();
```

Means different things in C and C++! In C it means "could take any number of parameters of unknown types", and in C++ it means the same as foo(void).

Question-47   What is the difference between *String* and *StringBuffer* classes in *Java*?

Answer: *Java* provides the StringBuffer and String classes, and the String class is used to manipulate character strings that cannot be changed. Simply stated, objects of type String are read only and immutable. The *StringBuffer* class is used to represent characters that can be modified.

The significant performance difference between these two classes is that *StringBuffer* is faster than *String* when performing simple concatenations. In *String* manipulation code, character strings are routinely concatenated. Using the *String* class, concatenations are typically performed as follows:

```
String str = new String ("Testing the ");
str += "strings!!";
```

If we were to use *StringBuffer* to perform the same concatenation, we would need code that looks like this:

```
StringBuffer str = new StringBuffer ("Testing the ");
str.append("strings!!");
```

Developers usually assume that the first example above is more efficient because they think that the second example, which uses the append method for concatenation, is more costly than the first example, which uses the + operator to concatenate two *String* objects.

Question-48   What is the difference between "==" and *equals(...)* method in *Java*? What is the difference between shallow comparison and deep comparison of objects?

Answer: The == returns true, if the variable reference points to the same object in memory. This is a "shallow comparison". The *equals*() - returns the results of running the *equals*() method of a user supplied class, which compares the attribute values.

The *equals*() method provides "deep comparison" by checking if two objects are logically equal as opposed to the shallow comparison provided by the operator ==. If *equals*() method does not exist in a user supplied class than the inherited Object class's *equals*() method is run which evaluates if the references point to the same object in memory. The object.equals() works just like the "==" operator (i.e. shallow comparison).

Question-49   What is serialization? How would you exclude a field of a class from serialization or what is a transient variable?

Answer: Serialization is a process of reading or writing an object. It is a process of saving an object's state to a sequence of bytes, as well as a process of rebuilding those bytes back into a live object at some future time. An object is marked serializable by implementing the *java.io.Serializable* interface, which is only a marker interface -- it simply allows the serialization mechanism to verify that the class can be persisted, typically to a file.

Transient variables cannot be serialized. The fields marked transient in a serializable object will not be transmitted in the byte stream. An example would be a file handle, a database connection, a system thread etc. Such objects are only meaningful locally. So they should be marked as transient in a serializable class.

Question-50   What is the difference between *final*, *finally* and *finalize()* in *Java*?

Answer: *final* - constant declaration. *Final* class cannot be inherited and final mehod cannot be overridden. *finally* handles exception. The finally block is optional and provides a mechanism to clean up regardless of what happens within the try block (except *System.exit*(0) call). Use the *finally* block to close files or to release other system resources like database connections, statements etc.

finalize() - method helps in garbage collection. A method that is invoked before an object is discarded by the garbage collector, allowing it to clean up its state. Should not be used to release non-memory resources like file handles, sockets, database connections etc. because Java has only a finite number of these resources and you do not know when the garbage collection is going to kick in to release these non-memory resources through the finalize() method.

Question-51   What do you know about the *Java garbage collector*?

Answer: Each time an object is created in Java, it goes into the area of memory known as heap. The Java heap is called the *garbage collectable heap*. The garbage collection cannot be forced. The garbage collector runs in low memory situations. When it runs, it releases the memory allocated by an unreachable object. The garbage collector runs on a low priority daemon (i.e. background) thread. We can nicely ask the garbage collector to collect garbage by calling *System.gc*() but we can't force it.

An object's life has no meaning unless something has reference to it. If we can't reach it then we can't ask it to do anything. Then the object becomes unreachable and the garbage collector will figure it out. Java automatically collects all the unreachable objects periodically and releases the memory consumed by those unreachable objects to be used by the future reachable objects.

Question-52   What is the diamond problem? Does it exist in Java? If so, how can it be avoided?

Answer: Taking a look at the figure below helps in explaining the diamond problem. In the diagram above, we have 2 classes B and C that derive from the same class – which would be class A in the diagram above. We also have class D that derives from both B and C by using multiple inheritance. You can see in the figure above that the classes essentially form the shape of a diamond – which is why this problem is called the diamond problem.

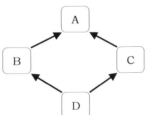

The problem with having an inheritance hierarchy like the one shown in the diagram above is that when we instantiate an object of class D, any calls to method definitions in class A will be ambiguous – because it's not sure whether to call the version of the method derived from class B or class C.

Java does not have multiple inheritance

But, wait one second. Java does not have multiple inheritance! This means that Java is not at risk of suffering the consequences of the diamond problem. However, C++ does have multiple inheritance, and if you want to read more about the diamond problem in C++, check this out: Diamond problem in C++.

Java uses interfaces to support multiple inheritance

Java has interfaces which do allow it to mimic multiple inheritance. Although interfaces give us something similar to multiple inheritance, the implementation of those interfaces is singly (as opposed to multiple) inherited. This means that problems like the diamond problem – in which the compiler is confused as to which method to use – will not occur in Java.

Question-53   What is the difference between declaring a variable and defining a variable?

Answer: In declaration we just mention the type of the variable and its name. We do not initialize it. But defining means declaration and initialization. For example, *String s;* is just a declaration while *String s = new String* ("*abcd*"); and *String s* = "*abcd*"; are both definitions.

Question-54   What is serialization?

Answer: Serialization is a mechanism by which you can save the state of an object by converting it to a byte stream.

Question-55   How do we serialize an object to a file?

1.13 Basic Concepts of OOPS

Answer: The class whose instances are to be serialized should implement an interface *Serializable*. Then you pass the instance to the *ObjectOutputStream* which is connected to a *fileoutputstream*. This will save the object to a file.

Question-56   Explain JDBC.

Answer: JDBC is the short for Java Database Connectivity. It is a Java API that enables Java programs to execute SQL statements. This allows Java programs to interact with any SQL-compliant database. Since nearly all relational database management systems (DBMSs) support SQL, and because Java itself runs on most platforms, JDBC makes it possible to write a single database application that can run on different platforms and interact with different DBMSs.

JDBC is similar to ODBC (Open DataBase Connectivity), but is designed specifically for Java programs, whereas ODBC is language-independent. ODBC a standard database access method developed by the SQL Access group in 1992. The goal of ODBC is to make it possible to access any data from any application, regardless of which database management system (DBMS) is handling the data.

ODBC manages this by inserting a middle layer, called a *database driver*, between an application and the DBMS. The purpose of this layer is to translate the application's data queries into commands that the DBMS understands. For this to work, both the application and the DBMS must be ODBC-compliant -- that is, the application must be capable of issuing ODBC commands and the DBMS must be capable of responding to them.

Creating JDBC Application

There are six steps involved in building a JDBC application which we are going to discuss in this section:

Step 1: Import The Packages

This requires that you include the packages containing the JDBC classes needed for database programming. Most often, using import java.sql.* will suffice as follows:

```
import java.sql.*;
```

Step 2: Register The JDBC Driver

This requires that you initialize a driver so you can open a communications channel with the database. Following is the code snippet to achieve this:

```
Class.forName("com.mysql.jdbc.Driver");
```

Step 3: Open a Connection

This requires using the DriverManager.getConnection() method to create a Connection object, which represents a physical connection with the database as follows:

```
// Privide authentication parameters
static final String USER = "username";
static final String PASS = "password";
System.out.println("Connecting to database...");
conn = DriverManager.getConnection(DB_URL,USER,PASS);
```

Step 4: Execute a Query

This requires using an object of type Statement or PreparedStatement for building and submitting an SQL statement to the database as follows:

```
System.out.println("Creating statement...");
stmt = conn.createStatement();
String sql;
sql = "SELECT id, firstName, lastName, age FROM Students";
ResultSet rs = stmt.executeQuery(sql);
```

If there is an SQL UPDATE,INSERT or DELETE statement required, then following code snippet would be required:

```
System.out.println("Creating statement...");
stmt = conn.createStatement();
String sql;
sql = "DELETE FROM Students";
ResultSet rs = stmt.executeUpdate(sql);
```

Step 5: Extract Data From Result Set

This step is required in case you are fetching data from the database. You can use the appropriate ResultSet.getXXX() method to retrieve the data from the result set as follows:

```
while(rs.next()){
   //Retrieve by column name
   int id  = rs.getInt("id");
```

1.13 Basic Concepts of OOPS

```
    int age = rs.getInt("age");
    String firstName = rs.getString("first");
    String lastName = rs.getString("last");

    //Display values
    System.out.print("ID: " + id);
    System.out.print(", Age: " + age);
    System.out.print(", First Name: " + firstName);
    System.out.println(", Last Name: " + lastName);
}
```

Step 6: Clean Up The Environment

You should explicitly close all database resources versus relying on the JVM's garbage collection as follows:

```
//Step 6: Clean-up environment
rs.close();
stmt.close();
conn.close();
```

Sample JDBC Program

Based on the above steps, we can have following consolidated sample code which we can use as a template while writing our JDBC code:

```
//Step 1. Import required packages
import java.sql.*;
public class FirstExample {
    // JDBC driver name and database URL
    static final String JDBC_DRIVER = "com.mysql.jdbc.Driver";
    static final String DB_URL = "jdbc:mysql://localhost/EMP";

    // Database credentials
    static final String USER = "username";
    static final String PASS = "password";

    public static void main(String[] args) {
    Connection conn = null;
    Statement stmt = null;
    try{
        //Step 2: Register JDBC driver
        Class.forName("com.mysql.jdbc.Driver");

        //Step 3: Open a connection
        System.out.println("Connecting to database...");
        conn = DriverManager.getConnection(DB_URL,USER,PASS);

        //Step 4: Execute a query
        System.out.println("Creating statement...");
        stmt = conn.createStatement();
        String sql;
        sql = "SELECT id, first, last, age FROM Students";
        ResultSet rs = stmt.executeQuery(sql);

        //Step 5: Extract data from result set
        while(rs.next()){
            //Retrieve by column name
            int id  = rs.getInt("id");
            int age = rs.getInt("age");
            String firstName = rs.getString("firstName");
            String lastName = rs.getString("lastName");

            //Displaying values
            System.out.print("ID: " + id);
            System.out.print(", Age: " + age);
            System.out.print(", First Name: " + firstName);
            System.out.println(", Last Name: " + lastName);
        }
        //Step 6: Clean-up environment
        rs.close();
            stmt.close();
    conn.close();
    }catch(SQLException se){
        //Handle errors for JDBC
```

```
          se.printStackTrace();
      }catch(Exception e){
        //Handle errors for Class.forName
        e.printStackTrace();
      }finally{
        //finally block used to close resources
        try{
          if(stmt!=null)
            stmt.close();
        }catch(SQLException se2){
        }
        try{
          if(conn!=null)
            conn.close();
        }catch(SQLException se){
          se.printStackTrace();
        }
      }
    }
  }
}
```

Question-57   What is the difference between const int*, const int * const, int const * in C/C++?

Answer: Read it backwards...

int*	pointer to int
int const *	pointer to const int
int * const	const pointer to int
int const * const	const pointer to const int

For example, consider the following declarations:

"const Item* ptr", "Item* const ptr" and "const Item* const ptr"

We have to read pointer declarations right-to-left.

1. *const Item * ptr* means "ptr points to an Item that is const" — that is, the Item object can't be changed via ptr.
2. *Item * const ptr* means "ptr is a const pointer to an Item" — that is, you can change the Item object via ptr, but you can't change the pointer ptr itself.
3. *const Item * const ptr* means "ptr is a const pointer to a const Item" — that is, you can't change the pointer ptr itself, nor can you change the Item object via ptr.

Now the first const can be on either side of the type so:

```
const int * == int const *
const int * const == int const * const
```

Question-58   What are the differences between .dll and .lib?

Answer: A *dll* is a library of functions that are shared among other executable programs. Just look in your windows/system32 directory and you will find many of them. When your program creates a *dll* it also normally creates a lib file so that the application *.exe program can resolve symbols that are declared in the *dll*.

A .lib is a library of functions that are statically linked to a program. They are not shared by other programs. Each program that links with a *.lib file has all the code in that file. If you have two programs *X.exe* and *Y.exe* that link with *Z.lib* then each *X* and *Y* will both contain the code in *Z.lib*.

How you create dlls and libs depend on the compiler you use. Each compiler does it differently.

Question-59   What is the difference between big and little endian?

Answer: The big-endian and little-endian refer to which bytes are most significant in multi-byte data types and describe the order in which a sequence of bytes is stored in a computer memory.

If the hardware is built so that the lowest, least significant byte of a multi-byte scalar is stored *first*, at the lowest memory address, then the hardware is said to be *little-endian*; the *little* end of the integer gets stored first, and the next bytes get stored in higher (increasing) memory locations. Little-Endian byte order is "littlest end goes first (to the littlest address)".

Machines such as the Intel/AMD x86, Digital VAX, and Digital Alpha, handle scalars in Little-Endian form.

If the hardware is built so that the highest, most significant byte of a multi-byte scalar is stored *first*, at the lowest memory address, then the hardware is said to be *big-endian*; the *big* end of the integer gets stored first, and the next bytes get stored in higher (increasing) memory locations. Big-Endian byte order is "biggest end goes first (to the lowest address)".

1.13 Basic Concepts of OOPS

Machines such as IBM mainframes, the Motorola 680x0, Sun SPARC, PowerPC, and most RISC machines, handle scalars in Big-Endian form.

Four-byte Integer Example

Consider the four-byte integer 0x44332211. The "*little*" end byte, the lowest or least significant byte, is 0x11, and the "*big*" end byte, the highest or most significant byte, is 0x44. The two memory storage patterns for the four bytes are:

Four-Byte Integer: 0x44332211

Memory address	Big-Endian byte value	Little-Endian byte value
104	11	44
103	22	33
102	33	22
101	44	11

Here is sample code to determine what is the type of your machine

```
#include <stdio.h>
int main(void) {
    int num = 1;
    if(*(char *)&num == 1){
        printf("\nLittle-Endian\n");
    }
    else {
        printf("Big-Endian\n");
    }
    return 0;
}
```

Question-60   Explain the concept of C++ Containers and STL.

Answer: The C++ STL (Standard Template Library) is a set of C++ template classes to provides general-purpose templatized classes and functions that implement many popular and commonly used algorithms and data structures like vectors, lists, queues, and stacks. A container is an object that stores a collection of other objects (its elements). They are implemented as class templates, which allows a great flexibility in the types supported as elements.

The container manages the storage space for its elements and provides member functions to access them, either directly or through iterators (reference objects with similar properties to pointers).

Containers replicate structures very commonly used in programming: dynamic arrays (vector), queues (queue), stacks (stack), heaps (priority_queue), linked lists (list), trees (set), associative arrays (map), etc...

Many containers have several member functions in common, and share functionalities. The decision of which type of container to use for a specific need does not generally depend only on the functionality offered by the container, but also on the efficiency of some of its members (complexity). This is especially true for linear containers, which offer different trade-offs in complexity between inserting/removing elements and accessing them.

Container Classes	
Sequences	• *vector*: Vectors are sequence containers representing arrays that can change in size. • *deque*: Array which supports insertion/removal of elements at beginning or end of array. It is a double ended queue with pop and push at both ends. • *list*: Linked list of variables, struct or objects. It is a randomly changing sequence of items.
Associative Containers	• *set* (duplicate data not allowed in set), multiset (duplication allowed): It is an unordered collection of items. • *map* (unique keys), multimap (duplicate keys allowed): Associative key-value pair held in balanced binary tree structure. An collection of pairs of items indexed by the first one.
Container Adapters	• *stack* [LIFO]: A sequence of items with pop and push at one end only. • *queue* [FIFO]: A Sequence of items with pop and push at opposite ends. • *priority$_{queue}$*: It returns element with highest priority.
String	• *string*: Character strings and manipulation. • *rope*: String storage and manipulation.
Bits	• *bitset*: Contains a more intuitive method of storing and manipulating bits.
Operations/Utilities	• *iterator*: STL class to represent position in an STL container. An iterator is declared to be associated with a single container class type. • *algorithm*: Routines to find, count, sort, search, ... elements in container classes. • *auto_ptr*: Class to manage memory pointers and avoid memory leaks.

Sample Code:

```cpp
#include <iostream>
#include <vector>
#include <string>
using namespace std;
main(){
  vector<string> stk;
  stk.push_back("The number is 100");
  stk.push_back("The number is 200");
  stk.push_back("The number is 300");
  cout << "Loop by index:" << endl;
  int i;
  for(i=0; i < stk.size(); i++){
    cout << stk[i] << endl;
  }
  cout << endl << "Constant Iterator:" << endl;
  vector<string>::const_iterator ci;
  for(ci=stk.begin(); ci!=stk.end(); ci++){
    cout << *ci << endl;
  }
  cout << endl << "Reverse Iterator:" << endl;
  vector<string>::reverse_iterator ri;
  for(ri=stk.rbegin(); ri!=stk.rend(); ++ri){
    cout << *ri << endl;
  }
  cout << endl << "Output:" << endl;
  cout << stk.size() << endl;
  cout << stk[2] << endl;
  swap(stk[0], stk[2]);
  cout << stk[2] << endl;
}
```

Question-61   Explain the concept of smart pointers in C++.

Answer: The power of C++ comes with pointers and objects. In C++, pointers are very commonly used, but the built-in pointers may give unexpected results if they were not used properly. When a built-in pointer is created, it is not automatically set to NULL. If an uninitialized pointer is then compared to NULL (*pointer == NULL*) the test will pass, and any dereferencing will result in undefined behavior.

It's fairly easy to remember to set a pointer to NULL when you create it, so this issue isn't that important, but what if you call a function that returns a pointer? If the memory was allocated on the heap (i.e. came from a call to *new* or *malloc*) then someone has to delete it, or it will be a memory leak. It's up to the programmer to read the documentation and figure it out.

What about in a multi-threaded environment? It's very easy for two threads to share the same data, but what if both of them are using the same pointer, and one thread calls delete on the pointer while the other thread is still using it?

Finally, if you're using exceptions, you've probably had a pretty hard time making sure that each time an exception is thrown, all of the allocated memory gets freed. Take the following code:

```cpp
try{
  int* ptr = new int;
  Foo();
  .
  .
  delete ptr;
}
```

What if *Foo* throws an exception? You have to make sure that each and every exception that *Foo* (or any function called by *Foo*) throws will be caught, in order to *delete ptr*; otherwise you'll have a memory leak. Certainly there must be a better solution than using these built-in pointers. The answer for such problems is smart pointers.

The idea behind this *smart pointer* implementation is to have a set of objects that wrap the functionality of a built-in pointer. These smart pointers either *point* to an object or they equal NULL (they never point to memory that has been deleted and they are always initialized).

- The pointers must always point to valid memory, or be NULL
- The pointers will be reference counted and handle freeing the memory being pointed to (so they can be exception safe while at the same time eliminating memory leaks)
- The pointers should be as similar to the built-in pointers as possible

Also, in order for the *smart pointers* to act like the built-in types, it was necessary for the implementation to be non-intrusive. An intrusive smart pointer is one that requires a common base class be used in any object that will be pointed to. When you create your custom objects, you would have to inherit from a base class the gives reference counting functionality to your object. This approach only works for user defined types, and the *smart pointers* would never be able to point to built-in types (like int and float). A non-intrusive approach requires no changes to a defined type (whether built-in or user defined) because the pointer has a more intelligent means of keeping track of the reference count.

With smart pointers, the programmer doesn't have to worry about memory management (never see the word *delete* again!), the pointers are copy safe, thread safe, exception safe, and they never point to memory that has already been deleted. If used properly, they avoid circular references, and they work almost identically to the built-in pointers.

Question-62   Explain the concept of auto_ptr in C++.

Answer: The standard C++ library comes with a smart pointer called auto_ptr, for "automatic pointer." The auto_ptr smart pointer owns the object it holds a pointer to. That is, it releases the memory associated to it upon destruction; it does not do any allocation by itself, nor does it keep a reference counter of the memory involved.

The auto_ptr class overloads the * and -> operators so as to allow transparent access to the dynamic object. To access the raw pointer itself, use the get method. Consider a simple example:

```
std::auto_ptr<int> ptr1(new int(5));
*ptr1 = 4;
std::cout << *ptr1 << std::endl;
int* ptr2 = ptr1.get();
*ptr2 = 3;
std::cout << *ptr1 << ", " << *ptr2 << std::endl;
```

It is important to note in the example above that auto_ptr's constructor cannot fail (it is declared as throws()) If it could, the code would need to be more complex in order to catch those failures, defeating in part the purpose of the smart pointer. The automatic pointer also provides the release method, which detaches itself from the memory object, returning a raw pointer to it. This allows the use of an automatic pointer in a critical section only, falling back to manual management once that delicate code is over. As an example, imagine a function that returns a raw pointer to a dynamically allocated object. This function needs to do multiple initialization tasks and has several exit points if errors happen. You can use an automatic pointer to simplify its code:

```
foo * get_new_foo(void){
    std::auto_ptr<foo> obj(new foo);
    // The following two operations can raise an exception.
    // We need not care about it thanks to the smart pointer.
    obj->do_something();
    obj->do_something_else();
    // We are done. The caller is only interested in the raw
    // pointer, which we can safely return now.
    return obj.release();
}
```

Automatic pointers are not copyable. If the developer attempts to copy an instance of auto_ptr, the object it points to will be transferred to the new smart pointer, invalidating the old one. Therefore, using this class together with STL collections is dangerous; don't do it, because it does not follow the required semantics.

```
std::auto_ptr<int> ptr1(new int(5));
// ptr1 is valid and can be accessed.
*ptr1 = 4;
std::auto_ptr<int> ptr2(ptr1);
// ptr2 now owns the dynamically allocated integer, so we can access it.
*ptr2 = 3;
// However, ptr1 is now longer valid; the following crashes the program.
*ptr1 = 2;
// At last, the following has undefined behavior.
int* i = new int(1);
std::auto_ptr<int> ptr3(i);
std::auto_ptr<int> ptr4(i);
```

Furthermore, if two automatic pointers hold a reference to the same memory object, the behavior is undefined (but typically the application will simply crash).

Note: In the C++11 standard, $std::unique\_ptr$ is used instead of $std::auto\_ptr$.

Question-63   What is Serialization and Deserialization in Java?

Answer: We can convert a Java object to an Stream that is called *Serialization*. Once an object is converted to Stream, it can be saved to file or send over the network or used in socket connections. The object should implement Serializable interface and we can use java.io.ObjectOutputStream to write object to file or to any OutputStream object. The process of converting stream data created through serialization to Object is called *deserialization*.

Question-64   Why Java is not pure Object Oriented language?

Answer: Java is not said to be pure object oriented because it support primitive types such as int, byte, short, long etc. I believe it brings simplicity to the language while writing our code. Obviously java could have wrapper objects for the primitive types but just for the representation, they would not have provided any benefit.

As we know, for all the primitive types we have wrapper classes such as Integer, Long etc. that provides some additional methods.

Question-65   What is difference between *path* and *classpath* variables?

Answer: PATH is an environment variable used by operating system to locate the executable. That's why when we install Java or want any executable to be found by OS, we need to add the directory location in the PATH variable.

Classpath is specific to java and used by java executables to locate class files. We can provide the classpath location while running java application and it can be a directory, ZIP files, JAR files etc.

Question-66   Can we have multiple public classes in a java source file?

Answer: We can't have more than one public class in a single java source file. A single source file can have multiple classes that are not public.

Question-67   What is final keyword?

Answer: *final* keyword is used with Class to make sure no other class can extend it, for example String class is final and we can't extend it.

We can use *final* keyword with methods to make sure child classes can't override it.

final keyword can be used with variables to make sure that it can be assigned only once. However the state of the variable can be changed, for example we can assign a final variable to an object only once but the object variables can change later on.

Java interface variables are by default *final* and *static*.

Question-68   What is static keyword?

Answer: *static* keyword can be used with class level variables to make it global i.e all the objects will share the same variable.

static keyword can be used with methods also. A *static method* can access only static variables of class and invoke only static methods of the class.

Question-69   What is finally and finalize in Java?

Answer: *finally* block is used with try-catch to put the code that you want to get executed always, even if any exception is thrown by the try-catch block. finally block is mostly used to release resources created in the try block.

finalize() is a special method in Object class that we can override in our classes. This method gets called by garbage collector when the object is getting garbage collected. This method is usually overridden to release system resources when object is garbage collected.

Question-70   Can we declare a class as static?

Answer: We can't declare a top-level class as static however an inner class can be declared as static. If inner class is declared as static, it's called static nested class.
Static nested class is same as any other top-level class and is nested for only packaging convenience.

Question-71   What is *static* import?

Answer: If we have to use any static variable or method from other class, usually we import the class and then use the method/variable with class name.

```
import java.lang.Math;
//inside class
double test = Math.PI * 5;
```

We can do the same thing by importing the static method or variable only and then use it in the class as if it belongs to it.

```
import static java.lang.Math.PI;
//no need to refer class now
double test = PI * 5;
```

Use of static import can cause confusion, so it's better to avoid it. Overuse of static import can make your program unreadable and unmaintainable.

1.13 Basic Concepts of OOPS

Question-72   What is Java *Annotations*?

Answer: Java Annotations provide information about the code and they have no direct effect on the code they annotate. Annotations are introduced in Java 5. Annotation is metadata about the program embedded in the program itself.

It can be parsed by the annotation parsing tool or by compiler. We can also specify annotation availability to either compile time only or till runtime also. Java Built-in annotations are @Override, @Deprecated and @SuppressWarnings.

Question-73   What is *anonymous inner* class?

Answer: A local inner class without name is known as anonymous inner class. An anonymous class is defined and instantiated in a single statement. Anonymous inner class always extend a class or implement an interface. Since an anonymous class has no name, it is not possible to define a constructor for an anonymous class. Anonymous inner classes are accessible only at the point where it is defined.

Question-74   What is *Classloader* in Java?

Answer: Java Classloader is the program that loads byte code program into memory when we want to access any class. We can create our own classloader by extending ClassLoader class and overriding loadClass(String name) method.

Question-75   What is this keyword?

Answer: this keyword provides reference to the current object and it's mostly used to make sure that object variables are used, not the local variables having same name.

```
//constructor
public Point(int x, int y) {
    this.x = x;
    this.y = y;
}
```

We can also use this keyword to invoke other constructors from a constructor.

```
public Rectangle() {
    this(0, 0, 0, 0);
}
public Rectangle(int width, int height) {
    this(0, 0, width, height);
}
public Rectangle(int x, int y, int width, int height) {
    this.x = x;
    this.y = y;
    this.width = width;
    this.height = height;
}
```

Question-76   What is the use of *System* class?

Answer: Java System Class is one of the core classes. One of the easiest way to log information for debugging is System.out.print() method.

System class is final and static so that we can't subclass and override it's behavior through inheritance. System class doesn't provide any public constructors, so we can't instantiate this class and that's why all of its methods are static.

Some of the utility methods of System class are for array copy, get current time, reading environment variables.

Question-77   What is *instanceof* keyword?

Answer: We can use *instanceof* keyword to check if an object belongs to a class or not. We should avoid it's usage as much as possible. Sample usage is:

```
public static void main(String args[]){
    Object str = new String("Test");
    if(str instanceof String){
        System.out.println("String value:"+str);
    }
    if(str instanceof Integer){
        System.out.println("Integer value:"+str);
    }
}
```

Since str is of type String at runtime, first *if* statement evaluates to true and second one to false.

Question-78   Can we have try without catch block in Java?

Answer: Yes, we can have try-finally statement and hence avoiding catch block.

1.13 Basic Concepts of OOPS

Question-79   What does super keyword do?

Answer: super keyword can be used to access *super* class method when you have overridden the method in the child class.

We can use *super* keyword to invoke super class constructor in child class constructor but in this case it should be the first statement in the constructor method.

```
package com.journaldev.access;
public class SuperClass {
    public SuperClass(){
    }
    public SuperClass(int i){}
    public void test(){
        System.out.println("super class test method");
    }
}
```

Use of super keyword can be seen in below child class implementation.

```
package com.journaldev.access;
public class ChildClass extends SuperClass {
    public ChildClass(String str){
        //access super class constructor with super keyword
        super();
        //access child class method
        test();
        //use super to access super class method
        super.test();
    }
    @Override
    public void test(){
        System.out.println("child class test method");
    }
}
```

Question-80   Explain the concepts of Java Servlets and JavaServer Pages (JSP).

Answer: JavaServer Pages (JSP) is a technology for developing web pages that support dynamic content which helps developers insert java code in HTML pages by making use of special JSP tags, most of which start with <% and end with %>.

A JavaServer Pages component is a type of Java servlet that is designed to fulfill the role of a user interface for a Java web application. Web developers write JSPs as text files that combine HTML or XHTML code, XML elements, and embedded JSP actions and commands.

Using JSP, you can collect input from users through web page forms, present records from a database or another source, and create web pages dynamically.

JSP tags can be used for a variety of purposes, such as retrieving information from a database or registering user preferences, accessing JavaBeans components, passing control between pages and sharing information between requests, pages etc.

JavaServer Pages often serve the same purpose as programs implemented using the Common Gateway Interface (CGI). But JSP offer several advantages in comparison with the CGI.

- Performance is significantly better because JSP allows embedding Dynamic Elements in HTML Pages itself instead of having a separate CGI files.
- JSP are always compiled before it's processed by the server unlike CGI/Perl which requires the server to load an interpreter and the target script each time the page is requested.
- JavaServer Pages are built on top of the Java Servlets API, so like Servlets, JSP also has access to all the powerful Enterprise Java APIs, including JDBC, JNDI, EJB, JAXP etc.
- JSP pages can be used in combination with servlets that handle the business logic, the model supported by Java servlet template engines.

Finally, JSP is an integral part of Java EE, a complete platform for enterprise class applications. This means that JSP can play a part in the simplest applications to the most complex and demanding.

How it works?

The web server (such as Apache) needs a JSP engine ie. container to process JSP pages. The JSP container (such as WebLogic) is responsible for intercepting requests for JSP pages. This tutorial makes use of Apache which has built-in JSP container to support JSP pages development.

A JSP container works with the Web server to provide the runtime environment and other services a JSP needs. It knows how to understand the special elements that are part of JSPs.

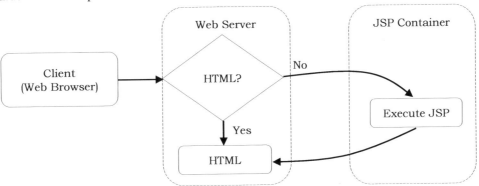

The following steps explain how the web server creates the web page using JSP:

- As with a normal page, your browser sends an HTTP request to the web server.
- The web server recognizes that the HTTP request is for a JSP page and forwards it to a JSP engine. This is done by using the URL or JSP page which ends with .jsp instead of .html.
- The JSP engine loads the JSP page from disk and converts it into a servlet content. This conversion is very simple in which all template text is converted to println( ) statements and all JSP elements are converted to Java code that implements the corresponding dynamic behavior of the page.
- The JSP engine compiles the servlet into an executable class and forwards the original request to a servlet engine.
- A part of the web server called the servlet engine loads the Servlet class and executes it. During execution, the servlet produces an output in HTML format, which the servlet engine passes to the web server inside an HTTP response.
- The web server forwards the HTTP response to your browser in terms of static HTML content.
- Finally web browser handles the dynamically generated HTML page inside the HTTP response exactly as if it were a static page.

JSP Life Cycle

A JSP life cycle can be defined as the entire process from its creation till the destruction which is similar to a servlet life cycle with an additional step which is required to compile a JSP into servlet. The following are the paths followed by a JSP.

- Compilation
- Initialization
- Execution
- Cleanup

1. *JSP Compilation*: When a browser asks for a JSP, the JSP engine first checks to see whether it needs to compile the page. If the page has never been compiled, or if the JSP has been modified since it was last compiled, the JSP engine compiles the page. The compilation process involves three steps:

- Parsing the JSP.
- Turning the JSP into a servlet.
- Compiling the servlet.

2. *JSP Initialization*: When a container loads a JSP it invokes the jspInit() method before servicing any requests. If you need to perform JSP-specific initialization, override the jspInit() method:

```
public void jspInit(){
  // Initialization code...
}
```

Typically initialization is performed only once and as with the servlet *init* method, you generally initialize database connections, open files, and create lookup tables in the jspInit method.

3. *JSP Execution*: This phase of the JSP life cycle represents all interactions with requests until the JSP is destroyed. Whenever a browser requests a JSP and the page has been loaded and initialized, the JSP engine invokes the _jspService() method in the JSP. The _jspService() method takes an HttpServletRequest and an HttpServletResponse as its parameters as follows:

```
void _jspService(HttpServletRequest request, HttpServletResponse response){
  // Service handling code...
}
```

The _jspService() method of a JSP is invoked once per a request and is responsible for generating the response for that request and this method is also responsible for generating responses to all seven of the HTTP methods ie. GET, POST, DELETE etc.

4.*JSP Cleanup*: The destruction phase of the JSP life cycle represents when a JSP is being removed from use by a container. The jspDestroy() method is the JSP equivalent of the destroy method for servlets. Override jspDestroy when you need to perform any cleanup, such as releasing database connections or closing open files. The jspDestroy() method has the following form:

```
public void jspDestroy(){
  // cleanup code
}
```

jspInit(), _jspService() and jspDestroy() are called the life cycle methods of the JSP.

Question-81   What are Javabeans?

Answer: Like Java applets, JavaBeans components (or "Beans") can be used to give World Wide Web pages (or other applications) interactive capabilities such as computing interest rates or varying page content based on user or browser characteristics.

From a user's point-of-view, a component can be a button that you interact with or a small calculating program that gets initiated when you press the button. From a developer's point-of-view, the button component and the calculator component are created separately and can then be used together or in different combinations with other components in different applications or situations.

When the components or Beans are in use, the properties of a Bean (for example, the background color of a window) are visible to other Beans and Beans that haven't "met" before can learn each other's properties dynamically and interact accordingly.

Beans are developed with a Beans Development Kit (BDK) from Oracle and can be run on any major operating system platform inside a number of application environments (called containers), including browsers, word processors, and other applications.

To build a component with JavaBeans, you write language statements using Oracle's Java programming language and include JavaBeans statements that describe component properties such as user interface characteristics and events that trigger a bean to communicate with other beans in the same container or elsewhere in the network. The enterprise version of Javabeans are usually called *EJB*.

Question-82   What is Hibernate Framework?

Answer: Hibernate is an object-relational mapping library for the Java language, providing a framework for mapping an object-oriented domain model to a traditional relational database.

Mapping Java classes to database tables is accomplished through the configuration of an XML file or by using Java Annotations.

Hibernate's primary feature is mapping from Java classes to database tables (and from Java data types to SQL data types). Hibernate also provides data query and retrieval facilities. It generates SQL calls and relieves the developer from manual result set handling and object conversion.

Question-83   What are Java Struts?

Answer: Struts is the most popular framework for developing Java based web applications. Struts is being developed as an open source project started by Apache. Struts framework is based on Model View Controller (MVC) architecture.

Question-84   Explain Java Spring Framework.

Answer: Spring is a Framework that provides comprehensive infrastructure support for developing Java applications. Spring handles the infrastructure so we can focus on our application.

Spring enables us to build applications from "plain old Java objects" (POJOs) and to apply enterprise services non-invasively to POJOs. This capability applies to the Java SE programming model and to full and partial Java EE.

Spring framework advantages:

- Make a Java method execute in a database transaction without having to deal with transaction APIs.
- Make a local Java method a remote procedure without having to deal with remote APIs.
- Make a local Java method a management operation without having to deal with JMX APIs.
- Make a local Java method a message handler without having to deal with JMS APIs.

Chapter-2

SCRIPTING LANGUAGES

2.1 Interpreter versus Compiler

By now, you might have understood that, any programming language is essentially a human-friendly formalism for writing instructions for a computer to follow. These instructions are at some point translated into machine language, which is what the computer really *understands*. Let's introduce at this point some concepts of execution of programs written in high level programming languages. As we have already seen, the only language that a computer can understand is the so called *machine language*. These languages are composed of a set of basic operations whose execution is implemented in the hardware of the processor.

A *Compiler* and *Interpreter* both carry out the same purpose – convert a high level language (like C, Java) instructions into the binary form which is understandable by computer hardware. However both compiler and interpreter have the same objective but they differ in the way they accomplish their task.

2.1.1 Compiler

A compiler is defined as a computer program that is used to convert high level instructions or language into a form that can be understood by the computer. Since computer can understand only in binary numbers so a compiler is used to fill the gap otherwise it would have been difficult for a human to find info in the 0 and 1 form.

Earlier the compilers were simple programs which were used to convert symbols into bits. The programs were also very simple and they contained a series of steps translated by hand into the data. However, this was a very time consuming process. So, some parts were programmed or automated. This formed the first compiler.

More sophisticated compliers are created using the simpler ones. With every new version, more rules added to it and a more natural language environment is created for the human programmer. The complier programs are evolving in this way which improves their ease of use.

There are specific compliers for certain specific languages or tasks. Compliers can be multiple or multistage pass. The first pass can convert the high level language into a language that is closer to computer language. Then the further passes can convert it into final stage for the purpose of execution.

2.1.2 Interpreter

The programs created in high level languages can be executed by using two different ways. The first one is the use of compiler and the other method is to use an interpreter. High level instruction or language is converted into intermediate from by an interpreter. The advantage of using an interpreter is that the high level instruction does not goes through compilation stage which can be a time consuming method. So, by using an interpreter, the high level program is executed directly. That is the reason why some programmers use interpreters while making small sections as this saves time.

Almost all high level programming languages have compilers and interpreters. But some languages like LISP and BASIC are designed in such a way that the programs made using them are executed by an interpreter.

2.1.3 Difference between compiler and interpreter

- A complier converts the high level instruction into machine language while an interpreter converts the high level instruction into an intermediate form.
- Before execution, entire program is executed by the compiler whereas after translating the first line, an interpreter then executes it and so on.
- List of errors is created by the compiler after the compilation process while an interpreter stops translating after the first error.
- An independent executable file is created by the compiler whereas interpreter is required by an interpreted program each time.

2.2 What Are Scripting Languages?

Languages like C and C++ allow a programmer to write code at a very detailed level which has *good execution* speed. But in many applications sometimes we would prefer to write at a higher level. For example, for text processing applications, the basic unit in C/C++ is a character, while for languages like *Perl* and *Python* the basic units are lines of text and words within lines. We can work with lines and words in C/C++, but one must go to greater effort to accomplish the same thing. C/C++ might give better speed, but if speed is *not* an issue, the convenience of a scripting language is very attractive.

The term scripting language has never been formally defined, but here are the typical characteristics:

- Used often for system administration.
- Very casual with regard to typing of variables, e.g. no distinction between integer, floating-point or string variables.
- Lots of high-level operations intrinsic to the language, e.g. stack push/pop.
- *Interpreted*, rather than being compiled to the instruction set of the host machine.

Today many people prefer *Python*, as it is much cleaner and more elegant. Our introduction here assumes knowledge of C/C++ programming. There will be a couple of places in which we describe things briefly in a Unix context, so some Unix knowledge would be helpful.

In this chapter we look at three scripting languages: Shell, PERL and Python.

2.3 Shell Scripting

Steve Bourne wrote the *Bourne* shell that appeared in the Bell Labs research version for Unix. Since then, many other shells have been written. The most commonly used shells are SH(Bourne SHell) CSH(C SHell) and KSH(*Korn* SHell), most of the other shells you encounter will be variants of these shells and will share the same syntax.

The various shells all have built in functions which allow for the creation of shell scripts, that is, the putting together of shell commands and constructs to automate what can be automated in order to make life easier for the user. We can specify the shell we want to interpret our shell script within the script itself by including the following in the first line.

```
#!/path/to/shell
```

Usually anything following (#) is *interpreted* as a comment and ignored but if it occurs on the first line with a (!) following it is treated as being special and the filename following the (!) is considered to point to the location of the shell that should interpret the script. When a script is *executed* it is being interpreted by an invocation of the shell that is running it. Hence the shell is said to be running non-interactively, when the shell is used *normally* it is said to be running interactively.

2.3.1 Command Redirection and Pipelines

By default a normal command accepts input from standard input, which we call *stdin*, standard input is the command line in the form of arguments passed to the command. By default a normal command directs its output to standard output, which we abbreviate to stdout, standard output is usually the console display.

For some commands this may be the desired action but other times we may wish to get our input for a command from somewhere other than stdin and direct our output to somewhere other than stdout. This is done by redirection:

- We use > to *redirect stdout* to a *file*, for instance, if we wanted to redirect a directory listing generated by the ls we could do the following:
  ```
  ls > file
  ```

- We use < to specify that we want the command immediately before the redirection symbol to get its *input* from the source specified immediately after the symbol, for instance, we could redirect the input to grep(which searches for strings within files) so that it comes from a file like this:
  ```
  grep searchterm < file
  ```

- We use >> to *append* stdout to a *file*, for instance, if we wanted to append the date to the end of a file we could redirect the output from date like so:
  ```
  date >> file
  ```

- One can redirect standard *error* (stderr) to a file by using 2>, if we wanted to redirect the standard error from commandA to a file we would use:
  ```
  commmandA 2>
  ```

Pipelines are another form of redirection that are used to chain commands so that powerful composite commands can be constructed, the pipe symbol '|' takes the stdout from the command preceding it and redirects it to the command following it:

```
ls -l | grep searchword | sort -r
```

The example above firsts requests a long (-l directory listing of the current directory using the *ls* command, the output from this is then piped to *grep* which filters out all the listings containing the searchword and then finally pipes this through to sort which then sorts the output in reverse (-r, sort then passes the output on normally to stdout.

2.3.2 Variables

When a script starts, all environment variables are turned into shell variables. New variables can be instantiated like this:

```
name=value
```

You must do it exactly like that, with *no spaces* either side of the equals sign, the name must only be made up of alphabetic characters, numeric characters and underscores, it cannot begin with a numeric character. Variables are referenced like this: $name, here is an example:

```
#!/bin/sh
msg1=Hello
msg2=World!
echo $msg1 $msg2
```

This would echo "Hello World!" to the console display, if you want to assign a string to a variable and the string contains spaces you should enclose the string in double quotes ("), the double quotes tell the shell to take the contents literally and ignore keywords, however, a few keywords are still processed. You can still use $ within a (") quoted string to include variables:

```
#!/bin/sh
msg1="one"
msg2="$msg1 two"
msg3="$msg2 three"
echo $msg3
```

Would echo "one two three" to the screen. The escape character can also be used within a double quoted section to output special characters, the escape character is "\", it outputs the character immediately following it literally so \\ would output \.

A special case is when the escape character is followed by a newline, the shell ignores the newline character which allows the spreading of long commands that must be executed on a single line in reality over multiple lines within the script. The escape character can be used anywhere else too.

Except within single quotes. Surrounding anything within single quotes causes it to be treated as literal text that is it will be passed on exactly as intended, this can be useful for sending command sequences to other files in order to create new scripts because the text between the single quotes will remain untouched. For example:

```
#!/bin/sh
echo 'msg="Hello World!"' > hello
echo 'echo $msg' >> hello
chmod 700 hello
./hello
```

This would cause "msg="Hello World!"" to be echoed and redirected to the file hello, "echo $msg" would then be echoed and redirected to the file hello but this time appended to the end. The chmod line changes the file permissions of hello so that we can execute it. The final line executes hello causing it output "Hello World". If we had not used literal quotes we never would have had to use escape characters to ensure that ($) and (") were echoed to the file, this makes the code a little clearer. A variable may be referenced like so ${VARIABLENAME}, this allows one to place characters immediately preceding the variable like ${VARIABLENAME}aaa without the shell interpreting *aaa* as being part of the variable name.

2.3.3 Command Line Arguments

Command line arguments are treated as special variables within the script, the reason I am calling them variables is because they can be changed with the shift command. The command line arguments are enumerated in the following manner $0, $1, $2, $3, $4, $5, $6, $7, $8 and $9. $0 is special in that it corresponds to the name of the script itself. $1 is the first argument, $2 is the second argument and so on.

To reference after the ninth argument you must enclose the number in brackets like this ${nn}. You can use the shift command to shift the arguments 1 variable to the left so that $2 becomes $1, $1 becomes $0 and so on, $0 gets scrapped because it has nowhere to go, this can be useful to process all the arguments using a loop, using one variable to reference the first argument and shifting until you have exhausted the arguments list.

As well as the command-line arguments there are some special built-in variables:

- $# represents the parameter count. Useful for controlling loop constructs that need to process each parameter.

- $@ expands to all the parameters separated by spaces. Useful for passing all the parameters to some other function or program.

- $- expands to the flags (options) the shell was invoked with. Useful for controlling program flow based on the flags set.

- $$ expands to the process id of the shell innovated to run the script. Useful for creating unique temporary filenames relative to this instantiation of the script.

2.3.4 Command Substitution

In the words of the shell manual "Command substitution allows the output of a command to be substituted in place of the command name itself". There are two ways this can be done. The first is to enclose the command like this:

```
$(command)
```

The second is to enclose the command in back quotes like this:

```
`command`
```

The command will be executed in a sub-shell environment and the standard output of the shell will replace the command substitution when the command completes.

2.3.5 Arithmetic Expansion

Arithmetic expansion is also allowed and comes in the form:

```
$((expression))
```

The value of the expression will replace the substitution. Eg:

```
!#/bin/sh
echo $((1 + 3 + 4))
```

Will ccho "8" to stdout.

2.3.6 Control Constructs

The flow of control within shell scripts is done via four main constructs; if...then...elif..else, do...while, for and case.

2.3.6.1 If..Then..Elif..Else

This construct takes the following generic form. The parts enclosed within ([) and (]) are optional:

```
if list
     then list
[elif list
     then list] ...
[else list]
fi
```

When a Unix command exits it exits with what is known as an *exit status*, this indicates to anyone who wants to know the degree of success the command had in performing whatever task it was supposed to do, usually when a command executes without error it terminates with an exit status of zero. An exit status of some other value would indicate that some error had occurred, the details of which would be specific to the command.

The commands' manual pages detail the exit status messages that they produce. A list is defined in the shell as "a sequence of zero or more commands separated by newlines, semicolons, or ampersands, and optionally terminated by one of these three characters.", hence in the generic definition of the if above the list will determine which of the execution paths the script takes.

For example, there is a command called test on Unix which evaluates an expression and if it evaluates to true will return zero and will return one otherwise, this is how we can test conditions in the list part(s) of the if construct because test is a command.

We do not actually have to type the test command directly into the list to use it, it can be implied by encasing the test case within ([) and (]) characters, as illustrated by the following (silly) example:

```
#!/bin/sh
if [ "$1" = "1" ]
then
     echo "The first option is nice"
elif [ "$1" = "2" ]
then
     echo "The second option is just as nice"
```

```
elif [ "$1" = "3" ]
then
    echo "The third option is excellent"
else
    echo "I see you were wise enough not to choose"
    echo "You win"
fi
```

What this example does is compare the first parameter (command line argument in this case) with the strings "1", "2" and "3" using tests' (=) test which compares two strings for equality, if any of them match it prints out the corresponding message. If none of them match it prints out the final case. OK the example is silly and actually flawed (the user still wins even if they type in (4) or something) but it illustrates how the if statement works.

Notice that there are spaces between (if) and ([), ([) and the test and the test and (]), these spaces must be present otherwise the shell will complain. There must also be spaces between the operator and operands of the test otherwise it will not work properly.

Notice how it starts with (if) and ends with (fi), also, notice how (then) is on a separate line to the test above it and that (else) does not require a (then) statement. You must construct this construct exactly like this for it to work properly.

It is also possible to integrate logical AND and OR into the testing, by using two tests separated by either "&&" or "||" respectively. For example we could replace the third test case in the example above with:

```
elif [ "$1" = "3"] || [ "$1" = "4" ]
then echo "The third choi...
```

The script would print out "The third choice is excellent" if the first parameter was either "3" OR "4". To illustrate the use of "&&

```
elif [ "$1" = "3"] || [ "$2" = "4" ]
then echo "The third choi...
```

The script would print out "The third choice is excellent" if and only if the first parameter was "3" AND the second parameter was "4".

"&&" and "||" are both lazily evaluating which means that in the case of "&&", if the first test fails it won't bother evaluating the second because the list will only be true if they BOTH pass and since one has already failed there is no point wasting time evaluating the second. In the case of "||" if the first test passes it won't bother evaluating the second test because we only need ONE of the tests to pass for the whole list to pass.

2.3.6.2 Do...While

The Do...While takes the following generic form:

```
while list
    do list
done
```

In the words of the SH manual "The two lists are executed repeatedly while the exit status of the first list is zero." there is a variation on this that uses until in place of while which executes until the exit status of the first list is zero. Here is an example use of the while statement:

```
#!/bin/sh
count=$1                          # Initialize count to first parameter
while [ $count -gt 0 ]            # while count is greater than 10 do
do
    echo $count seconds till supper time!
    count=$(expr $count -1)       # decrement count by 1
    sleep 1                       # sleep for a second using the Unix sleep command
done
echo Supper time!!, YEAH!!        # were finished
```

If called from the commandline with an argument of 4 this script will output

```
4 seconds till supper time!
3 seconds till supper time!
2 seconds till supper time!
1 seconds till supper time!
Supper time!!, YEAH!!
```

You can see that this time we have used the -gt of the test command implicitly called via '[' and ']', which stands for greater than. Pay careful attention to the formatting and spacing.

2.3.6.3 For Loop

The syntax of the for command is:

```
for variable in word ...
    do list
done
```

The shell manual states "The words are expanded, and then the list is executed repeatedly with the variable set to each word in turn.". A word is essentially some other variable that contains a list of values of some sort, the for construct assigns each of the values in the word to variable and then variable can be used within the body of the construct, upon completion of the body variable will be assigned the next value in word until there are no more values in word. An example should make this clearer:

```
#!/bin/sh
fruitlist="Apple Pear Tomato Peach Grape"
for fruit in $fruitlist
do
    if [ "$fruit" = "Tomato" ] || [ "$fruit" = "Peach" ]
    then
        echo "I like ${fruit}es"
    else
        echo "I like ${fruit}s"
    fi
done
```

In this example, fruitlist is word, fruit is variable and the body of the statement outputs how much this person loves various fruits but includes an if...then..else statement to deal with the correct addition of letters to describe the plural version of the fruit, notice that the variable fruit was expressed like ${fruit} because otherwise the shell would have interpreted the preceding letter(s) as being part of the variable and echoed nothing because we have not defined the variables fruits and fruites. When executed this script will output:

```
I like Apples
I like Pears
I like Tomatoes
I like Peachs
I like Grapes
```

Within the for construct, do and done may be replaced by '{' and '}'. This is not allowed for while.

2.3.6.4 Case

The case construct has the following syntax:

```
case word in
    pattern) list ;;
    ...
esac
```

An example of this should make things clearer:

```
!#/bin/sh
case $1 in
    1) echo 'First Choice';;
    2) echo 'Second Choice';;
    *) echo 'Other Choice';;
esac
```

"1", "2" and "*" are patterns, word is compared to each pattern and if a match is found the body of the corresponding pattern is executed, we have used "*" to represent everything, since this is checked last we will still catch "1" and "2" because they are checked first.

In our example word is "$1", the first parameter, hence if the script is ran with the argument "1" it will output "First Choice", "2" "Second Choice" and anything else "Other Choice". In this example we compared against numbers (essentially still a string comparison however) but the pattern can be more complex, see the SH man page for more information.

2.3.7 Functions

The syntax of an shell function is defined as follows:

```
name () command
```

It is usually laid out like this:

```
name() {
    commands
}
```

A function will return with a default exit status of zero, one can return different exit status' by using the notation return exit status. Variables can be defined locally within a function using local name=value. The example below shows the use of a user defined increment function:

Example 1. Increment Function Example

```
#!/bin/sh
inc() {                     # The increment is defined first so we can use it
    echo $(($1 + $2))       # We echo the result of the first
                            # parameter plus the second parameter
}
# We check to see that all the command line arguments are present
if [ "$1" "" ] || [ "$2" = "" ] || [ "$3" = "" ]
then
    echo USAGE:
    echo " counter startvalue incrementvalue endvalue"
    else
    count=$1                        # Rename are variables with clearer names
    value=$2
    end=$3
    while [ $count -lt $end ]        # Loop while count is less than end
    do
        echo $count
        count=$(inc $count $value) # Call increment with count and value as parameters
    done    # so that count is incremented by value
fi
inc() {
    echo $(($1 + $2))
}
```

The function is defined and opened with inc() {, the line echo $(($1 + $2)) uses the notation for arithmetic expression substitution which is $((expression)) to enclose the expression, $1 + $2 which adds the first and second parameters passed to the function together, the echo bit at the start echoes them to standard output, we can catch this value by assigning the function call to a variable, as is illustrated by the function call.

```
count=$(inc $count $value)
```

We use command substitution which substitutes the value of a command to substitute the value of the function call whereupon it is assigned to the count variable. The command within the command substitution block is inc $count $value, the last two values being its parameters. Which are then referenced from within the function using $1 and $2. We could have used the other command substitution notation to call the function if we had wanted:

```
count=`inc $count $value`
```

Example 2. Variable Scope, Example

We will show another quick example to illustrate the scope of variables:

```
#!/bin/sh
inc() {
    local value=4
    echo "value is $value within the function\\n"
    echo "\\b\$1 is $1 within the function"
}
value=5
echo value is $value before the function
echo "\$1 is $1 before the function"
echo
echo -e $(inc $value)
echo
echo value is $value after the function
echo "\$1 is $1 after the function"
inc() {
    local value=4
    echo "value is $value within the function\\n"
    echo "\\b\$1 is $1 within the function"
}
```

We assign a local value to the variable value of 4. The next three lines construct the output we would like, remember that this is being echoed to some buffer and will be replace the function call with all the stuff that was passed to stdout within the function when the function exits. So the calling code will be replaced with whatever we direct to standard output within the function. The function is called like this:

```
echo -e $(inc $value)
```

We have passed the option -e to the echo command which causes it to process C-style backslash escape characters, so we can process any backslash escape characters which the string generated by the function call contains.

If we just echo the lines we want to be returned by the function it will not pass the newline character onto the buffer even if we explicitly include it with an escape character reference so what we do is actually include the sequence of characters that will produce a new line within the string so that when it is echoed by the calling code with the -e the escape characters will be processed and the newlines will be placed where we want them.

```
echo "value is $value within the function\\n"
```

Notice how the newline has been inserted with \\n, the first two backslashes indicate that we want to echo a backslash because within double quotes a backslash indicates to process the next character literally, we have to do this because we are only between double quotes and not the literal-text single quotes.

If we had used single quotes we would had have to echo the bit with the newline in separately from the bit that contains $value otherwise $value would not be expanded.

```
echo "\\b\$1 is $1 within the function"
```

This is our second line, and is contained within double quotes so that the variable $1 will be expanded, \\b is included so that \b will be placed in the echoed line and our calling code will process this as a backspace character. We have to do this because for some reason the shell prefixes a space to the second line if we do not, the backspace removes this space. The output from this script called with 2 as the first argument is:

```
alue is 5 before the function
$1 is 2 before the function
value is 4 within the function
$1 is 5 within the function
value is 5 after the function
$1 is 2 after the function
```

2.4 PERL [Practical Extraction and Report Language]

Perl (or PERL) is an acronym, short for Practical Extraction and Report Language. Perl is a scripting language with powerful text processing capabilities. Because of these, Perl has become a very popular language in the context of web servers.

Perl is an interpreted language. That means, program code is interpreted at run time. Code is compiled by the interpreter before it is actually executed. It was designed By *Larry Wall* as a tool for writing programs in the UNIX environment.

Perl is a very feature-rich language, which clearly cannot be discussed in full detail here. Instead, our goals here are to
- Enable the reader to quickly become proficient at writing simple Perl programs and
- Prepare the reader to consult full Perl books (or Perl tutorials on the Web) for further details of whatever Perl constructs he/she needs for a particular application.

2.4.1 Starting with "Hello world!"

Perl *script* is a text file with default extension *.pl*. As an example let us consider the text of *helloworld.pl* given below:

```
#!/usr/bin/perl
# This is my first Perl program!
print ("Hello World!\n");
print ("This is my first Perl program.\n\n");
```

Perl scripts are interpreted by the Perl interpreter: perl, or perl.exe.

```
perl helloworld.pl [arg0 [arg1 [arg2 ...]]]
```

In the above code, *print()* is a function that displays text to the screen. \n prints a new line to the screen; i.e. it goes to the start of the next line. The symbol # indicates beginning of the comment – everything after it will be ignored. Perl has no block comment syntax. The semicolon (;) separates the Perl statements from one another. Statements do not have to occur on separate lines.

2.4.2 Perl Command Line Arguments

When you run a program, it is often desired to use different data. We will now update the helloworld program to use command line arguments that can be used to set different options for a program. In this specific example, we will allow the user to enter in their name, which then gets printed to the screen.

Edit the hello.pl file so it now looks like the following:

```
#!/usr/bin/perl
use Getopt::Long;

#usage: perl helloCommandLine.pl –name <YourName>
&GetOptions("name=s" => \$Name);
# The above line lets the user enter in their name
print ("Hello $Name \n");
print ("This is a perl program using command line arguments \n\n");
```

Once you have finished, save this file as *helloCommandLine.pl* and then run it by typing:

```
perl helloCommandLine.pl –name <yourname>
```

In the above code, for now assume that *use Getopt::Long;* is used whenever we want to retrieve command line arguments. Basically this line tells the perl interpreter that we are using a function that is already defined in another location. *&GetOptions()* is a function that retrieves the command line options.

In this example, it retrieves the value directly after the *–name* when the program is run. It stores the value entered in in a variable called *$Name*. This value can be retrieved any time in the program. We will talk about variables more in the next perl session.

2.4.3 Perl Datatypes and Variables

Perl is loosely typed language. In Perl, there is no need to specify a type for your data, the Perl interpreter will choose the type based on the context of the data itself. Before we can proceed much further with Perl, we'll need some understanding of variables.

A variable is a container that holds one or more values that can change throughout a program. Perl variables come in three types: *scalars*, *arrays* and *hashes*. Variables in Perl are always preceded with a sign called a *sigil*. These signs are $ for scalars, @ for arrays, and % for hashes.

2.4.3.1 Scalar Variables

Scalars are simple variables. They are preceded by a dollar sign ($). A scalar is either a number, a string, or a reference. A reference is actually an address of a variable. Here is a simple example of using scalar variables:

```
#!/usr/bin/perl
$age = 31;                  # An integer assignment
$name = "Srinivas Mary";    # A string
$salary = 1999.50;          # A floating point

print "Age = $age\n";
print "Name = $name\n";
print "Salary = $salary\n";
```

This will produce following result:

```
Age = 31
Name = Srinivas Mary
Salary = 1999.50
```

The '.' is used to concatenate strings. For example,

```
$x = $x . "abc"
```

would add the string "abc" to $x.

2.4.3.2 Array Variables

An array is a variable that stores an ordered list of scalar values. Array variables are preceded by an "at" (@) sign. To refer to a single element of an array, you will use the dollar sign ($) with the variable name followed by the index of the element in square brackets. Array indices are integers beginning at 0. Here is a simple example of using array variables:

```
#!/usr/bin/perl
@ages = (32, 20, 21);
@names = ("Rama Krishna", "Mary", "Ahmed");
```

```
print "\$ages[0] = $ages[0]\n";
print "\$ages[1] = $ages[1]\n";
print "\$ages[2] = $ages[2]\n";
print "\$names[0] = $names[0]\n";
print "\$names[1] = $names[1]\n";
print "\$names[2] = $names[2]\n";
```

Here we used escape sign (\) before $ sign just to print it other Perl will understand it as a variable and will print its value. When exected, this will produce following result:

```
$ages[0] = 32
$ages[1] = 20
$ages[2] = 21
$names[0] = Rama Krishna
$names[1] = Mary
$names[2] = Ahmed
```

Array elements can only be scalars, and not for instance other arrays. For example

```
@wt = (1,(2,3),4);
```

would have the same effect as

```
@wt = (1,2,3,4);
```

Since array elements are scalars, their names begin with $, not @, e.g.

```
@wt = (1,2,3,4);
print $wt[2]; # prints 3
```

Arrays are referenced for the most part as in C, but in a more flexible manner. Their lengths are not declared, and they grow or shrink dynamically, without "warning," i.e. the programmer does not "ask for permission" in growing an array. For example, if the array x currently has 7 elements, i.e. ends at $x[6], then the statement

```
$x[7] = 12;
```

changes the array length to 8. For that matter, we could have assigned to element 99 instead of to element 7, resulting in an array length of 100.

The programmer can treat an array as a *queue* data structure, using the Perl operations push and shift (usage of the latter is especially common in the Perl idiom), or treat it as a stack by using push and pop. We'll see the details below.

An array without a name is called a *list*. For example, in

```
@x = (88,12,"abc");
```

we assign the array name @x to the list (88,12,"abc"). We will then have $x[0] = 88, etc. One of the big uses of lists and arrays is in loops, e.g.:

```
# prints out 1, 2 and 4
for $i ((1,2,4)) {
    print $i, "\n";
}
```

The length of an array or list is obtained calling scalar() or by simply using the array name (though not a list) in a scalar context.

Operations

```
$x[0] = 15; # don't have to warn Perl that x is an array first
$x[1] = 16;
$y = shift @x; # "output" of shift is the element shifted out
print $y, "\n"; # prints 15
print $x[0], "\n"; # prints 16

push(@x,9); # sets $x[1] to 9
print scalar(@x), "\n"; # prints 2
print @x, "\n"; # prints 169 (16 and 9 with no space)

$k = @x;

print $k, "\n"; # prints 2
@x = (); # @x will now be empty
print scalar(@x), "\n"; # prints 0

@rt = ('abc',15,20,95);
delete $rt[2]; # $rt[2] now = undef

print "scalar(@rt) \n"; # prints 4
print @rt, "\n"; # prints abc1595
```

```
print "@rt\n"; # prints abc 15 95, due to quotes
print "$rt[-1]\n"; # prints 95
$m = @rt;
print $m, "\n"; # prints 4
 ($m) = @rt; # 4-element array truncated to a 1-element array
print $m, "\n"; # prints abc
```

A useful operation is array slicing. Subsets of arrays may be accessed—"sliced"—via commas and a .. range operator. For example:

```
@z = (5,12,13,125);
@w = @z[1..3];              # @w will be (12,13,125)
@q = @z[0..1];             # @q will be (5,12)
@y = @z[0,2];              # @y will be (5,13)
@w[0,2] = @w[2,0];          # swaps elements 0 and 2
@g = @z[0,2..3];           # can mix "," and
print "@g\n"               # prints 0 13 125
```

2.4.3.3 Hash Variables

A hash is a set of key/value pairs. Hash variables are preceded by a percent (%) sign. To refer to a single element of a hash, you will use the hash variable name followed by the *key* associated with the value in curly brackets. Here is a simple example of using hash variables:

```
#!/usr/bin/perl
%data = ('Rama Krishna', 32, 'Mary', 30, 'Ahmed', 40);
print "\$data{'Rama Krishna'} = $data{'Rama Krishna'}\n";
print "\$data{'Mary'} = $data{'Mary'}\n";
print "\$data{'Ahmed'} = $data{'Ahmed'}\n";
```

This will produce following result:

```
$data{'Rama Krishna'} = 32
$data{'Mary'} = 30
$data{'Ahmed'} = 40
```

In the code above, if we add the line

```
print %data, "\n";
```

the output of that statement will be

```
Rama Krishna32Mary30Ahmed40
```

2.4.4 References

References are like C pointers. They are considered scalar variables, and thus have names beginning with $. They are dereferenced by prepending the symbol for the variable type, e.g. prepending a $ for a scalar, a @ for an array, etc.:

```
# set up a reference to a scalar
$r = \3; # \ means "reference to," like & means "pointer to" in C
# now print it; $r is a reference to a scalar, so $$r denotes that scalar
print $$r, "\n"; # prints 3
@x = (1,2,4,8,16);
$s = \@x;
# an array element is a scalar, so prepend a $
print $$s[3], "\n"; # prints 8
# for the whole array, prepend a @
print scalar(@$s), "\n"; # prints 5
```

In Line 4, for example, you should view $$r as $($r), meaning take the reference $r and dereference it. Since the result of dereferencing is a scalar, we get another dollar sign on the left.

2.4.5 Declaration of Variables

A variable need not be explicitly declared; its *declaration* consists of its first usage. For example, if the statement

```
$var = 5;
```

were the first reference to $var, then this would both declare $var and assign 5 to it. If you wish to make a separate declaration, you can do so, e.g.

```
$var;
...
$var = 5;
```

If you wish to have protection against accidentally using a variable which has not been previously defined, say due to a misspelling, include a line

```
use strict;
```

at the top of your source code.

2.4.6 Scope of Variables

Variables in Perl are global by default. To make a variable local to subroutine or block, the my construct is used. For instance,

```
my $x;
my $y;
```

would make the scope of $x and $y only the subroutine or block in which these statements appear. You can also combine the above two statements, using a list:

```
my ($x,$y);
```

Other than the scope aspect, the effect of my is the same as if this keyword were not there. Thus for example

```
my $z = 3;
```

is the same as

```
my $z;
...
$z = 3;
```

and

```
my($x) = @rt;
```

would assign $rt[0] to $x.

Note that my does apply at the block level. This can lead to subtle bugs if you forget about it. For example,

```
if ($x == 2) {
    my $y = 5;
}
print $y, "\n";
will print 0.
```

There are other scope possibilities, e.g. namespaces of packages and the local keyword.

2.4.7 String Literals

In perl there are two ways to represent string literals: single-quoted strings and double-quoted strings.

2.4.7.1 Single-Quoted Strings

Single quoted are a sequence of characters that begin and end with a single quote. These quotes are not a part of the string they just mark the beginning and end for the Perl interpreter. If you want a ' inside of your string you need to preclude it with a \ like this \' as you'll see below. Let's see how this works below.

```
'five'              #has four letters in the string
'can\'t'            #has five characters and represents "can't"
'hi\there'          #has eight characters and represents"hi\\there" (one \ in the string)
'mam\\blah'         #has nine characters and represents "mam\\blah" (one \ in the string)
```

If you want to put a new line in a single-quoted string it goes something like this

```
'line1
line2'      #has eleven characters line1, newline character, and then line2
```

Single-quoted strings don't interpret \n as a newline.

2.4.7.2 Double-Quoted Strings

Double quoted strings act more like strings in C or C++ the backslash allows you to represent control characters. Another nice feature Double-Quoted strings offers is variable interpolation this substitutes the value of a variable into the string. Some examples are below:

```
$word="hello";                    #$word becomes hello
$statement="$word world!";        #variable interpolation, $statement becomes "hello world!"
"Hello World!\n";                 #"Hello World!" followed by a newline
```

2.4.8 PERL Standard Input

As an example, consider the script below.

```
#!/usr/bin/perl
$title = "PERL Programming";
print "Hello there.  What is your name?\n";
$name = <STDIN>;
chomp($name);
print "Hello, $you. Welcome to $title.\n";
```

The script will prompt you for your name, and read your name using the following line:

```
$name = <STDIN>;
```

STDIN is standard input. This is the default input channel for your script; if you're running your script in the shell, STDIN is whatever you type as the script runs. The program will print "Hello there. What is your name?", then pause and wait for you to type something in. Whatever you typed is stored in the scalar variable $name. Since $name also contains the carriage return itself, we use

```
chomp($name);
```

to remove the carriage return from the end of the string you typed in. The following print statement:

```
print "Hello, $name. Welcome to $classname.\n";
```

substitutes the value of $name that you entered. The "\n" at the end if the line is the perl syntax for a carriage return.

2.4.9 PERL Operators

2.4.9.1 Numeric PERL Operators

2.4.9.1.1 Arithmetic PERL Operators

In the table below you see the Perl operators used in arithmetic operations.

Symbol	Name	Definition
+	addition	It's a binary operator that returns the sum of two operands. Example: $v1 = 22; $v2 = 6; $v = $v1+$v2; print "$v (expected 28)\n";
-	subtraction	It's a binary operator that returns the difference of two operands. Example: $v1 = 12; $v2 = 5; $v = $v1-$v2; print "$v (expected 7)\n";
-	negation	I's a unary operator that performs arithmetic negation. Example: $v1 = 12; $v2 = -$v1; print "$v2 (expected -12)\n";
*	multiplication	It's a binary operator that multiplies two operands. Example: $v1 = 12; $v2 = 5; $v = $v1 * $v2; print "$v (expected 60)\n";
/	division	It's a binary operator that divides left value by right value. Example: $v1 = 12; $v2 = 5; $v = $v1 / $v2; print "$v (expected 2.4)\n";
**	exponentiation	It's a binary operator that raises the left value to the power of the right value. Example: $v1 = 12; $v2 = 2; $v = $v1 ** $v2; print "$v (expected 144)\n";
%	modulus	It's a binary operator that returns the remainder of dividing left value by right value. Example: $v1 = 12; $v2 = 5; $v = $v1 % $v2; print "$v (expected 2)\n";

++	auto increment	If you place this unary operator before/after a variable, the variable will be incremented before/after returning the alue. Example: $v1 = 10; $v2 = ++$v1; print "$v1 $v2(expected 11 11)\n"; $v1 = 10; $v2 = $v1++; print "$v1 $v2(expected 11 10)\n";
--	auto decrement	If you place this unary operator before/after a variable, the variable will be decremented before/after returning the alue. Example: $v1 = 10; $v2 = --$v1; print "$v1 $v2(expected 9 9)\n"; $v1 = 10; $v2 = $v1--; print "$v1 $v2(expected 9 10)\n";

2.4.9.1.2 Numeric Relational PERL Operators

The numeric relational Perl operators compare two numbers and determine the validity of a relationship.

Symbol	Name	Definition

<	less than	The *less than* operator indicates if the value of the left operand is less than the value of the right one.
		
		Example:
		($v1, $v2) = (5, 7);
		if($v1 < $v2){
		  print "OK (expected)\n";
		}

<=	less than or equal to	The *less than or equal to* operator indicates if the value of the left operand is less than or equal to the value of the right one.
		
		Example:
		($v1, $v2) = (5, 5);
		if($v1 <= $v2){
		  print "OK (expected)\n";
		}

>	greater than	The *greater than* operator indicates if the value of the left operand is greater than the value of the right one.
		
		Example:
		($v1, $v2) = (5, 7);
		if($v2 > $v1){
		  print "OK (expected)\n";
		}

>=	greater than or equal to	The *greater than or equal to* operator indicates if the value of the left operand is greater than or equal to the value of the right one.
		
		Example:
		($v1, $v2) = (5, 5);
		if($v2 >= $v1){
		  print "OK (expected)\n";
		}

==	equal	The *equal* operator returns true if the left operand is equal to the right one.
		
		Example:
		($v1, $v2) = (5, 5);
		if($v1 == $v2){
		  print "OK (expected)\n";
		}

!=	not equal to	The *not equal to* operator returns true if the left operand is not equal to the right one.
		
		Example:
		($v1, $v2) = (5, 7);
		if($v1 != $v2){
		  print "OK (expected)\n";
		}

<=>	numeric comparison	This binary operator returns -1, 0, or 1 if the left operand is less than, equal to or greater than the right one. Example: ($v1, $v2) = (5, 7); $v = $v1 <=> $v2; print "$v\n"; # displays -1;

2.4.9.1.3 Numerical Logical PERL Operators

The numeric logical Perl operators are generally derived from boolean algebra and they are mainly used to control program flow, finding them as part of an if, a while or some other control statement. See in the table below the logical numerical Perl operators.

Symbol	Name	Definition
!	negation	This unary operator evaluates an operand and return true if the operand has the false value (0) and false otherwise. Example: $v1 = !25; $v2 = !0; print "v1=$v1,v2=$v2\n"; # displays v1=,v2=1
not	not	It has the same meaning as the "!" operator, described above.

and, &&	and	The *and* operator returns the logical conjunction of two operands.
		
		Example:
		($v1, $v2) = (5, 7);
		if($v1 == 5 && $v2 == 7) {
		  print "OK (expected)\n";
		}

or, ||	or	The *or* operator returns the logical disjunction of two operands.
		
		Example:
		($v1, $v2) = (5, 7);
		if($v1 == 5 || $v2 == 0) {
		  print "OK (expected)\n";
		}

xor	exclusive or	The *exclusive or* operator returns the logical exclusive-or of two operands (the result is true if either but not both of the operands is true). Example: ($v1, $v2) = (5, 7); print ($v1==5 xor $v2==3); # displays 1 print ($v1==5 xor $v2==7); # displays
?	conditional operator	This ternary operator is like the symbolic if ... then ... else clause from the C language. It returns the second operand if the leftmost operand is true and the third operand otherwise. Example: $v = (2 == 2) ? "Equal\n" : "Not equal\n"; print $v; # displays Equal

2.4.9.1.4 Numeric Bitwise PERL Operations

Numeric bitwise Perl operators are similar to the logical operators, but they work on the binary representation of data. They are used to change individual bits in an operand. Please note that both operands associated with bitwise operators are integers.

Symbol	Name	Definition
<<	shift left	The *shift left* << operator is a binary operator that shifts the bits to the left. Its first operand specifies the integer value to be shifted meanwhile the second one specifies the number of position that the bits in the value will be shifted. The rightmost bits of the integer value will be assigned with 0 and the leftmost bits will be discarded. Example: $v = 25 << 3; print "$v (expected 200)\n";
>>	shift right	The *shift right* >> operator is a binary operator that shifts the bits to the right. Its first operand specifies the integer value to be shifted meanwhile the second one specifies the number of position that the bits in the value will be shifted. The leftmost bits of the integer value will be assigned with 0 and the rightmost bits will be discarded. Example: $v = 32 >> 3; print "$v (expected 4)\n";
&	and	The *and* operator sets a bit to 1 if both of the corresponding bits in its operands are 1, and 0 otherwise. Example: $v = 32 & 16; print "$v (expected 0)\n";
|	or	The *or* operator sets a bit to 0 if both of the corresponding bits in its operands are 0, and 1 otherwise. Example: $v = 32 \| 16; print "$v (expected 48)\n";
^	exclusive or	The *exclusive or* operator sets a bit to 1 if the corresponding bits in its operands are

		different, and 0 otherwise.
		Example: $v = 3 ^ 9; print "$v (expected 10)\n";
~	not	The unary *not* operator inverts each bit in the operand, changing all the ones to zeros and zeros to ones.
		Example: $v = ~1024;

2.4.9.1.5 Other Numeric PERL Operations

See in the table below other numeric Perl operators:

Symbol	Name	Definition

,	comma	In scalar context this binary operator evaluates its left argument, discards this value, then evaluates its right argument and returns that value. In a list context, it's just a separator and inserts both its arguments into the list.
		
		Example (in scalar context):
		    $v1 = 2; $v2 = 4; $v3 = $v1 == $v2;
		    $v = ($v3, 5 == 5);
		    print(" $v3(expected)\n");
		    print(" $v(expected 1)\n");

=>	comma	It has the same function like the comma operator described above.
..	Range operator	In scalar context, this operator returns false as long as its left operand is false. When the left operand becomes true, the range operator returns true until the right operator remains true, after which it becomes false again. In a list context, this operator will return an array with contiguous sequences of items, beginning with the left operand value and ending with the right operand value (the items can be characters or numbers). Example (in a list context): print ('a'..'zz'); print ('1'..'10');

2.4.9.1.6 Numeric Assignment PERL Operations

Numeric assignment Perl operators perform some type of numeric operation and then assign the value to the existing variable.

Symbol	Name	Definition

=	assignment	This is the ordinary assignment operator. In a scalar context, it assigns the right operand's value to the left operand. In a list context, it assigns multiple values to the left array operand if the right operand is a list.
		
		Example:
		    $v = 15; print $v, "\n"; # displays 15
		    @array = (10, 20, 30);
		    print "@array\n"; # displays 10 20 30

+=	addition	It adds the right operand's value to the left operand. Example: $v = 10; $v += 15; print "$v (expected 25)\n";
-=	subtraction	It subtracts the right operand from the left operand Example: $v = 25; $v -= 15; print "$v (expected 10)\n";
*=	multiplication	It multiplies the left operand's value by the right operand's value. Example: $v = 10; $v *= 15; print "$v (expected 150)\n";
/=	division	It divides the left operand's value by the right operand's value. Example: $v = 150; $v /= 15; print "$v (expected 10)\n";
**=	exponentiation	It raises the left operand's value to the power of the right operand's value. Example: $v = 12; $v **= 2; print "$v (expected 144)\n";
&&=	logical and	It's a combination between the logical "&&" and the assignment operators. Example: $v = 1; $v &&= 7 == 7; print "$v (expected 1)\n";
%=	modulus	It divides the left operand value by the right operand value and assigns the remainder to the left operand. Example: $v = 12; $v %= 5; print "$v (expected 2)\n";
||=	logical or	It's a combination between the logical "||" and the assignment operators. Example:

		$v = 0; $v \| \|= 7 == 7; print "$v (expected 1)\n";
<<=	bitwise shift left	It's a bitwise left shift assign. example: $v = 25; $v <<= 3; print "$v (expected 200)\n";
>>=	bitwise shift right	It's a bitwise right shift assign. Example: $v = 32; $v >>= 3; print "$v (expected 4)\n";
&=	bitwise and	It's a bitwise AND assign. Example: $v = 32; $v &= 16; print "$v (expected 0)\n";
|=	bitwise or	It's a bitwise OR assign. Example: $v = 32; $v \|= 16; print "$v (expected 48)\n";
^=	bitwise exclusive or	It's a bitwise XOR assign. Example: $v = 3; $v ^= 9; print "$v (expected 10)\n";

2.4.9.2 String PERL Operators

2.4.9.2.1 String Relational PERL Operators

The string relational Perl operators compare two strings and determine the validity of a relationship.

Symbol	Name	Definition

lt	less than	It returns true if the left operand is string wise less then the right one.
		
		Example:
		($v1, $v2) = ("abc", "abz");
		if($v1 lt $v2){
		  print ("$v1 is less than $v2\n");
		}

le	less than or equal to	It returns true if the left operand is string wise less than or equal to the right one.
		
		Example:
		($v1, $v2) = ("abc", "abc");
		if($v1 le $v2){
		  print("$v1 is less than or equal to $v2");
		  print "\n";
		}

gt	greater than	It returns true if the left operand is string wise greater then the right one.
		
		Example:
		($v1, $v2) = ("abc", "abz");
		if($v2 gt $v1){
		  print ("$v2 is greater than $v1 \n");
		}

gc	greater than or equal to	It returns true if the left operand is string wise greater than or equal to the right one.
		
		Example:
		($v1, $v2) = ("abc", "abc");
		if($v1 ge $v2){
		  print("$v1 is greater than or equal to $v2");
		  print "\n";
		}

eq	equality	It returns true if the left operand is string wise equal to the right one.
		
		Example:
		($v1, $v2) = ("abc", "abc");
		if($v1 eq $v2){
		  print ("$v1 is equal to $v2\n");
		}

ne	not equal to	It returns true if the left operand is string wise not equal to the right one.
		
		Example:
		($v1, $v2) = ("abc", "ab1");
		if($v1 ne $v2){
		  print ("$v1 is not equal to $v2\n");
		}

cmp	comparison	It returns -1, 0, or 1 if the left operand is string wise less than, equal to or

		greater than the right one.

		Example:
		  ($v1, $v2) = ("am", "ak");
		  $v = $v1 cmp $v2;
		  print ("$v(expected 1)\n");

2.4.9.2.2 String Logical PERL Operators

The string logical Perl operators are generally derived from boolean algebra and they are mainly used to control program flow, finding them as part of an if, a while or some other control statement. See in the table below the logical string Perl operators.

Symbol	Name	Definition
!	not	It returns true if the operand is a null string or an undefined value and false otherwise. Example: $v1 = !'some string here'; $v2 = !''; The $v1 variable will return false and the $v2 variable will return true.
not	not	The same meaning as above, but it is a lower-precedence version.

&&	and	This operator is used to determine if both operands are true.
		
		Example:
		  ($v1, $v2) = ('abc', 'abzu');
		  $v = $v1 == 'abc' && $v2 == 'abzu';
		  print "$v (expected 1)";

and	and	Same as above.

||	or	This operator is used to determine if either of the operands is true.
		
		Example:
		  ($v1, $v2) = ('hello', 'good');
		  $v = $v1 == 'hello' || $v2 == 'hello';
		  print "$v (expected 1)";

or	or	Same as above.

xor	exclusive or	It returns true if either but not both of the operands is true.
		
		Example:
		  ($v1, $v2) = ('hello', 'good');
		  $v = $v1 == 'hello' xor $v2 == 'world';
		  print "$v (expected 1)";

?	conditional operator	This is a ternary operator and it works like an if ... then ... else clause from the C language. If the left operand is true, it will return the central operand, otherwise the right operand.
		
		Example:
		  $v = ("abc" eq "abd") ? "It's equal.\n" :
		     "It's not equal. (expected)\n";
		  print $v;

2.4.9.2.3 Other String PERL Operations

See in the table below other string Perl operators:

Symbol	Name	Definition

,	comma	In a scalar context, the comma operator evaluates each element from left to right and returns the value of the rightmost element. In a list context, the comma operator separates the elements of a literal list.
		
		Example:
		  # scalar context
		  $colors = ('blue', 'red', 'yellow');
		  print "$colors (expected yellow)\n";
		  # list context
		  @colors = ('blue', 'red', 'yellow');
		  print "@colors[1] (expected red)\n";

=>	comma	This operator is a special type of comma, for example ('dog', 'cat') is similar to (dog => 'cat'). Or it can be used to separate key/value pairs in a hash structure: %petColors = (dog => 'brown', cat => 'white');
-	negation	If the string operand begins with a plus or minus sign, the string negation operator returns a string with the opposite sign. Example: $v = "-abcd"; print (-$v, "(expected +abcd)\n");
.	concatenation	This operator joins two or more strings like in the example below. Example:

		$v = "Hello" . " World" . "!"; print $v, " (expected Hello World!)\n";
..	range operator	The range operator, in a list context, produces the range of values from the left value through the right value in increments of 1. Example: @v = ('ab' .. 'ae'); print @v, " (expected abacadae)\n";
x	repetition	The repetition operator returns the first operand (which is a string) repeated by the number of times specified by the second operand (which is an integer). Example: @v = 'ab' x 3; print @v, " (expected ababab)\n";

2.4.9.2.4 String Assignment PERL Operations

String assignment Perl operators perform some type of string operation and then assign the value to the existing variable.

Symbol	Name	Definition
=	Assignment	This is the ordinary assignment operator. Example: $v = 'Hello World!'; print $v, " (expected Hello World!)\n";
&&=	logical and	It's a combination between the logical "&&" and the assignment operators. Example: $v = 1; $v &&= 'abc' eq 'abc'; print $v, " (expected 1)\n";
||=	logical or	It's a combination between the logical "||" and the assignment operators. Example: $v = 0; $v ||= 'abc' eq 'abc'; print $v, " (expected 1)\n";
.=	concatenation	It's a combination between the concatenation "." and the assignment operators. Example: $v = "Hello "; $v .= 'World!'; print $v, " (expected Hello World!)\n";
x=	repetition	It's a repetition assignment operator. Example: $v = "true "; $v x= 2; print $v, " (expected true true)\n";

2.4.9.3 Special PERL Operations

See in the table below the special Perl operators:

Symbol	Name	Definition
\	reference	We call reference the scalar value that contains a memory address. In order to reference a variable, we use the operator. Look at the below snippet code to see how to use it. Example: $v="Hello World!"; $ref_v=\$v; print $$ref_v, " (expected Hello World!)\n";
->	dereference	The dereference operator was used for the first time in the Perl 5 language. This operator let us to access and manipulate the elements of an array, hash, object of a class data structure. If you use the reference operator to reference a scalar variable, before you use it you must dereference the reference variable. Example: @v = ('black', 'white', 'blue', 'orange'); $vRef = \@v; # the reference variable print $v[1], " (expected white)\n"; $vRef->[1] = 'red'; # dereference before use print $v[1], " (expected red)\n";

=~	pattern binding	This binary operator binds a string expression to a pattern match. The string which is intend to bind is put on the left meanwhile the operator itself is put on the right. We use the pattern binding operator in the case we have a string which is not stored in the $_ variable and we need to perform some matches or substitutions of that string.
		
		Example:
		$v = "black and white";
		if($v =~ m/white/) {
		  print "Yes (expected)\n";
		}
		$v =~ s/black and white/red/;
		print $v, " (expected red)\n";

!~	pattern binding (not)	This operator is similar the operator above, but the return value is negated logically. Example:

		$v = "black and white";
		if($v =! m/yellow/) {
		    print "Yes (expected)\n";
		}

2.4.10 PERL Conditional Statements

In this section, we will see how to use the if statement in Perl scripts. The if statement let you execute a block of statements between two curly braces if a boolean condition is evaluated true, otherwise the execution continues with the following block, either an elsif/else block or after the end of the if statement.

2.4.10.1 if used as a modifier

`Statement if (Expr)`

In this first form we used Perl *if* as a modifier of a statement. *Expr* is a condition which must be evaluate in order to execute the Perl *if* statement. By writing code like this, you can put the important part of the statement at the beginning, in order to monitor it. The next code sample shows you how to use it when you need to print the values of certain variables in order to debug your Perl script:

```
$debug = 1;
$a = 1; $b = 2;
# ... some statements here
print "a = $a\n" if $debug;   # check the $a value
# ... other statements
print "b = $b\n" if $debug;   # check the $b value
# the rest of script statements
```

If we want to print the debug messages, at the beginning of the script we set the $debug variable value to 1, otherwise we set it to 0. The next example will show you how to use the regular expressions in the Perl if condition (the =~ operator):

```
$vari = "An example with the if modifier";
print "\$v contains the word \'example\'\n" if ($vari =~ /example/);
# it prints: $v contains the word 'example'
$vari = "";
```

This code will execute the print statement only if the $vari string variable matches the 'example' word. If it doesn't, the script will continue with the next statement (i.e. $v = "").

2.4.10.2 General if statement

The second syntax form is more general:

`if (Expr) Block elsif (Expr) Block ... else Block`

where:
- Expr represents a Boolean conditional expression
- The elsif and else clauses are optional and are used if you want to check a certain sequence of conditional expressions and find out which one of them is true
- Block consists of one or more statements enclosed in curly braces; in the construction of a block, the curly braces are always required.

We can split the general conditional Perl if statement as follows:

2.4.10.2.1 A simple if statement

`if (Expr) Block`

Perl will evaluate the *Expr* and if it is true, it will execute the code between the curly braces of the block. Otherwise, the script will continue with the next statement after the block. Neither *elsif* nor *else* clauses are used in the above format. See the next snippet code example:

```
$a = -1;
if($a < 0) {
    $a += 2;
}
print "a = $a\n";   # it outputs a = 1
```

The Perl interpreter will check the condition between parentheses and if the result is true, it will increment the $a scalar variable value with 2. It is possible that *Expr* doesn't represent a condition, like in the following example:

`if(1) {`

```
    $a = 1;
}
```

Because the expression is true, the Perl interpreter will continue with the execution of the block, i.e. it will assign the value 1 to the $a scalar variable. As you guess, in this example you don't need to use the Perl if statement at all, the assign statement $a = 1 is sufficient to do the job.

2.4.10.2.2 if-else

if (Expr) Block else Block

The Perl interpreter will evaluate the conditional expression and if the result is true, the execution of the script will continue with the block that follows the conditional expression; otherwise, the script execution will skip inside the block that is after the else clause. Let's look at a simple example where we need to find the maximum of two numbers:

```
$a = 15;
$b = 27;
if($a > $b) {
    print "max($a, $b) = $a\n";
} else {
    print "max($a, $b) = $b\n";
}
# it prints: max(15, 27) = 27
```

Well, there is a shorter way to do this by using the ? logical ternary operator - also called the conditional operator. I remind you briefly that the ternary operator (named ternary because it uses three operands) is like an if-else compound statement both included into an expression.

Please note that this operator is an expression that returns a value based on the conditional sentence it evaluates. It can be used by following the syntax:

Expr ? true-value : false-value

The logical ternary operator evaluates its first argument (*Expr*) and if this is true, it returns the second argument (true-value), otherwise it returns the third argument (false-value). With the ternary operator, we can rewrite the above code like so:

```
$a = 15; $b = 27;
print "max($a, $b) = ", $a > $b ? $a : $b,"\n";
```

The output obtained after running this code will be the same as in the previous example, where we used Perl if statement. Now I'll discuss a bit about the case when in a Perl *if* statement we have an empty block after the expression, like in the following snippet code example:

```
$a = 12; $b = -25;
if($a*$b >= 0 && $a + $b >= 0) {
    # do nothing
} else {
    print "at least $a or $b is negative\n";
}
```

There are at least two ways to get rid of the empty if block. One way is to use the Perl unless statement instead of the Perl *if* statement:

```
$a = 12; $b = -25;
unless($a*$b >= 0 && $a + $b >= 0) {
    print "at least $a or $b is negative\n";
}
```

In writing the conditional statements, you can swap as you wish between Perl *if* and Perl *unless* in order to make your code more readable. Another way is to rewrite the conditional expression enclosed between the parentheses that follow the if keyword: ($a*$b >= 0 && $a + $b >= 0). This is a boolean expression and as you expect Perl provides you with the logical AND operator (&&) and the logical OR operator (||) in order to manipulate the boolean expressions.

When you use the && and || operators be careful not to include any spaces between the symbols ("& &" or "| |" is wrong) because you'll get something you couldn't expect. So than we can rewrite the above condition in order to get rid of the empty block:

```
$a = 12; $b = -25;
if($a*$b < 0) {
    print "at least $a or $b is negative\n";
}
```

2.4.10.2.3 if-elsif-else

```
if (Expr) Block elsif (Expr) Block ... else Block
```

This form uses the elsif clause that allows you to check as many conditional expressions as are required. The else clause from the end of the form is still optional but you can use it at the end of the *if* statement if all other tests fail – with other words, the block of the final else will be executed if none of the conditions are true.

The next snippet code shows you an example about how to use if in connection with the elsif and else clauses:

```perl
chomp ($line = <STDIN>);
$line = lc($line);
if($line eq "index"){
    print "index function\n";
} elsif ($line eq "chomp") {
    print "chomp function\n";
} elsif ($line eq "hex") {
    print "hex function\n";
} elsif ($line eq "substr") {
    print "substr function\n";
} else {
    print "$line: unknown function\n";
}
```

In this example we read a line from <STDIN>, remove the last newline with the chomp function and convert all the characters in lowercases. Next we check if the text read from <STDIN> is the name of index, chomp, hex or substr functions. If we don't find any occurrence, the script program will execute the block that follows the else clause.

2.4.11 PERL Loops

2.4.11.1 For Loop

A *for* loop goes through the loop a certain number of times. Here is the general form of a for loop:

```perl
for (starting assignment; test condition; increment){
    code to repeat
}
```

Well, that's great, but it doesn't tell us much about what happens. Instead, let's use a real example. Let's say we wanted to print the word "Hi" ten times in a row. We could use a for loop like this:

```perl
for ($count=1; $count<6; $count++){
    print "Hi\n";
}
```

You'll notice above we created a variable named $count to test the condition each time through. In this case, we only used it to test the condition and not inside the loop itself. The first time through $count is 1 since we have that as our starting condition.

The loop will keep repeating until count finishes the 6th time through. When it tries to go through as 6, it is stopped because it fails the test condition— 6 is not less than 6. So, what we get is this repetitive list:

```
Hi
Hi
Hi
Hi
Hi
```

You could also use the $count variable inside the *for* loop to change what is printed. This comes in handy when we get to arrays, but for now we will just print the value of $count each time through. This will print a list of numbers from one to five:

```perl
for ($count=1; $count<6; $count++){
    print "$count\n";
}
```

Now you will get this:

```
1
2
3
4
5
```

2.4.11.2 While Loop

The *while* loop repeats a portion of code, but it repeats it until the condition you provide comes back *false*. Here is the general syntax for the while loop:

```
while (test condition){
    code to repeat
}
```

So, we could print out that list of numbers from one to ten with the while loop instead. Be sure to define your test variable (in our case $count) before the loop begins. You will also need to be sure to increment the test variable inside the loop. Here is the code for the number list with a while loop:

```
$count=1;
while ($count<6){
    print "$count\n";
    $count++;
}
```

For some things, this is easier to use than the *for* loop. It just depends on what action you wish to perform.

2.4.11.3 Foreach Loop

The *foreach* loop is one that is often used with some sort of array. If you have an understanding of arrays, this will make a bit more sense:

```
foreach variable_name (array_name){
    code to repeat
}
```

An array is a way of storing a group of variables that makes them easy to access and manipulate later. The *foreach* loop takes each element of the array and uses it with your code. Let's say we had an array named @bank (The @ sign signals an array). Using the *foreach* loop, we could print out each element of the array. If we use the variable $dollar to represent an element in the array, we could print out every $dollar we have in the @bank, so to speak!

```
foreach $dollar (@bank){
    print "$dollar\n";
}
```

2.4.12 Subroutines

2.4.12.1 Arguments, Return Values

Arguments for a subroutine are passed via an array @. Note once again that the @ sign tells us this is an array; we can think of the array name as being , with the @ sign then telling us it is an array. Here are some examples:

```
# read in two numbers from the command line (note: the duality of
# numbers and strings in Perl means no need for atoi()!)
$x = $ARGV[0];
$y = $ARGV[1];
# call subroutine which finds the minimum and print the latter
$z = min($x,$y);
print $z, "\n";
sub min {
    if ($_[0] < $_[1]) {return $_[0];}
    else {return $_[1];}
}
```

A common Perl idiom is to have a subroutine use shift on @ to get the arguments and assign them to local variables.

Arguments must be pass-by-value, but this small restriction is more than compensated by the facts that (a) arguments can be references, and (b) the return value can also be a list. Here is an example illustrating all this:

```
$x = $ARGV[0];
$y = $ARGV[1];
($mn,$mx) = minmax($x,$y);
print $mn, " ", $mx, "\n";
sub minmax {
    $s = shift @_; # get first argument
    $t = shift @_ ; # get second argument
    if ($s < $t) {return ($s,$t);} # return a list
        else {return ($t,$s);}
```

```
}
```

Or, one could use array assignment:

```
($s,$t) = @_
```

However, this won't work for subroutines having a variable number of arguments.

Any subroutine, even if it has no return, will return the last value computed. So for instance in the minmax() example above, it would still work even if we were to remove the two return keywords. This is a common aspect of many scripting languages, such as the R data manipulation language and the Yacas symbolic mathematics language.

If any of the arguments in a call are arrays, all of the arguments are flattened into one huge array, @_ . For example, in the call to f() here,

```
$n = 10;
@x = (5,12,13);
f($n,@x);
$_[2] would be 12.
```

2.4.12.2 Some Remarks on Notation

Instead of enclosing arguments within parentheses, as in C, one can simply write them in "command-line arguments" fashion. For example, the call

```
($mn,$mx) = minmax($x,$y);
```

can be written as

```
($mn,$mx) = minmax $x,$y;
```

In fact, we've been doing this in all our previous examples, in our calls to print(). This style is often clearer. In any case, you will often encounter this in Perl code, especially in usage of Perl's built-in functions, such as the print() example we just mentioned.

On the other hand, if the subroutine, say x(), has no arguments make sure to use the parentheses in your call:

```
x();
```

rather than

```
x;
```

In the latter case, the Perl interpreter will treat this as the "declaration" of a variable x, not a call to x().

2.4.12.3 Passing Subroutines As Arguments

Older versions of Perl required that subroutines be referenced through an ampersand preceding the name, e.g.

```
($mn,$mx) = &minmax $x,$y;
```

In some cases we must still do so, such as when we need to pass a subroutine name to a subroutine. The reason this need arises is that we may write a packaged program which calls a user-written subroutine. Here is an example of how to do it;

```
sub x {
    print "this is x\n";
}
sub y {
    print "this is y\n";
}
sub w {
    $r = shift;
    &$r();
}
w \&x; # prints "this is x"
w \&y; # prints "this is y"
```

Here w() calls r(), with the latter actually being either x() or y().

2.4.13 String Manipulation in Perl

One major category of Perl string constructs involves searching and possibly replacing strings. For example, the following program acts like the Unix *grep* command, reporting all lines found in a given file which contain a given string (the file name and the string are given on the command line):

```
open(INFILE,$ARGV[0]);
while ($line = <INFILE>) {
   if ($line =~ /$ARGV[1]/) {
      print $line;
   }
}
```

Here the Perl expression

```
($line =~ /$ARGV[1]/)
```

checks $line for the given string, resulting in a true value if the string is found. In this string-matching operation Perl allows many different types of regular expression conditions.3 For example,

```
open(INFILE,$ARGV[0]);
while ($line = <INFILE>) {
   if ($line =~ /us[ei]/) {
      print $line;
   }
}
```

would print out all the lines in the file which contain either the string "use" or "usi". Substitution is another common operation. For example, the code

```
open(INFILE,$ARGV[0]);
while ($line = <INFILE>) {
   if ($line =~ s/abc/xyz/) {
      print $line;
   }
}
```

would pull out all lines in the file which contain the string "abc", replace the first instance of that string in each such line by "xyz", and then print out those changed lines. There are many more string operations in the Perl repertoire. As mentioned earlier, Perl uses eq to test string equality; it uses ne to test string inequality.

A popular Perl operator is chop, which removes the last character of a string. This is typically used to remove an end-of-line character. For example,

```
chop $line;
```

removes the last character in $line, and reassigns the result to $line. Since chop is actually a function, and in fact one that has $ as its default argument, if $line had been read in from STDIN, we could write the above code as

```
chop;
```

2.4.14 Perl Packages/Modules

In the spirit of modular programming, it's good to break up our program into separate files, or packages. Perl specialized the packages notion to modules, and it will be the latter that will be our focus here. Except for the top-level file (the one containing the analog of main() in C/C++), a file must have the suffix .pm ("Perl module") in its name and have as its first noncomment/nonblank line a package statement, named after the file name. For example the module X.pm would begin with

```
package X;
```

The files which draw upon X.pm would have a line

```
use X;
```

near the beginning.

The :: symbol is used to denote membership. For example, the expression $X::y refers to the scalar $y in the file X.pm, while @X::z refers to the array @z in that file. The top-level file is referred to as main from within other modules. As you can see, packages give one a separate namespace. Modules which are grouped together as a library are placed in the same directory, or the same directory tree.

2.5 Python

2.5.1 What is Python?

Python is an *interpreted, object-oriented, high-level programming* language with dynamic semantics. Its high-level built in data structures, combined with dynamic typing and dynamic binding, make it very attractive for Rapid Application

Development, as well as for use as a scripting or glue language to connect existing components together. Python's simple, easy to learn syntax emphasizes readability and therefore reduces the cost of program maintenance.

Python supports modules and packages, which encourages program modularity and code reuse. The Python interpreter and the extensive standard library are available in source or binary form without charge for all major platforms, and can be freely distributed.

Often, programmers fall in love with Python because of the increased productivity it provides. Since there is no compilation step, the edit-test-debug cycle is incredibly fast. *Debugging Python* programs is easy: a bug or bad input will never cause a segmentation fault. Instead, when the interpreter discovers an error, it raises an exception. When the program doesn't catch the exception, the interpreter prints a stack trace.

A source level debugger allows inspection of local and global variables, evaluation of arbitrary expressions, setting breakpoints, stepping through the code a line at a time, and so on. The debugger is written in Python itself, testifying to Python's introspective power. On the other hand, often the quickest way to debug a program is to add a few print statements to the source: the fast edit-test-debug cycle makes this simple approach very effective.

2.5.2 Booleans

The *Boolean* constants are *True* and *False*, and the six relational operators work on all primitives, including strings. !, ||, and && have been replaced by the more expressive not, or, and and. Also, we can chain relational tests like *min < mean < max* make perfect sense.

```
>>> 4 > 0
True
>>> "apple" == "bear"
False
>>> "apple" < "bear" < "candy cane" < "dill"
True
>>> x = y = 7
>>> x <= y and y <= x
True
>>> not x >= y
False
```

2.5.3 Whole Numbers

Integers work as you'd expect, though you're insulated almost entirely from the fact that small numbers exist as four-byte figures and super big numbers are managed as longs,
without the memory limits:

```
>>> 1 * -2 * 3 * -4 * 5 * -6
-720
>>> factorial(6)
720
>>> factorial(5)
120
>>> factorial(10)
3628800
>>> factorial(15)
1307674368000L
>>> factorial(40)
815915283247897734345611269596115894272000000000L
```

When the number is big, you're reminded how big by the big fat L at the end. Also, assume that we defined the factorial function, because it's not a built-in.

2.5.4 Strings

String constants can be delimited using either double or single quotes. Substring selection, concatenation, and repetition are all supported.

```
>>> interjection = "ohplease"
>>> interjection[2:6]
'plea'
>>> interjection[4:]
'ease'
>>> interjection[:2]
'oh'
>>> interjection[:]
```

```
'ohplease'
>>> interjection * 4
'ohpleaseohpleaseohpleaseohplease'
>>> oldmaidsays = "pickme" + interjection * 3
>>> oldmaidsays
'pickmeohpleaseohpleaseohplease'
>>> 'abcdefghijklmnop'[-5:] # negative indices count from the end!
'lmnop'
```

The quirky syntax that's likely new to you is the slicing, ala [start:stop]. The [2:6] identifies the substring of interest: character data from position 2 up through but not including position 6. Leave out the start index and it's taken to be 0.

Leave out the stop index, it's the full string length. Leave them both out, and you get the whole string. (Python doesn't burden us with a separate character type. We just use one-character strings where we'd normally use a character, and everything works just swell.)

Strings are really objects, and there are good number of methods. Rather than exhaustively document them here, I'll just illustrate how some of them work. In general, you should expect the set of methods to more or less imitate what strings in other objectoriented languages do.

You can expect methods like find, startswith, endswith, replace, and so forth, because a string class would be a pretty dumb string class without them. Python's string provides a bunch of additional methods that make it all the more useful in scripting and WWW capacities—methods like capitalize, split, join, expandtabs, and encode. Here's are some examples:

```
>>> 'abcdefghij'.find('ef')
4
>>> 'abcdefghij'.find('ijk')
-1
>>> 'yodelady-yodelo'.count('y')
3
>>> 'google'.endswith('ggle')
False
>>> 'lItTle ThIrTeEn YeAr OlD gIrl'.capitalize()
'Little thirteen year old girl'
>>>
>>> 'Spiderman 3'.istitle()
True
>>> '1234567890'.isdigit()
True
>>> '12345aeiuo'.isdigit()
False
>>> '12345abcde'.isalnum()
True
>>> 'sad'.replace('s', 'gl')
'glad'
>>> 'This is a test.'.split(' ')
['This', 'is', 'a', 'test.']
>>> '-'.join(['ee','eye','ee','eye','oh'])
'ee-eye-ee-eye-oh'
```

2.5.5 Lists and Tuples

Python has two types of sequential containers: lists (which are read-write) and tuples (which are immutable, read-only). Lists are delimited by square brackets, whereas tuples are delimited by parentheses. Here are some examples:

```
>>> streets = ["Castro", "Noe", "Sanchez", "Church",
"Dolores", "Van Ness", "Folsom"]
>>> streets[0]
'Castro'
>>> streets[5]
'Van Ness'
>>> len(streets)
7
>>> streets[len(streets) - 1]
'Folsom'
```

The same slicing that was available to us with strings actually works with lists too:

```
>>> streets[1:6]
```

```
['Noe', 'Sanchez', 'Church', 'Dolores', 'Van Ness']
>>> streets[:2]
['Castro', 'Noe']
>>> streets[5:5]
[]
```

Coolest feature ever: you can splice into the middle of a list by identifying the slice that should be replaced:

```
>>> streets
['Castro', 'Noe', 'Sanchez', 'Church', 'Dolores', 'Van Ness', 'Folsom']
>>> streets[5:5] = ["Guerrero", "Valencia", "Mission"]
>>> streets
['Castro', 'Noe', 'Sanchez', 'Church', 'Dolores', 'Guerrero',
'Valencia', 'Mission', 'Van Ness', 'Folsom']
>>> streets[0:1] = ["Eureka", "Collingswood", "Castro"]
>>> streets
['Eureka', 'Collingswood', 'Castro', 'Noe', 'Sanchez', 'Church',
'Dolores', 'Guerrero', 'Valencia', 'Mission', 'Van Ness', 'Folsom']
>>> streets.append("Harrison")
>>> streets
['Eureka', 'Collingswood', 'Castro', 'Noe', 'Sanchez', 'Church',
'Dolores', 'Guerrero', 'Valencia', 'Mission', 'Van Ness', 'Folsom', 'Harrison']
```

The first splice states that the empty region between items 5 and 6—or in [5, 5], in interval notation—should be replaced with the list constant on the right hand side. The second splice states that streets[0:1]—which is the sublist ['Castro']—should be overwritten with the sequence ['Eureka', 'Collingswood', 'Castro']. And naturally there's an append method.

Note: lists need not be homogenous. If you want, you can model a record using a list, provided you remember what slot stores what data.

```
>>> prop = ["355 Noe Street", 3, 1.5, 2460,
[[1988, 385000],[2004, 1380000]]]
>>> print("The house at %s was built in %d." % (prop[0], prop[4][0][0]))
```

The house at 355 Noe Street was built in 1988. The list's more conservative brother is the tuple, which is more or less an immutable list constant that's delimited by parentheses instead of square brackets. It's supports readonly slicing, but no clever insertions:

```
>>> cto = ("Will Shulman", 154000, "BSCS Stanford, 1997")
>>> cto[0]
'Will Shulman'
>>> cto[2]
'BSCS Stanford, 1997'
>>> cto[1:2]
(154000,)
>>> cto[0:2]
('Will Shulman', 154000)
>>> cto[1:2] = 158000
Traceback (most recent call last):
File "<stdin>", line 1, in ?
TypeError: object doesn't support slice assignment
```

2.5.6 Functions

In practice, I'd say that Python walks the fence between the procedural and objectoriented paradigms. Here's an implementation of a standalone gatherDivisors function. This illustrates if tests, for-loop iteration, and most importantly, the dependence on white space and indentation to specify block structure:

```
# Function: gatherDivisors
# ----------------------
# Accepts the specified number and produces
# a list of all numbers that divide evenly
# into it.
def gatherDivisors(num):
    """Synthesizes a list of all the positive numbers
    that evenly divide into the specified num."""
    divisors = []
    for d in xrange(1, num/2 + 1):
        if (num % d == 0):
            divisors.append(d)
```

```
    return divisors
```

The syntax takes some getting used to. We don't really miss the semicolons (and they're often ignored if you put them in by mistake). You'll notice that certain parts of the implementation are indented one, two, even three times. The indentation (which comes in the form of either a tab or four space characters) makes it clear who owns whom. You'll notice that def, for, and if statements are punctuated by colons: this means at least one statement and possibly many will fall under the its jurisdiction.

Note the following:

- The # marks everything from it to the end of the line as a comment. I bet you figured that out already.
- None of the variables—neither parameters nor locals—are strongly typed. Of course, Python supports the notion of numbers, floating points, strings, and so forth. But it doesn't require you state why type of data need be stored in any particular variable. Identifiers can be bound to any type of data at any time, and it needn't be associated with the same type of data forever. Although there's rarely a good reason to do this, a variable called data could be set to 5, and reassigned to "five", and later reassigned to [5, "five", 5, [5]] and Python would approve.
- The triply double-quote delimited string is understood to be a string constant that's allowed to span multiple lines. In particular, if a string constant is the first expression within a def, it's taken to be a documentation string explanation the function to the client. It's not designed to be an implementation comment—just a user comment so they know what it does.
- The for loop is different than it is in other language. Rather than counting a specific numbers of times, for loops iterate over what are called iterables. The iterator (which in the gatherDivisors function is d) is bound to each element within the iterable until it's seen every one. Iterables take on several forms, but the list is probably the most common. We can also iterate over strings, over sequences (which are read-only lists, really), and over dictionaries (which are Python's version of the C++ hash_map)

2.5.7 Packaging Code In Modules

Once you're solving a problem that's large enough to require procedural decomposition, you'll want to place the implementations of functions in files—files that operate either as modules (sort of like Java packages, C++ libraries, etc) or as scripts.

This gatherDivisors function above might be packaged up in a file called divisors.py. If so, and you launch python from the directory storing the divisors.py file, then you can import the divisors module, and you can even import actual functions from within the module. Look here:

```
bash-3.2$ python
Python 2.5.1 (r251:54863, Oct 5 2007, 21:08:09)
[GCC 4.0.1 (Apple Inc. build 5465)] on darwin
Type "help", "copyright", "credits" or "license" for more information.
>>> import divisors
>>> divisors.gatherDivisors(54)
[1, 2, 3, 6, 9, 18, 27]
>>> gatherDivisors(216)
Traceback (most recent call last):
File "<stdin>", line 1, in ?
NameError: name 'gatherDivisors' is not defined
>>> from divisors import gatherDivisors
>>> gatherDivisors(216)
[1, 2, 3, 4, 6, 8, 9, 12, 18, 24, 27, 36, 54, 72, 108]
>>> "neat"
'neat'
```

If everything you write is designed to be run as a standalone script—in other words, an independent interpreted program—then you can bundle the collection of meaningful functions into a single file, save the file, and mark the file as something that's executable (i.e. chmod a+x narcissist.py).

Design Interview Questions

Chapter-3

3.1 Glossary

- A *design pattern* is a general repeatable solution to a commonly occurring problem in software design. A design pattern is not a finished design that can be transformed directly into code. It is a description or template for how to solve a problem that can be used in many different situations. Because design patterns consist of proven reusable architectural concepts, they are reliable and they speed up software development process. In simple words, there are a lot of common problems which a lot of developers have faced over time. These common problems ideally should have a common solution too. It is this solution when documented and used over and over becomes a design pattern.

- We cannot always apply the same solution to different problems. Design patterns would study the different problems at hand and suggest different design patterns to be used. However, the type of code to be written in that design pattern is solely the discretion of the Project Manager who is handling that project.

- Design patterns should present a higher abstraction level though it might include details of the solution. However, these details are lower abstractions and are called *strategies*. There may be more than one way to apply these strategies in implementing the patterns.

- To use design patterns in our application:
  1. We need to understand the problem at hand. Break it down to fine grained problems. Each design pattern is meant to solve certain kinds of problems. This would narrow down our search for design patterns.
  2. Read the problem statement again along with the solution which the design pattern will provide. This may instigate to change a few patterns that we are to use.
  3. Now figure out the interrelations between different patterns. Also decide what all patterns will remain stable in the application and what all need to change.

- *Refactoring*: Refactoring is a disciplined technique for restructuring an existing body of code, altering its internal structure without changing its external behavior. Learning different design patterns is not sufficient to becoming a good designer. We have to understand these patterns and use them where they have more benefits. Using too many patterns (more than required) would be over-engineering and using less design patterns than required would be under-engineering. In both these scenarios we use refactoring. Refactoring is a change made to the internal structure of the software to make it easier to understand and cheaper to modify, without changing its observable behavior.

- Patterns: There are 23 design patterns [given by *Gang of Four*]. These patterns are grouped under three categories:
  - *Creational* Patterns: These patterns deal with object creation mechanisms. The basic form of object creation could result in design problems and adds complexity to the design. Creational design patterns solve this problem by somehow controlling this object creation. Creational design patterns are further categorized into *Object*-creational patterns and *Class*-creational patterns, where Object-creational patterns deal with Object creation and Class-creational deal with Class-instantiation.
    - *Examples*: Factory, Abstract Factory, Builder, Prototype and Singleton patterns
  - *Structural* Patterns: Structural Patterns describe how objects and classes can be combined to form larger structures. The difference between class patterns and object patterns is that class patterns describe abstraction with the help of inheritance and how it can be used to provide more useful program interface. Object patterns, on other hand, describe how objects can be associated and composed to form larger, more complex structures.
    - *Examples*: Adapter, Bridge, Composite, Decorator, Facade, Flyweight and Proxy patterns
  - *Behavioral* Patterns: Behavioral patterns are those which are concerned with interactions between the objects. They identify common communication patterns between objects and realize these patterns.
    - *Examples*: Chain of Responsibility, Command, Interpreter, Iterator, Mediator, Memento, Observer, State, Strategy, Template and Visitor patterns

3.2 Tips

- Provide consistent and intuitive class interface: Clients which uses the class only need to know how to use the class and should not be forced to know how the functionality if provided.
- Provide common properties of classes in base class: Common properties of various classes should be identified and should be provided in a common base class (which may be an abstract, concrete or a pure interface class). Placing virtual methods in the base class interface is the basis of runtime polymorphism; it also avoids code duplication and unnecessary downcasts.
- Do not expose implementation details in the public interface of the class: If the class interface exposes any implementation details of the class, it violates the rules of abstraction. Also, any changes to internal details of the class can affect the interface of the class, which is not desirable.
- Consider providing helper classes while designing large classes.
- Keep the data members private.
- Provide lowest possible access to methods.
- Try to keep *loose* coupling between classes: Classes should be either independent of other classes or they should use only the public interface of other classes. Strive for such loose coupling between the classes because such classes are easy to understand, use, maintain and modify.
- While designing the classes beware of order of initialization as they are provided by the compiler or the implementation.
- Avoid calling virtual functions in constructors: Constructors do not support runtime polymorphism fully as the derived objects are still in construction when base class constructor executes. So, avoid calling virtual functions from base class constructors, which might result bugs in the code.
- Consider providing *factory* methods (refer *Problems* section).
- Make constructor *private* if there are *only* static members in the class: When there are only static members in the class, there is no need to instantiate it.
- Avoid creating useless temporary objects.
- Prefer virtual function over *RTTI* (RunTime Type Identification): Extensive use of RTTI can potentially make the code difficult to manage. Whenever you find cascading *if − else* statements for matching particular types to take actions, consider redesigning it by using virtual functions.
- Write unit test cases for classes.
- Overload functions only if the functions semantically do the same thing.
- Do not use inheritance when only values are different among classes.
- Hierarchically partition the namespace.
- Try eliminating all forms of code *duplication*.
- Use *design patterns* whenever *appropriate*.
- Know and make best use of the standard library.
- Provide catch handlers for specific exceptions before general exceptions.
- Forget about inheritance when you're modeling objects. It's just one way of implementing common code. When you're modeling objects just pretend you're looking at each object through an interface that describes what it can be asked to do. Don't make decisions about inheritance relationships based on names.
- Learn about test-driven development. Nobody gets their object model right up front but if we do test-driven development we're putting in the groundwork to make sure our object model does what it needs to and making it safe to refactor when things change later.
- Create loosely coupled classes: Often times when we give each object only one responsibility, the objects tightly couple together. This is a mistake, because it makes reuse harder later on.
- Practice as many problems as possible. This gives more experience and control in designing the better objects.

Problems and Questions with Answers

Note: For some design problems we have used *Java* classes to make the discussion simple. If you are not a *Java* professional, feel free to download the *C + +* code online or try designing your own classes.

Question-1   Explain Singleton design pattern.

Answer: There are only two points in the definition of a singleton design pattern,
- There should be only one instance allowed for a class and
- We should allow global point of access to that single instance.

The key is not the problem and definition. In singleton pattern, trickier part is implementation and management of that single instance.

Strategy for Singleton instance creation: We suppress the constructor (by making it *private*) and don't allow even a single instance for the class. But we declare an attribute for that same class inside, create instance for that and return it.

```
class Singleton {
    public:
        static Singleton* getInstance(){
            if (instance == 0) {
```

```
            instance = new Singleton();
        }
        return instance;
    }
    private:
        Singleton(){}
        static Singleton* instance;
};
```

We need to be careful with multiple threads. In a single-threaded environment, this works fine. If we don't synchronize the method which is going to return the instance, there is a possibility of allowing multiple instances in a multi-threaded scenario. Making the classic *Singleton* implementation thread safe is easy. Just acquire a lock before testing the instance.

```
class Singleton {
    public:
        static Singleton* getInstance(){
            Lock lock; // acquire lock (parameters omitted for simplicity)
            if (instance == 0) {
                instance = new Singleton();
            }
            return instance;
        }
    private:
        Singleton(){}
        static Singleton* instance;
};
```

The problem with this solution is that it may be expensive. Each access to the Singleton requires acquisition of a lock, but in reality, we need a lock only when initializing *instance*. That should occur only the first time instance is called. If the *instance* is called n times during the course of a program run, we need the lock only for the first call. To solve this problem, we generally go for *double-checked locking* mechanism.

```
class Singleton {
    public:
        static Singleton* getInstance(){
            if (instance == 0) {
                Lock lock; // acquire lock (parameterss omitted for simplicity)
                if (instance == 0) {
                    instance = new Singleton;
                }
            }
            return instance;
        }
    private:
        Singleton(){}
        static Singleton* instance;
};
```

In the above example for singleton pattern, we can see that it is thread-safe.

Early and lazy instantiation in singleton pattern: The above example code is a sample for *lazy* instantiation for singleton design pattern. The single instance will be created at the time of first call of the *getInstance*() method. We can also implement the same singleton design pattern in a simpler way but that would instantiate the single instance early at the time of loading the class. Following example code describes how we can instantiate early. It also takes care of the multithreading scenario.

```
class Singleton {
    static Singleton instance = new Singleton();
    Singleton() {}
    public:
        static Singleton getInstance() {
            return instance;
        }
};
```

Question-2   Explain *factory* method design pattern.

Answer: *Factory* method is just a fancy name for a method that instantiates objects. Like a factory, the job of the *factory method* is to create (or manufacture) objects. A *factory* method pattern is a *creational* pattern. It is used to instantiate an object from one among a set of classes based on some *logic*. *Factory* methods have many advantages over constructors. Depending on the situation, consider providing *factory* methods instead of constructors or in addition to existing constructors. The usual approach to create new objects is by calling constructors. *Factory* methods provide alternative approach for this.

Assume that we have a set of classes which extends a common super class or interface. Now we will create a concrete class with a method which accepts one or more arguments. This method is our *factory* method. What it does is, based on the arguments passed *factory* method does logical operations and decides on which subclass to instantiate. This *factory* method will have the super class as its return type. *Factory* methods can not only return the object of the same type as its class, but also the objects of its derived class types.

Another point to note here is that, we cannot make constructors as *virtual* but *factory* methods can be declared as *virtual*. For the same reason, *factory* methods design patterns are also called as *virtual constructors*. Now, let us implementation the factory method with a sample application.

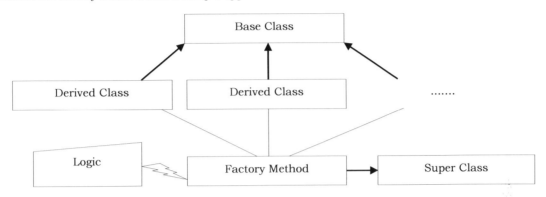

```
//Base class that serves as type to be instantiated for factory method pattern
class Pet {
    public:
        virtual void petSound() = 0;
};
//Derived class 1 that might get instantiated        //Derived class 2 that might get instantiated
//by a factory method pattern                        //by a factory method pattern
class Dog: public Pet{                               class Cat: public Pet{
  public:                                              public:
    void petSound(){                                     void petSound(){
      cout << "Bow Bow...\n";                              cout << "Meaw Meaw...\n";
    }                                                    }
};                                                   };
//Factory method pattern implementation that instantiates objects based on logic
class PetFactory {
    public:
        Pet* getPet(int petType) {
          Pet *pet = NULL;

          // Based on business logic factory instantiates an object
          if (petType == 1)
              pet = new Dog();
          else if (petType == 2)
              pet = new Cat();
          return pet;
        }
};
```

Now, let us create the factory method to instantiate

```
//using the factory method pattern
int main(){
    //creating the factory
    PetFactory *petFactory = new PetFactory();
    //factory instantiates an object
    Pet pet = petFactory→getPet(2);
    //you don't know which object factory created
    cout <<"Pet Sound: ";
    pet→petSound();
}
```

Question-3   Explain prototype design pattern.

Answer: The prototype means making a clone. *Cloning* is the operation of replicating an object. The cloned object, the copy, is initialized with the current state of the object on which clone was invoked. *Cloning* an object is based on the concepts of *shallow* and *deep* copying.

- *Shallow* Copying: When the original object is changed, the new object is changed as well. This is due to the fact that the shallow copy makes copies of only the references, and not the objects to which they refer.
- *Deep* Copying:When the original object is modified, the new object remains unaffected, since the entire set of objects to which the original object refers to were copied as well.

This implies cloning of an object avoids creation. If the cost of creating a new object is large and creation is resource intensive, we clone the object. For example, we can consider construction of a home. *Home* is the final end product (object) that is to be returned as the output of the construction process. It will have many steps, like basement construction, wall construction, roof construction and so on. Finally the whole *home* object is returned. In *Java*, we use the interface *Cloneable* and call its method *clone*() to clone the object.

To implement the prototype design pattern, we just have to copy the existing instance in hand. Simple way is, clone the existing instance in hand and then make the required update to the cloned instance so that you will get the object you need. Always remember while using clone to copy, whether you need a shallow copy or deep copy and decide based on your business needs. Using clone to copy is entirely a design decision while implementing the prototype design pattern. *Clone* is not a mandatory choice for prototype pattern.

Implementation: We declare an abstract base class that specifies a pure virtual *clone*() method. The client code first invokes the factory method. This factory method, depending on the parameter, finds out concrete class. On this concrete class call to the *clone*() method is called and the object is returned by the factory method. In the below example *Quotation* class is an abstract class that has a pure virtual method *clone*(). *CarQuotation* and *BikeQuotation* are concrete implementation of a *Quotation* class.

```cpp
class Quotation{
    protected:
        string type;
        int value;
    public:
        virtual Quotation* clone() = 0;
        string getType(){
            return type;
        }
        int getValue(){
            return value;
        }
};
```

```cpp
class CarQuotation : public Quotation{
    public:
        CarQuotation(int number){
            type = "Car";
            value = number;
        }
        Quotation* clone(){
            return new CarQuotation(*this);
        }
};
class BikeQuotation : public Quotation{
    public:
        BikeQuotation(int number){
            type = "Bike";
            value = number;
        }
        Quotation* clone(){
            return new BikeQuotation(*this);
        }
};
```

QuotationFactory is a class that has *factory* method *CreateQuotation*(...). This method requires a parameter and depending on this parameter it returns the concrete implementation of *Quotation* class.

```cpp
class QuotationFactory{
    private :
        Quotation *carQuotation;
        Quotation *bikeQuotation;
    public :
    QuotationFactory(){
        carQuotation  = new CarQuotation(10);
        bikeQuotation = new BikeQuotation(20);
    }
    ~QuotationFactory(){
        delete bikeQuotation;
        delete carQuotation;
    }
    Quotation* createQuotation(int typeID) {
        if(typeID == 1)
            return carQuotation→clone();
        else return bikeQuotation→clone();
    }
};
```

For the above discussion, a test code can be given as:

```
int main(){
  QuotationFactory* qf = new QuotationFactory();

  Quotation* q;
  q = qf→createQuotation(1);
  delete q;

  q = qf→createQuotation(2);
  delete q;
  delete qf;
  return 0;
}
```

Java has a built-in clone method in native code. This method is defined by the parent class, *Object*, and presents the following behaviour: *clone*() takes a block of memory from the *Java* heap. The block size is the same size as the original object. It then performs a bitwise copy of all fields from the original object into fields in the cloned object. This kind of operation is known as a *shallow* copy.

When copying involves primitive types, i.e. a byte, modifying either the original or the new copy will not modify the other object. This occurs because shallow copying of primitive types values result in separate values being stored in the cloned object. However, when a clone involves reference types, the pointer is copied. As a result, the original and the copy objects will contain pointers to the same object.

Following sample *Java* source code demonstrates the prototype pattern. We have a basic *Animal* in hand and to make a different object (clonedAnimal), we copy the existing instance. Then make necessary modifications to the copied instance.

```
public Animal clone() {
    Animal clonedAnimal = NULL;
    try {
        clonedAnimal = (Animal) super.clone();
        clonedAnimal.setDescription(description);
        clonedAnimal.setNumberOfLegs(numberOfLegs);
        clonedAnimal.setName(name);
    } catch (CloneNotSupportedException e) {
        e.printStackTrace();
    }
    return clonedAnimal;
}
```

In addition to the above, *C + +* and *Java* have a similar behaviour regarding cloning objects. A clear difference is that *C + +* does not provide any built-in clone method as *Java* does. Despite of this fact, *C + +* is such a powerful language that with the use of a custom-maid copy constructor and pure virtual functions the same behavior can be accomplished.

Question-4   Explain decorator design pattern.

Answer: Decorator design pattern is used to extend or modify the behavior of an *instance* at runtime. Inheritance can used to extend the abilities of a *class* (for all instances of class). Unlike inheritance, we can choose any single object of a class and modify its behavior leaving the other instances unmodified. In implementing the decorator pattern we construct a wrapper around an object by extending its behavior. The wrapper will do its job either before or after and delegate the call to the wrapped instance.

We start with an interface (pure virtual functions) which creates a blue print for the class which will have decorators. Then implement that interface with basic functionalities. Till now we have got an interface and an implementation concrete class. Now, create an abstract class that contains (aggregation relationship) an attribute type of the interface. The constructor of this class assigns the interface type instance to that attribute. This class is the decorator base class. Now we can extend this class and create as many concrete decorator classes we want. The concrete decorator class will add its own methods. Either after or before executing its own method the concrete decorator will call the base instance's method. Key to this decorator design pattern is the binding of method and the base instance happens at runtime based on the object passed as parameter to the constructor. Its dynamically customizes the behavior of that specific instance alone.

Following given example is an implementation of decorator design pattern. *House* is a classic example for decorator design pattern. We create a basic *House* and then add decorations like colors, lights etc. to it as we prefer. The added decorations change the look and feel of the basic house. We can add as many decorations as we want. This sample scenario is implemented below.

```
class House {
  public:
      virtual string makeHouse() = 0;
};
```

The above is an interface depicting a house. I have kept things as simple as possible so that the focus will be on understanding the design pattern. Following class is a concrete implementation of this interface. This is the base class on which the decorators will be added.

```
class SimpleHouse: public House {
    public:
        string makeHouse() {
            return "Base House";
        }
};
```

Following class is the decorator base class. It is the core of the decorator design pattern. It contains an attribute for the type of interface (*House*). Instance is assigned dynamically at the creation of decorator using its constructor. Once assigned that instance method will be invoked.

```
class HouseDecorator: public House {
    House *house;
    public:
        HouseDecorator(House *housePtr) {
        house = housePtr;
        }
        string makeHouse() {
            return house→makeHouse();
        }
};
```

Following two classes are similar. These are two decorators, concrete class implementing the abstract decorator. When the decorator is created the base instance is passed using the constructor and is assigned to the super class. In the makeHouse method we call the base method followed by its own method *addColors()*. This *addColors()* extends the behavior by adding its own steps.

```
class ColorHouseDecorator: public HouseDecorator {
    private:
    string addColors() {
        return " + Colors";
    }
    public:
    ColorHouseDecorator(House *housePtr): HouseDecorator(housePtr) {
    }
    string makeHouse() {
        return HouseDecorator::makeHouse() + addColors();
    }
};
class LightsDecorator: public HouseDecorator {
    private:
    string addLights() {
        return " + Lights";
    }
    public:
    LightsDecorator(House *housePtr) : HouseDecorator(housePtr) {
    }
    string makeHouse() {
        return HouseDecorator::makeHouse() + addLights();
    }
};
```

Execution of the decorator pattern: To test the pattern we can create a simple house and decorate that with colors and lights. We can use as many decorators in any order we want. This excellent flexibility and changing the behavior of an instance of our choice at runtime is the main advantage of the decorator design pattern.

```
int main() {
    House *house = new LightsDecorator(new ColorHouseDecorator(new SimpleHouse()));
    cout<<house→makeHouse();
}
```

Question-5   What is the difference between inheritance and decorator pattern? Can't we add extra functionality with inheritance?

Answer: In the previous problem, to add colors and lights for decoration we can simply create a subclasses to *House*. If we wish to add colors and lights to all houses then it make sense create a subclass to *House*. Decorator pattern is an alternative to subclassing. Subclassing adds behavior at compile time, and the change affects all instances of the original class, decorating can provide new behavior at run-time for individual objects.

The major point of the pattern is to enable run-time changes: we may not know how we want the house to look until the program is running, and this allows us to easily modify it. Granted, this can be done via the subclassing, but not as nicely.

Question-6   Explain builder design pattern.

Answer: Builder pattern is a creational pattern used to construct a complex object step by step and the final step will return the object. The process of constructing an object should be generic so that it can be used to create different representations of the same object.

For example, we can consider construction of a car. *Car* is the final end product (object) that is to be returned as the output of the construction process. It will have many steps, like settting base, wheels, mirrors, lights, engine, roof, interior and so on. Finally, the whole car object is returned. We can build cars with different properties. In Java API, *StringBuffer* and *StringBuilder* are some examples of builder pattern. Following is the interface that will be returned as the product from the builder.

```
class CarPlan {
    public:
    virtual void setBase(string basement) = 0;
    virtual void setWheels(string structure) = 0;
    virtual void setEngine(string structure) = 0;
    virtual void setRoof(string structure) = 0;
    virtual void setMirrors(string roof) = 0;
    virtual void setLights(string roof) = 0;
    virtual void setInterior(string interior) = 0;
};
```

Concrete class for the above interface: The builder constructs an implementation for the following class.

```
class Car: public CarPlan {
    private:
    string base, wheels, engine, roof, mirrors, lights, interior;
    public:
    void setBase(string base) {
        this→base = base;
    }
    void setWheels(string wheels) {
        this→wheels = wheels;
    }
    void setEngine(string engine) {
        this→engine = engine;
    }
    void setRoof(string roof) {
        this→roof = roof;
    }
    void setMirrors(string mirrors) {
        this→mirrors = mirrors;
    }
    void setLights(string lights) {
        this→lights = lights;
    }
    void setInterior(string interior) {
        this→interior = interior;
    }
};
```

Now, we will define the builder interface with multiple different implementation of this interface in order to facilitate, the same construction process to create different representations.

```
class CarBuilder {
    public:
    virtual void buildBase() = 0;
    virtual void buildWheels() = 0;
    virtual void bulidEngine() = 0;
    virtual void bulidRoof() = 0;
    virtual void bulidMirrors() = 0;
    virtual void bulidLights() = 0;
    virtual void buildInterior() = 0;
    virtual Car* getCar() = 0;
};
```

First implementation of a builder.   *Second* implementation of a builder.

```
class LowPriceCarBuilder: public CarBuilder {
    private:
            Car *car;
    public:
            LowPriceCarBuilder() {
                car = new Car();
            }
            void buildBase() {
                car→setBase ("Low priced base");
            }
            void buildWheels() {
                car→setWheels("Cheap Tyres");
            }
            void bulidEngine() {
                car→setEngine("Low Quality Engine");
            }
            void bulidRoof() {
                car→setRoof("No flexible roof");
            }
            void bulidMirrors(){
                car→setMirrors("Cheap Mirrors");
            }
            void bulidLights(){
                car→setLights("Cheap Lights");
            }
            void buildInterior(){
                car→setInterior("Cheap Iterior");
            }
            Car* getCar() {
                return this→car;
            }
};
```

```
class HighEndCarBuilder: public CarBuilder {
    private:
            Car *car;
    public:
            HighEndCarBuilder() {
                car = new Car();
            }
            void buildBase() {
                car→setBase("Quality base");
            }
            void buildWheels() {
                car→setWheels("Quality Tyres");
            }
            void bulidEngine() {
                car→setEngine("High-end Engine");
            }
            void bulidRoof() {
                car→setRoof("Flexible roof");
            }
            void bulidMirrors(){
                car→setMirrors("Quality Mirrors");
            }
            void bulidLights(){
                car→setLights("Quality Lights");
            }
            void buildInterior(){
                car→setInterior("High-end Iterior");
            }
            Car* getCar() {
                return this→car;
            }
};
```

Following class constructs the car and most importantly, this maintains the building sequence of object.

```
class MechanicalEngineer {
    private:
            CarBuilder *carBuilder;
    public:
    MechanicalEngineer(CarBuilder *carBuilder){
        this→carBuilder = carBuilder;
    }
    Car *getCar() {
        return carBuilder→getCar();
    }
    void buildCar() {
        carBuilder→buildBase();
        carBuilder→buildWheels();
        carBuilder→bulidEngine();
        carBuilder→bulidRoof();
        carBuilder→bulidMirrors();
        carBuilder→bulidLights();
        carBuilder→buildInterior();
    }
};
```

Testing the sample builder design pattern.

```
int main() {
    CarBuilder *lowPriceCarBuilder = new LowPriceCarBuilder();
    MechanicalEngineer *engineer = new MechanicalEngineer(lowPriceCarBuilder);
    engineer→buildCar();
    Car *car = engineer→getCar();
    cout<<"Builder constructed: " + car;
}
```

Question-7   Explain abstract factory design pattern.

Answer: This pattern is one level of abstraction higher than factory pattern. This means that the abstract factory returns the factory of classes. Like Factory pattern (returns one of the several sub-classes), this returns such factory which later will return one of the sub-classes.

Let's understand this pattern with the help of an example. Suppose we need to get the specification of various parts of a car. The different parts of car are, say wheels, mirrors, engine and body. The different types of cars are BenQ, BMW, GeneralMotors and so on. So, here we have an abstract base class *Car*.

```
class Car {
  public:
      Parts *getWheels() = 0;
      Parts *getMirrors() = 0;
      Parts *getEngine() = 0;
      Parts *getBody() = 0;
};
```

This class, as you can see, has four methods all returning different parts of car. They all return an object called *Parts*. The specification of *Parts* will be different for different types of cars. Let's have a look at the class *Parts*.

```
class Parts {
  public:
      string specification;
      Parts(string specification) {
              this→specification = specification;
      }
      string getSpecification() {
              return specification;
      }
};
```

And now let's go to the sub-classes of *Car*. They are *BenQ*, *BMW* and *GeneralMotors*.

```
class BenQ: public Car {                        class BMW: public Car {
  public:                                         public:
      Parts *getWheels() {                            Parts *getWheels() {
          return new Parts("BenQ Wheels");                return new Parts("BMW Wheels");
      }                                               }
      Parts *getMirrors() {                           Parts *getMirrors() {
          return new Parts("BenQ Mirrors");               return new Parts("BMW Mirrors");
      }                                               }
      Parts *getEngine() {                            Parts *getEngine() {
          return new Parts("BenQ Engine");                return new Parts("BMW Engine");
      }                                               }
      Parts *getBody() {                              Parts *getBody() {
          return new Parts("BenQ Body");                  return new Parts("BMW Body");
      }                                               }
};                                              };
```

```
                    class GeneralMotors: public Car {
                      public:
                          Parts *getWheels() {
                              return new Parts("GeneralMotors Wheels");
                          }
                          Parts *getMirrors() {
                              return new Parts("GeneralMotors Mirrors");
                          }
                          Parts *getEngine() {
                              return new Parts("GeneralMotors Engine");
                          }
                          Parts *getBody() {
                              return new Parts("GeneralMotors Body");
                          }
                    };
```

Now let's have a look at the *Abstract* factory which returns a factory "Car". We call the class CarType.

```
class CarType {
  private:
      Car *car;

  public:
      void mainFunction() {
              CarType *type = new CarType();
              Car *car = type→getCar("BenQ");
              cout<<"Wheels: " << car→getWheels()→getSpecification();
              cout<<"Mirrors: " << car→getMirrors()→getSpecification();
              cout<<"Engine: " << car→getEngine()→getSpecification();
```

```
                    cout<<"Body: " << car→getBody()→getSpecification();
            }
      Car *getCar(string carType) {
            if (carType.compare("BenQ"))
            car = new BenQ();
            else if(carType.compare("BMW"))
            car = new BMW();
            else if(carType.compare("GeneralMotors"))
            car = new GeneralMotors();
            return car;
      }
};
```

When to use Abstract Factory Pattern? One of the main advantages of *Abstract Factory Pattern* is that it isolates the concrete classes that are generated. The names of actual implementing classes are not needed to be known at the client side. Because of the isolation, we can change the implementation from one factory to another.

Question-8   Difference between abstract factory & builder pattern?

Answer: Abstract factory may also be used to construct a complex object, and then what is the difference with builder pattern? In builder pattern emphasis is on 'step by step'. Builder pattern will have many number of small steps. Those steps will have small units of logic enclosed in it. There will also be a sequence involved. It will start from step 1 and will go on up to step *n* and the final step is returning the object. In these steps, every step will add some value in construction of the object. That is you can imagine that the object grows stage by stage. Builder will return the object in last step. But in abstract factory how complex the built object might be, it will not have step by step object construction.

Question-9   Explain adapter design pattern.

Answer: Adapter pattern converts the existing interfaces to a new interface to achieve compatibility and reusability of the unrelated classes in one application. Adapter pattern is also known as Wrapper pattern. An adapter allows classes to work together that normally could not because of incompatible interfaces. The adapter is also responsible for transforming data into appropriate forms. When a client specifies its requirements in an interface, we can usually create a new class that implements the interface and subclasses an existing class. This approach creates a class adapter that translates a client's calls into calls to the existing class's methods.

Have you ever faced any problem with power sockets of 2 pin and 3 pin? If we have a 3-pin cable and a 2-pin power socket, then we use an intermediate expansion box and fit the 3-pin cable to it and attach the cable of expansion box to 2-pin power socket. In similar way this design pattern works.

There are two ways of implementing the *Adapter* Pattern, either use the Inheritance or use the composition. Let us do it with the approach of Inheritance. The first step in implementation is defining the *Cable* object which has the different specification (3 − *Pin*) to that of Socket.

```
class Cable {
   private:
       string specification;
       string getInput() {
          return specification;
       }
   public:
       Cable(){
          specification = "3-Pin";
       }
};
```

At very minimal, we can define the Socket interface and a sample concrete adapter for it as:

```
class Socket {                          class ExpansionAdapter: public Socket {
   public;                                  Cable *cable;
       virtual string & getOutput() = 0;        public:
};                                                  string & getOutput() {
                                                        cable = new Cable();
                                                        string & output = cable→getInput();
                                                        return output;
                                                    }
                                          };
```

Observe that, we are having two different methods for *Cable* (getInput()) and *Socket* (getOutput()). To test the pattern, we can simply create a *Socket* and use adapter class to convert the interface.

```
class Client {
   Socket *socket;
   public:
     void funtionTest() {
```

```
            socket = new ExpansionAdapter();
            socket→getOutput();
        }
};
```

Question-10   Explain facade design pattern.

Answer: Let us consider a simple example for understanding the pattern. While walking past the road, we can only see this glass face of the building. We do not know anything about it, the wiring, the pipes and other complexities. The face hides all the complexities of the building and displays a good looking front. This is how facade pattern is used. It hides the complexities of the system and provides a simple interface to the client from where the client can access the system. In Java, the interface JDBC is an example of facade pattern. We as users or clients create connection using the "java.sql.Connection" interface, the implementation of which we are not concerned about. The implementation is left to the vendor of driver.

Let's try to understand the facade pattern using a simple example (Graphical User Interface, GUI). Any typical GUI will have a title, menu items and content to be shown in the middle content area. To provide these features we can have different classes as shown below.

```
class GUIMenu{                                   class GUIContent{
   public:                                          public:
       void drawMenuButtons() {}                         void showButtons() {}
};                                                        void showTextFields() {}
                                                          void setDefaultValues() {}
class GUITitleBar{                               };
   public:
       void showTitleBar(const string & caption) {}
};
```

Now, to create a simple GUI the users have to think about all these classes. To make it simple, what we can do is create another class which combines all these into a single interface (facade).

```
class MyGUI{
   private:
       GUIMenu* menu;
       GUITitleBar* titleBar;
       GUIContent* content;
   public:
       MyGUI(){
           menu = new GUIMenu();
           titleBar = new GUITitleBar();
           content = new GUIContent();
       }
       ~MyGUI()  {
           delete menu;
           delete titleBar;
           delete content;
       }
       void drawGUI()  {
           content→showButtons();
           content→showTextFields();
           content→setDefaultValues();
           menu→drawMenuButtons();
           titleBar→showTitleBar("Title of the GUI");
       }
};
```

To create a GUI, users can simply use the MyGUI class with one simple call as shown below.

```
int main(){
   MyGUI* facade = new MyGUI();
   facade→drawGUI();
   return 0;
}
```

In this way the implementation is left to the façade. The client is given just one interface and can access only that. This hides all the complexities. All in all, the *Façade* pattern hides the complexities of system from the client and provides a simpler interface. Looking from other side, the facade also provides the implementation to be changed without affecting the client code.

Question-11   Explain visitor design pattern.

Answer: *Visitor* pattern is useful if we want to perform operations on a collection of objects of different types. One approach is to iterate through each element in the collection and then do something specific to each element, based on its class. If we just wanted to print out the elements in the collection, we could write a simple method like:

```
public void visitElements(vector<string> collection) {
    for(vector<string>::const_iterator iterator = collection.begin(); iterator!= collection.end(); ++ iterator)
        // print objects data
}
```

If we don't know what type of objects are in the collection then that can get pretty tricky. The above approach will not work if the objects are from different classes. I mean, what if, for example, we have a vector of hashtables? In this case, we might need to check the type of object dynamically at runtime as shown below. For each of the type in the collections we need to put a separate conditional statement. If we keep on adding if-else conditions, then the code will lose its maintainability.

```
Class AbstractElement{
    //some operations
};
class ConcreteFirstElement: public AbstractElement {       class ConcreteSecondElement: public AbstractElement {
    public:                                                    public:
        void operationOne() {                                      void operationTwo() {
            //operation on ConcreteFirstElemcnt objects.               //operation on ConcreteFirstElement objects.
        }                                                          }
};                                                         };

        void visitElements(vector<AbstractElement*>& elements) const{
            vector<AbstractElement*>& elems = elements.getElements();
            for(vector<AbstractElement*>::iterator it = elems.begin(); it != elems.end(); ++it ){
                if (typeid(*it).name() == "ConcreteFirstElement"){
                    //Some processing for type1
                }
                else if (typeid(*it).name() == "ConcreteSecondElement"){
                    //Some different processing for type-2
                }
            }
        }
```

The purpose of the *Visitor* pattern is to encapsulate an operation that we want to perform on the elements of a data structure. In this way, we can change the operation being performed on a structure without the need of changing the classes of the elements that we are operating on. Using a *Visitor* pattern allows us to decouple the classes for the data structure and the algorithms used upon them.

Each node in the data structure *accepts* a visitor, which sends a message to the visitor which includes the node's class. The visitor will then execute its algorithm for that element. This process is known as *double dispatching*. The node makes a call to the visitor, passing itself in, and the visitor executes its algorithm on the node. In double dispatching, the call made depends upon the type of the visitor and of the host (data structure node), not just of one component.

Now, let us concentrate on implementing *Visitor* pattern. Let us consider a very simple abstract data structure, *AbstractElement* and its two possible concrete classes, *ConcreteFirstElement* and *ConcreteSecondElement*. The data structure provides functions that any processing algorithm might use to manipulate the data. Note that these operations, represented here simply as the *operationOne()* and *operationTwo()* methods, are the atomic operations for manipulating the data upon which all more complex operations are built.

```
Class AbstractElement{
    virtual void accept (AbstractVisitor& v) = 0;
};
class ConcreteFirstElement: public AbstractElement {       class ConcreteSecondElement: public AbstractElement {
    public:                                                    public:
        void accept(AbstractVisitor& v) {                          void accept(AbstractVisitor& v) {
            v.visitConcreteFirstElement(*this);                        v.visitConcreteSecondElement(*this);
        }                                                          }
        void operationOne() {                                      void operationTwo() {
            // operation on ConcreteFirstElement                       // operation on ConcreteFirstElement
            // objects.                                                // objects
        }                                                          }
};                                                         };
```

The algorithms (*Visitor's*) on the data are represented by the abstract *AbstractVisitor* interface and its two possible algorithms *ConcreteFirstVisitor* and *ConcreteSecondVisitor*. In many traditional data processing algorithm architectures, *dumb* data is passed to a processing algorithm, which determines the specific type of the data and then processes it accordingly. In the *Visitor* design pattern, the data is given the ability to determine how it is processed. Instead of requiring the algorithm to query the data object to dynamically determine its type, the visitor pattern recognizes that each data type, *ConcreteFirstElement* and *ConcreteSecondElement* here, already intrinsically knows its own type.

The key is the *accept()* method in the ConcreteElement classes. The body of this method shows the double dispatching call, where the visitor is passed in to the accept method, and that visitor is told to execute its visit method, and is handed the element by the element itself. This makes for very robust code, since all of the decision making as to what to execute where and when it taken care of by the dispatching. Nobody ever needs to check anything: they just do what it is that they do, with whatever they're handed.

```
class AbstractVisitor{
    virtual void visit(ConcreteFirstElement& first) const = 0;
    virtual void visit(ConcreteSecondElement& second) const = 0;
    virtual ~AbstractVisitor() {}
};

class ConcreteFirstVisitor: public AbstractVisitor{
  public:
    void visit(ConcreteFirstElement& first) const {
    }
    void visit(ConcreteSecondElement& second) const{
    }
};
class ConcreteSecondVisitor: public AbstractVisitor{
  public:
    void visit(ConcreteFirstElement& first) const {
    }
    void visit(ConcreteSecondElement& second) const{
    }
};
```

The visitor simply provides methods for processing each respective data type and lets the data object determine which method to call. Since the data object intrinsically knows its own type, the determination of which method on the visitor algorithm to call is trivial. Thus the overall processing of the data involves a dispatch through the data object and then a subsequent dispatch into the appropriate processing method of the visitor. This is called *double dispatching*.

One key advantage of using the Visitor Pattern is that adding new operations to perform upon our data structure is very easy. All we have to do is create a new visitor and define the operation there. The problem with the visitor pattern is that because the each visitor is required to have a method to service every possible concrete data, the number and type of concrete classes cannot be easily altered once the visitor pattern is implemented.

Question-12   Explain iterator design pattern.

Answer: The *Iterator* pattern is one of the most simple and frequently used design patterns. The iterator pattern is a behavioral object design pattern. The iterator pattern allows the traversal through the elements in a group of objects. The Iterator Pattern is very useful for allowing iteration through data structures without having to worry about how the data structure is stored. In C++ there are iterator types associated with each container. Using these types is fine if we are iterating inside the class which defined the data structure. However, clients of class should not be exposed to the underlying data structure. For example, if a class returned a list of names, stored as a vector, the client of that class might iterate through the vector like this:

```
vector<string> names = myClassObj.getNames();
for(vector<string>::iterator itr = names.begin(); itr != names.end(); ++itr){
    // do something
}
```

In this case, the client of class now depends on the underlying data structure of *items*. If the data structure should ever change, the client must also be changed. The *Iterator* pattern makes the client *loosely* coupled to the *myClassObj*, and the code for iterating through a list of names might look like this:

```
MyClass::NameIterator nameItr = myClassObj.getNameIterator();
while(nameItr.hasNext()){
    // do something
}
```

An alternative to the Iterator pattern we are about to see would be to typedef the iterator type in MyClass like this:

```
class MyClass{
    // ...
    typedef vector<string>::iterator NameIterator;
};
```

However, this has the disadvantage of relying on the data structure to either be part of the standard library containers or conform to one of the standard library iterator interfaces. You could not, for example, create an iterator over a raw array or a *vector<bool>*.

We can write our own iterator by implementing methods like *hasNext()*, *next()*, and so on.

```
template <typename T>
class Iterator{
  public:
```

```
        typedef T value_type;
        virtual bool hasNext() const = 0;
        virtual T next() = 0;
};
```

Our interface is parameterized by *T*, which is the value type of the iterator (that is, it is the type we want to return from next, which is also the underlying data type of the container). There's nothing too special about this. Just note that next increments the iterator when calling it.

When writing an iterator for a class, it is very common for the iterator class to be an inner class of the class that we would like to iterate through. Here is example *NameManager* class. It has a list of names of type *vector :: string*. Names can be added via the *addName*() method. The *getNameIterator*() method returns an iterator of names. The *NameIterator* class is an *inner* class of *NameManager* that implements the *Iterator* interface for names objects. It contains basic implementations of the *hasNext*() and *next*() methods.

```
class NameManager {
    typedef std::vector<std::string> NameCollection;
    NameCollection m_names;
    public:
    class NameIterator: public Iterator< NameCollection::value_type >{
        // only NameManager should be allowed access to the constructor
        friend class NameManager;
    private:
        NameManager::NameCollection & m_names;
        NameManager::NameCollection::iterator m_itr;
        NameIterator(NameManager::NameCollection & names) :
        m_names(names), m_itr(m_names.begin()) {}
    public:
        virtual bool hasNext(void){
            return m_itr != m_names.end();
        }
        virtual NameIterator::value_type next(void){
            NameIterator::value_type value = (*m_itr);
            ++m_itr;
            return value;
        }
    };
    void addName(NameCollection::value_type name){
        m_names.push_back(name);
    }
    NameIterator getNameIterator(void){
        return NameIterator(m_names);
    }
};
```

The *below* code demonstrates the iterator pattern. It creates three names and adds them to the *nameMgr* object. Next, it gets an name iterator from the *nameMgr* object and iterates over them.

```
int main(void) {
    NameManager nameMgr;
    nameMgr.addName("Jobs");
    nameMgr.addName("Bill");
    nameMgr.addName("Larry");

    NameManager::NameIterator nameItr = nameMgr.getNameIterator();

    while(nameItr.hasNext()){
        cout << nameItr.next() << std::endl;
    }
}
```

Question-13   Explain command design pattern.

Answer: *Command* pattern is an object behavioral pattern. This allows us to achieve complete decoupling between the sender and the receiver. A *sender* is an object that invokes an operation, and a *receiver* is an object that receives the request to execute a certain operation. With decoupling, the sender has no knowledge of the receiver's interface. The term *request* refers to the command that is to be executed.

This pattern is different from the *Chain of Responsibility* in a way that, in the earlier one, the request passes through each of the classes (in the hierarchy) before finding an object that can take the responsibility. The command pattern however finds the particular object according to the command and invokes only that one.

A classic example of this pattern is *switch*. In this example we configure the switch with 2 commands: to turn the air conditioner *on* and to turn *off* the air conditioner. Let's have a look at this example with $C++$ code. Below code shows the *receiver* class.

```cpp
/*Receiver class*/
class AirConditioner {
 public:
    AirConditioner() { }
    void start() {
        cout << "The Air Conditioner is on" << endl;
    }
    void stop() {
        cout << "The Air Conditioner is off" << endl;
    }
};
```

The *Command* pattern convert the request itself into an object. This object can be stored and passed like other objects. The key to command pattern is a *Command* interface. Command interface declares an interface for executing operations.

```cpp
/*the Command interface*/
class Command {
    public:
    virtual void execute()=0;
};
```

A benefit of this particular implementation of the command pattern is that the switch can be used with any device, not just an air conditioner - the *Switch* in the following example turns a air conditioner on and off, but the *Switch's* constructor is able to accept any subclasses of *Command*(acts as *invoker*) for its 2 parameters. For example, we could configure the *Switch* to start a *motor*.

Our objective is to develop a *Switch* that can turn either object on or off. We see that the *AirConditioner* have different interfaces, which means the *Switch* has to be independent of the *receiver* interface. To solve this problem, we need to parameterize each of the *Switchs* with the appropriate command. When the *start()* and *stop()* operations are called, they will simply make the appropriate command to *execute( )*. The *Switch* will have no idea what happens as a result of *execute( )* being called. *Switch* is called the invoker because it invokes the execute operation in the command interface.

```cpp
class Switch {
public:
    Switch(Command& startCmd, Command& stopCmd)
            :startCommand(startCmd), stopCommand(stopCmd){
    }
    void start(){
        startCommand.execute();
    }
    void stop(){
        stopCommand.execute();
    }
 private:
    Command& startCommand;
    Command& stopCommand;
};
```

Each concrete *Command* class specifies a receiver-action by storing the receiver (*AirConditioner*) as an instance variable. It provides different implementations of the *execute()* method to invoke the request. The receiver has the knowledge required to carry out the request.

The concrete commands, *StartCommand* and *StopCommand*, implements the execute operation of the command interface. It has the knowledge to call the appropriate receiver object's operation. It acts as an adapter in this case. By the term adapter, I mean that the concrete *Command* object is a simple connector, connecting the *invoker* and the *receiver* with different interfaces.

```cpp
/*the Command for turning on the Air Conditioner*/
class StartCommand: public Command {
    public:
    StartCommand(AirConditioner& airConditioner):
            theAirConditioner(airConditioner) {
    }
    virtual void execute(){
        theAirConditioner.start();
    }
    private:
```

```
        AirConditioner& theAirConditioner;
};
/*the Command for turning off the Air Conditioner*/
class StopCommand: public Command{
  public:
    StopCommand(AirConditioner& airConditioner)
                :theAirConditioner(airConditioner){
    }
    virtual void execute() {
        theAirConditioner.stop();
    }
    private:
     AirConditioner& theAirConditioner;
};
/*The test class or client*/
int main() {
    AirConditioner ac;
    StartCommand switchUp(ac);
    StopCommand switchDown(ac);

    Switch s(switchUp, switchDown);
    s.start();
    s.stop();
}
```

Notice in the code example above that the *Command* pattern completely decouples the object that invokes the operation (*Switch*) from the ones having the knowledge to perform it (*AirConditioner*).

Question-14   Explain memento design pattern.

Answer:

```
class Memento {                                    class Caretaker {
    private:                                            private:
        string state;                                       list<Memento*> savedStates;
    public:                                             public:
        Memento(string& stateToSave) {                      void addMemento(Memento* m) {
            state = stateToSave;                                savedStates.push_back(m);
        }                                                   }
        string& getSavedState() {                           Memento* getMemento() {
            return state;                                       return savedStates.back();
        }                                                   }
};                                                 };
class Originator {                                 int main() {
    private:                                            Caretaker *caretaker = new Caretaker();
        string state;                                   Originator *originator = new Originator();
    public:                                             Originator→setState("State1");
        void setState(string& state) {                  originator→setState("State2");
            cout << "Setting state to " << state;       caretaker→addMemento(
            this→state = state;                             originator→saveToMemento() );
        }                                               originator→setState("State3");
        Memento* saveToMemento() {                      caretaker→addMemento(
            cout<<"Saving to Memento.";                     originator→saveToMemento() );
            return new Memento(state);                      originator→restoreFromMemento(
        }                                                       caretaker→getMemento());
        void restoreFromMemento(Memento* m) {      }
            state = m→getSavedState();
            cout<<"Restoring state
                    from Memento:"<<state;
        }
};
```

We all use this pattern at least once every day. *Memento* pattern provides an ability to restore an object to its previous state (undo via rollback). *Memento* pattern is used by two objects: originator and a caretaker. The originator is some object that has an internal state. *Caretaker* is going to perform some action to the originator, but wants to be able to undo the change.

❖   Identify a class that needs to be able to take a snapshot of its state (originator role.)
❖   Design a class that does nothing more than accept and return this snapshot (memento role).
❖   *Caretaker* role asks the *Originator* to return a Memento and cause the *Originator's* previous state to be restored of desired.

❖ Notion of undo or rollback has now been objectified (i.e. promoted to full object status).

Client requests a *Memento* from the source object when it needs to checkpoint the source object's state. Source object initializes the *Memento* with its state. The client is the care taker of the *Memento*, but only the source object can store and retrieve information from the *Memento*. If the client subsequently needs to "rollback" the source object's state, it hands the *Memento* back to the source object for reinstatement.

An unlimited "undo" and "redo" capability can be readily implemented with a stack of command objects and a stack of *Memento* objects.

Question-15   Explain strategy design pattern.

Answer: *Strategy* pattern is an example for behavioral pattern and is used when we want different algorithms needs to be applied on values (objects). That means, *Strategy* design pattern defines a set of algorithms and make them interchangeable. *Strategy* lets the algorithm vary independently from clients that use it. The strategy pattern is also known as the *Policy* pattern. We can apply *Strategy* pattern when we need different variants of an algorithm (each algorithm can be assumed as a separate class) and these related classes differ only in their behavior.

Let us consider a real-time example for understanding the pattern. Assume we have a *vector or an array* container. To sort the items in that list, we can use bubble sort, quick sort, heap sort etc... But we can use only one algorithm at a time out of all the possible. As a first step we need to define the *Strategy*(algorithms) and *Context*(vector *or* array container) interfaces. Context pass data to Strategy. Strategy has point to *Context* to get data from *Context*. Strategies can be used as template parameters (*Template* design pattern) if strategy can be selected at compile-time and does not change at run-time.

```
class SortInterface {
    public:
        virtual void sort(int[], int) = 0;
};
```

The concrete implementations of the SortInterface can be given as:

```
class QuickSort: public SortInterface {
    public:
        void sort(int array[], int size) {
            //Quick sort logic
        }
};
```
```
class BubbleSort: public SortInterface {
    public:
        void sort(int array[], int size) {
            //Bubble sort logic
        }
};
```

The dependent abstract *Context* class and its dependent concrete class can be given as:

```
class Sorter {
    private:
        SortInterface* strategy;
    public:
        void setSorter(SortInterface* strategy) {
            this→strategy = strategy;
        }
        SortInterface* getSorter() {
            return this→strategy;
        }
        virtual void doSort(int listToSort[], int size) = 0;
};
```
```
class MySorter: public Sorter {
    public:
        void doSort(int listToSort[], int size) {
            getSorter()→sort(listToSort, size);
            // other processing here
        }
};
```

Sample Client Code:

```
int main() {
    int listToBeSoted[] = {18, 26, 26, 12, 127, 47, 62, 82, 3, 236, 84, 5};
    int listSize = sizeof(listToBeSoted)/sizeof(int);
    MySorter *mysorter = new MySorter();
    Mysorter→setSorter(new BubbleSort());
    mysorter→doSort(listToBeSoted, listSize);
    mysorter→setSorter(new QuickSort());
    mysorter→doSort(listToBeSoted, listSize);
}
```

Question-16   Explain state design pattern.

Answer: *State* pattern allows objects to behave in different ways depending on internal state (*Context*). The *Context* can have a number of internal states, whenever the *request*() method is called on the *Context*, the message is delegated to the *State* to handle. The *State* interface defines a common interface for all concrete states, encapsulating all behaviour associated with a particular state. The concrete state provides its own implementation for the request. When a Context changes state, what really happens is that we have a different *ConcreteState* associated with it.

This is all quite similar to the *Strategy* pattern, except the changes happen at runtime rather than the client deciding. *State* saves us from lots of conditional code in *Context*: by changing the *ConcreteState*object used, we can change the behavior of the context. Let us consider a real-time example for understanding the pattern (Music player). Similar to *Strategy* pattern here also we have *Context* and a *State* interface.

```cpp
class State {
    public:
        virtual void pressPlay(MusicPlayerContextInterface* context) = 0;
};
```

The concrete implementations of the *State* interface can be given as:

```cpp
class StandbyState: public State{
        public:
                void pressPlay(
                    MusicPlayerContextInterface *context){
                    context→setState(new PlayingState());
                }
};
class PlayingState: public State {
        public:
                void pressPlay(
                    MusicPlayerContextInterface *context){
                    context→setState(new StandbyState());
                }
};
```

A dependent abstract *Context* class and its dependent concrete class can be given as:

```cpp
//Context Interface
class MusicPlayerContextInterface{
    State *state;
    public:
        virtual void requestPlay() = 0;
        virtual void setState(State *state) = 0;
        virtual State* getState() = 0;
};
//Sample Test Code
int main(){
    MusicPlayerContext* musicPlayer = new
            MusicPlayerContext(new StandbyState());
    musicPlayer→requestPlay();
    musicPlayer→requestPlay();
    musicPlayer→requestPlay();
    musicPlayer→requestPlay();
    return 0;
}
```

```cpp
//Concrete Context
class MusicPlayerContext: public
                        MusicPlayerContextInterface{
    State *state;
    public:
        MusicPlayerContext(State *state){
            this→state= state;
        }
        void requestPlay(){
            state→pressPlay(this);
        }
        void setState(State *state){
            this→state = state;
        }
        State* getState(){
            return state;
        }
};
```

This shows how the state pattern works at a simple level. Few advantages of *State* pattern are.

- State pattern provides a clear state representation of an object
- It allows a clean way for an object to partially change its type at runtime

Question-17   Explain observer design pattern.

Answer: Have you ever used RSS feeds? If so, you already know about *Observer* pattern. The *Observer* pattern defines a link between objects so that when one object's state changes, all dependent objects are updated automatically (Producer/Consumer problem which we coded in *Java* is also a classic example). There is always an *Observer* (also called *Listeners*) and *Observable* (also called *Providers*) object around us. We are an *Observer*, TV is an *Observable* object. That means, *Observer* pattern is designed to help cope with one to many relationships between objects, allowing changes in an object to update many associated objects. This is a behavioral pattern.

To implement *Observer* pattern, we define the interfaces for *Listener* and *Observer*. Note that, *Listener* has methods *addObserver* and *removeObserver* to keep track of observers.

```cpp
class Listener {
    public:
    virtual void addObserver(Observer* o)=0;
    virtual void removeObserver(Observer* o) =0;
    virtual string& getState()=0;
    virtual void setState(string state) = 0;
    virtual void notifyObservers() = 0;
};
```

```cpp
class Observer {
    public:
        virtual void update(Listener* l)=0;
};
```

For simplicity, let us assume that the changes are notified as strings. To support multiple observers we used *list*. One possible implementation of above interfaces can be given as:

```
class ObserverImpl: public Observer {
    string state = "";
    public:
        void update(Listener *l) {
            state = l→getState();
            cout<<"Update received from
                        Listener: " << state<< endl;
        }
};
class ListenerImpl: public Listener {
    list<Observer*> observers ;
    string state = "";
    public:
        string& getState() {
            return state;
        }
        void setState(string &state) {
            this→state = state;
            notifyObservers();
        }
        void addObserver(Observer *obsr) {
            observers→push_back(obsr);
        }
        void removeObserver(Observer *obsr) {
            observers→remove(obsr);
        }
        void notifyObservers() {
            for(list<Observer*>::iterator it = observers.begin(),
                    itend = observers.end(); it != itend; ++it )
                (*it)→update(this);
        }
};
```

Now, to test the pattern we can create a listener object and any number of *Observer* objects as shown below.

```
int main() {
    Observer obsr = new ObserverImpl();
    Listener listener = new ListenerImpl();
    listener.addObserver(obsr);
    listener.setState("New State");
}
```

Question-18   Explain proxy design pattern.

Answer: *Proxy* means *in place of*. In attendance call, we give proxy for our friends in college, right? *Representing* or *in place of* or *on behalf of* are literal meanings of proxy and that directly explains proxy design pattern. It is one of the simplest and straight forward design pattern. Proxy pattern is an example of *structural* design patterns. There are many different flavors of *Proxy*, depending on its purpose. We may have a *protection* proxy, to control access rights to an object. A *virtual* proxy handles the case where an object might be expensive to create, and a *remote* proxy controls access to a remote object.

The proxy pattern is used when we need to represent a complex object with a simpler one. If creation of object is expensive, its creation can be postponed till the very need arises and till then, a simple object can represent it. This simple object is called the *Proxy* for the complex object.

For better understanding, let's take an example. Say, we want to attach an image with the email. Now, suppose this email has to be sent to millions of consumers in an ad-campaign. Attaching the image and sending along with the email will be a very heavy operation. What we can do instead is, send the image as a link to one of the servlet. The place holder of the image will be sent. Once the email reaches the consumer, the image place holder will call the servlet and load the image at run time straight from the server. First, we should create a common interface for the real and proxy implementations to use:

```
class Image{
    public:
        virtual void showImage() = 0;
};
```

- The RealImage implementation of this interface works as you would expect:
- Now the Proxy implementation can be written, which provides access to the RealImage class. Note that it's

```
class RealImage: public Image{
public:
    RealImage(URL *url)  {
        //load the image
        loadImage(url);
    }
    void showImage()  {
        //display the loaded image
    }
    //a method that only the real image
has
    void loadImage(URL *url){
        // complex operations to load image
    }
};
```

only when we call the displayImage() method that it actually uses the RealImage. Until then, we don't need the data.

```
class ProxyImage : public Image{
private:
    URL *url;
public:
    ProxyImage(URL *url)  {
        this→url = url;
    }
    //this method delegates to the real image
    void showImage() {
        RealImage *real = new RealImage(url);
        Real→showImage();
    }
};
```

Question-19   Explain composite design pattern.

Answer: A *Composite* is a tree structure consisting of individual objects mixed with compositions of objects, that is, objects that have other objects as their children. A classic example of this is a tree structure which we saw in *Trees* chapter. A tree consists of nodes and leaves. Leaves could represent a simple individual object, while nodes have branches with additional leaves and could for this reason described as collection of objects. The goal of the *Composite* pattern is to be able to *treat* individual objects (individual nodes or leaves) and compositions of objects (subtrees) the same way. All objects in the *Composite* are derived from *Composite* itself.

Another classic example is a file structure in an operating system (either *Linux* or *Windows*). As we know, any file system can have files, directories or combination of both. To begin with, we can create an interface for file-system object which just prints the name of it.

```
class FilesystemObject{
public:
    virtual void print() = 0;
};
```

To define the *File* object, we can simply create a concrete class for *FilesystemObject* and implement the print function.

```
class File : public FilesystemObject{
public:
    File(const string& filename) : fileName(filename) {}
    void print()   {
        cout << fileName << endl;
    }
private:
    string fileName;
};
```

Since directory is a collection of file-system objects, we can use a list to store them. In the below code observe that, we have a list which stores *FilesystemObjects*.

```
class Directory : public FilesystemObject{
public:
    Directory(const string& path) : dirPath(path) {}
    ~ Directory()   {
        for_each(children_.begin(), children_.end(), FilesystemObjectDeallocator() );
    }
    void print()   {
        cout << "Printing Directoy File Names" << dirPath << endl;
        for (list<FilesystemObject*>::iterator it = children_.begin(), itend = children_.end();
            it != itend; ++it)
        (*it)→print();
    }
    //Adds the object to the composition.
    void add(FilesystemObject* object)   {
        children_.push_back(object);
    }
    //Removes the object from the composition.
    void remove(FilesystemObject* object)   {
        list<FilesystemObject*>::iterator found = find(children_.begin(), children_.end(), object);
        if( found != children_.end() )
            children_.erase(found);
    }
```

```
    private:
        list<FilesystemObject*> children_;   //Collection of children
        string dirPath;
        struct FilesystemObjectDeallocator   {
            void operator()(FilesystemObject*& p) { delete p; p = 0; }
        };
};
```

Sample client code for testing could be: note that we are adding *directories* as *children* to *other* directoy.

```
int main(int argc, char *argv[]){
    File* file1 = new File("test1");
    File* file2 = new File("test2");
    File* file3 = new File("test3");

    Directory* directory1 = new Directory("/root");
    Directory* directory2 = new Directory("/username");

    //Compose the directories
    directory2→add(file1);
    directory2→add(file2);
    directory1→add(file3);

    directory1→add(directory2);
    directory2→add(directory1);

    directory1→print();

    return 0;
}
```

Question-20   Can you give brief about other patterns?

Answer: In the previous problems, we tried to understand different patterns which we encounter frequently in interviews. Now, let us take a look at remaining patterns to get an overview of what they do.

Creational patterns

Abstract Factory: Refer Question-7   *Builder*: Refer Question-6

Factory Method: Refer Question-2   *Prototype*: Refer Question-3

Singleton: Refer Question-1

Structural patterns

- *Adapter*: Refer Question-9
- *Bridge* decouples an abstraction from its implementation so that the two can vary independently.
- *Composite*: Refer Question-19
- *Decorator*: Refer Question-4
- *Façade*: Refer Question-10
- *Flyweight* reduces the cost of creating and manipulating a large number of similar objects. Consider for example a game of war, where there is a large number of soldier objects. Assume a Soldier object maintain the graphical representation of a soldier, soldier behavior such as motion, and firing weapons, in addition soldiers health and location on the war terrain. Creating a large number of soldier objects is a necessity however it would incur a huge memory cost. To solve these kind of issues Flyweight pattern is used.
- *Proxy*: Refer Question-18

Behavioral patterns

Most of these design patterns are specifically concerned with communication between objects.

- *Chain of responsibility* delegates commands to a chain of processing objects.
- *Command*: Refer Question-13
- *Interpreter* implements a specialized language.
- *Iterator*: Refer Question-12
- *Mediator* gives loose coupling among classes by being the only class that has detailed information of their methods.
- *Memento*: Refer Question-14
- *Observer*: Refer Question-17
- *Strategy*: Refer 0
- *State*: Refer Question-16
- *Template method* defines the skeleton of an algorithm as an abstract class and allows its subclasses to provide concrete behavior.
- *Visitor*: Question-11

Question-21   What is the difference between architectural patterns and design patterns?

Answer: Architectural Patterns are concerned with strategic aspects of a system. They have a global impact on the whole implementation of a system. Design Patterns are concerned with technical aspects of an implementation. They have a local impact on specific parts of the implementation of a system. Architectural Patterns are on a higher level of abstraction than Design Patterns.

There are *many* other *types* of patterns (like UI patterns which deals with presentation of UI) depending on domain. If you are appearing for architect position, I would request you refer those resources to fill the domain gap.

Question-22   Explain MVC pattern.

Answer: Model–View–Controller (*MVC*) is an architectural pattern. In MVC Design Pattern, the application is divided into three components known as *Model*, *View* and *Controller*. The pattern aims at separating out the inputs to the application (*Controller*), the business processing logic (*Model*) and the output format logic (*View*).

- Controller associates the user input to a Model and a View
- Model fetches the data to be presented from persistent storage
- View deals with how the fetched data is presented to the user

Controller can be considered as a middle man between user and processing (*Model*) and formatting (*View*) logic. It is an entry point for all the user requests or inputs to the application. The controller accepts the user inputs, parses them and decides which type of *Model* and *View* should be invoked. Accordingly, it invokes the chosen *Model* and then the chosen *View* to provide to the user what it requested.

Model represents the business processing logic of the application. This component would be an encapsulated version of the application logic. *Model* is also responsible for working with the databases and performing operations like *Insertion*, *Update* and *Deletion*. Every model is meant to provide a certain kind of data to the controller, when invoked. Further, a single model can return different variants of the same kind of data based on which method of the *Model* gets called. What exactly gets returned to the controller, could be controlled by passing arguments to a given method of the model.

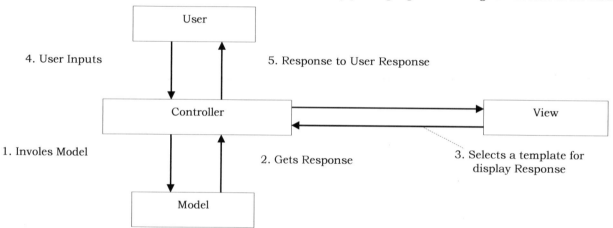

View, also known as *presentation* layer, is responsible for displaying the results obtained by the controller from the model component in a way that user wants them to see or a pre-determined format. The format in which the data can be visible to users can be of any *type* like HTML or XML. It is responsibility of the controller to choose a view to display data to the user. Type of view could be chosen based on the model chosen, user configuration etc.

Question-23   *Grading* a *class*: Assume that we are given a file of students data and the objective of this problem is to write a report of student grades in a class. Assume that each line of the students data file consists of a name, a mark for the midterm, a mark for the final, and marks for assignments. The number of assignments is not fixed; students do as many as they want to. The name is a single name with no embedded blanks. A line of the output file is similar to a line of the input file, but the first number is the total mark, computed as 25% of the midterm mark plus 55% of the final mark plus the median of the assignments. The output is written twice, once sorted by name, and once sorted by total mark.

Sample Input:	*Sample Output:*
Gates 47 83 9 8 4 7 6 9 8	*Sorted by student name:*
Jobs 36 88 8 6 7 4 9 7 8 7	Jobs 67.5 36 88 8 6 7 4 9 7 8 7
...	Gates 67.2 47 83 9 8 4 7 6 9 8
	...
	Sorted by student marks:
	Gates 67.2 47 83 9 8 4 7 6 9 8
	Jobs 67.5 36 88 8 6 7 4 9 7 8 7
	...

Answer: Goal of the design is to use an object to store a student record and to put as much problem-specific information as possible into the corresponding class. Below code shows the action items of the problem. The first paragraph takes a file name and tries to open the file. The second paragraph declares the principal data object of the program, a vector of *Students*. From this paragraph, we can tell that the *Student* class must provide a reading capability (>>) and a method process to compute the final mark. The last part of the program opens an output file and writes the data to it twice, first sorted by name and then sorted by total marks. From this section, we understand that the *Student* class must provide two sorting functions, *sortByNames* and *sortByMarks*.

```cpp
int main(){
    string inputFileName;
    cout << "Please enter class file name: ";
    cin >> inputFileName;
    ifstream ifs(inputFileName.c_str());
    if (!ifs){
        cerr << "Failed to open " << inputFileName << endl;
        return 1;
    }
    vector<Student> classData;
    Student stud;
    while (ifs >> stud){
        stud.process();
        classData.push_back(stud);
    }
    ofstream ofs("StudentGrades.txt");
    sort(classData.begin(), classData.end(), sortByNames);
    ofs << "Sorted by name:\n";
    showClass(ofs, classData);
    sort(classData.begin(), classData.end(), sortByMarks);
    ofs << "\nSorted by marks:\n";
    showClass(ofs, classData);
}
```

The function *showClass* is straightforward and uses an iterator to traverse the vector of marks data.

```cpp
void showClass(ostream & os, const vector<Student> & classData){
    for ( vector<Student>::const_iterator it = classData.begin(); it != classData.end(); ++it )
        os << *it << endl;
}
```

Below code shows the declaration for class *Student*.

```cpp
class Student{
    friend ostream & operator<<(ostream & os, const Student & stud);
    friend istream & operator>>(istream & is, Student & stud);
    friend bool sortByNames(const Student & left, const Student & right);
    friend bool sortByMarks(const Student & left, const Student & right);
    public:
        void process();
        string getName();
        void getName(string newName);
    private:
        static string::size_type maxNameLen;
        string name;
        int midterm;
        int final;
        vector<int> assignments;
        double total;
};
```

There is a public method, *process*, which performs any necessary computation on the data read from the marks file. The private data includes the information that is read from the marks file (*name*, *midterm*, *final*, and *assignments*) and computed information, *total*. For formatting the output, we need to know the length of the longest name. This is an attribute of the class, not the object, and so it is declared as a static data member. We need methods for input (>>) and output (<<); these are declared as *friends*. We need comparison functions that will be used for sorting: *sortByNames* orders by students names, and *sortByMarks* orders by students total marks. There is an important design choice here. The four friend functions cannot be member functions, because of the way they are called.

The next step is to complete the implementation of class *Student* by providing definitions for functions and initial values for static variables. The static data member can be initialized like this:

```cpp
int Student::maxNameLen = 0;
```

The public function *process* calculates the total mark. Calculating the total mark requires finding the median of the assignments. The median is meaningless for an empty vector, and the median function requires a non-empty vector as its argument. Thus process, calls median only if the student has done at least one assignment.

```
void Student::process(){
   if (maxNameLen < name.size())
      maxNameLen = name.size();
   total = 0.25 * midterm + 0.55 * final;
   if (assignments.size() > 0)
      total += median(assignments);
}
```

The *median* calculation is performed by the function shown below. The main design issue for this function is how to pass the vector of scores. Since we have to sort the vector in order to find the median, we cannot pass it by constant reference. If we pass it by reference, the caller will get back a sorted vector. Although this does not matter much for this program, a function should not in general change the data it is given unless the caller needs the changed value. Consequently, we choose to pass the vector by value, incurring the cost of copying it.

```
// Requires: scores.size() > 0.
double median(vector<int> scores) {
   typedef vector<int>::size_type szt;
   szt size = scores.size();
   assert(size > 0);
   sort(scores.begin(), scores.end());
   szt mid = size / 2;
   return size % 2 == 0 ? 0.5 * (scores[mid] + scores[mid+1]) : scores[mid];
}
```

Below code shows the comparison functions that we need for sorting. The parameter lists of these functions are determined by the requirements of the sort algorithm: there must be two parameters of the same type, both passed by constant reference. Since we have declared these functions as friends of Student, they have access to Student's private data members. The type of name is string and the type of total is double; both of these types provide the comparison operator <. After sorting, the records will be arranged in increasing order for the keys. Names will be alphabetical: Anne, Bo, Colleen, Dingbat, etc. Records sorted by marks will go from lowest mark to highest mark. To reverse this order, putting the students with highest marks at the "top" of the class, all we have to do is change < to >.

```
bool sortByNames(const Student & left, const Student & right){
   return left.name < right.name;
}
bool sortByMarks(const Student & left, const Student & right){
   return left.total < right.total;
}
```

The compiler has to perform a number of steps to determine that these functions are called by the statements

```
sort(classData.begin(), classData.end(), sortByNames);
sort(classData.begin(), classData.end(), sortByMarks);
```

Finally, below functions shows the extractor and inserter for class Student.

```
istream & operator>>(istream & ifs, Student & stud){
   if (ifs >> stud.name){
      ifs >> stud.midterm >> stud.final;
      int mark;
      stud.assignments.clear();
      while (ifs >> mark)
         stud.assignments.push_back(mark);
      ifs.clear();
   }
   return ifs;
}
ostream & operator<<(ostream & os, const Student & stud){
   os <<
   left << setw(static_cast<streamsize>(Student::maxNameLen)) <<
   stud.name << right <<
   fixed << setprecision(1) << setw(6) << stud.total <<
   setw(3) << stud.midterm <<
   setw(3) << stud.final;
   for ( vector<int>::const_iterator it = stud.assignments.begin(); it != stud.assignments.end(); ++it )
      os << setw(3) << *it;
   return os;
}
```

The extractor (input function, >>) is a bit tricky, because we rely on the failure management of input streams. The key problem is this: since students complete different numbers of assignments, how do we know when we have read all the assignments? The method we use depends on what follows the last assignment: it is either the name of the next student or the end of the file. If we attempt to read assignments as numbers, either of these will cause reading to fail. Consequently, we can use the following code to read the assignments:

```
while (ifs >> mark)
    stud.assignments.push_back(mark);
```

However, we must not leave the stream in a bad state, because this would prevent anything else being read. Therefore, when the loop terminates, we call

```
ifs.clear();
```

to reset the state of the input stream.

We assume that, if a student name can be read successfully, the rest of the record is also readable. If the name is not read successfully, the function immediately returns the input stream in a bad state, telling the user that we have encountered end of file. What happens if there is a format error in the input? Some markers, although they are asked to provide integer marks only, include fractions. Suppose that the input file contains this line:

```
Ram 45 76 9 9 8.5 9 9 8 8 9
```

The corresponding output file contains these lines:

```
Ram 63.6 45 76 9 9 8
.5 15.2 9 9 8 8 9
```

We see that *Ram* has lost all his assignment marks after 8.5 and we have a new student named ".5". It is clear that, if this was a production program, we would have to do more input validation.

There are many ways of solving this problem. If we are not given input file then we can ask the users to give input as shown below.

```
// This method is use to register one student
void RegisterStudent(){
    string name;
    double English, Maths, CompSc; //we can add other subjects as required
    cout << "\nPlease register the student\n";
    cout << "\nEnter the student's information\n";
    cout << "English Subject Marks: "; cin >> English;
    cout << "Mathematics Subject Marks: "; cin >> Maths;
    cout << "Comp Science Subject Marks: "; cin >> CompSc;
    //...
}
```

Question-24   Simulate a supermarket (grocery store).

Answer: Before creating the objects let us understand the use cases for simulating a grocery store. At very top level, a customer walks into a grocery store, picks up a few items, pays for them, and leaves. To make the problem simple we will discard the corner cases (like, what if customer forget to bring money after billing etc..). The obvious objects of any grocery store are:

- A customer
- A store
- Grocery items of various sorts
- A cashier

One doubt that may arise here is: Do we need to subclass the grocery items (beauty, health, cook etc..)? The answer is no, because these items don't have different behaviors. There is no obvious reason for any of these to be a superclass (or subclass) of any of the others. Another doubt that may arise here is: Should we make a class Person and use it as a superclass of *Customer* and *Cashier*? To make it simple let us not do that. We can always do it later, if we find some data or actions that *Customer* and *Cashier* should both have.

Now, let us start creating classes. The grocery items should be in the *store*, and initially only the store needs to know about them, so we will let the *store* create those. The *Customer* and the *Cashier* both need to know about the *store* (but the *store* kind of just sits there). So, we probably should create the store first. This is because, when we create the *Cashier* and the *Customer*, we want to create them with knowledge of the *store*.

The store is the central idea of this program, so let's put a main method in the *store* to kick things off. Let us call our main class as *GroceryStore*. What does our main method need to do?

- Create a GroceryStore
- Create a Cashier for the store
- Create a Customer who knows about the store
- Tell the Customer to "shop"

```
class GroceryStore {
    public static void main(String args[]) {
        GroceryStore store = new GroceryStore();
        Cashier cashier = new Cashier(store);
```

```
        Customer customer = new Customer(store);
        customer.shop();
    }
}
```

With the above code, the customer only shops in this one store. This is adequate for our program, but it's very restrictive and it's trivial to fix. So, the Customer needs to shop: this includes selecting groceries and paying for them.

```
class Customer {
    public void shop(GroceryStore store) {
        selectGroceries(store); // because the store holds the groceries
        checkOut(???); // who or what do we pay?
    }
}
```

Obviously, the Customer should pay the Cashier. But how does the Customer know about the Cashier? The Customer knows about (can reference) the GroceryStore and the Cashier knows about the GroceryStore. Neither the GroceryStore nor the Customer knows about the Cashier. To fix this, the Customer do not know about the Cashier as they don't know any clerks personally. Buy the GroceryStore know about the Cashier and the Cashier still needs to know about the GroceryStore. So, the customer class can be changed as:

```
class Customer {
    public void shop(GroceryStore store) {
        selectGroceries(store);
        checkOut(store);
    }
}
```

At this point, we understand that the Customer knows about the GroceryStore, the GroceryStore knows about the Cashier and hence, the Customer can ask the GroceryStore about the Cashier.

```
class GroceryStore {                              class Customer {
    GroceryStore() {...} // Constructor               public void shop(GroceryStore store) {...}
    public static void main(String args[]) {...}      public void selectGroceries(GroceryStore store) {...}
    public void hire(Clerk clerk) {...}               checkOut(GroceryStore  store) {...}
    public Clerk getClerk() {...}                 }
}
```

There's just one Cashier, whom we hired like this:

```
GroceryStore store = new GroceryStore();
Cashier Cashier = new Cashier();
store.hire(Cashier);
```

So we need to write the hire method. Also, don't forget the store and Cashier need to know about each other.

```
class GroceryStore {                              class Cashier {
    Cashier myCashier;                                GroceryStore myStore;
    public void hire(Cashier Cashier) {               public void takePosition(GroceryStore store) {
        myCashier = Cashier;                              myStore = store;
        Cashier.takePosition(this);                   }
    }                                             }
}
```

The Customer call get the Cashier from GroceryStore as:

```
class Store {
    Cashier myCashier;
    ...
    public Cashier getCashier() {
        return myCashier;
    }
    ...
}
```

Next, construct a Store containing an array of GroceryItems (along with how many of each).

```
// instance variables
public int KINDS_OF_ITEMS = 4;
public GroceryItem[ ] item = new GroceryItem[KINDS_OF_ITEMS];
public int[ ] itemCount = new int[KINDS_OF_ITEMS];

// constructor
GroceryStore() {
    item[0] = new GroceryItem("milk", 2.12);
    item[1] = new GroceryItem("butter", 2.50);
    item[2] = new GroceryItem("eggs", 0.89);
```

```
      item[3] = new GroceryItem("bread", 1.59);
      for (int i = 0; i < KINDS_OF_ITEMS; i++) {
          itemCount[i] = 50;  // the store has lots of everything
      }
  }
}
```

Customer selects the items as:

```
  GroceryItem[ ] myShoppingBasket = new GroceryItem[20];
  Random random = new Random();
  public void selectGroceries(GroceryStore store) {
        int itemsInMyBasket = 0;
        for (int i = 0; i < store.KINDS_OF_ITEMS; i++) {
                // for each kind of item
                for (int j = 0; j < 3; j++) {
                        // choose up to 3 of it
                        if (random.nextInt(2) == 1) {
                                myShoppingBasket[itemsInMyBasket] = store.item[i];
                                store.itemCount[i] = store.itemCount[i] - 1;
                                itemsInMyBasket = itemsInMyBasket + 1;
                        }
                }
        }
  }
```

The Customer can checkout as:

```
  void checkOut(GroceryStore  store) {
      Cashier Cashier = store.getCashier();
      double total = Cashier.getBill(myShoppingBasket);
      myMoney = myMoney - total;
      Cashier.pay(total);
  }
```

The final code for our discussion is:

```
public class GroceryStore {
  // instance variables
  Cashier myCashier;
  public int KINDS_OF_ITEMS = 4;
  public GroceryItem[ ] item = new GroceryItem[KINDS_OF_ITEMS];
  public int[ ] itemCount = new int[KINDS_OF_ITEMS];
  double money = 1000.00;
  // constructor
  GroceryStore() {
    item[0] = new GroceryItem("milk", 2.12);
    item[1] = new GroceryItem("butter", 2.50);
    item[2] = new GroceryItem("eggs", 0.89);
    item[3] = new GroceryItem("bread", 1.59);
    for (int i = 0; i < KINDS_OF_ITEMS; i++) {
        itemCount[i] = 50;  // the store has lots of everything
    }
  }
  public static void main(String args[]) {
    GroceryStore store = new GroceryStore();
    Cashier Cashier = new Cashier();
    store.hire(Cashier);
    Customer customer = new Customer();
    customer.shop(store);
  }
  public void hire(Cashier Cashier) {
    myCashier = Cashier;
    Cashier.takePosition(this); // "this" = this store
  }
  public Cashier getCashier() {
    return myCashier;
  }
}
public class Customer {
  GroceryItem[ ] myShoppingBasket = new GroceryItem[20];
  Random random = new Random();
```

```
    double myMoney = 100.00;
    public void shop(GroceryStore store) {
      selectGroceries(store); // because the store holds the groceries
      checkOut(store);
    }
    public void selectGroceries(GroceryStore store) {
      int itemsInMyBasket = 0;
      for (int i = 0; i < store.KINDS_OF_ITEMS; i++) { // for each kind of item
        for (int j = 0; j < 3; j++) {          // choose up to 3 of it
          if (random.nextInt(2) == 1) {
            myShoppingBasket[itemsInMyBasket] = store.item[i];
            store.itemCount[i] = store.itemCount[i] - 1;
            itemsInMyBasket = itemsInMyBasket + 1;
          }
        }
      }
    }
    void checkOut(GroceryStore store) {
      Cashier Cashier = store.getCashier();
      double total = Cashier.getBill(myShoppingBasket);
      myMoney = myMoney - total;
      Cashier.pay(total);
    }
}
public class Cashier {
    GroceryStore myStore;
    public void takePosition(GroceryStore store) {
      myStore = store;
    }
    public double getBill(GroceryItem[] item) {
      double total = 0;
      int itemNumber = 0;
      while (item[itemNumber] != null) {
        total = total + item[itemNumber].price;
        System.out.println(item[itemNumber].name + "    " + item[itemNumber].price);
        itemNumber = itemNumber + 1;
      }
      System.out.println("TOTAL    " + total);
      return total;
    }
    public void pay(double amount) {
      myStore.money = myStore.money + amount;
    }
}
public class GroceryItem {
    // Instance variables
    public String name;
    public double price;
    // Constructor
    GroceryItem(String name, double price) {
      this.name = name;
      this.price = price;
    }
}
```

In addition to above discussion, it is worth mentioning the other points for extensions:
1. Providing interface for changing the prices of items.
2. Providing discount coupons while checkouts.
3. Categorizing the store employees and assigning roles and many more.

Question-25   Consider a company which wants to process salary hikes of its employees during recession period. As a precautionary measure, instead of hiking all employees salaries it decided to hike only for the employees who met at least any two of the criteria. Can you design the classes and functions to help the company for processing the hike letters?

- Published at least two research papers.
- Got star of the year award.
- Completed at least 5 years of experience.

Answer: As the problem states, the two basic objects of the problem are: *Employee* and *Company*. For each employee, we need to maintain additional information such as number of papers published by employee, whether the employee got the award or not, and also the number of years he spend in current company. To maintain that information, we can define the interface of Employee as:

```
public interface Employee{
    public int getName();        // returns name of employee
    public int getAge();         // returns age of employee
    public int getYearsOnJob();  // returns number of years on job
    public double getSalary();   // returns salary in dollars
    public int getID();          // returns unique employee ID number
    public boolean gotAward();   // checks whether the employee got the award or not
    public int getCountPublished();// returns number of papers published by employee
}
```

One possible implementation for the employee would be:

```
public class EmployeeImpl implements Employee{
    private int myName;
    private int myAge;
    private int myYearsExp;
    private double mySalary;
    private int myID;
    private boolean gotAward;
    private int papersPublished;
    public EmployeeImpl(String name, int age, int yearsExp, double salary,
                        int id, boolean award, int papersCount){
        myName = name;
        myAge = age;
        myYearsExp = yearsExp;
        mySalary = salary;
        myID = id;
        gotAward = award;
        papersPublished = papersCount;
    }
    public String getName(){
        return myName;
    }
    public int getAge() {
        return myAge;
    }
    public int getYearsOnJob(){
        return myYearsExp;
    }
    public double getSalary(){
        return mySalary;
    }
    public int getID(){
        return myID;
    }
    public boolean gotAward(){
        return gotAward;
    }
    public int getCountPublished(){
        return papersPublished;
    }
}
```

We are done with *Employee* class and let us start defining the *Company* class. For simplicity we can discard the unrelated functionality (for example, adding new employees, changing name of employee etc..). We can assume that the Company class is the main class for our problem (which means, Company class takes care of adding employees with the values defined). Once, it generates the employee list we can use that and process for salary hikes.

```
public class Company{
    private final static int MIN_PUBLISH_COUNT  = 2;
    private final static int MIN_EXP = 5;
    private ArrayList myEmployees;
    private Employee[] empList = {
        new EmployeeImpl("James Bond", 25,3,12000,1, true, 3),
        new EmployeeImpl("Steve Jobs",35,6,13000,2,false, 4),
```

```
        new EmployeeImpl("Bill Gates",30,2,14000,true, 1),
        new EmployeeImpl("Jeff",23,1,9999,4, true, 5),
        new EmployeeImpl("Steve Gates",57,15,20000,5, true, 10)
    };
    private double myTotalSalary;
    //set myTotalSalary as total budget = sum of all salaries
    private void calcSalaries(){
        myTotalSalary = 0;
        Iterator it = myEmployees.iterator();
        while (it.hasNext()){
            Employee e = (Employee) it.next();
            myTotalSalary += e.getSalary();
        }
    }
    Company(){
        myEmployees = new ArrayList();
        myEmployees.addAll(Arrays.asList(empList));
        calcSalaries();
    }
    //returns total of all employee salaries
    public double getBudget(){
        return myTotalSalary;
    }
    //prints information about all employees
    public void printAll(){
        System.out.println("Number of employees = " + myEmployees.size());
        for(int k=0; k < myEmployees.size(); k++){
            Employee e = (Employee) myEmployees.get(k);
            System.out.println(k + ".\t id = " + e.getID()+ "\t$"+e.getSalary());
        }
        System.out.println("total budget = "+getBudget());
    }
    private boolean employeeIsEligible(Employee emp){
      return (emp.getCountPublished() >= MIN_PUBLISH_COUNT &&  emp.gotAward()) ||
          (emp.getCountPublished() >= MIN_PUBLISH_COUNT && emp.getYearsOnJob() >= MIN_EXP) ||
          (emp.getYearsOnJob() >= MIN_EXP &&  emp.gotAward());
    }
    public void processRetirements(){
        Iterator it = myEmployees.iterator();
        while (it.hasNext()){
            Employee e = (Employee) it.next();
            if (employeeIsEligible(e)){
                System.out.println(e.getID() + " is eligible for salary hike \n");
            }
        }
    }
}
```

Question-26   Design the library management system.

Answer: We all know how a library system works. The basic components of the library are: library items (like books, CDs, journals etc..), and a mechanism for giving books to users. The interface for LibraryItem is straightforward except for the decision to return a boolean for the method checkOut. To simplify our discussion, we can confine ourselves to only books. The book class can be defined as:

```
public class Book{
    private String theAuthor, theTitle,
                        pageCount, year, edition;

    public Book(String author, String title){
       theAuthor = author;
       theTitle = title;
       pageCount = pages;
       year = yearPublished;
       edition = bookEdition;
    }
    public String getAuthor(){
      return theAuthor;
    }
    public String getTitle(){
```

```
public interface LibraryItem{
    public String getID(); // return id of this item
     //return true if checking out (no holder) possible
    //and assign a new holder
    //otherwise (existing holder) return false
    public boolean checkOut(String holder);
    public String getHolder();//return current holder
    // We can add more functions
    // based on requirement
}
```

```
            return theTitle;
        }
        public String getPageCount(){
            return pageCount;
        }
        public String getYear(){
            return year;
        }
        public String getEdition(){
            return edition;
        }
}
```

Now, to create a library book we can simply implement the LibraryItem interface and extend the book class. It shouldn't duplicate state from the Book class (so no author/title, those are accessible via super.getXX methods), but a LibraryBook needs an ID and a holder, so those instance variables are required.

```
public class LibraryBook extends Book implements LibraryItem{
    private String theID;
    private String theHolder;
    public LibraryBook(String author, String title, String id,  int pageCount, int year, int edition){
        super(author, title, pageCount, year, edition);
        theID = id;
    }
    public String getHolder(){
        return theHolder;
    }
    public boolean checkOut(String holder){
        if (theHolder == null){
            theHolder = holder;
            return true;
        }
        return false;
    }
    public String getID(){
        return theID;
    }
}
```

Now, let us define the library class which maintains the library items as a collection. The problem statement pretty much requires a mapping of IDs to LibraryItems to facilitate efficient implementation of the checkOut and getHolder methods. For this, we can use a hash map.

```
public class Library{
    private Map items;

    public Library(){
        items = new HashMap();
    }
    public void add(LibraryItem theItem){
        items.put(theItem.getID(), theItem);
    }
    public void checkout(String id, String holder){
        LibraryItem item = (LibraryItem) items.get(id);
        item.checkOut(holder); // ignore return value here
    }
    public String getHolder(String id){
        LibraryItem item = (LibraryItem) items.get(id);
        return item.getHolder(); // precondition: item in library
    }
}
```

Question-27   Design an elevator system at a shopping complex using Java threads to support multithreading.

Answer: Let us understand the scenarios which need to be considered while designing an elevator system. Shoppers arrive in the building at random times. During the time a shopper is in the building he may request elevator service from the floor where he is currently located. The request always specifies a direction, *up* or *down*. Shoppers on the lowest floor may only request up service; those on the top floor may only request down service; all others may request either service.

On entering an elevator a shopper selects a destination floor. The elevator then closes its doors and moves to that destination floor, possibly stopping on intermediate floors to deliver other shoppers who may have selected intermediate floors. When an elevator arrives at a destination floor it stops, opens its doors, and discharges any shoppers who have selected that floor. Having stopped, opened its doors and unloaded its passengers, the elevator then admits any shoppers who may be waiting for service in the direction the elevator may be currently moving, subject to the restriction that the elevator may not exceed its capacity to carry passengers. Shoppers who do not succeed in boarding the elevator because it is full must make a fresh request to obtain service at the floor on which they are waiting.

For our implementation, we can assume that the elevator moves passengers from floor to floor in simulation. The basic objects of the system are: *Elevator*, *Person*, *Building* and the *Simulator* which controls the elevators. *Elevator* class keeps track of current state of it (whether it is moving up or down), its capacity, service time required at each floor and time required to move to next floor, current number of passengers on elevator, number of passengers getting off at each floor while moving etc... Operations on Elevator object are synchronized to make the system thread safe.

```java
public class Elevator extends Thread {
    private final String name; // name of elevator
    private final int capacity;  // number of people that will fit
    private int currentFloor;        // where elevator is now
    private bool goingUp = true;
    private Building thisBuilding;      // Building containing elevator
    private long floorServiceTime;      // How long takes at each floor
    private long travelTime;            // How long it takes between floors
    private int numPassengers;          // number of passengers on elevator
    private Vector[] passengers;        // Names of passengers getting off at each floor
    private int numberFloors; // number of floors in building
    private bool running = true;        // whether elevators are running

    public Elevator(string name, int numberOfFloors, int startingFloor, int capacity, Building office,
                long floorServiceTime, long travelTime) {
        name = name;
        numberFloors = numberOfFloors;
        currentFloor = startingFloor;
        thisBuilding = office;
        floorServiceTime = floorServiceTime;
        travelTime = travelTime;
        numPassengers = 0;
        capacity = capacity;
    }

    //stops elevator from running
    public void stopElevator() {
        running = false;
    }

    // returns floor where elevator is
    public synchronized int getCurrentFloor() {
        return currentFloor;
    }

    // run elevator up and down in building, picking up and depositing passengers.
    public void run() {
        System.out.println(toString() + " starting");
        while (running) {
            System.out.println(toString()+" now on floor "+currentFloor +
                                        at time "+ System.currentTimeMillis());
            // Should elevator change direction
            if (currentFloor == numberFloors-1){
                goingUp = false;
            } else if (currentFloor == 0) {
                goingUp = true;
            }
            // tell passengers so they can exit or load
            notifyPassengers();
            thisBuilding.tellAt();
            try{    // wait for passengers to leave and new ones to load
                sleep(floorServiceTime);
            } catch (InterruptedException exc) {
                System.out.println(toString() + " sleep interrupted");
            }
            System.out.println(toString() + " now leaving floor "+currentFloor
                    +" at time "+ System.currentTimeMillis());
```

```
                    // Go to next floor
                    if (goingUp) {
                        currentFloor++;
                    } else {
                        currentFloor--;
                    }
                    try{    // wait for elevator to arrive at next floor
                            sleep(travelTime);
                    } catch (InterruptedException exc) {
                            System.out.println(toString() + " sleep interrupted");
                    }
            }
    }

    //If elevator on currFloor and there is room for new passenger
    //     then return destFloor, otherwise return currFloor.
    public synchronized int takeElevator(int destFloor, int currFloor, Person waiter) {
            if (currentFloor == currFloor && numPassengers < capacity) {
                    numPassengers++;
                    System.out.println(waiter + " getting on " + toString() +
                                    " on floor " + currFloor+" at time "+ System.currentTimeMillis());
                    while (currentFloor != destFloor){
                            try{    // wait is in loop in case someone else sneaks in
                                wait();
                            } catch (InterruptedException ie){
                                System.out.println(toString()+" interrupted: "+ie.toString());
                            }
                    }
                    numPassengers--;
                    return destFloor;
            } else {
                    return currFloor;
            }
    }

    //Woke up all passengers who may be waiting for elevator
    private synchronized void notifyPassengers(){
            notifyAll();
    }

    // post: return name of elevator
    public String toString(){
            return name;
    }

    public bool isGoingUp(){
            return goingUp;
    }
}
```

Each building is associated with a number of floors and can have multiple elevators. This class takes care of starting/stopping the elevators. Whenever a passenger adds a request, it finds the elevator which reaches the passenger floor first and updates the status of elevators.

```
public class Building {
    public final int NUM_FLOORS;        // number of floors in building
    public final int NUM_ELEVATORS;  // number of elevators in building
    private Elevator[] lift;             // array of elevators

    public Building(int numFloors, int numElevators, int elevatorCapacity, int serviceFloor, int travelTime) {
            NUM_FLOORS = numFloors;
            NUM_ELEVATORS = numElevators;
            lift = new Elevator[numElevators];
            for (int liftNum = 0; liftNum < numElevators; liftNum++) {
                    lift[liftNum] = new Elevator("lift "+liftNum, NUM_FLOORS,
                                    liftNum % numFloors, elevatorCapacity, this, serviceFloor, travelTime);
            }
    }

    // start all of the elevators running
    public void startElevators(){
            for (int liftNum = 0; liftNum < NUM_ELEVATORS; liftNum++) {
```

```
                    lift[liftNum].start();
            }
    }
    // stop all of the elevators from running
    public void stopElevators(){
            for (int liftNum = 0; liftNum < NUM_ELEVATORS; liftNum++) {
                    lift[liftNum].stopElevator();
            }
    }

    //notified all of those waiting that an elevator has arrived at currentFloor
    public synchronized void tellAt() {
            notifyAll();
    }

    // Returns the first elevator to reach the current floor that is going the right direction.
    // Wait if necessary for one to arrive.
    public synchronized Elevator callElevator(int personFloor, bool goingUp){
            while (true) {
                    for (int liftNum = 0; liftNum < NUM_ELEVATORS; liftNum++) {
                            if(lift[liftNum].getCurrentFloor() == personFloor &&
                                    lift[liftNum].isGoingUp() == goingUp) {
                                    return lift[liftNum];
                            }
                    }
                    try {
                            wait();
                    } catch (InterruptedException e) {
                            e.printStackTrace();
                    }
            }
    }

    public synchronized void waitForElevatorToCome() {
            try{
                    wait();
            } catch  (InterruptedException e) {
                    e.printStackTrace();
            }
    }
}
```

Now, let us concentrate on passenger class. The shopper maintains the information about his state. To link the shopper and building, we can pass the building information to shopper (*Person* class) constructor.

```
public class Person extends Thread {
    private static final int WAITING = 0;
    private static final int SHOPPING = 1;
    private static final int ON_ELEVATOR = 2;
    private static final int DONE = 3;
    private int status = WAITING;          // what person is doing
    private final int[] itinerary;         // floors that shopper must visit
    private final String name;             // name of shopper
    private final int busyTime;            // how long it takes to shop on one floor
    private final Building building;       // where shopping takes place
    private int itemNumber;                // index of floor in itinerary shopping in now
    private int currentFloor;              // floor shopping in now
    public Person(String name, int[] itinerary,int busyTime, int startingFloor, Building building): {
            super("Person " + name);
            this.name = name;
            this.itinerary = itinerary;
            this.busyTime = busyTime;
            this.itemNumber = 0;
            this.currentFloor = startingFloor;
            this.building = building;
            // sanity checking that parameters are OK
            for (int i = 0; i < itinerary.length; i++)
                    checkFloor(itinerary[i], building);
            checkFloor(currentFloor, building);
            if (busyTime < 0)
```

```
                        busyTime = 0;
        }
        // if floor not legal floor in building office then throw exception
        private void checkFloor(int floor, Building office) {
                if (floor < 0 || floor >= office.NUM_FLOORS)
                        throw new RuntimeException("Illegal floor " + floor);
        }
        // Have shopper move through store using elevators to get to new floors.  Prints out all changes
        public void run() {
                while (itemNumber < itinerary.length) {
                        int dest = itinerary[itemNumber];
                        // If I'm on elevator, check to see if on the floor I want to be on to get off
                        if (dest == currentFloor && status == ON_ELEVATOR) {
                                System.out.println(name+" exiting elevator on floor "+dest
                                                +" at time "+ System.currentTimeMillis());
                                shopOnFloor();
                                System.out.println(name+" done shopping on floor "+dest
                                                +" at time "+ System.currentTimeMillis());
                                itemNumber++;
                        }
                        // take the next elevator to my floor
                        else {
                                System.out.println( name + " waiting on " + currentFloor
                                                + " for floor " + dest+" at time "+ System.currentTimeMillis());

                                // wait for an elevator
                                Elevator elevatorHere = building.callElevator(currentFloor, dest > currentFloor);

                                // found one --- try to get on
                                System.out.println(name + " tries to get on " + elevatorHere + " to floor "
                                                + dest+" at time "+ System.currentTimeMillis());
                                status = ON_ELEVATOR;
                                currentFloor = elevatorHere.takeElevator(dest, currentFloor, this);

                                if (currentFloor != dest) { // no room for me
                                        status = WAITING;
                                        System.out.println(
                                                "oops! " + name + " didn't make it onto elevator to " + dest);
                                        building.waitForElevatorToCome();
                                }
                        }
                }
                System.out.println(name + " is done shopping");
        }
        // printed message about starting shopping and then shop for busyTimeSecs.
        private void shopOnFloor() {
                System.out.println(name + " arrived at floor " + currentFloor
                                +" at time "+ System.currentTimeMillis());
                status = SHOPPING;
                try {
                        Thread.sleep(busyTime);
                } catch (InterruptedException e) {
                        System.exit(1); // just die
                }
                status = WAITING;
        }
        // return name of shopper
        public String toString() {
                return name;
        }
}
```

Finally, the *Simulator* class creates necessary objects for running the elevator. It gives sample inputs to all the classes defined earlier as given below.

```
public class Simulator {
        // how long it takes to get to next floor
        private static final int TRAVEL_TIME = 1000;
        // how long elevator stays on a floor
```

```
        private static final int FLOOR_TIME = 500;
        // time shopper is shopping on a floor
        private static final int BUSY_TIME = 3000;
        // number of elevators in building
        private static final int NUM_ELEVATORS = 2;
        // number of people that each elevator can hold
        private static final int ELEVATOR_CAPACITY = 2;
        // number of floors in building
        private static final int NUM_FLOORS = 3;

        // Report all events of simulations, including length of
        //      simulation.
        public static void main(String args[]) throws InterruptedException {
                // Create building
                Building shoppingComplex = new Building(NUM_FLOORS, NUM_ELEVATORS,
                        ELEVATOR_CAPACITY, FLOOR_TIME, TRAVEL_TIME);

                // create itineraries for shoppers
                int[] p1Itinerary = { 1, 2, 0 };
                int[] p2Itinerary = { 2, 1, 0 };

                // create shoppers
                Person Steve = new Person("Steve", p1Itinerary, BUSY_TIME, 0, shoppingComplex);
                Person Jeff = new Person("Jeff", p2Itinerary, BUSY_TIME, 0, shoppingComplex);
                Person Bill = new Person("Bill", p1Itinerary, BUSY_TIME, 0, shoppingComplex);
                Person Einstene = new Person("Einstene", p2Itinerary, BUSY_TIME, 0, shoppingComplex);

                // start all threads running
                shoppingComplex.startElevators();
                Steve.start();
                Jeff.start();
                Bill.start();
                Einstene.start();

                // Keep track of when we started
                long startTime = System.currentTimeMillis();

                Steve.join();          // Don't continue until all threads complete
                Jeff.join();
                Bill.join();
                Einstene.join();
                shoppingComplex.stopElevators();

                // Report time that simulation ran
                long elapsedTime = System.currentTimeMillis() - startTime;
                System.out.println("Total simulation time: " + elapsedTime + " ms");
        }
}
```

Question-28   Design a cache mechanism which uses LRU (Least Recently Used) in *Java*.

Answer: The processing costs for selecting a value from a database-table are fairly high compared to the costs having the value already in memory. So, it seems preferable to use some smart caching-mechanism that keeps often used values in your application instead of retrieving these values from resources somewhere *outside*.

A critical factor when using caches in Java is the size of the cache; when the cache grows too big, the Java Garbage Collector has to cleanup more often (which consumes time) or our application even crashes with a *out of memory* error. One way to control the memory-consumption of caches is to by implementing a caching-strategy like e.g. LRU. Instead of reinventing the wheel, Java provides an easy way to implement a LRU cache.: the *LinkedHashMap*. *LinkedHashMap* class allows us to implement both an LRU and FIFO queues almost without coding. Instantiating *LinkedHashMap* with the third parameter passed as true in this constuctor:

```
public LinkedHashMap(int initialCapacity, float loadFactor, boolean accessOrder)
```

causes the map to become an LRU map. That's because the map is ordered by access-order. But passing the third parameter as false makes it a FIFO, because the map is ordered by insertion order. So if you want to use it as an LRU, do the following:

```
HashMap  map = new LinkedHashMap(0, 0.75F, true);
```

One such possible implementation could be given as:

```
import java.util.LinkedHashMap;
import java.util.Map.Entry;
public class LRUCache extends LinkedHashMap {
    private static final long serialVersionUID = 1L;
```

```
    private final int capacity;
    private long accessCount = 0;
    private long hitCount = 0;

    public LRUCache(int capacity) {
        super(capacity + 1, 1.1f, true);
        this→capacity = capacity;
    }

    @Override
    public Object get(Object key) {
        accessCount++;
        if (super.containsKey(key)) {
            hitCount++;
        }
        Object value = super.get(key);
        return value;
    }

    @Override
    public boolean containsKey(Object key) {
        accessCount++;
        if (super.containsKey(key)) {
            hitCount++;
            return true;
        }else{
            return false;
        }
    }

    protected boolean removeEldestEntry(Entry eldest) {
        return size() > capacity;
    }

    public long getAccessCount() {
        return accessCount;
    }

    public long getHitCount() {
        return hitCount;
    }
}
```

What if the interviewer does not allow us to use LinkedHashMap? An LRU cache solution needs at least two main operations add and search:

- add(key, value): Adds a key-value pair into the cache. If the cache has reached its capacity then remove the least recently used entry and add the given entry. If the cache is not full then check if the given key-value pair is already in the cache. If it is, then the entry needs to be updated such that it becomes the most recently used entry. In the default case just add entry into the cache and make it the most recently used entry.
- search(key): Search cache for an entry with the given key. If an entry exist, then make it the most recently used entry and return its value otherwise return null.

Now on to the exciting part of how it works internally. The cache works with two data structures, a HashMap and doubly linked list. HashMap facilitates a constant time look up for a given key. Its value is a CacheEntry object that internally stores the key and value (yes, key is stored twice but we'll get to that). CacheEntry objects also have pointers to previous and next cache entries which forms a doubly linked list. The cache has access to head and tail dummy nodes of the doubly linked list to easily add entries in front and remove from the end.

In the below implementation we are storing the key twice: once in a HashMap (for constant-time lookups) and another time in CacheEntry object. Reason for storing the key in a CacheEntry object is being able to remove the eldest entry from the list and subsequently from the map to keep them consistent with each other. Following is the code.

```
class CacheEntry {
    private CacheEntry prev, next;
    private String key, value;

    CacheEntry(String key, String value) {
        this→key = key;
        this→value = value;
    }
    public String getKey() {
        return key;
    }
}
```

```java
  public String getValue() {
    return value;
  }
  public void setValue(String value) {
    this→value = value;
  }
  public CacheEntry getPrev() {
    return prev;
  }
  public void setPrev(CacheEntry prev) {
    this→prev = prev;
  }
  public CacheEntry getNext() {
    return next;
  }
  public void setNext(CacheEntry next) {
    this→next = next;
  }
}
class LRUCache {
  private Map<String, CacheEntry> map;
  private CacheEntry head, tail;
  private int maxSize;
  // maxSize specify maximum size of the cache
  public LRUCache(int maxSize) {
    if(maxSize < 1) {
      throw new IllegalArgumentException("Cache maxSize has to be at least 1");
    }
    this→map = new HashMap<String, CacheEntry>();
    head = new CacheEntry("head", NULL);
    tail = new CacheEntry("tail", NULL);
    head.setNext(tail);
    tail.setPrev(head);
    this→maxSize = maxSize;
  }
  public void add(String key, String value) {
    CacheEntry entry = map.get(key);
    if(entry == NULL) {
      // the key is not stored
      entry = new CacheEntry(key, value);
      if(map.size() == maxSize) {
        // max number of elements in cache reached, delete the eldest entry
        CacheEntry deleteEntry = tail.getPrev();
        // remove from the map
        map.remove(deleteEntry.getKey());
        // remove from the queue
        remove(deleteEntry);
      }
      // add entry to the queue
      addFront(entry);
      //add to the map
      map.put(entry.getKey(), entry);
    } else {
      // update the value incase it is different
      entry.setValue(value);
      // access the entry
      accessed(entry);
    }
  }

  public String search(String key) {
    CacheEntry entry = map.get(key);
    if(entry == NULL) {
      return NULL;
    }
    // update the access
    accessed(entry);
```

```
        return entry.getValue();
}
public void accessed(CacheEntry entry) {
  if (entry.getPrev() != head) {
    // remove from its current location in queue
    remove(entry);
    addFront(entry);
  }
}

private void remove(CacheEntry entry) {
  if (entry == head || entry == tail) {
    return;          // error
  }
  entry.getPrev().setNext(entry.getNext());
  if (entry.getNext() != NULL) {
    entry.getNext().setPrev(entry.getPrev());
  }
}

private void addFront(CacheEntry entry) {
  // add the new entry in queue at head
  CacheEntry nextEntry = head.getNext();
  head.setNext(entry);
  entry.setPrev(head);
  entry.setNext(nextEntry);
  if (nextEntry != NULL) {
     nextEntry.setPrev(entry);
  }
}

// prints the content of the cache
public void print() {
  CacheEntry entry = head.getNext();
  while(entry != tail) {
    System.out.println("{" + entry.getKey() + ":" + entry.getValue() + "}");
    entry = entry.getNext();
  }
  System.out.println();
}
}
```

Question-29   Design a simple address book which stores the contacts.

Answer: The basic functionality of any phonebook are adding a contact, searching for a contact, editing a contact, deleting a contact, viewing contact details and so on. Let us assume that *Contact* struct holds information for one contact entry and contacts with *no* first name will be recognised as deleted.

```
struct Contact{
    char firstName[20];      /*First Name*/
    char lastName[30];       /*Last Name*/
    char areaCode[6];        /*Area Code*/
    char phoneNumber[10];     /*Telephone Number*/
    char email[60];          /*E-Mail*/
    char webaddr[60];        /*website*/
    char address[60];        /*Home Address*/
};
```

Now, let us define the class to support the above functionality.

```
class PhoneBook{
    Contact contact;
  public:
      //ensures that the first name is not empty.
      bool CreateMe(){ //ensures that the first name is not empty.
              if(contact.first[0]=='\\')
                    return true;
              else return false;
      };
      void EditContact();
      void DeleteContact();
```

```
        void PrintContact(bool showall);
        bool SearchContact(char SearchThis[60]);
};
```

SearchContact() prompts the user to enter a string and locates the entry matching that string in *phonebook*. If a matching entry is found, it returns true else returns false. To make the search operation efficient, we can match the given data with any of the details of contact (with preference given to name, area code, phone number, mail, website and home address).

```
bool PhoneBook::SearchContact(char searchThis[60]){
    if(!strcmp(contact.first, searchThis)){ return true; }
    else if(!strcmp(contact.last, searchThis)){ return true; }
    /* --SEARCHING A PERSON WITH ONLY HIS AREA CODE  ISN'T LOGICAL--
            But, we can use this to show who are in our area... */
    else if(!strcmp(contact.areacode, searchThis)){ return true; }
    else if(!strcmp(contact.number, searchThis)){ return true; }
    else if(!strcmp(contact.email, searchThis)){ return true; }
    else if(!strcmp(contact.webaddr, searchThis)){ return true; }
    else if(!strcmp(contact.address, searchThis)){ return true; }
    else {return false;};
}
```

To edit the contact we can simply read the data from user and see whether we have any such contact in phonebook or not. If so, we can edit the contact by taking new values from user. *EditContact*() prompts the user to the details for that name. If *phonebook* contains an entry mathcing the entered string, the details for that entry is changed to the new data. If no entry matching the entered string is found, *phonebook* is unchanged.

```
void PhoneBook::EditContact(){
    cout << endl << "First Name: "; cin >> contact.firstName;
    cout << endl << "Last Name: "; cin >> contact.lastName;
    cout << endl << "Area Code: "; cin >> contact.areaCode;
    cout << endl << "Phone Number: "; cin >> contact.phoneNumber;
    cout << endl << "E-mail: "; cin >> contact.email;
    cout << endl << "WebAddress: "; cin >> contact.webaddr;
    cout << endl << "HomeAddress: "; cin >> contact.address;
    cout << "OK." << endl;
}
```

DeleteContact() makes the first name of contact empty and it indicates the non-existence of contact in phonebook.

```
void PhoneBook::DeleteContact{
    contact.first[0]='\\';
}
```

PrintContact() prints the current contact first name and last name. If we pass true as argument to it, it prints all details of the contact as shown below.

```
void PhoneBook::PrintContact(bool showall){
    cout << endl << "First Name: " << contact.first
        << endl << "Last Name: " << contact.last;
    if(showall){
        cout << endl << "Area Code: " << contact.areacode
            << endl << "Phone Number: " << contact.number
            << endl << "E-mail: " << contact.email
            << endl << "WebAddress: " << contact.webaddr
            << endl << "HomeAddress: " << contact.address
            << endl << "---" << endl <<  "OK." << endl;
    }
}
```

clearscreen() clears the screen and put the header.

```
inline void clearscreen(){
    system("CLS"); /* Clear the screen */
    cout << "Simple PhoneBook " << endl
        << "-------------------------------" << endl << endl;
}
```

Now, let us put all the above discussion together and write sample code to test the functionality. For simplicity, let us assume that user selects a menu option and based on his/her selection we call the corresponding functions as show below.

```
#define MAX_CONTACTS 100
int main(){
```

```
                /*Definitions and preparations*/
                PhoneBook book[MAX_CONTACTS];
           char menuOption='0';
           int i;
           char buff[60];
           bool found;
           for(int j=0; j<MAX_CONTACTS; j++)
                      book[j].Delete();

           clearscreen();
           while(PhoneBook != '6'){
                            found=false;
                            i=0;
                            cout << "1. Create New Contact" << endl;
                            cout << "2. Edit Contact's data" << endl;
                            cout << "3. Delete a Contact" << endl;
                            cout << "4. Search a Contact" << endl;
                            cout << "5. Save All Data" << endl;
                            cout << "6. Terminate program" << endl;

                    cout << endl << "Selection: ";
                    cin >> menuOption;

                    switch(menuOption){
                            case '1':
                                do{
                                        if(book[i].CreateMe()){
                                                book[i].Edit();
                                                found = true;
                                        }
                                        i++;
                                }while(i < MAX_CONTACTS && !found);
                                break;
                            case '2':
                                cout << "Please, give me a name or sth..." << endl;
                                cin >> buff;
                                if(book[i].SearchContact(buff) && !book[i].CreateMe()){
                                        cout << endl << "EDITING: ";
                                        book[i].Print(false);
                                        book[i].Edit();
                                }
                                else{
                                        i++;
                                }
                                break;
                            case '3':
                                cout << "Please, give me a name or sth..." << endl;
                                cin >> buff;
                                if(book[i].SearchContact(buff) && !book[i].CreateMe()){
                                        cout << endl << "DELETING: ";
                                        book[i].Print(true);
                                        cout << endl << "Are you sure? (y/n)";
                                        cin >> buff[0];
                                        if(buff[0]=='y') book[i].Delete();
                                }
                                else{
                                        i++;
                                }
                                break;
                            case '4':
                                cout << endl << "Search: " << endl;
                                cin >> buff;
                                if(book[i].SearchContact(buff) && !book[i].CreateMe()){
                                        book[i].Print(true);
                                        cout << endl;
                                }
                                else{
                                        i++;
                                }
                                break;
```

```
                        cout << endl << "Type a number to continue ";
                        cin >> i;
                case '5':
                        /*SAVE Data*/
                        break;
        }
    }
    cout << endl << endl << "END. " << endl;
    system("PAUSE");
    return 0;
}
```

Before ending the discussion, we can further note down a list of additional functionality that can be added to above list.

*   *ImportPhoneBook*() reads contacts from the text file.
*   *ExportPhoneBook*() writes contacts from the text file.
*   *MatchContacts*() matches multiple contacts with regular expressions.
*   *SortContacts*() sorts contacts based on given parameter.

3.3 Sample Design Questions For Practice

*   Design a billing and auctioning system similar to eBay.
*   Design the flight take-off control system.
*   Design question answer system similar to *StackOverFlow*.com and *CareerMonk*.com.
*   Design the hospital management system.
*   Design the library management system.
*   Design the book management system.
*   Design the system similar to CricInfo.com [score boards].
*   Design the online ticket reservation system.
*   Design the objects for constructing the house.
*   Design the traffic control system.
*   Design a system for car service.

OPERATING SYSTEM CONCEPTS

Chapter-4

4.1 Glossary

- The operating system is a program which controls the software and hardware so that the device behaves in a flexible and also in predictable way. The main operating system components are:
    - o Process management
    - o Memory management: Primary and Second Memory
    - o File management
    - o Device management
- The process of fetching a program from the secondary memory and placing it in main memory is called *job scheduling*. The current program which is running in main memory is called *process*.
- There are different types of operating systems:
    - o *Batched operating systems*: In batched operating systems users give their jobs to the operator. Operator sorts the programs based on their requirements and executes them. This is time consuming but makes the CPU busy all the time.
    - o *Multi − programmed operating systems*: These operating systems can execute a number of programs concurrently. They fetch a group of programs from the secondary memory and place them in the main memory. Then it selects a program from the ready queue and gives them to CPU for execution. While a executing program, if they needs some I/O operation then the operating system fetches another program and gives it to the CPU for execution and makes CPU busy all the time.
    - o *Timesharing operating systems*: In these operating systems, CPU executes multiple jobs by switching between them, but the switches occur so frequently that the user feels as if the operating system is running only onc (his) program.
    - o *Multi − processor systems or Parallel systems*: They contain a number of processors to increase the speed of execution, and reliability, and economy. They are of two types:
        - ▪ *Symmetric multiprocessing*: each processor runs an identical copy of the OS and they communicate with each other as and when needed.
        - ▪ *Asymmetric multiprocessing*: each processor is assigned a specific task.
    - o *Distributed operating systems*: Distributed systems work in a network. They can share the network resources, communicate with each other
    - o *Real − time operating systems*: These are used when rigid time requirement have been placed on the operation of a processor or on the flow of data. They are used as a control device in a dedicated application. They are of two types:
        - ▪ *Hard real time OS*: has a well-defined fixed time constraint.
        - ▪ *Soft real time OS*: have less stringent timing constraints.
- *System call*: A System call is a mechanism used by applications for requesting a service from the OS. For example, allocation and deallocation of memory, reporting of current date and time etc. These services can be used by an application with the help of system calls.
- *Kernel*: An operating system kernel is the piece or pieces of software that is responsible for servicing resource requests from applications and the management of resources. Kernels use system calls to handshake with applications.
- *Context switching*: Transferring the control from one process to other process requires saving the state of the old process and loading the saved state for new process. This task is called *context switching*. Context-switch time is overhead, because the system does no useful work while switching. Its speed varies from machine to machine, depending on the memory speed, the number of registers which must be copied, the existed of special instructions (such as a single instruction to load or store all registers).
- *Co − operating processes*: The processes which share system resources as data among each other. Also the processes can communicate with each other via interprocess communication facility (generally used in distributed systems). Example: chat programs.
- *Thread*: A thread is a program line under execution. Thread sometimes called a light-weight process, is a basic unit of CPU utilization, it comprises a thread id, a program counter, a register set, and a stack.
    - o *User thread*: User threads are easy to create and use but the disadvantage is that if they perform a blocking system calls the kernel is engaged completely to the single user thread blocking other processes. They are created in user space.
    - o *Kernel thread*: Kernel threads are supported directly by the operating system. They are slower to create and manage.

- *Process synchronization*: Process synchronization is required when several processes access and manipulate the same data concurrently and the outcome of the execution depends on the particular order in which the access takes place (is called *race condition*). To guard against the race condition we need to ensure that only one process at a time can be manipulating the same data. The technique used for this is called process synchronization.
- *Critical section problem*: Critical section is the code segment of a process in which the process may be changing common variables, updating tables, writing a file and so on. Only one process is allowed to go into critical section at any given time (*mutually exclusive*).The critical section problem is to design a protocol that the processes can use to co-operate. The three basic requirements of critical section are:
  - Mutual exclusion
  - Progress
  - Bounded waiting

  Note: *Bakery* algorithm is one of the solutions to CS problem.
- *Deadlock*: Suppose a process request resources, if the resources are not available at that time the process enters into a wait state. A waiting process may never again change state, because the resources they have requested are held by some other waiting processes. This situation is called *deadlock*.
- *Semaphor*: It is a synchronization tool used to solve complex critical section problems. A semaphore is an integer variable that, apart from initialization, is accessed only through two standard atomic operations: *Wait* and *Signal*.
- *Virtual memory*: A virtual memory is hardware technique where the system appears to have more memory that it actually does. This is done by time-sharing, the physical memory and storage parts of the memory one disk when they are not actively being used
- *Cache memory*: Cache memory is random access memory (RAM) that a computer microprocessor can access more quickly than it can access regular RAM. As the microprocessor processes data, it looks first in the cache memory and if it finds the data there (from a previous reading of data), it does not have to do the more time-consuming reading of data
- *Paging*: Paging is solution to external fragmentation problem which is to permit the logical address space of a process to be noncontiguous, thus allowing a process to be allocating physical memory wherever the latter is available.
- *Complier and Interpreter*: An interpreter reads one instruction at a time and execute that instruction. It does not perform any translation. But a compiler translates the entire instructions.
- *Preemptive and non – preemptive scheduling*: Consider any system where people use some kind of resources and compete for them. The non-computer examples for preemptive scheduling the traffic on the single lane road if there is emergency or there is an ambulance on the road the other vehicles give path to the vehicles that are in need. The example for preemptive scheduling is people standing in queue for tickets.
- *Starvation and aging*:
  - *Starvation*: Starvation is a resource management problem where a process does not get the resources it needs for a long time because the resources are being allocated to other processes.
  - *Aging*: Aging is a technique to avoid starvation in a scheduling system. It works by adding an aging factor to the priority of each request. The aging factor must increase the request's priority as time passes and must ensure that a request will eventually be the highest priority request (after it has waited long enough).

4.2 Questions on Operating System Concepts

Question-1   What is marshaling?

Answer: Marshaling is the process of gathering data from one or more applications (or sources) in computer storage, putting them into a message buffer, and converting it into a format that is prescribed for a particular receiver or programming interface. Marshaling is usually required when passing the output parameters of a program written in one language as input to a program written in another language.

Question-2   What are the basic functions of an operating system?

Answer: Operating system controls and coordinates the use of the hardware among the various applications programs for various uses. Operating system acts as resource allocator and manager. Since there are many possibly conflicting requests for resources the operating system must decide which requests are allocated resources to operating the computer system efficiently and fairly. Also operating system is a control program which controls the user programs to prevent errors and improper use of the computer. It is especially concerned with the operation and control of I/O devices.

Question-3   Why paging is used?

Answer: Paging is solution to external fragmentation problem which is to permit the logical address space of a process to be noncontiguous, thus allowing a process to be allocating physical memory wherever the latter is available.

Question-4   What resources are used when a thread created? How they differ when a process is created?

Answer: When a thread is created the threads does not require any new resources to execute the thread shares the resources like memory of the process to which they belong to. The benefit of code sharing is that it allows an application to have several different threads of activity all within the same address space. Whereas if a new process creation is very heavyweight because it always requires new address space to be created and even if they share the memory then the inter process communication is expensive when compared to the communication between the threads.

Question-5   What is virtual memory?

Answer: Virtual memory is hardware technique where the system appears to have more memory that it actually does. This is done by time-sharing, the physical memory and storage parts of the memory one disk when they are not actively being used.

Question-6   What is Throughput, Turnaround time, Waiting time and Response time?

Answer: *Throughput*: number of processes that complete their execution per time unit. *Turnaround* time: amount of time to execute a particular process. *Waiting* time: amount of time a process has been waiting in the ready queue. *Response* time: amount of time it takes from when a request was submitted until the first response is produced, not output (for time-sharing environment).

Question-7   What is the important aspect of a real-time system or mission critical systems?

Answer: A real time operating system has well defined fixed time constraints. Process must be done within the defined constraints or the system will fail. An example is the operating system for a flight control computer or an advanced jet airplane. Often used as a control device in a dedicated application such as controlling scientific experiments, medical imaging systems, industrial control systems, and some display systems. Real-Time systems may be either hard or soft real-time.

Hard real-time: Secondary storage limited or absent, data stored in short term memory, or read-only memory (ROM), Conflicts with time-sharing systems, not supported by general-purpose operating systems. *Soft* real-time: Limited utility in industrial control of robotics, Useful in applications (multimedia, virtual reality) requiring advanced operating-system features.

Question-8   What is the difference between Hard and Soft real-time systems?

Answer: A hard real-time system guarantees that critical tasks complete on time. This goal requires that all delays in the system be bounded from the retrieval of the stored data to the time that it takes the operating system to finish any request made of it. A soft real time system where a critical real-time task gets priority over other tasks and retains that priority until it completes. As in hard real time systems kernel delays need to be bounded.

Question-9   What is the cause of thrashing? How does the system detect thrashing? Once it detects thrashing, what can the system do to eliminate this problem?

Answer: Thrashing is caused by under allocation of the minimum number of pages required by a process, forcing it to continuously page fault. The system can detect thrashing by evaluating the level of CPU utilization as compared to the level of multiprogramming. It can be eliminated by reducing the level of multiprogramming.

Question-10   What is multi-tasking, multi programming, multi-threading?

Answer: Multi programming: Multiprogramming is the technique of running several programs at a time using timesharing. It allows a computer to do several things at the same time. Multiprogramming creates logical parallelism. The concept of multiprogramming is that the operating system keeps several jobs in memory simultaneously. The operating system selects a job from the job pool and starts executing a job, when that job needs to wait for any i/o operations the CPU is switched to another job. So the main idea here is that the CPU is never idle. Multi-tasking: Multitasking is the logical extension of multiprogramming.

The concept of multitasking is quite similar to multiprogramming but difference is that the switching between jobs occurs so frequently that the users can interact with each program while it is running. This concept is also known as time-sharing systems. A time-shared operating system uses CPU scheduling and multiprogramming to provide each user with a small portion of time-shared system. Multi-threading: An application typically is implemented as a separate process with several threads of control.

In some situations a single application may be required to perform several similar tasks for example a web server accepts client requests for web pages, images, sound, and so forth. A busy web server may have several of clients concurrently accessing it. If the web server ran as a traditional single-threaded process, it would be able to service only one client at a time. The amount of time that a client might have to wait for its request to be serviced could be enormous. So it is efficient to have one process that contains multiple threads to serve the same purpose. This approach would multithread the web-server process, the server would create a separate thread that would listen for client requests when a request was made rather than creating another process it would create another thread to service the request. To get the advantages like responsiveness, Resource sharing economy and utilization of multiprocessor architectures multithreading concept can be used.

Question-11   What is fragmentation? Different types of fragmentation?

Answer: Fragmentation occurs in a dynamic memory allocation system when many of the free blocks are too small to satisfy any request. External Fragmentation: External Fragmentation happens when a dynamic memory allocation algorithm allocates some memory and a small piece is left over that cannot be effectively used. If too much external fragmentation occurs, the amount of usable memory is drastically reduced. Total memory space exists to satisfy a request, but it is not contiguous. Internal Fragmentation: Internal fragmentation is the space wasted inside of allocated memory blocks because of restriction on the allowed sizes of allocated blocks. Allocated memory may be slightly larger than requested memory; this size difference is memory internal to a partition, but not being used.

4.2 Questions on Operating System Concepts

Question-12   Solve producer/consumer problem using *Java* threads.

Answer: The use of the implicit monitors in Java objects is powerful, but we can achieve a more subtle level of control through inter-process communication. Multithreading replaces event loop programming by dividing the tasks into discrete and logical units. Threads also provide a secondary benefit: they do away with polling. *Polling* is usually implemented by a loop that is used to check some condition repeatedly. Once the condition is true, appropriate action is taken. This wastes CPU time.

For example, consider the classic queuing problem, where one thread is producing some data and another is consuming it. To make the problem more interesting, suppose that the producer has to wait until the consumer is finished before it generates more data. In a polling system, the consumer would waste many CPU cycles while it waited for the producer to produce. Once the producer was finished, it would start polling, wasting more CPU cycles waiting for the consumer to finish, and so on. Clearly, this situation is undesirable.

To avoid polling, Java includes an elegant inter-process communication mechanism via the wait( ), notify( ), and notifyAll( ) methods. These methods are implemented as final methods in Object, so all classes have them. All three methods can be called only from within a synchronized method. Although conceptually advanced from a computer science perspective, the rules for using these methods are actually quite simple:

1.   wait( ) tells the calling thread to give up the monitor and go to sleep until some other thread enters the same monitor and calls notify( ).
2.   notify( ) wakes up the first thread that called wait( ) on the same object.
3.   notifyAll( ) wakes up all the threads that called wait( ) on the same object. The highest priority thread will run first.

These methods are declared within Object, as shown here:

```
final void wait( ) throws InterruptedException
final void notify( )
final void notifyAll( )
```

Additional forms of wait( ) exist that allow you to specify a period of time to wait. The following sample program incorrectly implements a simple form of the producer/consumer problem. It consists of four classes: Q, the queue that you're trying to synchronize; Producer, the threaded object that is producing queue entries; Consumer, the threaded object that is consuming queue entries; and PC, the tiny class that creates the single Q, Producer, and Consumer.

```
import java.util.*;
import java.io.*;
public class ProdCons {
  protected LinkedList list = new LinkedList();
  protected int MAX = 10;
  protected boolean done = false; // Also protected by lock on list.
  /** Inner class representing the Producer side */
  class Producer extends Thread {
    public void run() {
      while (true) {
        synchronized(list) {
          while (list.size() == MAX) // queue "full"
          try {     System.out.println("Producer WAITING");
            list.wait();   // Limit the size
          } catch (InterruptedException ex) {
            System.out.println("Producer INTERRUPTED");
          }
          list.addFirst(justProduced);
          list.notifyAll();  // must own the lock
          System.out.println("Produced 1; List size now " + list.size());
        }
      }
    }
  }
  class Consumer extends Thread {
    public void run() {
      while (true) {
        Object obj = null;
        synchronized(list) {
          while (list.size() == 0) {
            try {
              System.out.println("CONSUMER WAITING");
              list.wait(); // must own the lock
            } catch (InterruptedException ex) {
              System.out.println("CONSUMER INTERRUPTED");
```

```
        }
      }
      obj = list.removeLast();
      list.notifyAll();
      int len = list.size();
      System.out.println("List size now " + len);
    }
   }
  }
}

ProdCons(int nP, int nC) {
  for (int i=0; i<nP; i++)
    new Producer().start();
  for (int i=0; i<nC; i++)
    new Consumer().start();
}

public static void main(String[] args) throws IOException, InterruptedException {

  // Start producers and consumers
  int numProducers = 4;
  int numConsumers = 3;
  ProdCons pc = new ProdCons(numProducers, numConsumers);

  Thread.sleep(10*1000); // Let it run for, say, 10 seconds

  // End of simulation - shut down gracefully
  synchronized(pc.list) {
    pc.done = true;
    pc.list.notifyAll();
  }
 }
}
```

Question-13   What is stack unwinding?

Answer: When an exception is thrown and control passes from a try block to a handler, the $C++$ run time calls destructors for all automatic objects constructed since the beginning of the try block. This process is called *stack unwinding*. The automatic objects are destroyed in reverse order of their construction. Automatic objects are local objects that have been declared auto or register, or not declared static or extern. An automatic object x is deleted whenever the program exits the block in which x is declared.

If an exception is thrown during construction of an object consisting of subobjects or array elements, destructors are only called for those subobjects or array elements successfully constructed before the exception was thrown. A destructor for a local static object will only be called if the object was successfully constructed.

As you create objects statically (on the stack as opposed to allocating them in the heap memory) and perform function calls, they are *stacked up*. When a scope (anything delimited by { and }) is exited (by using return XXX;, reaching the end of the scope or throwing an exception) everything within that scope is destroyed (destructors are called for everything). This process of destroying local objects and calling destructors is called stack unwinding. (Exiting a code block using *goto* will not unwind the stack which is one of the reasons you should never use *goto* in $C++$).

If any destructor throws an exception during stack unwinding we end up in the land of undefined behavior which could cause your program to terminate unexpectedly.

COMPUTER NETWORKING BASICS	Chapter-5

5.1 Introduction

More and more, it is networks that connect us. People communicate online from everywhere. We focus on these aspects of the information network:

- Devices that make up the network (work stations, laptops, file servers, web servers, network printers, VoIP phones, security cameras, PDAs, etc..)
- Media that connect the devices
- Messages that are carried over the network
- Rules (protocols) and processes that control network communications
- Tools and commands for constructing and maintaining networks

Communication begins with a message that must be sent from one individual/device to another. People exchange ideas using many different communication methods. All of these methods have *three* elements in common. The first of these elements is the message *source/sender*. Message sources are people, or electronic devices, that need to send a message to other individuals/devices.

The second element of communication is the *destination/receiver*, of the message. The destination receives the message and interprets it. A third element, called a *channel*, consists of the media that provides the pathway over which the message can travel from source to destination.

5.2 LAN vs. WAN

An individual network usually spans a single geographical area, providing services and applications to people within a common organizational structure, such as a single business, campus or region. This type of network is called a *Local Area Network* (LAN). A LAN is usually administered by a single organization. The administrative control that governs the security and access control policies are enforced on the network level.

	LAN	WAN
Definition:	LAN (Local Area Network) is a computer network covering a small geographic area, like a home, office, schools, or group of buildings.	WAN (Wide Area Network) is a computer network that covers a broad area (e.g., any network whose communications links cross metropolitan, regional, or national boundaries over a long distance
Maintenance costs:	Because it covers a relatively small geographical area, LAN is easier to maintain at relatively low costs.	Maintaining WAN is difficult because of its wider geographical coverage and higher maintenance costs.
Fault Tolerance:	LANs tend to have less problems associated with them, as there are a smaller number of systems to deal with.	WANs tend to be less fault tolerant. as it consists of a large number of systems there is a lower amount of fault tolerance.
Example:	Network in an organization can be a LAN	Internet is the best example of a WAN
Geographical spread:	LANs will have a small geographical range and do not need any leased telecommunication lines	WANs generally spread across boundaries and need leased telecommunication lines
Set-up costs:	If there is a need to set-up a couple of extra devices on the network, it is not very expensive to do that	In this case since networks in remote areas have to be connected hence the set-up costs are higher. However WANs using public networks can be setup very cheaply, just software (VPN etc.)
Ownership:	Typically owned, controlled, and managed by a single person or organization	WANs (like the Internet) are not owned by any one organization but rather exist under collective or distributed ownership and management over long distances
Components:	Layer 2 devices like switches, bridges. layer1 devices like hubs , repeaters	Layers 3 devices Routers, Multi-layer Switches and Technology specific devices like ATM or Frame-relay Switches etc.

Data transfer rates:	LANs have a high data transfer rate	WANs have a lower data transfer rate as compared to LANs
Technology:	Tend to use certain connectivity technologies, primarily Ethernet and Token Ring	WANs tend to use technology like MPLS, ATM, Frame Relay and X.25 for connectivity over the longer distances
Connection:	One LAN can be connected to other LANs over any distance via telephone lines and radio waves	Computers connected to a WAN are often connected through public networks, such as the telephone system. They can also be connected through leased lines or satellites
Speed:	High speed(1000mbps)	Less speed(150mbps)

5.2 Segmentation and Multiplexing

In theory, a single communication, such as a music video or an e-mail message, could be sent across a network from a source to a destination as one massive continuous stream of bits. If messages were actually transmitted in this manner, it would mean that no other device would be able to send or receive messages on the same network while this data transfer was in progress. These large streams of data would result in significant delays. Further, if a link in the interconnected network infrastructure failed during the transmission, the complete message would be lost and have to be retransmitted in full.

A better approach is to divide the data into smaller, more manageable pieces to send over the network. This division of the data stream into smaller pieces is called *segmentation*. Segmenting messages has two primary benefits. First, by sending smaller individual pieces from source to destination, many different conversations can be interleaved on the network. The process used to interleave the pieces of separate conversations together on the network is called *multiplexing*.

Second, segmentation can increase the reliability of network communications. The separate pieces of each message need not travel the same pathway across the network from source to destination. If a particular path becomes congested with data traffic or fails, individual pieces of the message can still be directed to the destination using alternate pathways. If part of the message fails to make it to the destination, only the missing parts need to be retransmitted.

5.3 End Devices

In modern networks, a host can act as a client, a server, or both. Software installed on the host determines which role it plays on the network. Servers are hosts that have software installed that enables them to provide information and services, like e-mail or web pages, to other hosts on the network.

5.4 Intermediary Devices

In addition to the end devices that people are familiar with, networks rely on intermediary devices to provide connectivity and to work behind the scenes to ensure that data flows across the network. These devices connect the individual hosts to the network and can connect multiple individual networks to form an internetwork. Examples of intermediary network devices are:

- Network Access Devices (hubs, switches, and wireless access points)
- Internetworking Devices (routers)
- Communication Servers and Modems
- Security Devices (firewalls)

The management of data as it flows through the network is also a role of the intermediary devices. These devices use the destination host address, in conjunction with information about the network interconnections, to determine the path that messages should take through the network. Processes running on the intermediary network devices perform these functions:

- Regenerate and retransmit data signals
- Maintain information about what pathways exist through the network and internetwork
- Notify other devices of errors and communication failures
- Direct data along alternate pathways when there is a link failure
- Classify and direct messages according to priorities
- Permit or deny the flow of data, based on security settings

5.5 Hub, Switch, and Router Defined

Hub: A common connection point for devices in a network. Hubs are commonly used to connect segments of a LAN. A hub contains multiple ports. When a packet arrives at one port, it is copied to the other ports so that all segments of the LAN can see all packets.

Switch: In networks, a device that filters and forwards packets between LAN segments. Switches operate at the data link layer (layer 2) and sometimes the network layer (layer 3) of the OSI Reference Model and therefore support any packet protocol. LANs that use switches to join segments are called switched LANs or, in the case of Ethernet networks, switched Ethernet LANs.

Router: A device that forwards data packets along networks. A router is connected to at least two networks, commonly two LANs or WANs or a LAN and its ISPs network. Routers are located at gateways, the places where two or more networks connect. Routers use headers and forwarding tables to determine the best path for forwarding the packets, and they use protocols such as ICMP (*Internet Connection Management Protocol*) to communicate with each other and configure the best route between any two hosts.

Differences between Hubs, Switches, and Routers

Today most routers have something combining the features and functionality of a router and switch/hub into a single unit. So conversations regarding these devices can be a bit misleading — especially to someone new to computer networking.

The functions of a router, hub and a switch are all quite different from one another, even if at times they are all integrated into a single device. Let's start with the hub and the switch since these two devices have similar roles on the network. Each serves as a central connection for all of your network equipment and handles a data type known as frames. Frames carry the data. When a frame is received, it is amplified and then transmitted on to the port of the destination PC. The big difference between these two devices is in the method in which frames are being delivered.

In a hub, a frame *broadcasts* to every one of its ports. It doesn't matter that the frame is only destined for one port. The hub cannot distinguish which port a frame should be sent to. Broadcasting it on every port ensures that it will reach its intended destination. This places a lot of traffic on the network and can lead to poor network response times.

Additionally, a 10/100Mbps hub must share its bandwidth with each and every one of its ports. So, when only one PC is broadcasting, it will have access to the maximum available bandwidth. If, however, multiple PCs are broadcasting, then that bandwidth will need to be divided among all of those systems, which will degrade performance.

A switch, however, keeps a record of the MAC addresses of all the devices connected to it. With this information, a switch can identify which system is sitting on which port. So, when a frame is received, it knows exactly which port to send it to, without significantly increasing network response times. And, unlike a hub, a 10/100Mbps switch will allocate a full 10/100Mbps to each of its ports. So regardless of the number of PCs transmitting, users will always have access to the maximum amount of bandwidth. It's for these reasons why a switch is considered to be a much better choice than a hub.

Routers are completely different devices. Where a hub or switch is concerned with transmitting frames, a router's job, as its name implies, is to route packets to other networks until that packet ultimately reaches its destination. One of the key features of a packet is that it not only contains data, but the destination address of where it's going.

A router is typically connected to at least two networks, commonly two Local Area Networks (LANs) or Wide Area Networks (WAN) or a LAN and its ISP's network, for example, your PC or workgroup and EarthLink. Routers are located at gateways, the places where two or more networks connect. Using headers and forwarding tables, routers determine the best path for forwarding the packets. Router use protocols such as ICMP to communicate with each other and configure the best route between any two hosts.

5.6 Medium

Communication across a network is carried on a *medium*. The medium provides the channel over which the message travels from source to destination. Modern networks primarily use three types of media to interconnect devices and to provide the pathway over which data can be transmitted. These media are:

- Metallic wires within cables
- Glass or plastic fibers (fiber optic cable)
- Wireless transmission

Different types of network media have different features and benefits. Not all network media has the same characteristics and is appropriate for the same purpose.

5.7 Peer-to-peer and Client/server networks

Peer − to − peer networks are more commonly implemented where less than ten computers are involved and where strict security is not necessary. All computers have the same status, hence the term *peer*, and they communicate with each other on an equal footing. Files, such as word processing or spreadsheet documents, can be shared across the network and all the computers on the network can share devices, such as printers or scanners, which are connected to any one computer [figure on left side].

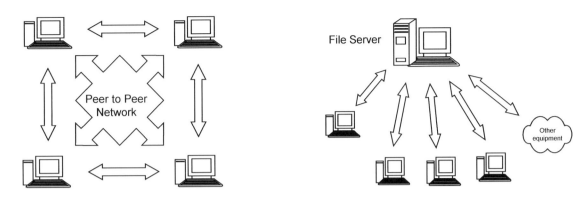

Client/Server networks are more suitable for larger networks. A central computer, or *server*, acts as the storage location for files and applications shared on the network. Usually the server is a higher than average performance computer. The server also controls the network access of the other computers which are referred to as the 'client' computers. Typically, teachers and students in a school will use the client computers for their work and only the network administrator (usually a designated staff member) will have access rights to the server [figure on right side].

5.8 How does Internet works?

There are a set of protocols that support network. These protocols are known as *Internet protocol suite* and include the *Internet Protocol* (IP), the *Transport Control Protocol* (TCP), and the *User Datagram Protocol* (UDP) as well as other, less-prominent supporting protocols. Computers on the Internet communicate by exchanging packets of data, called as Internet Protocol (IP), packets. IP is the network protocol used to send information from one computer to another over the Internet. All computers on the Internet communicate using IP. IP moves information contained in IP packets. The IP packets are routed via special routing algorithms from a source to destination. The routing algorithms figure out the best way to send the packets from source to destination.

In order for IP to send packets from a source computer to a destination computer, it must have some way of identifying these computers. All computers on the Internet are identified using one or more IP addresses. A computer may have more than one IP address if it has more than one interface to computers that are connected to the Internet.

IP addresses are 32-bit numbers. They may be written in decimal, hexadecimal, or other formats, but the most common format is dotted decimal notation. This format breaks the 32-bit address up into four bytes and writes each byte of the address as unsigned decimal integers separated by dots. For example, one of *CareerMonk.com* IP addresses is 0xccD499C1. Since, 0xcc = 204, 0xD4 = 212, 0x99 = 153, and 0xC1 = 193, *CareerMonk.com* IP address in dotted decimal form is 204.212.153.193.

IP addresses are not easy to remember, even using dotted decimal notation. The Internet has adopted a mechanism, referred to as the *Domain Name System* (DNS), whereby computer names can be associated with IP addresses. These computer names are referred to as *domain names*. The DNS has several rules that determine how domain names are constructed and how they relate to one another. The mapping of domain names to IP addresses is maintained by a system of *domain name servers*. These servers are able to look up the IP address corresponding to a domain name. They also provide the capability to look up the domain name associated with a particular IP address, if one exists.

Computers running on the Internet communicate to each other using either the Transmission Control Protocol (TCP) or the User Datagram Protocol (UDP). When we write *Java* programs that communicate over the network, we are programming at the application layer. Typically, we don't need to concern with the TCP and UDP layers. Instead, we can use the classes in the java.net package. These classes provide system-independent network communication. However, to decide which *Java* classes our programs should use, we do need to understand how TCP and UDP differ.

TCP: When two applications want to communicate to each other reliably, they establish a connection and send data back and forth over that connection. This is analogous to making a telephone call. If we want to speak to a person who is in another country, a connection is established when we dial the phone number and the other party answers. We send data back and forth over the connection by speaking to one another over the phone lines. Like the phone company, TCP guarantees that data sent from one end of the connection actually gets to the other end and in the same order it was sent. Otherwise, an error is reported.

TCP provides a point-to-point channel for applications that require reliable communications. The Hypertext Transfer Protocol (HTTP), File Transfer Protocol (FTP), and Telnet are all examples of applications that require a reliable communication channel. The order in which the data is sent and received over the network is critical to the success of these applications. When HTTP is used to read from a URL, the data must be received in the order in which it was sent. Otherwise, we end up with a jumbled HTML file, a corrupt zip file, or some other invalid information.

| Application: HTTP, ftp, telnet, SMTP,... |
| Transport: TCP, UDP,... |

| Network: IP,... |
| Link: Device driver,... |

Definition: TCP (Transmission Control Protocol) is a connection-based protocol that provides a reliable flow of data between two computers.

Transport protocols are used to deliver information from one port to another and thereby enable communication between application programs. They use either a connection-oriented or connectionless method of communication. TCP is a connection-oriented protocol and UDP is a connectionless transport protocol.

The TCP connection-oriented protocol establishes a communication link between a source port/IP address and a destination port/IP address. The ports are bound together via this link until the connection is terminated and the link is broken. An example of a connection-oriented protocol is a telephone conversation. A telephone connection is established, communication takes place, and then the connection is terminated.

The reliability of the communication between the source and destination programs is ensured through error-detection and error-correction mechanisms that are implemented within TCP. TCP implements the connection as a stream of bytes from source to destination. This feature allows the use of the stream I/O classes provided by java.io.

UDP: The UDP protocol provides for communication that is not guaranteed between two applications on the network. UDP is not connection-based like TCP. Rather, it sends independent packets of data, called datagrams, from one application to another. Sending datagrams is much like sending a letter through the postal service: The order of delivery is not important and is not guaranteed, and each message is independent of any other.

Definition: UDP (User Datagram Protocol) is a protocol that sends independent packets of data, called *datagrams*, from one computer to another with no guarantees about arrival. UDP is not connection-based like TCP.

For many applications, the guarantee of reliability is critical to the success of the transfer of information from one end of the connection to the other. However, other forms of communication don't require such strict standards. In fact, they may be slowed down by the extra overhead or the reliable connection may invalidate the service altogether.

Consider, for example, a clock server that sends the current time to its client when requested to do so. If the client misses a packet, it doesn't really make sense to resend it because the time will be incorrect when the client receives it on the second try. If the client makes two requests and receives packets from the server out of order, it doesn't really matter because the client can figure out that the packets are out of order and make another request. The reliability of TCP is unnecessary in this instance because it causes performance degradation and may hinder the usefulness of the service.

Another example of a service that doesn't need the guarantee of a reliable channel is the ping command. The purpose of the ping command is to test the communication between two programs over the network. In fact, ping needs to know about dropped or out-of-order packets to determine how good or bad the connection is. A reliable channel would invalidate this service altogether.

The UDP protocol provides for communication that is not guaranteed between two applications on the network. UDP is not connection-based like TCP. Rather, it sends independent packets of data from one application to another. Sending datagrams is much like sending a letter through the mail service: The order of delivery is not important and is not guaranteed, and each message is independent of any others.

The UDP connectionless protocol differs from the TCP connection-oriented protocol in that it does not establish a link for the duration of the connection. An example of a connectionless protocol is postal mail. To mail something, you just write down a destination address (and an optional return address) on the envelope of the item you're sending and drop it in a mailbox. When using UDP, an application program writes the destination port and IP address on a datagram and then sends the datagram to its destination. UDP is less reliable than TCP because there are no delivery-assurance or error-detection and error-correction mechanisms built into the protocol.

Application protocols such as FTP, SMTP, and HTTP use TCP to provide reliable, stream-based communication between client and server programs. Other protocols, such as the Time Protocol, use UDP because speed of delivery is more important than end-to-end reliability.

Understanding Ports: Generally speaking, a computer has a single physical connection to the network. All data destined for a particular computer arrives through that connection. However, the data may be intended for different applications running on the computer. So, how does the computer know to which application to forward the data? Through the use of ports.

Data transmitted over the Internet is accompanied by addressing information that identifies the computer and the port for which it is destined. The computer is identified by its 32-bit IP address, which IP uses to deliver data to the right computer on the network. Ports are identified by a 16-bit number, which TCP and UDP use to deliver the data to the right application.

In connection-based communication such as TCP, a server application binds a socket to a specific port number. This has the effect of registering the server with the system to receive all data destined for that port. A client can then rendezvous with the server at the server's port, as illustrated here:

Definition: The TCP and UDP protocols use ports to map incoming data to a particular process running on a computer.

In datagram-based communication such as UDP, the datagram packet contains the port number of its destination and UDP routes the packet to the appropriate application, as illustrated in this figure:

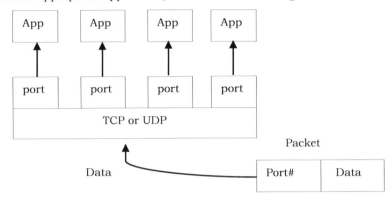

Port numbers range from 0 to 65,535 because ports are represented by 16-bit numbers. The port numbers ranging from 0 - 1023 are restricted; they are reserved for use by well-known services such as HTTP and FTP and other system services. These ports are called well – known ports. Your applications should not attempt to bind to them.

Port	Protocol
21	File Transfer Protocol
23	Telnet Protocol
25	Simple Mail Transfer Protocol
80	Hypertext Transfer Protocol

5.9 Difference between OSI and TCP/IP models

The Internet Protocol suite, like many protocol suites, may be viewed as a set of layers. Each layer solves a set of problems involving the transmission of data, and provides a well-defined service to the upper layer protocols based on using services from some lower layers. Upper layers are logically closer to the user and deal with more abstract data, relying on lower layer protocols to translate data into forms that can eventually be physically transmitted.

Layer #	Name	Encapsulation Units	Devices or Components	Keywords/Description
7	Application	data	PC	Network services for application processes, such as file, print, messaging, database services
6	Presentation	data		Standard interface to data for the application layer. MIME encoding, data encryption, conversion, formatting, compression
5	Session	data		Inter host communication. Establishes, manages and terminates connection between applications
4	Transport	segments		End-to-end connections and reliability. Segmentation/desegmentation of data in proper sequence. Flow control
3	Network	packets	router	Logical addressing and path determination. Routing. Reporting delivery errors
2	Data Link	frames	bridge, switch, NIC	Physical addressing and access to media. Two sublayers: Logical Link Control (LLC) and Media Access Control (MAC)

1	Physical	bits	repeater, hub, transceiver	Binary transmission signals and encoding. Layout of pins, voltages, cable specifications, modulation

OSI comparison with TCP/IP Protocol Stack

OSI #	OSI Layer Name	TCP/IP #	TCP/IP Layer Name	Encapsulation Units	TCP/IP Protocols
7	Application	4	Application	data	FTP, HTTP, POP3, IMAP, telnet, SMTP, DNS, TFTP
6	Presentation			data	
5	Session			data	
4	Transport	3	Transport	segments	TCP, UDP
3	Network	2	Internet	packets	IP
2	Data Link	1	Network Access	frames	
1	Physical			bits	

The main differences between the two models are as follows:

- OSI is a reference model and TCP/IP is an implementation of OSI model.
- TCP/IP protocols are considered to be standards around which the internet has developed. The OSI model however is a *generic, protocol-independent* standard.
- TCP/IP combines the presentation and session layer issues into its application layer.
- TCP/IP combines the OSI data link and physical layers into the network access layer.
- TCP/IP appears to be a simpler model and this is mainly due to the fact that it has fewer layers.
- TCP/IP is considered to be a more credible model- This is mainly due to the fact because TCP/IP protocols are the standards around which the internet was developed therefore it mainly gains creditability due to this reason. Where as in contrast networks are not usually built around the OSI model as it is merely used as a guidance tool.
- The OSI model consists of 7 architectural layers whereas the TCP/IP only has 4 layers.

5.10 Client/Server Computing and the Internet

The Internet provides a variety of services including e-mail, newsgroups, file transfer, remote login, and the Web. Internet services are organized according to a client/server architecture. Client programs, such as Web browsers and file transfer programs, create connections to servers, such as Web and FTP servers. The clients make requests of the server, and the server responds to the requests by providing the service requested by the client.

The Web provides a good example of client/server computing. Web browsers are the clients and Web servers are the servers. Browsers request HTML files from Web servers on your behalf by establishing a connection with a Web server and submitting file requests to the server. The server receives the file requests, retrieves the files, and sends them to the browser over the established connection. The browser receives the files and displays them to your browser window.

Sockets and Client/Server Communication: Clients and servers establish connections and communicate via *sockets*. Connections are communication links that are created over the Internet using TCP. Some client/server applications are also built around the connectionless UDP. These applications also use sockets to communicate.

Sockets are the endpoints of Internet communication. Clients create client sockets and connect them to server sockets. Sockets are associated with a host address and a port address. The host address is the IP address of the host where the client or server program is located. The port address is the communication port used by the client or server program. Server programs use the well-known port number associated with their application protocol.

A client communicates with a server by establishing a connection to the socket of the server. The client and server then exchange data over the connection. Connection-oriented communication is more reliable than connectionless communication because the underlying TCP provides message-acknowledgment, error-detection, and error-recovery services. When a connectionless protocol is used, the client and server communicate by sending datagrams to each other's socket. The UDP is used for connectionless protocols. It does not support reliable communication like TCP.

5.11 ARP and RARP

RARP (Reverse Address Resolution Protocol) is a protocol used to get IP address from given MAC address. Generally, a network administrator creates an Address Resolution Protocol (ARP) table in a local area networks gateway router that maps the physical machine (MAC address) addresses to corresponding Internet Protocol addresses (IP address). When a new machine is set up, its RARP client program requests from the RARP server on the router to be sent its IP address. Assuming that an entry has been set up in the router table, the RARP server will return the IP address to the machine which can store it for future use.

Address Resolution Protocol (ARP) provides a completely different function to the network than Reverse Address Resolution Protocol (RARP). ARP is used to resolve the MAC address from an IP address in order to construct an Ethernet packet around an IP data packet. The layer 3 address is a logical address and layer 2 address is a physical address. A computer can have any number of layer 3 addresses but it will only have one layer 2 address per LAN interface. At layer 3, the data is addressed to the host that the data is destined for. At layer 2 though, the data is addressed to the next hop. This is handy because we only need to know a host's layer 3 address (which can be found out by using DNS for instance) but we won't need to know the hardware. The layer 3 packet (addressed to the destination host) will be encapsulated within a layer 2 frame (addressed to the next hop).

ARP operation for a local host: When the data gets to the *network* layer it will put on the destination IP address. All of this info is passed down to the data link layer where it is taken and placed within a data link frame. Based on the IP address, computer should be able to figure out if the destination IP is a local IP or not. If the IP is local, computer will look in its ARP table (a table where the responses to previous ARP requests are cached) to find the MAC address. If it is not there, then computer will broadcast an ARP request to find out the MAC address for the destination IP. Since this request is broadcast, all machines on the LAN will receive it and examine the contents. If the IP address in the request is their own, they will reply. On receiving this information, the computer will update its ARP table to include the new information and will then send out the frame (addressed with the destination host's MAC address).

ARP operation for a remote host: If the IP is not local then the gateway (router) will see this (remember, the ARP request is broadcast so all hosts on the LAN will see the request). The router will look in its routing table and if it has a route to the destination network, then it will reply with its *own* MAC address.

This is only the case if the computer doesn't know anything about the network topology. In most cases, computer knows the subnet mask and has a default gateway set. Because of this, the computer can figure out for itself that the packet is not destined for the local network. Instead, the computer will use the MAC address of the default gateway (which it will either have in its ARP table or have to send out an ARP request for as outlined above). When the default gateway (router) receives the frame it will see that the MAC address matches its own, so the frame must be for it. The routers will un-encapsulate the data link frame and pass the data part up to the network layer.

At the network layer, the router will see that the destination IP address (contained in the header of the IP packet) does not match its own (remember, the IP address has not been touched at all in this process since the computer created the IP packet). The router will realize that this is a packet that is supposed to be routed. The router will look in its routing table for the closest match to the destination IP in order to figure out which interface to send the packet out on. When a match is found, the router will create a new data link frame addressed to the next hop (and if the router doesn't know the hardware address for the next hop it will request it using the appropriate means for the technology in question). The data portion of this frame will contain the complete IP packet (where the destination IP address remains unchanged) and is sent out the appropriate interface.

This process will continue at each router along the way until the information reaches a router connected to the destination network. It will see that the packet is addressed to a host that's on a directly connected network (the closest match we can get for an address, short of the packet being addressed to us). It will send out an ARP request for MAC address of the destination IP (assuming it doesn't already have it in its table) and then address it to the destination's MAC address.

5.12 Subnetting

Subnetting helps in reducing the traffic on the LAN. Subnets are created to separate areas of network for security and/or to hold down broadcasts. Computers constantly communicate to each other. If we have a network of 10 computers, broadcasting packets that are sent out during networking is not much traffic at all. However, if we have 10,000 computers talking and passing data, we will have thousands of computers passing data and the network will slow down from all of the information.

A subnet or sub-network is usually utilized to break large networks into logical groups. One of those groups might be the accounting department. The members of a subnet exist on the same logical router. That router will look at traffic from each device on the subnet and if it recognizes the recipient as being on the same subnet sends the information directly to that recipient. If the recipient is not on the subnet, the data is sent over the entire network and possibly out over the Internet.

5.13 How Routing Works?

Assume that our computer has an address of 200.0.1.2, and it is connected to the 200.0.1.0 network (also, assume the subnet mask as 255.255.255.0, and call this *Network* 1) which is an ethernet network. Default gateway is a router (Router R_1) which has an address of 200.0.1.1. That router is connected to the 200.0.1.0 network and the 200.0.2.0 (*Network* 2) network (the interface connected to the 200.0.2.0 network will have an address of 200.0.2.1). The *Network* 2 is also an ethernet network. Also connected to *Network* 2 is another router (*Router* R_2) which has the address (for the interface connected to *Network* 2 at least) of 200.0.2.2. Router R_2 is also connected to *Network* 3 (200.0.3.0). Router R_2's interface on *Network* 3 has the address of 200.0.3.1. Here's a diagram to illustrate:

```
          Router              Router
           R₁                  R₂
  -----------O-------------------------O------------
     Network 1        Network 2       Network 3
     (200.0.1.0)      (200.0.2.0)     (200.0.3.0)
```

Now, if the computer (on *Network* 1 with an address of 200.0.1.2) wants to send some data to a computer on *Network* 3 (with an address of 200.0.3.2). We'll assume that none of the info in already cached in an ARP table on any of the machines or routers. The computer will create an IP packet addressed to 200.0.3.2. That packet will be sent to the data link layer where it needs a MAC address. Based on the subnet mask, the computer will know that the destination computer isn't on the same local network. So, the computer will send out an ARP request for the default gateway's MAC address (i.e., what's the MAC for 200.0.1.1?). On receiving the MAC address, the computer will send out the IP packet (still addressed to 200.0.3.2) encapsulated within a data link frame that is addressed to the MAC address of router R_1's interface on *Network* 1 (because routers have more than 1 interface they can have more than 1 MAC address, in this case each router has 2 Ethernet interface each with its own unique MAC address).

Router R_1 will receive this frame and send the data portion up to the network layer (layer 3). At the network layer, router a will see that the packet (which is addressed to 200.0.3.2) is not addressed to router R_1. Router R_1 will look in its routing table to find out where to send the packet. The routing table will show that network 3 (the closest match to 200.0.3.2) is reachable via network 2. The routing table will also show the IP address for the next hop is 200.0.2.2. Router R_1 will send out an ARP request onto Network 2 asking for router R_2's MAC address (well at least for the interface connected to Network 2). On receiving this, router R_1 will send the IP packet (still addressed to 200.0.3.2, nothing's changed here) encapsulated in a data link frame addressed to router R_2's MAC address. When router R_2 receives this frame it will do the same thing that router R_1 did, it will send the IP packet up to the network layer and see that the packet is not addressed to router R_2 (the packet is still addressed to 200.0.3.2).

Router R_2 will then look up in its routing table for the closest match and see that it is directly connected to network 3, so there isn't a next hop router to send it to. Router R_2 will send out an ARP request to learn the MAC address for 200.0.3.2. When this is received, router b will send out the IP packet (again, this is still addressed to 200.0.3.2) encapsulated within a data link frame that is addressed to the MAC address of the destination computer. The destination computer will see that the data link frame is addressed to it and will pass the IP packet to the network layer. At the network layer, the IP address will also match that of the computer and the data from the IP packet will be passed up to the transport layer. Each layer will examine the header and determine where to pass it up to until eventually, the data reaches the application running on the destination computer that has been waiting for the data.

What you'll notice through this whole process is that the IP address never changes. The IP packet is always addressed to 200.0.3.2. However, at the data link layer, the address used changes at each hop (it's always addressed to the next hop). As you go up through the layers, you get more and more specific about where the data is supposed to be going. At the data link layer this is very vague, it's basically just, "here's who to pass it on to, they should know what to do with it". At the network layer you get more specific (this is the exact computer I want to send this to). Above that you get more specific (is it TCP or UDP?, what port?, etc.)

5.14 Unicast, Broadcast and Multicast

Unicast: Unicast packets are sent from host to host. The communication is from a single host to another single host. There is one device transmitting a message destined for one receiver. Examples of Unicast transmission are http, smtp, telnet, ssh, pop3 where the request for information is directed from one sender to only one receiver at the other end.

Broadcast: Broadcast is when a single device is transmitting a message to all other devices in a given address range. This broadcast could reach all hosts on the subnet, all subnets, or all hosts on all subnets. Broadcast packets have the host (and/or subnet) portion of the address set to all ones. By design, most modern routers will block IP broadcast traffic and restrict it to the local subnet. Broadcast transmission is supported on most LANs (e.g. Ethernet), and may be used to send the same message to all computers on the LAN (e.g. the address resolution protocol (arp) uses this to send an address resolution query to all computers on a LAN).

Multicast: Multicast is a special protocol for use with IP. Multicast enables a single device to communicate with a specific set of hosts, not defined by any standard IP address and mask combination. This allows for communication that resembles a conference call. Anyone from anywhere can join the conference, and everyone at the conference hears what the speaker has to say. The speaker's message isn't broadcasted everywhere, but only to those in the conference call itself. A special set of addresses is used for multicast communication. One good example of Multicast based network is video transmission network in which one computer needs to transmit video channel to a specific group of computers.

5.15 How traceroute (or tracert) and ping works?

Tracert (and ping) are both command line utilities that are built into Windows (traceroute and ping for Linux operating systems) computer systems. The basic tracert command syntax is "tracert hostname". For example, "tracert CareerMonk.com" and the output might look like:

```
1 51 ms 59 ms 49 ms 10.176.119.1
2 66 ms 50 ms 38 ms 172.31.242.57
```

3 54 ms 69 ms 60 ms 172.31.78.130

Discover the path: Tracert sends an ICMP echo packet, but it takes advantage of the fact that most Internet routers will send back an ICMP *'TTL expired in transit'* message if the TTL field is ever decremented to zero by a router. Using this knowledge, we can discover the path taken by IP Packets.

How tracert works: Tracert sends out an ICMP echo packet to the named host, but with a TTL of 1; then with a TTL of 2; then with a TTL of 3 and so on. Tracert will then get *'TTL expired in transit'* message back from routers until the destination host computer finally is reached and it responds with the standard ICMP *'echo reply'* packet.

Round Trip Times: Each millisecond (ms) time in the table is the round-trip time that it took (to send the ICMP packet and to get the ICMP reply packet). The faster (smaller) the times the better. *ms* times of 0 mean that the reply was faster than the computers timer of 10 milliseconds, so the time is actually somewhere between 0 and 10 milliseconds.

Packet Loss: Packet loss kills throughput. So, having no packet loss is critical to having a connection to the Internet that responds well. A slower connection with zero packet loss can easily outperform a faster connection with some packet loss. Also, packet loss on the last hop, the destination, is what is most important. Sometimes routers in-between will not send ICMP *'TTL expired in transit'* messages, causing what looks to be high packet loss at a particular hop, but all it means is that the particular router is not responding to ICMP echo.

Ping: The basic ping command syntax is *"ping hostname"*. For example, "ping visualroute.com" and the output might look like:

Pinging careermonk.com [182.50.143.69] with 32 bytes of data:
Reply from 182.50.143.69: bytes=32 time=130ms TTL=116
Reply from 182.50.143.69: bytes=32 time=130ms TTL=116
Reply from 182.50.143.69: bytes=32 time=137ms TTL=116

How ping works?

1. The source host generates an ICMP protocol data unit.
2. The ICMP PDU is encapsulated in an IP datagram, with the source and destination IP addresses in the IP header. At this point the datagram is most properly referred to as an ICMP ECHO datagram, but we will call it an IP datagram from here on since that's what it looks like to the networks it is sent over.
3. The source host notes the local time on its clock as it transmits the IP datagram towards the destination. Each host that receives the IP datagram checks the destination address to see if it matches their own address or is the all hosts address (all 1's in the host field of the IP address).
4. If the destination IP address in the IP datagram does not match the local host's address, the IP datagram is forwarded to the network where the IP address resides.
5. The destination host receives the IP datagram, finds a match between itself and the destination address in the IP datagram.
6. The destination host notes the ICMP ECHO information in the IP datagram performs any necessary work then destroys the original IP/ICMP ECHO datagram.
7. The destination host creates an ICMP ECHO REPLY, encapsulates it in an IP datagram placing its own IP address in the source IP address field, and the original sender's IP address in the destination field of the IP datagram.
8. The new IP datagram is routed back to the originator of the PING. The host receives it, notes the time on the clock and finally prints PING output information, including the elapsed time
9. The process above is repeated until all requested ICMP ECHO packets have been sent and their responses have been received or the default 2-second timeout expired. The default 2-second timeout is local to the host initiating the PING and is NOT the Time-To-Live value in the datagram.

5.16 What is QoS?

QoS (Quality of Service) refers to a broad collection of networking technologies and techniques. The goal of QoS is to provide guarantees on the ability of a network to deliver predictable results. Elements of network performance within the scope of QoS generally includes availability (uptime), bandwidth (throughput), latency (delay), and error rate.

QoS involves prioritization of network traffic. QoS can be targeted at a network interface, toward a given server or router's performance, or in terms of specific applications. A network monitoring system must typically be deployed as part of QoS, to insure that networks are performing at the desired level.

QoS is especially important for the new generation of Internet applications such as VoIP, video-on-demand and other consumer services. Some core networking technologies like Ethernet were not designed to support prioritized traffic or guaranteed performance levels, making it much more difficult to implement QoS solutions across the Internet.

Chapter-6

DATABASE CONCEPTS

6.1 Glossary

Database: A database is a collection of data organized in a particular way. Databases can be of many types such as Flat File Databases, Relational Databases, Distributed Databases etc.

A relational database uses the concept of linked two-dimensional tables which comprise of rows and columns. A user can draw relationships between multiple tables and present the output as a table again. A user of a relational database need not understand the representation of data in order to retrieve it. Relational programming is non-procedural.

Procedural and non − procedural: Programming languages are procedural if they use programming elements such as conditional statements (if-then-else, do-while etc.). SQL (Structured Query Language) has none of these types of statements and is an example for non-procedural.

SQL: SQL is the language used to query all databases. It's simple to learn and appears to do very little but is the heart of a successful database application. Understanding SQL and using it efficiently is highly imperative in designing an efficient database application. The better our understanding of SQL the more versatile we'll be in getting information out of databases.

DBMS: MySQL and mSQL are database management systems (DBMS). These software packages are used to manipulate a database. All DBMSs use their own implementation of SQL.

Data Definition and *Manipulation*: DBMS makes use of a Data Definition Language (DDL) and a Data Manipulation Language (DML). The DML enables the specification of data types, structures and constraints that should be part of the database. All specifications defined by the DDL are stored in the database.

The DML enables those with access to the database to insert, update, delete and retrieve data from it. Structured Query Language (SQL) is the standard DML used today. SQL is a non-procedural language.

Normalization: Normalization is the process where a database is designed in a way that removes redundancies, and increases the clarity in organizing data in a database. In simple terms, it means taking similar stuff out of a collection of data and placing them into tables. Keep doing this for each new table recursively and we will have a *normalized* database.

The important thing here is to know when to normalize and when to be practical. That will come with experience. Normalization of a database helps in modifying the design at later times and helps in being prepared if a change is required in the database design. Normalization raises the efficiency of the database in terms of management, data storage and scalability. Now normalization of a Database is achieved by following a set of rules called *normal forms* in creating the database. These rules are 5 in number (with one extra one stuck in-between 3 & 4) and they are:

1st Normal Form or 1NF	Each Column Type is Unique
2nd Normal Form or 2NF	The entity under consideration should already be in the 1NF and all attributes within the entity should depend solely on the entity's unique identifier.
3rd Normal Form or 3NF	The entity should already be in the 2NF and no column entry should be dependent on any other entry (value) other than the key for the table. If such an entity exists, move it outside into a new table. Now if these 3NF are achieved, the database is considered normalized.
BCNF (Boyce & Codd):	The database should be in 3NF and all tables can have only one primary key.
4NF	Tables cannot have multi-valued dependencies on a Primary Key.
5NF	There should be no cyclic dependencies in a composite key.

Well this is a highly simplified explanation for database normalization. One can study this process extensively though. After working with databases for some time we'll automatically create normalized databases. For now, don't worry too much about above definitions. Much of database design depends on how we want to keep the data. In real life situations often you may find it more convenient to store data in tables designed in a way that does fall a bit short of keeping all the NFs happy. But that's what databases are all about.

***Pros* and *Cons* of a *Normalized* database design**: Normalized databases fair very well under conditions where the applications are write-intensive and the write-load is more than the read-load. This is because of the following reasons:

- Normalized tables are generally smaller in size and have a smaller foot-print as the data is divided vertically among many tables. This allows them to perform better as they are small enough to get fit into the buffer.
- The updates are very fast as the data to be updated is located at a single place and there are no duplicates.
- Similarly the inserts are very fast as the data has to be inserted at a single place and does not have to be duplicated.
- The selects are fast in cases where data has to be fetched from a single table, because normally normalized tables are small enough to get fit into the buffer.
- Because the data is not duplicated so there is less need for heavy duty group by or distinct queries.

Although there seems to be much in favor of normalized tables, with all the pros outlined above, but the main cause of concern with fully normalized tables is that normalized data means *joins* between tables. And this joining means that read operations have to suffer because indexing strategies do not go well with table joins.

Pros **and** ***Cons*** **of a denormalized database design:** Denormalized databases fair well under heavy read-load and when the application is read intensive. This is because of the following reasons:

- The data is present in the same table so there is *no* need for any joins, hence the selects are very fast.
- A single table with all the required data allows much more efficient index usage. If the columns are indexed properly, then results can be filtered and sorted by utilizing the same index. While in the case of a normalized table, since the data would be spread out in different tables, this would not be possible.

Although for reasons mentioned above selects can be very fast on denormalized tables, but because the data is duplicated, the updates and inserts become complex and costly.

Having said that neither one of the approach can be entirely neglected, because a real world application is going to have both read-loads and write-loads. Hence the correct way would be to utilize both the normalized and denormalized approaches depending on situations.

6.2 Questions on Database Concepts

Question-1   What is SELECT statement?

Answer: The SELECT statement lets users to select a set of values from a table in a database. The values selected from the database table would depend on the various conditions that are specified in the SQL query.

Question-2   How can we compare a part of the name rather than the entire name?

Answer: SELECT * FROM people WHERE empname LIKE '%na%'; This would return a recordset with records consisting empname the sequence *'na'* in empname .

Question-3   What is the INSERT statement?

Answer: The INSERT statement lets users to insert information into a database.

Question-4   How do you delete a record from a database?

Answer: Use the DELETE statement to remove records or any particular column values from a database.

Question-5   How could we get distinct entries from a table?

Answer: The SELECT statement in conjunction with DISTINCT lets users to select a set of distinct values from a table in a database. The values selected from the database table would of course depend on the various conditions that are specified in the SQL query. Example: SELECT DISTINCT empname FROM emptable

Question-6   How to get the results of a Query sorted in any order?

Answer: We can sort the results and return the sorted results to our program by using ORDER BY keyword thus saving us the pain of carrying out the sorting. The ORDER BY keyword is used for sorting.

SELECT empname, age, city FROM emptable ORDER BY empname

Question-7   How can we find the total number of records in a table?

Answer: We could use the COUNT keyword , example: SELECT COUNT(*) FROM emp WHERE age > 40

Question-8   What is GROUP BY?

Answer: The GROUP BY keywords have been added to SQL because aggregate functions (like SUM) return the aggregate of all column values every time they are called. Without the GROUP BY functionality, finding the sum for each individual group of column values was not possible.

Question-9   What is the difference "dropping a table", "truncating a table" and "deleting all records" from a table.

Answer: DELETE TABLE is a logged operation, so the deletion of each row gets logged in the transaction log, which makes it slow. TRUNCATE TABLE also deletes all the rows in a table, but it will not log the deletion of each row, instead it logs the de-allocation of the data pages of the table, which makes it faster. Of course, TRUNCATE TABLE can be rolled back.

Question-10   Difference between a *where* clause and a *having* clause.

Answer: *Having* clause is used only with group functions whereas *Where* is not used with.

Question-11   What's the difference between a primary key and a unique key?

Answer: Both primary key and unique enforce uniqueness of the column on which they are defined. But by default primary key creates a clustered index on the column, whereas unique creates a nonclustered index by default. Another major difference is that, primary key doesn't allow NULLs, but unique key allows one NULL only.

Question-12   What are cursors? Explain different types of cursors. What are the disadvantages of cursors? How can you avoid cursors?

Answer: Cursors allow row-by-row processing of the result sets. Types of cursors: Static, Dynamic, Forward-only, Keyset-driven. *Disadvantages* of cursors: Each time you fetch a row from the cursor, it results in a network roundtrip, where as a normal SELECT query makes only one round trip, however large the resultset is. Cursors are also costly because they require more resources and temporary storage (results in more IO operations). Further, there are restrictions on the SELECT statements that can be used with some types of cursors. Most of the times, set based operations can be used instead of cursors. Here is an example: If you have to give a flat hike to your employees using the following criteria:

```
Salary between 30000 and 40000 -- 5000 hike
Salary between 40000 and 55000 -- 7000 hike
Salary between 55000 and 65000 -- 9000 hike
```

In this situation many developers tend to use a cursor, determine each employee's salary and update his salary according to the above formula. But the same can be achieved by multiple update statements or can be combined in a single UPDATE statement as shown below:

```
UPDATE tbl_emp SET salary =
CASE WHEN salary BETWEEN 30000 AND 40000 THEN salary + 5000
WHEN salary BETWEEN 40000 AND 55000 THEN salary + 7000
WHEN salary BETWEEN 55000 AND 65000 THEN salary + 10000
END
```

Another situation in which developers tend to use cursors: We need to call a stored procedure when a column in a particular row meets certain condition. We don't have to use cursors for this. This can be achieved using WHILE loop, as long as there is a unique key to identify each row.

Question-13   What are triggers? How to invoke a trigger on demand?

Answer: Triggers are special kind of stored procedures that get executed automatically when an INSERT, UPDATE or DELETE operation takes place on a table. Triggers can't be invoked on demand. They get triggered only when an associated action (INSERT, UPDATE, DELETE) happens on the table on which they are defined. Triggers are generally used to implement business rules, auditing. Triggers can also be used to extend the referential integrity checks, but wherever possible, use constraints for this purpose, instead of triggers, as constraints are much faster.

Question-14   What is a join and explain different types of joins.

Answer: Joins are used in queries to explain how different tables are related. Joins also let you select data from a table depending upon data from another table. *Types* of joins: INNER JOINs, OUTER JOINs, CROSS JOINs. OUTER JOINs are further classified as LEFT OUTER JOINS, RIGHT OUTER JOINS and FULL OUTER JOINS.

Question-15   What is a self-join?

Answer: Self join is just like any other join, except that two instances of the same table will be joined in the query.

Question-16   What is de-normalization and when would you go for it?

Answer: As the name indicates, de-normalization is the reverse process of normalization. It is the controlled introduction of redundancy in to the database design. It helps improve the query performance as the number of joins could be reduced.

Question-17   How to implement one-to-one, one-to-many & many-to-many relationships while designing tables?

Answer: One-to-One relationship can be implemented as a single table and rarely as two tables with primary and foreign key relationships. One-to-Many relationships are implemented by splitting the data into two tables with primary key and foreign key relationships. Many-to-Many relationships are implemented using a junction table with the keys from both the tables forming the composite primary key of the junction table.

Question-18   What's the difference between a primary key and a unique key?

Answer: Both primary key and unique enforce uniqueness of the column on which they are defined. But by default primary key creates a clustered index on the column, where are unique creates a non-clustered index by default. Another major difference is that, primary key does not allow NULLs, but unique key allows one NULL only.

Question-19   What are user defined data types and when you should go for them?

Answer: User defined data types let you extend the base SQL Server data types by providing a descriptive name, and format to the database.

Question-20   Define candidate key, alternate key, composite key.

Answer: A candidate key is one that can identify each row of a table uniquely. Generally a candidate key becomes the primary key of the table. If the table has more than one candidate key, one of them will become the primary key, and the rest are called alternate keys. A key formed by combining at least two or more columns is called composite key.

Question-21   What are defaults? Is there a column to which a default cannot be bound?

Answer: A default is a value that will be used by a column, if no value is supplied to that column while inserting data. IDENTITY columns and timestamp columns can't have defaults bound to them.

Question-22   What is a transaction and what are ACID properties?

Answer: A transaction is a logical unit of work in which, all the steps must be performed or none. ACID stands for Atomicity, Consistency, Isolation, Durability. These are the properties of a transaction.

Question-23   What is Lock Escalation?

Solution: Lock escalation is the process of converting a lot of low level locks (like row locks, page locks) into higher level locks (like table locks). Every lock is a memory structure too many locks would mean, more memory being occupied by locks. To prevent this from happening, SQL Server escalates the many fine-grain locks to fewer coarse-grain locks.

Question-24   What are constraints? Explain different types of constraints.

Answer: Constraints enable the RDBMS enforce the integrity of the database automatically, without needing us to create triggers, rule or defaults. *Types* of constraints: NOT NULL, CHECK, UNIQUE, PRIMARY KEY, FOREIGN KEY.

Question-25   What is an index? What are the types of indexes? How many clustered indexes can be created on a table? If we create a separate index on each column of a table, what are the advantages and disadvantages?

Answer: Indexes in SQL Server are similar to the indexes in books. They help SQL Server retrieve the data quicker. Indexes are of two types: Clustered indexes and non-clustered indexes. When you create a clustered index on a table, all the rows in the table are stored in the order of the clustered index key. So, there can be only one clustered index per table. Non-clustered indexes have their own storage separate from the table data storage.

Non-clustered indexes are stored as B-tree structures (so do clustered indexes), with the leaf level nodes having the index key and it's row locater. The row located could be the RID or the Clustered index key, depending up on the absence or presence of clustered index on the table.

If you create an index on each column of a table, it improves the query performance, as the query optimizer can choose from all the existing indexes to come up with an efficient execution plan. At the same time, data modification operations (such as INSERT, UPDATE, DELETE) will become slow, as every time data changes in the table, all the indexes need to be updated. Another disadvantage is that, indexes need disk space, the more indexes you have, more disk space is used.

Question-26   What is a join and explain different types of joins?

Answer: Let us assume that we are joining on columns with no duplicates:
- An inner join of Table-1 and Table-2 gives the result of Table-1 intersect Table-2, i.e. the inner part of a Venn diagram intersection.
- An outer join of Table-1 and Table-2 gives the results of Table-1 union Table-2, i.e. the outer parts of a Venn diagram union.

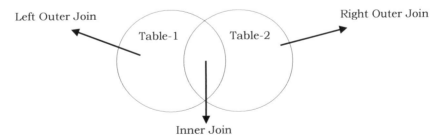

Suppose we have two tables, with a single column each, and data as follows: note that (1,2) are unique to Table-1, (3,4) are common, and (5,6) are unique to Table-2.

Table-1, Column:A
1
2
3
4

Table-2, Column: B
3
4
5
6

Inner join: An inner join using either of the equivalent queries gives the intersection of the two tables, i.e. the two rows they have in common.

```
select * from Table-1 INNER JOIN Table-2 on Table-1.A = Table-1.B;
```

A	B
3	3
4	4

Left outer join: A left outer join will give all rows in Table-1, plus any common rows in Table-2.

select * from Table-1 LEFT OUTER JOIN Table-2 on Table-1.A = Table-1.B;

A	B
1	null
2	null
3	3
4	4

Right outer join: A right outer join will give all rows in Table-2, plus any common rows in Table-1.

select * from Table-1 RIGHT OUTER JOIN Table-2 on Table-1.A = Table-1.B;

A	B
3	3
4	4
null	5
null	6

Full outer join: A full outer join will give you the union of Table-1 and Table-2, i.e. All the rows in Table-1 and all the rows in Table-2. If something in Table-1 doesn't have a corresponding datum in Table-2, then the Table-2 portion is null, and vice versa.

select * from Table-1 FULL OUTER JOIN Table-2 on Table-1.A = Table-2.B;

A	B
1	null
2	null
3	3
4	4
null	5
null	6

Question-27   What is RAID and what are different types of RAID configurations?

Answer: RAID stands for Redundant Array of Inexpensive Disks, used to provide fault tolerance to database servers. There are six RAID levels 0 through 5 offering different levels of performance, fault tolerance.

Question-28   What is a deadlock and what is a live lock? How will you go about resolving deadlocks?

Answer: Deadlock is a situation when two processes, each having a lock on one piece of data, attempt to acquire a lock on the other's piece. Each process would wait indefinitely for the other to release the lock, unless one of the user processes is terminated. SQL Server detects deadlocks and terminates one user's process. A livelock is one, where a request for an exclusive lock is repeatedly denied because a series of overlapping shared locks keeps interfering. SQL Server detects the situation after four denials and refuses further shared locks. A livelock also occurs when read transactions monopolize a table or page, forcing a write transaction to wait indefinitely.

Question-29   What is blocking?

Answer: Blocking happens when one connection from an application holds a lock and a second connection requires a conflicting lock type. This forces the second connection to wait, blocked on the first.

BRAIN TEASERS	Chapter-7

7.1 Questions on Brain Teasers

Question-1 **Hats Problem:** Three wise men are told to stand in a straight line, one in front of the other. A hat is put on each of their heads. They are told that each of these hats was selected from a group of five hats: two black hats and three white hats. The first man, standing at the front of the line, can't see either of the men behind him or their hats. The second man, in the middle, can see only the first man and his hat. The last man, at the rear, can see both other men and their hats.

None of the men can see the hat on his own head. They are asked to deduce its color. Some time goes by as the wise men ponder the puzzle in silence. Finally the first one, at the front of the line, makes an announcement: "My hat is white." He is correct. How did he come to this conclusion?

Answer: If the two front hats were black, the third wise man would have called out the color of his hat as white immediately. If the first hat was black, and the third man did not call out any color, the second wise man could deduce that his hat was white. Since neither man called out a color, the first wise man would know that his hat is white, which is the only color that does not allow either the second or third man to guess the color of their own hat.

Question-2 **Weighing:** You have got a 4 liter jug and a 9 liter jug and got a pool of water. What is the fewest number of steps it takes to come up with exactly 6 liters of water? You cannot pour some water into the 9 liter jug and then guess. Nor can you fill each jug up half way or something. You have to be exact. A step is defined as pouring water into or out of a jug. For instance, filling the 4 liter jug and then pouring it into the 9 liter jug, and emptying the 9 liter into the pool is 3 steps.

Answer: One possible full answer is as follows:
- Fill up the 9 liter jug from the pool.
- Fill up the 4 liter jug from the 9 liter jug (leaving 5 liters in the 9 liter jug).
- Empty the 4 liter jug into the pool.
- Fill the 4 liter jug again from the 9 liter jug (leaving 1 liter in the 9 liter jug).
- Empty the 4 liter jug into the pool.
- Put the 1 liter from the 9 liter jug into the 4 liter.
- Fill the 9 liter jug from the pool.
- Fill up the 4 liter jug from the 9 liter jug. There was 1 liter in the 4 liter jug, so 3 liters will fill it. This leaves, in the 9 liter jug, exactly 6 *liters*.

Question-3 **Careful Farmer:** A farmer returns from the market, where he bought a goat, a cabbage and a wolf. On the way home he must cross a river. His boat is small and won't fit more than one of his purchases. He cannot leave the goat alone with the cabbage (because the goat would eat it), nor he can leave the goat alone with the wolf (because the goat would be eaten). How can the farmer get everything on the other side in this river crossing puzzle?

Answer: Take the goat to the other side. Go back, take cabbage, unload it on the other side where you load the goat, go back and unload it. Take the wolf to the other side where you unload it. Go back for the goat.

Question-4 **Algorithmic Weighing:** Weighing in a Harder Way· You've got 27 coin, each of them is 10 g, except for 1. The 1 different coin is 9 g or 11 g (heavier, or lighter by 1 g). You should use balance scale that compares what's in the two pans. You can get the answer by just comparing groups of coins. What is the minimum number weighing's that can always guarantee to determine the different coin.

Answer: Separate the coins into 3 stacks of 9 (A, B, C). Weigh stack A against B and then A against C. Take the stack with the different weight (note lighter or heavier) and break it into 3 stacks of 3 (D, E, F). Weigh stack D against E. If D and E are equal, then F is the odd stack. If D and E are not equal, the lighter or heavier (based on the A, B, C comparison) is the odd stack. You now have three coins (G, H, I). Weigh G and H. If G equals H, then I is the odd and is lighter or heavier (based on the A, B, C comparison). If G and H are not equal, then the lighter or heavier (based on the A, B, C comparison) is the odd coin.

Note: for algorithmic solution refer *Divide* and *Conquer* chapter.

Question-5 Having 2 sandglasses: one 7-minute and the second one 4-minute, how can you correctly time 9 minutes?

Answer: Turn both sand-glasses. After 4 minutes turn upside down the 4-min sand-glass. When the 7-min sand-glass spills the last grain, turn the 7-min upside down. Then you have 1 minute in the 4-min sand-glass left and after spilling everything, in the 7-min sand-glass there will be 1 minute of sand down (already spilt). Turn the 7-min sand-glass upside down and let the 1 minute go back. And that's it. 4 + 3 + 1 + 1 = 9.

Question-6   You are travelling down a country lane to a distant village. You reach a fork in the road and find a pair of identical twin sisters standing there.

- Fork in the road riddle One standing on the road to village and the other standing on the road to neverland (of course, you don't know or see where each road leads).
- One of the sisters always tells the truth and the other always lies (of course, you don't know who is lying).
- Both sisters know where the roads go.

If you are allowed to ask only one question to one of the sisters to find the correct road to the village, what is your question?

Solution: This is one of the most famous logic problems which can be solved by using classic logic operations. You may have heard a few variations of this puzzle before but still, it's one of the best brain teasers. There are a few types of logic questions:

- Indirect question: "Hello there beauty, what would your sister say, if I asked her where this road leads?" The answer is always negated.
- Tricky question: "Excuse me lady, does a truth telling person stand on the road to the village?" The answer will be YES, if I am asking a truth teller who is standing at the road to village, or if I am asking a liar standing again on the same road. So I can go that way. A similar deduction can be made for negative answer.
- Complicated question: "Hey you, what would you say, if I asked you ...?" A truth teller is clear, but a liar should lie. However, she is forced by the question to lie two times and thus speak the truth.

Question-7   **Super Observer**: There are three switches in a room on the first floor and a lamp on the third floor. Each one is labeled On and Off. One (and only one) of the switches controls the lamp. There is no possible way for you to see whether the light is on or off from the first floor. You are alone in the house.
- You are allowed to turn on and off the switches as often and as long as you'd like.
- However, you can only go upstairs once to check on the status of the lamp.
- Determine which switch controls the lamp.

Answer: If the lamp contains a normal bulb that produces heat when turned on, you can turn on the 1st switch for 5 minutes or so then turn it off. Immediately turn on the 2nd light switch and run upstairs to check the light. If the light is on then it is the 2nd switch which controls the light. If it is off but the bulb is still hot/warm then it is the 1st switch. If it is off but cool then it is the 3rd. If the bulb is a fluorescent or LED bulb which gives off less heat then you may not be able to tell.

Question-8   Ten Stacks of Coins: You have ten stacks of ten coins. 9 of the 10 stacks contain coins that weigh 1.0 grams each. The 10th stack contains 1.1 grams. You also have a scale which returns the number of grams of the weighed items. Using the scale once, locate the stack with the 1.1 gram coins.

Answer: Take 1 coin from the first stack, 2 from the second, 3 from the third, ..., and 10 from the tenth stack and weigh them all together. If the weight of these coins is 55.1 grams then you know it is the 1st stack since $1.1 + 2 + 3 + 4 + 5 + 6 + 7 + 8 + 9 + 10 = 55.1$. If it is 55.2 then it is the second stack, 55.3 is the third, etc.. If the coins weigh 56 grams then it is the tenth stack which holds the 1.1g coins.

Note: There were huge number of brainteasers and it is very difficult to cover all of them in a technical book. I would suggest you to refer other books specifically designed for those kind of questions.

Chapter-8

ALGORITHMS INTRODUCTION

Objective of this chapter is to explain the importance of analysis of algorithms, their notations, relationships and solving as many problems as possible. We first concentrate on understanding the basic elements of algorithms, importance of analysis and then slowly move towards analyzing the algorithms with different notations and finally the problems.

After completion of this chapter you should be able to find the complexity of any given algorithm (especially recursive functions).

8.1 What is an Algorithm?

Let us consider the problem of preparing an omelette. For preparing omelette, we follow the steps as given below:
1) Get the frying pan.
2) Get the oil.
   a. Do we have oil?
      i. If yes, put it in the pan.
      ii. If no, do we want to buy oil?
         1. If yes, then go out and buy.
         2. If no, we can terminate.
3) Turn on the stove, etc...

What we are doing is, for a given problem (preparing an omelette), giving step by step procedure for solving it. Formal definition of an algorithm can be given as:

> An algorithm is the step-by-step instructions to solve a given problem.

Note: we do not have to prove each step of the algorithm.

8.2 Why Analysis of Algorithms?

To go from city *"A"* to city *"B"*, there can be many ways of accomplishing this: by flight, by bus, by train and also by bicycle. Depending on the availability and convenience we choose the one that suits us. Similarly, in computer science multiple algorithms are available for solving the same problem (for example, sorting problem has many algorithms like insertion sort, selection sort, quick sort and many more). Algorithm analysis helps us determining which of them is efficient in terms of time and space consumed.

8.3 Goal of Analysis of Algorithms

The goal of *analysis of algorithms* is to compare algorithms (or solutions) mainly in terms of running time but also in terms of other factors (e.g., memory, developers effort etc.)

8.4 What is Running Time Analysis?

It is the process of determining how processing time increases as the size of the problem (input size) increases. Input size is the number of elements in the input and depending on the problem type the input may be of different types. The following are the common types of inputs.

* Size of an array
* Polynomial degree
* Number of elements in a matrix
* Number of bits in binary representation of the input
* Vertices and edges in a graph

8.5 How to Compare Algorithms?

To compare algorithms, let us define few *objective measures*:

Execution times? *Not a good measure* as execution times are specific to a particular computer.

Number of statements executed? *Not a good measure*, since the number of statements varies with the programming language as well as the style of the individual programmer.

Ideal Solution? Let us assume that we expressed running time of given algorithm as a function of the input size n (i.e., $f(n)$) and compare these different functions corresponding to running times. This kind of comparison is independent of machine time, programming style, etc.

8.6 What is Rate of Growth?

The rate at which the running time increases as a function of input is called *rate of growth*. Let us assume that you went to a shop to buy a car and a cycle. If your friend sees you there and asks what you are buying then in general you say *buying a car*. This is because, cost of car is too big compared to cost of cycle (approximating the cost of cycle to cost of car).

$$Total\ Cost = cost\_of\_car + cost\_of\_cycle$$
$$Total\ Cost \approx cost\_of\_car\ (approximation)$$

For the above-mentioned example, we can represent the cost of car and cost of cycle in terms of function and for a given function ignore the low order terms that are relatively insignificant (for large value of input size, n). As an example in the case below, n^4, $2n^2$, $100n$ and 500 are the individual costs of some function and approximate it to n^4. Since, n^4 is the highest rate of growth.

$$n^4 + 2n^2 + 100n + 500 \approx n^4$$

8.7 Commonly used Rate of Growths

Given below is the list of rate of growths which come across in remaining chapters.

Time complexity	Name	Example
1	Constant	Adding an element to the front of a linked list
$logn$	Logarithmic	Finding an element in a sorted array
n	Linear	Finding an element in an unsorted array
$nlogn$	Linear Logarithmic	Sorting n items by 'divide-and-conquer'-Mergesort
n^2	Quadratic	Shortest path between two nodes in a graph
n^3	Cubic	Matrix Multiplication
2^n	Exponential	The Towers of Hanoi problem

Diagram [refer next page] shows the relationship between different rates of growth.

8.8 Types of Analysis

To analyze the given algorithm we need to know on what inputs the algorithm takes less time (performing well) and on what inputs the algorithm takes long time. We have already seen that an algorithm can be represented in the form of an expression. That means we represent the algorithm with multiple expressions: one for the case where it takes less time and other for the case where it takes the more time. In general the first case is called the *best case* and second case is called the *worst case* of the algorithm. To analyze an algorithm we need some kind of syntax and that forms the base for asymptotic analysis/notation. There are three types of analysis:

- **Worst case**
    - o Defines the input for which the algorithm takes long time.
    - o Input is the one for which the algorithm runs the slower.
- **Best case**
    - o Defines the input for which the algorithm takes lowest time.
    - o Input is the one for which the algorithm runs the fastest.
- **Average case**
    - o Provides a prediction about the running time of the algorithm
    - o Assumes that the input is random

$$Lower\ Bound \leq Average\ Time \leq Upper\ Bound$$

For a given algorithm, we can represent the best, worst and average cases in the form of expressions. As an example, let $f(n)$ be the function, which represents the given algorithm.

$f(n) = n^2 + 500$, for worst case
$f(n) = n + 100n + 500$, for best case

Similarly, for average case too. The expression defines the inputs with which the algorithm takes the average running time (or memory).

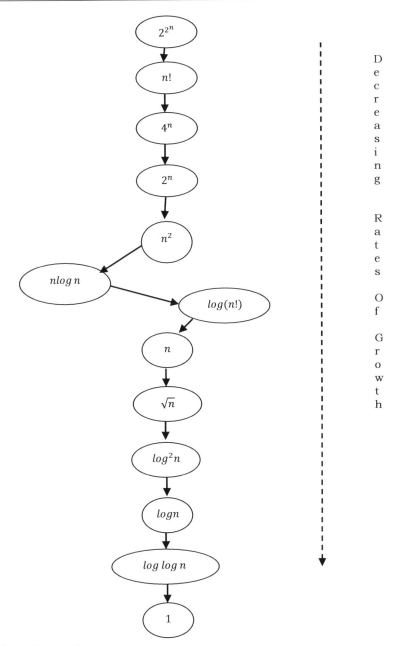

8.9 Asymptotic Notation

Having the expressions for the best, average case and worst cases, for all the three cases we need to identify the upper and lower bounds. To represent these upper and lower bounds we need some kind of syntax and that is the subject of the following discussion. Let us assume that the given algorithm is represented in the form of function $f(n)$.

8.10 Big-O Notation

This notation gives the *tight* upper bound of the given function. Generally, it is represented as $f(n) = O(g(n))$. That means, at larger values of n, the upper bound of $f(n)$ is $g(n)$. For example, if $f(n) = n^4 + 100n^2 + 10n + 50$ is the given algorithm, then n^4 is $g(n)$. That means, $g(n)$ gives the maximum rate of growth for $f(n)$ at larger values of n.

Let us see the O−notation with little more detail. O−notation defined as $O(g(n)) = \{f(n)$: there exist positive constants c and n_0 such that $0 \leq f(n) \leq cg(n)$ for all $n \geq n_0\}$. $g(n)$ is an asymptotic tight upper bound for $f(n)$. Our objective is to give smallest rate of growth $g(n)$ which is greater than or equal to given algorithms rate of growth $f(n)$.

Generally we discard lower values of n. That means the rate of growth at lower values of n is not important. In the figure below, n_0 is the point from which we need to consider the rate of growths for a given algorithm. Below n_0 the rate of growths could be different.

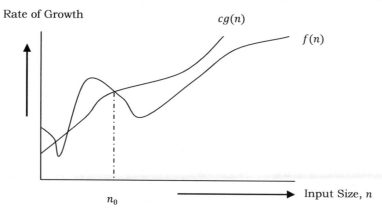

Big-O Visualization

$O(g(n))$ is the set of functions with smaller or same order of growth as $g(n)$. For example, $O(n^2)$ includes $O(1), O(n), O(nlogn)$ etc.

Note: Analyze the algorithms at larger values of n only. What this means is, below n_0 we do not care for rate of growth.

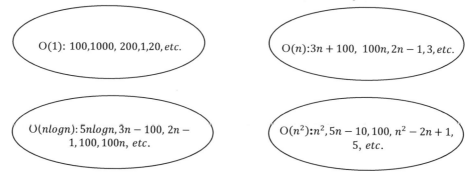

Big-O Examples

Example-1 Find upper bound for $f(n) = 3n + 8$

Solution: $3n + 8 \leq 4n$, for all $n \geq 8$
∴ $3n + 8 = O(n)$ with c = 4 and $n_0 = 8$

Example-2 Find upper bound for $f(n) = n^2 + 1$

Solution: $n^2 + 1 \leq 2n^2$, for all $n \geq 1$
∴ $n^2 + 1 = O(n^2)$ with $c = 2$ and $n_0 = 1$

Example-3 Find upper bound for $f(n) = n^4 + 100n^2 + 50$

Solution: $n^4 + 100n^2 + 50 \leq 2n^4$, for all $n \geq 11$
∴ $n^4 + 100n^2 + 50 = O(n^4)$ with $c = 2$ and $n_0 = 11$

Example-4 Find upper bound for $f(n) = 2n^3 - 2n^2$

Solution: $2n^3 - 2n^2 \leq 2n^3$, for all $n \geq 1$
∴ $2n^3 - 2n^2 = O(2n^3)$ with $c = 2$ and $n_0 = 1$

Example-5 Find upper bound for $f(n) = n$

Solution: $n \leq n^2$, for all $n \geq 1$
∴ $n = O(n^2)$ with $c = 1$ and $n_0 = 1$

Example-6 Find upper bound for $f(n) = 410$

Solution: $410 \leq 410$, for all $n \geq 1$
∴ $410 = O(1)$ with $c = 1$ and $n_0 = 1$

No Uniqueness?

There are no unique set of values for n_0 and c in proving the asymptotic bounds. Let us consider, $100n + 5 = O(n)$. For this function there are multiple n_0 and c values possible.

Solution1: $100n + 5 \leq 100n + n = 101n \leq 101n$, for all $n \geq 5$, $n_0 = 5$ and $c = 101$ is a solution.

Solution2: $100n + 5 \leq 100n + 5n = 105n \leq 105n$, for all $n \geq 1, n_0 = 1$ *and* $c = 105$ is also a solution.

8.15 Omega-Ω Notation

Similar to O discussion, this notation gives the tighter lower bound of the given algorithm and we represent it as $f(n) = \Omega(g(n))$. That means, at larger values of n, the tighter lower bound of $f(n)$ is $g(n)$. For example, if $f(n) = 100n^2 + 10n + 50$, $g(n)$ is $\Omega(n^2)$.

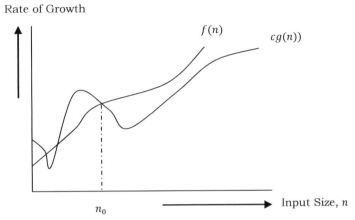

The Ω notation can be defined as $\Omega(g(n)) = \{f(n):$ there exist positive constants c and n_0 such that $0 \le cg(n) \le f(n)$ for all $n \ge n_0\}$. $g(n)$ is an asymptotic tight lower bound for $f(n)$. Our objective is to give largest rate of growth $g(n)$ which is less than or equal to given algorithms rate of growth $f(n)$.

Ω Examples

Example-1 Find lower bound for $f(n) = 5n^2$

Solution: $\exists c,\ n_0$ Such that: $0 \le cn^2 \le 5n^2 \Rightarrow cn^2 \le 5n^2 \Rightarrow c = 1$ and $n_0 = 1$
$\therefore 5n^2 = \Omega(n^2)$ with $c = 1$ and $n_0 = 1$

Example-2 Prove $f(n) = 100n + 5 \ne \Omega(n^2)$

Solution: $\exists c,\ n_0$ Such that: $0 \le cn^2 \le 100n + 5$
$100n + 5 \le 100n + 5n\ (\forall n \ge 1) = 105n$
$cn^2 \le 105n \Rightarrow n(cn - 105) \le 0$
Since n is positive $\Rightarrow cn - 105 \le 0 \Rightarrow n \le 105/c$
$\Rightarrow$ Contradiction: n cannot be smaller than a constant

Example-3 $2n = \Omega(n)$, $n^3 = \Omega(n^3)$, $logn = \Omega(logn)$

8.16 Theta-Θ Notation

This notation decides whether the upper and lower bounds of a given function (algorithm) are same. The average running time of algorithm is always between lower bound and upper bound. If the upper bound (O) and lower bound (Ω) give the same result then Θ notation will also have the same rate of growth. As an example, let us assume that $f(n) = 10n + n$ is the expression. Then, its tight upper bound $g(n)$ is O(n). The rate of growth in best case is $g(n) = $O($n$).

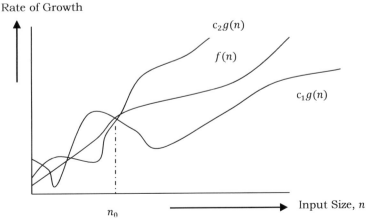

In this case, rate of growths in the best case and worst are same. As a result, the average case will also be same. For a given function (algorithm), if the rate of growths (bounds) for O and Ω are not same then the rate of growth Θ case may not be same. In this case, we need to consider all possible time complexities and take average of those (for example, quick sort average case, refer *Sorting* chapter).

Now consider the definition of Θ notation. It is defined as $\Theta(g(n)) = \{f(n):$ there exist positive constants c_1, c_2 and n_0 such that $0 \le c_1 g(n) \le f(n) \le c_2 g(n)$ for all $n \ge n_0\}$. $g(n)$ is an asymptotic tight bound for $f(n)$. $\Theta(g(n))$ is the set of functions with the same order of growth as $g(n)$.

Θ Examples

Example-1 Find Θ bound for $f(n) = \frac{n^2}{2} - \frac{n}{2}$

Solution: $\frac{n^2}{5} \le \frac{n^2}{2} - \frac{n}{2} \le n^2$, for all, $n \ge 1$ $\quad \therefore \frac{n^2}{2} - \frac{n}{2} = \Theta(n^2)$ with $c_1 = 1/5, c_2 = 1$ and $n_0 = 1$

Example-2 Prove $n \ne \Theta(n^2)$

Solution: $c_1 n^2 \le n \le c_2 n^2 \Rightarrow$ only holds for: $n \le 1/c_1$ $\therefore n \ne \Theta(n^2)$

Example-3 Prove $6n^3 \ne \Theta(n^2)$

Solution: $c_1 n^2 \le 6n^3 \le c_2 n^2 \Rightarrow$ only holds for: $n \le c_2/6$ $\therefore 6n^3 \ne \Theta(n^2)$

Example-4 Prove $n \ne \Theta(logn)$

Solution: $c_1 logn \le n \le c_2 log n \Rightarrow c_2 \ge \frac{n}{\log n}, \forall n \ge n_0$ – Impossible

Important Notes

For analysis (best case, worst case and average) we try to give upper bound (O) and lower bound (Ω) and average running time (Θ). From the above examples, it should also be clear that, for a given function (algorithm) getting upper bound (O) and lower bound (Ω) and average running time (Θ) may not be possible always. For example, if we are discussing the best case of an algorithm, then we try to give upper bound (O) and lower bound (Ω) and average running time (Θ).

In the remaining chapters we generally focus on upper bound (O) because knowing lower bound (Ω) of an algorithm is of no practical importance and we use Θ notation if upper bound (O) and lower bound (Ω) are same.

8.17 Why is it called Asymptotic Analysis?

From the discussion above (for all the three notations: worst case, best case and average case), we can easily understand that, in every case for a given function $f(n)$ we are trying to find other function $g(n)$ which approximates $f(n)$ at higher values of n. That means, $g(n)$ is also a curve which approximates $f(n)$ at higher values of n. In mathematics we call such curve as *asymptotic curve*. In other terms, $g(n)$ is the asymptotic curve for $f(n)$. For this reason, we call algorithm analysis as *asymptotic analysis*.

8.18 Guidelines for Asymptotic Analysis

There are some general rules to help us determine the running time of an algorithm.

1) **Loops**: The running time of a loop is, at most, the running time of the statements inside the loop (including tests) multiplied by the number of iterations.
   ```
   // executes n times
   for (i=1; i<=n; i++)
       m = m + 2; // constant time, c
   Total time = a constant c × n = c n = O(n).
   ```

2) **Nested loops:** Analyze from inside out. Total running time is the product of the sizes of all the loops.
   ```
   //outer loop executed n times
   for (i=1; i<=n; i++) {
       // inner loop executed n times
       for (j=1; j<=n; j++)
               k = k+1; //constant time
   }
   Total time = c × n × n = cn² = O(n²).
   ```

3) **Consecutive statements:** Add the time complexities of each statement.
   ```
   x = x +1; //constant time
   // executed n times
   for (i=1; i<=n; i++)
       m = m + 2; //constant time
   //outer loop executed n times
   for (i=1; i<=n; i++) {
       //inner loop executed n times
   ```

```
        for (j=1; j<=n; j++)
                k = k+1; //constant time
}
Total time = c_0 + c_1 n + c_2 n^2 = O(n^2).
```

Total time $= c_0 + c_1 n + c_2 n^2 = O(n^2)$.

4) **If-then-else statements:** Worst-case running time: the test, plus *either* the *then* part *or* the *else* part (whichever is the larger).

```
//test: constant
if(length( ) == 0 ) {
        return false; //then part: constant
}
else {// else part: (constant + constant) * n
        for (int n = 0; n < length( ); n++) {
                // another if : constant + constant (no else part)
                if(!list[n].equals(otherList.list[n]))
                        //constant
                        return false;
        }
}
```

Total time $= c_0 + c_1 + (c_2 + c_3) * n = O(n)$.

5) **Logarithmic complexity:** An algorithm is O($logn$) if it takes a constant time to cut the problem size by a fraction (usually by ½).

As an example let us consider the following program:
```
        for (i=1; i<=n;)
                i = i*2;
```

If we observe carefully, the value of i is doubling every time. Initially $i = 1$, in next step $i = 2$, and in subsequent steps $i = 4, 8$ and so on. Let us assume that the loop is executing some k times. At k^{th} step $2^k = n$ and we come out of loop. Taking logarithm on both sides, gives

$log(2^k) = logn$
$klog2 = logn$
$k = logn$ //if we assume base-2
Total time = O($logn$).

Note: Similarly, for the case below also, worst case rate of growth is O($logn$). The same discussion holds good for decreasing sequence as well.

```
        for (i=n; i>=1;)
                i = i/2;
```

Another example: binary search (finding a word in a dictionary of n pages)

- Look at the center point in the dictionary
- Is word towards left or right of center?
- Repeat process with left or right part of dictionary until the word is found

8.19 Properties of Notations

- Transitivity: $f(n) = \Theta(g(n))$ and $g(n) = \Theta(h(n)) \Rightarrow f(n) = \Theta(h(n))$. Valid for O and Ω as well.
- Reflexivity: $f(n) = \Theta(f(n))$. Valid for O and Ω also.
- Symmetry: $f(n) = \Theta(g(n))$ if and only if $g(n) = \Theta(f(n))$.
- Transpose symmetry: $f(n) = O(g(n))$ if and only if $g(n) = \Omega(f(n))$.

8.20 Commonly used Logarithms and Summations

Logarithms

$log\,x^y = y\,log\,x$ $log\,n = log_{10}^n$ $log\,xy = logx + logy$

$log^k n = (logn)^k$ $log\,logn = log(logn)$ $log\frac{x}{y} = logx - logy$

$a^{log_b^x} = x^{log_b^a}$ $log_b^x = \frac{log_a^x}{log_a^b}$

Arithmetic series

$$\sum_{K=1}^{n} k = 1 + 2 + \cdots + n = \frac{n(n+1)}{2}$$

Geometric series

$$\sum_{k=0}^{n} x^k = 1 + x + x^2 \dots + x^n = \frac{x^{n+1}-1}{x-1}(x \neq 1)$$

Harmonic series

$$\sum_{k=1}^{n} \frac{1}{k} = 1 + \frac{1}{2} + \dots + \frac{1}{n} \approx \log n$$

Other important formulae

$$\sum_{k=1}^{n} \log k \approx n\log n \qquad \sum_{k=1}^{n} k^p = 1^p + 2^p + \dots + n^p \approx \frac{1}{p+1}n^{p+1}$$

8.21 Master Theorem for Divide and Conquer

All divide and conquer algorithms (Also discussed in detail in the *Divide and Conquer* chapter) divide the problem into sub-problems, each of which is part of the original problem, and then perform some additional work to compute the final answer. As an example, merge sort algorithm [for details, refer *Sorting* chapter] operates on two sub-problems, each of which is half the size of the original and then performs O(n) additional work for merging. This gives the running time equation: $T(n) = 2T\left(\frac{n}{2}\right) + O(n)$

The following theorem can be used to determine the running time of divide and conquer algorithms. For a given program (algorithm), first we try to find the recurrence relation for the problem. If the recurrence is of the below form then we can directly give the answer without fully solving it. If the recurrence is of the form $T(n) = aT\left(\frac{n}{b}\right) + \Theta(n^k log^p n)$, where $a \geq 1, b > 1, k \geq 0$ and p is a real number, then:

1) If $a > b^k$, then $T(n) = \Theta\left(n^{log_b^a}\right)$
2) If $a = b^k$
   a. If $p > -1$, then $T(n) = \Theta\left(n^{log_b^a} log^{p+1}n\right)$
   b. If $p = -1$, then $T(n) = \Theta\left(n^{log_b^a} loglogn\right)$
   c. If $p < -1$, then $T(n) = \Theta\left(n^{log_b^a}\right)$
3) If $a < b^k$
   a. If $p \geq 0$, then $T(n) = \Theta(n^k log^p n)$
   b. If $p < 0$, then $T(n) = O(n^k)$

8.22 Problems on Divide and Conquer Master Theorem

For each of the following recurrences, give an expression for the runtime $T(n)$ if the recurrence can be solved with the Master Theorem. Otherwise, indicate that the Master Theorem does not apply.

Problem-1 $\quad T(n) = 3T(n/2) + n^2$

Solution: $T(n) = 3T(n/2) + n^2 => T(n) = \Theta(n^2)$ (Master Theorem Case 3.a)

Problem-2 $\quad T(n) = 4T(n/2) + n^2$

Solution: $T(n) = 4T(n/2) + n^2 => T(n) = \Theta(n^2 logn)$ (Master Theorem Case 2.a)

Problem-3 $\quad T(n) = T(n/2) + n^2$

Solution: $T(n) = T(n/2) + n^2 => \Theta(n^2)$ (Master Theorem Case 3.a)

Problem-4 $\quad T(n) = 2^n T(n/2) + n^n$

Solution: $T(n) = 2^n T(n/2) + n^n =>$ Does not apply (a is not constant)

Problem-5 $\quad T(n) = 16T(n/4) + n$

Solution: $T(n) = 16T(n/4) + n => T(n) = \Theta(n^2)$ (Master Theorem Case 1)

Problem-6 $\quad T(n) = 2T(n/2) + nlogn$

Solution: $T(n) = 2T(n/2) + nlogn => T(n) = \Theta(nlog^2 n)$ (Master Theorem Case 2.a)

Problem-7 $\quad T(n) = 2T(n/2) + n/logn$

Solution: $T(n) = 2T(n/2) + n/logn => T(n) = \Theta(nloglogn)$ (Master Theorem Case 2.b)

Problem-8 $\quad T(n) = 2T(n/4) + n^{0.51}$

Solution: $T(n) = 2T(n/4) + n^{0.51} => T(n) = \Theta(n^{0.51})$ (Master Theorem Case 3.b)

Problem-9 $\quad T(n) = 0.5T(n/2) + 1/n$

Solution: $T(n) = 0.5T(n/2) + 1/n =>$ Does not apply ($a < 1$)

Problem-10 $\quad T(n) = 6T(n/3) + n^2 logn$

Solution: $T(n) = 6T(n/3) + n^2 logn => T(n) = \Theta(n^2 logn)$ (Master Theorem Case 3.a)

Problem-11 $T(n) = 64T(n/8) - n^2 logn$

Solution: $T(n) = 64T(n/8) - n^2 logn =>$ Does not apply (function is not positive)

Problem-12 $T(n) = 7T(n/3) + n^2$

Solution: $T(n) = 7T(n/3) + n^2 => T(n) = \Theta(n^2)$ (Master Theorem Case 3.as)

Problem-13 $T(n) = 4T(n/2) + logn$

Solution: $T(n) = 4T(n/2) + logn => T(n) = \Theta(n^2)$ (Master Theorem Case 1)

Problem-14 $T(n) = 16T(n/4) + n!$

Solution: $T(n) = 16T(n/4) + n! => T(n) = \Theta(n!)$ (Master Theorem Case 3.a)

Problem-15 $T(n) = \sqrt{2}T(n/2) + logn$

Solution: $T(n) = \sqrt{2}T(n/2) + logn => T(n) = \Theta(\sqrt{n})$ (Master Theorem Case 1)

Problem-16 $T(n) = 3T(n/2) + n$

Solution: $T(n) = 3T(n/2) + n => T(n) = \Theta(n^{log3})$ (Master Theorem Case 1)

Problem-17 $T(n) = 3T(n/3) + \sqrt{n}$

Solution: $T(n) = 3T(n/3) + \sqrt{n} => T(n) = \Theta(n)$ (Master Theorem Case 1)

Problem-18 $T(n) = 4T(n/2) + cn$

Solution: $T(n) = 4T(n/2) + cn => T(n) = \Theta(n^2)$ (Master Theorem Case 1)

Problem-19 $T(n) = 3T(n/4) + nlogn$

Solution: $T(n) = 3T(n/4) + nlogn => T(n) = \Theta(nlogn)$ (Master Theorem Case 3.a)

Problem-20 $T(n) = 3T(n/3) + n/2$

Solution: $T(n) = 3T(n/3) + n/2 => T(n) = \Theta(nlogn)$ (Master Theorem Case 2.a)

8.23 Master Theorem for Subtract and Conquer Recurrences

Let $T(n)$ be a function defined on positive n, and having the property

$$T(n) = \begin{cases} c, & \text{if } n \leq 1 \\ aT(n-b) + f(n), & \text{if } n > 1 \end{cases}$$

for some constants $c, a > 0, b > 0, k \geq 0$, and function $f(n)$. If $f(n)$ is in $O(n^k)$, then

$$T(n) = \begin{cases} O(n^k), & \text{if } a < 1 \\ O(n^{k+1}), & \text{if } a = 1 \\ O\left(n^k a^{\frac{n}{b}}\right), & \text{if } a > 1 \end{cases}$$

8.24 Variant of subtraction and conquer master theorem

The solution to the equation $T(n) = T(\alpha n) + T((1 - \alpha)n) + \beta n$, where $0 < \alpha < 1$ and $\beta > 0$ are constants, is $O(nlogn)$.

8.25 Problems on Algorithms Analysis

Note: From the following problems, try to understand the cases which give different complexities $(O(n), O(logn), O(loglogn)$ etc...).

Problem-21   Find the complexity of the recurrence: $T(n) = \begin{cases} 3T(n-1), \text{if } n > 0, \\ 1, \qquad otherwise \end{cases}$

Solution: Let us try solving this function with substitution.

$T(n) = 3T(n-1)$

$T(n) = 3(3T(n-2)) = 3^2T(n-2)$

$T(n) = 3^2(3T(n-3))$

.

.

$T(n) = 3^nT(n-n) = 3^nT(0) = 3^n$

This clearly shows that the complexity of this function is $O(3^n)$.

Note: We can use the *Subtraction and Conquer* master theorem for this problem.

Problem-22 Find the complexity of the recurrence: $T(n) = \begin{cases} 2T(n-1) - 1, if \ n > 0, \\ 1, \qquad\qquad otherwise \end{cases}$

Solution: Let us try solving this function with substitution.

$$T(n) = 2T(n-1) - 1$$

$$T(n) = 2(2T(n-2) - 1) - 1 = 2^2 T(n-2) - 2 - 1$$

$$T(n) = 2^2(2T(n-3) - 2 - 1) - 1 = 2^3 T(n-4) - 2^2 - 2^1 - 2^0$$

$$T(n) = 2^n T(n-n) - 2^{n-1} - 2^{n-2} - 2^{n-3} \dots 2^2 - 2^1 - 2^0$$

$$T(n) = 2^n - 2^{n-1} - 2^{n-2} - 2^{n-3} \dots 2^2 - 2^1 - 2^0$$

$$T(n) = 2^n - (2^n - 1) \ [note: 2^{n-1} + 2^{n-2} + \dots + 2^0 = 2^n]$$

$$T(n) = 1$$

Time Complexity is O(1). Note that while the recurrence relation looks exponential the solution to the recurrence relation here gives a different result.

Problem-23 What is the running time of the following function?
```
void Function(int n) {
        int i=1, s=1;
        while( s <= n) {
            i++;
            s= s+i;
           printf("*");
        }
}
```

Solution: Consider the comments in below function:
```
void Function (int n) {
        int i-1, s-1;
        // s is increasing not at rate 1 but i
        while( s <= n) {
            i++;
            s= s+i;
            printf("*");
        }
}
```

We can define the terms 's' according to the relation $s_i = s_{i-1} + i$. The value of 'i' increases by 1 for each iteration. The value contained in 's' at the ith iteration is the sum of the first 'i' positive integers. If k is the total number of iterations taken by the program, then *while* loop terminates if: $1 + 2 + \dots + k = \frac{k(k+1)}{2} > n \Rightarrow k = O(\sqrt{n})$.

Problem-24 Find the complexity of the function given below.
```
void Function(int n) {
      int i, count =0;
      for(i-1; i*i<-n; i++)
            count++;
}
```
Solution:
```
void Function(int n) {
      int i, count =0;
      for(i=1; i*i<=n; i++)
            count++;
}
```
In the above-mentioned function the loop will end, if $i^2 \le n \Rightarrow T(n) = O(\sqrt{n})$. The reasoning is same as that of Problem-23.

Problem-25 What is the complexity of the program given below:
```
void function(int n) {
      int i, j, k , count =0;
      for(i=n/2; i<=n; i++)
            for(j=1; j + n/2<=n; j= j++)
                  for(k=1; k<=n; k= k * 2)
                        count++;
}
```
Solution: Consider the comments in the following function.
```
void function(int n) {
```

```
        int i, j, k , count =0;
        //outer loop execute n/2 times
        for(i=n/2; i<=n; i++)
                //Middle loop executes n/2 times
                for(j=1; j + n/2<=n; j= j++)
                        //outer loop execute logn times
                        for(k=1; k<=n; k= k * 2)
                                count++;
}
```

The complexity of the above function is $O(n^2 logn)$.

Problem-26   What is the complexity of the program given below:

```
void function(int n) {
        int i, j, k , count =0;
        for(i=n/2; i<=n; i++)
                for(j=1; j<=n; j= 2 * j)
                        for(k=1; k<=n; k= k * 2)
                                count++;
}
```

Solution: Consider the comments in the following function.

```
void function(int n) {
        int i, j, k , count =0;
        //outer loop execute n/2 times
        for(i=n/2; i<=n; i++)
                //Middle loop executes logn times
                for(j=1; j<=n; j= 2 * j)
                        //outer loop execute logn times
                        for(k=1; k<=n; k= k*2)
                                count++;
}
```

The complexity of the above function is $O(nlog^2 n)$.

Problem-27   Find the complexity of the program below.

```
function( int n ) {
        if(n == 1) return;
        for(int i = 1 ; i <= n ; i + + ) {
                for(int j= 1 ; j <= n ; j + + )            {
                        printf("*" );
                        break;
                }
        }
}
```

Solution: Consider the comments in the function below.

```
function( int n ) {
        //constant time
        if( n == 1 ) return;
        //outer loop execute n times
        for(int i = 1 ; i <= n ; i + + ) {
                // inner loop executes only time due to break statement.
                for(int j= 1 ; j <= n ; j + + )            {
                        printf("*" );
                        break;
                }
        }
}
```

The complexity of the above function is $O(n)$. Even though the inner loop is bounded by n, but due to the break statement it is executing only once.

Problem-28   Write a recursive function for the running time $T(n)$ of the function given below. Prove using the iterative method that $T(n) = \Theta(n^3)$.

```
        function( int n ) {
                if( n == 1 ) return;
                for(int i = 1 ; i <= n ; i + + )
                        for(int j = 1 ; j <= n ; j + + )
                                printf("ʌ" ) ;
                function( n-3 );
        }
```

Solution: Consider the comments in the function below:

```
function (int n) {
        //constant time
        if( n == 1 ) return;
        //outer loop execute n times
        for(int i = 1 ; i <= n ; i + + )
                //inner loop executes n times
                for(int j = 1 ; j <= n ; j + + )
                        //constant time
                        printf("*") ;
        function( n-3 );
}
```

The recurrence for this code is clearly $T(n) = T(n-3) + cn^2$ for some constant $c > 0$ since each call prints out n^2 asterisks and calls itself recursively on n - 3. Using the iterative method we get: $T(n) = T(n-3) + cn^2$. Using the *Subtraction and Conquer* master theorem, we get $T(n) = \Theta(n^3)$.

Problem-29   Determine Θ bounds for the recurrence relation: $T(n) = 2T\left(\frac{n}{2}\right) + nlogn$.

Solution: Using Divide and Conquer master theorem, we get $O(nlog^2n)$.

Problem-30   Determine Θ bounds for the recurrence: $T(n) = T\left(\frac{n}{2}\right) + T\left(\frac{n}{4}\right) + T\left(\frac{n}{8}\right) + n$.

Solution: Substituting in recurrence gives: $T(n) \leq c1 * \frac{n}{2} + c2 * \frac{n}{4} + c3 * \frac{n}{8} + cn \leq k * n$, k is a constant.

Problem-31   Determine Θ bounds for the recurrence relation: $T(n) = T(\lceil n/2 \rceil) + 7$.

Solution: Using Master Theorem we get $\Theta(logn)$.

Problem-32   Prove that the running time of the code below is $\Omega(logn)$.

```
Read(int n) {
        int k = 1;
        while( k < n )
                k = 3k;
}
```

Solution: The *while* loop will terminate once the value of 'k' is greater than or equal to the value of 'n'. In each iteration the value of 'k' is multiplied by 3. If i is the number of iterations, then 'k' has the value of 3i after i iterations. The loop is terminated upon reaching i iterations when $3^i \geq$ n $\leftrightarrow i \geq \log_3 n$, which shows that $i = \Omega (logn)$.

Problem-33   Solve the recurrence. $T(n) = \begin{cases} 1, & if\ n = 1 \\ T(n-1) + n(n-1), & if\ n \geq 2 \end{cases}$

Solution: By iteration:

$$T(n) = T(n-2) + (n-1)(n-2) + n(n-1)$$
$$...$$
$$T(n) = T(1) + \sum_{i=1}^{n} i(i-1)$$
$$T(n) - T(1) + \sum_{i=1}^{n} i^? - \sum_{i=1}^{n} i$$
$$T(n) = 1 + \frac{n((n+1)(2n+1)}{6} - \frac{n(n+1)}{2}$$
$$T(n) = \theta(n^3)$$

Note: We can use the *Subtraction and Conquer* master theorem for this problem.

Problem-34   Consider the following program:

```
Fib[n]
if(n==0) then return 0
else if(n==1) then return 1
else return Fib[n-1]+Fib[n-2]
```

Solution: The recurrence relation for running time of this program is $T(n) = T(n-1) + T(n-2) + c$. Notice T(n) has two recurrence calls indicating a binary tree. Each step recursively calls the program for n reduced by 1 and 2, so the depth of the recurrence tree is $O(n)$. The number of leaves at depth n is 2^n since this is a full binary tree, and each leaf takes at least $O(1)$ computation for the constant factor. Running time is clearly exponential in n.

Problem-35   Running time of following program?

```
function(n) {
        for(int i = 1 ; i <= n ; i + + )
                for(int j = 1 ; j <= n ; j+ = i )
                        printf( "*" ) ;
}
```

Solution: Consider the comments in below function:

```
function (n) {
        //this loop executes n times
        for(int i = 1 ; i <= n ; i + + )
                //this loop executes j times with j increase by the rate of i
                for(int j = 1 ; j <= n ; j+ = i )
                        printf("*") ;
}
```

In the above program, the inner loop executes n/i times for each value of i. Its running time is $n \times (\sum_{i=1}^{n} n/i) = O(nlogn)$.

Problem-36   What is the complexity of $\sum_{i=1}^{n} log\, i$?

Solution: Using the logarithmic property, $logxy = logx + logy$, we can see that this problem is equivalent to

$$\sum_{i=1}^{n} logi = log\,1 + log\,2 + \cdots + log\,n = log(1 \times 2 \times ... \times n) = log(n!) \leq log(n^n) \leq nlogn$$

This shows that that the time complexity = O($nlogn$).

Problem-37   What is the running time of the following recursive function (specified as a function of the input value n)? First write the recurrence formula and then find its complexity.

```
function(int n) {
        if(n <= 1)
                return;
        for (int i=1 ; i <= 3; i++ )
                f(⌈n/3⌉);
}
```

Solution: Consider the comments in below function:

```
function (int n) {
        //constant time
        if(n <= 1)  return;
        //this loop executes with recursive loop of n/3 value
        for (int i=1 ; i <= 3; i++ )
                f(⌈n/3⌉);
}
```

We can assume that for asymptotical analysis $k = \lceil k \rceil$ for every integer $k \geq 1$. The recurrence for this code is $T(n) = 3T(\frac{n}{3}) + \Theta(1)$. Using master theorem, we get $T(n) = \Theta(n)$.

Problem-38   What is the running time of the following recursive function (specified as a function of the input value n)? First write a recurrence formula, and show its solution using induction.

```
function(int n) {
        if(n <= 1)
                return;
        for (int i=1 ; i <= 3 ; i++ )
                function (n - 1).
}
```

Solution: Consider the comments in below function:

```
function (int n) {
        //constant time
        if(n <= 1)
                return;
        //this loop executes 3 times with recursive call of n-1 value
        for (int i=1 ; i <= 3 ; i++ )
                function (n - 1).
}
```

The *if* statement requires constant time (O(1)). With the *for* loop, we neglect the loop overhead and only count three times that the function is called recursively. This implies a time complexity recurrence:

$$T(n) = c, if\, n \leq 1;$$
$$= c + 3T(n - 1), if\, n > 1.$$

Using the *Subtraction and Conquer* master theorem, we get $T(n) = \Theta(3^n)$.

Problem-39   Write a recursion formula for the running time $T(n)$ of the function f, whose code is below. What is the running time of *function*, as a function of n?

```
function (int n) {
        if(n <= 1)
                return;
```

```
            for(int i = 1; i < n; i + +)
                    printf("*");
            function ( 0.8n ) ;
    }
```

Solution: Consider the comments in below function:
```
function (int n) {
        //constant time
        if(n <= 1)
                return;
        // this loop executes n times with constant time loop
        for(int i = 1; i < n; i + +)
                printf("*");
        //recursive call with 0.8n
        function ( 0.8n ) ;
}
```

The recurrence for this piece of code is $T(n) = T(.8n) + O(n) = T\left(\frac{4}{5}n\right) + O(n) = \frac{4}{5}T(n) + O(n)$. Applying master theorem, we get $T(n) = O(n)$.

Problem-40   Find the complexity of the recurrence: $T(n) = 2T(\sqrt{n}) + logn$

Solution: The given recurrence is not in the master theorem form. Let us try to convert this to master theorem format by assuming $n = 2^m$. Applying logarithm on both sides gives, $logn = mlog2 \Rightarrow m = logn$. Now, the given function becomes,

$$T(n) = T(2^m) = 2T\left(\sqrt{2^m}\right) + m = 2T\left(2^{\frac{m}{2}}\right) + m.$$

To make it simple we assume $S(m) = T(2^m) \Rightarrow S(\frac{m}{2}) = T(2^{\frac{m}{2}}) \Rightarrow S(m) = 2S\left(\frac{m}{2}\right) + m$.
Applying the master theorem would result $S(m) = O(mlogm)$. If we substitute $m = logn$ back, $T(n) = S(logn) = O((logn) loglogn)$.

Problem-41   Find the complexity of the recurrence: $T(n) = T(\sqrt{n}) + 1$

Solution: Applying the logic of Problem-40, gives $S(m) = S\left(\frac{m}{2}\right) + 1$. Applying the master theorem would result $S(m) = O(logm)$. Substituting $m = logn$, gives $T(n) = S(log\,n) = O(loglogn)$.

Problem-42   Find the complexity of the recurrence: $T(n) = 2T(\sqrt{n}) + 1$

Solution: Applying the logic of Problem-40, gives: $S(m) = 2S\left(\frac{m}{2}\right) + 1$. Using the master theorem results $S(m) = O\left(m^{log_2^2}\right) = O(m)$. Substituting $m = logn$ gives $T(n) = O(logn)$.

Problem-43   Find the complexity of the below function.
```
    int Function (int n) {
            if(n <= 2)
                    return 1;
            else return (Function (floor(sqrt(n))) + 1);
    }
```

Solution: Consider the comments in below function:
```
int Function (int n) {
        //constant time
        if(n <= 2)
            return 1;
        else      // executes √n + 1 times
            return (Function (floor(sqrt(n))) + 1);
}
```
For the above function, the recurrence function can be given as: $T(n) = T(\sqrt{n}) + 1$. This is same as Problem-41.

Problem-44   Analyze the running time of the following recursive pseudo-code as a function of n.
```
    void function(int n) {
            if( n < 2 )
                    return;
            else counter = 0;
            for i = 1 to 8 do
                    function (n/2);
            for i =1 to n³ do
                    counter = counter + 1;
    }
```

Solution: Consider the comments in below pseudo-code and call running time of function(n) as $T(n)$.
```
    void function(int n) {
```

```
if( n < 2 )
    return;    //constant time
else
    counter = 0;
// this loop executes 8 times with n value half in every call
for i = 1 to 8 do
    function (n/2);
    // this loop executes n³ times with constant time loop
    for i =1 to n³ do
        counter = counter + 1;

}
```

$T(n)$ can be defined as follows:

$$T(n) = 1 \; if \; n < 2,$$
$$= 8T(\frac{n}{2}) + n^3 + 1 \; otherwise.$$

Using the master theorem gives, $T(n) = \Theta(n^{log_2^8} \log n) = \Theta(n^3 \log n)$.

Problem-45 Find the complexity of the below pseudo-code.

```
temp = 1
repeat
        for i = 1 to n
                temp = temp + 1;
        n = n/2;
until n <= 1
```

Solution: Consider the comments in below pseudo-code:

```
temp = 1  //const time
repeat    // this loops executes n times
        for i = 1 to n
                temp = temp + 1;
        //recursive call with n/2 value
        n = n/2;
until n <= 1
```

The recurrence for this function is T(n) = T(n/2) + n. Using master theorem we get, $T(n) = O(n)$.

Problem-46 Running time of following program?

```
function(int n) {
        for(int i = 1 ; i <= n ; i + + )
                for(int j = 1 ; j <= n ; j * = 2 )
                        printf( "*" );
}
```

Solution: Consider the comments in below function:

```
function(int n) {
        for(int i = 1 ; i <= n ; i + + ) // this loops executes n times
                // this loops executes logn times from our logarithms guideline
                for(int j = 1 ; j <= n ; j * = 2 )
                        printf( "*" );
}
```

Complexity of above program is : $O(nlogn)$.

Problem-47 Running time of following program?

```
function(int n) {
        for(int i = 1 ; ı <= n/3 ; i + + )
                for(int j = 1 ; j <= n ; j += 4 )
                        printf( "*" );
}
```

Solution: Consider the comments in below function:

```
function(int n) {  // this loops executes n/3 times
        for(int i = 1 ; i <= n/3 ; i + + )
                // this loops executes n/4 times
                for(int j = 1 ; j <= n ; j += 4)
                        printf( "*" );
}
```

The time complexity of this program is : $O(n^2)$.

Problem-48 Find the complexity of the below function.

```
void function(int n) {
        if(n <=  1)
                return;
        if(n > 1) {
                printf ("*");
                    function( n/2 );
                    function( n/2 );
        }
}
```

Solution: Consider the comments in below function:

```
void function(int n) {
        //constant time
        if(n <= 1)
                return;
        if(n > 1) {   //constant time
                printf ("*");
                //recursion with n/2 value
                function( n/2 );
                //recursion with n/2 value
                function( n/2 );
        }
}
```

The recurrence for this function is: $T(n) = 2T\left(\frac{n}{2}\right) + 1$. Using master theorem, we get $T(n) = O(n)$.

Problem-49   Find the complexity of the below function.

```
function(int n) {
        int i=1;
        while (i < n) {
                int j=n;
                while(j > 0)
                        j = j/2;
                i=2*i;
        } // i
}
```

Solution:

```
function(int n) {
        int i=1;
        while (i < n) {
                int j=n;
                while(j > 0)
                        j = j/2;   //logn code
                i=2*i; //logn times
        } // i
}
```

Time Complexity: $O(logn * logn) = O(log^2 n)$.

Problem-50   Find the complexity of the below function.

```
function(int n) {
    for (int i = 0; i<n; i++)
        for(int j=i; j<i*i; j++)
            if (j %i == 0){
                for (int k = 0; k < j; k++)
                    printf(" * ");
            }
}
```

Solution:

```
function(int n) {
    for (int i = 0; i<n; i++)              // Executes n times
        for(int j=i; j<i*i; j++)           // Executes n*n times
            if (j %i == 0){
                for (int k = 0; k < j; k++) // Executes j times = (n*n) times
                    printf(" * ");
            }
}
```

Time Complexity: $O(n^5)$.

Problem-51   To calculate 9^n, give algorithm and discuss its complexity.

Solution: Start with 1 and multiply by 9 until reaching 9^n.

Time Complexity: There are $n-1$ multiplications and each takes constant time giving a $\Theta(n)$ algorithm.

Problem-52   For Problem-51, can we improve the time complexity?

Solution: Refer *Divide and Conquer* chapter.

Problem-53   Find the complexity of the below function.

```
function(int n) {
    int sum = 0;
    for (int i = 0; i<n; i++)
        if (i>j)
            sum = sum +1;
        else {
            for (int k = 0; k < n; k++)
                sum = sum -1;
        }
    }
}
```

Solution: Consider the worst-case.

```
function(int n) {
    int sum = 0;
    for (int i = 0; i<n; i++)             // Executes n times
        if (i>j)
            sum = sum +1;                 // Executes n times
        else {
            for (int k = 0; k < n; k++)   // Executes n times
                sum = sum -1;
        }
    }
}
```

Time Complexity: $O(n^2)$.

RECURSION AND BACKTRACKING

Chapter-9

9.1 Introduction

In this chapter, we will look at one of the important topics "*recursion*", which will be used in almost every chapter and also its relative "*backtracking*".

9.2 What is Recursion?

Any function which calls itself is called *recursive*. A recursive method solves a problem by calling a copy of itself to work on a smaller problem. This is called the recursion step. The recursion step can result in many more such recursive calls. It is important to ensure that the recursion terminates. Each time the function calls itself with a slightly simpler version of the original problem. The sequence of smaller problems must eventually converge on the base case.

9.3 Why Recursion?

Recursion is a useful technique borrowed from mathematics. Recursive code is generally shorter and easier to write than iterative code. Generally, loops are turned into recursive functions when they are compiled or interpreted. Recursion is most useful for tasks that can be defined in terms of similar subtasks. For example, sort, search, and traversal problems often have simple recursive solutions.

9.4 Format of a Recursive Function

A recursive function performs a task in part by calling itself to perform the subtasks. At some point, the function encounters a subtask that it can perform without calling itself. This case, where the function does not recur, is called the *base case,* the former, where the function calls itself to perform a subtask, is referred to as the *recursive case.* We can write all recursive functions using the format:

```
if(test for the base case)
    return some base case value
else if(test for another base case)
    return some other base case value
// the recursive case
else
    return (some work and then a recursive call)
```

As an example consider the factorial function: $n!$ is the product of all integers between n and 1. Definition of recursive factorial looks like:

$$n! = 1, \qquad \text{if } n = 0$$
$$n! = n * (n-1)! \quad \text{if } n > 0$$

This definition can easily be converted to recursive implementation. Here the problem is determining the value of $n!$, and the subproblem is determining the value of $(n-l)!$. In the recursive case, when n is greater than 1, the function calls itself to determine the value of $(n-l)!$ and multiplies that with n. In the base case, when n is 0 or 1, the function simply returns 1. This looks like the following:

```
// calculates factorial of a positive integer
int Fact(int n) {
    // base cases: fact of 0 or 1 is 1
    if(n == 1)
        return 1;
    else if(n == 0)
        return 1;
    // recursive case: multiply n by (n − 1) factorial
    else    return n*Fact(n-1);
}
```

9.5 Recursion and Memory (Visualization)

Each recursive call makes a new copy of that method (actually only the variables) in memory. Once a method ends (that is, returns some data), the copy of that returning method is removed from memory. The recursive solutions look simple but visualization and tracing takes times. For better understanding, let us consider the following example.

```
int Print(int n) { //print numbers 1 to n backward
    if( n == 0) // this is the terminating base case
        return 0;
    else {
        printf ("%d",n);
        return Print(n-1); // recursive call to itself again
    }
}
```

For this example, if we call the print function with n=4, visually our memory assignments may look like:

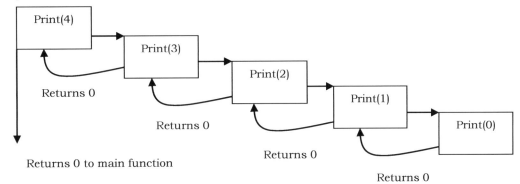

Now, let us consider our factorial function. The visualization of factorial function with n=4 will look like:

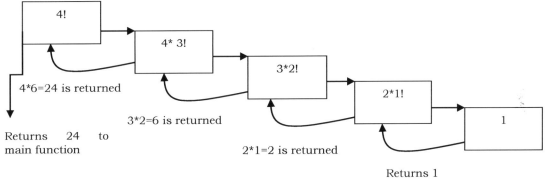

9.6 Recursion versus Iteration

While discussing recursion the basic question that comes to mind is, which way is better? – Iteration or recursion? Answer to this question depends on what we are trying to do. A recursive approach mirrors the problem that we are trying to solve. A recursive approach makes it simpler to solve a problem, which may not have the most obvious of answers. But, recursion adds overhead for each recursive call (needs space on the stack frame).

Recursion

- Terminates when a base case is reached.
- Each recursive call requires extra space on the stack frame (memory).
- If we get infinite recursion, the program may run out of memory and gives stack overflow.
- Solutions to some problems are easier to formulate recursively.

Iteration

- Terminates when a condition is proven to be false.
- Each iteration does not require any extra space.
- An infinite loop could loop forever since there is no extra memory being created.
- Iterative solutions to a problem may not always be as obvious as a recursive solution.

9.7 Notes on Recursion

- Recursive algorithms have two types of cases, recursive cases and base cases.

- Every recursive function case must terminate at base case.
- Generally iterative solutions are more efficient than recursive solutions [due to the overhead of function calls].
- A recursive algorithm can be implemented without recursive function calls using a stack, but it's usually more trouble than its worth. That means any problem that can be solved recursively can also be solved iteratively.
- For some problems, there are no obvious iterative algorithms.
- Some problems are best suited for recursive solutions while others are not.

9.8 Example Algorithms of Recursion

- Fibonacci Series, Factorial Finding
- Merge Sort, Quick Sort
- Binary Search
- Tree Traversals and many Tree Problems: InOrder, PreOrder PostOrder
- Graph Traversals: DFS [Depth First Search] and BFS [Breadth First Search]
- Dynamic Programming Examples
- Divide and Conquer Algorithms
- Towers of Hanoi
- Backtracking algorithms [we will discuss in next section]

9.9 Problems on Recursion

In this chapter we cover few problems on recursion and will discuss the rest in other chapters. By the time you complete the reading of entire book you will encounter many problems on recursion.

Problem-1   Discuss Towers of Hanoi puzzle.

Solution: The Tower of Hanoi is a mathematical puzzle. It consists of three rods (or pegs or towers), and a number of disks of different sizes which can slide onto any rod. The puzzle starts with the disks on one rod in ascending order of size, the smallest at the top, thus making a conical shape. The objective of the puzzle is to move the entire stack to another rod, satisfying the following rules:

- Only one disk may be moved at a time.
- Each move consists of taking the upper disk from one of the rods and sliding it onto another rod, on top of the other disks that may already be present on that rod.
- No disk may be placed on top of a smaller disk.

Algorithm

- Move the top $n-1$ disks from *Source* to *Auxiliary* tower,
- Move the nth disk from *Source* to *Destination* tower,
- Move the $n-1$ disks from Auxiliary tower to *Destination* tower.
- Transferring the top $n-1$ disks from *Source* to *Auxiliary* tower can again be thought as a fresh problem and can be solved in the same manner. Once we solve *Tower of Hanoi* with three disks, we can solve it with any number of disks with the above algorithm.

```
void TowersOfHanoi(int n, char frompeg, char topeg, char auxpeg) {
    /* If only 1 disk, make the move and return */
    if(n==1) {
        printf("Move disk 1 from peg %c to peg %c",frompeg, topeg);
        return;
    }
    /* Move top n-1 disks from A to B, using C as auxiliary */
    TowersOfHanoi(n-1, frompeg, auxpeg, topeg);

    /* Move remaining disks from A to C */
    printf("\nMove disk %d from peg %c to peg %c", n, frompeg, topeg);

    /* Move n-1 disks from B to C using A as auxiliary */
    TowersOfHanoi(n-1, auxpeg, topeg, frompeg);
}
```

Problem-2   Given an array, check whether the array is in sorted order with recursion.

Solution:
```
int isArrayInSortedOrder(int A[],int n){
    if(n == 1)
        return 1;
    return (A[n-1] < A[n-2])?0:isArrayInSortedOrder(A,n-1);
}
```

Time Complexity: O(n). Space Complexity: O(n) for recursive stack space

Problem-3 **Permutations of a string [anagrams]:** Give an algorithm for printing all possible permutations of the characters in a string. Unlike combinations, two permutations are considered distinct if they contain the same characters, but in a different order. For simplicity assume that each occurrence of a repeated character is a distinct character. That is, if the input is "aaa", the output should be six repetitions of "aaa". The permutations may be output in any order.

Solution: Refer *String Algorithms* chapter.

Problem-4 **Combinations of a String:** Unlike permutations, two combinations are considered to be the same if they contain the same characters, but may be in a different order. Give an algorithm that prints all possible combinations of the characters in a string. For example, "*ac*" and "*ab*" are different combinations from the input string "*abc*", but "*ab*" is the same as "*ba*".

Solution: Refer *String Algorithms* chapter.

9.10 What is Backtracking?

Backtracking is a method of exhaustive search using divide and conquer.

- Sometimes the best algorithm for a problem is to try all possibilities.
- This is always slow, but there are standard tools that can be used to help.
- Tools: algorithms for generating basic objects, such as binary strings [2^n possibilities for n-bit string], permutations [$n!$], combinations [$n!/r!\,(n-r)!$], general strings [k $-$ ary strings of length n has k^n possibilities], etc...
- Backtracking speeds the exhaustive search by pruning.

9.11 Example Algorithms of Backtracking

- Binary Strings: generating all binary strings
- Generating k-ary Strings
- The Knapsack Problem
- Generalized Strings
- Hamiltonian Cycles [refer *Graphs* chapter]
- Graph Coloring Problem

9.12 Problems on Backtracking

Problem-5 Generate all the strings of n bits. Assume $A[0..n-1]$ is an array of size n.

Solution:

```
void Binary(int n) {
    if(n < 1 )
        printf("%s", A);          //Assume array A is a global variable
    else {
        A[n-1] = 0;
        Binary(n - 1);
        A[n-1] = 1;
        Binary(n - 1);
    }
}
```

Let $T(n)$ be the running time of $binary(n)$. Assume function $printf$ takes time O(1).

$$T(n) = \begin{cases} c, & \text{if } n < 0 \\ 2T(n-1) + d, & \text{otherwise} \end{cases}$$

Using Subtraction and Conquer Master theorem we get, $T(n) =$ O(2^n). This means that the algorithm for generating bit-strings is optimal.

Problem-6 Generate all the strings of length n drawn from $0...k-1$.

Solution: Let us assume we keep current k-ary string in an array $A[0..n-1]$. Call function $k\text{-}string$(n, k):

```
void k-string(int n, int k) {
    //process all k-ary strings of length m
    if(n < 1 )
        printf("%s",A);          //Assume array A is a global variable
    else {
        for (int j = 0 ; j < k ; j++) {
            A[n-1] = j;
            k-string(n- 1, k);
        }
    }
}
```

```
        }
    }
```

Let $T(n)$ be the running time of $k - string(n)$. Then,

$$T(n) = \begin{cases} c, & if\ n < 0 \\ kT(n-1) + d, otherwise \end{cases}$$

Using Subtraction and Conquer Master theorem we get, $T(n) = O(k^n)$.

Note: For more problems, refer *String Algorithms* chapter.

Problem-7   Given a string pattern of 0s, 1s, and ?s (wildcards), generate all 0-1 strings that match this pattern. Sample Input: 1?00?101 Sample Output: 10000101, 10001101, 11000101, 11001101

Solution: The only difference to this problem and Problem-5 and 6 is, we should consider changing only the wildcard characters and keep the 0s and 1s same.

```cpp
#include <iostream>
#include <string>
#include <vector>
using namespace std;
void RegularExpressions(string inputPattern, string & src, int index){
    if(index == inputPattern.size()){
        cout<<inputPattern<<"  ";
        return;
    }
    if(inputPattern[index] == '?'){
        inputPattern[index] = '0';
        RegularExpressions(inputPattern, src, index + 1);
        inputPattern[index] = '1';
        RegularExpressions(inputPattern, src, index + 1);
    }
    else{
        RegularExpressions(inputPattern, src, index + 1);
    }
}
int main(int argc, char* argv[]){
    string testCase;
    string output;
    testCase = "01?0?101";
    cout << "The pattern is " << testCase<< endl;
    RegularExpressions(testCase, output, 1);
    return 0;
}
```

Problem-8   **Finding the length of connected cells of 1s (regions) in an matrix of 0s and 1s**: Given a matrix, each of which may be 1 or 0. The filled cells that are connected form a region. Two cells are said to be connected if they are adjacent to each other horizontally, vertically or diagonally. There may be several regions in the matrix. How do you find the largest region (in terms of number of cells) in the matrix?

Sample Input: 11000   **Sample Output**:5
                    01100
                    00101
                    10001
                    01011

Solution: The simplest idea is, for each location traverse in all 8 directions and in each of those directions keep track of maximum region found.

```cpp
int getval(int (*A)[5],int i,int j,int L, int H){
    if (i< 0 || i >= L || j< 0 || j >= H)
        return 0;
    else
        return A[i][j];
}
void findMaxBlock(int (*A)[5], int r, int c,int L,int H,int size, bool **cntarr,int &maxsize){
    if ( r >= L || c >= H)
        return;
    cntarr[r][c]=true;
    size++;
    if (size > maxsize)
```

```
            maxsize = size;
        //search in eight directions
        int direction[][2]={{-1,0},{-1,-1},{0,-1},{1,-1},{1,0},{1,1},{0,1},{-1,1}};
        for(int i=0; i<8; i++)          {
            int newi =r+direction[i][0];
            int newj=c+direction[i][1];
            int val=getval (A,newi,newj,L,H);
            if (val>0  && (cntarr[newi][newj]==false)){
                findMaxBlock(A,newi,newj,L,H,size,cntarr,maxsize);
            }
        }
        cntarr[r][c]=false;
    }
    int getMaxOnes(int (*A)[5], int rmax, int colmax){
        int maxsize=0;
        int size=0;
        bool **cntarr=create2darr(rmax,colmax);
        for(int i=0; i< rmax; i++){
            for(int j=0; j< colmax; j++){
                if (A[i][j] == 1){
                    findMaxBlock(A,i,j,rmax,colmax, 0,cntarr,maxsize);
                }

            }
        }
        return maxsize;
    }
```

Sample Call:

```
    int zarr[][5]={{1,1,0,0,0},{0,1,1,0,1},{0,0,0,1,1},{1,0,0,1,1},{0,1,0,1,1}};
    cout << "Number of maximum 1s are " << getMaxOnes(zarr,5,5) << endl;
```

Chapter-10

LINKED LISTS

10.1 What is a Linked List?

Linked list is a data structure used for storing collections of data. Linked list has the following properties.

- Successive elements are connected by pointers
- Last element points to NULL
- Can grow or shrink in size during execution of a program
- Can be made just as long as required (until systems memory exhausts)
- It does not waste memory space (but takes some extra memory for pointers)

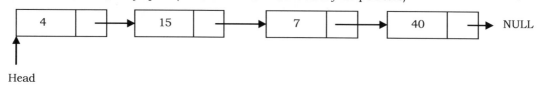

10.2 Linked Lists ADT

The following operations make linked lists an ADT:

Main Linked Lists Operations

- Insert: inserts an element into the list
- Delete: removes and returns the specified position element from the list

Auxiliary Linked Lists Operations

- Delete List: removes all elements of the list (disposes the list)
- Count: returns the number of elements in the list
- Find n^{th} node from the end of the list

10.3 Why Linked Lists?

There are many other data structures (say, *arrays*) that does the same as that of linked lists. Before discussing linked lists, it is important to understand the difference between linked lists and arrays. Both linked lists and arrays are used to store collections of data. Since both are used for the same purpose, we need to differentiate their usage. That means, in which cases *arrays* are suitable and in which cases *linked lists* are suitable.

10.4 Arrays Overview

One memory block is allocated for the entire array to hold elements of the array. The array elements can be accessed in a constant time by using the index of the particular element as the subscript.

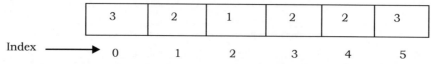

Why Constant Time for Accessing Array Elements?

To access an array element, address of an element is computed as an offset from the base address of the array and one multiplication is needed to compute what is supposed to be added to the base address to get the memory address of the element. First, the size of an element of that data type is calculated and then it is multiplied with the index of the element to get the value to be added to the base address.

This process takes one multiplication and one addition. Since these two operations take constant time, we can say the array access can be performed in constant time.

Advantages of Arrays

- Simple and easy to use
- Faster access to the elements (constant access)

Disadvantages of Arrays

- **Fixed size:** The size of the array is static (specify the array size before using it).
- **One block allocation**: To allocate the array at the beginning itself, sometimes it may not be possible to get the memory for the complete array (if the array size is big).
- **Complex position-based insertion**: To insert an element at a given position we may need to shift the existing elements. This will create a position for us to insert the new element at the desired position. If the position at which we want to add an element is at the beginning then the shifting operation is more expensive.

Dynamic Arrays

Dynamic array (also called as *growable array, resizable array, dynamic table*, or *array list*) is a random access, variable-size list data structure that allows elements to be added or removed. One simple way of implementing dynamic arrays is, initially start with some fixed size array. As soon as that array becomes full, create the new array of size double than the original array. Similarly, reduce the array size to half if the elements in the array are less than half.

Note: We will see the implementation for *dynamic arrays* in the *Stacks*, *Queues* and *Hashing* chapters.

Advantages of Linked Lists

Linked lists have both advantages and disadvantages. The advantage of linked lists is that they can be *expanded* in constant time. To create an array we must allocate memory for a certain number of elements. To add more elements to the array then we must create a new array and copy the old array into the new array. This can take lot of time. We can prevent this by allocating lots of space initially but then you might allocate more than you need and wasting memory. With a linked list we can start with space for just one element allocated and *add* on new elements easily without the need to do any copying and reallocating.

Issues with Linked Lists (Disadvantages)

There are a number of issues in linked lists. The main disadvantage of linked lists is *access time* to individual elements. Array is random-access, which means it takes $O(1)$ to access any element in the array. Linked lists takes $O(n)$ for access to an element in the list in the worst case. Another advantage of arrays in access time is *spacial locality* in memory. Arrays are defined as contiguous blocks of memory, and so any array element will be physically near its neighbors. This greatly benefits from modern CPU caching methods.

Although the dynamic allocation of storage is a great advantage, the *overhead* with storing and retrieving data can make a big difference. Sometimes linked lists are *hard* to *manipulate*. If the last item is deleted, the last but one must now have its pointer changed to hold a NULL reference. This requires that the list is traversed to find the last but one link, and its pointer set to a NULL reference. Finally, linked lists wastes memory in terms of extra reference points.

10.5 Comparison of Linked Lists with Arrays & Dynamic Arrays

Parameter	Linked list	Array	Dynamic array
Indexing	$O(n)$	$O(1)$	$O(1)$
Insertion/deletion at beginning	$O(1)$	$O(n)$, if array is not full (for shifting the elements)	$O(n)$
Insertion at ending	$O(n)$	$O(1)$, if array is not full	$O(1)$, if array is not full $O(n)$, if array is full
Deletion at ending	$O(n)$	$O(1)$	$O(n)$
Insertion in middle	$O(n)$	$O(n)$, if array is not full (for shifting the elements)	$O(n)$
Deletion in middle	$O(n)$	$O(n)$, if array is not full (for shifting the elements)	$O(n)$
Wasted space	$O(n)$	0	$O(n)$

10.6 Singly Linked Lists

Generally "linked list" means a singly linked list. This list consists of a number of nodes in which each node has a *next* pointer to the following element. The link of the last node in the list is NULL, which indicates end of the list.

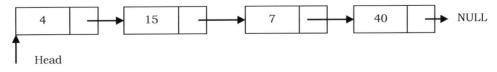

Following is a type declaration for a linked list of integers:

```
struct ListNode {
    int data;
    struct ListNode *next;
};
```

Basic Operations on a List

- Traversing the list
- Inserting an item in the list
- Deleting an item from the list

Traversing the Linked List

Let us assume that the *head* points to the first node of the list. To traverse the list we do the following.

- Follow the pointers.
- Display the contents of the nodes (or count) as they are traversed.
- Stop when the next pointer points to NULL.

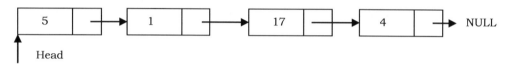

Head

The ListLength() function takes a linked list as input and counts the number of nodes in the list. The function given below can be used for printing the list data with extra *print* function.

```
int ListLength(struct ListNode *head) {
    struct ListNode *current = head;
    int count = 0;

    while (current != NULL) {
        count++;
        current = current→next;
    }

    return count;
}
```

Time Complexity: O(n), for scanning the complete list of size n.
Space Complexity: O(1), for one temporary variable.

Singly Linked List Insertion

Insertion into a singly-linked list has three cases:

- Inserting a new node before the head (at the beginning)
- Inserting a new node after the tail (at the end of the list)
- Inserting a new node at the middle of the list (random location)

Note: To insert an element in the linked list at some position p, assume that after inserting the element the position of this new node is p.

Inserting a Node in Singly Linked List at the Beginning

In this case, a new node is inserted before the current head node. *Only one next pointer* needs to be modified (new node's next pointer) and it can be done in two steps:

- Update the next pointer of new node, to point to the current head.

New node

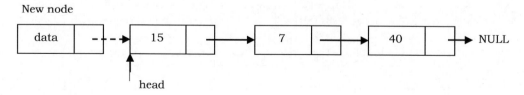

head

- Update head pointer to point to the new node.

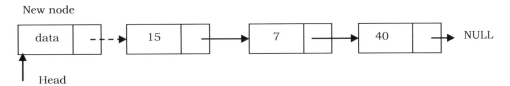

Inserting a Node in Singly Linked List at the Ending

In this case, we need to modify *two next pointers* (last nodes next pointer and new nodes next pointer).

- New nodes next pointer points to NULL.

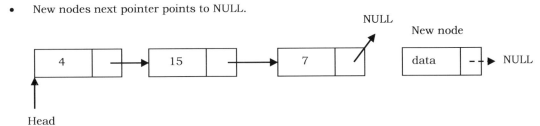

- Last nodes next pointer points to the new node.

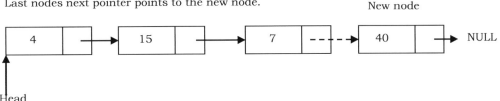

Inserting a Node in Singly Linked List at the Middle

Let us assume that we are given a position where we want to insert the new node. In this case also, we need to modify two next pointers.

- If we want to add an element at position 5 then we stop at position 2. That means we traverse 2 nodes and insert the new node. For simplicity let us assume that second node is called *position* node. New node points to the next node of the position where we want to add this node.

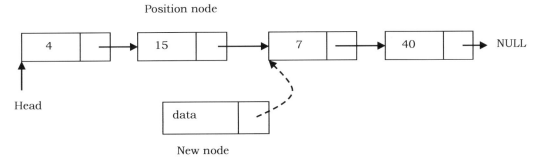

- Position nodes next pointer now points to the new node.

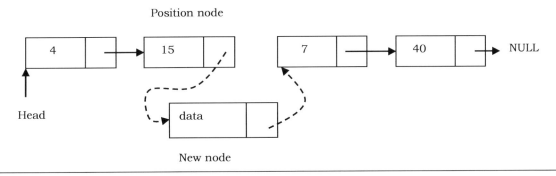

Let us write the code for all these three cases. We must update the first element pointer in the calling function, not just in the called function. For this reason we need to send double pointer. The following code inserts a node in the singly linked list.

```c
void InsertInLinkedList(struct ListNode **head,int data,int position) {
    int k=1;
    struct ListNode *p,*q,*newNode;
    newNode = (ListNode *)malloc(sizeof(struct ListNode));

    if(!newNode){
        printf("Memory Error");
        return;
    }

    newNode→data=data;
    p=*head;

    //Inserting at the beginning
    if(position == 1){
        newNode→next=p;
        *head=newNode;
    }
    else{
        //Traverse the list until the position where we want to insert
        while((p!=NULL) && (k<position)){
            k++;
            q=p;
            p=p→next;
        }
        q→next=newNode;   //more optimum way to do this
        newNode→next=p;
    }
}
```

Note: We can implement the three variations of the *insert* operation separately.

Time Complexity: $O(n)$. Since, in the worst we may need to insert the node at end of the list.
Space Complexity: $O(1)$, for creating one temporary variable.

Singly Linked List Deletion

As similar to insertion here also we have three cases.

- Deleting the first node
- Deleting the last node
- Deleting an intermediate node

Deleting the First Node in Singly Linked List

First node (current head node) is removed from the list. It can be done in two steps:

- Create a temporary node which will point to same node as that of head.

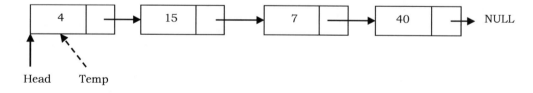

- Now, move the head nodes pointer to the next node and dispose the temporary node.

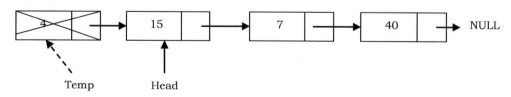

Deleting the Last Node in Singly Linked List

In this case, last node is removed from the list. This operation is a bit trickier than removing the first node, because algorithm should find a node, which is previous to the tail first. It can be done in three steps:

- Traverse the list and while traversing maintain the previous node address also. By the time we reach the end of list, we will have two pointers one pointing to the *tail* node and other pointing to the node *before* tail node.

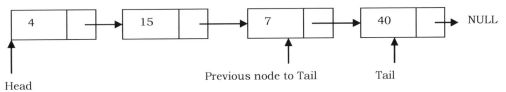

- Update previous nodes next pointer with NULL.

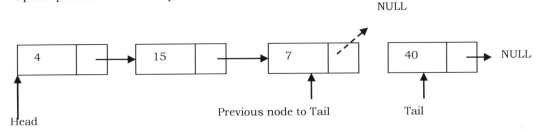

- Dispose the tail node.

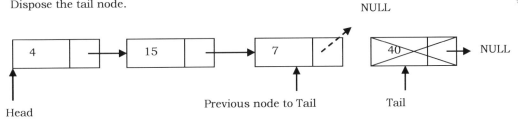

Deleting an Intermediate Node in Singly Linked List

In this case, node to be removed is *always located between* two nodes. Head and tail links are not updated in this case. Such a removal can be done in two steps:

- As similar to previous case, maintain previous node while traversing the list. Once we found the node to be deleted, change the previous nodes next pointer to next pointer of the node to be deleted.

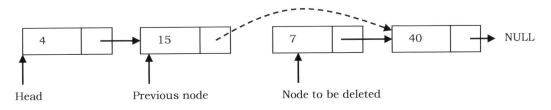

- Dispose the current node to be deleted.

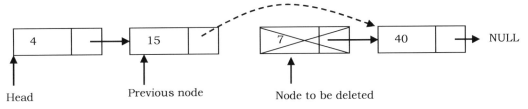

```
void DeleteNodeFromLinkedList (struct ListNode **head, int position) {
    int k = 1;
    struct ListNode *p, *q;
    if(*head == NULL) {
        printf ("List Empty");
```

```
            return;
    }
    p = *head;
    if(position == 1) {                          /* from the beginning */
            *head = (*head)→next;
            free (p);
                return;
    }
    else {
            //Traverse the list until the position from which we want to delete
            while ((p != NULL) && (k < position)) {
                k++;   q = p;
               p = p→next;
            }
            if(p == NULL)                        /* At the end */
                printf ("Position does not exist.");
            else {                               /* From the middle */
                q→next = p→next;
                free(p);
            }
    }
}
```

Time Complexity: O(n). In the worst we may need to delete the node at the end of the list.
Space Complexity: O(1). Since, we are creating only one temporary variable.

Deleting Singly Linked List

This works by storing the current node in some temporary variable and freeing the current node. After freeing the current node go to next node with temporary variable and repeat this process for all nodes.

```
void DeleteLinkedList(struct ListNode **head) {
    struct ListNode *auxilaryNode, *iterator;
    iterator = *head;

    while (iterator) {
        auxilaryNode = iterator→next;
        free(iterator);
        iterator = auxilaryNode;
    }
    *head = NULL;                    // to affect the real head back in the caller.
}
```

Time Complexity: O(n), for scanning the complete list of size n.
Space Complexity: O(1), for one temporary variable.

10.7 Doubly Linked Lists

The *advantage* of a doubly linked list (also called *two − way linked list*) is that given a node in the list, we can navigate in both directions. A node in a singly linked list can't be removed unless we have the pointer to its predecessor. But in doubly linked list we can delete a node even if we don't have previous nodes address (since, each node has left pointer pointing to previous node and we can move backward). The primary *disadvantages* of doubly linked lists are:

- Each node requires an extra pointer, requiring more space.
- The insertion or deletion of a node takes a bit longer (more pointer operations).

As similar to singly linked list, let us implement the operations of doubly linked lists. If you understand the singly linked list operations then doubly linked list operations are very obvious. Following is a type declaration for a doubly linked list of integers:

```
struct DLLNode {
    int data;
    struct DLLNode *next;
    struct DLLNode *prev;
};
```

Doubly Linked List Insertion

Insertion into a doubly-linked list has three cases (same as singly linked list):

- Inserting a new node before the head.

- Inserting a new node after the tail (at the end of the list).
- Inserting a new node at the middle of the list.

Inserting a Node in Doubly Linked List at the Beginning

In this case, new node is inserted before the head node. Previous and next pointers need to be modified and it can be done in two steps:

- Update the right pointer of new node to point to the current head node (dotted link in below figure) and also make left pointer of new node as NULL.

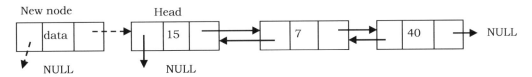

- Update head nodes left pointer to point to the new node and make new node as head.

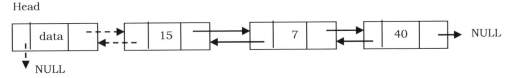

Inserting a Node in Doubly Linked List at the Ending

In this case, traverse the list till the end and insert the new node.

- New node right pointer points to NULL and left pointer points to the end of the list.

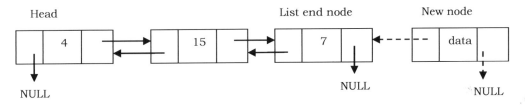

- Update right of pointer of last node to point to new node.

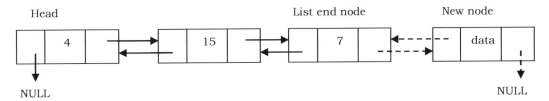

Inserting a Node in Doubly Linked List at the Middle

As discussed in singly linked lists, traverse the list till the position node and insert the new node.

- *New node* right pointer points to the next node of the *position node* where we want to insert the new node. Also, *new node* left pointer points to the *position node*.

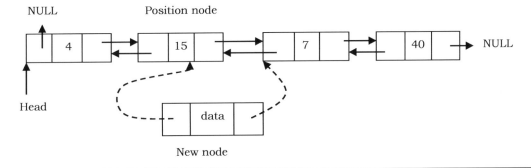

- Position node right pointer points to the new node and the *next node* of position nodes left pointer points to new node.

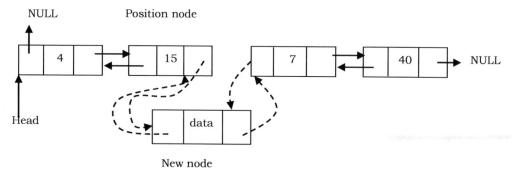

New node

Now, let us write the code for all these three cases. We must update the first element pointer in the calling function, not just in the called function. For this reason we need to send double pointer. The following code inserts a node in the doubly linked list.

```
void DLLInsert(struct DLLNode **head, int data, int position) {
    int k = 1;
    struct DLLNode *temp, *newNode;

    newNode = (struct DLLNode *) malloc(sizeof ( struct DLLNode ));

    if(!newNode) {                        //Always check for memory errors
        printf ("Memory Error");
        return;
    }
    newNode→data = data;

    if(position == 1) {                   //Inserting a node at the beginning
        newNode→next = *head;
        newNode→prev = NULL;
        if(*head)
            (*head)→prev = newNode;
        *head = newNode;
        return;
    }

    temp = *head;

    //After this loop, the temp will point to either last node or the previous node
    //of the position at which we want to insert a node
    while ( (k < position) && temp→next!=NULL) {
        temp = temp→next;
        k++;
    }

    if(k!=position){
        printf("Desired position does not exist\n");
    }
    newNode→next=temp→next;
    newNode→prev=temp;
    if(temp→next)
        temp→next→prev=newNode;

    temp→next=newNode;

    return;
}
```

Time Complexity: O(n). In the worst we may need to insert the node at the end of the list.
Space Complexity: O(1), for creating one temporary variable.

Doubly Linked List Deletion

As similar to singly linked list deletion, here also we have three cases:

- Deleting the first node
- Deleting the last node
- Deleting an intermediate node

Deleting the First Node in Doubly Linked List

In this case, first node (current head node) is removed from the list. It can be done in two steps:

- Create a temporary node which will point to same node as that of head.

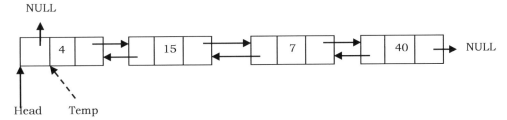

- Move the head nodes pointer to the next node and change the heads left pointer to NULL. Then, dispose the temporary node.

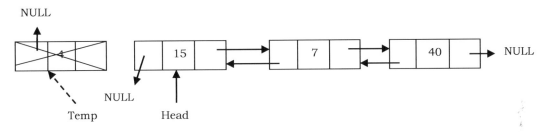

Deleting the Last Node in Doubly Linked List

This operation is a bit trickier than removing the first node as the algorithm should find a node, which is previous to the tail first. This can be done in three steps:

- Traverse the list and while traversing maintain the previous node address as well. By the time we reach the end of list, we will have two pointers one pointing to the tail and other pointing to the node before tail node.

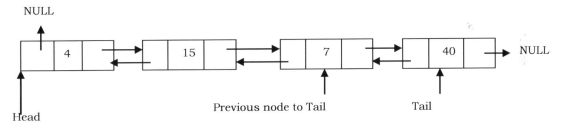

- Update tail nodes previous nodes next pointer with NULL.

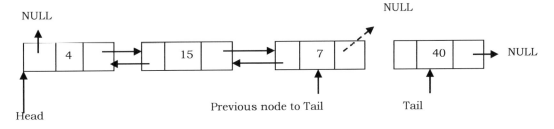

- Dispose the tail node.

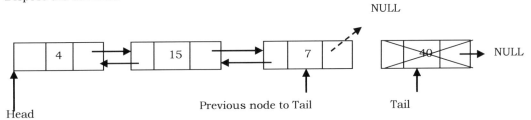

Deleting an Intermediate Node in Doubly Linked List

In this case, node to be removed is *always located between* two nodes. Head and tail links are not updated in this case. Such a removal can be done in two steps:

- Similar to previous case, maintain previous node also while traversing the list. Once we found the node to be deleted, change the previous nodes next pointer to the next node of the node to be deleted.

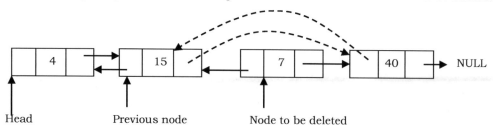

- Dispose the current node to be deleted.

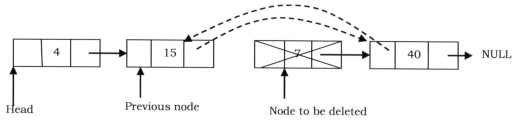

```
void DLLDelete(struct DLLNode **head, int position) {
        struct DLLNode *temp, *temp2, temp = *head;
        int k = 1;
        if(*head == NULL) {
                printf("List is empty");
                return;
        }
        if(position == 1) {
                *head = *head→next;
                if(*head != NULL)
                        *head→prev = NULL;
                free(temp);
                return;
        }
        while((k < position - 1) && temp→next!=NULL) {
                temp = temp→next;
                k++;
        }
        if(k!=position-1){
                printf("Desired position does not exist\n");
        }
        temp2=temp→prev;
        temp2→next=temp→next;
        if(temp→next) // Deletion from Intermediate Node
                temp→next→prev=temp2;
        free(temp);
        return;
}
```

Time Complexity: O(n), for scanning the complete list of size n.
Space Complexity: O(1), for creating one temporary variable.

10.8 Circular Linked Lists

In singly linked lists and doubly linked lists the end of lists are indicated with NULL value. But circular linked lists do not have ends. While traversing the circular linked lists we should be careful otherwise we will be traversing the list infinitely. In circular linked lists each node has a successor. Note that unlike singly linked lists, there is no node with NULL pointer in a circularly linked list. In some situations, circular linked lists are useful. For example, when several processes are using the same computer resource (CPU) for the same amount of time, we have to assure that no process accesses the resource before all other processes did (round robin algorithm). The following is a type declaration for a circular linked list of integers:

```
struct CLLNode {
    int data;
    struct ListNode *next;
};
```

In circular linked list we access the elements using the *head* node (similar to *head* node in singly linked list and doubly linked lists).

Counting Nodes in a Circular List

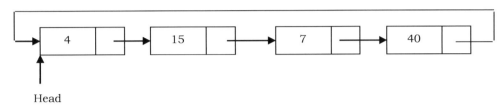

Head

The circular list is accessible through the node marked *head*. To count the nodes, the list has to be traversed from node marked *head*, with the help of a dummy node *current* and stop the counting when *current* reaches the starting node *head*. If the list is empty, *head* will be NULL, and in that case set *count* = 0. Otherwise, set the current pointer to the first node, and keep on counting till the current pointer reaches the starting node.

```
int CircularListLength(struct CLLNode *head) {
    struct CLLNode *current = head;
    int count = 0;
    if(head == NULL)
        return 0;
    do {
        current = current→next;
        count++;
    } while (current != head);
    return count;
}
```

Time Complexity: O(n), for scanning the complete list of size n.
Space Complexity: O(1), for creating one temporary variable.

Printing the Contents of a Circular List

We assume here that the list is being accessed by its *head* node. Since all the nodes are arranged in a circular fashion, the *tail* node of the list will be the node previous to the *head* node. Let us assume we want to print the contents of the nodes starting with the *head* node. Print its contents, move to the next node and continue printing till we reach the *head* node again.

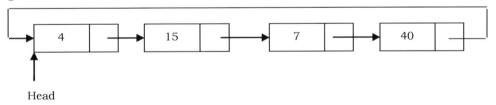

Head

```
void PrintCircularListData(struct CLLNode *head) {
    struct CLLNode *current = head;
    if(head == NULL)
        return;
    do {
        printf ("%d", current→data);
        current = current→next;
    } while (current != head);
}
```

Time Complexity: O(n), for scanning the complete list of size n.
Space Complexity: O(1), for creating one temporary variable.

Inserting a Node at the End of a Circular Linked List

Let us add a node containing *data*, at the end of a list (circular list) headed by *head*. The new node will be placed just after the tail node (which is the last node of the list), which means it will have to be inserted in between the tail node and the first node.

- Create a new node and initially keep its next pointer points to itself.

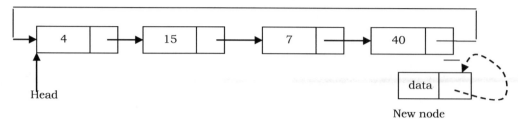

Head

New node

- Update the next pointer of new node with head node and also traverse the list until the tail. That means in circular list we should stop at a node whose next node is head.

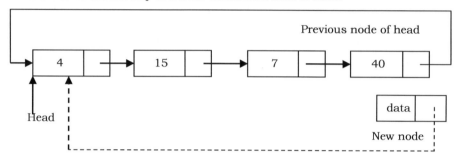

Previous node of head

Head

data

New node

- Update the next pointer of previous node to point to new nod and we get the list as shown below.

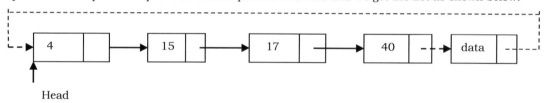

Head

```
void InsertAtEndInCLL (struct CLLNode **head, int data) {
    struct CLLNode *current = *head;
    struct CLLNode *newNode = (struct CLLNode *) (malloc(sizeof(struct CLLNode)));
    if(!newNode) {
        printf("Memory Error");
        return;
    }
    newNode→data = data;
    while (current→next != head)
        current = current→next;
    newNode→next = newNode;
    if(*head ==NULL)
        *head = newNode;
    else {
        newNode→next = *head;
        current→next = newNode;
    }
}
```

Time Complexity: O(n), for scanning the complete list of size n.
Space Complexity: O(1), for creating one temporary variable.

Inserting a Node at Front of a Circular Linked List

The only difference between inserting a node at the beginning and at the ending is that, after inserting the new node we just need to update the pointer. The steps for doing this is given below:

- Create a new node and initially keep its next pointer points to itself.

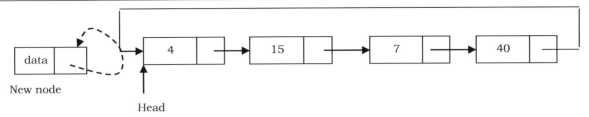

New node
Head

- Update the next pointer of new node with head node and also traverse the list until the tail. That means in circular list we should stop at the node which is its previous node in the list.

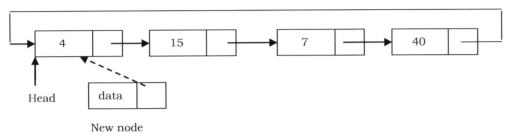

Head
data
New node

- Update the previous node of head in the list to point to new node.

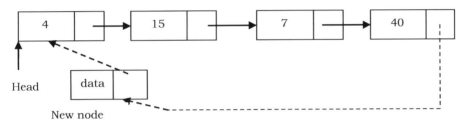

Head
data
New node

- Make new node as head.

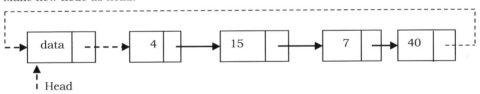

data
Head

```
void InsertAtBeginInCLL (struct CLLNode **head, int data) {
    struct CLLNode *current = *head;
    struct CLLNode * newNode = (struct CLLNode *) (malloc(sizeof(struct CLLNode)));
    if(!newNode) {
        printf("Memory Error");
        return;
    }
    newNode→data = data;
    while (current→next != head)
        current = current→next;
    newNode→next = newNode;
    *head = newNode;
    else {
        newNode→next = *head;
        current→next = newNode;
        *head = newNode;
    }
    return;
}
```

Time Complexity: O(n), for scanning the complete list of size n.
Space Complexity: O(1), for one temporary variable.

Deleting the Last Node in a Circular List

The list has to be traversed to reach the last but one node. This has to be named as the tail node, and its next field has to point to the first node. Consider the following list. To delete the last node 40, the list has to be traversed till you reach 7. The next field of 7 has to be changed to point to 60, and this node must be renamed *pTail*.

- Traverse the list and find the tail node and its previous node.

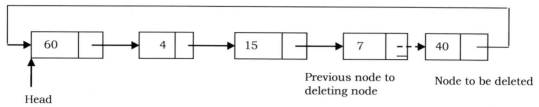

Head

Previous node to deleting node

Node to be deleted

- Update the tail nodes previous node next pointer to point to head.

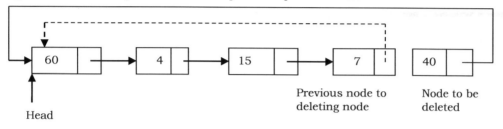

Head

Previous node to deleting node

Node to be deleted

- Dispose the tail node.

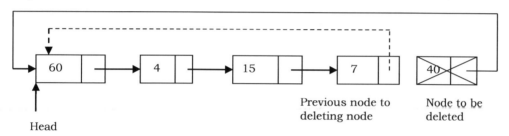

Head

Previous node to deleting node

Node to be deleted

```
void DeleteLastNodeFromCLL (struct CLLNode **head) {
    struct CLLNode *temp = *head, *current = *head;

    if(*head == NULL) {
        printf( "List Empty");
        return;
    }

    while (current→next != head) {
        temp = current;
        current = current→next;
    }
    temp→next = current→next;
    free(current);
    return;
}
```

Time Complexity: O(n), for scanning the complete list of size n.
Space Complexity: O(1), for temporary variable.

Deleting the First Node in a Circular List

The first node can be deleted by simply replacing the next field of tail node with the next field of the first node.

- Find the tail node of the linked list by traversing the list. Tail node is the previous node to the head node which we want to delete.

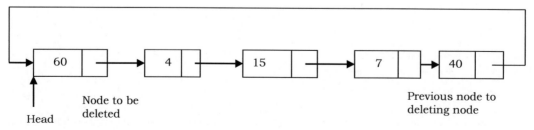

Head

Node to be deleted

Previous node to deleting node

- Create a temporary node which will point to head. Also, update the tail nodes next pointer to point to next node of head (as shown below).

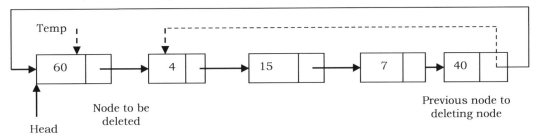

- Now, move the head pointer to next node. Create a temporary node which will point to head. Also, update the tail nodes next pointer to point to next node of head (as shown below).

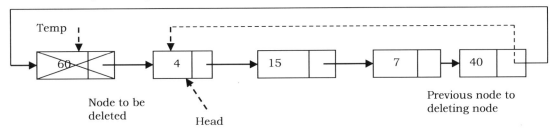

```
void DeleteFrontNodeFromCLL (struct CLLNode **head) {
    struct CLLNode *temp = *head;
    struct CLLNode *current = *head;
    if(*head == NULL) {
        printf("List Empty");
        return;
    }
    while (current→next != head)
        current = current→next;
    current→ next = *head→next;
    *head = *head→next;
    free(temp);
    return;
}
```

Time Complexity: O(n), for scanning the complete list of size n.
Space Complexity: O(1), for one temporary variable.

Applications of Circular List

Circular linked lists are used in managing the computing resources of a computer. We can use circular lists for implementing stacks and queues.

10.9 Memory-Efficient Doubly Linked List

In conventional implementation, we need to keep a forward pointer to the next item on the list and a backward pointer to the previous item. That means, elements in doubly linked list implementations consist of data, a pointer to the next node and a pointer to the previous node in the list as shown below.

Conventional Node Definition

```
struct ListNode {
    int data;
    struct ListNode * prev;
    struct ListNode * next;
};
```

Recently, a journal (Sinha) presented an alternative implementation of the doubly linked list ADT, with insertion, traversal and deletion operations. This implementation is based on *pointer difference*. Each node uses only one pointer field to traverse the list back and forth.

New Node Definition

```
struct ListNode {
    int data;
```

```
        struct ListNode * ptrdiff;
};
```

The *ptrdiff* pointer field contains the difference between the pointer to the next node and the pointer to the previous node. The pointer difference is calculated by using exclusive-or ($\oplus$) operation.

$$ptrdiff = pointer\ to\ previous\ node \oplus pointer\ to\ next\ node.$$

The *ptrdiff* of the start node (head node) is the $\oplus$ of NULL and *next* node (next node to head). Similarly, the *ptrdiff* of end node is the $\oplus$ of *previous* node (previous to end node) and NULL. As an example, consider the following linked list.

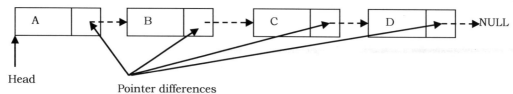

In the example above,

- The next pointer of A is: NULL $\oplus$ B
- The next pointer of B is: A $\oplus$ C
- The next pointer of C is: B $\oplus$ D
- The next pointer of D is: C $\oplus$ NULL

Why does it work?

To have answer for this question let us consider the properties of $\oplus$:

$$X \oplus X = 0$$
$$X \oplus 0 = X$$
$$X \oplus Y = Y \oplus X \text{ (symmetric)}$$
$$(X \oplus Y) \oplus Z = X \oplus (Y \oplus Z) \text{ (transitive)}$$

For the example above, let us assume that we are at C node and want to move to B. We know that Cs *ptrdiff* is defined as B $\oplus$ D. If we want to move to B, performing $\oplus$ on Cs *ptrdiff* with D would give B. This is due to fact that,

$$(B \oplus D) \oplus D = B \text{ (since, } D \oplus D=0)$$

Similarly, if we want to move to D, then we have to apply $\oplus$ to Cs *ptrdiff* with B would give D.

$$(B \oplus D) \oplus B = D \text{ (since, } B \oplus B=0)$$

From the above discussion we can see that just by using single pointer, we can move back and forth. A memory-efficient implementation of a doubly linked list is possible without compromising much timing efficiency.

10.10 Unrolled Linked Lists

One of the biggest advantages of linked lists over arrays is that inserting an element at any location takes only O(1) time. However, it takes O(n) to search for an element in a linked list. There is a simple variation of the singly linked list called *unrolled linked lists*.

An unrolled linked list stores multiple elements in each node (let us call it a block for our convenience). In each block, a circular linked list is used to connect all nodes.

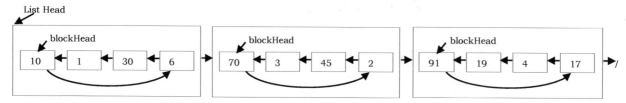

Assume that there will be no more than n elements in the unrolled linked list at any time. To simplify this problem, all blocks, except the last one, should contain exactly $\lceil\sqrt{n}\rceil$ elements. Thus, there will be no more than $\lfloor\sqrt{n}\rfloor$ blocks at any time.

Searching for an element in Unrolled Linked Lists

In unrolled linked lists, we can find the kth element in O($\sqrt{n}$):

- Traverse on the *list of blocks* to the one that contains the kth node, i.e., the $\left\lceil\frac{k}{\lceil\sqrt{n}\rceil}\right\rceil^{th}$ block. It takes O($\sqrt{n}$) since we may find it by going through no more than $\sqrt{n}$ blocks.

- Find the $(k \bmod \lceil\sqrt{n}\rceil)^{\text{th}}$ node in the circular linked list of this block. It also takes $O(\sqrt{n})$ since there are no more than $\lceil\sqrt{n}\rceil$ nodes in a single block.

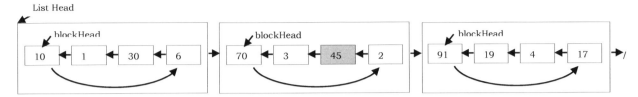

Inserting an element in Unrolled Linked Lists

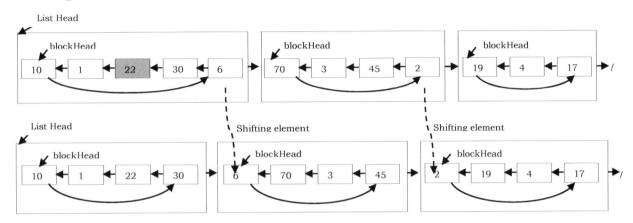

When inserting a node, we have to re-arrange the nodes in the unrolled linked list to maintain the properties previously mentioned, that each block contains $\lceil\sqrt{n}\rceil$ nodes. Suppose that we insert a node x after the ith node, and x should be placed in the jth block. Nodes in the jth block and in the blocks after the jth block have to be shifted toward the tail of the list so that each of them still have $\lceil\sqrt{n}\rceil$ nodes. In addition, a new block needs to be added to the tail if the last block of the list is out of space, i.e., it has more than $\lceil\sqrt{n}\rceil$ nodes.

Performing Shift Operation

Note that each *shift* operation, which includes removing a node from the tail of the circular linked list in a block and inserting a node to the head of the circular linked list in the block after, takes only $O(1)$. The total time complexity of an insertion operation for unrolled linked lists is therefore $O(\sqrt{n})$; there are at most $O(\sqrt{n})$ blocks and therefore at most $O(\sqrt{n})$ shift operations.

- A temporary pointer is needed to store the tail of A.

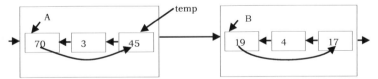

- In block A, move the next pointer of the head node to point to the second to-the-last node, so that the tail node of A can be removed.

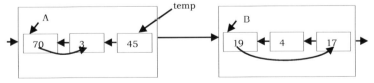

- Let the next pointer of the node which will be shifted (the tail node of A) point to the tail node of B.

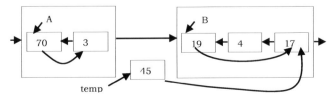

- Let the next pointer of the head node of *B* point to the node temp points to.

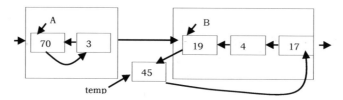

- Finally, set the head pointer of *B* to point to the node temp points to. Now the node temp points to become the new head node of *B*.

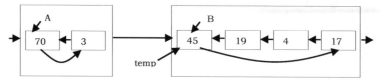

- *temp* pointer can be thrown away. We have completed the shift operation to move the original tail node of *A* to become the new head node of *B*.

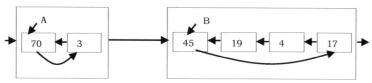

Performance

With unrolled linked lists, there are a couple of advantages, one in speed and one in space.

First, if the number of elements in each block is appropriately sized (e.g., at most the size of one cache line), we get noticeably better cache performance from the improved memory locality.

Second, since we have $O(n/m)$ links, where n is the number of elements in the unrolled linked list and m is the number of elements we can store in any block, we can also save an appreciable amount of space, which is particularly noticeable if each element is small.

Comparing Linked Lists and Unrolled Linked Lists

To compare the overhead for an unrolled list, elements in doubly linked list implementations consist of data, a pointer to the next node and a pointer to the previous node in the list as shown below.

```
struct ListNode {
    int data;
    struct ListNode *prev;
    struct ListNode *next;
};
```

Assuming we have got 4 byte pointers, each node is going to take 8 bytes. But the allocation overhead for the node could be anywhere between 8 and 16 bytes. Let's go with the best case and assume it will be 8 bytes. So, if we want to store 1K items in this list, we are going to have 16KB of overhead.

Now, let's think about an unrolled linked list node (let us call it *LinkedBlock*). It will look something like this:

```
struct LinkedBlock{
    struct LinkedBlock *next;
    struct ListNode *head;
    int nodeCount;
};
```

Therefore, allocating a single node (12 bytes + 8 bytes of overhead) with an array of 100 elements (400 bytes + 8 bytes of overhead) will now cost 428 bytes, or 4.28 bytes per element. Thinking about our 1K items from above, it would take about 4.2KB of overhead, ,which is close to 4x better than our original list. Even if the list becomes severely fragmented and the item arrays are only 1/2 full on average, this is still an improvement. Also, note that we can tune the array size to whatever gets we the best overhead for our application.

Implementation

```
#include <stdio.h>
#include <string.h>
#include <stdlib.h>
```

```
#include <math.h>
#include <time.h>
int blockSize; //max number of nodes in a block
struct ListNode{
    struct ListNode* next;
    int value;
};
struct LinkedBlock{
    struct LinkedBlock *next;
    struct ListNode *head;
    int nodeCount;
};
struct LinkedBlock* blockHead;

//create an empty block
struct LinkedBlock* newLinkedBlock(){
    struct LinkedBlock* block=(struct LinkedBlock*)malloc(sizeof(struct LinkedBlock));
    block→next=NULL;
    block→head=NULL;
    block→nodeCount=0;
    return block;
}

struct ListNode* newListNode(int value){
    struct ListNode* temp=(struct ListNode*)malloc(sizeof(struct ListNode));
    temp→next=NULL;
    temp→value=value;
    return temp;
}

void searchElement(int k,struct LinkedBlock **fLinkedBlock,struct ListNode **fListNode){
    //find the block
    int j=(k+blockSize-1)/blockSize; //k-th node is in the j-th block
    struct LinkedBlock* p=blockHead;
    while(--j){
        p=p→next;
    }
    *fLinkedBlock=p;
    //find the node
    struct ListNode* q=p→head;
    k=k%blockSize;
    if(k==0) k=blockSize;
    k=p→nodeCount+1-k;
    while(k--){
        q=q→next;
    }
    *fListNode=q;
}
//start shift operation from block *p
void shift(struct LinkedBlock *A){
    struct LinkedBlock *B;
    struct ListNode* temp;
    while(A→nodeCount > blockSize){ //if this block still have to shift
        if(A→next==NULL){ //reach the end. A little different
            A→next=newLinkedBlock();
            B=A→next;
            temp=A→head→next;
            A→head→next=A→head→next→next;
            B→head=temp;
            temp→next=temp;
            A→nodeCount--;
            B→nodeCount++;
        }else{
            B=A→next;
            temp=A→head→next;
            A→head→next=A→head→next→next;
            temp→next=B→head→next;
            B→head→next=temp;
            B→head=temp
```

```
                  A→nodeCount--;
                  B→nodeCount++;
              }
          A=B;
          }
      }
      void addElement(int k,int x){
          struct ListNode *p,*q;
          struct LinkedBlock *r;
          if(!blockHead){ //initial, first node and block
              blockHead=newLinkedBlock();
              blockHead→head=newListNode(x);
              blockHead→head→next=blockHead→head;
              blockHead→nodeCount++;
          }else{
              if(k==0){ //special case for k=0.
              p=blockHead→head;
              q=p→next;
              p→next=newListNode(x);
              p→next→next=q;
              blockHead→head=p→next;
              blockHead→nodeCount++;
              shift(blockHead);
              }else{
                  searchElement(k,&r,&p);
                  q=p;
                  while(q→next!=p) q=q→next;
                  q→next=newListNode(x);
                  q→next→next=p;
                  r→nodeCount++;
                  shift(r);
              }
          }
      }
      int searchElement(int k){
          struct ListNode *p;
          struct LinkedBlock *q;
          searchElement(k,&q,&p);
          return p→value;
      }
      int testUnRolledLinkedList(){
          int tt=clock();
          int m,i,k,x;
          char cmd[10];
          scanf("%d",&m);
          blockSize=(int)(sqrt(m-0.001))+1;
          for( i=0; i<m; i++ ){
              scanf("%s",cmd);
              if(strcmp(cmd,"add")==0){
                  scanf("%d %d",&k,&x);
                  addElement(k,x);
              }else if(strcmp(cmd,"search")==0){
                  scanf("%d",&k);
                  printf("%d\n",searchElement(k));
              }else{
                  fprintf(stderr,"Wrong Input\n");
              }
          }
          return 0;
      }
```

10.11 Skip Lists

Binary trees can be used for representing abstract data types such as dictionaries and ordered lists. They work well when the elements are inserted in a random order. Some sequences of operations, such as inserting the elements in order, produce degenerate data structures that give very poor performance. If it were possible to randomly permute the list of items to be inserted, trees would work well with high probability for any input sequence. In most cases queries must be answered on-line, so randomly permuting the input is impractical. Balanced tree algorithms re-arrange the tree as operations are performed to maintain certain balance conditions and assure good performance.

Skip lists are a probabilistic alternative to balanced trees. Skip list is a data structure that can be used as an alternative to balanced binary trees (refer *Trees* chapter). As compared to a binary tree, skip lists allow quick search, insertions and deletions of elements. This is achieved by using probabilistic balancing rather than strictly enforce balancing. It is basically a linked list with additional pointers such that intermediate nodes can be skipped. It uses a random number generator to make some decisions.

In an ordinary sorted linked list, search, insert, and delete are in O(*n*) because the list must be scanned node-by-node from the head to find the relevant node. If somehow we could scan down the list in bigger steps (skip down, as it were), we would reduce the cost of scanning. This is the fundamental idea behind Skip Lists.

Skip Lists with One Level

Skip Lists with Two Levels

Skip Lists with Three Levels

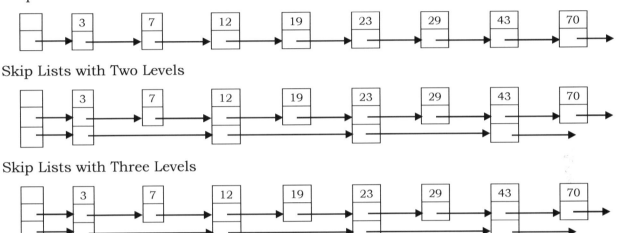

This section gives algorithms to search for, insert and delete elements in a dictionary or symbol table. The Search operation returns the contents of the value associated with the desired key or failure if the key is not present. The Insert operation associates a specified key with a new value (inserting the key if it had not already been present). The Delete operation deletes the specified key. It is easy to support additional operations such as "find the minimum key" or "find the next key".

Each element is represented by a node, the level of which is chosen randomly when the node is inserted without regard for the number of elements in the data structure. A level i node has i forward pointers, indexed 1 through i. We do not need to store the level of a node in the node. Levels are capped at some appropriate constant MaxLevel. The level of a list is the maximum level currently in the list (or 1 if the list is empty). The header of a list has forward pointers at levels one through MaxLevel. The forward pointers of the header at levels higher than the current maximum level of the list point to NULL.

Initialization

An element NIL is allocated and given a key greater than any legal key. All levels of all skip lists are terminated with NIL. A new list is initialized so that the the level of the list is equal to 1 and all forward pointers of the list's header point to NIL.

Search for an element

We search for an element by traversing forward pointers that do not overshoot the node containing the element being searched for. When no more progress can be made at the current level of forward pointers, the search moves down to the next level. When we can make no more progress at level 1, we must be immediately in front of the node that contains the desired element (if it is in the list).

Insertion and Deletion Algorithms

To insert or delete a node, we simply search and splice. A vector update is maintained so that when the search is complete (and we are ready to perform the splice), update[i] contains a pointer to the rightmost node of level i or higher that is to the left of the location of the insertion/deletion. If an insertion generates a node with a level greater than the previous maximum level of the list, we update the maximum level of the list and initialize the appropriate portions of the update vector. After each deletion, we check if we have deleted the maximum element of the list and if so, decrease the maximum level of the list.

Choosing a Random Level

Initially, we discussed a probability distribution where half of the nodes that have level i pointers also have level i+1 pointers. To get away from magic constants, we say that a fraction p of the nodes with level i pointers also have level i+1 pointers. (for our original discussion, p = 1/2). Levels are generated randomly by an algorithm. Levels are generated without reference to the number of elements in the list

Performance

In a simple linked list that consists of n elements, to perform a search n comparisons are required in the worst case. If a second pointer pointing two nodes ahead is added to every node, the number of comparisons goes down to $n/2 + 1$ in the worst case.

Adding one more pointer to every fourth node and making them point to the fourth node ahead reduces the number of comparisons to $\lceil n/2 \rceil + 2$. If this strategy is continued so that every node with i pointers points to $2*i - 1$ nodes ahead, O($logn$) performance is obtained and the number of pointers has only doubled ($n + n/2 + n/4 + n/8 + n/16 + ... = 2n$).

The find, insert, and remove operations on ordinary binary search trees are efficient, O($logn$), when the input data is random; but less efficient, O(n), when the input data are ordered. Skip List performance for these same operations and for any data set is about as good as that of randomly-built binary search trees - namely O($logn$).

Comparing Skip Lists and Unrolled Linked Lists

In simple terms, Skip Lists are sorted linked lists with two differences:

- The nodes in an ordinary list have *one next* reference. The nodes in a Skip List have many *next* references (also called *forward* references).
- The number of forward references for a given node is determined probabilistically.

We speak of a Skip List node having levels, one level per forward reference. The number of levels in a node is called the *size* of the node. In an ordinary sorted list, insert, remove, and find operations require sequential traversal of the list. This results in O(n) performance per operation. Skip Lists allow intermediate nodes in the list to be skipped during a traversal   resulting in an expected performance of O($logn$) per operation.

Implementation

```
#include <stdio.h>
#include <stdlib.h>
#define MAXSKIPLEVEL 5

struct ListNode {
    int data;
    struct ListNode *next[1];
};
struct SkipList {
    struct ListNode *header;
    int listLevel;           //current level of list */
};
struct SkipList list;

struct ListNode *insertElement(int data) {
    int i, newLevel;
    struct ListNode *update[MAXSKIPLEVEL+1];
    struct ListNode *temp;
    temp = list.header;
    for (i = list.listLevel; i >= 0; i--) {
        while (temp->next[i] !=list.header && temp->next[i]->data < data)
            temp = temp->next[i];
        update[i] = temp;
    }
    temp = temp->next[0];
    if (temp != list.header && temp->data == data) return(temp);

    //determine level
    for (newLevel = 0; rand() < RAND_MAX/2 && newLevel < MAXSKIPLEVEL; newLevel++);

    if (newLevel > list.listLevel) {
        for (i = list.listLevel + 1; i <= newLevel; i++)
            update[i] = list.header;
        list.listLevel = newLevel;
    }
    // make new node
    if ((temp = malloc(sizeof(Node) +
```

```
            newLevel*sizeof(Node *))) == 0) {
        printf ("insufficient memory (insertElement)\n");
        exit(1);
    }
    temp->data = data;
    // update next links
    for (i = 0; i <= newLevel; i++) {
        temp->next[i] = update[i]->next[i];
        update[i]->next[i] = temp;
    }
    return(temp);
}
// delete node containing data
void deleteElement(int data) {
    int i;
    struct ListNode *update[MAXSKIPLEVEL+1], *temp;

    temp = list.header;
    for (i = list.listLevel; i >= 0; i--) {
        while (temp->next[i] != list.header && temp->next[i]->data < data)
            temp = temp->next[i];
        update[i] = temp;
    }
    temp = temp->next[0];
    if (temp == list.header || !(temp->data == data) return;

    //adjust next pointers
    for (i = 0; i <= list.listLevel; i++) {
        if (update[i]->next[i] != temp) break;
        update[i]->next[i] = temp->next[i];
    }
    free (temp);

    //adjust header level
    while ((list.listLevel > 0) && (list.header->next[list.listLevel] == list.header))
        list.listLevel--;
}
// find node containing data
struct ListNode *findElement(int data) {
    int i;
    struct ListNode *temp = list.header;
    for (i = list.listLevel; i >= 0; i--) {
        while (temp->next[i] != list.header
            && temp->next[i]->data < data)
            temp = temp->next[i];
    }
    temp = temp->next[0];
    if (temp != list.header && temp->data == data) return (temp);
    return(0);
}
// initialize skip list
void initList() {
    int i;
    if ((list.header = malloc(sizeof(struct ListNode) + MAXSKIPLEVEL*sizeof(struct ListNode *))) == 0) {
        printf ("Memory Error\n");
        exit(1);
    }
    for (i = 0; i <= MAXSKIPLEVEL; i++)
        list.header->next[i] = list.header;
    list.listLevel = 0;
}
/* command-line: skipList maxnum
    skipList 2000: process 2000 sequential records */
int main(int argc, char **argv) {
    int i, *a, maxnum = atoi(argv[1]);

    initList();
    if ((a = malloc(maxnum * sizeof(*a))) == 0) {
```

```
            fprintf (stderr, "insufficient memory (a)\n");
            exit(1);
        }
    for (i = 0; i < maxnum; i++) a[i] = rand();
        printf ("Random, %d items\n", maxnum);

    for (i = 0; i < maxnum; i++) {
        insertElement(a[i]);
    }
    for (i = maxnum-1; i >= 0; i--) {
        findElement(a[i]);
    }
    for (i = maxnum-1; i >= 0; i--) {
        deleteElement(a[i]);
    }
    return 0;
}
```

10.12 Problems on Linked Lists

Problem-1   Implement Stack using Linked List

Solution: Refer *Stacks* chapter.

Problem-2   Find n^{th} node from the end of a Linked List.

Solution: Brute-Force Approach: In this method, start with the first node count the number of nodes present after that node. If the number of nodes are $< n - 1$ then return saying "fewer number of nodes in the list". If the number of nodes are $> n - 1$ then go to next node. Continue this until the numbers of nodes after current node are $n - 1$.

Time Complexity: $O(n^2)$, for scanning the remaining list (from the current node) for each node.
Space Complexity: O(1).

Problem-3   Can we improve the complexity of Problem-2?

Solution: Yes, using hash table. As an example consider the following list.

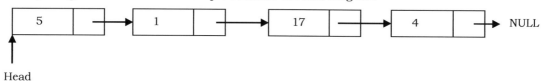

Head

In this approach, create a hash table whose entries are $< position\ of\ node,\ node\ address >$. That means, key is the position of the node in the list and value is the address of that node.

Position in List	Address of Node
1	Address of 5 node
2	Address of 1 node
3	Address of 17 node
4	Address of 4 node

By the time we traverse the complete list (for creating hash table), we can find the list length. Let us say, the list length is M. To find n^{th} from end of linked list, we can convert this to $M- n + 1^{th}$ from the beginning. Since we already know the length of the list, it's just a matter of returning $M- n + 1^{th}$ key value from the hash table.

Time Complexity: Time for creating the hash table. Therefore, $T(m) = O(m)$.
Space Complexity: $O(m)$. Since, we need to create a hash table of size m.

Problem-4   Can we use Problem-3 approach for solving Problem-2 without creating the hash table?

Solution: Yes. If we observe the Problem-3 solution, what actually we are doing is finding the size of the linked list. That means, we are using hash table to find the size of the linked list. We can find the length of the linked list just by starting at the head node and traversing the list. So, we can find the length of the list without creating the hash table. After finding the length, compute $M - n + 1$ and with one more scan we can get the $M - n + 1^{th}$ node from the beginning. This solution needs two scans: one for finding the length of list and other for finding $M - n + 1^{th}$ node from the beginning.

Time Complexity: Time for finding the length + Time for finding the $M- n + 1^{th}$ node from the beginning. Therefore, $T(n = O(n) + O(n) \approx O(n)$.
Space Complexity: O(1). Since, no need of creating the hash table.

Problem-5   Can we solve Problem-2 in one scan?

Solution: Yes. Efficient Approach: Use two pointers *pNthNode* and *pTemp*. Initially, both points to head node of the list. *pNthNode* starts moving only after *pTemp* made *n* moves. From there both moves forward until *pTemp* reaches end of the list. As a result *pNthNode* points to n^{th} node from end of the linked list.

Note: at any point of time both moves one node at time.

```
struct ListNode *NthNodeFromEnd(struct ListNode *head, int NthNode){
    struct ListNode *pNthNode = NULL, *pTemp = head;
    for(int count =1; count< NthNode;count++) {
        if(pTemp)
            pTemp = pTemp→next;
    }
    while(pTemp) {
        if(pNthNode == NULL)
            pNthNode = head;
        else
            pNthNode = pNthNode→next;
        pTemp = pTemp→next;
    }
    if(pNthNode)
        return pNthNode;
    return NULL;
}
```

Time Complexity: O(*n*). Space Complexity: O(1).

Problem-6   Check whether the given linked list is either NULL-terminated or ends in a cycle (cyclic)

Solution: Brute-Force Approach. As an example consider the following linked list which has a loop in it. The difference between this list and the regular list is that, in this list there are two nodes whose next pointers are same. In regular singly linked lists (without loop) each nodes next pointer is unique. That means, the repetition of next pointers indicates the existence of loop.

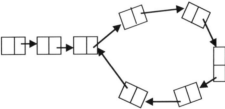

One simple and brute force way of solving this is, start with the first node and see whether there is any node whose next pointer is current node's address. If there is a node with same address then that indicates that some other node is pointing to the current node and we can say loops exists. Continue this process for all the nodes of the linked list.

Does this method works? As per the algorithm we are checking for the next pointer addresses, but how do we find the end of the linked list (otherwise we will end up in infinite loop)?

Note: If we start with a node in loop, this method may work depending on the size of the loop.

Problem-7   Can we use hashing technique for solving Problem-6?

Solution: Yes. Using Hash Tables we can solve this problem.

Algorithm:
- Traverse the linked list nodes one by one.
- Check if the address of the node is available in the hash table or not.
- If it is already available in the hash table then that indicates that we are visiting the node that was already visited. This is possible only if the given linked list has a loop in it.
- If the address of the node is not available in the hash table then insert that nodes address into the hash table.
- Continue this process until we reach end of the linked list *or* we find loop.

Time Complexity: O(*n*) for scanning the linked list. Note that we are doing only scan of the input. Space Complexity: O(*n*) for hash table.

Problem-8   Can we solve the Problem-6 using sorting technique?

Solution: No. Consider the following algorithm which is based on sorting. And then, we see why this algorithm fails.

Algorithm:
- Traverse the linked list nodes one by one and take all the next pointer values into some array.
- Sort the array that has next node pointers.
- If there is a loop in the linked list, definitely two nodes next pointers will pointing to the same node.

- After sorting if there is a loop in the list, the nodes whose next pointers are same will come adjacent in the sorted list.
- If any such pair exists in the sorted list then we say the linked list has loop in it.

Time Complexity: O($nlogn$) for sorting the next pointers array.
Space Complexity: O(n) for the next pointers array.

Problem with above algorithm?

The above algorithm works only if we can find the length of the list. But if the list is having loop then we may end up in infinite loop. Due to this reason the algorithm fails.

Problem-9   Can we solve the Problem-6 in O(n)?

Solution: Yes. Efficient Approach (Memory less Approach): This problem was solved by *Floyd*. The solution is named as Floyd cycle finding algorithm. It uses 2 pointers moving at different speeds to walk the linked list. Once they enter the loop they are expected to meet, which denotes that there is a loop. This works because the only way a faster moving pointer would point to the same location as a slower moving pointer is, if somehow the entire list or a part of it is circular.

Think of a tortoise and a hare running on a track. The faster running hare will catch up with the tortoise if they are running in a loop. As an example, consider the following example and trace out the Floyd algorithm. From the diagrams below we can see that after the final step they are meeting at some point in the loop which may not be the starting of the loop.

Note: *slowPtr* (*tortoise*) moves one pointer at a time and *fastPtr* (*hare*) moves two pointers at a time.

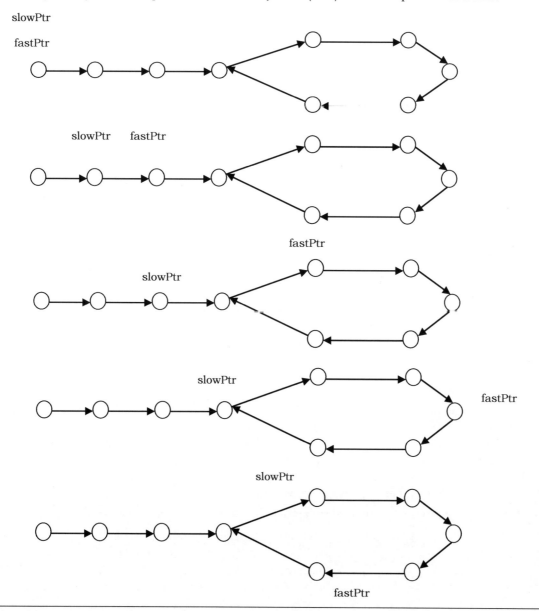

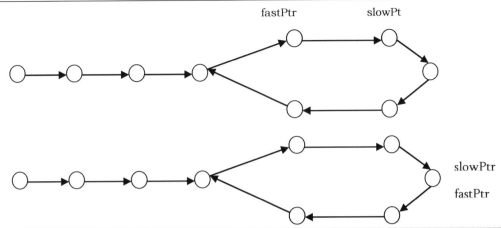

```
int DoesLinkedListContainsLoop(struct ListNode * head) {
    struct ListNode *slowPtr = head, *fastPtr = head;
    while (slowPtr && fastPtr && fastPtr→next) {
        slowPtr = slowPtr→next;
        fastPtr = fastPtr→next→next;
        if (slowPtr == fastPtr)
            return 1;
    }
    return 0;
}
```

Time Complexity: O(n). Space Complexity: O(1).

Problem-10   You are given a pointer to the first element of a linked list L. There are two possibilities for L, it either ends (snake) or its last element points back to one of the earlier elements in the list (snail). Task is to devise an algorithm that tests whether a given list L is a snake or a snail.

Solution: It is same as Problem-6.

Problem-11   Check whether the given linked list is either NULL-terminated or not. If there is a cycle find the start node of the loop.

Solution: The solution is an extension to the previous solution (Problem-9). After finding the loop in the linked list, we initialize the *slowPtr* to head of the linked list. From that point onwards both *slowPtr* and *fastPtr* moves only one node at a time. The point at which they meet is the start of the loop. Generally we use this method for removing the loops.

```
int FindBeginofLoop(struct ListNode * head) {
    struct ListNode *slowPtr = head, *fastPtr = head;
    int loopExists = 0;
        while (slowPtr && fastPtr && fastPtr→next) {
        slowPtr = slowPtr→next;
        fastPtr = fastPtr→next→next;
        if (slowPtr == fastPtr){
            loopExists = 1;
            break;
        }
    }
    if(loopExists) {
        slowPtr = head;
        while(slowPtr != fastPtr) {
            fastPtr = fastPtr→next;
            slowPtr = slowPtr→next;
        }
        return slowPtr;
    }
    return NULL;
}
```

Time Complexity: O(n). Space Complexity: O(1).

Problem-12   From the previous discussion and problems we understand that the meeting of tortoise and hare meeting concludes the existence of loop, but how does moving tortoise to beginning of linked list while keeping the hare at meeting place, followed by moving both one step at a time make them meet at starting point of cycle?

Solution: This problem is the heart of number theory. In Floyd cycle finding algorithm, notice that the tortoise and the hare will meet when they are $n \times L$, where L is the loop length. Furthermore, the tortoise is at the midpoint between the hare and the beginning of the sequence, because of the way they move. Therefore the tortoise is $n \times L$ away from the beginning of the sequence as well.

If we move both one step at a time, from the position of tortoise and from the start of the sequence, we know that they will meet as soon as both are in the loop, since they are $n \times L$, a multiple of the loop length, apart. One of them is already in the loop, so we just move the other one in single step until it enters the loop, keeping the other $n \times L$ away from it at all times.

Problem-13 In Floyd cycle finding algorithm, does it work if we use the steps 2 and 3 instead of 1 and 2?

Solution: Yes, but the complexity might be high. Trace out some example.

Problem-14 Check whether the given linked list is NULL-terminated. If there is a cycle find the length of the loop.

Solution: This solution is also an extension to the basic cycle detection problem. After finding the loop in the linked list, keep the *slowPtr* as it is. *fastPtr* keeps on moving until it again comes back to *slowPtr*. While moving *fastPtr*, use a counter variable which increments at the rate of 1.

```
int FindLoopLength(struct ListNode * head) {
    struct ListNode *slowPtr = head, *fastPtr = head;
    int loopExists = 0, counter = 0;
    while (slowPtr && fastPtr && fastPtr→next) {
        slowPtr = slowPtr→next;
        fastPtr = fastPtr→next→next;
        if (slowPtr == fastPtr){
            loopExists = 1;
            break;
        }
    }
    if(loopExists) {
        fastPtr = fastPtr→next;
        while(slowPtr != fastPtr) {
            fastPtr = fastPtr→next;
            counter++;
        }
        return counter;
    }
    return 0;                          //If no loops exists
}
```

Time Complexity: O(n). Space Complexity: O(1).

Problem-15 Insert a node in a sorted linked list

Solution: Traverse the list and find a position for the element and insert it.

```
struct ListNode *InsertInSortedList(struct ListNode * head, struct ListNode * newNode) {
    struct ListNode *current = head, temp;
    if(!head)  return newNode;
    // traverse the list until you find item bigger the new node value
    while (current != NULL && current→data < newNode→data){
        temp = current;
        current = current→next;
    }
    //  insert the new node before the big item
    newNode→next = current;
    temp→next = newNode;
    return head;
}
```

Time Complexity: O(n). Space Complexity: O(1).

Problem-16 Reverse a singly linked list

Solution: // iterative version
```
struct ListNode *ReverseList(struct ListNode *head ) {
    struct ListNode *temp = NULL, *nextNode = NULL;
    while (head) {
        nextNode = head→next;
        head→next = temp;
        temp = head;
        head = nextNode;
    }
    return temp;
```

}

Time Complexity: O(n). Space Complexity: O(1).

Problem-17   Suppose there are two singly linked lists both of which intersect at some point and become a single linked list. The head or start pointers of both the lists are known, but the intersecting node is not known. Also, the number of nodes in each of the list before they intersect are unknown and both list may have it different. *List*1 may have n nodes before it reaches intersection point and *List*2 might have m nodes before it reaches intersection point where m and n may be $m = n, m < n$ or $m > n$. Give an algorithm for finding the merging point.

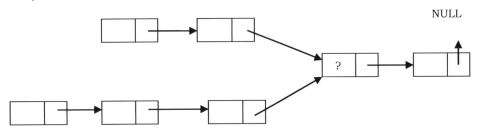

Solution: Brute-Force Approach: One easy solution is to compare every node pointer in the first list with every other node pointer in the second list by which the matching node pointers will lead us to the intersecting node. But, the time complexity in this case will O(mn) which will be high.

Time Complexity: O(mn). Space Complexity: O(1).

Problem-18   Can we solve Problem-17 using sorting technique?

Solution: No. Consider the following algorithm which is based on sorting and see why this algorithm fails.

Algorithm
- Take first list node pointers and keep in some array and sort them.
- Take second list node pointers and keep in some array and sort them.
- After sorting, use two indexes: one for first sorted array and other for second sorted array.
- Start comparing values at the indexes and increment the index whichever has lower value (increment only if the values are not equal).
- At any point, if we were able to find two indexes whose values are same then that indicates that those two nodes are pointing to the same node and we return that node.

Time Complexity: Time for sorting lists + Time for scanning (for comparing)=O($mlogm$) + O($nlogn$) + O($m+n$). We need to consider the one that gives the maximum value. Space Complexity: O(1).

Any problem with the above algorithm? Yes. In the algorithm, we are storing all the node pointers of both the lists and sorting. But we are forgetting the fact that, there can be many repeated elements. This is because after the merging point all node pointers are same for both the lists. The algorithm works fine only in one case and it is when both lists have ending node at their merge point.

Problem-19   Can we solve Problem-17 using hash tables?

Solution: Yes.

Algorithm:
- Select a list which has less number of nodes (If we do not know the lengths beforehand then select one list randomly).
- Now, traverse the other list and for each node pointer of this list check whether the same node pointer exists in the hash table.
- If there is a merge point for the given lists then we will definitely encounter the node pointer in the hash table.

Time Complexity: Time for creating the hash table + Time for scanning the second list =O(m)+ O(n) (or O(n) + O(m), depends on which list we select for creating the hash table). But in both cases the time complexity is same. Space Complexity: O(n) or O(m).

Problem-20   Can we use stacks for solving the Problem-17?

Solution: Yes.

Algorithm:
- Create two stacks: one for the first list and one for the second list.
- Traverse the first list and push all the node address on to the first stack.
- Traverse the second list and push all the node address on to the second stack.
- Now both stacks contain the node address of the corresponding lists.
- Now, compare the top node address of both stacks.
- If they are same, then pop the top elements from both the stacks and keep in some temporary variable (since both node addresses are node, it is enough if we use one temporary variable).
- Continue this process until top node addresses of the stacks are not same.

- This point is the one where the lists merge into single list.
- Return the value of the temporary variable.

Time Complexity: $O(m + n)$, for scanning both the lists. Space Complexity: $O(m + n)$, for creating two stacks for both the lists.

Problem-21   Is there any other way of solving the Problem-17?

Solution: Yes. Using "finding the first repeating number" approach in an array (for algorithm refer *Searching* chapter).

Algorithm:
- Create an array A and keep all the next pointers of both the lists in the array.
- In the array find the first repeating element in the array [Refer *Searching* chapter for algorithm].
- The first repeating number indicates the merging point of the both lists.

Time Complexity: $O(m + n)$. Space Complexity: $O(m + n)$.

Problem-22   Can we still think of finding an alternative solution for the Problem-17?

Solution: Yes. By combining sorting and search techniques we can reduce the complexity.

Algorithm:
- Create an array A and keep all the next pointers of the first list in the array.
- Sort these array elements.
- Then, for each of the second list element, search in the sorted array (let us assume that we are using binary search which gives $O(logn)$).
- Since we are scanning the second list one by one, the first repeating element that appears in the first array is nothing but the merging point.

Time Complexity: Time for sorting + Time for searching = $O(Max(mlogm, nlogn))$. Space Complexity: $O(Max(m,n))$.

Problem-23   Can we improve the complexity for the Problem-17?

Solution: Yes.

Efficient Approach:
- Find lengths (L1 and L2) of both list -- $O(n) + O(m) = O(max(m,n))$.
- Take the difference d of the lengths -- $O(1)$.
- Make d steps in longer list -- $O(d)$.
- Step in both lists in parallel until links to next node match -- $O(min(m,n))$.
- Total time complexity = $O(max(m,n))$.
- Space Complexity = $O(1)$.

```
struct ListNode* FindIntersectingNode(struct ListNode* list1, struct ListNode* list2) {
    int L1=0, L2=0, diff=0;
    struct ListNode *head1 = list1, *head2 = list2;
    while(head1!= NULL) {
        L1++;
        head1 = head1→next;
    }
    while(head2!= NULL) {
        L2++;
        head2 = head2→next;
    }
    if(L1 < L2) {
        head1 = list2;
        head2 = list1;
        diff = L2 - L1;
    } else{
        head1 = list1;
        head2 = list2;
        diff = L1 – L2;
    }
    for(int i = 0; i < diff; i++)
            head1 = head1→next;
    while(head1 != NULL && head2 != NULL) {
        if(head1 == head2)
            return head1→data;
        head1= head1→next;
        head2= head2→next;
    }
    return NULL;
}
```

Problem-24   How will you find the middle of the linked list?

Solution: Efficient Approach: Use two pointers. Move one pointer at twice the speed of the second. When the first pointer reaches end of the list, the second pointer will be pointing to the middle node.

Note: If the list has even number of nodes, the middle node will be of $\lfloor n/2 \rfloor$.

```
struct ListNode * FindMiddle(struct ListNode *head) {
    struct ListNode *ptr1x, *ptr2x;
    ptr1x = ptr2x = head;
    int i=0;
    // keep looping until we reach the tail
    // (next will be NULL for the last node)
    while(ptr1x→next != NULL) {
        if(i == 0) {
            ptr1x = ptr1x→next; //increment only the 1st pointer
            i=1;
        }
        else if( i == 1) {
            ptr1x = ptr1x→next; //increment both pointers
            ptr2x = ptr2x→next;
            i = 0;
        }
    }
    return ptr2x;       //now return the ptr2 which points to the middle node
}
```

Time Complexity: O(n). Space Complexity: O(1).

Problem-25   How will you display a linked list from the end?

Solution: Traverse recursively till end of the linked list. While coming back, start printing the elements.

```
//This Function will print the linked list from end
void PrintListFromEnd(struct ListNode *head) {
    if(!head)
        return;
    PrintListFromEnd(head→next);
    printf("%d",head→data);
}
```

Time Complexity: O(n). Space Complexity: O(n)→ for Stack.

Problem-26   Check whether the given Linked List length is even or odd?

Solution: Use $2x$ pointer. Take a pointer that moves at $2x$ [two nodes at a time]. At the end, if the length is even then pointer will be NULL otherwise it will point to last node.

```
int IsLinkedListLengthEven(struct ListNode * listHead) {
    while(listHead && listHead→next)
        listHead = listHead→next→next;

    if(!listHead)
        return 0;
    return 1;
}
```

Time Complexity: O($\lfloor n/2 \rfloor$) $\approx$O(n). Space Complexity: O(1).

Problem-27   Is it possible to get O(1) access time for Linked Lists?

Solution: Yes. Create a linked list at the same time keep it in a hash table. For n elements we have to keep all the elements into hash table which gives preprocessing time of O(n). To read any element we require only constant time O(1) and to read n elements we require $n * 1$ unit of time = n units. Hence by using amortized analysis we can say that element access can be performed within O(1) time.

Time Complexity – O(1) [Amortized]. Space Complexity - O(n) for Hash.

Problem-28   Given two sorted Linked Lists, we need to merge them into the third list in sorted order.

Solution: Assume the size of lists are m and n.

Recursive:

```
struct ListNode *MergeSortedList(struct ListNode *a, struct ListNode *b) {
    struct ListNode *result = NULL;
    if(a == NULL)
```

```
                return b;
          if(b == NULL)
                return a;
          if(a→data <= b→data) {
                result =a;
                result→next = MergeSortedList(a→next, b);
          }
          else {
                result =b;
                result→next = MergeSortedList(b→next,a);
          }
          return result;
   }
```

Time Complexity – O($n + m$), where n and m are lengths of two lists.

Iterative:

```
struct ListNode *MergeSortedListIterative(struct ListNode *head1, struct ListNode *head2){
      struct ListNode * newNode = (struct ListNode*) (malloc(sizeof(struct ListNode)));
      struct ListNode *temp;
      newNode = new Node;
      newNode→next = NULL;
      temp = newNode;

      while (head1!=NULL and head2!=NULL){
            if (head1→data<=head2→data){
                  temp→next = head1;
                  temp = temp→next;
                  head1 = head1→next;
            }else{
                  temp→next = head2;
                  temp = temp→next;
                  head2 = head2→next;
            }
      }
      if (head1!=NULL)
            temp→next = head1;
      else
            temp→next = head2;

      temp = newNode→next;
      free(newNode);
      return temp;
}
```

Time Complexity – O($n + m$), where n and m are lengths of two lists.

Problem-29   Reverse the linked list in pairs. If you have a linked list that holds $1 \to 2 \to 3 \to 4 \to X$, then after the function has been called the linked list would hold $2 \to 1 \to 4 \to 3 \to X$.

Solution:

```
//Recursive Version
struct ListNode *ReversePairRecursive(struct ListNode *head) {
    struct ListNode *temp;
    if(head ==NULL || head→next ==NULL)
            return;   //base case for empty or 1 element list
    else {
            //Reverse first pair
            temp = head→next;
            head→next = temp→next;
            temp→next = head;
            head = temp;

            //Call the method recursively for the rest of the list
            head→next→next = ReversePairRecursive(head→next→next);
            return head;
    }
}

/*Iterative version*/
```

```
struct ListNode *ReversePairIterative(struct ListNode *head) {
    struct ListNode *temp1=NULL, *temp2=NULL, *current = head;

    while(current != NULL && current→next != NULL) {
        if (temp1 != null) {
            temp1→next→next = current→next;
        }
        temp1 = current→next;
        current→next = current→next→next;
        temp1.next = current;
        if (temp2 == null)
            temp2 = temp1;
        current = current→next;
    }
    return temp2;
}
```

Time Complexity – O(n). Space Complexity - O(1).

Problem-30   Split a Circular Linked List into two equal parts. If the number of nodes in the list are odd then make first list one node extra than second list.

Solution:

Algorithm

- Store the mid and last pointers of the circular linked list using Floyd cycle finding algorithm.
- Make the second half circular.
- Make the first half circular.
- Set head pointers of the two linked lists.

As an example, consider the following circular list.

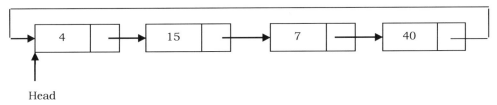

Head

After the split, the above list will look like:

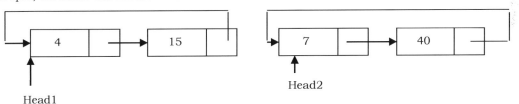

Head1   Head2

```
/* structure for a node */
struct ListNode {
    int data;
    struct ListNode *next;
};
void SplitList(struct ListNode *head, struct ListNode **head1, struct ListNode **head2) {
    struct ListNode *slowPtr = head;
    struct ListNode *fastPtr = head;
    if(head == NULL)
        return;
    /* If there are odd nodes in the circular list then fastPtr→next becomes
        head and for even nodes fastPtr→next→next becomes head */
    while(fastPtr→next != head && fastPtr→next→next != head)  {
        fastPtr = fastPtr→next→next;
        slowPtr = slowPtr→next;
    }
    /* If there are even elements in list then move fastPtr */
    if(fastPtr→next→next == head)
        fastPtr = fastPtr→next;
    /* Set the head pointer of first half */
    *head1 = head;
```

```
        /* Set the head pointer of second half */
        if(head→next != head)
                *head2 = slowPtr→next;
        /* Make second half circular */
        fastPtr→next = slowPtr→next;
        /* Make first half circular */
        slowPtr→next = head;
}
```

Time Complexity: $O(n)$. Space Complexity: $O(1)$.

Problem-30   How will you check if the linked list is palindrome or not?

Solution:

Algorithm
1. Get the middle of the linked list.
2. Reverse the second half of the linked list.
3. Compare the first half and second half.
4. Construct the original linked list by reversing the second half again and attaching it back to the first half.

Time Complexity: $O(n)$. Space Complexity: $O(1)$.

Problem-32   For a given K value ($K > 0$) reverse blocks of K nodes in a list.
    Example: Input: 1 2 3 4 5 6 7 8 9 10.
    Output for different K values:
        For K = 2: 2 1 4 3 6 5 8 7 10 9   For K = 3: 3 2 1 6 5 4 9 8 7 10   For K = 4: 4 3 2 1 8 7 6 5 9 10

Solution:

Algorithm: This is an extension of swapping nodes in a linked list.
1) Check if remaining list has K nodes.
    a.   If yes get the pointer of $K + 1^{th}$ node.
    b.   Else return.
2) Reverse first K nodes.
3) Set next of last node (after reversal) to $K + 1^{th}$ node.
4) Move to $K + 1^{th}$ node.
5) Go to step 1.
6) $K - 1^{th}$ node of first K nodes becomes the new head if available. Otherwise, we can return the head.

```
struct ListNode * GetKPlusOneThNode(int K, struct ListNode *head) {
    struct ListNode *Kth;
    int i = 0;
    if(!head)
        return head;
    for (i=0, Kth=head; Kth && (i < K); i++, Kth=Kth→next);
    if(i==K && Kth!=NULL)
        return Kth;
    return head→next;
}
int HasKnodes(struct ListNode *head, int K) {
    int i =0;
    for(i=0; head && (i < K); i++, head=head→next);
    if(i == K)
        return 1;
    return 0;
}
struct ListNode *ReverseBlockOfK-nodesInLinkedList(struct ListNode *head, int K) {
    struct ListNode *cur=head, *temp, *next, newHead;
    int i;
    if(K==0 || K==1)
        return head;
    if(HasKnodes(cur, K-1))
        newHead = GetKPlusOneThNode(K-1, cur);
    else newHead = head;
    while(cur && HasKnodes(cur, K)) {
        //Take care of below step
        temp = GetKPlusOneThNode(K, cur);
        i=0;
        while(i < K) {
            next = cur→next;
            cur→next=temp;
```

```
                    temp = cur;
                    cur = next;
                    i++;
            }
    }
    return newHead;
}
```

Problem-31   Is it possible to get O(1) access time for Linked Lists?

Solution: Yes. Create a linked list at the same time keep it in a hash table. For n elements we have to keep all the elements into hash table which gives preprocessing time of O(n). To read any element we require only constant time O(1) and to read n elements we require $n * 1$ unit of time = n units. Hence by using amortized analysis we can say that element access can be performed within O(1) time.

Time Complexity – O(1) [Amortized]. Space Complexity - O(n) for Hash.

Problem-32   **JosephusCircle:** N people have decided to elect a leader by arranging themselves in a circle and eliminating every M^{th} person around the circle, closing ranks as each person drops out. Find which person will be the last one remaining (with rank 1).

Solution: Assume the input is a circular linked list with N nodes and each node has a number (range 1 to N) associated with it. The head node has number 1 as data.

```
struct ListNode *GetJosephusPosition(){
    struct ListNode *p, *q;
    printf("Enter N (number of players): ");  scanf("%d", &N);
    printf("Enter M (every M-th payer gets eliminated): ");  scanf("%d", &M);
    // Create circular linked list containing all the players:
    p = q = malloc(sizeof(struct node));
    p→data = 1;
    for (int i = 2; i <= N; ++i) {
            p→next = malloc(sizeof(struct node));
            p = p→next;
            p→data = i;
    }
    p→next = q;  // Close the circular linked list by having the last node point to the first.
    // Eliminate every M-th player as long as more than one player remains:
    for (int count = N; count > 1; --count) {
            for (int i = 0; i < M - 1; ++i)
                    p = p→next;
            p→next = p→next→next;  // Remove the eiminated player from the circular linked list.
    }
    printf("Last player left standing (Josephus Position) is %d\n.", p→data);
}
```

Problem-33   Given a linked list consists of data, next pointer and also a random pointer which points to a random node of the list. Give an algorithm for cloning the list.

Solution: We can use the hash table to associate newly created nodes with the instances of node in the given list.

Algorithm:
- Scan the original list and for each node X, create a new node Y with data of X, then store the pair (X, Y) in hash table using X as a key. Note that during this scan we set $Y-> next$ and $Y-> random$ to $NULL$ and we will fix them in the next scan
- Now for each node X in the original list we have a copy Y stored in our hash table. We scan again the original list and set the pointers buildings the new list

```
struct ListNode *Clone(struct ListNode *head){
    struct ListNode *X, *Y;
    struct HashTable *HT = CreateHashTable();
    X = head;
    while (X != NULL) {
            Y = (struct ListNode *)malloc(sizeof(struct ListNode *));
            Y→data = X→data;
            Y→next = NULL;
            Y→random = NULL;
            HT.insert(X, Y);
            X = X→next;
    }
    X = head;
    while (X != NULL) {
```

```
            // get the node Y corresponding to X from the hash table
            Y = HT.get(X);
            Y→next = HT.get(X→next);
            Y.setRandom = HT.get(X→random);
            X = X→next;
        }
        // Return the head of the new list, that is the Node Y
        return HT.get(head);
    }
```

Time Complexity: $O(n)$. Space Complexity: $O(n)$.

Problem-34   Can we solve Problem-33 without any extra space?

Solution: Yes. Follow the comments in below code and trace out.

```
void Clone(struct ListNode *head){
    struct ListNode *temp, *temp2;
    // Step1: put temp→random in temp2→next,
    // so that we can reuse the temp→random field to point to temp2.
    temp = head;
    while (temp != NULL) {
        temp2 = (struct ListNode *)malloc(sizeof(struct ListNode *));
        temp2→data = temp→data;
        temp2→next = temp→random;
        temp→random = temp2;
        temp = temp→next;
    }
    //Step2: Setting temp2→random. temp2→next is the old copy of the node that
    // temp2→random should point to, so temp2→next→random is the new copy.
    temp = head;
    while (temp != NULL) {
        temp2 = temp→random;
        temp2→random = temp2→next→random;
        temp = temp→next;
    }
    //Step3: Repair damage to old list and fill in next pointer in new list.
    temp = head;
    while (temp != NULL) {
        temp2 = temp→random;
        temp→random = temp2→next;
        temp2→next = temp→next→random;
        temp = temp→next;*
    }
}
```

Time Complexity: $O(3n) \approx O(n)$. Space Complexity: $O(1)$.

Problem-35   **Find modular node:** Given a singly linked list, write a function to find the element whose $n\%k == 0$, where n is the number of elements in the list and k is an integer constant. For example, if $n = 19$ and $k = 3$ then we should return 18th node.

Solution: For this problem the value of n is not known in advance.

```
struct ListNode *modularNodes(struct ListNode *head, int k){
    struct ListNode *modularNode;
    int i=0;
    if(k<=0)
        return NULL;
    for (;head!= NULL; head = head→next){
        if(i%k == 0){
            modularNode = head;
        }
        i++;
    }
    return modularNode;
}
```

Time Complexity: $O(n)$. Space Complexity: $O(1)$.

Problem-36   Find modular node: Given a singly linked list, write a function to find the last element from the beginning whose $n\%k == 0$, where n is the number of elements in the list and k is an integer constant. For example, if $n = 19$ and $k = 3$ then we should return 16th node.

Solution: For this problem the value of n is not known in advance and it is same as finding the kth element from end of the linked list.

```
struct ListNode *modularNodes(struct ListNode *head, int k){
    struct ListNode *modularNode;
    int i=0, j=0;
    if(k<=0)
        return NULL;
    for (;head!= NULL; head = head→next){
        if(i%k == 0){
            modularNode = head;
        }
        i++;
    }
    for (j=0; j < i%k; j++){
        modularNode = modularNode→next;
    }
    return modularNode;
}
```

Time Complexity: O(n). Space Complexity: O(1).

Problem-37   Find fractional node: Given a singly linked list, write a function to find the $\frac{n}{k}th$ element, where n is the number of elements in the list. If $n = 19$ and $k = 3$ then we should return 16th node.

Solution: For this problem the value of n is not known in advance.

```
struct ListNode *modularNodes(struct ListNode *head, int k){
    struct ListNode *modularNode=NULL;
    int i=0;
    if(k<=0)
        return NULL;
    for (i=0; i < k; i++){
        if(head)
            head = head→next;
        else
            return NULL;
    }
    while(head!= NULL)
        modularNode = modularNode→next;
        head = head→next;
    }
    return modularNode;
}
```

Time Complexity: O(n). Space Complexity: O(1).

**Problem-38   ** Given two lists List1 = $\{A_1, A_2, \ldots, A_n\}$ and List2 = $\{B_1, B_2, \ldots, B_m\}$ with data (both lists) in ascending order. Merge them into the third list in ascending order so that the merged list will be:

$$\{A_1, B_1, A_2, B_2 \ldots A_m, B_m, A_{m+1} \ldots A_n\} \text{ if } n >= m$$
$$\{A_1, B_1, A_2, B_2 \ldots A_n, B_n, B_{n+1} \ldots B_m\} \text{ if } m >= n$$

Solution:

```
struct ListNode*AlternateMerge(struct ListNode *List1, struct ListNode *List2){
    struct ListNode *newNode = (struct ListNode*) (malloc(sizeof(struct ListNode)));
    struct ListNode *temp;
    newNode→next = NULL;
    temp = newNode;
    while (List1!=NULL and List2!=NULL){
        temp→next = List1;
        temp = temp→next;
        List1 = List1→next;
        temp→next = List2;
        List2 = List2→next;
        temp = temp→next;
    }
    if (List1!=NULL)
```

```
            temp→next = List1;
        else
            temp→next = List2;
        temp = newNode→next;
        free(newNode);
        return temp;
}
```

Time Complexity: The *while* loop takes $O(min(n,m))$ time as it will run for $min(n,m)$ times. The other steps run in $O(1)$. Therefore the total time complexity is $O(min(n,m))$. Space Complexity: $O(1)$.

Problem-39   Median in an infinite series of integers.

Solution: Median is the middle number in a sorted list of numbers (if we have odd number of elements). If we have even number of elements, median is the average of two middle numbers in a sorted list of numbers.

We can solve this problem with linked lists (with both sorted and unsorted linked lists).

First, let us try with *unsorted* linked list. In an unsorted linked list, we can insert the element either at the head or at the tail. The disadvantage with this approach is that, finding the median takes $O(n)$. Also, the insertion operation takes $O(1)$.

Now, let us with *sorted* linked list. We can find the median in $O(1)$ time if we keep track of the middle elements. Insertion to a particular location is also $O(1)$ in any linked list. But, finding the right location to insert is not $O(logn)$ as in sorted array, it is instead $O(n)$ because we can't perform binary search in a linked list even if it is sorted.

So, using a sorted linked list doesn't worth the effort, insertion is $O(n)$ and finding median is $O(1)$, same as the sorted array. In sorted array insertion is linear due to shifting, here it's linear because we can't do binary search in a linked list.

Note: For efficient algorithm refer *Priority Queues and Heaps* chapter.

Problem-40   Given a linked list, how do you modify it such that all even numbers appear before all the odd numbers in the modified linked list?

Solution:

```
struct ListNode *exchangeEvenOddList(struct ListNode *head){
    struct ListNode *oddList = NULL, *evenList =NULL;

    struct ListNode *oddListEnd = NULL, *evenListEnd = NULL;
    struct ListNode *itr=head;
    if( head == NULL ){
        return;
    }
    else{
        while( itr != NULL ){
            if( itr→data % 2 == 0 ){
                if( evenList == NULL ){
                    // first even node
                    evenList = evenListEnd = itr;
                }
                else{
                    // inserting the node at the end of linked list
                    evenListEnd→next = itr;
                    evenListEnd = itr;
                }
            }
            else{
                if( oddList == NULL ){
                    // first odd node
                    oddList = oddListEnd = itr;
                }
                else{
                    // inserting the node at the end of linked list
                    oddListEnd→next = itr;
                    oddListEnd = itr;
                }
            }
            itr = itr→next;
        }
        evenListEnd→next = oddList;
        return head;
    }
}
```

Time Complexity: O(n). Space Complexity: O(1).

Problem-41   Given two linked lists, each list node with one integer digit, add these two linked lists. Result should be stored in third linked list. Also note that the head node contains the most significant digit of the number.

Solution: Since the integer addition starts from the least significant digit, we first need to visit the last node of both the lists and add them up, create new node to store the result, take care of the carry if any and the link the result node to node which will be added to second least significant node and continue.

First of all, we need to take into account the difference in number of digits in two number. So before starting recursion, we need to do some calculation and move the longer list pointer to appropriate place so that we need the last node of both lists at same time. Other thing is we need to take care of is carry. If two digits add more than 10, we need to forward the carry to next node and add it to them. If most significant digit addition results in carry, we need to create an extra node to store carry.

Function below is actually a wrapper function which does all house keeping like calculating lengths of lists, calling recursive implementation, creating extra node for carry in most significant digit, and adding any remaining nodes left in longer list.

```c
void addListNumbersWrapper(struct ListNode *list1, struct ListNode *list2, int *carry, struct ListNode **result){
    int list1Length = 0, list2Length = 0, diff =0;
    struct ListNode *current = list1;
    while(current){
        current = current->next;
        list1Length++;
    }
    current = list2;
    while(current){
        current = current->next;
        list2Length++;
    }
    if(list1Length < list2Length){
        current = list1;
        list1 = list2;
        list2 = current;
    }
    diff = abs(list1Length-list2Length);
    current = list1;
    while(diff--)
        current = current->next;

    addListNumbers(current, list2, carry, result);
    diff = abs(list1Length-list2Length);
    addRemainingNumbers(list1, carry, result, diff);

    if(*carry){
        struct ListNode * temp = (struct ListNode *)malloc(sizeof(struct ListNode ));
        temp->next = (*result);
        *result = temp;

    }
    return;
}
void addListNumbers(struct ListNode *list1, struct ListNode *list2, int *carry, struct ListNode **result){
    int sum;
    if(!list1)
        return;

    addListNumbers(list1->next, list2->next, carry, result);

    //End of both lists, add them
    struct ListNode * temp = (struct ListNode *)malloc(sizeof(struct ListNode ));
    sum = list1->data + list2->data + (*carry);

    // Store carry
    *carry = sum/10;
    sum = sum%10;

    temp->data = sum;
    temp->next = (*result);
    *result = temp;

    return;
}
```

```
    void addRemainingNumbers(struct ListNode * list1, int *carry, struct ListNode **result, int diff){
        int sum =0;
        if(!list1 || diff == 0)
            return;

        addRemainingNumbers(list1->next, carry, result, diff-1);

        struct ListNode * temp = (struct ListNode *)malloc(sizeof(struct ListNode ));
        sum = list1->data + (*carry);
        *carry = sum/10;
        sum = sum%10;

        temp->data = sum;
        temp->next = (*result);
        *result = temp;

        return;
    }
```

Time Complexity: O($max(List1\ length, List2\ length)$).
Space Complexity: O($min(List1\ length, List2\ length)$) for recursive stack.

Note: It can also be solved using stacks.

Problem-42   Which sorting algorithm is easily adaptable to singly linked lists?

Solution: Simple Insertion sort is easily adabtable to singly linked list. To insert the an element, the linked list is traversed until the proper position is found, or until the end of the list is reached. It be inserted into the list by merely adjusting the pointers without shifting any elements unlike in the array. This reduces the time required for insertion but not the time required for searching for the proper position.

Chapter-11

STACKS

11.1 What is a Stack?

A *stack* is a simple data structure used for storing data (similar to Linked Lists). In stack, the order in which the data arrives is important. The pile of plates of a cafeteria is a good example of stack. The plates are added to the stack as they are cleaned. They are placed on the top. When a plate is required it is taken from the top of the stack. The first plate placed on the stack is the last one to be used.

Definition: A *stack* is an ordered list in which insertion and deletion are done at one end, called *top*. The last element inserted is the first one to be deleted. Hence, it is called Last in First out (LIFO) or First in Last out (FILO) list.

Special names are given to the two changes that can be made to a stack. When an element is inserted in a stack, the concept is called as *push*, and when an element is removed from the stack, the concept is called as *pop*. Trying to pop out an empty stack is called as *underflow* and trying to push an element in a full stack is called as *overflow*. Generally, we treat them as *exceptions*. As an example, consider the following snapshots of the stack.

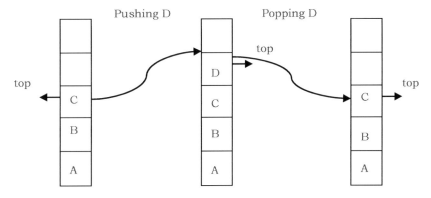

11.2 How Stacks are used?

Consider a working day in the office. Let us assume a developer is working on a long-term project. The manager then gives the developer a new task, which is more important. The developer places the long-term project aside and begins work on the new task. The phone rings, this is the highest priority, as it must be answered immediately. The developer pushes the present task into the pending tray and answers the phone. When the call is complete the task abandoned to answer the phone is retrieved from the pending tray and work progresses. To take another call, it may have to be handled in the same manner, but eventually the new task will be finished, and the developer can draw the long-term project from the pending tray and continue with that.

11.3 Stack ADT

The following operations make a stack an ADT. For simplicity, assume the data is of integer type.

Main stack operations

- Push (int data): Inserts *data* onto stack.
- int Pop(): Removes and returns the last inserted element from the stack.

Auxiliary stack operations

- int Top(): Returns the last inserted element without removing it.
- int Size(): Returns the number of elements stored in stack.
- int IsEmptyStack(): Indicates whether any elements are stored in stack or not.
- int IsFullStack(): Indicates whether the stack is full or not.

Exceptions

Attempting the execution of an operation may sometimes cause an error condition, called an exception. Exceptions are said to be "thrown" by an operation that cannot be executed. In the Stack ADT, operations pop and top cannot be performed if the stack is empty. Attempting the execution of pop (top) on an empty stack throws an exception. Trying to push an element in a full stack throws an exception.

11.4 Applications

Following are some of the applications in which stacks plays an important role.

Direct applications

- Balancing of symbols
- Infix-to-postfix conversion
- Evaluation of postfix expression
- Implementing function calls (including recursion)
- Finding of spans (finding spans in stock markets, refer *Problems* section)
- Page-visited history in a Web browser [Back Buttons]
- Undo sequence in a text editor
- Matching Tags in HTML and XML

Indirect applications

- Auxiliary data structure for other algorithms (Example: Tree traversal algorithms)
- Component of other data structures (Example: Simulating queues, refer *Queues* chapter)

11.5 Implementation

There are many ways of implementing stack ADT, given below are the commonly used methods.

- Simple array based implementation
- Dynamic array based implementation
- Linked lists implementation

Simple Array Implementation

This implementation of stack ADT uses an array. In the array, we add elements from left to right and use a variable to keep track of the index of the top element.

The array storing the stack elements may become full. A push operation will then throw a *full stack exception*. Similarly, if we try deleting an element from empty stack then it will throw *stack empty exception*.

```
struct ArrayStack {
    int top;
    int capacity;
    int *array;
};
struct ArrayStack *CreateStack() {
    struct ArrayStack *S = malloc(sizeof(struct ArrayStack));
    if(!S)
        return NULL;
    S→capacity = 1;
    S→top = -1;
    S→array= malloc(S→capacity * sizeof(int));
    if(!S→array)
        return NULL;
    return S;
}
int IsEmptyStack(struct ArrayStack *S) {
    return (S→top == -1);    // if the condition is true then 1 is returned else 0 is returned
}
int IsFullStack(struct ArrayStack *S){
    //if the condition is true then 1 is returned else 0 is returned
    return (S→top == S→capacity - 1);
```

```
        }
        void Push(struct ArrayStack *S, int data){
            /* S→top == capacity -1 indicates that the stack is full*/
            if(IsFullStack(S))
                printf( "Stack Overflow");
            else    /*Increasing the 'top' by 1 and storing the value at 'top' position*/
                S→ array[++S→top]= data;
        }
        int Pop(struct ArrayStack *S){
            if(IsEmptyStack(S)){    /* S→top == - 1 indicates empty stack*/
                    printf("Stack is Empty");
                    return 0;
            }
            else /* Removing element from 'top' of the array and reducing 'top' by 1*/
                    return (S→ array[S→top--]);
        }
        void DeleteStack(struct DynArrayStack *S){
            if(S) {
                if(S→array)
                    free(S→array);
                free(S);
            }
        }
```

Performance & Limitations

Performance

Let n be the number of elements in the stack. The complexities of stack operations with this representation can be given as:

Space Complexity (for n push operations)	$O(n)$
Time Complexity of Push()	$O(1)$
Time Complexity of Pop()	$O(1)$
Time Complexity of Size()	$O(1)$
Time Complexity of IsEmptyStack()	$O(1)$
Time Complexity of IsFullStack()	$O(1)$
Time Complexity of DeleteStack()	$O(1)$

Limitations

The maximum size of the stack must be defined in prior and cannot be changed. Trying to push a new element into a full stack causes an implementation-specific exception.

Dynamic Array Implementation

First, let's consider how we implemented a simple array based stack. We took one index variable *top* which points to the index of the most recently inserted element in the stack. To insert (or push) an element, we increment *top* index and then place the new element at that index. Similarly, to delete (or pop) an element we take the element at *top* index and then decrement the *top* index. We represent empty queue with *top* value equal to −1. The issue still need to be resolved is that what we do when all the slots in fixed size array stack are occupied?

First try

What if we increment the size of the array by 1 every time the stack is full?
- Push(): increase size of S[] by 1
- Pop(): decrease size of S[] by 1

Problems with this approach?

This way of incrementing the array size is too expensive. Let us a see the reason for this. For example, at $n = 1$, to push an element create a new array of size 2 and copy all the old array elements to new array and at the end add the new element. At $n = 2$, to push an element create a new array of size 3 and copy all the old array elements to new array and at the end add the new element.

Similarly, at $n = n - 1$, if we want to push an element create a new array of size n and copy all the old array elements to new array and at the end add the new element. After n push operations the total time $T(n)$ (number of copy operations) is proportional to $1 + 2 + ... + n \approx O(n^2)$.

Alternative Approach: Repeated Doubling

Let us improve the complexity by using array *doubling* technique. If the array is full, create a new array of twice the size, and copy items. With this approach, pushing n items takes time proportional to n (not n^2).

For simplicity, let us assume that initially we started with $n = 1$ and moved till $n = 32$. That means, we do the doubling at $1, 2, 4, 8, 16$. The other way of analyzing the same is, at $n = 1$, if we want to add (push) an element then double the current size of array and copy all the elements of old array to new array.

At, $n = 1$, we do 1 copy operation, at $n = 2$, we do 2 copy operations, and $n = 4$, we do 4 copy operations and so on. By the time we reach $n = 32$, the total number of copy operations is $1 + 2 + 4 + 8 + 16 = 31$ which is approximately equal to $2n$ value (32). If we observe carefully, we are doing the doubling operation $logn$ times.

Now, let us generalize the discussion. For n push operations we double the array size $logn$ times. That means, we will have $logn$ terms in the expression below. The total time $T(n)$ of a series of n push operations is proportional to

$$1 + 2 + 4 + 8 \dots + \frac{n}{4} + \frac{n}{2} + n = n + \frac{n}{2} + \frac{n}{4} + \frac{n}{8} \dots + 4 + 2 + 1$$
$$= n \left(1 + \frac{1}{2} + \frac{1}{4} + \frac{1}{8} \dots + \frac{4}{n} + \frac{2}{n} + \frac{1}{n}\right)$$
$$= n(2) \approx 2n = O(n)$$

$T(n)$ is $O(n)$ and the amortized time of a push operation is $O(1)$.

```
struct DynArrayStack {
    int top;
    int capacity;
    int *array;
};
struct DynArrayStack *CreateStack(){
    // allocate memory for structure
    struct DynArrayStack *S = malloc(sizeof(struct DynArrayStack));
    if(!S)
        return NULL;
    S→capacity = 1;
    S→top = -1;
    S→array = malloc(S→capacity * sizeof(int));        // allocate an array of size 1 initially
    if(!S→array)
        return NULL;
    return S;
}
int IsFullStack(struct DynArrayStack *S){
    return (S→top == S→capacity-1);
}
void DoubleStack(struct DynArrayStack *S){
    S→capacity *= 2;
    S→array = realloc(S→array, S→capacity);
}
void Push(struct DynArrayStack *S, int x){
    // No overflow in this implementation
    if(IsFullStack(S))
        DoubleStack(S);
    S→array[++S→top] = x;
}
int IsEmptyStack(struct DynArrayStack *S){
    return S→top == -1;
}
int Top(struct DynArrayStack *S){
    if(IsEmptyStack(S))
        return INT_MIN;
    return S→array[S→top];
}
int Pop(struct DynArrayStack *S){
    if(IsEmptyStack(S))
        return INT_MIN;
    return S→array[S→top--];
}
void DeleteStack(struct DynArrayStack *S){
    if(S) {
        if(S→array)
            free(S→array);
```

```
        free(S);
    }
}
```

Performance

Let n be the number of elements in the stack. The complexities for operations with this representation can be given as:

Space Complexity (for n push operations)	O(n)
Time Complexity of CreateStack()	O(1)
Time Complexity of Push()	O(1) (Average)
Time Complexity of Pop()	O(1)
Time Complexity of Top()	O(1)
Time Complexity of IsEmptyStack()	O(1))
Time Complexity of IsFullStack()	O(1)
Time Complexity of DeleteStack()	O(1)

Note: Too many doublings may cause memory overflow exception.

Linked List Implementation

The other way of implementing stacks is by using Linked lists. Push operation is implemented by inserting element at the beginning of the list. Pop operation is implemented by deleting the node from the beginning (the header/top node).

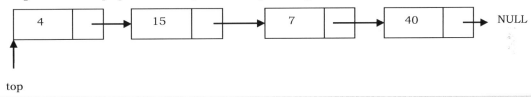

top

```
struct ListNode{
    int data;
    struct ListNode *next;
};
struct Stack *CreateStack(){
    return NULL;
}
void Push(struct Stack **top, int data){
    struct Stack *temp;
    temp = malloc(sizeof(struct Stack));
    if(!temp)
        return NULL;
    temp→data = data;
    temp→next = *top;
    *top = temp;
}
int IsEmptyStack(struct Stack *top){
    return top == NULL;
}
int Pop(struct Stack **top){
    int data;
    struct Stack *temp;
    if(IsEmptyStack(top))
        return INT_MIN;
    temp = * top;
    *top = * top→next;
    data = temp→data;
    free(temp);
    return data;
}
int Top(struct Stack * top){
    if(IsEmptyStack(top))
        return INT_MIN;
    return top→next→data;
}
void DeleteStack(struct Stack **top){
    struct Stack *temp, *p;
    p = *top;
```

```
        while( p→next) {
            temp = p→next;
            p→next = temp→next;
            free(temp);
        }
        free(p);
    }
```

Performance

Let n be the number of elements in the stack. Let n be the number of elements in the stack. The complexities for operations with this representation can be given as:

Space Complexity (for n push operations)	$O(n)$
Time Complexity of CreateStack()	$O(1)$
Time Complexity of Push()	$O(1)$ (Average)
Time Complexity of Pop()	$O(1)$
Time Complexity of Top()	$O(1)$
Time Complexity of IsEmptyStack()	$O(1)$
Time Complexity of DeleteStack()	$O(n)$

11.6 Comparison of Implementations

Comparing Incremental Strategy and Doubling Strategy

We compare the incremental strategy and doubling strategy by analyzing the total time $T(n)$ needed to perform a series of n push operations. We start with an empty stack represented by an array of size 1. We call *amortized* time of a push operation is the average time taken by a push over the series of operations, that is, $T(n)/n$.

Incremental Strategy

The amortized time (average time per operation) of a push operation is $O(n)$ [$O(n^2)/n$].

Doubling Strategy

In this method, the amortized time of a push operation is $O(1)$ [$O(n)/n$].

Note: For reasoning, refer the Implementation section.

Comparing Array Implementation and Linked List Implementation

Array Implementation

- Operations take constant time.
- Expensive doubling operation every once in a while.
- Any sequence of n operations (starting from empty stack) -- "amortized" bound takes time proportional to n.

Linked list Implementation

- Grows and shrinks gracefully.
- Every operation takes constant time $O(1)$.
- Every operation uses extra space and time to deal with references.

11.7 Problems on Stacks

Problem-1   Discuss how stacks can be used for checking balancing of symbols?

Solution: Stacks can be used to check whether the given expression has balanced symbols. This algorithm is very useful in compilers. Each time parser reads one character at a time. If the character is an opening delimiter such as (, {, or [- then it is written to the stack. When a closing delimiter is encountered like), }, or]- is encountered the stack is popped. The opening and closing delimiters are then compared. If they match, the parsing of the string continues. If they do not match, the parser indicates that there is an error on the line. A linear-time $O(n)$ algorithm based on stack can be given as:

Algorithm
- a)   Create a stack.
- b)   while (end of input is not reached) {

1) If the character read is not a symbol to be balanced, ignore it.
2) If the character is an opening symbol like (, [, {, push it onto the stack
3) If it is a closing symbol like),],}, then if the stack is empty report an error. Otherwise pop the stack.
4) If the symbol popped is not the corresponding opening symbol, report an error.
}
c) At end of input, if the stack is not empty report an error

Examples:

Example	Valid?	Description
(A+B)+(C-D)	Yes	The expression is having balanced symbol
((A+B)+(C-D)	No	One closing brace is missing
((A+B)+[C-D])	Yes	Opening and immediate closing braces correspond
((A+B)+[C-D]}	No	The last closing brace does not correspond with the first opening parenthesis

For tracing the algorithm let us assume that the input is: () (() [()])

Input Symbol, A[i]	Operation	Stack	Output
(	Push (	(	
)	Pop (Test if (and A[i] match? YES		
(	Push (	(	
(	Push (	((	
)	Pop (Test if(and A[i] match? YES	(	
[	Push [	([	
(	Push (	([(	
)	Pop (Test if(and A[i] match? YES	([	
]	Pop [Test if [and A[i] match? YES	(	
)	Pop (Test if(and A[i] match? YES		
	Test if stack is Empty? YES		TRUE

Time Complexity: O(n). Since, we are scanning the input only once. Space Complexity: O(n) [for stack].

Problem-2   Discuss infix to postfix conversion algorithm using stack.

Solution: Before discussing the algorithm, first let us see the definitions of infix, prefix and postfix expressions.

Infix: An infix expression is a single letter, or an operator, proceeded by one infix string and followed by another Infix string.

     A
     A+B
     (A+B)+ (C-D)

Prefix: A prefix expression is a single letter, or an operator, followed by two prefix strings. Every prefix string longer than a single variable contains an operator, first operand and second operand.

     A
     +AB
     ++AB-CD

Postfix: A postfix expression (also called Reverse Polish Notation) is a single letter or an operator, preceded by two postfix strings. Every postfix string longer than a single variable contains first and second operands followed by an operator.

     A
     AB+
     AB+CD-+

Prefix and postfix notions are methods of writing mathematical expressions without parenthesis. Time to evaluate a postfix and prefix expression is $O(n)$, were n is the number of elements in the array.

Infix	Prefix	Postfix
A+B	+AB	AB+

A+B-C	-+ABC	AB+C-
(A+B)*C-D	-*+ABCD	AB+C*D-

Now, let us focus on the algorithm. In infix expressions, the operator precedence is implicit unless we use parentheses. Therefore, for the infix to postfix conversion algorithm we have to define the operator precedence (or priority) inside the algorithm. The table shows the precedence and their associatively (order of evaluation) among operators.

Token	Operator	Precedence	Associatively
( ) [ ] → .	function call array element struct or union member	17	left-to-right
-- ++	increment, decrement	16	left-to-right
-- ++ ! ~ - + & * sizeof	decrement, increment logical not one's complement unary minus or plus address or indirection size (in bytes)	15	right-to-left
(type)	type cast	14	right-to-left
* / %	multiplicative	13	Left-to-right
+ -	binary add or subtract	12	left-to-right
<< >>	shift	11	left-to-right
> >= < <=	relational	10	left-to-right
== !=	equality	9	left-to-right
&	bitwise and	8	left-to-right
^	bitwise exclusive or	7	left-to-right
|	bitwise or	6	left-to-right
&&	logical and	5	left-to-right
||	logical or	4	left-to-right
?:	conditional	3	right-to-left
= += -= /= *= %= <<= >>= &= ^=	assignment	2	right-to-left
,	Comma	1	left-to-right

Important Properties

- Let us consider the infix expression 2 + 3 * 4 and its postfix equivalent 2 3 4 * +. Notice that between infix and postfix the order of the numbers (or operands) is unchanged. It is 2 3 4 in both cases. But the order of the operators * and + is affected in the two expressions.
- Only one stack is enough to convert an infix expression to postfix expression. The stack that we use in the algorithm will be used to change the order of operators from infix to postfix. The stack we use will only contain operators and the open parentheses symbol '('. Postfix expressions do not contain parentheses. We shall not output the parentheses in the postfix output.

Algorithm

a) Create a stack
b) for each character t in the input stream{
    if(t is an operand)
        output t
    else if(t is a right parenthesis){
        Pop and output tokens until a left parenthesis is popped (but not output)
    }

else // t is an operator or left parenthesis{
    pop and output tokens until one of lower priority than t is encountered or a left parenthesis is encountered or the stack is empty
    Push t
  }
}
c)   pop and output tokens until the stack is empty

For better understanding let us trace out some example: A * B- (C + D) + E

Input Character	Operation on Stack	Stack	Postfix Expression
A		Empty	A
*	Push	*	A
B		*	AB
-	Check and Push	-	AB*
(	Push	-(	AB*
C		-(	AB*C
+	Check and Push	-(+	AB*C
D			AB*CD
)	Pop and append to postfix till '('	-	AB*CD+
+	Check and Push	+	AB*CD+-
E		+	AB*CD+-E
End of input	Pop till empty		AB*CD+-E+

Problem-3   Discuss postfix evaluation using stacks?

Solution:

Algorithm

1   Scan the Postfix string from left to right.
2   Initialize an empty stack.
3   Repeat steps 4 and 5 till all the characters are scanned.
4   If the scanned character is an operand, push it onto the stack.
5   If the scanned character is an operator, and if the operator is unary operator then pop an element from the stack. If the operator is binary operator then pop two elements from the stack. After popping the elements, apply the operator to those popped elements. Let the result of this operation be retVal onto the stack.
6   After all characters are scanned, we will have only one element in the stack.
7   Return top of the stack as result.

Example: Let us see how the above-mentioned algorithm works using an example. Assume that the postfix string is 123*+5-. Initially the stack is empty. Now, the first three characters scanned are 1, 2 and 3, which are operands. They will be pushed into the stack in that order.

Next character scanned is "*", which is an operator. Thus, we pop the top two elements from the stack and perform the "*" operation with the two operands. The second operand will be the first element that is popped.

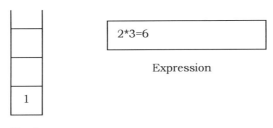

The value of the expression (2*3) that has been evaluated (6) is pushed into the stack.

```
┌───┬───┐          ┌─────────────────────┐
│   │   │          │                     │
│   │   │          │                     │
│   6   │          └─────────────────────┘
│   1   │                 Expression
└───┴───┘
  Stack
```

Next character scanned is "+", which is an operator. Thus, we pop the top two elements from the stack and perform the "+" operation with the two operands. The second operand will be the first element that is popped.

```
┌───┬───┐          ┌─────────────────────┐
│   │   │          │  1 + 6 = 7          │
│   │   │          │                     │
│   │   │          └─────────────────────┘
│   │   │                 Expression
└───┴───┘
  Stack
```

The value of the expression (1+6) that has been evaluated (7) is pushed into the stack.

```
┌───┬───┐          ┌─────────────────────┐
│   │   │          │                     │
│   │   │          │                     │
│   │   │          └─────────────────────┘
│   7   │                 Expression
└───┴───┘
  Stack
```

Next character scanned is "5", which is added to the stack.

```
┌───┬───┐          ┌─────────────────────┐
│   │   │          │                     │
│   │   │          │                     │
│   5   │                 Expression
│   7   │
└───┴───┘
  Stack
```

Next character scanned is "-", which is an operator. Thus, we pop the top two elements from the stack and perform the "-" operation with the two operands. The second operand will be the first element that is popped.

```
┌───┬───┐          ┌─────────────────────┐
│   │   │          │  7 - 5 = 2          │
│   │   │          │                     │
│   │   │          └─────────────────────┘
│   │   │                 Expression
└───┴───┘
  Stack
```

The value of the expression(7-5) that has been evaluated(23) is pushed into the stack.

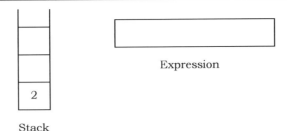

Expression

Stack

Now, since all the characters are scanned, the remaining element in the stack (there will be only one element in the stack) will be returned. End result:

- Postfix String : 123*+5-
- Result : 2

Problem-4   Can we evaluate the infix expression with stacks in one pass?

Solution: Using 2 stacks we can evaluate an infix expression in 1 pass without converting to postfix.

Algorithm

1) Create an empty operator stack
2) Create an empty operand stack
3) For each token in the input string
   a. Get the next token in the infix string
   b. If next token is an operand, place it on the operand stack
   c. If next token is an operator
      i. Evaluate the operator (next op)
4) While operator stack is not empty, pop operator and operands (left and right), evaluate left operator right and push result onto operand stack
5) Pop result from operator stack

Problem-5   How to design a stack such that GetMinimum( ) should be $O(1)$?

Solution: Take an auxiliary stack that maintains the minimum of all values in the stack. Also, assume that, each element of the stack is less than its below elements. For simplicity let us call the auxiliary stack as *min stack*.

When we *pop* the main stack, *pop* the min stack too. When we push the main stack, push either the new element or the current minimum, whichever is lower. At any point, if we want to get the minimum then we just need to return the top element from the min stack. Let us take some example and trace out. Initially let us assume that we have pushed 2, 6, 4, 1 and 5. Based on above-mentioned algorithm the *min stack* will look like:

Main stack	Min stack
5 → top	1 → top
1	1
4	2
6	2
2	2

After popping twice we get:

Main stack	Min stack
4 -→ top	2 → top
6	2
2	2

Based on the discussion above, now let us code the push, pop and GetMinimum() operations.

```
struct AdvancedStack{
    struct Stack elementStack;
    struct Stack minStack;
};
void Push(struct AdvancedStack *S, int data ){
    Push (S→elementStack, data);
    if(IsEmptyStack(S→minStack) || Top(S→minStack) >= data)
        Push (S→minStack, data);
    else
        Push (S→minStack, Top(S→minStack));
}
int Pop(struct AdvancedStack *S ){
    int temp;
    if(IsEmptyStack(S→elementStack))
        return -1;
    temp = Pop (S→elementStack);
```

```
        Pop (S→minStack);
        return temp;
    }
    int GetMinimum(struct AdvancedStack *S){
        return Top(S→minStack);
    }
    struct AdvancedStack *CreateAdvancedStack(){
        struct AdvancedStack *S = (struct AdvancedStack *)malloc(sizeof(struct AdvancedStack));
        if(!S)
            return NULL;
        S→elementStack = CreateStack();
        S→minStack = CreateStack();
        return S;
    }
```

Time complexity: O(1). Space complexity: O(n) [for Min stack]. This algorithm has much better space usage if we rarely get a "new minimum or equal".

Problem-6   For Problem-5 is it possible to improve the space complexity?

Solution: Yes. The main problem of the previous approach is, for each push operation we are pushing the element on to *min stack* also (either the new element or existing minimum element). That means, we are pushing the duplicate minimum elements on to the stack.

Now, let us change the algorithm to improve the space complexity. We still have the min stack, but we only pop from it when the value we pop from the main stack is equal to the one on the min stack. We only *push* to the min stack when the value being pushed onto the main stack is less than *or equal* to the current min value. In this modified algorithm also, if we want to get the minimum then we just need to return the top element from the min stack. For example, taking the original version and pushing 1 again, we'd get:

Main stack	Min stack
1 → top	
5	
1	
4	1 → top
6	1
2	2

Popping from the above pops from both stacks because 1 == 1, leaving:

Main stack	Min stack
5 → top	
1	
4	
6	1 → top
2	2

Popping again *only* pops from the main stack, because 5 > 1:

Main stack	Min stack
1 → top	
4	
6	1 → top
2	2

Popping again pops both stacks because 1 == 1:

Main stack	Min stack
4 → top	
6	
2	2 → top

Note: The difference is only in push & pop operations.

```
    struct AdvancedStack {
        struct Stack elementStack;
        struct Stack minStack;
    };
    void Push(struct AdvancedStack *S, int data){
        Push (S→elementStack, data);
        if(IsEmptyStack(S→minStack) || Top(S→minStack) >= data)
                Push (S→minStack, data);
    }
    int Pop(struct AdvancedStack *S ){
        int temp;
```

```
        if(IsEmptyStack(S→elementStack))
                return -1;
        temp = Top (S→elementStack);
        if(Top(S→minStack) == Pop(S→elementStack))
                Pop (S→minStack);
        return temp;
}
int GetMinimum(struct AdvancedStack *S){
        return Top(S→minStack);
}
struct AdvancedStack * AdvancedStack(){
        struct AdvancedStack *S = (struct AdvancedStack) malloc (sizeof (struct AdvancedStack));
        if(!S)
                return NULL;
        S→elementStack = CreateStack();
        S→minStack = CreateStack();
        return S;
}
```

Time complexity: O(1). Space complexity: O(n) [for Min stack]. But this algorithm has much better space usage if we rarely get a "new minimum or equal".

Problem-7   For a given array with n symbols how many stack permutations are possible?

Solution: The number of stack permutations with n symbols is represented by *Catalan number* and we will discuss this in *Dynamic Programming* chapter.

Problem-8   Given an array of characters formed with a's and b's. The string is marked with special character X which represents the middle of the list (for example: ababa...ababXbabab.....baaa). Check whether the string is palindrome.

Solution: This is one of the simplest algorithms. What we do is, start two indexes one at the beginning of the string and other at the ending of the string. Each time compare whether the values at both the indexes are same or not. If the values are not same then we say that the given string is not a palindrome. If the values are same then increment the left index and decrement the right index. Continue this process until both the indexes meet at the middle (at X) or if the string is not palindrome.

```
int IsPalindrome(char *A){
        int i=0, j = strlen(A)-1;
        while(i < j && A[i] == A[j]) {
                i++;
                j--;
        }
        if(i < j ) {
                printf("Not a Palindrome");
                return 0;
        }
        else {
                printf("Palindrome");
                return 1;
        }
}
```

Time Complexity: O(n). Space Complexity: O(1).

Problem-9   For Problem-8, if the input is in singly linked list then how do we check whether the list elements form a palindrome (That means, moving backward is not possible).

Solution: Refer *Linked Lists* chapter.

Problem-10   Can we solve Problem-8 using stacks?

Solution: Yes.

Algorithm
- Traverse the list till we encounter X as input element.
- During the traversal push all the elements (until X) on to the stack.
- For the second half of the list, compare each elements content with top of the stack. If they are same then pop the stack and go to the next element in the input list.
- If they are not same then the given string is not a palindrome.
- Continue this process until the stack is empty or the string is not a palindrome.

```
int IsPalindrome(char *A){
        int i=0;
```

```
        struct Stack S= CreateStack();
        while(A[i] != 'X') {
            Push(S, A[i]);
            i++;
        }
        i++;
        while(A[i]) {
                if(IsEmptyStack(S) || A[i] != Pop(S)) {
                    printf("Not a Palindrome");
                    return 0;
                }
                i++;
        }
        return IsEmptyStack(S);
}
```

Time Complexity: $O(n)$. Space Complexity: $O(n/2) \approx O(n)$.

Problem-11   Given a stack, how to reverse the elements of stack using only stack operations (push & pop)?

Solution: Algorithm
- First pop all the elements of the stack till it becomes empty.
- For each upward step in recursion, insert the element at the bottom of stack.

```
void ReverseStack(struct Stack *S){
    int data;
    if(IsEmptyStack(S))
        return;
    data = Pop(S);
    ReverseStack(S);
    InsertAtBottom(S, data);
}
void InsertAtBottom(struct Stack *S, int data){
    int temp;
    if(IsEmptyStack(S)) {
        Push(S, data);
        return;
    }
    temp = Pop(S);
    InsertAtBottom(S, data);
    Push(S, temp);
}
```

Time Complexity: $O(n^2)$. Space Complexity: $O(n)$, for recursive stack.

Problem-12   Show how to implement one queue efficiently using two stacks. Analyze the running time of the queue operations.

Solution: Refer *Queues* chapter.

Problem-13   Show how to implement one stack efficiently using two queues. Analyze the running time of the stack operations.

Solution: Refer *Queues* chapter.

Problem-14   How do we implement 2 stacks using only one array? Our stack routines should not indicate an exception unless every slot in the array is used?

Solution:

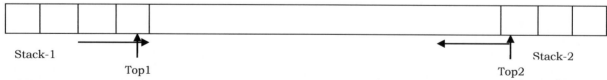

Stack-1   Top1   Top2   Stack-2

Algorithm:
- Start two indexes one at the left end and other at the right end.
- The left index simulates the first stack and the right index simulates the second stack.
- If we want to push an element into the first stack then put the element at left index.
- Similarly, if we want to push an element into the second stack then put the element at right index.
- First stack gets grows towards right, second stack grows towards left.

Time Complexity of push and pop for both stacks is $O(1)$. Space Complexity is $O(1)$.

Problem-15   3 stacks in one array: How to implement 3 stacks in one array?

Solution: For this problem, there could be other way of solving it. Given below is one such possibility and it works as long as there is an empty space in the array.

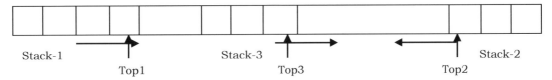

To implement 3 stacks we keep the following information.
- The index of the first stack (Top1): this indicates the size of the first stack.
- The index of the second stack (Top2): this indicates the size of the second stack.
- Starting index of the third stack (base address of third stack).
- Top index of the third stack.

Now, let us define the push and pop operations for this implementation.

Pushing:
- For pushing on to the first stack, we need to see if adding a new element causes it to bump into the third stack. If so, try to shift the third stack upwards. Insert the new element at (start1 + Top1).
- For pushing to the second stack, we need to see if adding a new element causes it to bump into the third stack. If so, try to shift the third stack downward. Insert the new element at (start2 – Top2).
- When pushing to the third stack, see if it bumps the second stack. If so, try to shift the third stack downward and try pushing again. Insert the new element at (start3 + Top3).

Time Complexity: O(n). Since, we may need to adjust the third stack. Space Complexity: O(1).

Popping: For popping, we don't need to shift, just decrement the size of the appropriate stack.

Time Complexity: O(1). Space Complexity: O(1).

```cpp
#include <iostream>
#include <vector>
using namespace std;

const int STACK_SIZE = 20;
static vector<int> stk;
static int stackLength[3] = {STACK_SIZE, STACK_SIZE, STACK_SIZE};

bool push(int stackNumber, int num){
    if(stackLength[stackNumber] == 0){
        cout << "Stack " << stackNumber << " is FULL " << endl;
        return false;
    }
    stackLength[stackNumber] --;
    stk.at(stackNumber * STACK_SIZE + stackLength[stackNumber]) = num;
    return true;
}
bool pop(int stackNumber, int &num){
    if(stackLength[stackNumber] == STACK_SIZE){
        cout << "Stack " << stackNumber << " is EMPTY " << endl;
        return false;
    }
    num = stk.at(stackNumber * STACK_SIZE + stackLength[stackNumber]);
    stackLength[stackNumber] ++;
    return true;
}
bool top(int stackNumber, int &num){
    if(stackLength[stackNumber] == STACK_SIZE){
        cout << "Stack " << stackNumber << " is EMPTY " << endl;
        return false;
    }
    num = stk.at(stackNumber * STACK_SIZE + stackLength[stackNumber]);
    return true;
}
int main(int argc, char* argv[]){
    stk.reserve(3 * STACK_SIZE);
    stk.resize(3 * STACK_SIZE);
    cout << "Total Stack size is: " << stk.capacity() << endl;
```

```
for(int i = 0; i < 25; i++){
    push(1, i);
}
int value;
for(int i = 0; i < 25; i++){
    top(1,value);
    cout << "Top value: " << value << endl;
    pop(1, value);
    cout << "Value: " << value << endl;
}
return 0;
}
```

Problem-16   For Problem-15, is there any other way implementing middle stack?

Solution: Yes. When either the left stack (which grows to the right) or the right stack (which grows to the left) bumps into the middle stack, we need to shift the entire middle stack to make room. The same happens if a push on the middle stack causes it to bump into the right stack. To solve the above-mentioned problem (number of shifts) what we can do is, alternating pushes could be added at alternating sides of the middle list (For example, even elements are pushed to the left, odd elements are pushed to the right). This would keep the middle stack balanced in the center of the array but it would still need to be shifted when it bumps into the left or right stack, whether by growing on its own or by the growth of a neighboring stack.

We can optimize the initial locations of the three stacks if they grow/shrink at different rates and if they have different average sizes. For example, suppose one stack doesn't change much. If you put it at the left then the middle stack will eventually get pushed against it and leave a gap between the middle and right stacks, which grow toward each other. If they collide, then it's likely you've run out of space in the array. There is no change in the time complexity but the average number of shifts will get reduced.

Problem-17   Multiple (m) stacks in one array: Similar to Problem-15, what if we want to implement m stacks in one array?

Solution: Let us assume that array indexes are from 1 to n. Similar to the discussion of Problem-15, to implement m stacks in one array, we divide the array into m parts (as shown below). The size of each part is $\frac{n}{m}$.

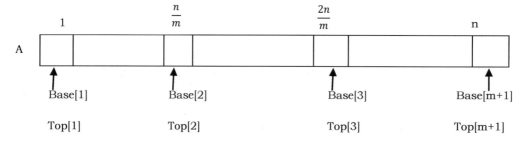

From the above representation we can see that, first stack is starting at index 1 (starting index is stored in Base[1]), second stack is starting at index $\frac{n}{m}$ (starting index is stored in Base[2]), third stack is starting at index $\frac{2n}{m}$ (starting index is stored in Base[3]) and so on. Similar to *Base* array, let us assume that *Top* array stores the top indexes for each of the stack. Consider the following terminology for the discussion.

- Top[i], for $1 \le i \le m$ will point to the topmost element of the stack i.
- If Base[i] == Top[i], then we can say the stack i is empty.
- If Top[i] == Base[i+1], then we can say the stack i is full.
  Initially Base[i] = Top[i] = $\frac{n}{m}(i-1)$, for $1 \le i \le m$.
- The ith stack grows from Base[i]+1 to Base[i+1].

Pushing on to i^{th} stack:

1) For pushing on to the ith stack, we check whether top of ith stack is pointing to Base[i+1] (this case defines that i^{th} stack is full). That means, we need to see if adding a new element causes it to bump into the $i+1^{th}$ stack. If so, try to shift the stacks from $i+1^{th}$ stack to m^{th} stack towards right. Insert the new element at (Base[i] + Top[i]).
2) If right shifting is not possible then try shifting the stacks from 1 to $i-1^{th}$ stack towards left.
3) If both of them are not possible then we can say that all stacks are full.

```
void Push(int StackID, int data) {
    if(Top[i] == Base[i+1])
        Print i^th Stack is full and does the necessary action (shifting);
    Top[i] = Top[i]+1;
    A[Top[i]] = data;
```

```
        }
```

Time Complexity: O(n). Since, we may need to adjust the stacks. Space Complexity: O(1).

Popping from i^{th} stack: For popping, we don't need to shift, just decrement the size of the appropriate stack. The only case to check is stack empty case.

```
int Pop(int StackID) {
    if(Top[i] == Base[i])
        Print i^{th} Stack is empty;
    return  A[Top[i]--];
}
```

Time Complexity: O(1). Space Complexity: O(1).

Problem-18   Consider an empty stack of integers. Let the numbers 1, 2, 3, 4, 5, 6 be pushed on to this stack only in the order they appeared from left to right. Let S indicates a push and X indicate a pop operation. Can they be permuted in to the order 325641(output) and order 154623? (If a permutation is possible give the order string of operations.

Solution: SSSXXSSXSXXX outputs 325641. 154623 cannot be output as 2 is pushed much before 3 so can appear only after 3 is output.

Problem-19   Suppose there are two singly linked lists, which intersect at some point and become a single linked list. The head or start pointers of both the lists are known, but the intersecting node is not known. Also, the number of nodes in each of the list before they intersect are unknown and both list may have it different. *List*1 may have n nodes before it reaches intersection point and *List*2 might have m nodes before it reaches intersection point where m and n may be $m = n, m < n$ or $m > n$. Can we find the merging point using stacks?

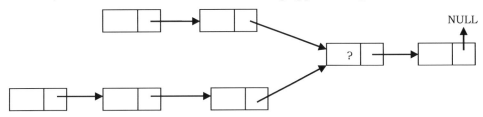

Solution: Yes. For algorithm refer *Linked Lists* chapter.

Problem-20   Earlier in this chapter, we discussed that for dynamic array implementation of stack, 'repeated doubling' approach is used. For the same problem what is the complexity if we create a new array whose size is $n + K$ instead of doubling?

Solution: Let us assume that the initial stack size is 0. For simplicity let us assume that $K = 10$. For inserting the element we create a new array whose size is $0 + 10 = 10$. Similarly, after 10 elements we again create a new array whose size is $10 + 10 = 20$ and this process continues at values: $30, 40 \ldots$ That means, for a given n value, we are creating the new arrays at: $\frac{n}{10}, \frac{n}{20}, \frac{n}{30}, \frac{n}{40} \ldots$ The total number of copy operations is:

$$= \frac{n}{10} + \frac{n}{20} + \frac{n}{30} + \cdots 1 = \frac{n}{10}\left(\frac{1}{1} + \frac{1}{2} + \frac{1}{3} + \cdots \frac{1}{n}\right) = \frac{n}{10} log n \approx O(nlogn)$$

If we are performing n push operations, the cost of per operation is O($log n$).

Problem-21   **Finding Spans:** Given an array A, the span $S[i]$ of $A[i]$ is the maximum number of consecutive elements $A[j]$ immediately preceding $A[i]$ and such that $A[j] \leq A[i]$?
    Otherway: Given an array A of integers, find the maximum of $i - j$ subjected to the constraint of $A[j] < A[i]$.

Solution:

Day: Index i	Input Array A[i]	S[i]: Span of A[i]
0	6	1
1	3	1
2	4	2
3	5	3
4	2	1

This is a very common problem in stock markets to find the peaks. Spans are used in financial analysis (E.g., stock at 52-week high). The span of a stock price on a certain day, i, is the maximum number of consecutive days (up to the current day) the price of the stock has been less than or equal to its price on i. As an example, let us consider the table and the corresponding spans diagram. In the figure the arrows indicates the length of the spans. Now, let us concentrate on the algorithm for finding the spans. One simple way is, each day, check how many contiguous days are with less stock price than current price.

Algorithm:

```
FindingSpans(int A[], int n) {
```

```
//Input: array A of n integers, Output: array S of spans of A
int i, j, S[n]; //new array of n integers;
for (i = 0; i < n; i++) {                              //Executes n times
    j = 1;                                             n
    while j <= i && A[i] > A[i-j]                      1 + 2 + ...+ (n − 1)
        j = j + 1;                                     1 + 2 + ...+ (n − 1)
    S[i] = j;                                          n
}
return S;                                              1
}
```

Time Complexity: $O(n^2)$. Space Complexity: $O(1)$.

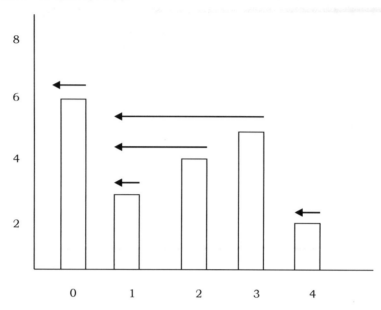

Problem-22   Can we improve the complexity of Problem-21?

Solution: From the example above, we can see that the span $S[i]$ on day i can be easily calculated if we know the closest day preceding i, such that the price is greater than on that day than the price on day i. Let us call such a day as P. If such a day exists then the span is now defined as $S[i] = i - P$.

Algorithm:

```
FindingSpans(int A[], int n) {
    struct stack *D = CreateStack();
    int P;
    for (int i = 0 i< n; i++) {
        while (!IsEmptyStack(D) && A[i] > A[Top(D)])
            Pop(D);
        if(IsEmptyStack(D))
            P = -1;
        else    P = Top(D);

        S[i] = i-P;
        Push(D, i);
    }
    return S;
}
```

Time Complexity: Each index of the array is pushed into the stack exactly one and also popped from the stack at most once. The statements in the while loop are executed at most n times. Even though the algorithm has nested loops, the complexity is $O(n)$ as the inner loop is executing only n times during the course of algorithm (trace out an example and see how many times the inner loop is becoming success). Space Complexity: $O(n)$ [for stack].

Problem-23   **Largest rectangle under histogram:** A histogram is a polygon composed of a sequence of rectangles aligned at a common base line. For simplicity, assume that the rectangles are having equal widths but may have different heights. For example, the figure on the left shows the histogram that consists of rectangles with the heights 3, 2, 5, 6, 1, 4, 4, measured in units where 1 is the width of the rectangles. Here our problem is: given an array with heights of rectangles (assuming width is 1), we need to find the largest rectabgle possible. For the given example the largest rectangle is the shared part.

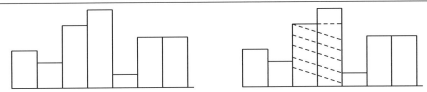

Solution: A straightforward answer is to go for each bar in the histogram and find the maximum possible area in histogram for it. Finally, find the maximum of these values. This will require $O(n^2)$.

Problem-24   For Problem-23, can we improve the time complexity?

Solution: Linear search using a stack of incomplete subproblems: There are many ways of solving this problem. *Judge* has given a nice algorithm for this problem which is based on stack. Process the elements in left-to-right order and maintain a stack of information about started but yet unfinished sub histograms.

If the stack is empty, open a new subproblem by pushing the element onto the stack. Otherwise compare it to the element on top of the stack. If the new one is greater we again push it. If the new one is equal we skip it. In all these cases, we continue with the next new element. If the new one is less, we finish the topmost subproblem by updating the maximum area with respect to the element at the top of the stack. Then, we discard the element at the top, and repeat the procedure keeping the current new element.

This way, all subproblems are finished until the stack becomes empty, or its top element is less than or equal to the new element, leading to the actions described above. If all elements have been processed, and the stack is not yet empty, we finish the remaining subproblems by updating the maximum area with respect to the elements at the top.

```
struct StackItem {
        int height;
        int index;
};
int MaxRectangleArea(int A[], int n) {
        int i, maxArea=-1, top = -1, left, currentArea;
        struct StackItem *S = (struct StackItem *) malloc(sizeof(struct StackItem) * n);
        for(i=0; i<=n; i++) {
                while(top >= 0 && (i==n || S[top]→data > A[i])) {
                        if(top > 0)
                                left = S[top-1]→index;
                        else  left = -1;
                        currentArea = (i – left-1) * S[top]→data;
                        --top;
                        if(currentArea > maxArea)
                                maxArea = currentArea;
                }
                if(i<n) {   ++top;
                        S[top]→data = A[i];
                        S[top]→index = i;
                }
        }
        return maxArea;
}
```

In first impression, this solution seems to be having $O(n^2)$ complexity. But if we look carefully, every element is pushed and popped at most once and in every step of the function at least one element is pushed or popped. Since the amount of work for the decisions and the update is constant, the complexity of the algorithm is $O(n)$ by amortized analysis. Space Complexity: $O(n)$ [for stack].

Problem-25   On a given machine, how do you check whether the stack grows up or down?

Solution: Try noting down the address of a local variable. Call another function with a local variable declared in it and check the address of that local variable and compare.

```
int testStackGrowth() {
    int temporary;
    stackGrowth(&temporary);
    exit(0);
}
void stackGrowth(int *temp){
    int temp2;
    printf("\nAddress of first local valirable: %u", temp);
    printf("\nAddress of second local: %u", &temp2);
    if(temp < &temp2)
        printf("\n Stack is growing downwards");
    else printf("\n Stack is growing upwards");
```

```
}
```

Time Complexity: O(1). Space Complexity: O(1).

Problem-26   Given a stack of integers, how do check whether each successive pair of numbers in the stack is consecutive or not. The pairs can be increasing or decreasing, and if the stack has an odd number of elements, the element at the top is left out of a pair. For example, if the stack of elements are [4, 5, -2, -3, 11, 10, 5, 6, 20], then the output should be true because each of the pairs (4, 5), (-2, -3), (11, 10), and (5, 6) consists of consecutive numbers.

Solution: Refer *Queues* chapter.

Problem-27   Recursively remove all adjacent duplicates: Given a string of characters, recursively remove adjacent duplicate characters from string. The output string should not have any adjacent duplicates.

Input: careermonk, *Output*: camonk	*Input*: Mississippi, *Output*: m

Solution: This solution runs with the concept of in-place stack. When element on stack doesn't match to the current character, we add it to stack. When it matches to stack top, we skip characters until the element match the top of stack and remove the element from stack.

```
void removeAdjacentDuplicates(char *str){
    int stkptr=-1;
    int i=0;
    int len=strlen(str);
    while (i<len){
        if (stkptr == -1 || str[stkptr]!=str[i]){
            stkptr++;
            str[stkptr]=str[i];
            i++;
        }else {
            while(i < len&& str[stkptr]==str[i])
                i++;
            stkptr--;
        }
    }
    str[stkptr+1]='\0';
}
```

Time Complexity: O(*n*). Space Complexity: O(1) as the stack simulation is done inplace.

Problem-28   Given an array of elements, replace every element with nearest greater element on the right of that element.

Solution: One simplest approach would involve scanning the array elements and for each of the element, scan the remaining elements and find the nearest greater element in that.

```
void replaceWithNearestGreaterElement(int A[], int n){
    int nextNearestGreater = INT_MIN;
    int i = 0, j = 0;
    for (i=0; i<n; i++){
        nextNearestGreater = -INT_MIN;
        for (j = i+1; j<n; j++){
            if (A[i] < A[j]){
                nextNearestGreater = A[j];
                break;
            }
        }
        printf("For the element %d, %d is the nearest greater element\n", A[i], nextNearestGreater);
    }
}
```

Time Complexity: O(n^2). Space Complexity: O(1).

Problem-29   For the Problem-28, can we improve the complexity?

Solution: Create a stack and push the first element. For rest of the elements, mark the current element as *nextNearestGreater*. If stack is not empty, then pop an element from stack and compare it with *nextNearestGreater*. If *nextNearestGreater* is greater than the popped element, then *nextNearestGreater* is the next greater element for the popped element. Keep popping from the stack while the popped element is smaller than nextNearestGreater. *nextNearestGreater* becomes the next greater element for all such popped elements. If *nextNearestGreater* is smaller than the popped element, then push the popped element back.

```
void replaceWithNearestGreaterElement(int A[], int n){
    int i = 0;
```

```
    struct Stack *S = CreateStack();
    int element, nextNearestGreater;
    Push(S, A[0]);
    for (i=1; i<n; i++){
        nextNearestGreater = A[i];
        if (!IsEmptyStack(S)){
            element = Pop(S);
          while (element < nextNearestGreater){
            printf("For the element %d, %d is the nearest greater element\n", A[i], nextNearestGreater);
            if(IsEmptyStack(S))
              break;
            element = Pop(S);
          }
          if (element > nextNearestGreater)
            Push(S, element);
        }
        Push(S, nextNearestGreater);
    }
    while (!IsEmptyStack(S)){
        element = Pop(S);
        nextNearestGreater = -INT_MIN;
        printf("For the element %d, %d is the nearest greater element\n", A[i], nextNearestGreater);
    }
}
```

Time Complexity: $O(n)$. Space Complexity: $O(n)$.

Problem-30   How do you sort a stack in increasing order using the operations push, pop, top, and empty?

Solution:

```
#include <iostream>
#include <stack>
using namespace std;
void sortingStack(stack<int> &stk){
    int data, min;
    stack<int> t;
    while(!stk.empty()){
        data = stk.top();
        stk.pop();
        t.push(data);
    }
    while(!t.empty()){
        min = t.top();
        t.pop();
        while(!stk.empty() && stk.top() > min){
            data = stk.top();
            stk.pop();
            t.push(data);
        }
        stk.push(min);
    }
}
int main(int argc, char* argv[]){
    stack<int> stk;
    stk.push(3);   stk.push(1);   stk.push(2);   stk.push(2);
    stk.push(-4);   stk.push(-6);   stk.push(6);   stk.push(9);
    sortingStack(stk);
    while(!stk.empty()){
        int data;
        data = stk.top();
        stk.pop();
        cout << data << endl;
    }
    return 0;
}
```

Chapter-12

QUEUES

12.1 What is a Queue?

A queue is a data structure used for storing data (similar to Linked Lists and Stacks). In queue, the order in which data arrives is important. In general, a queue is a line of people or things waiting to be served in sequential order starting at the beginning of the line or sequence.

Definition: A *queue* is an ordered list in which insertions are done at one end (*rear*) and deletions are done at other end (*front*). The first element to be inserted is the first one to be deleted. Hence, it is called First in First out (FIFO) or Last in Last out (LILO) list.

Similar to *Stacks*, special names are given to the two changes that can be made to a queue. When an element is inserted in a queue, the concept is called *EnQueue*, and when an element is removed from the queue, the concept is called *DeQueue*. *DeQueueing* an empty queue is called *underflow* and *EnQueuing* an element in a full queue is called *overflow*. Generally, we treat them as exceptions. As an example, consider the snapshot of the queue.

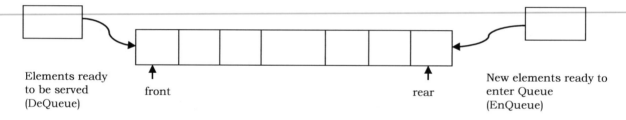

Elements ready
to be served   front   rear   New elements ready to
(DeQueue)   enter Queue
                                                                                                   (EnQueue)

12.2 How are Queues Used?

The concept of a queue can be explained by observing a line at a reservation counter. When we enter the line we stand at the end of the line and the person who is at the front of the line is the one who will be served next. He will exit the queue and be served.

As this happens, the next person will come at head of the line, will exit the queue and will be served. As each person at the head of the line keeps exiting the queue we move towards the head of the line. Finally we will reach head of the line and we will exit the queue and be served. This behavior is very useful in cases where there is a need to maintain the order of arrival.

12.3 Queue ADT

The following operations make a queue an ADT. Insertions and deletions in queue must follow the FIFO scheme. For simplicity we assume the elements are integers.

Main Queue Operations

- EnQueue(int data): Inserts an element at the end of the queue
- int DeQueue(): Removes and returns the element at the front of the queue

Auxiliary Queue Operations

- int Front(): Returns the element at front without removing it
- int QueueSize(): Returns the number of elements stored in the queue
- int IsEmptyQueue(): Indicates whether no elements are stored in the queue or not

12.4 Exceptions

Similar to other ADTs, executing *DeQueue* on an empty queue throws an *"Empty Queue Exception"* and executing *EnQueue* on a full queue throws an *"Full Queue Exception"*.

12.5 Applications

Following are the some of the applications that are using queues.

Direct Applications

- Operating systems schedule jobs (with equal priority) in the order of arrival (e.g., a print queue).
- Simulation of real-world queues such as lines at a ticket counter or any other first-come first-served scenario requires a queue.
- Multiprogramming.
- Asynchronous data transfer (file IO, pipes, sockets).
- Waiting times of customers at call center.
- Determining number of cashiers to have at a supermarket.

Indirect Applications

- Auxiliary data structure for algorithms
- Component of other data structures

12.6 Implementation

There are many ways (similar to Stacks) of implementing queue operations and some of the commonly used methods are listed below.

- Simple circular array based implementation
- Dynamic circular array based implementation
- Linked list implementation

Why Circular Arrays?

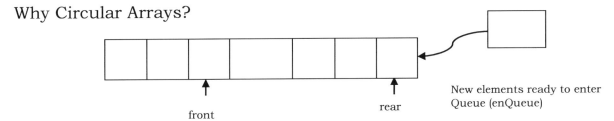

New elements ready to enter Queue (enQueue)

front   rear

First, let us see whether we can use simple arrays for implementing queues as we have done for stacks. We know that, in queues, the insertions are performed at one end and deletions are performed at other end. After performing some insertions and deletions the process becomes easy to understand. In the example shown below, it can be seen clearly that the initial slots of the array are getting wasted. So, simple array implementation for queue is not efficient. To solve this problem we assume the arrays as circular arrays. That means, we treat last element and first array elements as contiguous. With this representation, if there are any free slots at the beginning, the rear pointer can easily go to its next free slot.

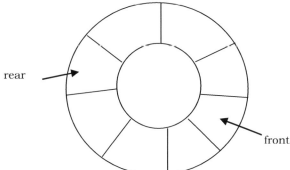

rear   front

With this representation, if there are any free slots at the beginning, the rear pointer can easily go to its next free slot.

Note: The simple circular array and dynamic circular array implementations are very similar to stack array implementations. Refer *Stacks* chapter for analysis of these implementations.

Simple Circular Array Implementation

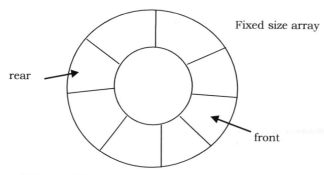

Fixed size array

rear

front

This simple implementation of Queue ADT uses an array. In the array, we add elements circularly and use two variables to keep track of start element and end element. Generally, *front* is used to indicate the start element and *rear* is used to indicate the end element in the queue. The array storing the queue elements may become full. An *EnQueue* operation will then throw a *full queue exception*. Similarly, if we try deleting an element from empty queue then it will throw *empty queue exception*.

Note: Initially, both front and rear points to -1 which indicates that the queue is empty.

```
struct ArrayQueue {
    int front, rear;
    int capacity;
    int *array;
};
struct ArrayQueue *Queue(int size) {
    struct ArrayQueue *Q = malloc(sizeof(struct ArrayQueue));
    if(!Q)
        return NULL;
    Q→capacity = size;
    Q→front = Q→rear = -1;
    Q→array= malloc(Q→capacity * sizeof(int));
    if(!Q→array) return NULL;
        return Q;
}
int IsEmptyQueue(struct ArrayQueue *Q) {
    // if the condition is true then 1 is returned else 0 is returned
    return (Q→front == -1);
}
int IsFullQueue(struct ArrayQueue *Q) {
    //if the condition is true then 1 is returned else 0 is returned
    return ((Q→rear +1) % Q→capacity == Q→front);
}
int QueueSize() {
    return (Q→capacity - Q→front + Q→rear + 1)% Q→capacity;
}
void EnQueue(struct ArrayQueue *Q, int data) {
    if(IsFullQueue(Q))
        printf("Queue Overflow");
    else {
        Q→rear = (Q→rear+1) % Q→capacity;
        Q→ array[Q→rear]= data;
        if(Q→front == -1)
            Q→front = Q→rear;
    }
}
int DeQueue(struct ArrayQueue *Q) {
    int data = 0;//or element which does not exist in Queue
    if(IsEmptyQueue(Q)) {
        printf("Queue is Empty");
        return 0;
    }
```

```
        else {
            data = Q→array[Q→front];
            if(Q→front== Q→rear)
                Q→front= Q→rear = -1;
            else Q→front = (Q→front+1) % Q→capacity;
        }
        return data;
    }
    void DeleteQueue(struct ArrayQueue *Q) {
        if(Q) {
            if(Q→array)
                free(Q→array);
            free(Q);
        }
    }
```

Performance and Limitations

Performance

Let n be the number of elements in the queue:

Space Complexity (for n EnQueue operations)	$O(n)$
Time Complexity of EnQueue()	$O(1)$
Time Complexity of DeQueue()	$O(1)$
Time Complexity of IsEmptyQueue()	$O(1)$
Time Complexity of IsFullQueue()	$O(1)$
Time Complexity of QueueSize()	$O(1)$
Time Complexity of DeleteQueue()	$O(1)$

Limitations: The maximum size of the queue must be defined a prior and cannot be changed. Trying to *EnQueue* a new element into a full queue causes an implementation-specific exception.

Dynamic Circular Array Implementation

```
    struct DynArrayQueue {
        int front, rear;
        int capacity;
        int *array;
    };
    struct DynArrayQueue *CreateDynQueue() {
        struct DynArrayQueue *Q = malloc(sizeof(struct DynArrayQueue));
        if(!Q)
            return NULL;
        Q→capacity = 1;
        Q→front = Q→rear = -1;
        Q→array= malloc(Q→capacity * sizeof(int));
        if(!Q→array)
            return NULL;
        return Q;
    }
    int IsEmptyQueue(struct DynArrayQueue *Q) {
        // if the condition is true then 1 is returned else 0 is returned
        return (Q→front == -1);
    }
    int IsFullQueue(struct DynArrayQueue *Q) {
        //if the condition is true then 1 is returned else 0 is returned
        return ((Q→rear +1) % Q→capacity == Q→front);
    }
    int QueueSize() {
        return (Q→capacity - Q→front + Q→rear + 1)% Q→capacity;
    }
    void EnQueue(struct DynArrayQueue *Q, int data) {
        if(IsFullQueue(Q))
            ResizeQueue(Q);
        Q→rear = (Q→rear+1)% Q→capacity;
```

```
            Q→ array[Q→rear]= data;
            if(Q→front == -1)
                Q→front = Q→rear;
        }
        void ResizeQueue(struct DynArrayQueue *Q) {
            int size = Q→capacity;
            Q→capacity = Q→capacity*2;
            Q→array = realloc (Q→array, Q→capacity);
            if(!Q→array) {
                printf("Memory Error");
                return;
            }
            if(Q→front > Q→rear ) {
                for(int i=0; i < Q→front; i++) {
                    Q→array[i+size] =Q→array[i];
                }
                Q→rear = Q→rear + size;
            }
        }
        int DeQueue(struct DynArrayQueue *Q) {
            int data = 0;//or element which does not exist in Queue
            if(IsEmptyQueue(Q)) {
                printf("Queue is Empty");
                return 0;
            }
            else {
                data = Q→array[Q→front];
                if(Q→front== Q→rear)
                    Q→front= Q→rear = -1;
                else
                    Q→front = (Q→front+1) % Q→capacity;
            }
            return data;
        }
        void DeleteQueue(struct DynArrayQueue *Q) {
            if(Q) {
                if(Q→array)
                    free(Q→array);
                free(Q→array);
            }
        }
```

Performance

Let n be the number of elements in the queue.

Space Complexity (for n EnQueue operations)	O(n)
Time Complexity of EnQueue()	O(1) (Average)
Time Complexity of DeQueue()	O(1)
Time Complexity of QueueSize()	O(1)
Time Complexity of IsEmptyQueue()	O(1)
Time Complexity of IsFullQueue()	O(1)
Time Complexity of QueueSize()	O(1)
Time Complexity of DeleteQueue()	O(1)

Linked List Implementation

Another way of implementing queues is by using Linked lists. *EnQueue* operation is implemented by inserting element at the ending of the list. *DeQueue* operation is implemented by deleting an element from the beginning of the list.

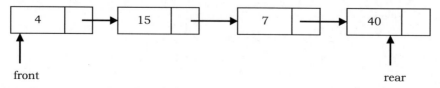

```
struct ListNode {                              struct Queue {
    int data;                                      struct ListNode *front;
    struct ListNode *next;                         struct ListNode *rear;
};                                             };

struct Queue *CreateQueue() {
    struct Queue *Q;
    struct ListNode *temp;
    Q = malloc(sizeof(struct Queue));
    if(!Q)
        return NULL;
    temp = malloc(sizeof(struct ListNode));
    Q→front = Q→rear = NULL;
    return Q;
}
int IsEmptyQueue(struct Queue *Q) {
    // if the condition is true then 1 is returned else 0 is returned
    return (Q→front == NULL);
}
void EnQueue(struct Queue *Q, int data) {
    struct ListNode *newNode;
    newNode = malloc(sizeof(struct ListNode));
    if(!newNode)
        return NULL;

    newNode→data = data;
    newNode→next = NULL;
    if(Q→rear) Q→rear→next = newNode;
    Q→rear = newNode;
    if(Q→front == NULL)
        Q→front = Q→rear;
}
int DeQueue(struct Queue *Q) {
    int data = 0;       //or element which does not exist in Queue
    struct ListNode *temp;
    if(IsEmptyQueue(Q)) {
        printf("Queue is empty");
        return 0;
    }
    else {
        temp = Q→front;
        data = Q→front→data;
        Q→front== Q→front→next;
        free(temp);
    }
    return data;
}
void DeleteQueue(struct Queue *Q) {
    struct ListNode *temp;
    while(Q) {
        temp = Q;
        Q = Q→next;
        free(temp);
    }
    free(Q);
}
```

Performance

Let n be the number of elements in the queue, then

Space Complexity (for n EnQueue operations)	O(n)
Time Complexity of EnQueue()	O(1) (Average)
Time Complexity of DeQueue()	O(1)
Time Complexity of IsEmptyQueue()	O(1)
Time Complexity of DeleteQueue()	O(1)

Comparison of Implementations

Note: Comparison is very similar to stack implementations and *Stacks* chapter.

12.7 Problems on Queues

Problem-1   Give an algorithm for reversing a queue Q. To access the queue, you are only allowed to use the methods of queue ADT.

Solution:

```
void ReverseQueue(struct Queue *Q) {
    struct Stack *S = CreateStack();
    while (!IsEmptyQueue(Q))
        Push(S, DeQueue(Q))
    while (!IsEmptyStack(S))
        EnQueue(Q, Pop(S));
}
```

Time Complexity: O(n).

Problem-2   How can you implement a queue using two stacks?

Solution: Let *stack*1 and *stack*2 be the two stacks to be used in the implementation of queue. All we have to do is to define the EnQueue and DeQueue operations for the queue.

EnQueue Algorithm

- Just push on to stack *stack*1

Time Complexity: O(1).

DeQueue Algorithm

- If stack S2 is not empty then pop from *stack*2 and return that element.
- If stack is empty, then transfer all elements from *stack*1 to *stack*2 and pop the top element from *stack*2 and return that popped element [we can optimize the code little by transferring only $n - 1$ elements from *stack*1 to *stack*2 and pop the nth element from *stack*1 and return that popped element].
- If stack *stack*1 is also empty then throw error.

Time Complexity: From the algorithm, if the stack *stack*2 is not empty then the complexity is O(1). If the stack *stack*2 is empty then, we need to transfer the elements from stack1 to *stack*2. But if we carefully observe, the number of transferred elements and the number of popped elements from *stack*2 are equal. Due to this the average complexity of pop operation in this case is O(1). Amortized complexity of pop operation is O(1).

```
#include <iostream>
#include <stack>
using namespace std;

stack<int> stack1;
stack<int> stack2;

bool enQueue(int value){
    stack1.push(value);
    return true;
}
bool deQueue(int &value){
    int data;
    if(!stack2.empty()){
        value = stack2.top();
        stack2.pop();
        return true;
    }
    while(!stack1.empty()){
        data = stack1.top();
        stack1.pop();
        stack2.push(data);
    }
    if(stack2.empty())
        return false;
    value = stack2.top();
    stack2.pop();
```

```
        return true;
    }
    bool que_peek(int &value){
        int data;
        while(!stack1.empty()){
            data = stack2.top();
            stack2.pop();
            stack1.push(data);
        }
        if(stack2.empty())
            return false;
        value = stack2.top();
        return true;
    }
    bool isQueueEmpty(){
        return (stack1.empty() && stack2.empty()) ? true : false;
    }
    int main(int argc, char* argv[]){
        enQueue(11);
        enQueue(22);
        enQueue(33);
        enQueue(44);
        int data;
        while(!isQueueEmpty()){
            deQueue(data);
            cout << data << endl;
        }
        return 0;
    }
```

Problem-3   Show how can you efficiently implement one stack using two queues. Analyze the running time of the stack operations.

Solution: Let S1 and S2 be the two stacks to be used in the implementation of queue. All we have to do is to define the push and pop operations for the stack.

```
struct Stack {
    struct Queue *Q1;
    struct Queue *Q2;
}
```

In the algorithms below, we make sure that one queue is always empty.

Push Operation Algorithm: Insert the element in whichever queue is not empty.
- Check whether queue Q1 is empty or not. If Q1 is empty then Enqueue the element into Q2.
- Otherwise EnQueue the element into Q1.

```
void Push(struct Stack *S, int data) {
    if(IsEmptyQueue(S→Q1))
            EnQueue(S→Q2, data);
    else    EnQueue(S→Q1, data);
}
```

Time Complexity: O(1).

Pop Operation Algorithm: Transfer $n-1$ elements to the other queue and delete last from queue for performing pop operation.
- If queue Q1 is not empty then transfer $n-1$ elements from Q1 to Q2 and then, DeQueue the last element of Q1 and return it.
- If queue Q2 is not empty then transfer $n-1$ elements from Q2 to Q1 and then, DeQueue the last element of Q2 and return it.

```
int Pop(struct Stack *S) {
    int i, size;
    if(IsEmptyQueue(S→Q2)) {
            size = size(S→Q1);
            i = 0;
```

```
                        while(i < size-1) {
                                EnQueue(S→Q2, DeQueue(S→Q1));
                                i++;
                        }
                        return DeQueue(S→Q1);
                }
            else {
                    size = size(S→Q2);
                    while(i < size-1) {
                            EnQueue(S→Q1, DeQueue(S→Q2));
                            i++;
                    }
                    return DeQueue(S→Q2);
            }
    }
```

Time Complexity: Running time of pop operation is $O(n)$ as each time pop is called, we are transferring all the elements from one queue to the other.

Problem-4   **Maximum sum in sliding window:** Given array A[] with sliding window of size w which is moving from the very left of the array to the very right. Assume that we can only see the w numbers in the window. Each time the sliding window moves rightwards by one position. For example: The array is [1 3 -1 -3 5 3 6 7], and w is 3.

Window position	Max
[1 3 -1] -3 5 3 6 7	3
1 [3 -1 -3] 5 3 6 7	3
1 3 [-1 -3 5] 3 6 7	5
1 3 -1 [-3 5 3] 6 7	5
1 3 -1 -3 [5 3 6] 7	6
1 3 -1 -3 5 [3 6 7]	7

Input: A long array A[], and a window width w.
Output: An array B[], B[i] is the maximum value from A[i] to A[i+w-1]
Requirement: Find a good optimal way to get B[i]

Solution: This problem can be solved with doubly ended queue (which support insertion and deletions at both ends). Refer *Priority Queues* chapter for algorithms.

Problem-5   What is the most appropriate data structure to print elements of queue in reverse order?

Solution: Stack.

Problem-6   Implement doubly ended queues. A double-ended queue is an abstract data structure that implements a queue for which elements can only be added to or removed from the front (head) or back (tail). It is also often called a head-tail linked list.

Solution:

```
void pushBackDEQ(struct ListNode **head, int data){
    struct ListNode *newNode = (struct ListNode*) malloc(sizeof(struct ListNode));
    newNode→data = data;
    if(*head == NULL){
        *head = newNode;
        (*head)→next = *head;
        (*head)→prev = *head;
    }
    else{
        newNode→prev = (*head)→prev;
        newNode→next = *head;
        (*head)→prev→next = newNode;
        (*head)→prev = newNode;
    }
}
void pushFrontDEQ(struct ListNode **head, int data){
    pushBackDEQ(head,data);
    *head = (*head)→prev;
}
int popBackDEQ(struct ListNode **head){
```

```
        int data;
        if( (*head)→prev == *head ){
            data = (*head)→data;
            free(*head);
            *head = NULL;
        }
        else{
            struct ListNode *newTail = (*head)→prev→prev;
            data = (*head)→prev→data;
            newTail→next = *head;
            free((*head)→prev);
            (*head) →prev = newTail;
        }
        return data;
    }
    int popFront(struct ListNode **head){
        int data;
        *head = (*head)→next;
        data = popBackDEQ(head);
        return data;
    }
```

Problem-7   Given a stack of integers, how do check whether each successive pair of numbers in the stack is consecutive or not. The pairs can be increasing or decreasing, and if the stack has an odd number of elements, the element at the top is left out of a pair. For example, if the stack of elements are [4, 5, -2, -3, 11, 10, 5, 6, 20], then the output should be true because each of the pairs (4, 5), (-2, -3), (11, 10), and (5, 6) consists of consecutive numbers.

Solution:

```
int checkStackPairwiseOrder(struct Stack *s) {
    struct Queue *q = CreateQueue();
    int pairwiseOrdered = 1;
    while (!isEmptyStack(s))
        EnQueue(q, Pop(s));
    while (!IsEmptyQueue(q))
        Push(s, DeQueue(q));
    while (!isEmptyStack(s)) {
        int n = Pop(s);
        EnQueue(q, n);
        if (!isEmptyStack(s)) {
            int m = Pop(s);
            EnQueue(q, m);
            if (abs(n - m) != 1) {
                pairwiseOrdered = 0;
            }
        }
    }
    while (!IsEmptyQueue(q))
        Push(s, DeQueue(q));
    return pairwiseOrdered;
}
```

Time Complexity: $O(n)$. Space Complexity: $O(n)$.

Problem-8   Given a queue of integers, rearrange the elements by interleaving the first half of the list with the second half of the list. For example, suppose a queue stores the following sequence of values: [11, 12, 13, 14, 15, 16, 17, 18, 19, 20]. Consider the two halves of this list: first half: [11, 12, 13, 14, 15] second half: [16, 17, 18, 19, 20]. These are combined in an alternating fashion to form a sequence of interleave pairs: the first values from each half (11 and 16), then the second values from each half (12 and 17), then the third values from each half (13 and 18), and so on. In each pair, the value from the first half appears before the value from the second half. Thus, after the call, the queue stores the following values: [11, 16, 12, 17, 13, 18, 14, 19, 15, 20].

Solution:

```
void interLeavingQueue(struct Queue *q) {
    if (Size(q) % 2 != 0)
        return;
    struct Stack *s = CreateStack();
    int halfSize = Size(q) / 2;
```

```
    for (int i = 0; i < halfSize; i++)
        Push(s, DeQueue(q));
    while (!isEmptyStack(s))
        EnQueue(q, Pop(s));
    for (int i = 0; i < halfSize; i++)
        EnQueue(q, DeQueue(q));
    for (int i = 0; i < halfSize; i++)
        Push(s, DeQueue(q));
    while (!isEmptyStack(s)) {
        EnQueue(q, Pop(s));
        EnQueue(q, DeQueue(q));
    }
}
```

Time Complexity: O(n). Space Complexity: O(n).

Problem-9   Given an integer k and a queue of integers, how do you reverse the order of the first k elements of the queue, leaving the other elements in the same relative order? For example, if k=4 and queue has the elements [10, 20, 30, 40, 50, 60, 70, 80, 90]; the output should be [40, 30, 20, 10, 50, 60, 70, 80, 90].

Solution:

```
void reverseQueueFirstKElements(int k, struct Queue *q) {
    if (q == Null || k > Size(q)) {
        return;
    }
    else if (k > 0) {
        struct Stack *s = CreateStack();
        for (int i = 0; i < k; i++) {
            Push(s, DeQueue(q));
        }
        while (!isEmptyStack(s)) {
            EnQueue(q, Pop(s));
        }
        for (int i = 0; i < Size(q) - k; i++) { // wrap around rest of elements
            EnQueue(q, DeQueue(q));
        }
    }
}
```

Time Complexity: O(n). Space Complexity: O(n).

Chapter-13

TREES

13.1 What is a Tree?

A *tree* is a data structure similar to a linked list but instead of each node pointing simply to the next node in a linear fashion, each node points to a number of nodes. Tree is an example of non-linear data structures. A *tree* structure is a way of representing the hierarchical nature of a structure in a graphical form.

In trees ADT (Abstract Data Type), order of the elements is not important. If we need ordering information linear data structures like linked lists, stacks, queues, etc. can be used.

13.2 Glossary

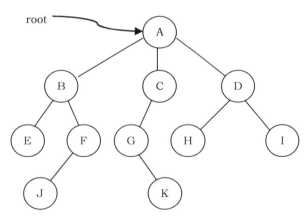

- The *root* of a tree is the node with no parents. There can be at most one root node in a tree (node *A* in the above example).

- An *edge* refers to the link from parent to child (all links in the figure).

- A node with no children is called *leaf* node (E, J, K, H and I).

- Children of same parent are called *siblings* (B, C, D are siblings of A and E, F are the siblings of B).

- A node p is an *ancestor* of node q if there exists a path from *root* to q and p appears on the path. The node q is called a *descendant* of p. For example, A, C and G are the ancestors of K.

- The *depth* of a node is the length of the path from the root to the node (depth of G is 2, $A - C - G$).

- The *height* of a node is the length of the path from that node to the deepest node. The height of a tree is the length of the path from the root to the deepest node in the tree. A (rooted) tree with only one node (the root) has a height of zero. In the previous example, height of B is 2 ($B - F - J$).

- *Height of the tree* is the maximum height among all the nodes in the tree and *depth of the tree* is the maximum depth among all the nodes in the tree. For a given tree depth and height returns the same value. But for individual nodes we may get different results.

- Size of a node is the number of descendants it has including itself (size of the subtree C is 3).

- Set of all nodes at a given depth is called *level* of the tree (B, C and D are same level). The root node is at level zero.

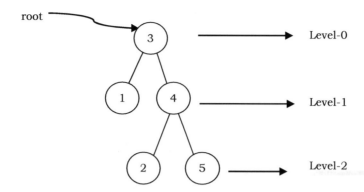

- If every node in a tree has only one child (except leaf nodes) then we call such trees *skew trees*. If every node has only left child then we call them as *left skew trees*. Similarly, if every node has only right child then we call them *right skew trees*.

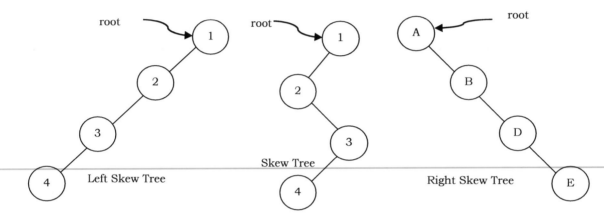

13.3 Binary Trees

A tree is called *binary tree* if each node has zero child, one child or two children. Empty tree is also a valid binary tree.

We can visualize a binary tree as consisting of a root and two disjoint binary trees, called the left and right subtrees of the root.

Generic Binary Tree

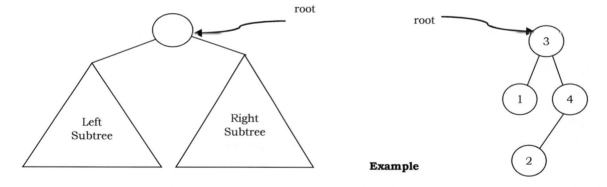

13.4 Types of Binary Trees

Strict Binary Tree: A binary tree is called *strict binary tree* if each node has exactly two children or no children.

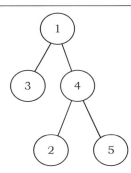

Full Binary Tree: A binary tree is called *full binary tree* if each node has exactly two children and all leaf nodes are at same level.

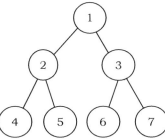

Complete Binary Tree: Before defining the *complete binary tree,* let us assume that the height of the binary tree is h. In complete binary trees, if we give numbering for the nodes by starting at root (let us say the root node has 1) then we get a complete sequence from 1 to number of nodes in the tree.

While traversing we should give numbering for NULL pointers also. A binary tree is called complete binary tree if all leaf nodes are at height h or $h-1$ and also without any missing number in the sequence.

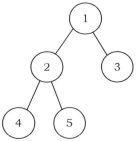

13.5 Properties of Binary Trees

For the following properties, let us assume that the height of the tree is h. Also, assume that root node is at height zero. From the below diagram we can infer the following properties:

- The number of nodes n in a full binary tree is $2^{h+1} - 1$. Since, there are h levels we need to add all nodes at each level $[2^0 + 2^1 + 2^2 + \cdots + 2^h = 2^{h+1} - 1]$.
- The number of nodes n in a complete binary tree is between 2^h (minimum) and $2^{h+1} - 1$ (maximum). For more information on this, refer *Priority Queues* chapter.
- The number of leaf nodes in a full binary tree is 2^h.
- The number of NULL links (wasted pointers) in a complete binary tree of n nodes is $n + 1$.

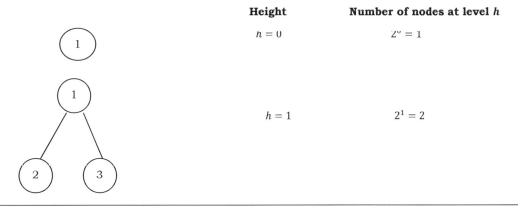

	Height	Number of nodes at level h
	$h = 0$	$2^0 = 1$
	$h = 1$	$2^1 = 2$

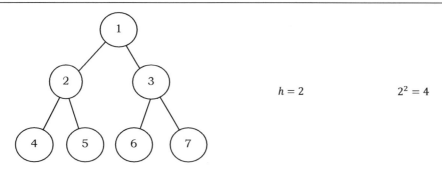

$h = 2$ $\qquad$ $2^2 = 4$

Structure of Binary Trees

Now let us define structure of the binary tree. For simplicity, assume that the data of the nodes are integers. One way to represent a node (which contains data) is to have two links which points to left and right children along with data fields as shown below:

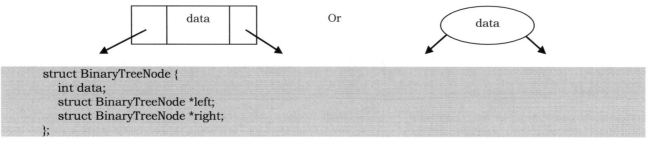

```
struct BinaryTreeNode {
    int data;
    struct BinaryTreeNode *left;
    struct BinaryTreeNode *right;
};
```

Note: In trees, the default flow is from parent to children and it is not mandatory to show directed branches. For our discussion, we assume both the representations shown below are same.

Operations on Binary Trees

Basic Operations

- Inserting an element into a tree
- Deleting an element from a tree
- Searching for an element
- Traversing the tree

Auxiliary Operations

- Finding size of the tree
- Finding height of the tree
- Finding the level which has maximum sum
- Finding least common ancestor (LCA) for a given pair of nodes and many more.

Applications of Binary Trees

Following are the some of the applications where *binary trees* play important role:

- Expression trees are used in compilers.
- Huffman coding trees that are used in data compression algorithms.
- Binary Search Tree (BST), which supports search, insertion and deletion on a collection of items in O(*logn*) (average).
- Priority Queues (PQ), which supports search and deletion of minimum(or maximum) on a collection of items in logarithmic time (in worst case).

13.6 Binary Tree Traversals

In order to process trees, we need a mechanism for traversing them and that forms the subject of this section. The process of visiting all nodes of a tree is called *tree traversal*. Each node is processed only once but it may be visited more than once. As we have already seen that in linear data structures (like linked lists, stacks, queues, etc.), the elements are visited in sequential order. But, in tree structures there are many different ways.

Tree traversal is like searching the tree except that in traversal the goal is to move through the tree in a particular order. In addition, all nodes are processed in the *traversal by searching* stops when the required node is found.

Traversal Possibilities

Starting at the root of a binary tree, there are three main steps that can be performed and the order in which they are performed defines the traversal type. These steps are: performing an action on the current node (referred to as "visiting" the node and denoted with *"D"*), traversing to the left child node (denoted with *"L"*), and traversing to the right child node (denoted with *"R"*). This process can be easily described through recursion. Based on the above definition there are 6 possibilities:

1. *LDR*: Process left subtree, process the current node data and then process right subtree
2. *LRD*: Process left subtree, process right subtree and then process the current node data
3. *DLR*: Process the current node data, process left subtree and then process right subtree
4. *DRL*: Process the current node data, process right subtree and then process left subtree
5. *RDL*: Process right subtree, process the current node data and then process left subtree
6. *RLD*: Process right subtree, process left subtree and then process the current node data

Classifying the Traversals

The sequence in which these entities (nodes) processed defines a particular traversal method. The classification is based on the order in which current node is processed. That means, if we are classifying based on current node (*D*) and if *D* comes in the middle then it does not matter whether *L* is on left side of *D* or *R* is on left side of *D*. Similarly, it does not matter whether *L* is on right side of *D* or *R* is on right side of *D*. Due to this, the total 6 possibilities are reduced to 3 and these are:

- Preorder (*DLR*) Traversal
- Inorder (*LDR*) Traversal
- Postorder (*LRD*) Traversal

There is another traversal method which does not depend on above orders and it is:

- Level Order Traversal: This method is inspired from Breadth First Traversal (BFS of Graph algorithms).

Let us use the diagram below for remaining discussion.

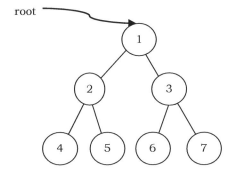

PreOrder Traversal

In pre-order traversal, each node is processed before (pre) either of its sub-trees. This is the simplest traversal to understand. However, even though each node is processed before the subtrees, it still requires that some information must be maintained while moving down the tree.

In the example above, 1 is processed first, then the left sub-tree, and this is followed by the right subtree. Therefore, processing must return to the right sub-tree after finishing the processing of the left subtree. To move to right subtree after processing left subtree, we must maintain the root information. The obvious ADT for such information is a stack. Because of its LIFO structure, it is possible to get the information about the right subtrees back in the reverse order.

Preorder traversal is defined as follows:

- Visit the root.
- Traverse the left subtree in Preorder.
- Traverse the right subtree in Preorder.

The nodes of tree would be visited in the order: 1 2 4 5 3 6 7

```
void PreOrder(struct BinaryTreeNode *root){
    if(root){
        printf("%d",root→data);
        PreOrder(root→left);
        PreOrder (root→right);
    }
}
```

```
        }
```

Time Complexity: O(n). Space Complexity: O(n).

Non-Recursive Preorder Traversal

In recursive version a stack is required as we need to remember the current node so that after completing the left subtree we can go to right subtree. To simulate the same, first we process the current node and before going to left subtree, we store the current node on stack. After completing the left subtree processing, *pop* the element and go to its right subtree. Continue this process until stack is nonempty.

```
void PreOrderNonRecursive(struct BinaryTreeNode *root){
    struct Stack *S = CreateStack();
    while(1) {
        while(root) {
            //Process current node
            printf("%d",root→data);
            Push(S,root);
            //If left subtree exists, add to stack
            root = root→left;
        }
        if(IsEmptyStack(S))
            break;
        root = Pop(S);
        //Indicates completion of left subtree and current node, now go to right subtree
        root = root→right;
    }
    DeleteStack(S);
}
```

Time Complexity: O(n). Space Complexity: O(n).

InOrder Traversal

In Inorder traversal the root is visited between the subtrees. Inorder traversal is defined as follows:

- Traverse the left subtree in Inorder.
- Visit the root.
- Traverse the right subtree in Inorder.

The nodes of tree would be visited in the order: 4 2 5 1 6 3 7

```
void InOrder(struct BinaryTreeNode *root){
    if(root) {
        InOrder(root→left);
        printf("%d",root→data);
        InOrder(root→right);
    }
}
```

Time Complexity: O(n). Space Complexity: O(n).

Non-Recursive Inorder Traversal

Non-recursive version of Inorder traversal is similar to Preorder. The only change is, instead of processing the node before going to left subtree, process it after popping (which indicates after completion of left subtree processing).

```
void InOrderNonRecursive(struct BinaryTreeNode *root){
    struct Stack *S = CreateStack();
    while(1) {
        while(root) {
            Push(S,root);
            //Got left subtree and keep on adding to stack
            root = root→left;
        }
        if(IsEmptyStack(S))
            break;
        root = Pop(S);
        printf("%d", root→data);          //After popping, process the current node
        //Indicates completion of left subtree and current node, now go to right subtree
        root = root→right;
```

```
        }
        DeleteStack(S);
    }
```

Time Complexity: O(n). Space Complexity: O(n).

PostOrder Traversal

In postorder traversal, the root is visited after both subtrees. Postorder traversal is defined as follows:
- Traverse the left subtree in Postorder.
- Traverse the right subtree in Postorder.
- Visit the root.

The nodes of tree would be visited in the order: 4 5 2 6 7 3 1

```
void PostOrder(struct BinaryTreeNode *root){
    if(root) {
            PostOrder(root→left);
            PostOrder(root→right);
            printf("%d",root→data);
    }
}
```

Time Complexity: O(n). Space Complexity: O(n).

Non-Recursive Postorder Traversal

In preorder and inorder traversals, after popping the stack element we do not need to visit the same vertex again. But in postorder traversal, each node is visited twice. That means, after processing left subtree we will visit the current node and after processing the right subtree we will visit the same current node. But we should be processing the node during the second visit. Here the problem is how to differentiate whether we are returning from left subtree or right subtree?

Trick to solving this problem is that after popping an element from stack, check whether that element and right of top of the stack are same or not. If they are same then we have completed the process of left subtree and right subtree. In this case we just need to pop the stack one more time and print its data.

```
void PostOrderNonRecursive(struct BinaryTreeNode *root){
    struct Stack *S = CreateStack();
    while (1) {
            if (root != NULL) {
                    Push(S,root);
                    root=root→left;
            }
            else {
                    if(IsEmptyStack(S)) {
                            printf("Stack is Empty");
                            return;
                    }
                    else if(Top(S)→right == NULL) {
                        root = Pop(S);
                        printf("%d",root→data);
                        if(root == Top(S)→right) {
                                printf("%d",Top(S)→data);
                                Pop(S);
                        }
                    }
                    if(!IsEmptyStack(S))
                        root=Top(S)→right;
                    else root=NULL;
            }
    }
    DeleteStack(S);
}
```

Time Complexity: O(n). Space Complexity: O(n).

Level Order Traversal

Level order traversal is defined as follows:

- Visit the root.
- While traversing level l, keep all the elements at level l+1 in queue.
- Go to the next level and visit all the nodes at that level.
- Repeat this until all levels are completed.

The nodes of tree would be visited in the order: 1 2 3 4 5 6 7

```
void LevelOrder(struct BinaryTreeNode *root){
    struct BinaryTreeNode *temp;
    struct Queue *Q = CreateQueue();
    if(!root)
        return;
    EnQueue(Q,root);
    while(!IsEmptyQueue(Q)) {
        temp = DeQueue(Q);
        //Process current node
        printf("%d", temp→data);
        if(temp→left)
            EnQueue(Q, temp→left);
        if(temp→right)
            EnQueue(Q, temp→right);
    }
    DeleteQueue(Q);
}
```

Time Complexity: O(n). Space Complexity: O(n). Since, in the worst case, all the nodes on the entire last level could be in the queue simultaneously.

Problems on Binary Trees

Problem-1   Give an algorithm for finding maximum element in binary tree.

Solution: One simple way of solving this problem is: find the maximum element in left subtree, find maximum element in right sub tree, compare them with root data and select the one which is giving the maximum value. This approach can be easily implemented with recursion.

```
int FindMax(struct BinaryTreeNode *root) {
    int root_val, left, right, max = INT_MIN;
    if(root !=NULL) {
        root_val = root→data;
        left = FindMax(root→left);
        right = FindMax(root→right);
        // Find the largest of the three values.
        if(left > right)
            max = left;
        else
            max = right;
        if(root_val > max)
            max = root_val;
    }
    return max;
}
```

Time Complexity: O(n). Space Complexity: O(n).

Problem-2   Give an algorithm for finding maximum element in binary tree without recursion.

Solution: Using level order traversal: just observe the elements data while deleting.

```
int FindMaxUsingLevelOrder(struct BinaryTreeNode *root){
    struct BinaryTreeNode *temp;
    int max = INT_MIN;
    struct Queue *Q = CreateQueue();
    EnQueue(Q,root);
    while(!IsEmptyQueue(Q)) {
        temp = DeQueue(Q);
        // largest of the three values
        if(max < temp→data)
            max = temp→data;
        if(temp→left)
            EnQueue (Q, temp→left);
```

```
                if(temp→right)
                    EnQueue (Q, temp→right);
        }
        DeleteQueue(Q);
        return max;
}
```

Time Complexity: O(n). Space Complexity: O(n).

Problem-3   Give an algorithm for searching an element in binary tree.

Solution: Given a binary tree, return true if a node with data is found in the tree. Recurse down the tree, choose the left or right branch by comparing data with each nodes data.

```
int FindInBinaryTreeUsingRecursion(struct BinaryTreeNode *root, int data) {
    int temp;
    // Base case == empty tree, in that case, the data is not found so return false
    if(root == NULL)
            return 0;
    else {    //see if found here
            if(data == root→data)
                    return true;
            else {    // otherwise recur down the correct subtree
                    temp = FindInBinaryTreeUsingRecursion (root→left, data)
                    if(temp != 0)
                            return temp;
                    else    return(FindInBinaryTreeUsingRecursion(root→right, data));
            }
    }
    return 0;
}
```

Time Complexity: O(n). Space Complexity: O(n).

Problem-4   Give an algorithm for searching an element in binary tree without recursion.

Solution: We can use level order traversal for solving this problem. The only change required in level order traversal is, instead of printing the data we just need to check whether the root data is equal to the element we want to search.

```
int SearchUsingLevelOrder(struct BinaryTreeNode *root, int data){
    struct BinaryTreeNode *temp;
    struct Queue *Q;
    if(!root)
        return -1;
    Q = CreateQueue();
    EnQueue(Q,root);
    while(!IsEmptyQueue(Q)) {
            temp = DeQueue(Q);
            //see if found here
            if(data == root→data)
                    return true;
            if(temp→left)
                    EnQueue (Q, temp→left);
            if(temp→right)
                    EnQueue (Q, temp→right);
    }
    DeleteQueue(Q);
    return 0;
}
```

Time Complexity: O(n). Space Complexity: O(n).

Problem-5   Give an algorithm for inserting an element into binary tree.

Solution: Since the given tree is a binary tree, we can insert the element wherever we want. To insert an element, we can use the level order traversal and insert the element wherever we found the node whose left or right child is NULL.

```
void InsertInBinaryTree(struct BinaryTreeNode *root, int data){
    struct Queue *Q;
    struct BinaryTreeNode *temp;
    struct BinaryTreeNode *newNode;
```

```
            newNode = (struct BinaryTreeNode *) malloc(sizeof(struct BinaryTreeNode));
            newNode→left = newNode→right = NULL;
            if(!newNode) {
                    printf("Memory Error");
                    return;
            }
            if(!root) {
                    root = newNode;
                    return;
            }
            Q = CreateQueue();
            EnQueue(Q,root);

            while(!IsEmptyQueue(Q)) {
                    temp = DeQueue(Q);
                    if(temp→left)
                            EnQueue(Q, temp→left);
                    else {
                        temp→left=newNode;
                        DeleteQueue(Q);
                        return;
                    }
                    if(temp→right)
                            EnQueue(Q, temp→right);
                    else {
                            temp→right=newNode;
                            DeleteQueue(Q);
                            return;
                    }
            }
            DeleteQueue(Q);
}
```

Time Complexity: O(n). Space Complexity: O(n).

Problem-6   Give an algorithm for finding the size of binary tree.

Solution: Calculate the size of left and right subtrees recursively, add 1 (current node) and return to its parent.

```
// Compute the number of nodes in a tree.
int SizeOfBinaryTree(struct BinaryTreeNode *root) {
    if(root==NULL)
            return 0;
    else    return(SizeOfBinaryTree(root→left) + 1 +  SizeOfBinaryTree(root→right));
}
```

Time Complexity: O(n). Space Complexity: O(n).

Problem-7   Can we solve Problem-6 without recursion?

Solution: Yes, using level order traversal.

```
int SizeofBTUsingLevelOrder(struct BinaryTreeNode *root){
    struct BinaryTreeNode *temp;
    struct Queue *Q;
    int count = 0;
    if(!root)
        return 0;

    Q = CreateQueue();
    EnQueue(Q,root);

    while(!IsEmptyQueue(Q)) {
            temp = DeQueue(Q);
            count++;

            if(temp→left)
                    EnQueue (Q, temp→left);
            if(temp→right)
                    EnQueue (Q, temp→right);
    }
    DeleteQueue(Q);
    return count;
```

}

Time Complexity: O(n). Space Complexity: O(n).

Problem-8   Give an algorithm for printing the level order data in reverse order. For example, the output for the below tree should be: 4 5 6 7 2 3 1

root

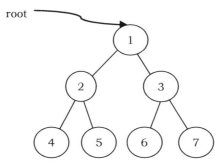

Solution:

```
void LevelOrderTraversalInReverse(struct BinaryTreeNode *root){
    struct Queue *Q;
    struct Stack *s = CreateStack();
    struct BinaryTreeNode *temp;
    if(!root)
        return;
    Q = CreateQueue();
    EnQueue(Q, root);
    while(!IsEmptyQueue(Q)) {
        temp = DeQueue(Q);
        if(temp→right)
            EnQueue(Q, temp→right);
        if(temp→left)
            EnQueue (Q, temp→left);
        Push(s, temp);
    }
    while(!IsEmptyStack(s))
        printf("%d",Pop(s)→data);
}
```

Time Complexity: O(n). Space Complexity: O(n).

Problem-9   Give an algorithm for deleting the tree.

Solution: To delete a tree we must traverse all the nodes of the tree and delete them one by one. So which traversal should we use Inorder, Preorder, Postorder or Level order Traversal?

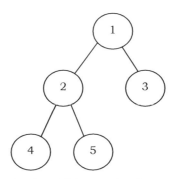

Before deleting the parent node we should delete its children nodes first. We can use postorder traversal as it does the work without storing anything. We can delete tree with other traversals also with extra space complexity. For the following tree nodes are deleted in order – 4, 5, 2, 3, 1.

```
void DeleteBinaryTree(struct BinaryTreeNode *root){
    if(root == NULL)
        return;
    /* first delete both subtrees */
    DeleteBinaryTree(root→left);
    DeleteBinaryTree(root→right);
    //Delete current node only after deleting subtrees
    free(root);
}
```

Time Complexity: O(n). Space Complexity: O(n).

Problem-10 Give an algorithm for finding the height (or depth) of the binary tree.

Solution: Recursively calculate height of left and right subtrees of a node and assign height to the node as max of the heights of two children plus 1. This is similar to *PreOrder* tree traversal (and *DFS* of Graph algorithms).

```
int HeightOfBinaryTree(struct BinaryTreeNode  *root){
    int leftheight, rightheight;
    if(root == NULL)
            return 0;
    else {   /* compute the depth of each subtree */
            leftheight = HeightOfBinaryTree (root→left);
            rightheight = HeightOfBinaryTree (root→right);
            if(leftheight > rightheight)
                    return(leftheight + 1);
            else      return(rightheight + 1);
    }
}
```

Time Complexity: O(n). Space Complexity: O(n).

Problem-11 Can we solve Problem-10 without recursion?

Solution: Yes, using level-order traversal. This is similar to *BFS* of Graph algorithms. End of level is identified with NULL.

```
int FindHeightofBinaryTree(struct BinaryTreeNode *root){
    int level=1;
    struct Queue *Q;
    if(!root)
            return 0;
    Q = CreateQueue();
    EnQueue(Q,root);
    // End of first level
    EnQueue(Q,NULL);
    while(!IsEmptyQueue(Q)) {
            root=DeQueue(Q);
            // Completion of current level.
            if(root==NULL) {
                    //Put another marker for next level.
                    if(!IsEmptyQueue(Q))
                            EnQueue(Q,NULL);
                    level++;
            }
            else {   if(root→left)
                            EnQueue(Q, root→left);
                    if(root→right)
                            EnQueue(Q, root→right);
            }
    }
    return level;
}
```

Time Complexity: O(n). Space Complexity: O(n).

Problem-12 Give an algorithm for finding the deepest node of the binary tree.

Solution:

```
struct BinaryTreeNode *DeepestNodeinBinaryTree(struct BinaryTreeNode *root){
    struct BinaryTreeNode *temp;
    struct Queue *Q;
    if(!root)  return 0;
    Q = CreateQueue();
    EnQueue(Q,root);
    while(!IsEmptyQueue(Q)) {
            temp = DeQueue(Q);
            if(temp→left)
                    EnQueue(Q, temp→left);
            if(temp→right)
                    EnQueue(Q, temp→right);
```

```
        }
        DeleteQueue(Q);
        return temp;
}
```

Time Complexity: O(n). Space Complexity: O(n).

Problem-13   Give an algorithm for deleting an element (assuming data is given) from binary tree.

Solution: The deletion of a node binary tree can be implemented as
* Starting at root, find the node which we want to delete.
* Find the deepest node in the tree.
* Replace the deepest nodes data with node to be deleted.
* Then delete the deepest node.

Problem-14   Give an algorithm for finding the number of leaves in the binary tree without using recursion.

Solution: The set of nodes whose both left and right children are NULL are called leaf nodes.

```
int NumberOfLeavesInBTusingLevelOrder(struct BinaryTreeNode *root){
    struct BinaryTreeNode *temp;
    struct Queue *Q;
    int count = 0;
    if(!root)
        return 0;
    Q = CreateQueue();
    EnQueue(Q,root);
    while(!IsEmptyQueue(Q)) {
        temp = DeQueue(Q);
        if(!temp→left && !temp→right)
            count++;
        else {
            if(temp→left)
                EnQueue(Q, temp→left);
            if(temp→right)
                EnQueue(Q, temp→right);
        }
    }
    DeleteQueue(Q);
    return count;
}
```

Time Complexity: O(n). Space Complexity: O(n).

Problem-15   Give an algorithm for finding the number of full nodes in the binary tree without using recursion.

Solution: The set of all nodes with both left and right children are called full nodes.

```
int NumberOfFullNodesInBTusingLevelOrder(struct BinaryTreeNode *root){
    struct BinaryTreeNode *temp;
    struct Queue *Q;
    int count = 0;
    if(!root)
        return 0;
    Q = CreateQueue();
    EnQueue(Q,root);
    while(!IsEmptyQueue(Q)) {
        temp = DeQueue(Q);
        if(temp→left && temp→right)
            count++;
        if(temp→left)
            EnQueue (Q, temp→left);
        if(temp→right)
            EnQueue (Q, temp→right);
    }
    DeleteQueue(Q);
    return count;
}
```

Time Complexity: O(n). Space Complexity: O(n).

Problem-16   Give an algorithm for finding the number of half nodes (nodes with only one child) in the binary tree without using recursion.

Solution: The set of all nodes with either left or either right child (but not both) are called half nodes.

```
int NumberOfHalfNodesInBTusingLevelOrder(struct BinaryTreeNode *root){
    struct BinaryTreeNode *temp;
    struct Queue *Q;
    int count = 0;
    if(!root)
            return 0;

    Q = CreateQueue();
    EnQueue(Q,root);

    while(!IsEmptyQueue(Q)) {
            temp = DeQueue(Q);
            //we can use this condition also instead of two temp→left ^ temp→right
            if(!temp→left && temp→right || temp→left && !temp→right)
                    count++;
            if(temp→left)
                    EnQueue (Q, temp→left);
            if(temp→right)
                    EnQueue (Q, temp→right);
    }
    DeleteQueue(Q);
    return count;
}
```

Time Complexity: O(n). Space Complexity: O(n).

Problem-17   Given two binary trees, return true if they are structurally identical.

Solution:

Algorithm:

- If both trees are NULL then return true.
- If both trees are not NULL, then compare data and recursively check left and right subtree structures.

```
//Return true if they are structurally identical.
int AreStructurullySameTrees(struct BinaryTreeNode *root1, struct BinaryTreeNode *root2) {
    // both empty→1
    if(root1==NULL && root2==NULL)
            return 1;
    if(root1==NULL || root2==NULL)
            return 0;
    // both non-empty→compare them
    return(root1→data == root2→data && AreStructurullySameTrees(root1→left, root2→left) &&
            AreStructurullySameTrees(root1→right, root2→right));
}
```

Time Complexity: O(n). Space Complexity: O(n), for recursive stack.

Problem-18   Give an algorithm for finding the diameter of the binary tree. The diameter of a tree (sometimes called the *width*) is the number of nodes on the longest path between two leaves in the tree.

Solution: To find the diameter of a tree, first calculate the diameter of left subtree and right sub trees recursively. Among these two values, we need to send maximum value along with current level (+1).

```
int DiameterOfTree(struct BinaryTreeNode *root, int *ptr){
    int left, right;
    if(!root)
         return 0;
    left = DiameterOfTree(root→left, ptr);
    right = DiameterOfTree(root→right, ptr);
    if(left + right > *ptr)
       *ptr = left + right;
    return Max(left, right)+1;
}
```

Time Complexity: O(n). Space Complexity: O(n).

Problem-19   Give an algorithm for finding the level that has the maximum sum in the binary tree.

Solution: The logic is very much similar to finding number of levels. The only change is, we need to keep track of sums as well.

```
int FindLevelwithMaxSum(struct BinaryTreeNode *root){
```

```
        struct BinaryTreeNode *temp;
        int level=0, maxLevel=0;
        struct Queue *Q;
        int currentSum = 0, maxSum = 0;
        if(!root)
                return 0;
        Q=CreateQueue();
        EnQueue(Q,root);
        EnQueue(Q,NULL);                        //End of first level.
        while(!IsEmptyQueue(Q)) {
                temp =DeQueue(Q);
                // If the current level is completed then compare sums
                if(temp == NULL) {
                        if(currentSum> maxSum) {
                                maxSum = currentSum;
                                maxLevel = level;
                        }
                        currentSum = 0;
                        //place the indicator for end of next level at the end of queue
                        if(!IsEmptyQueue(Q))
                                EnQueue(Q,NULL);
                        level++;
                }
                else  {
                        currentSum  += temp→data;
                        if(temp→left)
                                EnQueue(temp, temp→left);
                        if(root→right)
                                EnQueue(temp, temp→right);
                }
        }
        return maxLevel;
}
```

Time Complexity: O(n). Space Complexity: O(n).

Problem-20 Given a binary tree, print out all its root-to-leaf paths.

Solution: Refer comments in functions.

```
void PrintPathsRecur(struct BinaryTreeNode  * root, int path[], int pathLen) {
    if(root ==NULL)
    return;

    // append this node to the path array
    path[pathLen] = root→data;
    pathLen++;

    // it's a leaf, so print the path that led to here
    if(root→left==NULL && root→right==NULL)
        PrintArray(path, pathLen);
    else {    // otherwise try both subtrees
        PrintPathsRecur (root→left, path, pathLen);
        PrintPathsRecur (root→right, path, pathLen);
    }
}
// Function that prints out an array on a line.
void PrintArray(int ints[], int len) {
for (int i=0; i<len; i++)
        printf("%d",ints[i]);
}
```

Time Complexity: O(n). Space Complexity: O(n), for recursive stack.

Problem-21 Give an algorithm for checking the existence of path with given sum. That means, given a sum check whether there exists a path from root to any of the nodes.

Solution: For this problem, the strategy is: subtract the node value from the sum before calling its children recursively, and check to see if the sum is 0 when we run out of tree.

```
int HasPathSum(struct BinaryTreeNode  * root, int sum) {
    // return true if we run out of tree and sum==0
    if(root == NULL)
```

```
                return(sum == 0);
        else {          // otherwise check both subtrees
            int remainingSum = sum - root→data;

            if((root→left&& root→right)||(! root→left && ! root→right))
                return(HasPathSum (root→left, remainingSum) ||
                 HasPathSum (root→right, remainingSum));
            else if(root→left)
                    return HasPathSum (root→left, remainingSum);
            else
                return HasPathSum (root→right, remainingSum);
        }
    }
}
```

Time Complexity: O(n). Space Complexity: O(n).

Problem-22   Give an algorithm for finding the sum of all elements in binary tree.

Solution: Recursively, call left subtree sum, right subtree sum and add their values to current nodes data.

```
int Add(struct BinaryTreeNode  *root) {
    if(root == NULL)
        return 0;
    else
        return (root→data + Add(root→left) +  Add(root→right));
}
```

Time Complexity: O(n). Space Complexity: O(n).

Problem-23   Can we solve Problem-22 without recursion?

Solution: We can use level order traversal with simple change. Every time after deleting an element from queue, add the nodes data value to *sum* variable.

```
int SumofBTusingLevelOrder(struct BinaryTreeNode *root){
    struct BinaryTreeNode *temp;
    struct Queue *Q;
    int sum = 0;
    if(!root)
        return 0;
    Q = CreateQueue();
    EnQueue(Q,root);
    while(!IsEmptyQueue(Q)) {
            temp = DeQueue(Q);
            sum += temp→data;
            if(temp→left)
                EnQueue (Q, temp→left);
            if(temp→right)
                EnQueue (Q, temp→right);
    }
    DeleteQueue(Q);
    return sum;
}
```

Time Complexity: O(n). Space Complexity: O(n).

Problem-24   Give an algorithm for converting a tree to its mirror. Mirror of a tree is another tree with left and right children of all non-leaf nodes interchanged. The trees below are mirrors to each other.

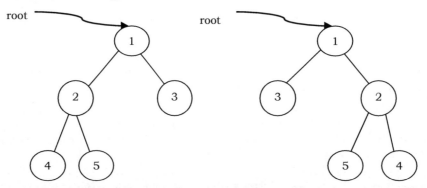

Solution:

```
    struct BinaryTreeNode *MirrorOfBinaryTree(struct BinaryTreeNode *root){
```

```
        struct BinaryTreeNode * temp;
        if(root) {
                MirrorOfBinaryTree(root→left);
                MirrorOfBinaryTree(root→right);
                /* swap the pointers in this node */
                temp   = root→left;
                root→left  = root→right;
                root→right = temp;
        }
        return root;
}
```

Time Complexity: O(n). Space Complexity: O(n).

Problem-25   Given two trees, give an algorithm for checking whether they are mirrors of each other.

Solution:

```
int AreMirrors(struct BinaryTreeNode * root1, struct BinaryTreeNode * root2) {
    if(root1 == NULL && root2 == NULL)
        return 1;
    if(root1 == NULL || root2 == NULL)
        return 0;
    if(root1→data != root2→data)
        return 0;
    else return AreMirrors(root1→left, root2→right) && AreMirrors(root1→right, root2→left);
}
```

Time Complexity: O(n). Space Complexity: O(n).

Problem-26   Give an algorithm for constructing binary tree from given Inorder and Preorder traversals.

Solution: Let us consider the traversals below:

Inorder sequence: D B E A F C
Preorder sequence: A B D E C F

In a Preorder sequence, leftmost element denotes the root of the tree. So we know 'A' is root for given sequences. By searching 'A' in Inorder sequence we can find out all elements on left side of 'A', which come under left subtree and elements right side of 'A', which come under right subtree. So we get the structure as given below.

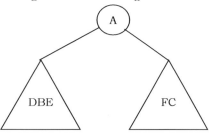

We recursively follow above steps and get the following tree.

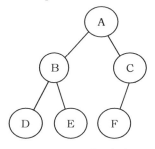

Algorithm: BuildTree()
1   Select an element from Preorder. Increment a Preorder index variable (preIndex in below code) to pick next element in next recursive call.
2   Create a new tree node (newNode) with the data as selected element.
3   Find the selected elements index in Inorder. Let the index be inIndex.
4   Call BuildBinaryTree for elements before inIndex and make the built tree as left subtree of newNode.
5   Call BuildBinaryTree for elements after inIndex and make the built tree as right subtree of newNode.
6   return newNode.

```
struct BinaryTreeNode *BuildBinaryTree(int inOrder[], int preOrder[], int inStrt, int inEnd){
    static int preIndex = 0;
```

```
      struct BinaryTreeNode *newNode
      if(inStrt > inEnd)
            return NULL;
      newNode = (struct BinaryTreeNode *) malloc (sizeof(struct BinaryTreeNode));
      if(!newNode) {
            printf("Memory Error");
            return NULL;
      }
      // Select current node from Preorder traversal using preIndex
      newNode→data = preOrder[preIndex];
      preIndex++;
      if(inStrt == inEnd)                    /* if this node has no children then return */
            return newNode;
      /* else find the index of this node in Inorder traversal */
      int inIndex = Search(inOrder, inStrt, inEnd, newNode→data);

      /* Using index in Inorder traversal, construct left and right subtress */
      newNode→left = BuildBinaryTree(inOrder, preOrder, inStrt, inIndex-1);
      newNode→right = BuildBinaryTree(inOrder, preOrder, inIndex+1, inEnd);
      return newNode;
}
```

Time Complexity: O(n). Space Complexity: O(n).

Problem-27   If we are given two traversal sequences, can we construct the binary tree uniquely?

Solution: It depends on what traversals are given. If one of the traversal methods is *Inorder* then the tree can be constructed uniquely, otherwise not.

Therefore, following combination can uniquely identify a tree:
- Inorder and Preorder
- Inorder and Postorder
- Inorder and Level-order

And following do not.
- Postorder and Preorder
- Preorder and Level-order
- Postorder and Level-order

For example, Preorder, Level-order and Postorder traversals are same for following trees:

    Preorder Traversal   = AB
    Postorder Traversal   = BA
    Level-order Traversal = AB

So, even if three of them (PreOrder, Level-Order and PostOrder) are given, the tree cannot be constructed uniquely.

Problem-28   Give an algorithm for printing all the ancestors of a node in a Binary tree. For the tree below, for 7 the ancestors are 1 3 7.

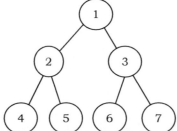

Solution: Apart from the Depth First Search of this tree, we can use the following recursive way to print the ancestors.

```
int PrintAllAncestors(struct BinaryTreeNode *root, struct BinaryTreeNode *node){
      if(root == NULL)
            return 0;
      if(root→left == node || root→right == node || PrintAllAncestors(root→left, node) ||
                              PrintAllAncestors(root→right, node)) {
            printf("%d", root→data);
```

```
                return 1;
        }
        return 0;
}
```

Time Complexity: O(*n*). Space Complexity: O(*n*) for recursion.

Problem-29   Give an algorithm for finding LCA (Least Common Ancestor) of two nodes in a Binary Tree.

Solution:

```
struct BinaryTreeNode *LCA(struct BinaryTreeNode *root, struct BinaryTreeNode *α, struct BinaryTreeNode *β){
        struct BinaryTreeNode *left, *right;
        if(root == NULL)
                return root;
        if(root == α || root == β)
                return root;
        left = LCA (root→left, α, β );
        right = LCA (root→right, α, β );
        if(left && right)
                return root;
        else     return (left? left: right)
}
```

Time Complexity: O(*n*). Space Complexity: O(*n*) for recursion.

Problem-30   **Zigzag Tree Traversal:** Give an algorithm to traverse a binary tree in Zigzag order. For example, the output for the tree below should be: 1 3 2 4 5 6 7

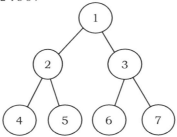

Solution: This problem can be solved easily using two stacks. Let us say the two stacks are: *currentLevel* and *nextLevel*. We would also need a variable to keep track of the current level order (whether it is left to right or right or left). We pop from *currentLevel* stack and print the nodes value. Whenever the current level order is from left to right, push the nodes left child, then its right child to stack *nextLevel*. Since a stack is a Last In First OUT (*LIFO*) structure, next time when nodes are popped off nextLevel, it will be in the reverse order. On the other hand, when the current level order is from right to left, we would push the nodes right child first, then its left child. Finally, don't forget to swap those two stacks at the end of each level (*i.e.*, when *currentLevel* is empty).

```
void ZigZagTraversal(struct BinaryTreeNode *root){
        struct BinaryTreeNode *temp;
        int leftToRight = 1;
        if(!root) return;
        struct Stack *currentLevel = CreateStack(), *nextLevel = CreateStack();
        Push(currentLevel, root);
        while(!IsEmptyStack(currentLevel)) {
                temp = Pop(currentLevel);
                if(temp) {
                        printf("%d",temp→data);
                        if(leftToRight) {
                                if(temp→left)
                                Push(nextLevel, temp→left);
                                if(temp→right)
                                Push(nextLevel, temp→right);
                        }
                        else {
                                if(temp→right)
                                Push(nextLevel, temp→right);
                                if(temp→left)
                                Push(nextLevel, temp→left);
                        }
                }
                if(IsEmptyStack(currentLevel)) {
```

```
                    leftToRight = 1-leftToRight;
                    swap(currentLevel, nextLevel);
            }
    }
}
```

Time Complexity: $O(n)$. Space Complexity: Space for two stacks = $O(n) + O(n) = O(n)$.

Problem-31   Give an algorithm for finding the vertical sum of a binary tree. For example,
The tree has 5 vertical lines
    Vertical-1: nodes-4 => vertical sum is 4
    Vertical-2: nodes-2 => vertical sum is 2
    Vertical-3: nodes-1,5,6 => vertical sum is $1 + 5 + 6 = 12$
    Vertical-4: nodes-3 => vertical sum is 3
    Vertical-5: nodes-7 => vertical sum is 7
    We need to output: 4 2 12 3 7

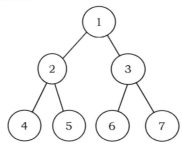

Solution: We can do an inorder traversal and hash the column. We call VerticalSumInBinaryTree(root, 0) which means the root is at column 0. While doing the traversal, hash the column and increase its value by $root \rightarrow data$.

```
void VerticalSumInBinaryTree (struct BinaryTreeNode *root, int column){
    if(root==NULL)
            return;
    VerticalSumInBinaryTree(root→left, column-1);

    //Refer Hashing chapter for implementation of hash table
    Hash[column] += root→data;

    VerticalSumInBinaryTree(root→right, column+1);
}
VerticalSumInBinaryTree(root, 0);
Print Hash;
```

Problem-32   How many different binary trees are possible with n nodes?

Solution: For example, consider a tree with 3 nodes ($n = 3$). It will have the maximum combination of 5 different (i.e., $2^3 - 3 = 5$) trees.

  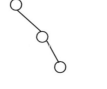

In general, if there are n nodes, there exist $2^n - n$ different trees.

Problem-33   Given a tree with a special property where leaves are represented with 'L' and internal node with 'I'. Also, assume that each node has either 0 or 2 children. Given preorder traversal of this tree, construct the tree.
    Example: Given preorder string => ILILL

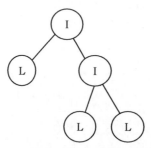

Solution: First, we should see how preorder traversal is arranged. Pre-order traversal means first put root node, then pre-order traversal of left subtree and then pre-order traversal of right subtree. In normal scenario, it's not possible to detect where left subtree ends and right subtree starts using only pre-order traversal. Since every node has either 2 children or no child, we can surely say that if a node exists then its sibling also exists. So every time when we are computing a subtree, we need to compute its sibling subtree as well.

Secondly, whenever we get 'L' in the input string, that is a leaf and we can stop for a particular subtree at that point. After this 'L' node (left child of its parent 'L'), its sibling starts. If 'L' node is right child of its parent, then we need to go up in the hierarchy to find next subtree to compute. Keeping above invariant in mind, we can easily determine when a subtree ends and the next one starts. It means that we can give any start node to our method and it can easily complete the subtree it generates going outside of its nodes. We just need to take care of passing correct start nodes to different sub-trees.

```
struct BinaryTreeNode *BuildTreeFromPreOrder(char* A, int *i){
    struct BinaryTreeNode *newNode;
    newNode = (struct BinaryTreeNode *) malloc(sizeof(struct BinaryTreeNode));
    newNode→data = A[*i];
    newNode→left = newNode→right = NULL;
    if(A == NULL){                          //Boundary Condition
            free(newNode);
            return NULL;
    }

    if(A[*i] == 'L')                        //On reaching leaf node, return
            return newNode;

    *i = *i + 1;                            //Populate left sub tree
    newNode→left = BuildTreeFromPreOrder(A, i);
    *i = *i + 1;                            //Populate right sub tree
    newNode→right = BuildTreeFromPreOrder(A, i);
    return newNode;
}
```

Time Complexity: O(n).

Problem-34   Given a binary tree with three pointers (left, right and nextSibling), give an algorithm for filling the *nextSibling* pointers assuming they are NULL initially.

Solution: We can use simple queue (similar to the solution of Problem-11). Let us assume that the structure of binary tree is:

```
struct BinaryTreeNode {
    struct BinaryTreeNode* left;
    struct BinaryTreeNode* right;
    struct BinaryTreeNode* nextSibling;
};
int FindHeightofBinaryTree(struct BinaryTreeNode *root){
    struct BinaryTreeNode *temp;
    struct Queue *Q;
    if(!root)   return 0;
    Q = CreateQueue();
    EnQueue(Q,root);
    EnQueue(Q,NULL);
    while(!IsEmptyQueue(Q)) {
            temp =DeQueue(Q);

            // Completion of current level.
            if(temp ==NULL) { //Put another marker for next level.
                    if(!IsEmptyQueue(Q))
                            EnQueue(Q,NULL);
            }
            else {
                    temp→nextSibling = QueueFront(Q);
                    if(root→left)
                            EnQueue(Q, temp→left);
                    if(root→right)
                            EnQueue(Q, temp→right);
            }
    }
}
```

Time Complexity: O(n). Space Complexity: O(n).

Problem-35   Is there any other way of solving Problem-34?

Solution: The trick is to re-use the populated *nextSibling* pointers. As mentioned earlier, we just need one more step for it to work. Before we passed the *left* and *right* to the recursion function itself, we connect the right childs *nextSibling* to the current nodes nextSibling left child. In order for this to work, the current node *nextSibling* pointer must be populated, which is true in this case.

```
void FillNextSiblings(struct BinaryTreeNode* root) {
    if (!root)
        return;
    if (root→left)
        root→left→nextSibling = root→right;
    if (root→right)
        root→right→nextSibling = (root→nextSibling) ? root→nextSibling→left : NULL;
    FillNextSiblings(root→left);
    FillNextSiblings(root→right);
}
```

Time Complexity: O(n).

13.7 Generic Trees (N-ary Trees)

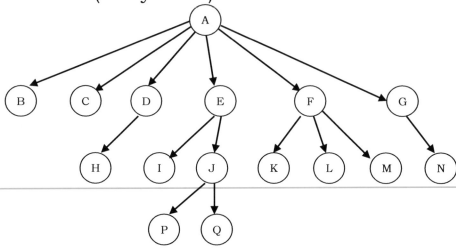

In the previous section we discussed binary trees where each node can have maximum of two children and these are represented easily with two pointers. But suppose if we have a tree with many children at every node and also if we do not know how many children a node can have, how do we represent them? For example, consider the tree shown above.

How do we represent the tree?

In the above tree, there are nodes with 6 children, with 3 children, 2 children, with 1 child, and with zero children (leaves). To present this tree we have to consider the worst case (6 children) and allocate those many child pointers for each node.

Based on this, the node representation can be given as:

```
struct TreeNode{
    int data;
    struct TreeNode *firstChild;
    struct TreeNode *secondChild;
    struct TreeNode *thirdChild;
    struct TreeNode *fourthChild;
    struct TreeNode *fifthChild;
    struct TreeNode *sixthChild;
};
```

Since we are not using all the pointers in all the cases there is a lot of memory wastage. Also, another problem is that, in advance we do not know the number of children for each node.

In order to solve this problem we need a representation that minimizes the wastage and also accept nodes with any number of children.

Representation of Generic Trees

Since our objective is to reach all nodes of the tree, a possible solution to this is as follows:

- At each node link children of same parent (siblings) from left to right.
- Remove the links from parent to all children except the first child.

What these above statements say is if we have a link between children then we do not need extra links from parent to all children. This is because we can traverse all the elements by starting at the first child of the parent.

So if we have link between parent and first child and also links between all children of same parent then it solves our problem.

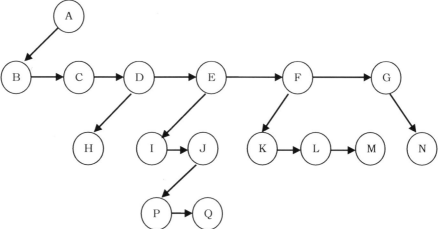

This representation is sometimes called first child/next sibling representation. First child/next sibling representation of the generic tree is shown above. The actual representation for this tree is:

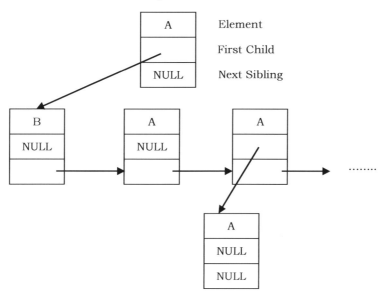

Based on this discussion, the tree node declaration for general tree can be given as:

```
struct TreeNode {
    int data;
    struct TreeNode *firstChild;
    struct TreeNode *nextSibling;
};
```

Note: Since we are able to represent any generic tree with binary representation, in practice we use only binary tree.

Problems on Generic Trees

Problem-36   Given a tree, give an algorithm for finding the sum of all the elements of the tree.

Solution: The solution is similar to what we have done for simple binary trees. That means, traverse the complete list and keep on adding the values. We can either use level order traversal or simple recursion.

```
int FindSum(struct TreeNode *root){
    if(!root)
        return 0;
    return root→data + FindSum(root→firstChild) + FindSum(root→nextSibling);
}
```

Time Complexity: O(n). Space Complexity: O(1) (if we do not consider stack space), otherwise O(n).

Note: All problems which we have discussed for binary trees are applicable for generic trees also. Instead of left and right pointers we just need to use firstChild and nextSibling.

Problem-37 For a 4-ary tree (each node can contain maximum of 4 children), what is the maximum possible height with 100 nodes? Assume height of a single node is 0.

Solution: In 4-ary tree each node can contain 0 to 4 children and to get maximum height, we need to keep only one child for each parent.

With 100 nodes the maximum possible height we can get is 99. If we have a restriction that at least one node has 4 children, then we keep one node with 4 children and remaining nodes with 1 child. In this case, the maximum possible height is 96. Similarly, with n nodes the maximum possible height is $n-4$.

Problem-38 For a 4-ary tree (each node can contain maximum of 4 children), what is the minimum possible height with n nodes?

Solution: Similar to above discussion, if we want to get minimum height, then we need to fill all nodes with maximum children (in this case 4). Now let's see the following table, which indicates the maximum number of nodes for a given height.

Height, h	Maximum Nodes at height, $h = 4^h$	Total Nodes height $h = \frac{4^{h+1}-1}{3}$
0	1	1
1	4	1+4
2	4 × 4	1+ 4 × 4
3	4 × 4 × 4	1+ 4 × 4 + 4 × 4 × 4

For a given height h the maximum possible nodes are: $\frac{4^{h+1}-1}{3}$. To get minimum height, take logarithm on both sides:

$$n = \frac{4^{h+1}-1}{3} \Rightarrow 4^{h+1} = 3n+1 \Rightarrow (h+1)log4 = log(3n+1)$$
$$\Rightarrow h+1 = \log_4(3n+1) \Rightarrow h = \log_4(3n+1) - 1$$

Problem-39 Given a parent array P, where $P[i]$ indicates the parent of ith node in the tree (assume parent of root node is indicated with -1). Give an algorithm for finding the height or depth of the tree.

Solution: From the problem definition, the given array represents the parent array. That means, we need to consider the tree for that array and find the depth of the tree.

For example: if the P is

-1	0	1	6	6	0	0	2	7
0	1	2	3	4	5	6	7	8

Its corresponding tree is:

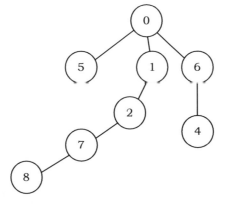

The depth of this given tree is 4. If we carefully observe, we just need to start at every node and keep going to its parent until we reach -1 and also keep track of the maximum depth among all nodes.

```
int FindDepthInGenericTree(int P[], int n){
    int maxDepth =-1, currentDepth =-1, j;
    for (int i = 0; i < n; i++)    {
        currentDepth = 0; j = i;
        while(P[j] != -1) {
            currentDepth++; j = P[j];
        }
        if(currentDepth > maxDepth)
            maxDepth = currentDepth;
    }
```

```
    return maxDepth;
}
```

Time Complexity: $O(n^2)$. For skew trees we will be re-calculating the same values. Space Complexity: $O(1)$.

Note: We can optimize the code by storing the previous calculated nodes depth in some hash table or other array. This reduces the time complexity but uses extra space.

Problem-40   Given a node in the generic tree, give an algorithm for counting the number of siblings for that node.

Solution: Since tree is represented with first child/next sibling method, the tree structure can be given as:

```
struct TreeNode{
    int data;
    struct TreeNode *firstChild;
    struct TreeNode *nextSibling;
};
```

For a given node in the tree, we just need to traverse all its nextsiblings.

```
int SiblingsCount(struct TreeNode *current){
    int count = 0;
    while(current)    {
            count++;
            current = current→nextSibling;
    }
    reutrn count;
}
```

Time Complexity: $O(n)$. Space Complexity: $O(1)$.

Problem-41   Given a node in the generic tree, give an algorithm to count the number of children for that node.

Solution: Since the tree is represented as first child/next sibling method, the tree structure can be given as:

```
struct TreeNode{
    int data;
    struct TreeNode *firstChild;
    struct TreeNode *nextSibling;
};
```

For a given node in the tree, we just need to point to its first child and keep traversing all its nextsiblings.

```
int ChildCount(struct TreeNode *current){
    int count = 0;
    current = current→firstChild;
    while(current)    {
            count++;
            current = current→nextSibling;
    }
    reutrn count;
}
```

Time Complexity: $O(n)$. Space Complexity: $O(1)$.

Problem-42   Given two trees how do we check whether the trees are isomorphic to each other or not?

Solution: Two binary trees $root1$ and $root2$ are isomorphic if they have the same structure. The values of the nodes does not affect whether two trees are isomorphic or not. In the diagram below, the tree in the middle is not isomorphic to the other trees, but the tree on the right is isomorphic to the tree on the left.

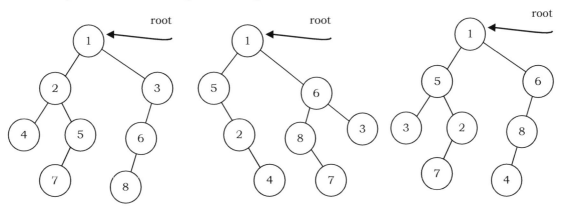

```
int IsIsomorphic(struct TreeNode *root1, struct TreeNode *root2){
    if(!root1 && !root2) return 1;
    if((!root1 && root2) || (root1 && !root2)) return 0;
    return (IsIsomorphic(root1→left, root2→left) && IsIsomorphic(root1→right, root2→right));
}
```

Time Complexity: O(n). Space Complexity: O(n).

Problem-43   Given two trees how do we check whether they are quasi-isomorphic to each other or not?

Solution:

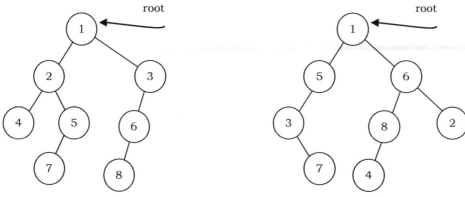

Two trees $root1$ and $root2$ are quasi-isomorphic if $root1$ can be transformed into $root2$ by swapping left and right children of some of the nodes of $root1$. Data in the nodes are not important in determining quasi-isomorphism, only the shape is important. The trees below are quasi-isomorphic because if the children of the nodes on the left are swapped, the tree on the right is obtained.

```
int QuasiIsomorphic(struct TreeNode *root1, struct TreeNode *root2){
    if(!root1 && !root2)  return true;
    if((!root1 && root2) || (root1 && !root2))
            return false;
    return (QuasiIsomorphic(root1→left, root2→left) && QuasiIsomorphic(root1→right, root2→right)
        || QuasiIsomorphic(root1→right, root2→left) && QuasiIsomorphic(root1→left, root2→right));
}
```

Time Complexity: O(n). Space Complexity: O(n).

Problem-44   A full k −ary tree is a tree where each node has either 0 or k children. Given an array which contains the preorder traversal of full k −ary tree, give an algorithm for constructing the full k −ary tree.

Solution: In k −ary tree, for a node at i^{th} position its children will be at $k * i + 1$ to $k * i + k$. For example, the example below is for full 3-ary tree.

As we have seen, in preorder traversal first left subtree is processed then followed by root node and right subtree. Because of this, to construct a full k-ary, we just need to keep on creating the nodes without bothering about the previous constructed nodes. We can use this trick to build the tree recursively by using one global index. Declaration for k ary tree can be given as:

```
struct K-aryTreeNode{
    char data;
    struct K-aryTreeNode *child[];
};
int *Ind = 0;
struct K-aryTreeNode *BuildK-aryTree(char A[], int n, int k){
    if(n<=0) return NULL;
    struct K-aryTreeNode *newNode = (struct K-aryTreeNode*) malloc(sizeof(struct K-aryTreeNode));
    if(!newNode) {
            printf("Memory Error"); return;
    }
    newNode→child = (struct K-aryTreeNode*) malloc( k * sizeof(struct K-aryTreeNode));
    if(!newNode→child) {
            printf("Memory Error"); return;
    }
    newNode→data = A[Ind];
    for (int i = 0; i<k; i++) {
        if(k * Ind + i <n) {
            Ind++;
            newNode→child[i] = BuildK-aryTree(A, n, k,Ind );
        }
```

```
        else  newNode→child[i] =NULL;
    }
    return newNode;
}
```

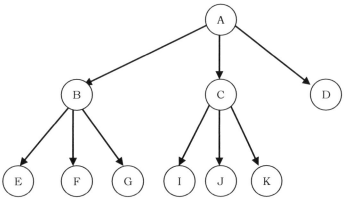

Time Complexity: O(n), where n is the size of the pre-order array. This is because we are moving sequentially and not visiting the already constructed nodes.

13.8 Threaded Binary Tree [Stack/Queue less] Traversals

In earlier sections we have seen that, *preorder, inorder and postorder* binary tree traversals used stacks and *level order* traversal used queues as an auxiliary data structure. In this section we will discuss new traversal algorithms which do not need both stacks and queues and such traversal algorithms are called *threaded binary tree traversals* or *stack/queue less traversals*.

Issues with Regular Binary Tree Traversals

* The storage space required for the stack and queue is large.
* The majority of pointers in any binary tree are NULL. For example, a binary tree with n nodes has $n + 1$ NULL pointers and these were wasted.

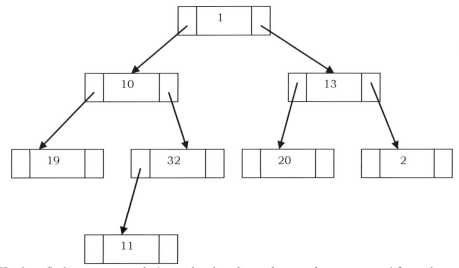

* It is difficult to find successor node (preorder, inorder and postorder successors) for a given node.

Motivation for Threaded Binary Trees

To solve these problems, one idea is to store some useful information in NULL pointers. If we observe previous traversals carefully, stack/queue is required because we have to record the current position in order to move to right subtree after processing the left subtree. If we store the useful information in NULL pointers, then we don't have to store such information in stack/queue. The binary trees which store such information in NULL pointers are called *threaded binary trees*. From the above discussion, let us assume that we want to store some useful information in NULL pointers. The next question is what to store? The common convention is to put predecessor/successor information. That means, if we are dealing with preorder traversals then for a given node, NULL left pointer will contain preorder predecessor information and NULL right pointer will contain preorder successor information. These special pointers are called *threads*.

Classifying Threaded Binary Trees

The classification is based on whether we are storing useful information in both NULL pointers or only in one of them.

- If we store predecessor information in NULL left pointers only then we call such binary trees as *left threaded binary trees*.
- If we store successor information in NULL right pointers only then we call such binary trees as *right threaded binary trees*.
- If we store predecessor information in NULL left pointers only then we call such binary trees as *fully threaded binary trees* or simply *threaded binary trees*.

Note: For the remaining discussion we consider only (*fully*) *threaded binary trees*.

Types of Threaded Binary Trees

Based on above discussion we get three representations for threaded binary trees.

- *Preorder Threaded Binary Trees*: NULL left pointer will contain PreOrder predecessor information and NULL right pointer will contain PreOrder successor information
- *Inorder Threaded Binary Trees*: NULL left pointer will contain InOrder predecessor information and NULL right pointer will contain InOrder successor information
- *Postorder Threaded Binary Trees*: NULL left pointer will contain PostOrder predecessor information and NULL right pointer will contain PostOrder successor information

Note: As the representations are similar, for the remaining discussion, we will use InOrder threaded binary trees.

Threaded Binary Tree structure

Any program examining the tree must be able to differentiate between a regular *left/right* pointer and a *thread*. To do this, we use two additional fields into each node giving us, for threaded trees, nodes of the following form:

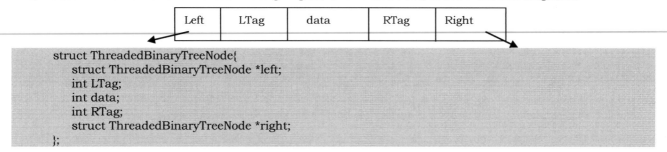

```
struct ThreadedBinaryTreeNode{
    struct ThreadedBinaryTreeNode *left;
    int LTag;
    int data;
    int RTag;
    struct ThreadedBinaryTreeNode *right;
};
```

Difference between Binary Tree and Threaded Binary Tree Structures

	Regular Binary Trees	Threaded Binary Trees
if LTag == 0	NULL	left points to the in-order predecessor
if LTag == 1	left points to the left child	left points to left child
if RTag == 0	NULL	right points to the in-order successor
if RTag == 1	right points to the right child	right points to the right child

Note: Similarly, we can define for preorder/postorder differences as well.

As an example, let us try representing a tree in inorder threaded binary tree form. The tree below shows what an inorder threaded binary tree will look like. The dotted arrows indicate the threads. If we observe, the left pointer of left most node (2) and right pointer of right most node (31) are hanging.

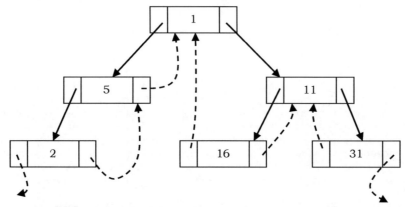

What should leftmost and rightmost pointers point to?

In the representation of a threaded binary tree, it is convenient to use a special node *Dummy* which is always present even for an empty tree. Note that right tag of dummy node is 1 and its right child points to itself.

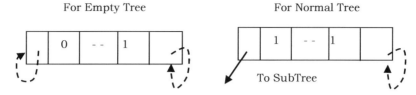

For Empty Tree   For Normal Tree

To SubTree

With this convention the above tree can be represented as:

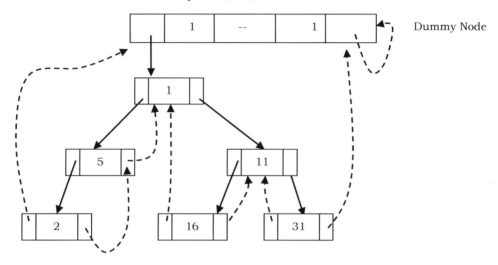

Dummy Node

Finding Inorder Successor in Inorder Threaded Binary Tree

To find inorder successor of a given node without using a stack, assume that the node for which we want to find the inorder successor is P.

Strategy: If P has a no right subtree, then return the right child of P. If P has right subtree, then return the left of the nearest node whose left subtree contains P.

```
struct ThreadedBinaryTreeNode* InorderSuccessor(struct ThreadedBinaryTreeNode *P){
    struct ThreadedBinaryTreeNode *Position;
    if(P→RTag == 0)
        return P→right;
    else {
        Position = P→right;
        while(Position→LTag == 1)
            Position = Position→left;
        return Position;
    }
}
```

Time Complexity: O(n). Space Complexity: O(1).

Inorder Traversal in Inorder Threaded Binary Tree

We can start with *dummy* node and call InorderSuccessor() to visit each node until we reach *dummy* node.

```
void InorderTraversal(struct ThreadedBinaryTreeNode *root){
    struct ThreadedBinaryTreeNode *P = InorderSuccessor(root);
    while(P != root) {
        P = InorderSuccessor(P);
        printf("%d",P→data);
    }
}
```

Other way of coding:

```
void InorderTraversal(struct ThreadedBinaryTreeNode *root){
```

```
    struct ThreadedBinaryTreeNode *P = root;
    while(1) {
            P = InorderSuccessor(P);
                if(P == root)
                    return;
                printf("%d",P→data);
        }
    }
```

Time Complexity: O(n). Space Complexity: O(1).

Finding PreOrder Successor in InOrder Threaded Binary Tree

Strategy: If *P* has a left subtree, then return the left child of *P*. If *P* has no left subtree, then return the right child of the nearest node whose right subtree contains *P*.

```
    struct ThreadedBinaryTreeNode* PreorderSuccessor(struct ThreadedBinaryTreeNode *P){
        struct ThreadedBinaryTreeNode *Position;
        if(P→LTag == 1)
                return P→left;
        else {
            Position = P;
                while(Position→RTag == 0)
                        Position = Position→right;
                return Position→right;
        }
    }
```

Time Complexity: O(n). Space Complexity: O(1).

PreOrder Traversal of InOrder Threaded Binary Tree

As in inorder traversal, start with *dummy* node and call PreorderSuccessor() to visit each node until we get *dummy* node again.

```
    void PreorderTraversal(struct ThreadedBinaryTreeNode *root){
        struct ThreadedBinaryTreeNode *P;
        P = PreorderSuccessor(root);
        while(P != root) {
                P = PreorderSuccessor(P);
                printf("%d",P→data);
        }
    }
```

Other way of coding:

```
    void PreorderTraversal(struct ThreadedBinaryTreeNode *root) {
        struct ThreadedBinaryTreeNode *P = root;
        while(1){
                P = PreorderSuccessor(P);
                if(P == root)
                        return;
                printf("%d",P→data);
        }
    }
```

Time Complexity: O(n). Space Complexity: O(1).

Note: From the above discussion, it should be clear that inorder and preorder successor finding is easy with threaded binary trees. But finding postorder successor is very difficult if we do not use stack.

Insertion of Nodes in InOrder Threaded Binary Trees

For simplicity, let us assume that there are two nodes *P* and *Q* and we want to attach *Q* to right of *P*. For this we will have two cases.

- Node *P* does not have right child: In this case we just need to attach *Q* to *P* and change its left and right pointers.

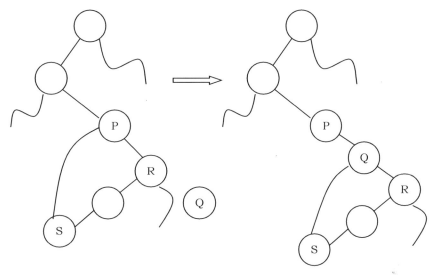

- Node *P* has right child (say, *R*): In this case we need to traverse *R's* left subtree and find the left most node and then update the left and right pointer of that node (as shown below).

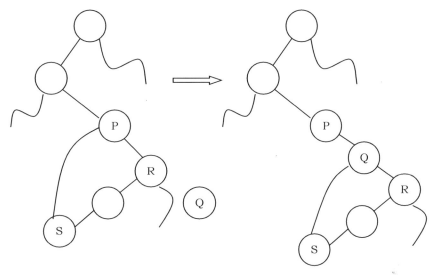

```
void InsertRightInInorderTBT(struct ThreadedBinaryTreeNode *P,  struct ThreadedBinaryTreeNode *Q){
    struct ThreadedBinaryTreeNode *Temp;
    Q→right = P→right;
    Q→RTag = P→RTag;
    Q→left = P;
    Q→LTag = 0;
    P→right = Q;
    P→RTag = 1;

    if(Q→RTag == 1) {                            //Case-2
            Temp = Q→right;
            while(Temp→LTag)
                    Temp = Temp→left;
            Temp→left = Q;
    }
}
```

Time Complexity: O(n). Space Complexity: O(1).

Problems on Threaded binary Trees

Problem-45   For a given binary tree (not threaded) how do we find the preorder successor?

Solution: For solving this problem, we need to use an auxiliary stack *S*. On the first call, the parameter node is a pointer to the head of the tree, thereafter its value is NULL. Since we are simply asking for the successor of the node we got last time we called the function. It is necessary that the contents of the stack *S* and the pointer *P* to the last node "visited" are preserved from one call of the function to the next; they are defined as static variables.

```
// pre-order successor for an unthreaded binary tree
struct BinaryTreeNode *PreorderSuccessor(struct BinaryTreeNode *node){
    static struct BinaryTreeNode *P;
    static Stack *S = CreateStack();
```

```
        if(node != NULL)
                P = node;
        if(P→left != NULL) {
            Push(S,P);
            P = P→left;
        }
        else {
                while (P→right == NULL)
                    P = Pop(S);
                P = P→right;
        }
        return P;
}
```

Problem-46   For a given binary tree (not threaded) how do we find the inorder successor?

Solution: Similar to above discussion, we can find the inorder successor of a node as:

```
// In-order successor for an unthreaded binary tree
struct BinaryTreeNode *InorderSuccssor(struct BinaryTreeNode *node){
    static struct BinaryTreeNode *P;
    static Stack *S = CreateStack();
    if(node != NULL)
            P = node;
    if(P→right == NULL)
            P = Pop(S);
    else {
            P = P→right;
            while (P→left != NULL)
                Push(S, P);
            P = P→left;
    }
    return P;
}
```

13.9 Expression Trees

A tree representing an expression is called an *expression tree*. In expression trees leaf nodes are operands and non-leaf nodes are operators. That means, an expression tree is a binary tree where internal nodes are operators and leaves are operands. Expression tree consists of binary expression. But for a u-nary operator, one subtree will be empty. The figure below shows a simple expression tree for (A + B * C) / D.

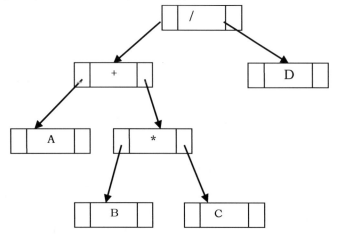

Algorithm for Building Expression Tree from Postfix Expression

```
struct BinaryTreeNode *BuildExprTree(char postfixExpr[], int size){
    struct Stack *S = Stack(size);

    for (int i = 0; i< size; i++) {
            if(postfixExpr[i] is an operand) {
                struct BinaryTreeNode newNode = (struct BinaryTreeNode*)
                    malloc( sizeof (struct BinaryTreeNode));
                if(!newNode) {
```

```
                              printf("Memory Error");
                              return NULL;
                    }
                    newNode→data =postfixExpr[i];
                    newNode→left = newNode→right = NULL;
                    Push(S, newNode);
        }
        else {
               struct BinaryTreeNode *T2 = Pop(S), *T1 = Pop(S);
               struct BinaryTreeNode newNode = (struct BinaryTreeNode*)
                         malloc(sizeof(struct BinaryTreeNode));
               if(!newNode) {
                      printf("Memory Error");
                      return NULL;
               }
               newNode→data = postfixExpr[i];
               //Make T2 as right child and T1 as left child for new node
               newNode→left = T1; newNode→right = T2;
               Push(S, newNode);
        }
    }
    return S;
}
```

Example

Assume that one symbol is read at a time. If the symbol is an operand, we create a tree node and push a pointer to it onto a stack. If the symbol is an operator, pop pointers to two trees T_1 and T_2 from the stack (T_1 is popped first) and forms a new tree whose root is the operator and whose left and right children point to T_2 and T_1 respectively. A pointer to this new tree is then pushed onto the stack. As an example, assume the input is A B C * + D /. The first three symbols are operands, so create tree nodes and push pointers to them onto a stack as shown below.

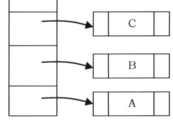

Next, an operator '*' is read, so two pointers to trees are popped, a new tree is formed and a pointer to it is pushed onto the stack.

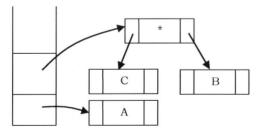

Next, an operator '+' is read, so two pointers to trees are popped, a new tree is formed and a pointer to it is pushed onto the stack.

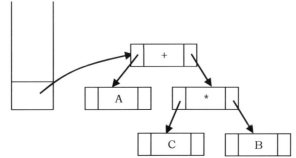

Next, an operand 'D' is read, a one-node tree is created and a pointer to the corresponding tree is pushed onto the stack.

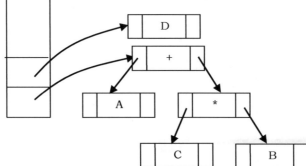

Finally, the last symbol ('/') is read, two trees are merged and a pointer to the final tree is left on the stack.

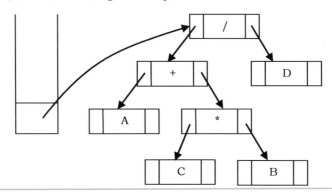

13.10 XOR Trees

This concept is similar to *memory efficient doubly linked lists* of *Linked Lists* chapter. Also, like threaded binary trees this representation does not need stacks or queues for traversing the trees. This representation is used for traversing back (to parent) and forth (to children) using $\oplus$ operation.

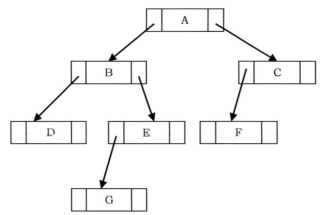

To represent the same in XOR trees, for each node below are the rules used for representation:

- Each nodes left will have the $\oplus$ of its parent and its left children.
- Each nodes right will have the $\oplus$ of its parent and its right children.
- The root nodes parent is NULL and also leaf nodes children are NULL nodes.

Based on the above rules and discussion the tree can be represented as shown in figure. The major objective of this presentation is ability to move to parent as well to children. Now, let us see how to use this representation for traversing the tree. For example, if we are at node B and want to move to its parent node A, then we just need to perform $\oplus$ on its left content with its left child address (we can use right child also for going to parent node).

Similarly, if we want to move to its child (say, left child D) then we have to perform $\oplus$ on its left content with its parent node address. One important point that we need to understand about this representation is: When we are at node B how do we know the address of its children D? Since the traversal starts at node root node, we can apply $\oplus$ on roots left content with NULL. As a result we get its left child, B. When we are at B, we can apply $\oplus$ on its left content with A address.

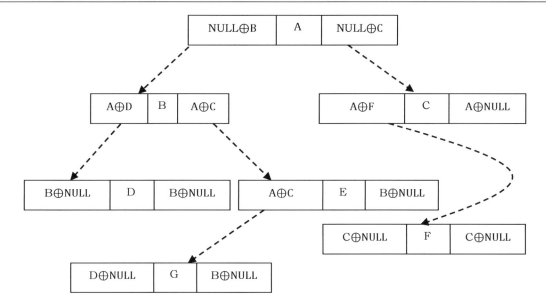

13.11 Binary Search Trees (BSTs)

Why Binary Search Trees?

In previous sections we have discussed different tree representations and in all of them we did not impose any restriction on the nodes data. As a result, to search for an element we need to check both in left subtree and in right subtree. Due to this, the worst case complexity of search operation is O(n).

In this section, we will discuss another variant of binary trees: Binary Search Trees (BSTs). As the name suggests, the main use of this representation is for *searching*. In this representation we impose restriction on the kind of data a node can contain. As a result, it reduces the worst case average search operation to O(*logn*).

Binary Search Tree Property

In binary search trees, all the left subtree elements should be less than root data and all the right subtree elements should be greater than root data. This is called binary search tree property. Note that, this property should be satisfied at every node in the tree.

- The left subtree of a node contains only nodes with keys less than the nodes key.
- The right subtree of a node contains only nodes with keys greater than the nodes key.
- Both the left and right subtrees must also be binary search trees.

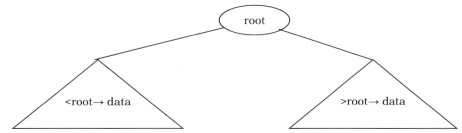

Example: The left tree is a binary search tree and right tree is not binary search tree (at node 6 it's not satisfying the binary search tree property).

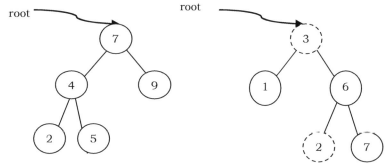

Binary Search Tree Declaration

There is no difference between regular binary tree declaration and binary search tree declaration. The difference is only in data but not in structure. But for our convenience we change the structure name as:

```
struct BinarySearchTreeNode{
    int data;
    struct BinarySearchTreeNode *left;
    struct BinarySearchTreeNode *right;
};
```

Operations on Binary Search Trees

Main operations

Following are the main operations that are supported by binary search trees:

- Find/ Find Minimum / Find Maximum element in binary search trees
- Inserting an element in binary search trees
- Deleting an element from binary search trees

Auxiliary operations

- Checking whether the given tree is a binary search tree or not
- Finding k^{th}-smallest element in tree
- Sorting the elements of binary search tree and many more

Important Notes on Binary Search Trees

- Since root data is always between left subtree data and right subtree data, performing inorder traversal on binary search tree produces a sorted list.
- While solving problems on binary search trees, first we process left subtree, then root data and finally we process right subtree. This means, depending on the problem only the intermediate step (processing root data) changes and we do not touch the first and third steps.
- If we are searching for an element and if the left subtree roots data is less than the element we want to search then skip it. Same is the case with right subtree.. Because of this binary search trees take less time for searching an element than regular binary trees. In other words, the binary search trees consider either left or right subtrees for searching an element but not both.

Finding an Element in Binary Search Trees

Find operation is straightforward in a BST. Start with the root and keep moving left or right using the BST property. If the data we are searching is same as nodes data then we return current node. If the data we are searching is less than nodes data then search left subtree of current node; otherwise search right subtree of current node. If the data is not present, we end up in a NULL link.

```
struct BinarySearchTreeNode *Find(struct BinarySearchTreeNode *root, int data ){
    // No elements in BST
    if( root == NULL )
        return NULL;
    if( data < root→data )
        return Find(root→left, data);
    else if( data > root→data )
        return( Find( root→right, data );
    return root;
}
```

Time Complexity: O(n), in worst case (when BST is a skew tree).
Space Complexity: O(n), for recursive stack.

Non recursive version of the above algorithm can be given as:

```
struct BinarySearchTreeNode *Find(struct BinarySearchTreeNode *root, int data ){
    // No elements in BST
    if( root == NULL )
        return NULL;
    while (root) {
        if(data == root→data)
            return root;
        else if(data > root→data)
            t = root→right;
```

```
        else root = root→left;
    }
    return NULL;
}
```

Time Complexity: O(n). Space Complexity: O(1).

Finding Minimum Element in Binary Search Trees

In BSTs, the minimum element is the left-most node, which does not has left child. In the BST below, the minimum element is **4**.

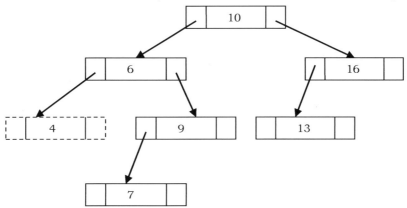

```
struct BinarySearchTreeNode *FindMin(struct BinarySearchTreeNode *root){
    if(root == NULL)  return NULL;
    else
        if( root→left == NULL )
            return root;
        else  return FindMin( root→left );
}
```

Time Complexity: O(n), in worst case (when BST is a *left skew* tree).
Space Complexity: O(n), for recursive stack.

Non recursive version of the above algorithm can be given as:

```
struct BinarySearchTreeNode *FindMin(struct BinarySearchTreeNode * root ) {
    if( root == NULL )
        return NULL;
    while( root→left != NULL )
        root = root→left;
    return root;
}
```

Time Complexity: O(n). Space Complexity: O(1).

Finding Maximum Element in Binary Search Trees

In BSTs, the maximum element is the right-most node, which does not have right child. In the BST below, the maximum element is **16**.

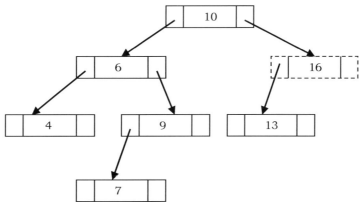

```
struct BinarySearchTreeNode *FindMax(struct BinarySearchTreeNode *root) {
    if( root == NULL )
        return NULL;
    else
        if( root→right == NULL )
            return root;
        else return FindMax( root→right );
}
```

Time Complexity: O(n), in worst case (when BST is a *right skew* tree).
Space Complexity: O(n), for recursive stack.

Non recursive version of the above algorithm can be given as:

```
struct BinarySearchTreeNode *FindMax(struct BinarySearchTreeNode * root ) {
    if( root == NULL )
        return NULL;
    while( root→right != NULL )
        root = root→right;
    return root;
}
```

Time Complexity: O(n). Space Complexity: O(1).

Where is Inorder Predecessor and Successor?

Where is the inorder predecessor and successor of node *X* in a binary search tree assuming all keys are distinct?

If *X* has two children then its inorder predecessor is the maximum value in its left subtree and its inorder successor the minimum value in its right subtree.

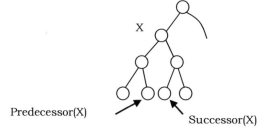

If it does not have a left child a nodes inorder predecessor is its first left ancestor.

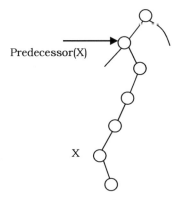

Inserting an Element from Binary Search Tree

To insert *data* into binary search tree, first we need to find the location for that element. We can find the location of insertion by following the same mechanism as that of *find* operation. While finding the location if the *data* is already there then we can simply neglect and come out. Otherwise, insert *data* at the last location on the path traversed. As an example let us consider the following tree. The dotted node indicates the element (5) to be inserted.

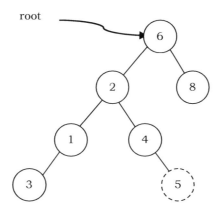

To insert 5, traverse the tree as using *find* function. At node with key 4, we need to go right, but there is no subtree, so 5 is not in the tree, and this is the correct location for insertion.

```
struct BinarySearchTreeNode *Insert(struct BinarySearchTreeNode *root, int data) {
    if( root == NULL ) {
        root = (struct BinarySearchTreeNode *) malloc(sizeof(struct  BinarySearchTreeNode));
        if( root == NULL ) {
            printf("Memory Error");
            return;
        }
        else {
            root→data = data;
            root→left = root→right = NULL;
        }
    }
    else {
        if( data < root→data )
            root→left = Insert(root→left,  data);
        else if( data > root→data )
            root→right = Insert(root→right,  data);
    }
    return root;
}
```

Note: In the above code, after inserting an element in subtrees, the tree is returned to its parent. As a result, the complete tree will get updated.

Time Complexity:$O(n)$.
Space Complexity:$O(n)$, for recursive stack. For iterative version, space complexity is O(1).

Deleting an Element from Binary Search Tree

The delete operation is more complicated than other operations. This is because the element to be deleted may not be the leaf node. In this operation also, first we need to find the location of the element which we want to delete. Once we have found the node to be deleted, consider the following cases:

- If the element to be deleted is a leaf node: return NULL to its parent. That means make the corresponding child pointer NULL. In the tree below to delete 5, set NULL to its parent node 2.

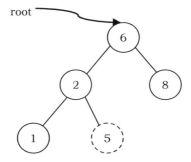

- If the element to be deleted has one child: In this case we just need to send the current nodes child to its parent. In the tree below, to delete 4, 4 left subtree is set to its parent node 2.

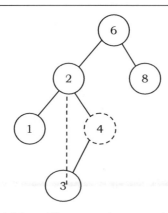

- If the element to be deleted has both children: The general strategy is to replace the key of this node with the largest element of the left subtree and recursively delete that node (which is now empty). The largest node in the left subtree cannot have a right child, the second *delete* is an easy one. As an example, let us consider the following tree. In the tree below, to delete 8, it is the right child of root. The key value is 8. It is replaced with the largest key in its left subtree (7), and then that node is deleted as before (second case).

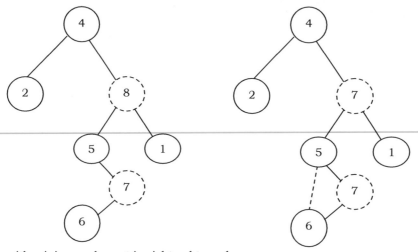

Note: We can replace with minimum element in right subtree also.

```
struct BinarySearchTreeNode *Delete(struct BinarySearchTreeNode *root, int data) {
    struct BinarySearchTreeNode *temp;
    if( root == NULL )
        printf("Element not there in tree");
    else if(data < root→data)
        root→left = Delete(root→left, data);
    else if(data > root→data)
        root→right = Delete(root→right, data);
    else {
        //Found element
        if( root→left && root→right ) {
            /* Replace with largest in left subtree */
            temp = FindMax( root→left );
            root→data = temp→data;
            root→left = Delete(root→left, root→data);
        }
        else {
            /* One child */
            temp = root;
            if( root→left == NULL )
                root = root→right;
            if( root→right == NULL )
                root = root→left;
            free( temp );
        }
```

```
        }
        return root;
    }
```

Time Complexity: O(n).

Space Complexity: O(n) for recursive stack. For iterative version, space complexity is O(1).

Problems on Binary Search Trees

Problem-47 Given pointers to two nodes in a binary search tree, find lowest common ancestor (*LCA*). Assume that both values already exist in the tree.

Solution: The main idea of the solution is: while traversing BST from root to bottom, the first node we encounter with value between α and β, i.e., $\alpha < node \rightarrow data < \beta$ is the Least Common Ancestor(LCA) of α and β (where $\alpha < \beta$). So just traverse the BST in pre-order, if we find a node with value in between α and β then that node is the LCA. If its value is greater than both α and β then LCA lies on left side of the node and if its value is smaller than both α and β then LCA lies on right side.

```
struct BinarySearchTreeNode *FindLCA(struct BinarySearchTreeNode *root,
        struct BinarySearchTreeNode *α, struct BinarySearchTreeNode * β) {
    while(1) {
        if((α→data < root→data && β→data > root→data) || (α→data > root→data && β→data < root→data))
            return root;
        if(α→data < root→data)
            root = root→left;
        else    root = root→right;
    }
}
```

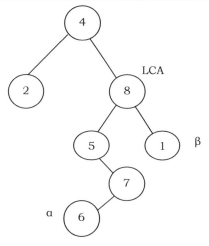

Time complexity: O(n). Space complexity: O(n), for skew trees.

Problem-48 Give an algorithm for finding the shortest path between two nodes in a BST.

Solution: It's nothing but finding the LCA of two nodes in BST.

Problem-49 Give an algorithm for counting the number of BSTs possible with n nodes.

Solution: This is a DP problem and refer to chapter on *Dynamic Programming* for algorithm.

Problem-50 Give an algorithm to check whether the given binary tree is a BST or not.

Solution: Consider the following simple program. For each node, check if node on its left is smaller and check if the node on its right is greater. This approach is wrong as this will return true for binary tree below. Checking only at current node is not enough.

```
int IsBST(struct BinaryTreeNode* root) {
    if(root == NULL) return 1;
    /* false if left is > than root */
    if(root→left != NULL && root→left→data > root→data)
        return 0;
    /* false if right is < than root */
    if(root→right != NULL && root→right→data < root→data)
        return 0;
    /* false if, recursively, the left or right is not a BST */
    if(!IsBST(root→left) || !IsBST(root→right))
        return 0;
    /* passing all that, it's a BST */
    return 1;
}
```

Problem-51   Can we think of getting the correct algorithm?

Solution: For each node, check if max value in left subtree is smaller than the current node data and min value in right subtree greater than the node data. It is assumed that we have helper functions *FindMin()* and *FindMax()* that return the min or max integer value from a non-empty tree.

```
/* Returns true if a binary tree is a binary search tree */
int IsBST(struct BinaryTreeNode* root) {
    if(root == NULL) return(1);
    /* false if the max of the left is > than root */
    if(root→left!=NULL && FindMax(root→left) > root→data)
        return 0;
    /* false if the min of the right is <= than root */
    if(root→right!=NULL && FindMin(root→right) < root→data)
        return 0;
    /* false if, recursively, the left or right is not a BST */
    if(!IsBST(root→left) || !IsBST(root→right))
        return0;
    /* passing all that, it's a BST */
    Return 1;
}
```

Time complexity: $O(n^2)$. Space Complexity: $O(n)$.

Problem-52   Can we improve the complexity of Problem-51?

Solution: Yes. A better solution looks at each node only once. The trick is to write a utility helper function IsBSTUtil(struct BinaryTreeNode* root, int min, int max) that traverses down the tree keeping track of the narrowing min and max allowed values as it goes, looking at each node only once. The initial values for min and max should be INT_MIN and INT_MAX — they narrow from there.

```
Initial call: IsBST(root, INT_MIN, INT_MAX);
int IsBST(struct BinaryTreeNode *root, int min, int max) {
    if(!root)
        return 1;
    return (root→data >min && root→data <max &&
            IsBSTUtil(root→left, min, root→data) && IsBSTUtil(root→right, root→data, max));
}
```

Time Complexity: $O(n)$. Space Complexity: $O(n)$, for stack space.

Problem-53   Can we further improve the complexity of Problem-51?

Solution: Yes, by using inorder traversal. The idea behind this solution is that, inorder traversal of BST produces sorted lists. While traversing the BST in inorder, at each node check the condition that its key value should be greater than the key value of its previous visited node. Also, we need to initialize the prev with possible minimum integer value (say, INT_MIN).

```
int prev = INT_MIN;
int IsBST(struct BinaryTreeNode *root, int *prev) {
    if(!root) return 1;
    if(!IsBST(root→left, prev))
        return 0;
    if(root→data < *prev)
        return 0;
    *prev = root→data;
    return IsBST(root→right, prev);
```

```
                    }
```

Time Complexity: O(n). Space Complexity: O(n), for stack space.

Problem-54 Give an algorithm for converting BST to circular DLL with space complexity O(1).

Solution: Convert left and right subtrees to DLLs and maintain end of those lists. Then, adjust the pointers.

```
struct BinarySearchTreeNode *BST2DLL(struct BinarySearchTreeNode *root,
                                     struct BinarySearchTreeNode **Ltail) {
    struct BinarySearchTreeNode *left, *ltail, *right, *rtail;
    if(!root) {
        * ltail = NULL;
        return NULL;
    }
    left = BST2DLL(root→left, &ltail);
    right = BST2DLL(root→right, &rtail);
    root→left = ltail;
    root→right = right;
    if(!right)
        * ltail = root;
    else {
        right→left = root;
        * ltail = rtail;
    }
    if(!left)
        return root;
    else {
        ltail→right = root;
        return left;
    }
}
```

Time Complexity: O(n).

Problem-55 Given a sorted doubly linked list, give an algorithm for converting it into balanced binary search tree.

Solution: Find the middle node and adjust the pointers.

```
struct DLLNode  * DLLtoBalancedBST(struct DLLNode *head) {
    struct DLLNode *temp, *p, *q;
    if( !head || !head→next)
        return head;
    temp = FindMiddleNode(head);
    p = head;
    while(p→next! = temp)
        p = p→next;
    p→next = NULL;
    q = temp→next;
    temp→next = NULL;
    temp→prev = DLLtoBalancedBST(head);
    temp→next = DLLtoBalancedBST(q);
    return temp;
}
```

Time Complexity: $2T(n/2) + O(n)$ [for finding the middle node]=O($nlogn$).

Note: For *FindMiddleNode* function refer *Linked Lists* chapter.

Problem-56 Given a sorted array, give an algorithm for converting the array to BST.

Solution: If we have to choose an array element to be the root of a balanced BST, which element should we pick? The root of a balanced BST should be the middle element from the sorted array. We would pick the middle element from the sorted array in each iteration. We then create a node in the tree initialized with this element. After the element is chosen, what is left? Could you identify the sub-problems within the problem?

There are two arrays left — The one on its left and the one on its right. These two arrays are the sub-problems of the original problem, since both of them are sorted. Furthermore, they are subtrees of the current node's left and right child.

The code below creates a balanced BST from the sorted array in $O(n)$ time (n is the number of elements in the array). Compare how similar the code is to a binary search algorithm. Both are using the divide and conquer methodology.

```
struct BinaryTreeNode  *BuildBST(int A[], int left, int right) {
    struct BinaryTreeNode  *newNode;
    int mid;
    if(left > right) return NULL;
    newNode = (struct BinaryTreeNode  *)malloc(sizeof(struct BinaryTreeNode));
    if(!newNode) {
            printf("Memory Error");
            return;
    }
    if(left == right) {
            newNode→data = A[left];
            newNode→left = newNode→right = NULL;
    }
    else {    mid = left + (right-left)/ 2;
            newNode→data = A[mid];
            newNode→left = BuildBST(A, left, mid - 1);
            newNode→right = BuildBST(A, mid + 1, right);
    }
    return newNode;
}
```

Time Complexity: $O(n)$. Space Complexity: $O(n)$, for stack space.

Problem-57   Given a singly linked list where elements are sorted in ascending order, convert it to a height balanced BST.

Solution: A naive way is to apply the Problem-55 solution directly. In each recursive call, we would have to traverse half of the list's length to find the middle element. The run time complexity is clearly $O(nlogn)$, where n is the total number of elements in the list. This is because each level of recursive call requires a total of $n/2$ traversal steps in the list, and there are a total of $logn$ number of levels (ie, the height of the balanced tree).

Problem-58   For Problem-57, can we improve the complexity?

Solution: Hint: How about inserting nodes following the list order? If we can achieve this, we no longer need to find the middle element, as we are able to traverse the list while inserting nodes to the tree.

Best Solution: As usual, the best solution requires us to think from another perspective. In other words, we no longer create nodes in the tree using the top-down approach. Create nodes bottom-up, and assign them to their parents. The bottom-up approach enables us to access the list in its order while creating nodes [42].

Isn't the bottom-up approach precise? Each time we are stuck with the top-down approach, give bottom-up a try. Although bottom-up approach is not the most natural way we think, it is helpful in some cases. However, we should prefer top-down instead of bottom-up in general, since the latter is more difficult to verify.

Below is the code for converting a singly linked list to a balanced BST. Please note that the algorithm requires the list length to be passed in as the function parameters. The list length could be found in $O(n)$ time by traversing the entire list once. The recursive calls traverse the list and create tree nodes by the list order, which also takes $O(n)$ time. Therefore, the overall run time complexity is still $O(n)$.

```
struct BinaryTreeNode* SortedListToBST(struct ListNode *& list, int start, int end) {
    if(start > end)
            return NULL;
    // same as (start+end)/2, avoids overflow
    int mid = start + (end - start) / 2;
    struct BinaryTreeNode *leftChild = SortedListToBST(list, start, mid-1);
    struct BinaryTreeNode * parent;
    parent = (struct BinaryTreeNode *)malloc(sizeof(struct BinaryTreeNode));
    if(!parent) {
      printf("Memory Error");
      return;
    }
    parent→data=list→data;
    parent→left = leftChild;
    list = list→next;
    parent→right = SortedListToBST(list, mid+1, end);
    return parent;
}
```

```
struct BinaryTreeNode * SortedListToBST(struct ListNode *head, int n) {
    return SortedListToBST(head, 0, n-1);
}
```

Problem-59   Give an algorithm for finding the kth smallest element in BST.

Solution: The idea behind this solution is that, inorder traversal of BST produces sorted lists. While traversing the BST in inorder, keep track of the number of elements visited.

```
struct BinarySearchTreeNode *kthSmallestInBST(struct BinarySearchTreeNode *root, int k, int *count){
    if(!root)
        return NULL;
    struct BinarySearchTreeNode *left = kthSmallestInBST(root→left, k, count);
    if( left )
        return left;
    if(++count == k)
        return root;
    return kthSmallestInBST(root→right, k, count);
}
```

Time Complexity: $O(n)$. Space Complexity: $O(1)$.

Problem-60   **Floor and ceiling:** If a given key is less than the key at the root of a BST then floor of key (the largest key in the BST less than or equal to key) must be in the left subtree. If key is greater than the key at the root then floor of key could be in the right subtree, but only if there is a key smaller than or equal to key in the right subtree; if not (or if key is equal to the key at the root) then the key at the root is the floor of key. Finding the ceiling is similar with interchanging right and left.For example, if the sorted with input array is {1, 2, 8, 10, 10, 12, 19}, then

For $x = 0$:   floor doesn't exist in array, ceil = 1, For $x = 1$:   floor = 1, ceil = 1
For $x = 5$:   floor = 2, ceil = 8, For $x = 20$:   floor = 19, ceil doesn't exist in array

Solution: The idea behind this solution is that, inorder traversal of BST produces sorted lists. While traversing the BST in inorder, keep track of the values being visited. If the roots data is greater than the given value then return the previous value which we have maintained during traversal. If the roots data is equal to the given data then return root data.

```
struct BinaryTreeNode *FloorInBST(struct BinaryTreeNode *root, int data){
    struct BinaryTreeNode *prev=NULL;
    return FloorInBSTUtil(root, prev, data);
}
struct BinaryTreeNode *FloorInBSTUtil(struct BinaryTreeNode *root, struct BinaryTreeNode *prev, int data){
    if(!root)
        return NULL;
    if(!FloorInBSTUtil(root→left, prev, data))
        return 0;
    if(root→data == data) return root;
    if(root→data > data)   return prev;
    prev = root;
    return FloorInBSTUtil(root→right, prev, data);
}
```

Time Complexity: $O(n)$. Space Complexity: $O(n)$, for stack space.

For ceiling, we just need to call the right subtree first and then followed by left subtree.

```
struct BinaryTreeNode *CeilingInBST(struct BinaryTreeNode *root, int data){
    struct BinaryTreeNode *prev=NULL;
    return CeilingInBSTUtil(root, prev, data);
}
struct BinaryTreeNode *CeilingInBSTUtil(struct BinaryTreeNode *root, struct BinaryTreeNode *prev, int data){
    if(!root) return NULL;
    if(!CeilingInBSTUtil(root→right, prev, data))
        return 0;
    if(root→data == data)
        return root;
    if(root→data < data)
        return prev;
    prev = root;
    return CeilingInBSTUtil(root→left, prev, data);
}
```

Time Complexity: $O(n)$. Space Complexity: $O(n)$, for stack space.

Problem-61   Give an algorithm for finding the union and intersection of BSTs. Assume parent pointers are available (say threaded binary trees). Also, assume the lengths of two BSTs are m and n respectively.

Solution: If parent pointers are available then the problem is same as merging of two sorted lists. This is because if we call inorder successor each time we get the next highest element. It's just a matter of which InorderSuccessor to call.

Time Complexity: $O(m + n)$. Space complexity: $O(1)$.

Problem-62   For Problem-61, what if parent pointers are not available?

Solution: If parent pointers are not available then, the BSTs can be converted to linked lists and then merged.
1   Convert both the BSTs into sorted doubly linked lists in $O(n + m)$ time. This produces 2 sorted lists.
2   Merge the two double linked lists into one and also maintain the count of total elements in $O(n + m)$ time.
3   Convert the sorted doubly linked list into height balanced tree in $O(n + m)$ time.

Problem-63   For Problem-61, is there any alternative way of solving the problem?

Solution: Yes, by using inorder traversal.
* Perform inorder traversal on one of the BST.
* While performing the traversal store them in table (hash table).
* After completion of the traversal of first *BST*, start traversal of the second *BST* and compare them with hash table contents.

Time Complexity: $O(m + n)$. Space Complexity: $O(Max(m, n))$.

Problem-64   Given a *BST* and two numbers $K1$ and $K2$, give an algorithm for printing all the elements of *BST* in the range $K1$ and $K2$.

Solution:
```
void RangePrinter(struct BinarySearchTreeNode *root, int K1, int K2) {
    f(root == NULL)  return;
    if(root→data >= K1)
        RangePrinter(root→left, K1, K2);
    if(root→data >= K1 && root→data <= K2)
        printf("%d", root→data);
    if(root→data <= K2)
        RangePrinter(root→right, K1, K2);
}
```

Time Complexity: $O(n)$. Space Complexity: $O(n)$, for stack space.

Problem-65   For Problem-64, is there any alternative way of solving the problem?

Solution: We can use level order traversal: while adding the elements to queue check for the range.

```
void  RangeSeachLevelOrder(struct BinarySearchTreeNode *root, int K1, int K2){
    struct BinarySearchTreeNode *temp;
    struct Queue *Q = CreateQueue();
    if(!root)  return NULL;
    Q = EnQueue(Q, root);
    while(!IsEmptyQueue(Q)) {
        temp=DeQueue(Q);
        if(temp→data >= K1 && temp→data <= K2)
            printf("%d",temp→data);
        if(temp→left && temp→data >= K1)
            EnQueue(Q, temp→left);
        if(temp→right && temp→data <= K2)
            EnQueue(Q, temp→right);
    }
    DeleteQueue(Q);
    return NULL;
}
```

Time Complexity: $O(n)$. Space Complexity: $O(n)$, for queue.

Problem-66   For Problem-64, can we still think of alternative way for solving the problem?

Solution: First locate $K1$ with normal binary search and after that use InOrder successor until we encounter $K2$. For algorithm, refer problems section of threaded binary trees.

Problem-67   Given root of a Binary Search tree, trim the tree, so that all elements in the new tree returned are between the inputs A and B.

Solution: It's just another way of asking the Problem-64.

Problem-68   Given two BSTs, check whether the elements of them are same or not. For example: two BSTs with data 10 5 20 15 30 and 10 20 15 30 5 should return true and the dataset with 10 5 20 15 30 and 10 15 30 20 5 should return false. **Note:** BSTs data can be in any order.

Solution: One simple way is performing a traversal on first tree and storing its data in hash table. As a second step perform traversal on second tree and check whether that data is already there in hash table or not. During the traversal of second tree if we find any mismatch return false.

Time Complexity: O($max(m,n)$), where m and n are the number of elements in first and second BST. Space Complexity: O($max(m,n)$). This depends on the size of the first tree.

Problem-69   For Problem-68, can we reduce the time complexity?

Solution: Instead of performing the traversals one after the other, we can perform $in-order$ traversal of both the trees in parallel. Since the $in-order$ traversal gives the sorted list, we can check whether both the trees are generating the same sequence or not.

Time Complexity: O($max(m,n)$). Space Complexity: O(1). This depends on the size of the first tree.

Problem-70   For the key values 1...n, how many structurally unique binary search trees are possible that store those keys.

Solution: Strategy: consider that each value could be the root. Recursively find the size of the left and right subtrees.

```
int CountTrees(int n) {
    if (n <= 1)
            return 1;
    else {
            // there will be one value at the root, with whatever remains on the left and right
            // each forming their own subtrees.Iterate through all the values that could be the root
            int sum = 0;
            int left, right, root;
            for (root=1; root<=n; root++) {
                    left = CountTrees(root - 1);
                    right = CountTrees(numKeys - root);
                    // number of possible trees with this root == left*right
                    sum += left*right;
            }
            return(sum);
    }
}
```

13.12 Balanced Binary Search Trees

In earlier sections we have seen different trees whose worst case complexity is O(n), where n is the number of nodes in the tree. This happens when the trees are skew trees. In this section we will try to reduce this worst case complexity to O($logn$) by imposing restrictions on the heights. In general, the height balanced trees are represented with $HB(k)$, where k is the difference between left subtree height and right subtree height. Sometimes k is called balance factor.

Full Balanced Binary Search Trees

In $HB(k)$, if $k = 0$ (if balance factor is zero), then we call such binary search trees as *full* balanced binary search trees. That means, in $HB(0)$ binary search tree, the difference between left subtree height and right subtree height should be at most zero. This ensures that the tree is a full binary tree. For example,

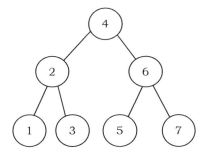

Note: For constructing $HB(0)$ tree refer problems section.

13.13 AVL (Adelson-Velskii and Landis) Trees

In $HB(k)$, if $k = 1$ (if balance factor is one), such binary search tree is called an AVL tree. That means an AVL tree is a binary search tree with a *balance* condition: the difference between left subtree height and right subtree height is at most 1.

Properties of AVL Trees

A binary tree is said to be an AVL tree, if:

- It is a binary search tree, and
- For any node X, the height of left subtree of X and height of right subtree of X differ by at most 1.

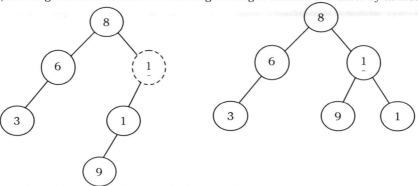

As an example among the above binary search trees, the left one is not an AVL tree, whereas the right binary search tree is an AVL tree.

Minimum/Maximum Number of Nodes in AVL Tree

For simplicity let us assume that the height of an AVL tree is h and $N(h)$ indicates the number of nodes in AVL tree with height h. To get minimum number of nodes with height h, we should fill the tree with as minimum nodes as possible. That means if we fill the left subtree with height $h - 1$ then we should fill the right subtree with height $h - 2$. As a result, the minimum number of nodes with height h is:

$$N(h) = N(h - 1) + N(h - 2) + 1$$

In the above equation:

- $N(h - 1)$ indicates the minimum number of nodes with height $h - 1$.
- $N(h - 2)$ indicates the minimum number of nodes with height $h - 2$.
- In the above expression, "1" indicates the current node.

We can give $N(h - 1)$ either for left subtree or right subtree. Solving the above recurrence gives:

$$N(h) = O(1.618^h) \Rightarrow h = 1.44logn \approx O(logn)$$

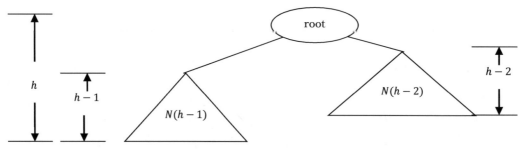

Where n is the number of nodes in AVL tree. Also, the above derivation says that the maximum height in AVL trees is $O(logn)$. Similarly, to get maximum number of nodes, we need to fill both left and right subtrees with height $h - 1$. As a result, we get $N(h) = N(h - 1) + N(h - 1) + 1 = 2N(h - 1) + 1$

The above expression defines the case of full binary tree. Solving the recurrence we get:

$$N(h) = O(2^h) \Rightarrow h = logn \approx O(logn)$$

$\therefore$ In both the cases, AVL tree property is ensuring that the height of an AVL tree with n nodes is $O(logn)$.

AVL Tree Declaration

Since AVL tree is a BST, the declaration of AVL is similar to that of BST. But just to simplify the operations, we include the height also as part of declaration.

```
struct AVLTreeNode{
```

```
        struct AVLTreeNode *left;
        int data;
        struct AVLTreeNode *right;
        int height;
};
```

Finding Height of an AVL tree

```
    int Height(struct AVLTreeNode *root ){
        if( !root) return -1;
        else return root→height;
    }
```

Time Complexity: O(1).

Rotations

When the tree structure changes (e.g., with insertion or deletion), we need to modify the tree to restore the AVL tree property. This can be done using single rotations or double rotations. Since an insertion/deletion involves adding/deleting a single node, this can only increase/decrease the height of some subtree by 1. So, if the AVL tree property is violated at a node X, it means that the heights of left(X) and right(X) differ by exactly 2. This is because, if we balance the AVL tree every time, then at any point, the difference in heights of left(X) and right(X) differ by exactly 2. Rotations is the technique used for restoring the AVL tree property. This means, we need to apply the rotations for the node X.

Observation

One important observation is that, after an insertion, only nodes that are on the path from the insertion point to the root might have their balances altered because only those nodes have their subtrees altered.

To restore the AVL tree property, we start at the insertion point and keep going to root of the tree. While moving to root, we need to consider the first node whichever is not satisfying the AVL property. From that node onwards every node on the path to root will have the issue.

Also, if we fix the issue for that first node, then all other nodes on the path to root will automatically satisfy the AVL tree property. That means we always need to care for the first node whichever is not satisfying the AVL property on the path from insertion point to root and fix it.

Types of Violations

Let us assume the node that must be rebalanced is X. Since any node has at most two children, and a height imbalance requires that $X's$ two subtree heights differ by two, we can easily observe that a violation might occur in four cases:
1. An insertion into the left subtree of the left child of X.
2. An insertion into the right subtree of the left child of X.
3. An insertion into the left subtree of the right child of X.
4. An insertion into the right subtree of the right child of X.

Cases 1 and 4 are symmetric and easily solved with single rotations. Similarly, cases 2 and 3 are also symmetric and can be solved with double rotations (needs two single rotations).

Single Rotations

Left Left Rotation (LL Rotation) [Case-1]: In the case below, at node X, the AVL tree property is not satisfying. As discussed earlier, rotation does not have to be done at the root of a tree. In general, we start at the node inserted and travel up the tree, updating the balance information at every node on the path.

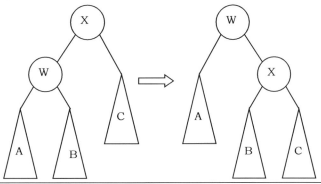

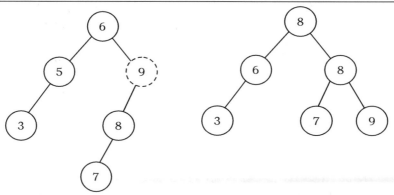

For example, in the figure above, after the insertion of 7 in the original AVL tree on the left, node 9 becomes unbalanced. So, we do a single left-left rotation at 9. As a result we get the tree on the right.

```
struct AVLTreeNode *SingleRotateLeft(struct AVLTreeNode *X ){
    struct AVLTreeNode *W = X→left;

    X→left = W→right;
    W→right = X;
    X→height = max( Height(X→left), Height(X→right) ) + 1;
    W→height = max( Height(W→left), X→height ) + 1;
    return W;  /* New root */
}
```

Time Complexity: O(1). Space Complexity: O(1).

Right Right Rotation (RR Rotation) [Case-4]: In this case, the node X is not satisfying the AVL tree property.

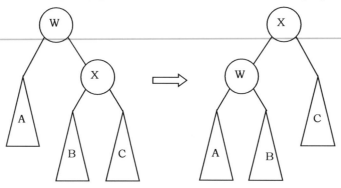

For example, in above figure, after the insertion of 29 in the original AVL tree on the left, node 15 becomes unbalanced. So, we do a single right-right rotation at 15. As a result we get the tree on the right.

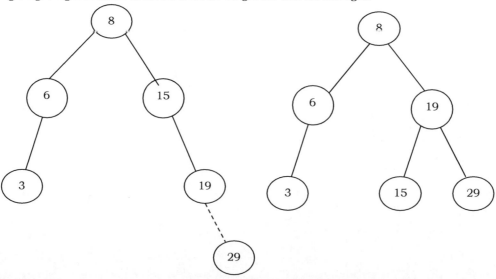

```
struct AVLTreeNode *SingleRotateRight(struct AVLTreeNode *W ) {
    struct AVLTreeNode *X  = W→right;
    W→right = X→left;
```

```
            X→left = W;
            W→height = max( Height(W→right), Height(W→left) ) + 1;
            X→height = max( Height(X→right), W→height) + 1;
            return X;
    }
```

Time Complexity: O(1). Space Complexity: O(1).

Double Rotations

Left Right Rotation (LR Rotation) [Case-2]: For case-2 and case-3 single rotation does not fix the problem. We need to perform two rotations.

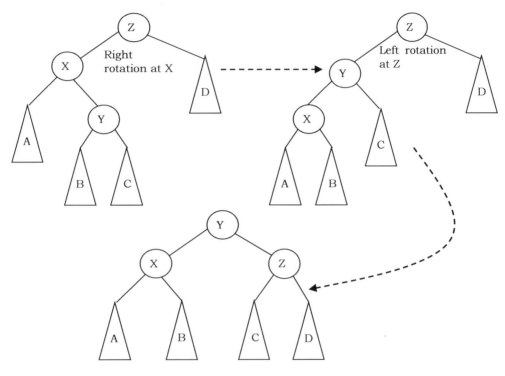

As an example, let us consider the following tree: Insertion of 7 is creating the case-2 scenario and right side tree is the one after double rotation.

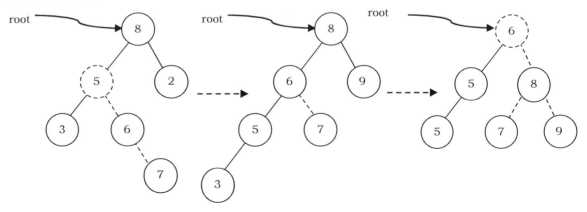

Code for left-right double rotation can be given as:

```
    struct AVLTreeNode *DoubleRotatewithLeft( struct AVLTreeNode *Z ){
        Z→left = SingleRotateRight( Z→left );
        return SingleRotateLeft(Z);
    }
```

Right Left Rotation (RL Rotation) [Case-3]: Similar to case-2, we need to perform two rotations for fixing this scenario.

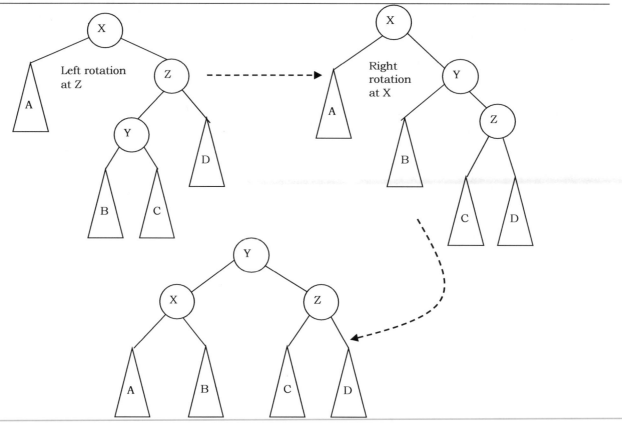

As an example, let us consider the following tree: Insertion of 6 is creating the case-3 scenario and right side tree is the one after double rotation.

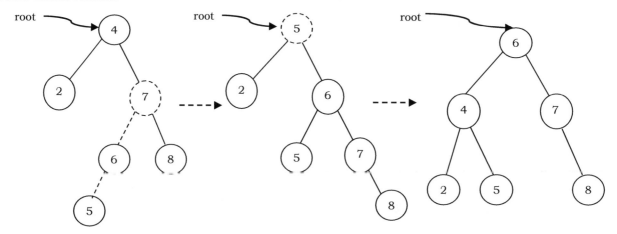

Insertion into an AVL tree

Insertion in AVL tree is similar to BST insertion. After inserting the element, we just need to check whether there is any height imbalance. If there is any imbalance, call the appropriate rotation functions.

```
struct AVLTreeNode *Insert( struct AVLTreeNode *root, struct AVLTreeNode *parent, int data){
    if( !root) {
        root = (struct AVLTreeNode*) malloc(sizeof (struct AVLTreeNode*) );
        if(!root) {
            printf("Memory Error");return NULL;
        }
        else {
            root→data = data;
            root→height = 0;
            root→left = root→right = NULL;
        }
    }
```

```
            else  if( data < root→data ) {
                root→left = Insert( root→left, root, data );
                if( ( Height( root→left ) - Height( root→right ) ) == 2 ) {
                    if( data < root→left→data )
                        root = SingleRotateLeft( root );
                    else root = DoubleRotateLeft( root );
                }
            }
            else  if( data > root→data ) {
                root→right = Insert( root→right, root, data );
                if( ( Height( root→right ) - Height( root→left ) ) == 2 ) {
                    if( data < root→right→data )
                        root = SingleRotateRight( root );
                    else root = DoubleRotateRight( root );
                }
            }
            //Else data is in the tree already. We'll do nothing
            root→height = max( Height(root→left), Height(root→right) ) + 1;
            return root;
        }
```

Time Complexity: $O(n)$. Space Complexity: $O(logn)$.

Problems on AVL Trees

Problem-71   Given a height h, give an algorithm for generating the $HB(0)$.

Solution: As we have discussed, $HB(0)$ is nothing but generating full binary tree. In full binary tree the number of nodes with height h are: $2^{h+1} - 1$ (let us assume that the height of a tree with one node is 0). As a result the nodes can be numbered as: 1 to $2^{h+1} - 1$.

```
struct BinarySearchTreeNode *BuildHB0(int h){
    struct BinarySearchTreeNode *temp;
    if(h == 0)
        return NULL;
    temp = (struct BinarySearchTreeNode *) malloc (sizeof(struct BinarySearchTreeNode));
    temp→left = BuildHB0 (h-1);
    temp→data = count++;                    //assume count is a global variable
    temp→right = BuildHB0 (h-1);
    return temp;
}
```

Time Complexity: $O(n)$.
Space Complexity: $O(logn)$, where $logn$ indicates the maximum stack size which is equal to height of tree.

Problem-72   Is there any alternative way of solving Problem-71?

Solution: Yes, we can following Mergesort logic. That means, instead of working with height, we can take the range. With this approach we do not need any global counter to be maintained.

```
Struct BinarySearchTreeNode *BuildHB0(int l, int r){
    struct BinarySearchTreeNode *temp;
    int mid = l + (r-l)/2;
    if( l > r ) return NULL;
    temp = (struct BinarySearchTreeNode *) malloc (sizeof(struct BinarySearchTreeNode));
    temp→data = mid;
    temp→left = BuildHB0(l, mid-1);
    temp→right = BuildHB0(mid+1, r);
    return temp;
}
```

The initial call to $BuildHB0$ function could be: $BuildHB0(1, 1 \ll h)$. $1 \ll h$ does the shift operation for calculating the $2^{h+1} - 1$.

Time Complexity: $O(n)$.
Space Complexity: $O(logn)$. Where $logn$ indicates maximum stack size which is equal to height of the tree.

Problem-73   Construct minimal AVL trees of height $0, 1, 2, 3, 4,$ and 5. What is the number of nodes in a minimal AVL tree of height 6?

Solution Let $N(h)$ be the number of nodes in a minimal AVL tree with height h.

$N(0) = 1$	o
$N(1) = 2$	
$N(h) = 1 + N(h-1) + N(h-2)$	
$N(2) = 1 + N(1) + N(0)$ $= 1 + 2 + 1 = 4$	
$N(3) = 1 + N(2) + N(1)$ $= 1 + 4 + 2 = 7$	
$N(4) = 1 + N(3) + N(2)$ $= 1 + 7 + 4 = 12$	
$N(5) = 1 + N(4) + N(3)$ $= 1 + 12 + 7 = 20$	...

Problem-74   For Problem-71, how many different shapes can there be of a minimal AVL tree of height?

Solution: Let $NS(h)$ be the number of different shapes of a minimal AVL tree of height h.

$NS(0) = 1$	o
$NS(1) = 2$	
$NS(2) = 2 * NS(1) * NS(0)$ $= 2 * 2 * 1 = 4$	
$NS(3) = 2 * NS(2) * NS(1)$ $= 2 * 4 * 1 = 8$	
	...
$NS(h) = 2 * NS(h-1) * NS(h-2)$	

Problem-75   Given a binary search tree check whether it is an AVL tree or not?

Solution: Let us assume that *IsAVL* is the function which checks whether the given binary search tree is an AVL tree or not. *IsAVL* returns -1 if the tree is not an AVL tree. During the checks each node sends height of it to their parent.

```
int IsAVL(struct BinarySearchTreeNode *root){
```

```
    int left, right;
    if(!root)
          return 0;

    left = IsAVL(root→left);
    if(left == -1)
          return left;

    right = IsAVL(root→right);

    if(right == -1)
          return right;

    if(abs(left-right)>1)
          return -1;

    return Max(left, right)+1;
}
```

Time Complexity: O(n). Space Complexity: O(n).

Problem-76   Given a height h, give an algorithm to generate an AVL tree with min number of nodes.

Solution: To get minimum number of nodes, fill one level with $h - 1$ and other with $h - 2$.

```
struct AVLTreeNode *GenerateAVLTree(int h){
    struct AVLTreeNode *temp;
    if(h == 0)
          return NULL;

    temp = (struct AVLTreeNode *)malloc (sizeof(struct AVLTreeNode));
    temp→left = GenerateAVLTree(h-1);
    temp→data = count++; //assume count is a global variable
    temp→right = GenerateAVLTree(h-2);
    temp→height = temp→left→height+1; // or temp→height = h;
    return temp;
}
```

Problem-77   Given an AVL tree with n integer items and two integers a and b, where a and b can be any integers with $a <= b$. Implement an algorithm to count the number of nodes in the range $[a, b]$.

Solution:

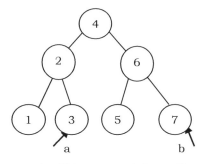

The idea is to make use of the recursive property of binary search trees. There are three cases to consider, whether the current node is in the range $[a, b]$, on the left side of the range $[a, b]$, or on the right side of the range $[a, b]$. Only subtrees that possibly contain the nodes will be processed under each of the three cases.

```
int RangeCount(struct AVLNode *root, int a, int b) {
    if(root == NULL)
          return 0;
    else if(root→data > b)
          return RangeCount(root→left, a, b);
    else if(root→data < a)
          return RangeCount(root→right, a, b);
    else if(root→data >= a && root→data <= b)
          return RangeCount(root→left, a, b) + RangeCount(root→right, a, b) + 1;
}
```

The complexity is similar to $in-order$ traversal of the tree but skipping left or right sub-trees when they do not contain any answers. So in the worst case, if the range covers all the nodes in the tree, we need to traverse all the n nodes to get the answer. The worst time complexity is therefore O(n).

If the range is small, which only covers few elements in a small subtree at the bottom of the tree, the time complexity will be O(h) = O($logn$), where h is the height of the tree. This is because only a single path is traversed to reach the small subtree at the bottom and many higher level subtrees have been pruned along the way.

Note: Refer similar problem in BST.

Problem-78   Given an BST (applicable to AVL trees as well) where each node contains two data elements (its data and also number of nodes in its subtrees) as shown below. Convert the tree to another BST by replacing the second data (number of nodes in its subtrees) with previous node data in inorder traversal. Note that, each node is merged with *inorder* previous node data. Also make sure that conversion happens in-place.

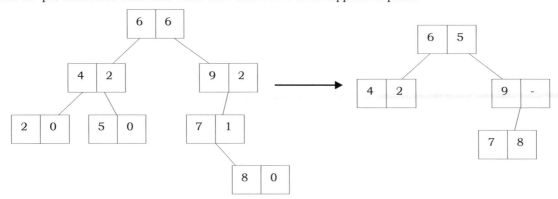

Solution: The simplest way is to use level order traversal. If the number of elements in left subtree is greater than number of elements in right subtree, find maximum element in left subtree and replace current node second data element with it. Similarly, if the number of elements in left subtree is lesser than number of elements in right subtree, find minimum element in right subtree and replace current node *second* data element with it.

```
struct BST *TreeCompression (struct BST *root){
    struct BST *temp, *temp2;
    struct Queue *Q = CreateQueue();
    if(!root)
        return NULL;

    EnQueue(Q, root);
    while(!IsEmptyQueue(Q)) {
            temp = DeQueue(Q);

                if(temp→left && temp→right && temp→left→data2 > temp→right→data2)
                    temp2 = FindMax(temp);
                else
                    temp2 = FindMin(temp);

            //Process current node
            temp→data2 = temp2→data2;

        //Remember to delete this node.
        DeleteNodeInBST(temp2);
            if(temp→left)
                    EnQueue(Q, temp→left);
            if(temp→right)
                    EnQueue(Q, temp→right);
    }
        DeleteQueue(Q);
}
```

Time Complexity: O(*nlogn*) on average since BST takes O(*logn*) on average to find maximum or minimum element. Space Complexity: O(*n*). Since, in the worst case, all the nodes on the entire last level could be in the queue simultaneously.

Problem-79   Can we reduce time complexity for the previous problem?

Solution: Let us try using an approach that is similar to what we followed in Problem-59. The idea behind this solution is that, inorder traversal of BST produces sorted lists. While traversing the BST in inorder, keep track elements visited and merge them.

```
struct BinarySearchTreeNode * TreeCompression(struct BinarySearchTreeNode *root,  int *previousNodeData){
    if(!root)
            return NULL;

    TreeCompression(root→left, previousNode);
    if(*previousNodeData == INT_MIN){
        *previousNodeData = root→data;
         free(root);
    }
```

13.13 AVL (Adelson-Velskii and Landis) Trees

```
        //Process current node
        if(*previousNodeData != INT_MIN){
            root→data2 = previousNodeData;
            *previousNodeData = INT_MIN;
        }
        return TreeCompression(root→right, previousNode);
}
```

Time Complexity: O(n).

Space Complexity: O(1). Note that, we are still having recursive stack space for inorder traversal.

Problem-80   Given a BST and a key, find the element in BST which is closest to the given key.

Solution: As a simple solution, we can use level-order traversal and for every element compute the different between given key and element's value. If that difference is less than previous maintained difference then update the difference with this new minimum value. With this approach, at the end of traversal we will get the element which is closest to given key.

```
int ClosestInBST(struct BinaryTreeNode *root, int key){
    struct BinaryTreeNode *temp, *element;
    struct Queue *Q;
    int difference = INT_MAX;
    if(!root)
        return 0;
    Q = CreateQueue();
    EnQueue(Q,root);
    while(!IsEmptyQueue(Q)) {
        temp = DeQueue(Q);
        if(difference > (abs(temp→data-key)){
            difference = abs(temp→data-key);
            element = temp;
        }
        if(temp→left)
            EnQueue (Q, temp→left);
        if(temp→right)
            EnQueue (Q, temp→right);
    }
    DeleteQueue(Q);
    return element→data;
}
```

Time Complexity: O(n). Space Complexity: O(n).

Problem-81   For Problem-80, can we solve using recursive approach?

Solution: The approach is similar to Problem-18. Following is a simple algorithm for finding closest Value in BST.

1. If root is NULL, then closest value is zero (or NULL).
2. If root's data matches the given key, then closest is root.
3. Else, consider root as closest and do following.
    a. If key is smaller than root data, find closest on left side tree of root recursively and call it temp.
    b. If key is larger than root data, find closest on right side tree of root recursively and call it temp.
4. Return root or temp depending on which ever is nearer to given key.

```
struct BinaryTreeNode * ClosestInBST(struct BinaryTreeNode *root, int key){
    struct BinaryTreeNode *temp;
    if(root == NULL)
        return root;
    if(root→data == key)
        return root;
    if(key < root→data){
        if(!root→left)
            return root;
        temp = ClosestInBST(root→left, key);
        return abs(temp→data-key) > abs(root→data-key) ? root : temp;
    }else{
        if(!root→right)
            return root;
        temp = ClosestInBST(root→right, key);
        return abs(temp→data-key) > abs(root→data-key) ? root : temp;
    }
}
```

13.13 AVL (Adelson-Velskii and Landis) Trees   317

```
    return NULL;
}
```

Time Complexity: O(n) in worst case and in average case it is O($logn$).
Space Complexity: O(n) in worst case and in average case it is O($logn$).

Problem-82   Median in an infinite series of integers

Solution: Median is the middle number in a sorted list of numbers (if we have odd number of elements). If we have even number of elements, median is the average of two middle numbers in a sorted list of numbers.

For solving this problem we can use binary search tree with additional information at each node, number of children on the left and right subtrees. We also keep the number of total nodes in the tree. Using this additional information we can find the median in O($logn$) time, taking the appropriate branch in the tree based on number of children on the left and right of the current node. But, the insertion complexity is O(n) because a standard binary search tree can degenerate into a linked list if we happen to receive the numbers in sorted order.

So, let's use a balanced binary search tree to avoid worst case behavior of standard binary search trees. For this problem, the balance factor is the number of nodes in the left subtree minus the number of nodes in the right subtree. And only the nodes with balance factor of +1 or 0 are considered to be balanced. So, the number of nodes on the left subtree is either equal to or 1 more than the number of nodes on the right subtree, but not less.

If we ensure this balance factor on every node in the tree, then the root of the tree is the median, if the number of elements is odd. In the even case, the median is the average of the root and its inorder successor, which is the leftmost descendent of its right subtree. So, complexity of insertion maintaining balance condition is O($logn$) and find median operation is O(1) assuming we calculate the inorder successor of the root at every insertion if the number of nodes is even. Insertion and balancing is very similar to AVL trees. Instead of updating the heights, we update the number of nodes information. Balanced binary search trees seem to be the most optimal solution, insertion is O($logn$) and find median is O(1).

Note: For efficient algorithm refer *Priority Queues and Heaps* chapter.

Problem-83   Given a binary tree, how do you remove all the half nodes (which has only one child)? Note that we should not touch leaves.

Solution: By using post-order traversal we can solve this problem efficiently. We first process the left children, then right children, and finally the node itself. So we form the new tree bottom up, starting from the leaves towards the root. By the time we process the current node, both its left and right subtrees were already processed.

```
struct BinaryTreeNode *removeHalfNodes(struct BinaryTreeNode *root){
    if (!root)
        return NULL;
    root→left=removeHalfNodes(root→left);
    root→right=removeHalfNodes(root→right);
    if (root→left == NULL && root→right == NULL)
        return root;
    if (root→left == NULL)
        return root→right;
    if (root→right == NULL)
        return root→left;
    return root;
}
```

Time Complexity: O(n).

Problem-84   Given a BST and two integers (minimum and maximum integers) as parameters, how do you remove (prune) elements from the tree any elements that are not within that range, inclusive.

Sample Tree

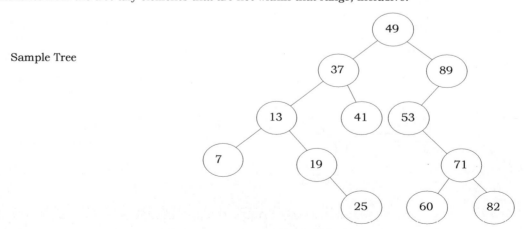

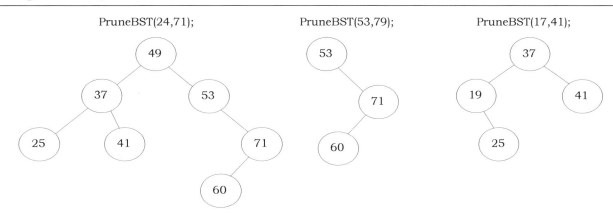

Solution: Observation: Since we need to check each and every element in tree and the subtree changes should reflect in parent, we can think of using post order traversal. So we process the nodes starting from the leaves towards the root. As a result while processing the node itself; both its left and right subtrees are valid pruned BSTs.

At each node we will return a pointer based on its value, which will then be assigned to its parent's left or right child pointer, depending on whether the current node is left or right child of the parent. If current node's value is between A and B ($A <= node's\ data <= B$) then there's no action need to be taken, so we return the reference to the node itself.

If current node's value is less than A, then we return the reference to its right subtree, and discard the left subtree. Because if a node's value is less than A, then its left children are definitely less than A since this is a binary search tree. But its right children may or may not be less than A we can't be sure, so we return the reference to it. Since we're performing bottom-up post-order traversal, its right subtree is already a trimmed valid binary search tree (possibly NULL), and left subtree is definitely NULL because those nodes were surely less than A and they were eliminated during the post-order traversal.

Similar situation occurs when node's value is greater than B, we now return the reference to its left subtree. Because if a node's value is greater than B, then its right children are definitely greater than B. But its left children may or may not be greater than B. So we discard the right subtree and return the reference to the already valid left subtree.

```
struct BinarySearchTreeNode* PruneBST(struct BinarySearchTreeNode *root, int A, int B){
    if(!root)  return NULL;
    root→left= PruneBST(root→left,A,B);
    root→right= PruneBST(root→right,A,B);

    if(A<=root→data && root→data<=B)
        return root;
    if(root→data<A)
        return root→right;
    if(root→data>B)
        return root→left;
}
```

Time Complexity: O(n) in worst case and in average case it is O($logn$).

Note: If the given BST is an AVL tree then O(n) is the average time complexity.

Problem-85   Given a binary tree, how do you remove leaves of it?

Solution: By using post-order traversal we can solve this problem (other traversals would also work).

```
struct BinaryTreeNode* removeLeaves(struct BinaryTreeNode* root) {
    if (root != NULL) {
        if (root→left == NULL && root→right == NULL) {
            free(root);  return NULL;
        } else {
            root→left = removeLeaves(root→left);
            root→right = removeLeaves(root→right);
        }
    }
    return root;
}
```

Time Complexity: O(n).

Problem-86   Given a binary tree, how do you connect all the adjacent nodes at the same level? Assume that given binary tree has next pointer along with left and right pointers as shown below.

```
struct BinaryTreeNode {
    int data;
    struct BinaryTreeNode *left;
```

```
      struct BinaryTreeNode *right;
      struct BinaryTreeNode *next;
};
```

Solution: One simple approach is to use level-order traversal and keep updating the next pointers. While traversing, we will link the nodes on next level. If the node has left and right node, we will link left to right. If node has next node, then link rightmost child of current node to leftmost child of next node.

```
void linkingNodesOfSameLevel(struct BinaryTreeNode *root){
    struct Queue *Q = CreateQueue();
    struct BinaryTreeNode *prev;     // Pointer to the previous node of the current level
    struct BinaryTreeNode *temp;
    int currentLevelNodeCount, nextLevelNodeCount;
    if(!root) return;
    EnQueue(Q, root);
    currentLevelNodeCount = 1;
    nextLevelNodeCount = 0;
    prev = NULL;
    while (!IsEmptyQueue(Q)) {
        temp = DeQueue(Q);
        if (temp→left){
            EnQueue(Q, temp→left);
            nextLevelNodeCount++;
        }
        if (temp→right){
            EnQueue(Q, temp→right);
            nextLevelNodeCount++;
        }
        // Link the previous node of the current level to this node
        if (prev)
            prev→next = temp;
        // Set the previous node to the current
        prev = temp;
        currentLevelNodeCount--;
        if (currentLevelNodeCount == 0) {   // if this is the last node of the current level
            currentLevelNodeCount = nextLevelNodeCount;
            nextLevelNodeCount = 0;
            prev = NULL;
        }
    }
}
```

Time Complexity: O(n). Space Complexity: O(n).

Problem-87   Can we improve space complexity for the Problem-86?

Solution: We can process the tree level by level, but without a queue. The logical part is that when we process the nodes of next level, we make sure that the current level has already been linked.

```
void linkingNodesOfSameLevel(struct BinaryTreeNode *root) {
    if(!root)
        return;
    struct BinaryTreeNode *rightMostNode = NULL, *nextHead = NULL, *temp = root;
    //connect next level of current root node level
    while(temp!= NULL){
        if(temp→left!= NULL)
            if(rightMostNode== NULL){
                rightMostNode=temp→left;
                nextHead=temp→left;
            }
            else{
                rightMostNode→next = temp→left;
                rightMostNode = rightMostNode→next;
            }
        if(temp→right!= NULL)
            if(rightMostNode== NULL){
                rightMostNode=temp→right;
                nextHead=temp→right;
            }
            else{
                rightMostNode→next = temp→right;
```

```
            rightMostNode = rightMostNode→next;
        }
    temp=temp→next;
    }
    linkingNodesOfSameLevel(nextHead);
}
```

Time Complexity: O(n). Space Complexity: O($depth\ of\ tree$) for stack space.

Problem-88   Assume that a set S of n numbers are stored in some form of balanced binary search tree; i.e. the depth of the tree is O($logn$). In addition to the key value and the pointers to children, assume that every node contains the number of nodes in its subtree. Specify a reason (s) why a balanced binary tree can be a better option than a complete binary tree for storing the set S.

Solution: Implementation of a balanced binary tree requires less RAM space as we do not need to keep complete tree in RAM (since they use pointers).

Problem-89   For the Problem-87, specify a reason (s) why a complete binary tree can be a better option than a balanced binary tree for storing the set S

Solution: A complete binary tree is more space efficient as we do not need any extra flags. A balanced binary tree usually takes more space since we need to store some flags. For example, in a Red-Black tree we need to store a bit for the color. Also, a complete binary tree can be stored in a RAM as an array without using pointers.

13.14 Other Variations in Trees

In this section, let us enumerate the other possible representations of trees. In the earlier sections, we have seen AVL trees which is a binary search tree (BST) with balancing property. Now, let us see few more balanced binary search trees: Red-Black Trees and Splay Trees.

13.14.1 Red-Black Trees

In red-black trees each node is associated with extra attribute: the color, which is either red or black. To get logarithmic complexity we impose the following restrictions.

Definition: A red-black tree is a binary search tree that satisfies the following properties:

- Root Property: the root is black
- External Property: every leaf is black
- Internal Property: the children of a red node are black
- Depth Property: all the leaves have the same black

Similar to AVL trees, if the Red-black tree becomes imbalanced then we perform rotations to reinforce the balancing property. With Red-black trees, we can perform the following operations in O($logn$) in worst case, where n is the number of nodes in the trees.

- Insertion, Deletion
- Finding predecessor, successor
- Finding minimum, maximum

13.14.2 Splay Trees

Splay-trees are BSTs with self-adjusting property. Another interesting property of splay-trees is: starting with empty tree, any sequence of K operations with maximum of n nodes takes O($Klogn$) time complexity in worst case.

Splay trees are easier to program and also ensures faster access to recently accessed items. Similar to AVL and Red-Black trees, at any point if the splay tree becomes imbalanced then we perform rotations to reinforce the balancing property.

Splay-trees cannot guarantee the O($logn$) complexity in worst case. But it gives amortized O($logn$) complexity. Even though individual operations can be expensive, any sequence of operations gets the complexity of logarithmic behavior. One operation may take more time (a single operation may take O(n) time) but the subsequent operations may not take worst case complexity and on the average $per\ operation$ complexity is O($logn$).

13.14.3 Augmented Trees

In earlier sections, we have seen the problems like finding K^{th} −smallest element in the tree and many other similar problems. For all those problems the worst complexity is O(n), where n is the number of nodes in the tree. To perform such operations in O($logn$) augmented trees are useful. In these trees, extra information is added to each node and that extra data depends on the problem we are trying to solve.

For example, to find K^{th} −smallest in binary search tree, let us see how augmented trees solve the problem.

Let us assume that we are using Red-Black trees as balanced BST (or any balanced BST) and augment the size information in the nodes data. For a given node X in Red-Black tree with a field $size(X)$ equal to the number of nodes in the subtree and can be calculated as:

$$size(X) = size(X \rightarrow left) + size(X \rightarrow right)) + 1$$

Example: With the extra size information, the augmented tree will look like:

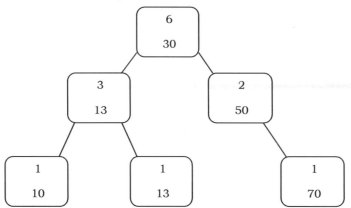

Kth-smallest operation can be defined as:

```
struct BinarySearcTreeNode *KthSmallest (struct BinarySearcTreeNode *X, int K) {
    int r = size(X→left) + 1;
    if(K == r)
        return X;
    if(K < r)
        return KthSmallest (X→left, K);
    if(K > r)
        return KthSmallest (X→right, K-r);
}
```

Time Complexity: O(*logn*). Space Complexity: O(*logn*).

13.14.4 Interval Trees

We often face questions that involve queries made in an array based on range. For example, for a given array of integers what is the maximum number in the range α to β, where α and β are of course within array limits. To iterate over those entries with intervals containing a particular value, we can use a simple array. But if we need more efficient access, we need a more sophisticated data structure.

An array-based storage scheme and a brute-force search through the entire array is acceptable only if a single search is to be performed or if the number of elements is small. For example, if you know all the array values of interest in advance, you need to make only one pass through the array. However, if you can interactively specify different search operations at different times, the brute-force search becomes impractical because every element in the array must be examined during each search operation.

If you sort the array in ascending order of the array values, you can terminate the sequential search when you reach the object whose low value is greater than element we are searching. Unfortunately, this technique becomes increasingly ineffective as the low increases, because fewer search operations are eliminated. That means, what if we have to answer a large number of queries like this, is brute force still a good option?

Another example is when we need to return sum in a given range. We can brute force this too, but the problem for large number of queries still remains. So, what can we do? Doing a bit of thinking we can come up with an approach like maintaining a separate array of n elements, where n is the size of the original array, where each index stores sum of all elements from 0 to that index. So essentially we have with a bit of preprocessing brought down the query time from a worst case O(*n*) to O(1). Now this is great as far as static arrays are concerned, but, what if we are required to perform updates on the array too.

The first approach gives us an O(*n*) query time, but an O(1) update time. The second approach, on the other hand gives us O(1) query time, but an O(*n*) update time. So, which one do we choose?

Interval trees are also binary search trees and store interval information in the node structure. That means, we maintain a set of n intervals $[i_1, i_2]$ such that one of the intervals containing a query point Q (if any) can be found efficiently. Interval trees are used for performing range queries efficiently.

A segment tree is a heap-like data structure that can be used for making update/query operations upon array intervals in logarithmical time. We define the segment tree for the interval $[i, j]$ in the following recursive manner:

- The root (first node in the array) node will hold the information for the interval $[i, j]$
- If $i < j$ the left and right children will hold the information for the intervals $[i, \frac{i+j}{2}]$ and $[\frac{i+j}{2}+1, j]$

Segment trees (also called as *segtrees* and *interval trees*) is a cool data structure, primarily used for range queries. It is a height balanced binary tree with a static structure. The nodes of segment tree correspond to various intervals, and can be augmented with appropriate information pertaining to those intervals. It is somewhat less powerful than balanced binary trees because of its static structure, but due to the recursive nature of operations on the segtree, it is incredibly easy to think about and code.

We can use segment trees to solve range minimum/maximum query Problems. The time complexity is T(*nlogn*) where O(n) is the time required to build the tree and each query takes O(*logn*) time.

Example: Given a set of intervals: S = {[2-5], [6-7], [6-10], [8-9], [12-15], [15-23], [25-30]}. A query with Q = 9 returns [6, 10] or [8, 9] (assume these are the intervals which contains 9 among all the intervals). A query with Q = 23 returns [15, 23].

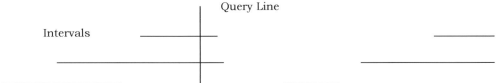

Construction of Interval Trees: Let us assume that we are given a set S of n intervals (called *segments*). These n intervals will have $2n$ endpoints. Now, let us see how to construct the interval tree.

Algorithm:

Recursively build tree on interval set S as follows:

- Sort the $2n$ endpoints
- Let X_{mid} be the median point

Time Complexity for building interval trees: O(*nlogn*). Since we are choosing the median, Interval Trees will be approximately balanced. This ensures that, we split the set of end points up in half each time. The depth of the tree is O(*logn*). To simplify the search process, generally X_{mid} is stored with each node.

Store intervals that cross X_{mid} in node n

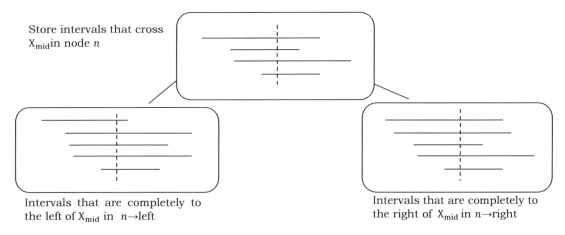

Intervals that are completely to the left of X_{mid} in $n \to$ left

Intervals that are completely to the right of X_{mid} in $n \to$ right

13.14.5 Scapegoat Trees

Scapegoat tree is a self-balancing binary search tree, discovered by Arne Andersson. It provides worst-case O(*logn*) search time, and O(*logn*) amortized (average) insertion and deletion time.

AVL tree rebalance whenever the heights of two sibling subtrees differ by more than one, scapegoat tree rebalance whenever the size of a child exceeds a certain ratio of its parent's, a ratio known as a. After inserting the element, we traverse back up the tree. If we find an imbalance where a child's size exceeds the parent's size times alpha, we must rebuild the subtree at the parent, the *scapegoat*.

There might be more than possible scapegoat, but we only have to pick one. The most optimal scapegoat is actually determined by height balance. When removing, we see if the total size of the tree is less than alpha of the largest size since the last rebuilding of the tree. If so, we rebuild the entire tree. The alpha for a scapegoat tree can be any number between 0.5 and 1.0. The value 0.5 will force perfect balance, while 1.0 will cause rebalancing to never occur, effectively turning it into a BST.

PRIORITY QUEUE AND HEAPS

Chapter-14

14.1 What is a Priority Queue?

In some situations we may need to find the minimum/maximum element among a collection of elements. We can do this with the help of Priority Queue ADT.A priority queue ADT is a data structure that supports the operations *Insert* and *DeleteMin* (which returns and removes the minimum element) or *DeleteMax* (which returns and removes the maximum element).

These operations are equivalent to *EnQueue* and *DeQueue* operations of a queue. The difference is that, in priority queues, the order in which the elements enter the queue may not be the same in which they were processed. An example application of a priority queue is job scheduling, which is prioritized instead of serving in first come first serve.

A priority queue is called an *ascending − priority* queue, if the item with smallest key has the highest priority (that means, delete smallest element always). Similarly, a priority queue is said to be a *descending − priority* queue if the item with largest key has the highest priority (delete maximum element always). Since these two types are symmetric we will be concentrating on one of them, say, ascending-priority queue.

14.2 Priority Queue ADT

The following operations make priority queues an ADT.

Main Priority Queues Operations

A priority queue is a container of elements, each having an associated key.

- Insert(key, data): Inserts data with *key* to the priority queue. Elements are ordered based on key.
- DeleteMin/DeleteMax: Remove and return the element with the smallest/largest key.
- GetMinimum/GetMaximum: Return the element with the smallest/largest key without deleting it.

Auxiliary Priority Queues Operations

- k^{th} −Smallest/k^{th} −Largest: Returns the kth −Smallest/k^{th} −Largest key in priority queue.
- Size: Returns number of elements in priority queue.
- Heap Sort: Sorts the elements in the priority queue based on priority (key).

14.3 Priority Queue Applications

Priority queues have many applications and few of them are listed below:

- Data compression: Huffman Coding algorithm
- Shortest path algorithms: Dijkstra's algorithm
- Minimum spanning tree algorithms: Prim's algorithm
- Event-driven simulation: customers in a line
- Selection problem: Finding k^{th}-smallest element

14.4 Priority Queue Implementations

Before discussing the actual implementation, let us enumerate the possible options.

Unordered Array Implementation

Elements are inserted into the array without bothering about the order. Deletions (DeleteMax) are performed by searching the key and then followed by deletion.

Insertions complexity: O(1). DeleteMin complexity: $O(n)$.

Unordered List Implementation

It is very much similar to array implementation, but instead of using arrays linked lists are used.

Insertions complexity: O(1). DeleteMin complexity: $O(n)$.

Ordered Array Implementation

Elements are inserted into the array in sorted order based on key field. Deletions are performed at only one end.

Insertions complexity: $O(n)$. DeleteMin complexity: O(1).

Ordered List Implementation

Elements are inserted into the list in sorted order based on key field. Deletions are performed at only one end, hence preserving the status of the priority queue. All other functionalities associated with a linked list ADT are performed without modification.

Insertions complexity: $O(n)$. DeleteMin complexity: O(1).

Binary Search Trees Implementation

Both insertions and deletions take $O(logn)$ on average if insertions are random (refer *Trees* chapter).

Balanced Binary Search Trees Implementation

Both insertions and deletion take $O(logn)$ in the worst case (refer *Trees* chapter).

Binary Heap Implementation

In subsequent sections we will discuss this in full detail. For now assume that binary heap implementation gives $O(logn)$ complexity for search, insertions and deletions and O(1) for finding the maximum or minimum element.

Comparing Implementations

Implementation	Insertion	Deletion (DeleteMax)	Find Min
Unordered array	1	n	n
Unordered list	1	n	n
Ordered array	n	1	1
Ordered list	n	1	1
Binary Search Trees	$logn$ (average)	$logn$ (average)	$logn$ (average)
Balanced Binary Search Trees	$logn$	$logn$	$logn$
Binary Heaps	$logn$	$logn$	1

14.5 Heaps and Binary Heap

What is a Heap?

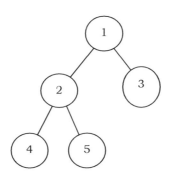

A heap is a tree with some special properties. The basic requirement of a heap is that the value of a node must be ≥ (or ≤) to the values of its children. This is called *heap property*. A heap also has the additional property that all leaves should be at h or $h - 1$ levels (where h is the height of the tree) for some $h > 0$ (*complete binary trees*). That means heap should form a *complete binary tree* (as shown below).

In the examples below, the left tree is a heap (each element is greater than its children) and right tree is not a heap (since, 11 is greater than 2).

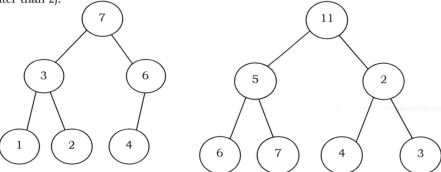

Types of Heaps?

Based on the property of a heap we can classify heaps into two types:

- **Min heap:** The value of a node must be less than or equal to the values of its children

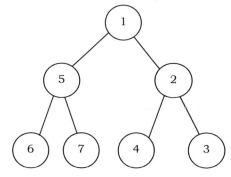

- **Max heap:** The value of a node must be greater than or equal to the values of its children

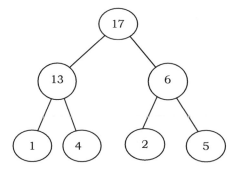

14.6 Binary Heaps

In binary heap each node may have up to two children. In practice, binary heaps are enough and we concentrate on binary min heaps and binary max heaps for remaining discussion.

Representing Heaps

Before looking at heap operations, let us see how heaps can be represented. One possibility is using arrays. Since heaps are forming complete binary trees, there will not be any wastage of locations. For the discussion below let us assume that elements are stored in arrays, which starts at index 0. The previous max heap can be represented as:

17	13	6	1	4	2	5
0	1	2	3	4	5	6

Note: For the remaining discussion let us assume that we are doing manipulations in max heap.

Declaration of Heap

```
struct Heap {
    int *array;
    int count;              // Number of elements in Heap
    int capacity;           // Size of the heap
    int heap_type;  // Min Heap or Max Heap
};
```

Creating Heap

```
struct Heap * CreateHeap(int capacity, int heap_type) {
    struct Heap * h = (struct Heap *)malloc(sizeof(struct Heap));
    if(h == NULL) {
        printf("Memory Error");
        return;
    }

    h→heap_type = heap_type;
    h→count = 0;
    h→capacity = capacity;

    h→array = (int *) malloc(sizeof(int) * h→capacity);

    if(h→array == NULL) {
        printf("Memory Error");
        return;
    }
    return h;
}
```

Time Complexity: O(1).

Parent of a Node

For a node at i^{th} location, its parent is at $\frac{i-1}{2}$ location. In the previous example, the element 6 is at second location and its parent is at 0th location.

```
int Parent (struct Heap * h, int i) {
    if(i <= 0 || i >= h→count)
        return -1;
    return i-1/2;
}
```

Time Complexity: O(1).

Children of a Node

Similar to above discussion for a node at i^{th} location, its children are at $2*i+1$ and $2*i+2$ locations. For example, in the above tree the element 6 is at second location and its children 2 and 5 are at 5 ($2*i+1 = 2*2+1$) and 6 ($2*i+2 = 2*2+2$) locations.

```
int LeftChild(struct Heap *h, int i) {
    int left = 2 * i + 1;
    if(left >= h→count)
        return -1;

    return left;
}
```

```
int RightChild(struct Heap *h, int i) {
    int right = 2 * i + 2;
    if(right >= h→count)
        return -1;

    return right;
}
```

Time Complexity: O(1).   Time Complexity: O(1).

Getting the Maximum Element

Since the maximum element in max heap is always at root, it will be stored at h→array[0].

```
int GetMaximum(Heap * h) {
    if(h→count == 0)
        return -1;

    return h→array[0];
}
```

Time Complexity: O(1).

Heapifying an Element

After inserting an element into heap, it may not satisfy the heap property. In that case we need to adjust the locations of the heap to make it heap again. This process is called *heapifying*.

In max-heap, to heapify an element, we have to find the maximum of its children and swap it with the current element and continue this process until the heap property is satisfied at every node.

Observation: One important property of heap is that, if an element is not satisfying the heap property then all the elements from that element to root will also have the same problem. In the example below, element 1 is not satisfying the heap property and its parent 31 is also having the issue.

Similarly, if we heapify an element then all the elements from that element to root will also satisfy the heap property automatically. Let us go through an example. In the above heap, the element 1 is not satisfying the heap property. Let us try heapifying this element.

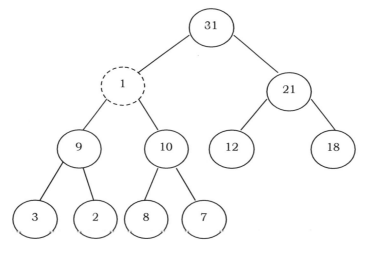

To heapify 1, find maximum of its children and swap with that.

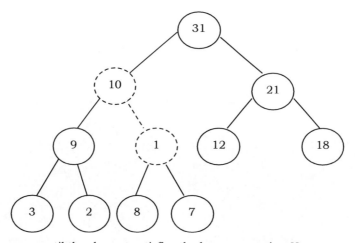

We need to continue this process until the element satisfies the heap properties. Now, swap 1 with 8.

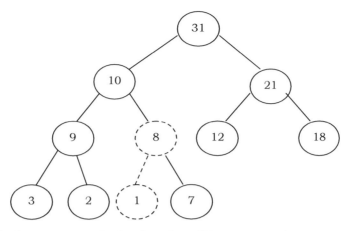

Now the tree is satisfying the heap property. In the above heapifying process, since we are moving from top to bottom, this process is sometimes called *percolate down*.

```
//Heapifying the element at location i.
void PercolateDown(struct Heap *h, int i) {
    int l, r, max, temp;

    l = LeftChild(h, i);
    r = RightChild(h, i);
    if(l != -1 && h→array[l] > h→array[i])
        max = l;
    else
        max = i;
    if(r != -1&& h→array[r] > h→array[max])
            max = r;
    if(max != i) {
        //Swap h→array[i] and  h→array[max];
        temp = h→array[i];
        h→array[i] = h→array[max];
        h→array[max] = temp;
    }
    PercolateDown(h, max);
}
```

Time Complexity: O($logn$). Heap is a complete binary tree and in the worst we start at root and coming down till the leaf. This is equal to the height of the complete binary tree. Space Complexity: O(1).

Deleting an Element

To delete an element from heap, we just need to delete the element from root. This is the only operation (maximum element) supported by standard heap. After deleting the root element, copy the last element of the heap (tree) and delete that last element. After replacing the last element the tree may not satisfy the heap property. To make it heap again, call *PercolateDown* function.

- Copy the first element into some variable
- Copy the last element into first element location
- *PercolateDown* the first element

```
int DeleteMax(struct Heap *h) {
    int data;
    if(h→count == 0)
        return -1;

    data = h→array[0];
    h→array[0] = h→array[h→count-1];
    h→count--; //reducing the heap size
    PercolateDown(h, 0);
    return data;

}
```

Note: Deleting an element uses *percolate down*.

Time Complexity: same as Heapify function and it is O($logn$).

Inserting an Element

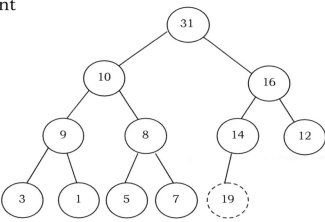

Insertion of an element is similar to heapify and deletion process.

- Increase the heap size
- Keep the new element at the end of the heap (tree)
- Heapify the element from bottom to top (root)

Before going through code, let us look at an example. We have inserted the element 19 at end of the heap and this is not satisfying the heap property.

In-order to heapify this element (19), we need to compare it with its parent and adjust them. Swapping 19 and 14 gives:

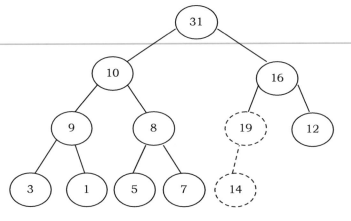

Again, swap 19 and16:

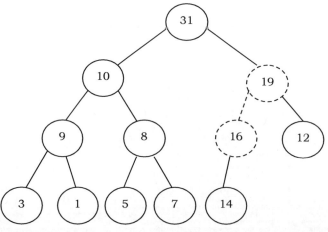

Now the tree is satisfying the heap property. Since we are following the bottom-up approach we sometimes call this process is *percolate up*.

```
int Insert(struct Heap *h, int data) {
    if(h→count == h→capacity)
        ResizeHeap(h);
    h→count++;          //increasing the heap size to hold this new item
```

```
        while(i>1 && data > h→array[(i-1)/2]) {
            h→array[i] = h→array[(i-1)/2];
            i = i-1/2;
        }
        h→array[i] = data;
    }
    void ResizeHeap(struct Heap * h) {
        int *array_old = h→array;
        h→array = (int *) malloc(sizeof(int) * h→capacity * 2);

        if(h→array == NULL) {
            printf("Memory Error");
            return;
        }

        for (int i = 0; i < h→capacity; i ++)
            h→array[i] = array_old[i];

        h→capacity *= 2;
        free(array_old);
    }
```

Time Complexity: O($logn$). The explanation is same as that of Heapify function.

Destroying Heap

```
    void DestroyHeap (struct Heap *h) {
        if(h == NULL)
            return;
        free(h→array);
        free(h);
        h = NULL;
    }
```

Heapifying the Array

One simple approach for building the heap is, take n input items and place them into an empty heap. This can be done with n successive inserts and takes O($nlogn$) in the worst case. This is due to the fact that each insert operation takes O($logn$).

Observation: Leaf nodes always satisfy the heap property and do not need to care for them. The leaf elements are always at the end and to heapify the given array it should be enough if we heapify the non-leaf nodes. Now let us concentrate on finding the first non-leaf node. The last element of the heap is at location $h \to count - 1$, and to find the first non-leaf node it is enough to find the parent of last element.

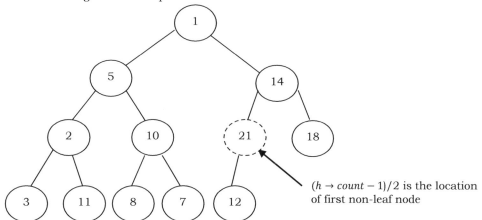

$(h \to count - 1)/2$ is the location of first non-leaf node

```
    void BuildHeap(struct Heap *h, int A[], int n) {
        if(h == NULL)
            return;
        while (len >= h→capacity)
            ResizeHeap(h);
        for (int i = 0; i < n; i ++)
            h→array[i] = A[i];
        h→count = n;
        for (int i = n/2 - 1; i >=0; i --)
```

```
            PercolateDown(h, i);
    }
```

Time Complexity: The linear time bound of building heap, can be shown by computing the sum of the heights of all the nodes. For a complete binary tree of height h containing $n = 2^{h+1} - 1$ nodes, the sum of the heights of the nodes is $n - h - 1 = n - \log n - 1$ (for proof refer *Problems Section*). That means, building heap operation can be done in linear time ($O(n)$) by applying a *PercolateDown* function to nodes in reverse level order.

Heapsort

One main application of heap ADT is sorting (heap sort). Heap sort algorithm inserts all elements (from an unsorted array) into a heap, then removes them from the root of a heap until the heap is empty. Note that heap sort can be done in place with the array to be sorted.

Instead of deleting an element, exchange the first element (maximum) with the last element and reduce the heap size (array size). Then, we heapify the first element. Continue this process until the number of remaining elements is one.

```
void Heapsort(int A[], in n) {
    struct Heap *h = CreateHeap(n);
    int old_size, i, temp;

    BuildHeap(h, A, n);
    old_size = h→count;

    for(i = n-1; i > 0; i++) {
        //h→array [0] is the largest element
        temp = h→array[0];
        h→array[0] = h→array[h→count-1];

        h→count--;
        PercolateDown(h,0);
    }
    h→count = old_size;
}
```

Time complexity: As we remove the elements from the heap, the values become sorted (since maximum elements are always *root* only). Since the time complexity of both the insertion algorithm and deletion algorithms is O($\log n$) (where n is the number of items in the heap), the time complexity of the heap sort algorithm is O($n\log n$).

14.7 Problems on Priority Queues [Heaps]

Problem-1   Is there a min-heap with seven distinct elements so that, the preorder traversal of it gives the elements in sorted order?

Solution: Yes. For the tree below, preorder traversal produces ascending order.

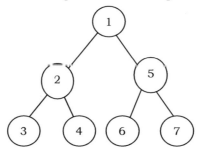

Problem-2   Is there a max-heap with seven distinct elements so that, the preorder traversal of it gives the elements in sorted order?

Solution: Yes. For the tree below, preorder traversal produces descending order.

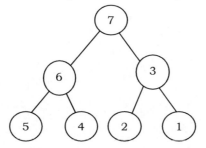

Problem-3   What are the minimum and maximum number of elements in a heap of height h?

Solution: Since heap is a complete binary tree (all levels contain full nodes except possibly the lowest level), it has at most $2^{h+1} - 1$ elements (if it is complete). This is because, to get maximum nodes, we need to fill all the h levels completely and the maximum number of nodes is nothing but sum of all nodes at all h levels.

To get minimum nodes, we should fill the $h-1$ levels fully and last level with only one element. As a result, the minimum number of nodes is nothing but sum of all nodes from $h-1$ levels plus 1 (for last level) and we get $2^h - 1 + 1 = 2^h$ elements (if the lowest level has just 1 element and all the other levels are complete).

Problem-4   Is there a min-heap/max-heap with seven distinct elements so that, the InOrder traversal of it gives the elements in sorted order?

Solution: No, since a heap must be either a min-heap or a max-heap, the root will hold the smallest element or the largest. An InOrder traversal will visit the root of tree as its second step, which is not the appropriate place if trees root contains the smallest or largest element.

Problem-5   Is there a min-heap/max-heap with seven distinct elements so that, the PostOrder traversal of it gives the elements in sorted order?

Solution: Yes, if tree is a max-heap and we want descending order (below left), or if tree is a min-heap and we want ascending order (below right).

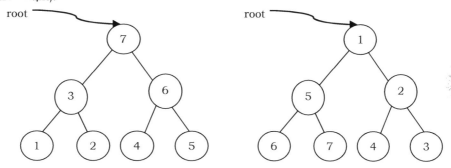

Problem-6   Show that the height of a heap with n elements is $logn$?

Solution: A heap is a complete binary tree. All the levels, except the lowest, are completely full. So the heap has at least 2^h element and atmost elements. $2^h \le n \le 2^{h+1} - 1$. This implies, $h \le logn \le h + 1$. Since h is integer, $h = logn$.

Problem-7   Given a min-heap, give an algorithm for finding the maximum element.

Solution:

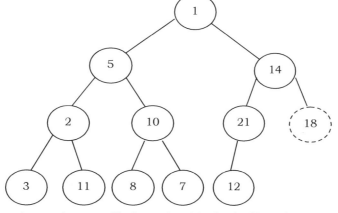

For a given min heap the maximum element will always be at leaf only. Now, the next question is how to find the leaf nodes in tree. If we carefully observe, the next node of last elements parent is the first leaf node. Since the last element is always at $h \to count - 1^{th}$ location, the next node of its parent (parent at location $\frac{h \to count - 1}{2}$) can be calculated as:

$$\frac{h \to count - 1}{2} + 1 \approx \frac{h \to count + 1}{2}$$

Now, the only step remaining is scanning the leaf nodes and finding the maximum among them.

```
int FindMaxInMinHeap(struct Heap *h) {
    int Max = -1;
    for(int i = (h→count+1)/2; i < h→count; i++)
        if(h→array[i] > Max)
            Max = h →array[i];
}
```

Time Complexity: $O(\frac{n}{2}) \approx O(n)$.

Problem-8 Give an algorithm for deleting an arbitrary element from min heap.

Solution: To delete an element, first we need to search for an element. Let us assume that we are using level order traversal for finding the element. After finding the element we need to follow the DeleteMin process.

Time Complexity = Time for finding the element + Time for deleting an element
$$= O(n) + O(logn) \approx O(n). //\text{Time for searching is dominated.}$$

Problem-9 Give an algorithm for deleting the ith indexed element in a given min-heap.

Solution:

```
int Delete(struct Heap *h, int i) {
    int key;
    if(n < i) {
        printf("Wrong position");
        return;
    }
    key = h→array[i];
    h→array[i]= h→array[h→count--];
    PercolateDown(h, i);
    return key;
}
```

Time Complexity = $O(logn)$.

Problem-10 Prove that, for a complete binary tree of height h the sum of the heights of all nodes is $O(n - h)$.

Solution: A complete binary tree has 2^i nodes on level i. Also, a node on level i has depth i and height $h - i$. Let us assume that S denotes the sum of the heights of all these nodes and S can be calculated as:

$$S = \sum_{i=0}^{h} 2^i(h - i)$$
$$S = h + 2(h - 1) + 4(h - 2) + \cdots + 2^{h-1}(1)$$

Multiplying with 2 on both sides gives: $2S = 2h + 4(h - 1) + 8(h - 2) + \cdots + 2^h(1)$
Now, subtract S from $2S$: $2S - S = -h + 2 + 4 + \cdots + 2^h \Rightarrow S = (2^{h+1} - 1) - (h - 1)$

But, we already know that the total number of nodes n in a complete binary tree with height h is $n = 2^{h+1} - 1$. This gives us: $h = \log(n + 1)$. Finally, replacing $2^{h+1} - 1$ with n, gives: $S = n - (h - 1) = O(n - logn) = O(n - h)$.

Problem-11 Give an algorithm to find all elements less than some value k in a binary heap.

Solution: Start from the root of the heap. If the value of the root is smaller than k then print its value and call recursively once for its left child and once for its right child. If the value of a node is greater or equal than k then the function stops without printing that value.

The complexity of this algorithm is $O(n)$, where n is the total number of nodes in the heap. This bound takes place in the worst case, where the value of every node in the heap will be smaller than k, so the function has to call each node of the heap.

Problem-12 Give an algorithm for merging two binary max-heaps. Let us assume that the size of first heap is $m + n$ and size of second heap is n.

Solution: One simple way of solving this problem is:

- Assume that elements of first array (with size $m + n$) are at the beginning. That means, first m cells are filled and remaining n cells are empty.
- Without changing the first heap, just append the second heap and heapify the array.
- Since the total number of elements in the new array are $m + n$, each heapify operation takes $O(log(m + n))$.

The complexity of this algorithm is : $O((m + n)log(m + n))$.

Problem-13 Can we improve the complexity of Problem-12?

Solution: Instead of heapifying all the elements of the $m + n$ array, we can use technique of "building heap with an array of elements (heapifying array)". We can start at non-leaf nodes and heapify them. The algorithm can be given as:

- Assume that elements of first array (with size $m + n$) are at the beginning. That means, first m cells are filled and remaining n cells are empty.
- Without changing the first heap, just append the second heap.
- Now, find the first non-leaf node and start heapifying from that element.

In theory section, we have already seen that, building a heap with n elements takes $O(n)$ complexity. The complexity of merging with this technique is: $O(m + n)$.

Problem-14 Is there an efficient algorithm for merging 2 max-heaps (stored as an array)? Assume both arrays have n elements.

Solution: The alternative solution for this problem depends on what type of heap it is. If it's a standard heap where every node has up to two children and which gets filled up that the leaves are on a maximum of two different rows, we cannot get better than O(n) for merge.

There is an O($logm \times logn$) algorithm for merging two binary heaps with sizes m and n. For $m = n$, this algorithm takes O(log^2n) time complexity. We will be skipping it due to its difficulty and scope.

For better merging performance, we can use another variant of binary heap like a *Fibonacci-Heap* which can merge in O(1) on average (*amortized*).

Problem-15 Give an algorithm for finding the kth smallest element in min-heap.

Solution: One simple solution to this problem is: perform deletion k times from min-heap.

```
int FindKthLargestEle(struct Heap *h, int k) {
    //Just delete first k-1 elements and return the kth element.
    for(int i=0;i<k-1;i++)
        DeleteMin(h);

    return DeleteMin(h);
}
```

Time Complexity: O($klogn$). Since we are performing deletion operation k times and each deletion takes O($logn$).

Problem-16 For the Problem-15, can we improve the time complexity?

Solution: Assume that the original min-heap is called *HOrig* and the auxiliary min-heap is named *HAux*. Initially, the element at the top of *HOrig*, the minimum one, is inserted into *HAux*. Here we don't do the operation of DeleteMin with *HOrig*.

```
Heap HOrig;
Heap HAux;
int FindKthLargestEle( int k ) {
    int heapeElement;//Assuming heap data is of integers
    int count=1;
    HAux.Insert(HOrig.Min());
    while( true ) {
        //return the minimum element and delete it from the HA heap
        heapeElement = HAux.DeleteMin();
        if(++count == k )
                return heapeElement;
        else {    //insert the left and right children in HO into the HA
                HAux.Insert(heapeElement.LeftChild());
                HAux.Insert(heapeElement.RightChild());
        }
    }
}
```

Every while-loop iteration gives the kth smallest element and we need k loops to get the kth smallest elements. Because the size of the auxiliary heap is always less than k, every while-loop iteration the size of the auxiliary heap increases by one, and the original heap *HOrig* has no operation during the finding, the running time is O($klogk$).

Problem-17 Find k max elements from max heap.

Solution: One simple solution to this problem is: build max-heap and perform deletion k times.
$$T(n) = \text{DeleteMin from heap } k \text{ times} = \Theta(klogn).$$

Problem-18 For Problem-17, is there any alternative solution?

Solution: We can use the Problem-16 solution. At the end the auxiliary heap contains the k-largest elements. Without deleting the elements we should keep on adding elements to *HAux*.

Problem-19 How do we implement stack using heap?

Solution: To implement a stack using a priority queue PQ (using min heap), let us assume that we are using one extra integer variable c. Also, assume that c is initialized equal to any known value (e.g. 0). The implementation of the stack ADT is given below. Here c is used as the priority while inserting/deleting the elements from PQ.

```
void Push(int element) {
    PQ.Insert(c, element);
    c--;
}
int Pop() {
    return PQ.DeleteMin();
```

```
    }
    int Top() {
        return PQ.Min();
    }
    int Size() {
        return PQ.Size();
    }
    int IsEmpty() {
        return PQ.IsEmpty();
    }
```

We could also increment c back when popping.

Observation: We could use the negative of the current system time instead of c (to avoid overflow). The implementation based on this can be given as:

```
    void Push(int element) {
        PQ.insert(-gettime(),element);
    }
```

Problem-20   How do we implement Queue using heap?

Solution: To implement a queue using a priority queue PQ (using min heap), as similar to stacks simulation, let us assume that we are using one extra integer variable, c. Also, assume that c is initialized equal to any known value (e.g. 0). The implementation of the queue ADT is given below. Here the c, is used as the priority while inserting/deleting the elements from PQ.

```
    void Push(int element) {
        PQ.Insert(c, element);
        c++;
    }
    int Pop() {
        return PQ.DeleteMin();
    }
    int Top() {
        return PQ.Min();
    }
    int Size() {
        return PQ.Size();
    }
    int IsEmpty() {
        return PQ.IsEmpty();
    }
```

Note: We could also decrement c when popping.

Observation: We could use just the negative of the current system time instead of c (to avoid overflow). The implementation based on this can be given as:

```
    void Push(int element) {
        PQ.insert(gettime(),element);
    }
```

Note: The only change is that we need to take positive c value instead of negative.

Problem-21   Given a big file containing billions of numbers. How can you find the the 10 maximum numbers from that file?

Solution: Always remember that when need to find max n elements, best data structure to use is priority queues.

One solution for this problem is to divide the data in sets of 1000 elements (let's say 1000), make a heap of them, and take 10 elements from each heap one by one. Finally heap sort all the sets of 10 elements and take top 10 among those. But the problem in this approach is where to store 10 elements from each heap. That may require a large amount of memory as we have billions of numbers.

Reusing top 10 elements from earlier heap in subsequent elements can solve this problem. That means to take first block of 1000 elements and subsequent blocks of 990 elements each.

Initially Heapsort first set of 1000 numbers, take max 10 elements and mix them with 990 elements of 2nd set. Again Heapsort these 1000 numbers (10 from first set and 990 from 2nd set), take 10 max element and mix those with 990 elements of 3rd set. Repeat till last set of 990 (or less) elements and take max 10 elements from final heap. These 10 elements will be your answer.

Time Complexity: $O(n) = n/1000 \times$(complexity of Heapsort 1000 elements) Since complexity of heap sorting 1000 elements will be a constant so the $O(n) = n$ i.e. linear complexity.

Problem-22 **Merge k sorted lists with total of n elements:** We are given k sorted lists with total n inputs in all the lists. Give an algorithm to merge them into one single sorted list.

Solution: Since there are k equal size lists with a total of n elements, size of each list is $\frac{n}{k}$. One simple way of solving this problem is:

1. Take the first list and merge it with second list. Since the size of each list is $\frac{n}{k}$, this step produces a sorted list with size $\frac{2n}{k}$. This is similar to merge sort logic. Time complexity of this step is: $\frac{2n}{k}$. This is because we need to scan all the elements of both the lists.

2. Then, merge the second list output with third list. As a result this step produces the sorted list with size $\frac{3n}{k}$. Time complexity of this step is: $\frac{3n}{k}$. This is because we need to scan all the elements of both the lists (one with size $\frac{2n}{k}$ and other with size $\frac{n}{k}$).

3. Continue this process until all the lists are merged to one list.

Total time complexity: $= \frac{2n}{k} + \frac{3n}{k} + \frac{4n}{k} + \cdots \cdot \frac{kn}{k} = \sum_{i=2}^{n} \frac{in}{k} = \frac{n}{k} \sum_{i=2}^{n} i \approx \frac{n(k^2)}{k} \approx O(nk)$.
Space Complexity: O(1).

Problem-23 For the Problem-22, can we improve the time complexity?

Solution:

1. Divide the lists into pairs and merge them. That means, first take two lists at a time and merge them so that the total elements parsed for all lists is $O(n)$. This operation gives $k/2$ lists.
2. Repeat step-1 until the number of lists becomes one.

Time complexity: Step-1 executes $logk$ times and each operation parses all n elements in all the lists for making $k/2$ lists. For example, if we have 8 lists then first pass would make 4 lists by parsing all n elements. Second pass would make 2 lists by parsing again n elements and third pass would give 1 list again by parsing n elements. As a result the total time complexity is $O(nlogn)$.
Space Complexity: $O(n)$.

Problem-24 For the Problem-23, can we improve the space complexity?

Solution: Let us use heaps for reducing the space complexity.

* Build the max-heap with all first elements from each list in $O(k)$.
* In each step extract the maximum element of the heap and add it at the end of the output.
* Add the next element from the list of the one extracted. That means, we need to select the next element of the list which contains the extracted element of the previous step.
* Repeat step-2 and step-3 until all the elements are completed from all the lists.

Time Complexity $= O(nlogk)$. At a time we have k elements max heap and for all n elements we have to read just the heap in $logk$ time so total time $= O(nlogk)$.
Space Complexity: $O(k)$ [for Max-heap].

Problem-25 Given 2 arrays A and B each with n elements. Give an algorithm for finding largest n pairs $(A[i], B[j])$.

Solution:

Algorithm:

1. Heapify A and B. This step takes $O(2n) \approx O(n)$.
2. Then keep on deleting the elements from both the heaps. Each step takes $O(2logn) \approx O(logn)$.
3.
Total Time complexity: $O(nlogn)$.

Problem-26 **Min-Max heap:** Give an algorithm that supports min and max in $O(1)$ time, insert, delete min, and delete max in $O(logn)$ time. That means, design a data structure which supports the following operations:

Operation	Complexity
Init	$O(n)$
Insert	$O(logn)$
FindMin	$O(1)$
FindMax	$O(1)$
DeleteMin	$O(logn)$
DeleteMax	$O(logn)$

Solution: This problem can be solved using two heaps. Let us say two heaps are: Minimum-Heap H_{min} and Maximum-Heap H_{max}. Also, assume that elements in both the arrays have mutual pointers. That means, an element in H_{min} will have a pointer to the same element in H_{max} and an element in H_{max} will have a pointer to the same element in H_{min}.

Init	Build H_{min} in $O(n)$ and H_{max} in $O(n)$
Insert(x)	Insert x to H_{min} in $O(logn)$. Insert x to H_{max} in $O(logn)$. Update the pointers in $O(1)$
FindMin()	Return root(H_{min}) in $O(1)$
FindMax	Return root(H_{max}) in $O(1)$
DeleteMin	Delete the minimum from H_{min} in $O(logn)$. Delete the same element from H_{max} by using the mutual pointer in $O(logn)$
DeleteMax	Delete the maximum from H_{max} in $O(logn)$. Delete the same element from H_{min} by using the mutual pointer in $O(logn)$

Problem-27   Dynamic median finding. Design a heap data structure that supports finding the median.

Solution: In a set of n elements, median is the middle element, such that the number of elements lesser than the median is equal to the number of elements larger than the median. If n is odd, we can find the median by sorting the set and taking the middle element. If n is even, the median is usually defined as the average of the two middle elements. This algorithm work even when some of the elements in the list are equal. For example, the median of the multiset $\{1, 1, 2, 3, 5\}$ is 2, and the median of the multiset $\{1, 1, 2, 3, 5, 8\}$ is 2.5.

"Median heaps" are the variant of heaps that give access to the median element. A median heap can be implemented using two heaps, each containing half the elements. One is a max-heap, containing the smallest elements, the other is a min-heap, containing the largest elements. The size of the max-heap may be equal to the size of the min-heap, if the total number of elements is even. In this case, the median is the average of the maximum element of the max-heap and the minimum element of the min-heap. If there are an odd number of elements, the max-heap will contain one more element than the min-heap. The median in this case is simply the maximum element of the max-heap.

Problem-28   **Maximum sum in sliding window:** Given array A[] with sliding window of size w which is moving from the very left of the array to the very right. Assume that we can only see the w numbers in the window. Each time the sliding window moves rightwards by one position. For example: The array is [1 3 -1 -3 5 3 6 7], and w is 3.

Window position	Max
[1 3 -1] -3 5 3 6 7	3
1 [3 -1 -3] 5 3 6 7	3
1 3 [-1 -3 5] 3 6 7	5
1 3 -1 [-3 5 3] 6 7	5
1 3 -1 -3 [5 3 6] 7	6
1 3 -1 -3 5 [3 6 7]	7

Input: A long array A[], and a window width w. **Output**: An array B[], B[i] is the maximum value of from A[i] to A[i+w-1]

Requirement: Find a good optimal way to get B[i]

Solution: Brute force solution is, every time the window is moved, we can search for a total of w elements in the window.

Time complexity: $O(nw)$.

Problem-29   For Problem-28, can we reduce the complexity?

Solution: Yes, we can use heap data structure. This reduces the time complexity to $O(nlogw)$. Insert operation takes $O(logw)$ time, where w is the size of the heap. However, getting the maximum value is cheap, it merely takes constant time as the maximum value is always kept in the root (head) of the heap. As the window slides to the right, some elements in the heap might not be valid anymore (range is outside of the current window). How should we remove them? We would need to be somewhat careful here. Since we only remove elements that are out of the window's range, we would need to keep track of the elements' indices too.

Problem-30   For Problem-28, can we further reduce the complexity?

Solution: Yes, The double-ended queue is the perfect data structure for this problem. It supports insertion/deletion from the front and back. The trick is to find a way such that the largest element in the window would always appear in the front of the queue. How would you maintain this requirement as you push and pop elements in and out of the queue?

Besides, you will notice that there are some redundant elements in the queue that we shouldn't even consider. For example, if the current queue has the elements: [10 5 3], and a new element in the window has the element 11. Now, we could have emptied the queue without considering elements 10, 5, and 3, and insert only element 11 into the queue.

Typically, most people try to maintain the queue size the same as the window's size. Try to break away from this thought and think out of the box. Removing redundant elements and storing only elements that need to be considered in the queue is the key to achieving the efficient $O(n)$ solution below. This is because each element in the list is being inserted and removed at most once. Therefore, the total number of insert + delete operations is $2n$.

```
void MaxSlidingWindow(int A[], int n, int w, int B[]) {
    struct DoubleEndQueue *Q = CreateDoubleEndQueue();
    for (int i = 0; i < w; i++) {
        while (!IsEmptyQueue(Q) && A[i] >= A[QBack(Q)])
            PopBack(Q);
        PushBack(Q, i);
    }
    for (int i = w; i < n; i++) {
        B[i-w] = A[QFront(Q)];
        while (!IsEmptyQueue(Q) && A[i] >= A[QBack(Q)])
            PopBack(Q);
        while (!IsEmptyQueue(Q) && QFront(Q) <= i-w)
            PopFront(Q);
        PushBack(Q, i);
    }
    B[n-w] = A[QFront(Q)];
}
```

Problem-31   A priority queue is a list of items in which each item has associated with it a priority. Items are withdrawn from a priority queue in order of their priorities starting with the highest priority item first. If the maximum priority item is required, then a heap is constructed such than priority of every node is greater than the priority of its children.

Design such a heap where the item with the middle priority is withdrawn first. If there are n items in the heap, then the number of items with the priority smaller than the middle priority is $\frac{n}{2}$ if n is odd, else $\frac{n}{2} \mp 1$.

Explain how the withdraw and insert operations work, calculate their complexity, and how the data structure is constructed.

Solution: We can use one min heap and one max heap such that root of the min heap is larger than the root of the max heap. The size of the min heap should be equal or one less than the size of the max heap. So the middle element is always the root of the max heap.

For the insert operation, if the new item is less than the root of max heap, then insert it into the max heap, else insert it into the min heap. After the withdraw or insert operation, if the size of heaps are not as specified above than transfer the root element of the max heap to min heap or vice-versa.

With this implementation, insert and withdraw operation will be in O(*logn*) time.

Problem-32   Given two heaps, how do you merge (union) them?

Solution: Binary heap supports various operations quickly: Find-min, insert, decrease-key. If we have two min-heaps, H1 and H2, there is no efficient way to combine them into a single min-heap.

For solving this problem efficiently, we can use mergeable heaps. Mergeable heaps support efficient union operation. It is a data structure that supports the following operations:

- Create-Heap(): creates an empty heap
- Insert(H,X,K) : insert an item x with key K into a heap H
- Find-Min(H) : return item with min key
- Delete-Min(H) : return and remove
- Union(H1, H2) : merge heaps H1 and H2

Examples of mergeable heaps are:

- Binomial Heaps
- Fibonacci Heaps

Both heaps also support:

1. Decrease-Key(H,X,K): assign item Y with a smaller key K
2. Delete(H,X) : remove item X

Binomial Heaps: Unlike binary heap which consists of a single tree, a *binomial* heap consists of a small set of component trees and no need to rebuild everything when union is performed. Each component tree is in a special format, called a *binomial tree*.

A binomial tree of order k, denoted by B_k is defined recursively as follows:

- B_0 is a tree with a single node
- For $k \geq 1$, B_k is formed by joining two B_{k-1}, such that the root of one tree becomes the leftmost child of the root of the other.

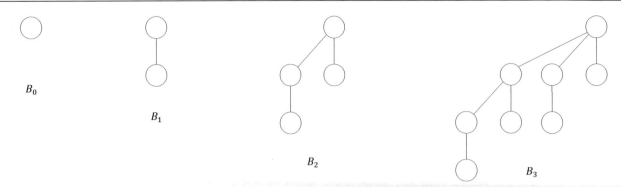

Fibonacci Heaps: Fibonacci heap is another example of mergeable heap. It has no good worst-case guarantee for any operation (except Insert/Create-Heap). Fibonacci Heaps have excellent amortized cost to perform each operation. Like *binomial* heap, *fibonacci* heap consists of a set of min-heap ordered component trees. However, unlike binomial heap, it has

- No limit on number of trees (up to $O(n)$), and
- No limit on height of a tree (up to $O(n)$)

Also, *Find-Min*, *Delete-Min*, *Union*, *Decrease-Key*, *Delete* all have worst-case $O(n)$ running time. However, in the amortized sense, each operation performs very quickly.

Operation	Binary Heap	Binomial Heap	Fibonacci Heap
Create-Heap	$\Theta(1)$	$\Theta(1)$	$\Theta(1)$
Find-Min	$\Theta(1)$	$\Theta(logn)$	$\Theta(1)$
Delete-Min	$\Theta(logn)$	$\Theta(logn)$	$\Theta(logn)$
Insert	$\Theta(logn)$	$\Theta(logn)$	$\Theta(1)$
Delete	$\Theta(logn)$	$\Theta(logn)$	$\Theta(logn)$
Decrease-Key	$\Theta(logn)$	$\Theta(logn)$	$\Theta(1)$
Union	$\Theta(n)$	$\Theta(logn)$	$\Theta(1)$

Problem-33   Median in an infinite series of integers

Solution: Median is the middle number in a sorted list of numbers (if we have odd number of elements). If we have even number of elements, median is the average of two middle numbers in a sorted list of numbers.

We can solve this problem efficiently by using 2 heaps: One MaxHeap and one MinHeap.

1. MaxHeap contains the smallest half of the received integers
2. MinHeap contains the largest half of the received integers

The integers in MaxHeap are always less than or equal to the integers in MinHeap. Also, the number of elements in MaxHeap is either equal to or 1 more than the number of elements in the MinHeap.

In the stream if we get $2n$ elements (at any point of time), MaxHeap and MinHeap will both contain equal number of elements (in this case, n elements in each heap). Otherwise, if we have received $2n + 1$ elements, MaxHeap will contain $n + 1$ and MinHeap n.

Let us find the Median: If we have $2n + 1$ elements (odd), the Median of received elements will be the largest element in the MaxHeap (nothing but the root of MaxHeap). Otherwise, the Median of received elements will be the average of largest element in the MaxHeap (nothing but the root of MaxHeap) and smallest element in the MinHeap (nothing but the root of MinHeap). This can be calculated in $O(1)$.

Inserting an element into heap can be done in $O(logn)$. Note that, any heap containing $n + 1$ elements might need one delete operation (and insertion to other heap) as well.

Example:

Insert 1: Insert to MaxHeap.
MaxHeap: {1}, MinHeap:{}
Insert 9: Insert to MinHeap. Since 9 is greater than 1 and MinHeap maintains the maximum elements.
MaxHeap: {1}, MinHeap:{9}
Insert 2: Insert MinHeap. Since 2 is less than all elements of MinHeap.
MaxHeap: {1,2}, MinHeap:{9}
Insert 0: Since MaxHeap already has more than half; we have to drop the max element from MaxHeap and insert it to MinHeap. So, we have to remove 2 and insert into MinHeap. With that it becomes:
MaxHeap: {1}, MinHeap:{2,9}
Now, insert 0 to MaxHeap.

Total Time Complexity: $O(logn)$.

## Chapter-15

GRAPH ALGORITHMS

15.1 Introduction

In real world, many problems are represented in terms of objects and connections between them. For example, in an airline route map, we might be interested in questions like: "What's the fastest way to go from Hyderabad to New York?" or "What is the cheapest way to go from Hyderabad to New York?" To answer these questions we need information about connections (airline routes) between objects (towns). Graphs are data structures used for solving these kinds of problems.

15.2 Glossary

Graph: A graph is a pair (V, E), where V is a set of nodes, called *vertices* and E is a collection of pairs of vertices, called *edges*.

- *Vertices* and *edges* are positions and store elements
- Definitions that we use:
  - *Directed edge*:
    - ordered pair of vertices (u, v)
    - first vertex u is the origin
    - second vertex v is the destination
    - Example: One-way road traffic

  - *Undirected edge*:
    - unordered pair of vertices (u, v)
    - Example: Railway lines

  - *Directed graph*:
    - all the edges are directed
    - Example: route network

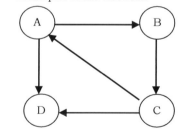

  - *Undirected graph*:
    - all the edges are undirected
    - Example: flight network

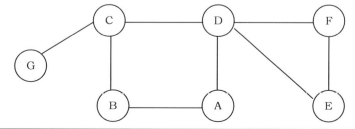

- When an edge connects two vertices, the vertices are said to be adjacent to each other and that the edge is incident on both vertices.
- A graph with no cycles is called a *tree*. A tree is an acyclic connected graph.

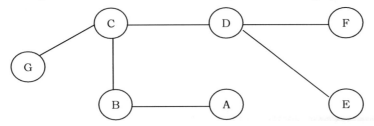

- A self loop is an edge that connects a vertex to itself.

- Two edges are parallel if they connect the same pair of vertices.

- *Degree* of a vertex is the number of edges incident on it.
- A subgraph is a subset of a graphs edges (with associated vertices) that forms a graph.
- A path in a graph is a sequence of adjacent vertices. *Simple* path is a path with no repeated vertices. In the graph below, dotted lines represent a path from *G* to *E*.

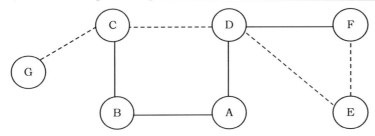

- A cycle is a path where first and last vertices are the same. A simple cycle is a cycle with no repeated vertices or edges (except the first and last vertices).

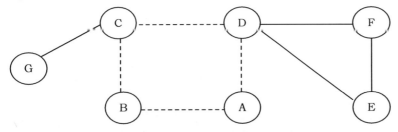

- We say that one vertex is connected to another if there is a path that contains both of them.
- A graph is connected if there is a path from *every* vertex to every other vertex.
- If a graph is not connected then it consists of a set of connected components.

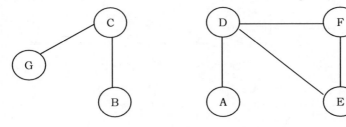

- A *directed* acyclic graph [DAG] is a directed graph with no cycles.

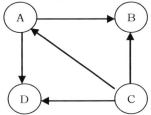

- A forest is a disjoint set of trees.
- A spanning tree of a connected graph is a subgraph that contains all of that graph's vertices and is a single tree. A spanning forest of a graph is the union of spanning trees of its connected components.
- A bipartite graph is a graph whose vertices can be divided into two sets such that all edges connect a vertex in one set with a vertex in the other set.

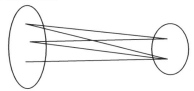

- In *weighted graphs* integers *(weights)* are assigned to each edge to represent (distances or costs).

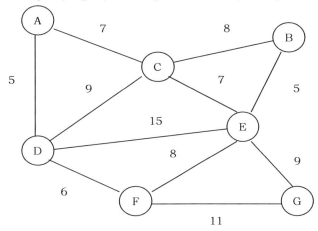

- We will denote the number of vertices in a given graph by $|V|$, the number of edges by $|E|$. Note that E can range anywhere from 0 to $|V|(|V| - 1)/2$ (in undirected graph). This is because each node can connect to every other node.
- Graphs with relatively few edges (generally if it edges $< |V| \log |V|$) are called *sparse graphs*.
- Graphs with relatively few of the possible edges missing are called *dense*.
- Directed weighted graphs are sometimes called *networks*.
- Graphs with all edges present are called *complete* graphs.

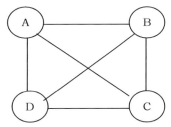

15.3 Applications of Graphs

- Representing relationships between components in electronic circuits
- Transportation networks: Highway network, Flight network
- Computer networks: Local area network, Internet, Web
- Databases: For representing ER (Entity Relationship) diagrams in databases, for representing dependency of tables in databases

15.4 Graph Representation

As in other ADTs, to manipulate graphs we need to represent them in some useful form. Basically, there are three ways of doing this:

- Adjacency Matrix
- Adjacency List
- Adjacency Set

Adjacency Matrix

Graph Declaration for Adjacency Matrix

First, let us see the components of the graph data structure. To represent graphs, we need number of vertices, number of edges and also their interconnections. So, the graph can be declared as:

```
struct Graph {
    int V;
    int E;
    int **Adj; //Since we need two dimensional matrix
};
```

Description

In this method, we use a matrix with size $V \times V$. The values of matrix are boolean. Let us assume the matrix is Adj. The value $Adj[u, v]$ set to 1 if there is an edge from vertex u to vertex v and 0 otherwise.

In the matrix, each edge is represented by two bits for undirected graphs. That means, an edge from u to v is represented by 1 values in both $Adj[u, v]$ and $Adj[u, v]$. To save time, we can process only half of this symmetric matrix. Also, we can assume that there is an "edge" from each vertex to itself. So, $Adj[u, u]$ is set to 1 for all vertices.

If the graph is a directed graph then we need to mark only one entry in the adjacency matrix. As an example, consider the directed graph below.

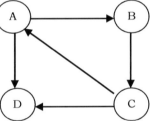

Adjacency matrix for this graph can be given as:

	A	B	C	D
A	0	1	0	1
B	0	0	1	0
C	1	0	0	1
D	0	0	0	0

Now, let us concentrate on the implementation. To read a graph, one way is to first read the vertex names and then read pairs of vertex names (edges). The code below reads an undirected graph.

```
//This code creates a graph with adj matrix representation
struct Graph *adjMatrixOfGraph() {
    int i, u, v;
    struct Graph *G = (struct Graph *) malloc(sizeof(struct Graph));
    if(!G) {
        printf("Memory Error");
        return;
    }
    scanf("Number of Vertices: %d, Number of Edges:%d", &G→V, &G→E);
    G→Adj = malloc(sizeof(G→V  * G→V));
    for(u = 0; u < G→V; u++)
        for(v = 0; v < G→V; v++)
            G→Adj[v][v] = 0;
    for(i = 0;  i < G→E; i++) {
        //Read an edge
        scanf("Reading Edge: %d %d", &u, &v);
        //For undirected graphs set both the bits
```

```
            G→ Adj[u][v] = 1;
            G→ Adj[v][u] = 1;
        }
        return G;
    }
```

The adjacency matrix representation is good if the graphs are dense. The matrix requires $O(V^2)$ bits of storage and $O(V^2)$ time for initialization. If the number of edges is proportional to V^2, then there is no problem because V^2 steps are required to read the edges. If the graph is sparse, since initializing the matrix takes V^2 and it dominates the running time of algorithm.

Adjacency List

Graph Declaration for Adjacency List

In this representation all the vertices connected to a vertex v are listed on an adjacency list for that vertex v. This can be easily implemented with linked lists. That means, for each vertex v we use a linked list and list nodes represents the connections between v and other vertices to which v has an edge. The total number of linked lists is equal to the number of vertices in the graph. The graph ADT can be declared as:

```
struct Graph {
    int V;
    int E;
    int *Adj; //head pointers to linked list
};
```

Description

Considering the same example as that of adjacency matrix, the adjacency list representation can be given as:

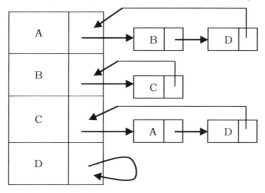

Since vertex A has an edge for B and D, we have added them in the adjacency list for A. Same is the case with other vertices as well.

```
//Nodes of the Linked List
struct ListNode {
    int vertexNumber;
    struct ListNode *next;
}
//This code creates a graph with adj list representation
struct Graph *adjListOfGraph() {
    int i, x, y;
    struct ListNode *temp;
    struct Graph *G = (struct Graph *) malloc(sizeof(struct Graph));
    if(!G) {
            printf("Memory Error");
            return;
    }
    scanf("Number of Vertices: %d, Number of Edges:%d", &G→V, &G→E);
    G→Adj = malloc(G→V * sizeof(struct ListNode));
    for(i = 0; i < G→V; i++) {
            G→Adj[i] = (struct ListNode *) malloc(sizeof(struct ListNode));
            G→Adj[i]→vertexNumber = i;
            G→Adj[i]→next = G→ Adj[i];
    }
    for(i = 0;  i < E; i++) {
```

```
        //Read an edge
        scanf("Reading Edge: %d %d", &x, &y);
        temp = (struct ListNode *) malloc(struct ListNode);
        temp→vertexNumber = y;
        temp→next = G→Adj[x];
        G→ Adj[x]→next = temp;
        temp = (struct ListNode *) malloc(struct ListNode);
        temp→vertexNumber = y;
        temp→next = G→ Adj[y];
        G→Adj[y]→ next= temp;
    }
    retutn G;
}
```

For this representation, the order of edges in the input is *important*. This is because they determine the order of the vertices on the adjacency lists. Same graph can be represented in many different ways in an adjacency list. The order in which edges appear on the adjacency list affects the order in which edges are processed by algorithms.

Disadvantages of Adjacency Lists

Using adjacency list representation we cannot perform some operations efficiently. As an example, consider the case of deleting a node. In adjacency list representation, if we delete a node from the adjacency list then that is enough. For each node on the adjacency list of that node specifies another vertex. We need to search other nodes linked list also for deleting it. This problem can be solved by linking the two list nodes which correspond to a particular edge and make the adjacency lists doubly linked. But all these extra links are risky to process.

Adjacency Set

It is very much similar to adjacency list but instead of using Linked lists, Disjoint Sets [Union-Find] are used. For more details refer *Disjoint Sets ADT* chapter.

Comparison of Graph Representations

Directed and undirected graphs are represented with same structures. For directed graphs, everything is the same, except that each edge is represented just once, an edge from x to y is represented by a 1 value in $Adj[x][y]$ in the adjacency matrix or by adding y on $x's$ adjacency list. For weighted graphs, everything is same except that fill the adjacency matrix with weights instead of boolean values.

Representation	Space	Checking edge between v and w?	Iterate over edges incident to v?
List of edges	E	E	E
Adj Matrix	V^2	1	V
Adj List	$E + V$	$Degree(v)$	$Degree(v)$
Adj Set	$E + V$	$log(Degree(v))$	$Degree(v)$

15.5 Graph Traversals

To solve problems on graphs, we need a mechanism for traversing the graphs. Graph traversal algorithms are also called as *graph search* algorithms. Like trees traversal algorithms (Inorder, Preorder, Postorder and Level-Order traversals), graph search algorithms can be thought of as starting at some source vertex in a graph, and "search" the graph by going through the edges and marking the vertices. Now, we will discuss two such algorithms for traversing the graphs.

* Depth First Search [DFS]
* Breadth First Search [BFS]

Depth First Search [DFS]

DFS algorithm works in a manner similar to preorder traversal of the trees. Like preorder traversal, internally this algorithm also uses stack. Let us consider the following example. Suppose a person is trapped inside a maze. To come out from that maze, the person visits each path and each intersection (in the worst case). Let us say the person uses two colors of paint, to mark the intersections already passed. When discovering a new intersection, it is marked grey, and he continues to go deeper. After reaching a "dead end" the person knows that there is no more unexplored path from the grey intersection, which now is completed and he marks it with black. This "dead end" is either an intersection which has already been marked grey or black, or simply a path that does not lead to an intersection.

Intersections of the maze are the vertices and the paths between the intersections are the edges of the graph. The process of returning from the "dead end" is called *backtracking*. We are trying to go away from starting vertex into the graph as deep as possible, until we have to backtrack to the preceding grey vertex. In DFS algorithm, we encounter the following types of edges.

Tree edge: encounter new vertex
Back edge: from descendent to ancestor
Forward edge: from ancestor to descendent
Cross edge: between a tree or subtrees

For most algorithms boolean classification unvisited/visited is enough (for three color implementation refer to problems section). That means, for some problems we need to use three colors, but for our discussion two colors are enough.

false   ⟶   Vertex is unvisited

true   ⟶   Vertex is visited

Initially all vertices are marked unvisited (false). DFS algorithm starts at a vertex u in graph. By starting at vertex u it considers the edges from u to other vertices. If the edge leads to an already visited vertex, then backtrack to current vertex u. If an edge leads to an unvisited vertex, then go to that vertex and start processing from that vertex. That means the new vertex becomes the current vertex. Follow this process until we reach the dead-end. At this point start *backtracking*. The process terminates when backtracking leads back to the start vertex. The algorithm based on this mechanism is given below: assume Visited[] is a global array.

```
int Visited[G→V];
void DFS(struct Graph *G, int u) {
    Visited[u] = 1;
    for( int v = 0; v < G→V; v++ ) {
        /* For example, if the adjacency matrix is used for representing the
        graph, then the condition to be used for finding unvisited adjacent
        vertex of u  is: if( !Visited[v] && G→Adj[u][v] ) */
            for each unvisited adjacent node v of u {
            DFS(G, v);
        }
    }
}
void DFSTraversal(struct Graph *G) {
    for (int i = 0; i< G→V;i++)
            Visited[i]=0;
    //This loop is required if the graph has more than one component
    for (int i = 0; i< G→V;i++)
            if(!Visited[i])
                    DFS(G, i);
}
```

As an example consider the following graph. We can see that sometimes an edge leads to an already discovered vertex. These edges are called *back edges,* and the other edges are called *tree edges* because deleting the back edges from the graph generates a tree. The final generated tree is called DFS tree and the order in which the vertices are processed is called *DFS numbers* of the vertices. In the graph below gray color indicates that the vertex is visited (there is no other significance). We need to see when Visited table is updated.

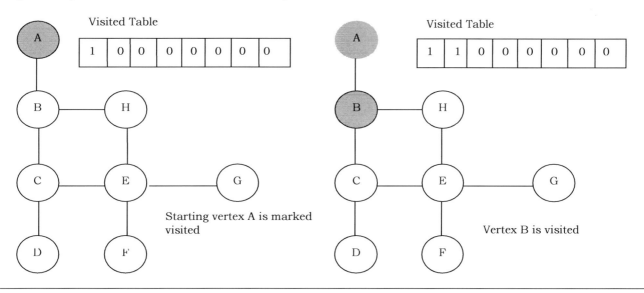

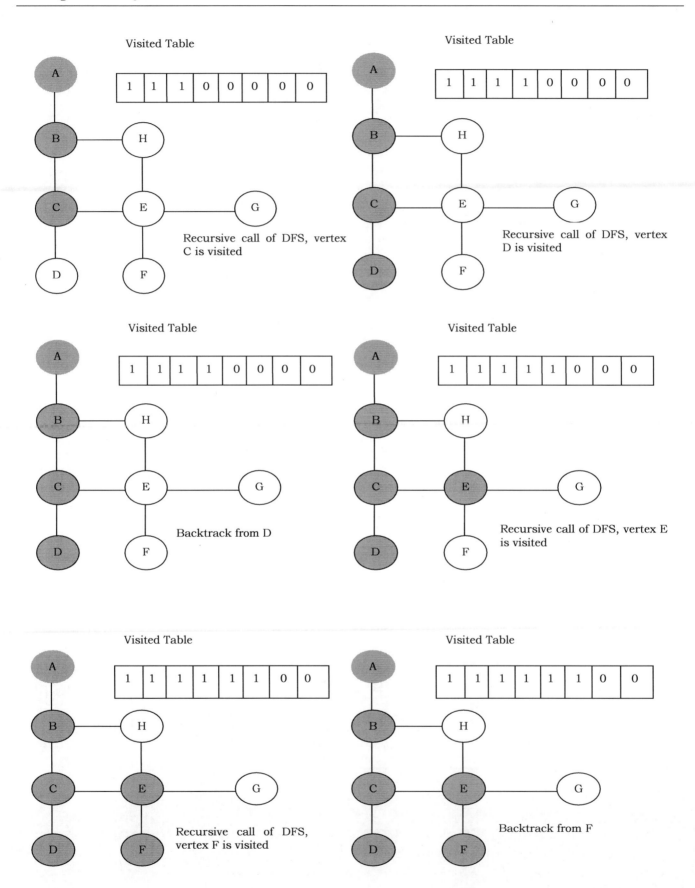

Visited Table

Recursive call of DFS, vertex C is visited

Visited Table

Recursive call of DFS, vertex D is visited

Visited Table

Backtrack from D

Visited Table

Recursive call of DFS, vertex E is visited

Visited Table

Recursive call of DFS, vertex F is visited

Visited Table

Backtrack from F

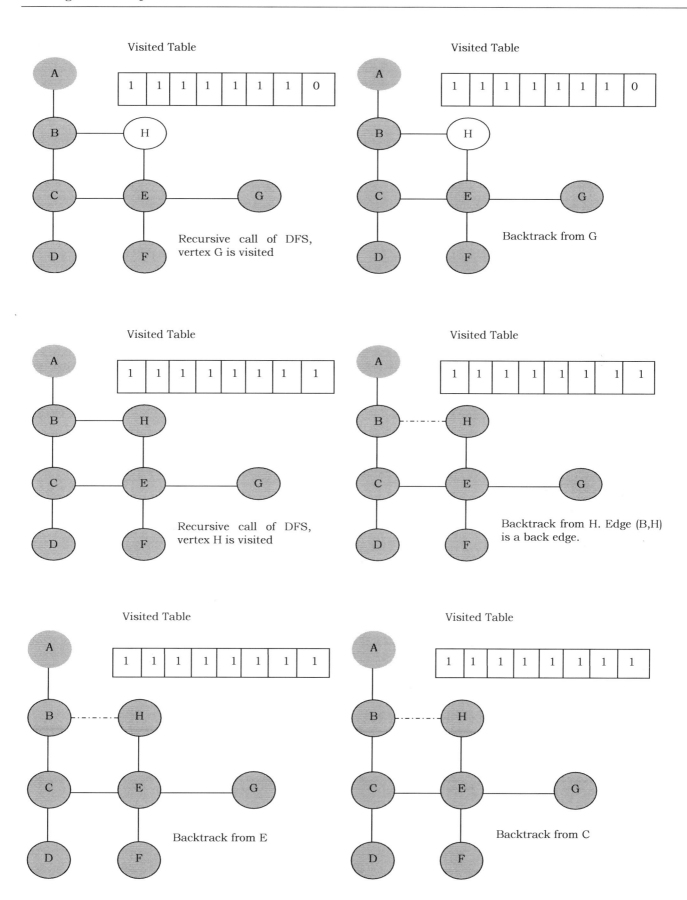

Visited Table

| 1 | 1 | 1 | 1 | 1 | 1 | 1 | 0 |

Recursive call of DFS, vertex G is visited

Visited Table

| 1 | 1 | 1 | 1 | 1 | 1 | 1 | 0 |

Backtrack from G

Visited Table

| 1 | 1 | 1 | 1 | 1 | 1 | 1 | 1 |

Recursive call of DFS, vertex H is visited

Visited Table

| 1 | 1 | 1 | 1 | 1 | 1 | 1 | 1 |

Backtrack from H. Edge (B,H) is a back edge.

Visited Table

| 1 | 1 | 1 | 1 | 1 | 1 | 1 | 1 |

Backtrack from E

Visited Table

| 1 | 1 | 1 | 1 | 1 | 1 | 1 | 1 |

Backtrack from C

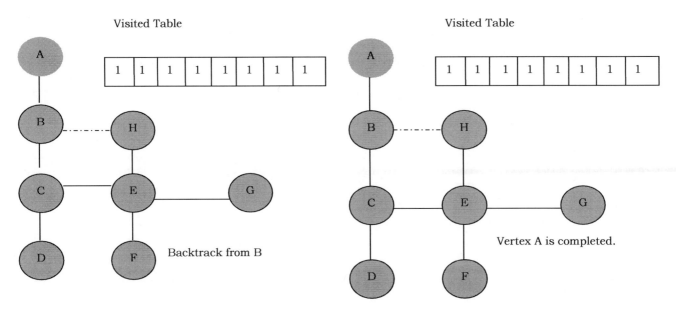

Backtrack from B

Vertex A is completed.

From the above diagrams, it can be seen that the DFS traversal creates a tree (without back edges) and we call such tree as *DFS tree*. The above algorithm works even if the given graph has connected components.

The time complexity of DFS is $O(V + E)$, if we use adjacency lists for representing the graphs. This is because we are starting at a vertex and processing the adjacent nodes only if they are not visited. Similarly, if an adjacency matrix is used for a graph representation, then all edges adjacent to a vertex can't be found efficiently, this gives $O(V^2)$ complexity.

Applications of DFS

- Topological sorting
- Finding connected components
- Finding articulation points (cut vertices) of the graph
- Finding strongly connected components
- Solving puzzles such as mazes

For algorithms refer *Problems Section*.

Breadth First Search [BFS]

BFS algorithm works similar to *level − order* traversal of the trees. Like *level − order* traversal BFS also uses queues. In fact, *level − order* traversal got inspired from BFS. BFS works level by level. Initially, BFS starts at a given vertex, which is at level 0. In the first stage it visits all vertices at level 1 (that means, vertices whose distance is 1 from start vertex of the graph). In the second stage, it visits all vertices at second level. These new vertices are the one which are adjacent to level 1 vertices. BFS continues this process until all the levels of the graph are completed. Generally *queue* data structure is used for storing the vertices of a level. As similar to DFS, assume that initially all vertices are marked *unvisited* (*false*). Vertices that have been processed and removed from the queue are marked *visited* (*true*). We use a queue to represent the visited set as it will keep the vertices in order of when they were first visited.

The implementation for the above discussion can be given as:

```
void BFS(struct Graph *G, int u) {
    int v;
    struct Queue *Q = CreateQueue();
    EnQueue(Q, u);
    while(!IsEmptyQueue(Q)) {
        u = DeQueue(Q);
        Process u; //For example, print
        Visited[s]=1;

        /* For example, if the adjacency matrix is used for representing the
            graph, then the condition be used for finding unvisited adjacent
            vertex of u  is: if( !Visited[v] && G→Adj[u][v] ) */
        for each unvisited adjacent node v of u {
            EnQueue(Q, v);
```

```
            }
        }
    }
    void BFSTraversal(struct Graph *G) {
        for (int i = 0; i< G→V;i++)
                Visited[i]=0;
        //This loop is required if the graph has more than one component
        for (int i = 0; i< G→V;i++)
                if(!Visited[i])
                        BFS(G, i);
    }
```

As an example, let us consider the same graph as that of DFS example. The BFS traversal can be shown as:

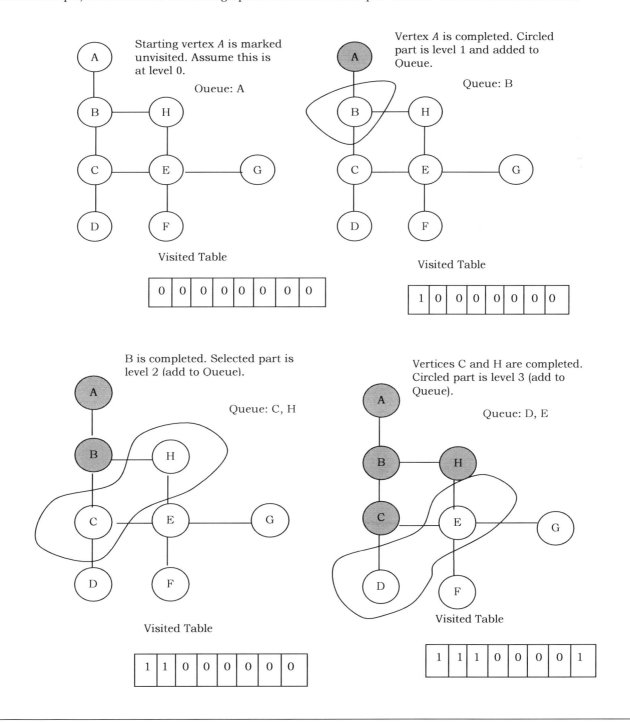

Starting vertex A is marked unvisited. Assume this is at level 0.

Queue: A

Visited Table

0	0	0	0	0	0	0	0

Vertex A is completed. Circled part is level 1 and added to Queue.

Queue: B

Visited Table

1	0	0	0	0	0	0	0

B is completed. Selected part is level 2 (add to Queue).

Queue: C, H

Visited Table

1	1	0	0	0	0	0	0

Vertices C and H are completed. Circled part is level 3 (add to Queue).

Queue: D, E

Visited Table

1	1	1	0	0	0	0	1

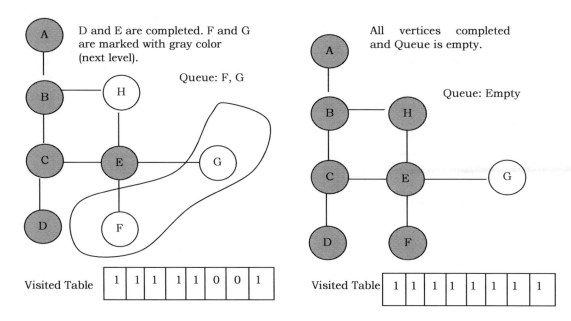

Visited Table | 1 | 1 | 1 | 1 | 1 | 0 | 0 | 1

Visited Table | 1 | 1 | 1 | 1 | 1 | 1 | 1 | 1

Time complexity of BFS is $O(V + E)$, if we use adjacency lists for representing the graphs and $O(V^2)$ for adjacency matrix representation.

Applications of BFS

- Finding all connected components in a graph
- Finding all nodes within one connected component
- Finding the shortest path between two nodes
- Testing a graph for bipartiteness

Comparing DFS and BFS

Comparing BFS and DFS, the big advantage of DFS is that it has much lower memory requirements than BFS, because it's not required to store all of the child pointers at each level. Depending on the data and what we are looking for, either DFS or BFS could be advantageous. For example, in a family tree if we are looking for someone who's still alive and if we assume that person would be at bottom of the tree then DFS is a better choice. BFS would take a very long time to reach that last level.

DFS algorithm finds the goal faster. Now, if we were looking for a family member who died a very long time ago, then that person would be closer to the top of the tree. In this case, BFS finds faster than DFS. So, the advantages of either vary depending on the data and what we are looking for.

DFS is related to preorder traversal of a tree. Like *preorder* traversal simply DFS visits each node before its children. BFS algorithm works similar to *level − order* traversal of the trees.

If someone asks whether DFS is better or BFS is better? The answer depends on the type of the problem that we are trying to solve. BFS visits each level one at a time, and if we know the solution we are searching for is at a low depth then BFS is good. DFS is better choice if the solution is at maximum depth. Below table shows the differences between DFS and BFS in terms of their applications.

Applications	DFS	BFS
Spanning forest, connected components, paths, cycles	Yes	Yes
Shortest paths		Yes
Minimal use of memory space	Yes	

15.6 Topological Sort

Topological sort is an ordering of vertices in a directed acyclic graph [DAG] in which each node comes before all nodes to which it has outgoing edges. As an example, consider the course prerequisite structure at universities. A directed *edge* (v, w) indicates that course v must be completed before course w. Topological ordering for this example is the sequence which does not violate the prerequisite requirement. Every DAG may have one or more topological orderings. Topological sort is not possible if the graph has a cycle, since for two vertices v and w on the cycle, v precedes w and w precedes v.

Topological sort has an interesting property that all pairs of consecutive vertices in the sorted order are connected by edges; then these edges form a directed Hamiltonian path [refer *Problems Section*] in the DAG. If a Hamiltonian path exists, the topological sort order is unique. If a topological sort does not form a Hamiltonian path, DAG can have two or more topological orderings. In the graph below: 7, 5, 3, 11, 8, 2, 9, 10 and 3, 5, 7, 8, 11, 2, 9, 10 are both topological orderings.

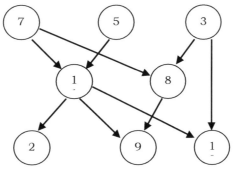

Initially, *indegree* is computed for all vertices and start with the vertices which are having indegree 0. That means consider the vertices which do not have any prerequisite. To keep track of vertices with indegree zero we can use a queue.

All vertices of indegree 0 are placed on queue. While the queue is not empty, a vertex v is removed, and all edges adjacent to v have their indegrees decremented. A vertex is put on the queue as soon as its indegree falls to 0. The topological ordering then is the order in which the vertices DeQueue. The time complexity of this algorithm is $O(|E| + |V|)$ if adjacency lists are used.

```
void TopologicalSort( struct Graph *G ) {
    struct Queue *Q;
    int v, w, counter = 0;
    Q = CreateQueue();
    for (v = 0; v< G→V; v++)
            if( indegree[v] ==  0 )
                    EnQueue( Q, v );
    while( !IsEmptyQueue( Q ) ) {
            v = DeQueue( Q );
            topologicalOrder[v] = ++counter;
            for each w adjacent to v
                    if( --indegree[w] == 0 )
                            EnQueue ( Q, w );
    }
    if( counter != G→V)
            printf("Graph has cycle");
    DeleteQueue( Q );
}
```

Total running time of topological sort is $O(V + E)$.

Note: Topological sorting problem can be solved with DFS. Refer *Problems Section* for algorithm.

Applications of Topological Sorting

- Representing course prerequisites
- In detecting deadlocks
- Pipeline of computing jobs
- Checking for symbolic link loop
- Evaluating formulae in spreadsheet

15.7 Shortest Path Algorithms

Let us consider the other important problem of graph. Given a graph $G = (V, E)$ and a distinguished vertex s, we need to find the shortest path from s to every other vertex in G. There are variations in the shortest path algorithms which depend on the type of the input graph and are given below.

Variations of Shortest Path Algorithms

Shortest path in unweighted graph
Shortest path in weighted graph
Shortest path in weighted graph with negative edges

Applications of Shortest Path Algorithms

- Finding fastest way to go from one place to another
- Finding cheapest way to fly/send data from one city to another

Shortest Path in Unweighted Graph

Let s be the input vertex from which we want to find shortest path to all other vertices. Unweighted graph is a special case of the weighted shortest-path problem, with all edges a weight of 1. The algorithm is similar to BFS and we need to use the following data structures:

- A distance table with three columns (each row corresponds to a vertex):
  - Distance from source vertex.
  - Path - contains the name of the vertex through which we get the shortest distance.
- A queue is used to implement breadth-first search. It contains vertices whose distance from the source node has been computed and their adjacent vertices are to be examined.

As an example, consider the following graph and its adjacency list representation.

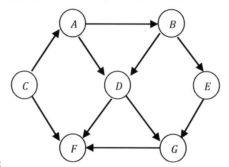

The adjacency list for this graph is:

$$A: B \to D$$
$$B: D \to E$$
$$C: A \to F$$
$$D: F \to G$$
$$E: G$$
$$F: -$$
$$G: F$$

Let $s = C$. The distance from C to C is 0. Initially, distances to all other nodes are not computed, and we initialize the second column in the distance table for all vertices (except C) with -1 as below.

Vertex	Distance[v]	Previous vertex which gave Distance[v]
A	-1	-
B	-1	-
C	0	-
D	-1	-
E	-1	-
F	-1	-
G	-1	-

Algorithm:

```
void UnweightedShortestPath(struct Graph *G, int s) {
    struct Queue *Q = CreateQueue();
    int v, w;
    EnQueue(Q, s);
    for (int i = 0; i< G→V;i++)
            Distance[i]=-1;
    Distance[s]= 0;
    while (!IsEmptyQueue(Q)) {
            v = DeQueue(Q);                          Each vertex examined at most once
            for each w adjacent to v
                    if(Distance[w] == -1)       {
                            Distance[w] = Distance[v] + 1;
                            Path[w] = v;
                            EnQueue(Q, w);
                    }                                 Each vertex EnQueue'd at most once
    }
}
```

```
        DeleteQueue(Q);
}
```

Running time: $O(|E| + |V|)$, if adjacency lists are used. In for loop, we are checking the outgoing edges for a given vertex and the sum of all examined edges in the while loop is equal to the number of edges which gives $O(|E|)$.

If we use matrix representation the complexity is $O(|V|^2)$, because we need to read an entire row in the matrix of length $|V|$ in order to find the adjacent vertices for a given vertex.

Shortest path in Weighted Graph [Dijkstra's]

A famous solution for shortest path problem was given by *Dijkstra*. *Dijkstra's* algorithm is a generalization of BFS algorithm. The regular BFS algorithm cannot solve the shortest path problem as it cannot guarantee that the vertex at the front of the queue is the vertex closest to source s. Before going to code let us understand how the algorithm works. As in unweighted shortest path algorithm, here too we use the distance table. The algorithm works by keeping the shortest distance of vertex v from the source in *Distance* table. The value *Distance[v]* holds the distance from s to v. The shortest distance of the source to itself is zero. *Distance* table for all other vertices is set to −1 to indicate that those vertices are not already processed.

Vertex	Distance[v]	Previous vertex which gave Distance[v]
A	-1	-
B	-1	-
C	0	-
D	-1	-
E	-1	-
F	-1	-
G	-1	-

After the algorithm finishes *Distance* table will have the shortest distance from source s to each other vertex v. To simplify the understanding of *Dijkstra's* algorithm, let us assume that the given vertices are maintained in two sets. Initially the first set contains only the source element and the second set contains all the remaining elements. After the kth iteration, the first set contains k vertices which are closest to the source. These k vertices are the ones for which we have already computed shortest distances from source.

Notes on Dijkstra's Algorithm

- It uses greedy method: Always pick the next closest vertex to the source.
- Uses priority queue to store unvisited vertices by distance from s.
- Does not work with negative weights.

Difference between Unweighted Shortest Path and Dijkstra's Algorithm

1) To represent weights in adjacency list, each vertex contains the weights of the edges (in addition to their identifier).
2) Instead of ordinary queue we use priority queue [distances are the priorities] and the vertex with the smallest distance is selected for processing.
3) The distance to a vertex is calculated by the sum of the weights of the edges on the path from the source to that vertex.
4) We update the distances in case the newly computed distance is smaller than old distance which we have already computed.

```
void Dijkstra(struct Graph *G, int s) {
        struct PriorityQueue *PQ = CreatePriorityQueue();
        int v, w;
        EnQueue(PQ, s);
        for (int i = 0; i< G→V;i++)
                Distance[i]=-1;
        Distance[s] = 0;
        while (!IsEmptyQueue(PQ)) {
            v = DeleteMin(PQ);
            for all adjacent vertices w of v {
                Compute new distance d= Distance[v] + weight[v][w];
                if(Distance[w] == -1) {
                    Distance[w] = new distance d;
                    Insert w in the priority queue with priority d
                    Path[w] = v;
                }
                if(Distance[w]  > new distance d) {
                    Distance[w] = new distance d;
                    Update priority of vertex w to be d;
                    Path[w] = v;
```

```
            }
          }
        }
      }
```

The above algorithm can be better understood through an example, which will explain each step that is taken and how *Distance* is calculated. The weighted graph below has 5 vertices from $A - E$. The value between the two vertices is known as the edge cost between two vertices. For example, the edge cost between A and C is 1. Dijkstra's algorithm can be used to find shortest path from source A to the remaining vertices in the graph.

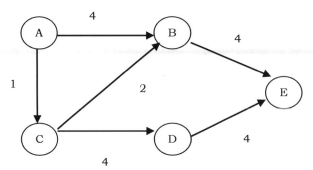

Initially the *Distance* table is:

Vertex	Distance[v]	Previous vertex which gave Distance[v]
A	0	-
B	-1	-
C	-1	-
D	-1	-
E	-1	-

After the first step, from vertex A, we can reach B and C. So, in the *Distance* table we update the reachability of B and C with their costs (as shown below).

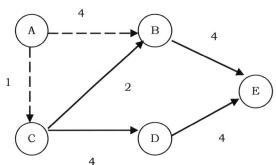

Shortest path from B, C from A

Now, let us select the minimum distance among all. The minimum distance vertex is C. That means, we have to reach other vertices from these two vertices (A and C). For example B can be reached from A and also from C. In this case we have to select the one which gives low cost. Since reaching B through C is giving minimum cost $(1 + 2)$, we update the *Distance* table for vertex B with cost 3 and the vertex from which we got this cost as C.

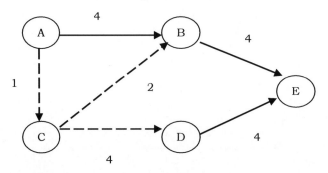

Shortest path to B, D using C as intermediate vertex

The only vertex remaining is E. To reach E, we have to see all the paths through which we can reach E and select the one which gives minimum cost. We can see that if we use B as intermediate vertex through C then we get the minimum cost.

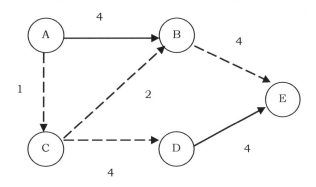

A	0	-
B	3	C
C	1	A
D	5	C
E	7	B

The final minimum cost tree which Dijkstra's algorithm generates is:

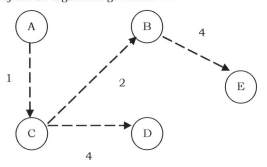

Performance

In Dijkstra's algorithm, the efficiency depends on the number of DeleteMins (V DeleteMins) and updates for priority queues (E updates) that were used. If a *standard binary heap* is used then the complexity is $O(ElogV)$. The term $ElogV$ comes from E updates (each update takes $logV$) for the standard heap. If the set used is an array then the complexity is $O(E + V^2)$.

Disadvantages of Dijkstra's Algorithm

- As discussed above, the major disadvantage of the algorithm is that it does a blind search thereby wasting time and necessary resources.
- Another disadvantage is that it cannot handle negative edges. This leads to acyclic graphs and most often cannot obtain the right shortest path.

Relatives of Dijkstra's Algorithm

- The *Bellman–Ford* algorithm computes single-source shortest paths in a weighted digraph. It uses the same concept as that of *Dijkstra's* algorithm but can handle negative edges as well. It has more running time than *Dijkstra's* algorithm.
- Prim's algorithm finds a minimum spanning tree for a connected weighted graph. It implies that a subset of edges that form a tree where the total weight of all the edges in the tree is minimized.

Bellman-Ford Algorithm

If the graph has negative edge costs, then *Dijkstra's* algorithm does not work. The problem is that once a vertex u is declared known, it is possible that from some other, unknown vertex v there is a path back to u that is very negative. In such a case, taking a path from s to v back to u is better than going from s to u without using v. A combination of Dijkstra's algorithm and unweighted algorithms will solve the problem. Initialize the queue with s. Then, at each stage, we *DeQueue* a vertex v. We find all vertices w adjacent to v such that,

$$distance\ to\ v\ +\ weight(v,w) < \text{old distance to w}$$

We update w old distance and path, and place w on a queue if it is not already there. A bit can be set for each vertex to indicate presence in the queue. We repeat the process until the queue is empty.

```
void BellmanFordAlgorithm(struct Graph *G, int s) {
    struct Queue *Q = CreateQueue();
    int v, w;
    EnQueue(Q, s);
    Distance[s] = 0;              // assume the Distance table is filled with INT_MAX
    while (!IsEmptyQueue(Q)) {
        v = DeQueue(Q);
        for all adjacent vertices w of v {
            Compute new distance d= Distance[v] + weight[v][w];
```

```
                    if(old distance to w > new distance d ) {
                        Distance[v] = (distance to v) + weight[v][w]);
                        Path[w] = v;
                        if(w is there in queue)
                            EnQueue(Q, w)
                    }
                }
            }
        }
```

This algorithm works if there are no negative-cost cycles. Each vertex can DeQueue at most $|V|$ times, so the running time is $O(|E|.|V|)$ if adjacency lists are used.

Overview of Shortest Path Algorithms

Shortest path in unweighted graph [*Modified BFS*]	$O(|E| + |V|)$
Shortest path in weighted graph [*Dijkstra's*]	$O(|E| \log |V|)$
Shortest path in weighted graph with negative edges [*Bellman − Ford*]	$O(|E|.|V|)$
Shortest path in weighted acyclic graph	$O(|E| + |V|)$

15.8 Minimal Spanning Tree

Spanning tree of a graph is a subgraph that contains all the vertices and is also a tree. A graph may have many spanning trees. As an example, consider a graph with 4 vertices as shown below. Let us assume that the corners of the graph are vertices.

For this simple graph, we can have multiple spanning trees as shown below.

The algorithm we will discuss now is *minimum spanning tree* in an undirected graph. We assume that the given graphs are weighted graph. If the graphs are unweighted graphs then we can still the weighted graph algorithms by treating all weights are equal. A *minimum spanning tree* of an undirected graph G is a tree formed from graph edges that connects all the vertices of G with minimum total cost (weights). A minimum spanning tree exists only if the graph is connected. There are two famous algorithms for this problem:

- *Prim's* Algorithm
- *Kruskal's* Algorithm

Prim's Algorithm

Prim's algorithm is almost same as Dijkstra's algorithm. Like in Dijkstra's algorithm, in Prim's algorithm also we keep values *distance* and *paths* in distance table. The only exception is that since the definition of *distance* is different and as a result the updating statement also changes little. The update statement is simpler than before.

```
void Prims(struct Graph *G, int s) {
    struct PriorityQueue *PQ = CreatePriorityQueue();
    int v, w;
    EnQueue(PQ, s);
    Distance[s] = 0;              // assume the Distance table is filled with -1
    while ((!IsEmptyQueue(PQ)) {
        v = DeleteMin(PQ);
        for all adjacent vertices w of v {
            Compute new distance d= Distance[v] + weight[v][w];
            if(Distance[w] == -1) {
                Distance[w] = weight[v][w];
                Insert w in the priority queue with priority d
                Path[w] = v;

            }
            if(Distance[w]  > new distance d) {
                Distance[w] = weight[v][w];
```

```
                    Update priority of vertex w to be d;
                    Path[w] = v;
                }
            }
        }
    }
```

The entire implementation of this algorithm is identical to that of Dijkstra's algorithm. The running time is $O(|V|^2)$ without heaps [good for dense graphs], and $O(ElogV)$ using binary heaps [good for sparse graphs].

Kruskal's Algorithm

The algorithm starts with V different trees (V is the vertices in graph). While constructing the minimum spanning tree, every time it selects the edge which has minimum weight and adds that edge if it doesn't creates a cycle. So, initially, there are $|V|$ single-node trees in the forest. Adding an edge merges two trees into one. When the algorithm is completed, there will be only one tree, and that is the minimum spanning tree. There are two ways of implementing Kruskal's algorithm:

- By using Disjoint Sets: Using UNION and FIND operations
- By using Priority Queues: Maintains weights in priority queue

The appropriate data structure is the UNION/FIND algorithm [for implementing forests]. Two vertices belong to the same set if and only if they are connected in the current spanning forest. Each vertex is initially in its own set. If u and v are in the same set, the edge is rejected, because it forms a cycle. Otherwise, the edge is accepted, and a UNION is performed on the two sets containing u and v. As an example, consider the following graph (edges shows the weights).

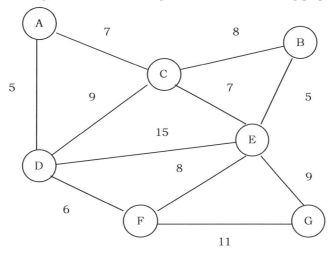

Now let us perform Kruskal's algorithm on this graph. We always select the edge which is having minimum weight (cost).

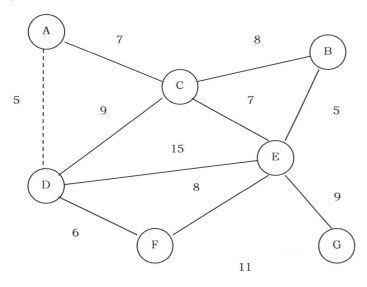

From the above graph, the edges which are having minimum weight (cost) are: AD and BE. Among these two we can select one of them and let us assume that we have selected AD (dotted line).

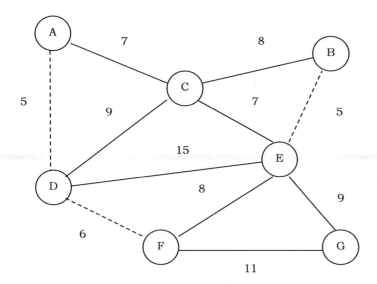

DF is the next edge which having the low cost (6).

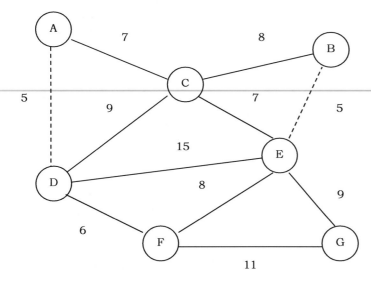

BE is now having the low cost among all and we select that (dotted lines indicates selected edges).

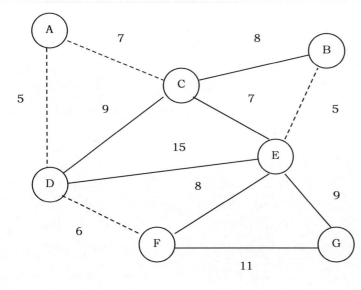

Next, AC and CE are having the low cost of 7 and let us assume that we have selected AC.

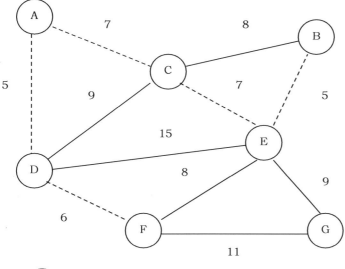

Select CE as its cost is 7 and does not form a cycle.

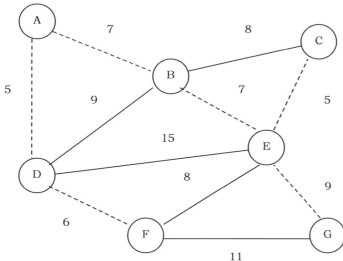

Next low cost edges are CB and EF. But if we select CB then it forms a cycle. So we discard that. Same is the case with EF also. So we should not select these 2. And the next low cost is 9 (BD and EG). Selecting BD forms a cycle and we discard that. Adding EG will not form a cycle and with this edge we complete all vertices of the graph.

```
void Kruskal(struct Graph *G) {
    S = φ;   // At the end S will contains the edges of minimum spanning trees
    for (int v = 0; v< G→V; v++)
        MakeSet (v);
    Sort edges of E by increasing weights w;
    for each edge (u, v) in E { //from sorted list
        if(FIND (u) ≠ FIND (v)) {
            S = S ∪ {(u, v)};
            UNION (u, v);
        }
    }
    return S;
}
```

Note: For implementation of UNION and FIND operations refer *Disjoint Sets ADT* chapter.

The worst-case running time of this algorithm is O(*ElogE*), which is dominated by the heap operations. That means, since we are constructing the heap with E edges we need $O(ElogE)$ time for doing that.

15.9 Problems on Graph Algorithms

Problem-1 In an undirected simple graph with n vertices, what is the maximum number of edges? Self loops are not allowed.

Solution: Since every node can connect to all other nodes, first node can connect o $n-1$ nodes. Second node can connect to $n-2$ nodes [since one edge is already there from first node]. The total number of edges is: $1 + 2 + 3 + \cdots + n - 1 = \frac{n(n-1)}{2}$ edges.

Problem-2   How many different adjacency matrices does a graph with n vertices and E edges have?

Solution: It's equal to the number of permutations of n elements. i.e., $n!$.

Problem-3   How many different adjacency lists does a graph with n vertices have?

Solution: It's equal to the number of permutations of edges. i.e., $E!$.

Problem-4   Which undirected graph representation is most appropriate for determining whether or not a vertex is isolated (is not connected to any other vertex)?

Solution: Adjacency List. If we use adjacency matrix then we need to check the complete row for determining whether that vertex has any edges or not. By using adjacency list it is very easy to check and it can be done just by checking whether that vertex has NULL for next pointer or not [NULL indicates that vertex is not connected to any other vertex].

Problem-5   For checking whether there is a path from source s to target t, which one is best among disjoint sets and DFS?

Solution: The table below shows the comparison between disjoint sets and DFS. The entries in table represent the case for any pair of nodes (for s and t).

Method	Processing Time	Query Time	Space
Union-Find	$V + E\ logV$	$logV$	V
DFS	$E + V$	1	$E + V$

Problem-6   What is the maximum number of edges a directed graph with n vertices can have and still not contain a directed cycle?

Solution: The number is $V\ (V - 1)/2$. Any directed graph can have at most n^2 edges. However, since the graph has no cycles it cannot contain a self loop and for any pair x, y of vertices at most one edge from (x, y) and (y, x) can be included. Therefore the number of edges can be at most $(V^2 - V)/2$ as desired. It is possible to achieve $V(V - 1)/2$ edges. Label n nodes $1, 2...n$ and add an edge (x, y) if and only if $x < y$. This graph has the appropriate number of edges and cannot contain a cycle (any path visits an increasing sequence of nodes).

Problem-7   Earlier in this chapter, we have discussed minimum spanning tree algorithms. Now, give an algorithm for finding the maximum-weight spanning tree in a graph?

Solution:

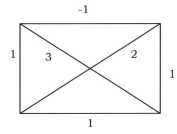

Given graph

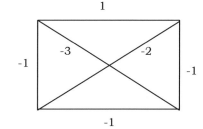

Transformed graph with negative edge weights

Problem-8   How many simple directed graphs with no parallel edges & self loops are possible as a function of V?
Solution: $(V) \times (V - 1)$. Since, each vertex can connect to $V - 1$ vertices without self loops.

Using the given graph, construct a new graph with same nodes and edges. But instead of using same weights take the negative of their weights. That means, weight of an edge = negative of weight of the corresponding edge in the given graph. Now, we can use existing *minimum spanning tree* algorithms on this new graph. As a result, we will get the maximum weight spanning tree in the original one.

Problem-9   Differences between DFS and BFS?

Solution:

DFS	BFS
Backtracking is possible from a dead end	Backtracking is not possible
Vertices from which exploration is incomplete are processed in a LIFO order LIFO order	The vertices to be explored are organized as a FIFO queue
Search is done in one particular direction	The vertices at the same level are maintained in parallel

Problem-10   How many topological sorts of the following dag are there?

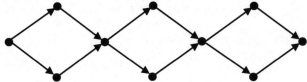

Solution: If we observer the above graph there are three stages with 2 vertices. In the early discussion of this chapter, we have seen that topological sort picks the elements with zero indegree at any point of time. At each of the two vertices stages, we can either first process the top vertex of bottom vertex. As a result at each of these stages we have two possibilities. So the total number of possibilities is the multiplication of possibilities at each stage and that is, $2 \times 2 \times 2 = 8$.

Problem-11   What is the difference between *Dijkstra's* and *Prim's* algorithm?

Solution: *Dijkstra's* algorithm is almost identical to that of *Prim's*. The algorithm begins at a specific vertex and extends outward within the graph, until all vertices have been reached. The only distinction is that *Prim's* algorithm stores a minimum cost edge whereas *Dijkstra's* algorithm stores the total cost from a source vertex to the current vertex. More simply, *Dijkstra's* algorithm stores a summation of minimum cost edges whereas *Prim's* algorithm stores at most one minimum cost edge.

Problem-12   Discuss Bipartite matchings?

Solution: In Bipartite graphs, we divide the graphs in to two disjoint sets and each edge connects a vertex from one set to a vertex in another subset (as shown in figure).

Definition: A simple graph $G = (V, E)$ is called bipartite graph if its vertices can be divided into two disjoint sets $V = V_1 \cup V_2$, such that every edge has the form $e = (a, b)$ where $a \in V_1$ and $b \in V_2$. One important condition is that no vertices both in V_1 or both in V_2 are connected.

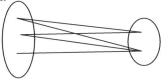

Properties of Bipartite Graphs

- A graph is called bipartite if and only if the given graph does not have an odd length cycle.
- A *complete bipartite graph* $K_{m,n}$ is a bipartite graph that has each vertex from one set adjacent to each vertex to another set.

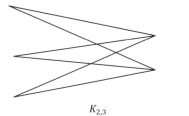

$K_{2,3}$

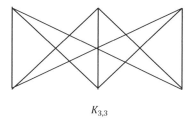

$K_{3,3}$

- A subset of edges $M \subset E$ is a *matching* if no two edges have a common vertex. As example, matching sets of edges are represented with dotted lines. A matching M is called *maximum* if it has a largest number of possible edges. In the graphs, the dotted edges represent the alternative matching for the given graph.

- A matching M is *perfect*, if it matches all vertices. We must have $V_1 = V_2$ in order to have perfect matching.
- An *alternating path* is a path whose edges alternate between matched and unmatched edges. If we find an alternating path then we can improve the matching. This is because an alternating path consists of matched and unmatched edges. The number of unmatched edges exceeds the number of matched edges by one. Therefore, an alternating path always increases the matching by one.

Next question is, how do we find a perfect matching? Based on the above theory and definition we can find the perfect matching with the following approximation algorithm.

Matching Algorithm (Hungarian algorithm)

1) Start at unmatched vertex.
2) Find an alternating path.
3) If it exists, change matching edges to no matching edges and conversely. If it does not exist, choose another unmatched vertex.

4) If the number of edges equals $V/2$ stop, otherwise proceed to step 1 and repeat as long all vertices have been examined without finding any alternating paths.

Time Complexity of the Matching Algorithm: The number of iterations is in $O(V)$. The complexity of finding an alternating path using BFS is $O(E)$. Therefore, the total time complexity is $O(V \times E)$.

Problem-13 Marriage and Personnel Problem?

Marriage Problem: There are X men and Y women who desire to get married. Participants indicate who among the opposite sex would be acceptable as a potential spouse. Every woman can be married to at most one man, and every man to at most one woman. How could we marry everybody to someone they liked?

Personnel Problem: You are the boss of a company. The company has M workers and N jobs. Each worker is qualified to do some jobs, but not others. How will you assign jobs to each worker?

Solution: This is just another way of asking about bipartite graphs and the solution is same as that of Problem-12.

Problem-14 How many edges will be there in complete bipartite graph $K_{m,n}$?

Solution: $m \times n$. This is because each vertex in first set can connect all vertices in second set.

Problem-15 A graph is called regular graph if it has no loops and multiple edges where each vertex has the same number of neighbors; i.e. every vertex has the same degree. Now, if $K_{m,n}$ is a regular graph what is the relation between m and n?

Solution: Since each vertex should have the same degree the relation should be $m = n$.

Problem-16 What is the maximum number of edges in the maximum matching of a bipartite graph with n vertices?

Solution: From the definition of *matching*, we should not have the edges with common vertices. So in bipartite graph, each vertex can connect to only one vertex. Since we divide the total vertices into two sets, we can get the maximum number of edges if we divide them into half. Finally the answer is $\frac{n}{2}$.

Problem-17 *Planar graphs* [Is it possible to draw the edges of a graph in such a way that edges do not cross]?

Solution: A graph G is said to be planar if it can be drawn in the plane in such a way that no two edges meet each other except at a vertex to which they are incident. Any such drawing is called a plane drawing of G. As an example consider the below graph:

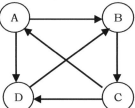

This graph we can easily convert to planar graph as below (without any cross edges).

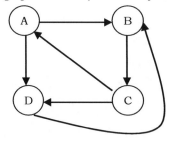

How do we decide whether a given graph is planar or not?

The solution to this problem is not simple. Instead some researchers found some interesting properties based on which we can decide whether the given graph is a planar graph or not.

Properties of Planar Graphs

- If a graph G is a connected planar simple graph with V vertices, where $V = 3$ and E edges then $E = 3V - 6$.
- K_5 is non-planar [K_5 stands for complete graph with 5 vertices].
- If a graph is a connected planar simple graph with V vertices, E edges, and no triangles then $E = 2V - 4$.

- $K_{3,3}$ is non-planar [$K_{3,3}$ stands for bipartite graph with 3 vertices on one side and other 3 vertices on other side. $K_{3,3}$ contains 6 vertices].
- If a graph G is connected planar simple graph then G contains at least one vertex of degree 5 or less.
- A graph is planar if and only if it does not contain a subgraph which has K_5 and $K_{3,3}$ as a contraction.
- If a graph G contains a nonplanar graph as a subgraph, then G is non-planar.
- If a graph G is a planar graph, then every subgraph of G is planar;
- For any connected planar graph $G = (V, E)$, the following formula should holds $V + F - E = 2$, where F stands for the number of faces.
- For any planar graph $G = (V, E)$ with K components, the following formula holds $V + F - E = 1 + K$.

Inorder to test planarity of a given graph we use these properties and decide whether it is planar graph or not. Note that all the above properties are only the necessary conditions but not sufficient.

Problem-18 How many faces do $K_{2,3}$ have?

Solution: From the above discussion, we know that $V + F - E = 2$ and from earlier problem we know that $E = m \times n = 2 \times 3 = 6$ and $V = m + n = 5$. $\therefore 5 + F - 6 = 2 \Rightarrow F = 3$.

SORTING

Chapter-16

16.1 What is Sorting?

Sorting is an algorithm that arranges the elements of a list in a certain order [either *ascending* or *descending*]. The output is a permutation or reordering of the input.

16.2 Why is Sorting necessary?

Sorting is one of the important categories of algorithms in computer science. Sometimes sorting significantly reduces the complexity of the problem. We can use sorting as a technique to reduce the search complexity. Great research went into this category of algorithms because of its importance. These algorithms are used in many computer algorithms [for example, searching elements], database algorithms and many more.

16.3 Classification of Sorting Algorithms

Sorting algorithms are generally categorized based on the following parameters.

By Number of Comparisons

In this method, sorting algorithms are classified based on the number of comparisons. For comparison based sorting algorithms best case behavior is O(*nlogn*) and worst case behavior is O(n^2). Comparison-based sorting algorithms evaluate the elements of the list by key comparison operation and need at least O(*nlogn*) comparisons for most inputs.

Later in this chapter we will discuss few *non − comparison* (*linear*) sorting algorithms like Counting sort, Bucket sort, and Radix sort, etc. Linear Sorting algorithms impose few restrictions on the inputs to improve the complexity.

By Number of Swaps

In this method, sorting algorithms are categorized by number of *swaps* (also called *inversions*).

By Memory Usage

Some sorting algorithms are "*in place*" and they need O(1) or O(*logn*) memory to create auxiliary locations for sorting the data temporarily.

By Recursion

Sorting algorithms are either recursive [quick sort] or non-recursive [selection sort, and insertion sort]. There are some algorithms which use both (merge sort).

By Stability

Sorting algorithm is *stable* if for all indices *i* and *j* such that the key *A*[*i*] equals key *A*[*j*], if record *R*[*i*] precedes record *R*[*j*] in the original file, record *R*[*i*] precedes record *R*[*j*] in the sorted list. Few sorting algorithms maintain the relative order of elements with equal keys (equivalent elements retain their relative positions even after sorting).

By Adaptability

Few sorting algorithms complexity changes based on presortedness [quick sort]: presortedness of the input affects the running time. Algorithms that take this into account are known to be adaptive.

16.4 Other Classifications

Another method of classifying sorting algorithms is:
- Internal Sort
- External Sort

Internal Sort

Sort algorithms that use main memory exclusively during the sort are called *internal* sorting algorithms. This kind of algorithm assumes high-speed random access to all memory.

External Sort

Sorting algorithms that use external memory, such as tape or disk, during the sort come under this category.

16.5 Bubble sort

Bubble sort is the simplest sorting algorithm. It works by iterating the input array from the first element to last, comparing each pair of elements and swapping them if needed. Bubble sort continues its iterations until no more swaps are needed. The algorithm gets its name from the way smaller elements "*bubble*" to the top of the list. Generally, insertion sort has better performance than bubble sort. Some researchers suggest that we should not teach bubble sort because of its simplicity and complexity. The only significant advantage that bubble sort has over other implementations is that it can detect whether the input list is already sorted or not.

Implementation

```
void BubbleSort(int A[], int n) {
    for (int pass = n - 1; pass >= 0; pass--)     {
        for (int i = 0; i <= pass - 1 ; i++)     {
            if(A[i] > A[i+1]) {
                // swap elements
                int temp = A[i];
                A[i] = A[i+1];
                A[i+1] = temp;
            }
        }
    }
}
```

Algorithm takes $O(n^2)$ (even in best case). We can improve it by using one extra flag. No more swaps indicate the completion of sorting. If the list is already sorted, we can use this flag to skip the remaining passes.

```
void BubbleSortImproved(int A[], int n) {
    int pass, i, temp, swapped = 1;
    for (pass = n - 1; pass >= 0 && swapped; pass--) {
        swapped = 0;
        for (i = 0; i <= pass - 1 ; i++) {
            if(A[i] > A[i+1]) {
                // swap elements
                temp = A[i];
                A[i] = A[i+1];
                A[i+1] =  temp;
                swapped = 1;
            }
        }
    }
}
```

This modified version improves the best case of bubble sort to $O(n)$.

16.5.1 Performance

Worst case complexity : $O(n^2)$
Best case complexity (Improved version) : $O(n)$
Average case complexity (Basic version) : $O(n^2)$
Worst case space complexity : $O(1)$ auxiliary

16.6 Selection Sort

Selection sort is an in-place sorting algorithm. Selection sort works well for small files. It is used for sorting the files with very large values and small keys. This is because selection is made based on keys and swaps are made only when required.

Advantages

- Easy to implement

- In-place sort (requires no additional storage space)

Disadvantages

- Doesn't scale well: $O(n^2)$

Algorithm

1. Find the minimum value in the list
2. Swap it with the value in the current position
3. Repeat this process for all the elements until the entire array is sorted

This algorithm is called *selection sort* since it repeatedly *selects* the smallest element.

Implementation

```
void Selection(int A [], int n) {
    int i, j, min, temp;
    for (i = 0; i < n - 1; i++) {
        min = i;
        for (j = i+1; j < n; j++) {
            if(A [j] < A [min])
            min = j;
        }
        // swap elements
        temp = A[min];
        A[min] = A[i];
        A[i] = temp;
    }
}
```

Performance

Worst case complexity : $O(n^2)$
Best case complexity : $O(n^2)$
Average case complexity : $O(n^2)$
Worst case space complexity: $O(1)$ auxiliary

16.7 Insertion sort

Insertion sort is a simple and efficient comparison sort. In this algorithm each iteration removes an element from the input data and inserts it into the correct position in the list being sorted. The choice of the element being removed from the input is random and this process is repeated until all input elements have gone through.

Advantages

- Simple implementation
- Efficient for small data
- Adaptive: If the input list is presorted [may not be completely] then insertions sort takes $O(n + d)$, where d is the number of inversions
- Practically more efficient than selection and bubble sorts even though all of them have $O(n^2)$ worst case complexity
- Stable: Maintains relative order of input data if the keys are same
- In-place: It requires only a constant amount $O(1)$ of additional memory space
- Online: Insertion sort can sort the list as it receives it

Algorithm

Every repetition of insertion sort removes an element from the input data, inserts it into the correct position in the already-sorted list until no input elements remain. Sorting is typically done in-place. The resulting array after k iterations has the property where the first $k + 1$ entries are sorted.

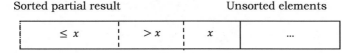

Sorted partial result			Unsorted elements
$\leq x$	$> x$	x	...

becomes

$\leq x$	x	$> x$	...

Sorted partial result | | | Unsorted elements

Each element greater than x copied to the right as it is compared against x.

Implementation

```
void InsertionSort(int A[], int n) {
    int i, j, v;
    for (i = 2; i <= n - 1; i++) {
        v = A[i];
        j = i;
        while (A[j-1] > v && j >= 1) {
            A[j] = A[j-1];
            j--;
        }
        A[j] = v;
    }
}
```

Example: Given an array: 6 8 1 4 5 3 7 2 and the goal is to put them in ascending order.

6 8 1 4 5 3 7 2 (Consider index 0)
6 8 1 4 5 3 7 2 (Consider indices 0 - 1)
1 6 8 4 5 3 7 2 (Consider indices 0 - 2: insertion places 1 in front of 6 and 8)
1 4 6 8 5 3 7 2 (Process same as above is repeated until array is sorted)
1 4 5 6 8 3 7 2
1 3 4 5 6 7 8 2
1 2 3 4 5 6 7 8 (The array is sorted!)

Analysis

Worst case analysis

Worst case occurs when for every i the inner loop has to move all elements $A[1], \ldots, A[i-1]$ (which happens when $A[i]$ = key is smaller than all of them), that takes $\Theta(i-1)$ time.

$$T(n) = \Theta(1) + \Theta(2) + \Theta(2) + \ldots\ldots + \Theta(n-1)$$
$$= \Theta(1 + 2 + 3 + \ldots + n - 1) = \Theta(\tfrac{n(n-1)}{2}) \approx \Theta(n^2)$$

Average case analysis

For the average case, the inner loop will insert $A[i]$ in the middle of $A[1], \ldots, A[i-1]$. This takes $\Theta(i/2)$ time.

$$T(n) = \sum_{i=1}^{n} \Theta(i/2) \approx \Theta(n^2)$$

Performance

Worst case complexity : $O(n^2)$
Best case complexity : $O(n^2)$
Average case complexity : $O(n^2)$
Worst case space complexity: $O(n^2)$ total, $O(1)$ auxiliary

16.7.1 Comparisons to Other Sorting Algorithms

Insertion sort is one of the elementary sorting algorithms with $O(n^2)$ worst-case time. Insertion sort is used when the data is nearly sorted (due to its adaptiveness) or when the input size is small (due to its low overhead). For these reasons and due to its stability, insertion sort is used as the recursive base case (when the problem size is small) for higher overhead divide-and-conquer sorting algorithms, such as merge sort or quick sort.

Note:

- Bubble sort takes $\frac{n^2}{2}$ comparisons and $\frac{n^2}{2}$ swaps (inversions) in both average case and in worst case.
- Selection sort takes $\frac{n^2}{2}$ comparisons and n swaps.
- Insertion sort takes $\frac{n^2}{4}$ comparisons and $\frac{n^2}{8}$ swaps in average case and in the worst case they are double.
- Insertion sort is almost linear for partially sorted input.
- Selection sort is best suits for elements with bigger values and small keys.

16.8 Shell sort

Shell sort (also called *diminishing increment sort*) was invented by *Donald Shell*. This sorting algorithm is a generalization of insertion sort. Insertion sort works efficiently on input that is already almost sorted. Shell sort is also known as *n*-gap insertion sort. Instead of comparing only adjacent pair, shell sort makes several passes and uses various gaps between adjacent elements (ending with the gap of 1 or classical insertion sort).

In insertion sort, comparisons are made between the adjacent elements. At most 1 inversion is eliminated for each comparison done with insertion sort. The variation used in shell sort is to avoid comparing adjacent elements until the last step of the algorithm. So, the last step of shell sort is effectively the insertion sort algorithm. It improves insertion sort by allowing the comparison and exchange of elements that are far away. This is the first algorithm which got less than quadratic complexity among comparison sort algorithms.

Shellsort is actually a simple extension for insertion sort. The primary difference is its capability of exchanging elements that are far apart, making it considerably faster for elements to get to where it should be. For example if the smallest element happens to be at the end of an array, with insertion sort it will require a full array steps to put this element at the beginning of the array. However with shellsort, this element can jump further instead of just one step a time and reach the proper destination in less exchanges.

The basic idea in shellsort is to exchange every h^{th} element in the array. Now this can be confusing so we'll talk more on this. h determine how far apart element exchange can happen, say for example take h as 13, the first element (index-0) is exchanged with the 14th element (index-13) if necessary (of course). The second element with the 15th element, and so on. Now if we take h as 1, it is exactly the same as a regular insertion sort.

Shellsort works by starting with big enough (but not larger than the array size) h as to allow elligible element exchanges that are far apart. Once a sort is complete with a particular h, the array can be said as h-sorted. The next step is to reduce h by a certain sequence, and again performing another complete h-sort. Once h is 1 and h-sorted, the array is completely sorted. Notice that the last sequence for h is 1 so the last sort is always an insertion sort, except by this time the array is already well-formed and easier to sort.

Shell sort uses a sequence $h1, h2, ..., ht$ called the *increment sequence*. Any increment sequence is fine as long as $h1 = 1$ and some choices are better than others. Shell sort makes multiple passes through input list and sorts a number of equally sized sets using the insertion sort. Shell sort improves the efficiency of insertion sort by *quickly* shifting values to their destination.

Implementation

```
void ShellSort(int A[], int array_size) {
    int i, j, h, v;
    for (h = 1; h = array_size/9; h = 3*h+1);

    for ( ; h > 0; h = h/3) {
        for (i = h+1; i = array_size; i += 1) {
            v = A[i];
            j = i;
            while (j > h && A[j-h] > v) {
                A[j] = A[j-h];
                j -= h;
            }
            A[j] = v;
        }
    }
}
```

Note that when $h == 1$, the algorithm makes a pass over the entire list, comparing adjacent elements, but doing very few element exchanges. For $h == 1$, shell sort works just like insertion sort, except the number of inversions that have to be eliminated is greatly reduced by the previous steps of the algorithm with $h > 1$.

Analysis

Shell sort is efficient for medium size lists. For bigger lists, the algorithm is not the best choice. It is the fastest of all $O(n^2)$ sorting algorithms.

The disadvantage of Shell sort is that it is a complex algorithm and not nearly as efficient as the merge, heap, and quick sorts. Shell sort is significantly slower than the merge, heap, and quick sorts, but is a relatively simple algorithm, which makes it a good choice for sorting lists of less than 5000 items unless speed is important. It is also a good choice for repetitive sorting of smaller lists.

The best case in Shell sort is when the array is already sorted in the right order. The number of comparisons is less. Running time of Shell sort depends on the choice of increment sequence.

Performance

Worst case complexity depends on gap sequence. Best known: $O(nlog^2 n)$	
Best case complexity: $O(n)$	
Average case complexity depends on gap sequence	
Worst case space complexity: $O(n)$	

16.9 Merge sort

Merge sort is an example of the divide and conquer.

Important Notes

- *Merging* is the process of combining two sorted files to make one bigger sorted file.
- *Selection* is the process of dividing a file into two parts: k smallest elements and $n - k$ largest elements.
- Selection and merging are opposite operations
    - selection splits a list into two lists
    - merging joins two files to make one file
- Merge sort is Quick sorts complement
- Merge sort accesses the data in a sequential manner
- This algorithm is used for sorting a linked list
- Merge sort is insensitive to the initial order of its input
- In Quick sort most of the work is done before the recursive calls. Quick sort starts with the largest subfile and finishes with the small ones and as a result it needs stack. Moreover, this algorithm is not stable. Merge sort divides the list into two parts; then each part is conquered individually. Merge sort starts with the small subfiles and finishes with the largest one. As a result it doesn't need stack. This algorithm is stable.

Implementation

```
void Mergesort(int A[], int temp[], int left, int right) {
    int mid;
    if(right > left) {
            mid = (right + left) / 2;
            Mergesort(A, temp, left, mid);
            Mergesort(A, temp, mid+1, right);
            Merge(A, temp, left, mid+1, right);
    }
}
void Merge(int A[], int temp[], int left, int mid, int right) {
    int i, left_end, size, temp_pos;
    left_end = mid - 1;
    temp_pos = left;
    size = right - left + 1;
    while ((left <= left_end) && (mid <= right)) {
            if(A[left] <= A[mid]) {
                    temp[temp_pos] = A[left];
                    temp_pos = temp_pos + 1;
                    left = left +1;
            }
            else {
                    temp[temp_pos] = A[mid];
                    temp_pos = temp_pos + 1;
                    mid = mid + 1;
            }
    }
    while (left <= left_end) {
            temp[temp_pos] = A[left];
            left = left + 1;
            temp_pos = temp_pos + 1;
    }
    while (mid <= right) {
            temp[temp_pos] = A[mid];
            mid = mid + 1;
            temp_pos = temp_pos + 1;
    }
```

```
        for (i = 0; i <= size; i++) {
                A[right] = temp[right];
                right = right - 1;
        }
}
```

Analysis

In Merge sort the input list is divided into two parts and these are solved recursively. After solving the sub problems they are merged by scanning the resultant sub problems. Let us assume $T(n)$ is the complexity of Merge sort with n elements. The recurrence for the Merge Sort can be defined as:

Recurrence for Mergesort is $T(n) = 2T(\frac{n}{2}) + \Theta(n)$.

Using Master theorem, we get, $T(n) = \Theta(nlogn)$.

Note: For more details, refer *Divide and Conquer* chapter.

Performance

Worst case complexity: $\Theta(nlogn)$
Best case complexity: $\Theta(nlogn)$
Average case complexity: $\Theta(nlogn)$
Worst case space complexity: $\Theta(n)$ auxiliary

16.10 Heapsort

Heapsort is a comparison-based sorting algorithm and is part of the selection sort family. Although somewhat slower in practice on most machines than a good implementation of Quick sort, it has the advantage of a more favorable worst-case $\Theta(n \, logn)$ runtime. Heapsort is an in-place algorithm but is not a stable sort.

Performance

Worst case performance: $\Theta(nlogn)$
Best case performance: $\Theta(nlogn)$
Average case performance: $\Theta(nlogn)$
Worst case space complexity: $\Theta(n)$ total, $\Theta(1)$ auxiliary

For other details on Heapsort refer *Priority Queues* chapter.

16.11 Quicksort

Quick sort is an example of divide-and-conquer algorithmic technique. It is also called *partition exchange sort*. It uses recursive calls for sorting the elements. It is one of famous algorithms among comparison-based sorting algorithms.

Divide: The array $A[low \dots high]$ is partitioned into two non-empty sub arrays $A[low \dots q]$ and $A[q+1 \dots high]$, such that each element of $A[low \dots high]$ is less than or equal to each element of $A[q+1 \dots high]$. The index q is computed as part of this partitioning procedure.

Conquer: The two sub arrays $A[low \dots q]$ and $A[q+1 \dots high]$ are sorted by recursive calls to Quick sort.

Algorithm

The recursive algorithm consists of four steps:
1) If there are one or no elements in the array to be sorted, return.
2) Pick an element in the array to serve as "*pivot*" point. (Usually the left-most element in the array is used.)
3) Split the array into two parts - one with elements larger than the pivot and the other with elements smaller than the pivot.
4) Recursively repeat the algorithm for both halves of the original array.

Implementation

```
void Quicksort( int A[], int low, int high ) {
        int pivot;
        /* Termination condition! */
        if( high > low ) {
                pivot = Partition( A, low, high );
                Quicksort( A, low, pivot-1 );
                Quicksort( A, pivot+1, high );
        }

}
int Partition( int A, int low, int high ) {
```

```
                int left, right, pivot_item = A[low];
                left = low;
                right = high;
                while ( left < right ) {
                        /* Move left while item < pivot */
                        while( A[left] <= pivot_item )
                                left++;
                        /* Move right while item > pivot */
                        while( A[right] > pivot_item )
                                right--;
                        if( left < right )
                                swap(A,left,right);
                }
                /* right is final position for the pivot */
                A[low] = A[right];
                A[right] = pivot_item;
                return right;
}
```

Analysis

Let us assume that $T(n)$ be the complexity of Quick sort and also assume that all elements are distinct. Recurrence for $T(n)$ depends on two subproblem sizes which depend on partition element. If pivot is i^{th} smallest element then exactly $(i - 1)$ items will be in left part and $(n - i)$ in right part. Let us call it as i −split. Since each element has equal probability of selecting it as pivot the probability of selecting i^{th} element is $\frac{1}{n}$.

Best Case: Each partition splits array in halves and gives

$$T(n) = 2T(\tfrac{n}{2}) + \Theta(n) = \Theta(nlogn), \text{ [using } Divide \text{ and } Conquer \text{ master theorem]}$$

Worst Case: Each partition gives unbalanced splits and we get

$$T(n) = T(n - 1) + \Theta(n) = \Theta(n^2) [using \ Subtraction \ and \ Conquer \ master \ theorem]$$

The worst-case occurs when the list is already sorted and last element chosen as pivot.

Average Case: In the average case of Quick sort, we do not know where the split happens. For this reason, we take all possible values of split locations, add all their complexities and divide with n to get the average case complexity.

$$T(n) = \sum_{i=1}^{n} \frac{1}{n}(runtime \ with \ i - split) + n + 1$$

$$= \frac{1}{n}\sum_{i=1}^{N}\big(T(i - 1) + T(n - i)\big) + n + 1$$

$$//since \ we \ are \ dealing \ with \ best \ case \ we \ can \ assume \ T(n - i) \ and \ T(i - 1) \ are \ equal$$

$$= \frac{2}{n}\sum_{i=1}^{n} T(i - 1) + n + 1$$

$$= \frac{2}{n}\sum_{i=0}^{n-1} T(i) + n + 1$$

Multiply both sides by n.

$$nT(n) = 2\sum_{i=0}^{n-1} T(i) + n^2 + n$$

Same formula for $n - 1$.

$$(n - 1)T(n - 1) = 2\sum_{i=0}^{n-2} T(i) + (n - 1)^2 + (n - 1)$$

Subtract the $n - 1$ formula from n.

$$nT(n) - (n - 1)T(n - 1) = 2\sum_{i=0}^{n-1} T(i) + n^2 + n - (2\sum_{i=0}^{n-2} T(i) + (n - 1)^2 + (n - 1))$$

$$nT(n) - (n - 1)T(n - 1) = 2T(n - 1) + 2n$$

$$nT(n) = (n + 1)T(n - 1) + 2n$$

Divide with $n(n + 1)$.

$$\frac{T(n)}{n + 1} = \frac{T(n - 1)}{n} + \frac{2}{n + 1}$$

$$= \frac{T(n-2)}{n-1} + \frac{2}{n} + \frac{2}{n+1}$$

.
.
.

$$= O(1) + 2\sum_{i=3}^{n}\frac{1}{i}$$
$$= O(1) + O(2logn)$$
$$\frac{T(n)}{n+1} = O(logn)$$
$$T(n) = O\big((n+1)\,logn\big) = O(nlogn)$$

Time Complexity, $T(n) = O(nlogn)$.

Performance

Worst case Complexity: $O(n^2)$
Best case Complexity: $O(nlogn)$
Average case Complexity: $O(nlogn)$
Worst case space Complexity: $O(1)$

16.11.1 Randomized Quick sort

In average-case behavior of Quicksort, we assumed that all permutations of the input numbers are equally likely. However, we cannot always expect it to hold. We can add randomization to an algorithm in order to reduce the probability of getting worst case in Quick sort.

There are two ways of adding randomization in Quick sort: either by randomly placing the input data in the array or by randomly choosing an element in the input data for pivot. The second choice is easier to analyze and implement. The change will only be done at the Partition algorithm.

In normal Quicksort, *pivot* element was always the leftmost element in the list to be sorted. Instead of always using $A[low]$ as *pivot*, we will use a randomly chosen element from the subarray $A[low..high]$ in the randomized version of Quicksort. It is done by exchanging element $A[low]$ with an element chosen at random from $A[low..high]$. This ensures that the *pivot* element is equally likely to be any of the $high - low + 1$ elements in the subarray. Since the pivot element is randomly chosen, we can expect the split of the input array to be reasonably well balanced on average. This can help in preventing the worst-case behavior of quick sort which occurs in unbalanced partitioning.

Even though, randomized version improves the worst case complexity, its worst case complexity is still $O(n^2)$. One way to improve *Randomized − QuickSort* is to choose the pivot for partitioning more carefully than by picking a random element from the array. One common approach is to choose the pivot as the median of a set of 3 elements randomly selected from the array.

16.12 Tree Sort

Tree sort uses a binary search tree. It involves scanning each element of the input and placing it into its proper position in a binary search tree. This has two phases:
- First phase is creating a binary search tree using the given array elements.
- Second phase is traversing the given binary search tree in inorder, thus resulting in a sorted array.

Performance

The average number of comparisons for this method is $O(nlogn)$. But in worst case, number of comparisons is reduced by $O(n^2)$, a case which arises when the sort tree is skew tree.

16.13 Comparison of Sorting Algorithms

Name	Average Case	Worst Case	Auxiliary Memory	Is Stable?	Other Notes
Bubble	$O(n^2)$	$O(n^2)$	1	yes	Small code
Selection	$O(n^2)$	$O(n^2)$	1	no	Stability depends on the implementation.
Insertion	$O(n^2)$	$O(n^2)$	1	yes	Average case is also $O(n+d)$, where d is the number of inversions
Shell	-	$O(nlog^2n)$	1	no	
Merge	$O(nlogn)$	$O(nlogn)$	depends	yes	
Heap	$O(nlogn)$	$O(nlogn)$	1	no	

Quick Sort	O($nlogn$)	O(n^2)	O($logn$)	depends	Can be implemented as a stable sort depending on how the pivot is handled.
Tree sort	O($nlogn$)	O(n^2)	O(n)	depends	Can be implemented as a stable sort.

Note: n denotes the number of elements in the input.

16.14 Linear Sorting Algorithms

In earlier sections, we have seen many examples on comparison-based sorting algorithms. Among them, the best comparison-based sorting can has the complexity O($nlogn$). In this section, we will discuss other types of algorithms: Linear Sorting Algorithms. To improve the time complexity of sorting these algorithms, make some assumptions about the input. Few examples of Linear Sorting Algorithms are:

- Counting Sort
- Bucket Sort
- Radix Sort

16.15 Counting Sort

Counting sort is not a comparison sort algorithm and gives O(n) complexity for sorting. To achieve O(n) complexity, *counting* sort assumes that each of the elements is an integer in the range 1 to K, for some integer K. When $K = O(n)$, the *counting*-sort runs in O(n) time. The basic idea of Counting sort is to determine, for each input element X, the number of elements less than X. This information can be used to place directly into its correct position. For example, if 10 elements are less than X, then X belongs to position 11 in output.

In the code below, $A[0..n-1]$ is the input array with length n. In counting sort we need two more arrays: let us assume array $B[0..n-1]$ contains the sorted output and the array $C[0..K-1]$ provides temporary storage.

```
void CountingSort (int A[], int n, int B[], int K) {
    int C[K], i, j;
    //Complexity: O(K)
    for (i =0 ; i<K; i++)
        C[i] = 0;

    //Complexity: O(n)
    for (j =0 ; j<n; j++)
        C[A[j]] = C[A[j]] + 1;

    //C[i] now contains the number of elements equal to i
    //Complexity: O(K)
    for (i =1 ; i<K; i++)
        C[i] = C[i] + C[i-1];

    // C[i] now contains the number of elements ≤ i
    //Complexity: O(n)
    for (j = n-1; j>=0; j--) {
        B[C[A[j]]] = A[j];
        C[A[j]] = C[A[j]] - 1;
    }
}
```

Total Complexity: O(K) + O(n) + O(K) + O(n) = O(n) if K =O(n). Space Complexity: O(n) if K =O(n).

Note: Counting works well if K =O(n). Otherwise, the complexity will be more.

16.16 Bucket sort [or Bin Sort]

Like *Counting* sort, *Bucket* sort also imposes restrictions on the input to improve the performance. In other words, Bucket sort works well if the input is drawn from fixed set. *Bucket* sort is the generalization of *Counting* Sort. For example, suppose that all the input elements from {0, 1, . . . , $K - 1$}, i.e., the set of integers in the interval [0, $K - 1$]. That means, K is the number of distant elements in the input. *Bucket* sort uses K counters. The ith counter keeps track of the number of occurrences of the ith element. Bucket sort with two buckets is effectively a version of Quick sort with two buckets.

```
#define BUCKETS 10
void BucketSort(int A[], int array_size) {
    int i, j, k;
    int buckets[BUCKETS];
    for(j =0; j < BUCKETS; j++)
        buckets[j] = 0;
    for(i =0; i < array_size; i++)
```

```
                ++ buckets[A[i]];
     for(i =0, j=0; j < BUCKETS; j++)
               for(k = buckets[j];k > 0; --k)
                    A[i++] = j;

}
```

Time Complexity: O(n). Space Complexity: O(n).

16.17 Radix sort

Similar to *Counting* sort and *Bucket* sort, this sorting algorithm also assumes some kind of information about the input elements. Suppose that the input values to be sorted are from base d. That means all numbers are d-digit numbers.

In radix sort, first sort the elements based on last digit [least significant digit]. These results were again sorted by second digit [next to least significant digits]. Continue this process for all digits until we reach most significant digits. Use some stable sort to sort them by last digit. Then stable sort them by the second least significant digit, then by the third, etc. If we use counting sort as the stable sort, the total time is O(nd) ≈O(n).

Algorithm:
1) Take the least significant digit of each element.
2) Sort the list of elements based on that digit, but keep the order of elements with the same digit (this is the definition of a stable sort).
3) Repeat the sort with each more significant digit.

The speed of Radix sort depends on the inner basic operations. If the operations are not efficient enough, Radix sort can be slower than other algorithms such as Quick sort and Merge sort. These operations include the insert and delete functions of the sub-lists and the process of isolating the digit we want. If the numbers were not of equal length then a test is needed to check for additional digits that need sorting. This can be one of the slowest parts of Radix sort and also one of the hardest to make efficient.

Since Radix sort depends on the digits or letters, it is less flexible than other sorts. For every different type of data, Radix sort needs to be rewritten and if the sorting order changes, the sort needs to be rewritten again. In short, Radix sort takes more time to write, and it is very difficult to write a general purpose Radix sort that can handle all kinds of data.

For many programs that need a fast sort, Radix sort is a good choice. Still, there are faster sorts, which is one reason why Radix sort is not used as much as some other sorts.

Time Complexity: O(nd) ≈O(n), if d is small.

16.18 Topological Sort

Refer *Graph Algorithms* Chapter.

16.19 External Sorting

External sorting is a generic term for a class of sorting algorithms that can handle massive amounts of data. These External sorting algorithms are useful when the files are too big and cannot fit into main memory.

Like internal sorting algorithms, there are number for algorithms for external sorting also. One such algorithm is External Mergesort. In practice these external sorting algorithms are being supplemented by internal sorts.

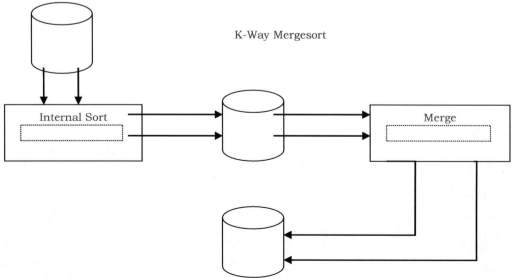

K-Way Mergesort

Simple External Mergesort

A number of records from each tape would be read into main memory and sorted using an internal sort and then output to the tape. For the sake of clarity, let us assume that 900 megabytes of data needs to be sorted using only 100 megabytes of RAM.

1) Read 100MB of the data into main memory and sort by some conventional method (let us say Quick sort).
2) Write the sorted data to disk.
3) Repeat steps 1 and 2 until all of the data is sorted in chunks of 100MB. Now we need to merge them into one single sorted output file.
4) Read the first 10MB of each sorted chunk (call them input buffers) in main memory (90MB total) and allocate the remaining 10MB for output buffer.
5) Perform a 9-way Mergesort and store the result in the output buffer. If the output buffer is full, write it to the final sorted file. If any of the 9 input buffers gets empty, fill it with the next 10MB of its associated 100MB sorted chunk or otherwise mark it as exhausted if there is no more data in the sorted chunk and do not use it for merging.

The above algorithm can be generalized by assuming that the amount of data to be sorted exceeds the available memory by a factor of K. Then, K chunks of data need to be sorted and a K-way merge has to be completed.

If X is the amount of main memory available, there will be K input buffers and 1 output buffer of size $X/(K+1)$ each. Depending on various factors (how fast is the hard drive?) better performance can be achieved if the output buffer is made larger (for example, twice as large as one input buffer). Complexity of the 2-way External Merge sort: In each pass we read + write each page in file. Let us assume that there are n pages in file. That means we need $\lceil logn \rceil + 1$ number of passes. The total cost is $2n(\lceil logn \rceil + 1)$.

16.20 Problems on Sorting

Problem-1   Given an array $A[0 \dots n-1]$ of n numbers containing repetition of some number. Give an algorithm for checking whether there are repeated elements or not. Assume that we are not allowed to use additional space (i.e., we can use a few temporary variables, O(1) storage).

Solution: Since we are not allowed to use any extra space, one simple way is to scan the elements one by one and for each element check whether that elements appears in the remaining elements. If we find a match we return true.

```
int CheckDuplicatesInArray(in A[], int n) {
    for (int i  =  0; i < n; i++)
    for (int j = i + 1; j < n; j++)
        if(A[i]==A[j])
                reutrn true;
    return false;
}
```

Each iteration of the inner, j-indexed loop uses O(1) space, and for a fixed value of i, the j loop executes $n - i$ times. The outer loop executes $n - 1$ times, so the entire function uses time proportional to

$$\sum_{i=1}^{n-1} n - i = n(n-1) - \sum_{i=1}^{n-1} i = n(n-1) - \frac{n(n-1)}{2} = \frac{n(n-1)}{2} = O(n^2)$$

Time Complexity: $O(n^2)$. Space Complexity: $O(1)$.

Problem-2   Can we improve the time complexity of Problem-1?

Solution: **Yes**, using sorting technique.

```
int CheckDuplicatesInArray(in A[], int n) {
    //for heap sort algorithm refer Priority Queues chapter
    Heapsort( A, n );
    for (int i  =  0; i < n-1; i++)
        if(A[i]==A[i+1])
                reutrn true;
    return false;
}
```

Heapsort function takes $O(n\,logn)$ time, and requires $O(1)$ space. The scan clearly takes for $n - 1$ iterations, each iteration using O(1) time. The overall time is $O(n\,logn + n) = O(n\,logn)$.

Time Complexity: $O(n\,logn)$. Space Complexity: $O(1)$.

Note: For variations of this problem, refer *Searching* chapter.

Problem-3   Given an array $A[0 \dots n-1]$, where each element of the array represents a vote in the election. Assume that each vote is given as an integer representing the ID of the chosen candidate. Give an algorithm for determining who wins the election.

Solution: This problem is nothing but finding the element which repeated maximum number of times. Solution is similar to Problem-1 solution: keep track of counter.

```
int CheckWhoWinsTheElection(in A[], int n) {
    int i, j, counter = 0, maxCounter = 0, candidate;
    candidate = A[0];
    for (i  =  0; i < n; i++) {
        candidate = A[i];
        counter = 0;
        for (j   = i + 1; j < n; j++) {
            if(A[i]==A[j]) counter++;
        }
        if(counter > maxCounter) {
            maxCounter = counter;
            candidate = A[i];

        }

    }
    return candidate;
}
```

Time Complexity: $O(n^2)$. Space Complexity: $O(1)$.

Note: For variations of this problem, refer *Searching* chapter.

Problem-4   Can we improve the time complexity of Problem-3? Assume we don't have any extra space.

Solution: Yes. The approach is to sort the votes based on candidate ID, then scan the sorted array and count up which candidate so far has the most votes. We only have to remember the winner, so we don't need a clever data structure. We can use heapsort as it is an in-place sorting algorithm.

```
int CheckWhoWinsTheElection(in A[], int n) {
    int i, j, currentCounter = 1, maxCounter = 1;
    int currentCandidate, maxCandidate;
    currentCandidate = maxCandidate= A[0];
    //for heap sort algorithm refer Priority Queues Chapter
    Heapsort( A, n );
    for (int i  =  1; i <= n; i++) {
        if( A[i] == currentCandidate)
            currentCounter ++;
        else {
            currentCandidate = A[i];
            currentCounter = 1;
        }
        if(currentCounter > maxCounter)
            maxCounter = currentCounter;
        else {   maxCandidate = currentCandidate;
            maxCounter = currentCounter;

        }

    }
    return candidate;
}
```

Since Heapsort time complexity is $O(n \log n)$ and in-place, so it only uses an additional $O(1)$ of storage in addition to the input array. The scan of the sorted array does a constant-time conditional $n - 1$ times, thus using $O(n)$ time. The overall time bound is $O(n \log n)$.

Problem-5   Can we further improve the time complexity of Problem-3?

Solution: In the given problem, number of candidates is less but the number of votes is significantly large. For this problem we can use counting sort.

Time Complexity: $O(n)$, n is the number of votes (elements) in array.
Space Complexity: $O(k)$, k is the number of candidates participated in election.

Problem-6   Given an array A of n elements, each of which is an integer in the range $[1, n^2]$. How do we sort the array in $O(n)$ time?

Solution: If we subtract each number by 1 then we get the range $[0, n^2 - 1]$. If we consider all number as 2 −digit base n. Each digit ranges from 0 to n^2 - 1. Sort this using radix sort. This uses only two calls to counting sort. Finally, add 1 to all the numbers. Since there are 2 calls, the complexity is $O(2n) \approx O(n)$.

Problem-7   For the Problem-6, what if the range is $[1 \ldots n^3]$?

Solution: If we subtract each number by 1 then we get the range $[0, n^3 - 1]$. Considering all number as 3-digit base n: each digit ranges from 0 to $n^3 - 1$. Sort this using radix sort. This uses only three calls to counting sort. Finally, add 1 to all the numbers. Since there are 3 calls, the complexity is $O(3n) \approx O(n)$.

Problem-8 Given an array with n integers each of value less than n^{100}, can it be sorted in linear time?

Solution: Yes. Reasoning is same as in of Problem-6 and Problem-7.

Problem-9 Let A and B be two arrays of n elements, each. Given a number K, give an $O(nlogn)$ time algorithm for determining whether there exists a $\in A$ and b $\in B$ such that $a + b = K$.

Solution: Since we need $O(n \, logn)$, it gives us a pointer that we need sorting. So, we will do that.

```
int Find( int A[], int B[], int n, K ) {
    int i, c;
    Heapsort( A, n );                    //O(nlogn)
    for (i =0; i< n; i++) {              //O(n)
        c = k-B[i];                      //O(1)
        if(BinarySearch(A, c))           //O(logn)
            return 1;
    }
    return 0;
}
```

Note: For variations of this problem, refer *Searching* chapter.

Problem-10 Given an array of n elements, can we output in sorted order the K elements following the median in sorted order in time $O(n + KlogK)$.

Solution: Yes. Find the median and partition about the median. With this we can find all the elements greater than it. Now find the Kth largest element in this set and partition about it; and get all the elements less than it. Output the sorted list of final set of elements. Clearly, this operation takes $O(n + KlogK)$ time.

Problem-11 Consider the sorting algorithms: Bubble Sort, Insertion Sort, Selection Sort, Merge Sort, Heap Sort, and Quick Sort. Which of these are stable?

Solution: Let us assume that A is the array to be sorted. Also, let us say R and S have the same key and R appears earlier in the array than S. That means, R is at $A[i]$ and S is at $A[j]$, with $i < j$. To show any stable algorithm, in the sorted output R must precede S.

Bubble sort: Yes. Elements change order only when a smaller record follows a larger. Since S is not smaller than R it cannot precede it.

Selection sort: No. It divides the array into sorted and unsorted portions and iteratively finds the minimum values in the unsorted portion. After finding a minimum x, if the algorithm moves x into the sorted portion of the array by means of a swap then the element swapped could be R which then could be moved behind S. This would invert the positions of R and S, so in general it is not stable. If swapping is avoided, it could be made stable but the cost in time would probably be very significant.

Insertion sort: Yes. As presented, when S is to be inserted into sorted subarray $A[1..j - 1]$, only records larger than S are shifted. Thus R would not be shifted during $S's$ insertion and hence would always precede it.

Merge sort: Yes, In the case of records with equal keys, the record in the left subarray gets preference. Those are the records that came first in the unsorted array. As a result, they will precede later records with the same key.

Heap sort: No. Suppose $i = 1$ and R and S happen to be the two records with the largest keys in the input. Then R will remain in location 1 after the array is heapified, and will be placed in location n in the first iteration of Heapsort. Thus S will precede R in the output.

Quick sort: No. The partitioning step can swap the location of records many times, and thus two records with equal keys could swap position in the final output.

Problem-12 Consider the same sorting algorithms as that of Problem-11. Which of them are in-place?

Solution:
Bubble sort: Yes, because only two integers are required.

Insertion sort: Yes, since we need to store two integers and a record.

Selection sort: Yes. This algorithm would likely need space for two integers and one record.

Merge sort: No. Arrays need to perform the merge. (If the data is in the form of a linked list, the sorting can be done in-place, but this is a nontrivial modification.)

Heap sort: Yes, since the heap and partially-sorted array occupy opposite ends of the input array.

Quicksort: No, since it is recursive and stores $O(logn)$ activation records on the stack. Modifying it to be non-recursive is feasible but nontrivial.

Problem-13   Among, Quick sort, Insertion sort, Selection sort, Heap sort algorithms, which one needs the minimum number of swaps?

Solution: Selected sort, it needs n swaps only (refer theory section).

Problem-14   What is the minimum number of comparisons required to determine if an integer appears more than $n/2$ times in a sorted array of n integers?

Solution: Refer *Searching* chapter.

Problem-15   **Sort an array of 0's, 1's and 2's:** Given an array A[] consisting $0's$, $1's$ and $2's$, give an algorithm for sorting A[]. The algorithm should put all $0's$ first, then all $1's$ and all $2's$ in last.
Example: Input = {0,1,1,0,1,2,1,2,0,0,0,1}, Output = {0, 0, 0, 0, 0, 1, 1, 1, 1, 1, 2, 2}

Solution: Use Counting Sort. Since there are only three elements and the maximum value is 2, we need a temporary array with 3 elements.

Time Complexity: O(n). Space Complexity: O(1).

Note: For variations of this problem, refer *Searching* chapter.

Problem-16   Is there any other way of solving Problem-16?

Solution: Using Quick Sort. Since we know that there are only 3 elements 0, 1 and 2 in the array, we can select 1 as a pivot element for Quick Sort. Quick Sort finds the correct place for 1 by moving all 0's to the left of 1 and all 2's to the right of 1. For doing this it uses only one scan.

Time Complexity: O(n). Space Complexity: O(1).

Note: For efficient algorithm, refer *Searching* chapter.

Problem-17   How do we find the number which appeared maximum number of times in an array?

Solution: One simple approach is to sort the given array and scan the sorted array. While scanning, keep track of the elements that occur the maximum number of times.

Algorithm:

```
QuickSort(A, n);
int i, j, count=1, Number=A[0], j=0;
for(i=0;i<n;i++) {
    if(A[j]==A) {
        count++;
        Number=A[j];
    }
    j=i;
}
printf("Number:%d, count:%d", Number, count);
```

Time Complexity = Time for Sorting + Time for Scan = O($nlogn$)+O(n) = O($nlogn$). Space Complexity: O(1).

Note: For variations of this problem, refer *Searching* chapter.

Problem-18   Is there any other way of solving the Problem-17?

Solution: Using Binary Tree. Create a binary tree with an extra field *count* which indicates the number of times an element appeared in the input. Let us say we have created a Binary Search Tree [BST]. Now, do the In-Order of the tree. In-Order traversal of BST produces sorted list. While doing In-Order traversal keep track of maximum element.

Time Complexity: O(n) +O(n) ≈ O(n). First parameter is for constructing the BST and the second parameter is for Inorder Traversal. Space Complexity: O($2n$) ≈O(n), since every node in BST needs two extra pointers.

Problem-19   Is there yet other way of solving the Problem-17?

Solution: Using Hash Table: For each element of the given array we use a counter and for each occurrence of the element we increment the corresponding counter. At the end we can just return the element which has the the maximum counter.

Time Complexity: O(n). Space Complexity: O(n). For constructing hash table we need O(n).

Note: For efficient algorithm, refer *Searching* chapter.

Problem-20   Given a 2 GB file with one string per line, which sorting algorithm would we use to sort the file and why?

Solution: When we have a size limit of 2GB, it means that we cannot bring all the data into main memory.

Algorithm: How much memory do we have available? Let's assume we have X MB of memory available. Divide the file into K chunks, where $X * K \sim 2\,GB$.
- Bring each chunk into memory and sort the lines as usual (any O($nlogn$) algorithm).
- Save the lines back to the file.

- Now bring next chunk into memory and sort.
- Once we're done, merge them one by one; in case of one set finish bring more data from concerned chunk.

The above algorithm is also known as external sort. Step $3 - 4$ is known as K-way merge. The idea behind going for external sort is the size of data. Since data is huge and we can't bring it to the memory, we need e to go for a disk based sorting algorithm.

Problem-21 **Nearly sorted:** Given an array of n elements, each which is at most K positions from its target position, devise an algorithm that sorts in O($n\ logK$) time.

Solution: Divide the elements into n/K groups of size K, and sort each piece in O($KlogK$) time, say using Mergesort. This preserves the property that no element is more than K elements out of position. Now, merge each block of K elements with the block to its left.

Problem-22 Is there any other way of solving Problem-21?

Solution: Insert the first K elements into a binary heap. Insert the next element from the array into the heap, and delete the minimum element from the heap. Repeat.

Problem-23 Can we improve the time complexity of Problem-21?

Solution: One method is to repeatedly pair up the lists, and merge each pair. This method can also be seen as a tail component of the execution merge sort, where the analysis is clear. This is called Tournament Method. Maximum depth of Tournament Method is logK and in each iteration we are scanning all the n elements.

Time Complexity: O($n$logK).

Problem-24 Is there any other way of solving the Problem-21?

Solution: Other method is to use a *min* priority queue for the minimum elements of each of the K lists. At each step, we output the extracted minimum of the priority queue, and determine from which of the K lists it came, and insert the next element from that list into the priority queue. Since we are using priority queue, that maximum depth of priority queue is *logK*.

Time Complexity: O($n$logK).

Problem-25 Given an array of $1,00,000$ pixel color values, each of which is an integer in the range [0,255]. Which sorting algorithm is preferable for sorting them?

Solution: Counting Sort. There are only 256 key values, so the auxiliary array would only be of size 256, and there would be only two passes through the data which would be very efficient in both time and space.

Problem-26 Similar to Problem-25, if we have a telephone directory with $1,00,000$ entries, which sorting algorithm is best?

Solution: Bucket sort. In Bucket sort the buckets are defined by the last 7 digits. This requires an auxiliary array of size 10 million, and has the advantage of requiring only one pass through the data on disk. Each bucket contains all telephone numbers with the same last 7 digits but different area codes. The buckets can then be sorted on area code by selection or insertion sort; there are only a handful of area codes.

Problem-27 Give an algorithm for merging K-sorted lists.

Solution: Refer *Priority Queues* chapter.

Chapter-17

SEARCHING

17.1 What is Searching?

In computer science, *searching* is the process of finding an item with specified properties from a collection of items. The items may be stored as records in a database, simple data elements in arrays, text in files, nodes in trees, vertices and edges in graphs, or may be elements of other search space.

17.2 Why do we need Searching?

Searching is one of core computer science algorithms. We know that today's computers store a lot of information. To retrieve this information proficiently we need very efficient searching algorithms.

There are certain ways of organizing the data which improves the searching process. That means, if we keep the data in a proper order, it is easy to search the required element. Sorting is one of the techniques for making the elements ordered. In this chapter we will see different searching algorithms.

17.3 Types of Searching

Following are the types of searches which we will be discussing in this book.

- Unordered Linear Search
- Sorted/Ordered Linear Search
- Binary Search
- Symbol Tables and Hashing
- String Searching Algorithms: Tries, Ternary Search and Suffix Trees

17.4 Unordered Linear Search

Let us assume that given an array whose elements order is not known. That means the elements of the array are not sorted. In this case if we want to search for an element then we have to scan the complete array and see if the element is there in the given list or not.

```
int UnOrderedLinearSearch (int A[], int n, int data) {
    for (int i = 0; i < n; i++) {
        if(A[i] == data)
            return i;
    }
    return -1;
}
```

Time complexity: O(*n*), in the worst case we need to scan the complete array. Space complexity: O(1).

17.5 Sorted/Ordered Linear Search

If the elements of the array are already sorted then in many cases we don't have to scan the complete array to see if the element is there in the given array or not. In the algorithm below, it can be seen that, at any point if the value at $A[i]$ is greater than *data* to be searched then we just return −1 without searching the remaining array.

```
int OrderedLinearSearch(int A[], int n, int data) {
    for (int i = 0; i < n; i++) {
        if(A[i] == data)
            return i;
        else if(A[i] > data)
            return -1;
    }
    return -1;
}
```

Time complexity of this algorithm is O(n). This is because in the worst case we need to scan the complete array. But in the average case it reduces the complexity even though the growth rate is same. Space complexity: O(1).

Note: For the above algorithm we can make further improvement by incrementing the index at faster rate (say, 2). This will reduce the number of comparisons for searching in the sorted list.

17.6 Binary Search

Let us consider the problem of searching a word in a dictionary. Typically, we directly go to some approximate page [say, middle page] start searching from that point. If the *name* that we are searching is same then the search is complete. If the page is before the selected pages then apply the same process for the first half otherwise apply the same process to the second half. Binary search also works in the same way. The algorithm applying such a strategy is referred to as *binary search* algorithm.

```
//Iterative Binary Search Algorithm
int BinarySearchIterative[int A[], int n, int data) {
    int low =  0;
    int high = n-1;
    while (low <= high) {
        mid  = low + (high-low)/2; //To avoid overflow
        if(A[mid] == data)
            return mid;
        else if(A[mid] < data)
            low =  mid + 1;
        else high =  mid - 1;
    }
    return -1;
}
//Recursive Binary Search Algorithm
int BinarySearchRecursive[int A[], int low, int high, int data) {
    int mid  = low + (high-low)/2; //To avoid overflow
    if(A[mid] == data)
        return mid;
    else if(A[mid] < data)
        return BinarySearchRecursive (A, mid + 1, high, data);
    else    return BinarySearchRecursive (A, low, mid - 1 , data);
    return -1;
}
```

Recurrence for binary search is $T(n) = T(\frac{n}{2}) + \Theta(1)$. This is because we are always considering only half of the input list and throwing out the other half. Using *Divide and Conquer* master theorem, we get, $T(n) = O(logn)$.

Time Complexity: O($logn$). Space Complexity: O(1) [for iterative algorithm].

17.7 Comparing Basic Searching Algorithms

Implementation	Search-Worst Case	Search-Avg. Case
Unordered Array	n	$\frac{n}{2}$
Ordered Array (Binary Search)	$logn$	$logn$
Unordered List	n	$\frac{n}{2}$
Ordered List	n	$\frac{n}{2}$
Binary Search Trees (for skew trees)	n	$logn$

Note: For discussion on binary search trees refer *Trees* chapter.

17.8 Symbol Tables and Hashing

Refer *Symbol Tables* and *Hashing* chapters.

17.9 String Searching Algorithms

Refer *String Algorithms* chapter.

17.10 Problems on Searching

Problem-1 Given an array of n numbers, give an algorithm for checking whether there are any duplicate elements in the array or not?

Solution: This is one of the simplest problems. One obvious answer to this is, exhaustively searching for duplicates in the array. That means, for each input element check whether there is any element with same value. This we can solve just by using two simple *for* loops. The code for this solution can be given as:

```
void CheckDuplicatesBruteForce(int A[], int n) {
    for(int i = 0; i < n; i++) {
        for(int j = i+1; j < n; j++) {
            if(A[i] == A[j]) {
                printf("Duplicates exist: %d", A[i]);
                return;
            }
        }
    }
    printf("No duplicates in given array.");
}
```

Time Complexity: $O(n^2)$, for two nested *for* loops. Space Complexity: O(1).

Problem-2 Can we improve the complexity of Problem-1's solution?

Solution: Yes. Sort the given array. After sorting all the elements with equal values come adjacent. Now, just do another scan on this sorted array and see if there are elements with same value and adjacent.

```
void CheckDuplicatesSorting(int A[], int n) {
    Sort(A, n);                    //sort the array
    for(int i = 0; i < n-1; i++) {
        if(A[i] == A[i+1]) {
            printf("Duplicates exist: %d", A[i]);
            return;
        }
    }
    printf("No duplicates in given array.");
}
```

Time Complexity: $O(nlogn)$, for sorting. Space Complexity: 0(1).

Problem-3 Is there any other way of solving Problem-1?

Solution: Yes, using hash table. Hash tables are a simple and effective method used to implement dictionaries. *Average* time to search for an element is O(1), while worst-case time is $O(n)$. Refer *Hashing* chapter for more details on hashing algorithms. As an example, consider the array, $A = \{3, 2, 1, 2, 2, 3\}$. Scan the input array and insert the elements into the hash. For each inserted element, keep the *counter* as 1 (assume initially all entires are filled with zeros). This indicates that the corresponding element has occurred already. For the given array, the hash table will look like (after inserting first three elements 3, 2 and 1):

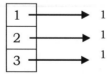

Now if we try inserting 2, since counter value of 2 is already 1, we can say the element has appeared twice.

Time Complexity: $O(n)$. Space Complexity: $O(n)$.

Problem-4 Can we further improve the complexity of Problem-1 solution?

Solution: Let us assume that the array elements are positive numbers and also all the elements are in the range 0 to $n - 1$. For each element $A[i]$, go to the array element whose index is $A[i]$. That means select $A[A[i]]$ and mark - $A[A[i]]$ (negate the value at $A[A[i]]$).

Continue this process until we encounter the element whose value is already negated. If one such element exists then we say duplicate elements exist in the given array. As an example, consider the array, $A = \{3, 2, 1, 2, 2, 3\}$.

Initially,

3	2	1	2	2	3
0	1	2	3	4	5

At step-1, negate A[abs(A[0])],

3	2	1	-2	2	3
0	1	2	3	4	5

At step-2, negate A[abs(A[1])],

3	2	-1	-2	2	3
0	1	2	3	4	5

At step-3, negate A[abs(A[2])],

3	-2	-1	-2	2	3
0	1	2	3	4	5

At step-4, negate A[abs(A[3])],

3	-2	-1	-2	2	3
0	1	2	3	4	5

At step-4, we can observe that $A[abs(A[3])]$ is already negative. That means we have encountered the same value twice.

```
void CheckDuplicates(int A[], int n) {
    for(int i = 0; i < n; i++) {
    if(A[abs(A[i])] < 0) {
            printf("Duplicates exist:%d", A[i]);
            return;
    }
    else    A[A[i]] = - A[A[i]];
    }
    printf("No duplicates in given array.");
}
```

Time Complexity: O(n). Since, only one scan is required. Space Complexity: O(1).

Notes:
- This solution does not work if the given array is read only.
- This solution will work only if all the array elements are positive.
- If the elements range is not in 0 to $n - 1$ then it may give exceptions.

Problem-5   Given an array of n numbers. Give an algorithm for finding the element which appears maximum number of times in the array?

Brute Force Solution: One simple solution to this is, for each input element check whether there is any element with same value and for each such occurrence, increment the counter. Each time, check the current counter with the max counter and update it if this value is greater than max counter. This we can solve just by using two simple *for* loops.

```
int CheckDuplicatesBruteForce(int A[], int n) {
    int counter =0, max=0;
    for(int i = 0; i < n; i++) {
        counter=0;
        for(int j = 0; j < n; j++) {
            if(A[i] == A[j])
                counter++;
        }
        if(counter > max)
            max = counter;
    }
    return max;
}
```

Time Complexity: O(n^2), for two nested *for* loops. Space Complexity: O(1).

Problem-6   Can we improve the complexity of Problem-5 solution?

Solution: Yes. Sort the given array. After sorting all the elements with equal values come adjacent. Now, just do another scan on this sorted array and see which element is appearing maximum number of times.

Time Complexity: O($nlogn$). (for sorting). Space Complexity: O(1).

Problem-7   Is there any other way of solving Problem-5?

Solution: Yes, using hash table. For each element of the input keep track of how many times that element appeared in the input. That means the counter value represents the number of occurrences for that element.

Time Complexity: O(n). Space Complexity: O(n).

Problem-8   For Problem-5, can we improve the time complexity? Assume that the elements range is 0 to $n-1$. That means all the elements are within this range only.

Solution: Yes. We can solve this problem in two scans. We *cannot* use the negation technique of Problem-3 for this problem because of number of repetitions. In the first scan, instead of negating add the value n. That means for each of occurrence of an element add the array size to that element. In the second scan, check the element value by dividing it with n and return the element whichever gives the maximum value. The code based on this method is given below.

```
void MaxRepititionsBruteForce(int A[], int n) {
    int i = 0, max = 0, maxIndex;
    for(i = 0; i < n; i++)
            A[A[i]%n] +=n;
    for(i = 0; i < n; i++)
        if(A[i]/n > max) {
            max = A[i]/n;
            maxIndex =i;
        }
    return maxIndex;
}
```

Notes:
- This solution does not work if the given array is read only.
- This solution will work only if the array elements are positive.
- If the elements range is not in 0 to $386386 - 1$ then it may give exceptions.

Time Complexity: O(n). Since no nested *for* loops are required. Space Complexity: O(1).

Problem-9   Given an array of n numbers, give an algorithm for finding the first element in the array which is repeated. For example, in the array, $A = \{3,2,1,2,2,3\}$ the first repeated number is 3 (not 2). That means, we need to return the first element among the repeated elements.

Solution: We can use the brute force solution that we used for Problem-1. For each element since it checks whether there is a duplicate for that element or not, whichever element duplicates first will be returned.

Problem-10   For Problem-9, can we use sorting technique?

Solution: No. For proving the failed case, let us consider the following array. For example, $A = \{3,2,1,2,2,3\}$. After sorting we get $A = \{1,2,2,2,3,3\}$. In this sorted array the first repeated element is 2 but the actual answer is 3.

Problem-11   For Problem-9, can we use hashing technique?

Solution: Yes. But the simple hashing technique which we used for Problem-3 will not work. For example, if we consider the input array as $A = \{3,2,1,2,3\}$, then first repeated element is 3 but using our simple hashing technique we get the answer as 2. This is because 2 is coming twice before 3. Now let us change the hashing table behavior so that we get the first repeated element.

Let us say, instead of storing 1 value, initially we store the position of the element in the array. As a result the hash table will look like (after inserting 3, 2 and 1):

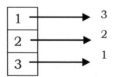

Now, if we see 2 again, we just negate the current value of 2 in the hash table. That means, we make its counter value as -2. The negative value in the hash table indicates that we have seen the same element two times. Similarly, for 3 (next element in input) also, we negate the current value of hash table and finally the hash table will look like:

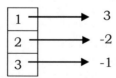

After processing the complete input array, scan the hash table and return the highest negative indexed value from it (i.e., -1 in our case). The highest negative value indicates that we have seen that element first (among repeated elements) and also repeating.

What if the element is repeated more than twice?

In this case, just skip the element if the corresponding value i already negative.

Problem-12   For Problem-9, can we use the technique that we used for Problem-3 (negation technique)?

Solution: No. As a contradiction example, for the array $A = \{3, 2, 1, 2, 2, 3\}$ the first repeated element is 3. But with negation technique the result is 2.

Problem-13   **Finding the Missing Number:** We are given a list of $n - 1$ integers and these integers are in the range of 1 to n. There are no duplicates in list. One of the integers is missing in the list. Given an algorithm to find the missing integer. **Example**: I/P: [1, 2, 4, 6, 3, 7, 8] O/P: 5

Brute Force Solution: One simple solution to this is, for each number in 1 to n check whether that number is in the given array or not.

```
int FindMissingNumber(int A[], int n) {
    int i, j, found=0;
    for (i = 1; i < =n; i ++) {
        found = 0;
        for (j = 0; j < n; j ++)
    if(A[j]==i)
                found = 1;
            if(!found) return i;
    }
    return -1;
}
```

Time Complexity: $O(n^2)$. Space Complexity: $O(1)$.

Problem-14   For Problem-13, can we use sorting technique?

Solution: Yes. Sorting the list will give the elements in increasing order and with another scan we can find the missing number.

Time Complexity: $O(nlogn)$, for sorting. Space Complexity: $O(1)$.

Problem-15   For Problem-13, can we use hashing technique?

Solution: Yes. Scan the input array and insert elements into the hash. For inserted element keep *counter* as 1 (assume initially all entires are filled with zeros). This indicates that the corresponding element has occurred already. Now, scan the hash table and return the element which has counter value zero.

Time Complexity: $O(n)$. Space Complexity: $O(n)$.

Problem-16   For Problem-13, can we improve the complexity?

Solution: Using summation formula
   1)   Get the sum of numbers, $sum = n*(n+1)/2$.
   2)   Subtract all the numbers from *sum* and you will get the missing number.

Time Complexity: $O(n)$, for scanning the complete array.

Problem-17   In Problem-13, if the sum of the numbers goes beyond maximum allowed integer, then there can be integer overflow and we may not get correct answer. Can we solve this problem?

Solution:
   1) XOR all the array elements, let the result of XOR be X.
   2) XOR all numbers from 1 to n, let XOR be Y.
   3) XOR of X and Y gives the missing number.

```
int FindMissingNumber(int A[], int n) {
    int i, X, Y;
    for (i = 0; i < n; i ++)
        X ^= A[i];
    for (i = 1; i <= n; i ++)
        Y ^= i;
    //In fact, one variable is enough.
    return X ^ Y;
}
```

Time Complexity: $O(n)$, for scanning the complete array. Space Complexity: $O(1)$.

Problem-18   **Find the Number Occurring Odd Number of Times:** Given an array of positive integers, all numbers occurs even number of times except one number which occurs odd number of times. Find the number in $O(n)$ time & constant space. **Example**:   I/P = [1, 2, 3, 2, 3, 1, 3] O/P = 3

Solution: Do a bitwise XOR of all the elements. We get the number which has odd occurrences. This is because, $A\ XOR\ A = 0$.

Time Complexity: O(n). Space Complexity: O(1).

Problem-19   **Find the two repeating elements in a given array:** Given an array with *size*, all elements of the array are in range 1 to n and also all elements occur only once except two numbers which occur twice. Find those two repeating numbers. For example: if the array is 4, 2, 4, 5, 2, 3, 1 with *size* = 7 and $n = 5$. This input has $n + 2 = 7$ elements with all elements occurring once except 2 and 4 which occur twice. So the output should be 4 2.

Solution: One simple way is to scan the complete array for each element of the input elements. That means use two loops. In the outer loop, select elements one by one and count the number of occurrences of the selected element in the inner loop. For the code below assume that *PrintRepeatedElements* is called with $n + 2$ to indicate the size.

```
void PrintRepeatedElements(int A[], int size) {
    for(int i = 0; i < size; i++)
        for(int j = i+1; j < size; j++)
            if(A[i] == A[j])
                printf("%d", A[i]);
}
```

Time Complexity: O(n^2). Space Complexity: O(1).

Problem-20   For Problem-19, can we improve the time complexity?

Solution: Sort the array using any comparison sorting algorithm and see if there are any elements which contiguous with same value.

Time Complexity: O($nlogn$). Space Complexity: O(1).

Problem-21   For Problem-19, can we improve the time complexity?

Solution: Use Count Array. This solution is like using a hash table. For simplicity we can use array for storing the counts. Traverse the array once and keep track of count of all elements in the array using a temp array *count*[] of size n. When we see an element whose count is already set, print it as duplicate. For the code below assume that *PrintRepeatedElements* is called with $n + 2$ to indicate the size.

```
void PrintRepeatedElements(int A[], int size) {
    int *count = (int *)calloc(sizeof(int), (size - 2));
    for(int i = 0; i < size; i++) {
        count[A[i]]++;
        if(count[A[i]] == 2)
            printf("%d", A[i]);
    }
}
```

Time Complexity: O(n). Space Complexity: O(n).

Problem-22   Consider Problem-19. Let us assume that the numbers are in the range 1 to n. Is there any other way of solving the problem?

Solution: Yes by using XOR Operation. Let the repeating numbers be X and Y, if we *XOR* all the elements in the array and also all integers from 1 to n, then the result will be X *XOR* Y. The 1's in binary representation of X *XOR* Y correspond to the different bits between X and Y. If the kth bit of X *XOR* Y is 1, we can *XOR* all the elements in the array and also all integers from 1 to n, whose k^{th} bits are 1. The result will be one of X and Y.

```
void PrintRepeatedElements (int A[], int size) {
    int XOR = A[0];
    int i, right_most_set_bit_no, X= 0, Y = 0;
    for(i = 0; i < size; i++)              /* Compute XOR of all elements in A[]*/
        XOR ^= A[i];
    for(i = 1; i <= n; i++)                /* Compute XOR of all elements {1, 2 ..n} */
        XOR ^= i;
    right_most_set_bit_no = XOR & ~( XOR -1);    // Get the rightmost set bit in right_most_set_bit_no

    /* Now divide elements in two sets by comparing rightmost set */
    for(i = 0; i < size; i++) {
        if(A[i] & right_most_set_bit_no)
            X = X^ A[i];        /*XOR of first set in A[] */
        else    Y = Y ^ A[i];        /*XOR of second set inA[] */
    }
    for(i = 1; i <= n; i++) {
        if(i & right_most_set_bit_no)
            X = X ^ i;        /*XOR of first set in A[] and {1, 2, ...n }*/
        else    Y = Y ^ i;        /*XOR of second set in A[] and {1, 2, ...n } */
    }
    printf("%d and %d",X, Y);
}
```

Time Complexity: O(n). Space Complexity: O(1).

Problem-23 Consider the Problem-19. Let us assume that the numbers are in the range 1 to n. Is there yet other way of solving the problem?

Solution: We can solve this by creating two simple mathematical equations. Let us assume that two numbers which we are going to find are X and Y. We know the sum of n numbers is $n(n+1)/2$ and product is $n!$. Make two equations using these sum and product formulae, and get values of two unknowns using the two equations. Let the summation of all numbers in array be S and product be P and the numbers which are being repeated are X and Y.

$$X + Y = S - \frac{n(n+1)}{2}$$
$$XY = P/n!$$

Using above two equations, we can find out X and Y. There can be addition and multiplication overflow problem with this approach.

Time Complexity: O(n). Space Complexity: O(1).

Problem-24 Similar to Problem-19, let us assume that the numbers are in the range 1 to n. Also, $n-1$ elements are repeating thrice and remaining element repeated twice. Find the element which is repeating twice.

Solution: If we *XOR* all the elements in the array and all integers from 1 to n, then all the elements which are thrice will become zero. This is because, since the element is repeating thrice and XOR another time from range makes that element appearing four times. As a result, output of $a\ XOR\ a\ XOR\ a\ XOR\ a = 0$. Same is case with all elements which repeated three times.

With the same logic, for the element which repeated twice, if we *XOR* the input elements and also the range, then the total number of appearances for that element are 3. As a result, output of $a\ XOR\ a\ XOR\ a = a$. Finally, we get the element which repeated twice.

Time Complexity: O(n). Space Complexity: O(1).

Problem-25 Given an array of n elements. Find two elements in the array such that their sum is equal to given element K?

Brute Force Solution: One simple solution to this is, for each input element check whether there is any element whose sum is K. This we can solve just by using two simple for loops. The code for this solution can be given as:

```
void BruteForceSearch[int A[], int n, int K) {
    for (int i = 0; i < n; i++) {
        for(int j = i; j < n; j++) {
            if(A[i]+A[j] == K) {
                printf("Items Found:%d %d", i, j);
                return;
            }
        }
    }
    printf("Items not found: No such elements");
}
```

Time Complexity: O(n^2). This is because of two nested for loops. Space Complexity: O(1).

Problem-26 For Problem-25, can we improve the time complexity?

Solution: Yes. Let us assume that we have sorted the given array. This operation takes O($n\ logn$). On the sorted array, maintain indices *loIndex* = 0 and hiIndex = $n-1$ and compute $A[loIndex] + A[hiIndex]$. If the sum equals K, then we are done with the solution. If the sum is less than K, decrement *hiIndex*, if the sum is greater than K, increment *loIndex*.

```
void Search[int A[], int n, int K) {
    int i, j, temp;
    Sort(A, n);
    for(i = 0, j = n-1; i < j) {
        temp = A[i] + A[j];
        if(temp == K) {
            printf("Elements Found: %d %d", i, j);
            return;
        }
        else if(temp < K)
            i = i + 1;
        else    j = j - 1;
    }
```

```
        return;
}
```

Time Complexity: O($nlogn$). If the given array is already sorted then the complexity is O(n).
Space Complexity: O(1).

Problem-27   Does the solution of Problem-25 work even if the array is not sorted?

Solution: Yes. Since we are checking all possibilities, the algorithm ensures that we get the pair of numbers if they exist.

Problem-28   Is there any other way of solving Problem-25?

Solution: Yes, using hash table. Since our objective is to find two indexes of the array whose sum is K. Let us say those indexes are X and Y. That means, $A[X] + A[Y] = K$.

What we need is, for each element of the input array $A[X]$, check whether $K - A[X]$ also exists in input array. Now, let us simplify that searching with hash table.

Algorithm:

- For each element of the input array, insert into the hash table. Let us say the current element is $A[X]$.
- Before proceeding to the next element we check whether $K - A[X]$ also exists in hash table or not.
- Existence of such number indicates that we are able to find the indexes.
- Otherwise proceed to the next input element.

Time Complexity: O(n). Space Complexity: O(n).

Problem-29   Given an array A of n elements. Find three indices, i, j & k such that $A[i]^2 + A[j]^2 = A[k]^2$?

Solution:

Algorithm:

- Sort the given array in-place.
- For each array index i compute $A[i]^2$ and store in array.
- Search for 2 numbers in array from 0 to $i-1$ which adds to $A[i]$ similar to Problem-25. This will give us the result in O(n) time. If we find such sum return true otherwise continue.

```
Sort(A); // Sort the input array
for (int i=0; i < n; i++)
      A[i] = A[i]*A[i];
for (i=n; i > 0; i--) {
      res = false;
      if(res) {
              //Problem-11/12 Solution
      }
}
```

Time Complexity:Time for sorting + $n \times$ (Time for finding the sum) = $O(nlogn) + n \times O(n) = n^2$. Space Complexity: $O(1)$.

Problem-30   Find two elements whose sum is closest to zero: Given an array with both positive and negative numbers, find the two elements such that their sum is closest to zero. For the below array, algorithm should give -80 and 85. Example: $1\ 60 - 10\ 70 - 80\ 85$

Brute Force Solution: For each element, find the sum with every other element in the array and compare sums. Finally, return the minimum sum.

```
void TwoElementsWithMinSum(int A[], int n) {
      int i, j, min_sum, sum, min_i, min_j, inv_count = 0;
      if(n < 2) {
              printf("Invalid Input");
              return;
      }
      /* Initialization of values */
      min_i = 0;
      min_j = 1;
      min_sum = A[0] + A[1];
      for(i= 0; i < n - 1; i ++)       {
              for(j = i + 1; j < n; j++)       {
                      sum = A[i] + A[j];
                      if(abs(min_sum) > abs(sum)) {
                              min_sum = sum;
                              min_i = i;
                              min_j = j;
                      }
```

```
            }
        }
        printf(" The two elements are %d and %d", arr[min_i], arr[min_j]);
}
```

Time complexity: $O(n^2)$. Space Complexity: $O(1)$.

Problem-31   Can we improve the time complexity of Problem-30?

Solution: Use Sorting.

Algorithm:

1. Sort all the elements of the given input array.
2. Maintain two indexes one at the beginning ($i = 0$) and other at the ending ($j = n - 1$). Also, maintains two variables to keep track of smallest positive sum closest to zero and smallest negative sum closest to zero.
3. While $i < j$:
   a. If the current pair sum is > zero and < postiveClosest then update the postiveClosest. Decrement j.
   b. If the current pair sum is < zero and > negativeClosest then update the negativeClosest. Increment i.
   c. Else, print the pair

```
void TwoElementsWithMinSum(int A[], int n) {
    int i = 0, j = n-1, temp, postiveClosest = INT_MAX, negativeClosest = INT_MIN;
    Sort(A, n);
    while(i < j) {
        temp  = A[i] + A[j];
        if(temp  > 0) {
            if (temp < postiveClosest)
                postiveClosest = temp;
            j--;
        }
        else if (temp  < 0) {
            if (temp > negativeClosest)
                negativeClosest = temp;
            i++;
        }
        else printf("Closest Sum: %d ", A[i] + A[j]);
    }
    return (abs(negativeClosest)> postiveClosest: postiveClosest: negativeClosest);
}
```

Time Complexity: $O(nlogn)$, for sorting. Space Complexity: $O(1)$.

Problem-32   Given an array of n elements. Find three elements in the array such that their sum is equal to given element K?

Brute Force Solution: The default solution to this is, for each pair of input elements check whether there is any element whose sum is K. This we can solve just by using three simple for loops. The code for this solution can be given as:

```
void BruteForceSearch[int A[], int n, int data) {
    for (int i = 0; i < n; i++) {
        for(int j = i+1; j < n; j++) {
            for(int k = j+1; k < n; k++)          {
                if(A[i] + A[j] + A[k]== data) {
                    printf("Items Found:%d %d %d", i, j, k);
                    return;
                }
            }
        }
    }
    printf("Items not found: No such elements");
}
```

Time Complexity: $O(n^3)$, for three nested *for* loops. Space Complexity: $O(1)$.

Problem-33   Does the solution of Problem-32 work even if the array is not sorted?

Solution: Yes. Since we are checking all possibilities, the algorithm ensures that we can find three numbers whose sum is K if they exist.

Problem-34   Can we use sorting technique for solving Problem-32?

Solution: Yes.

```
void Search[int A[], int n, int data) {
```

```
            Sort(A, n);
            for(int k = 0; k < n; k++) {
                    for(int i = k + 1, j = n-1; i < j;  ) {
                            if(A[k] + A[i] + A[j]  == data) {
                                    printf("Items Found:%d %d %d", i, j, k);
                                    return;
                            }
                            else if(A[k] + A[i] + A[j]  < data)
                                    i = i + 1;
                            else      j = j - 1;
                    }
            }
            return;
}
```

Time Complexity: Time for sorting + Time for searching in sorted list = $O(nlogn) + O(n^2) \approx O(n^2)$. This is because of two nested *for* loops. Space Complexity: $O(1)$.

Problem-35   Can we use hashing technique for solving Problem-32?

Solution: Yes. Since our objective is to find three indexes of the array whose sum is K. Let us say those indexes are X, Y and Z. That means, $A[X] + A[Y] + A[Z] = K$.

Let us assume that we have kept all possible sums along with their pairs in hash table. That means the key to hash table is $K - A[X]$ and values for $K - A[X]$ are all possible pairs of input whose sum is $K - A[X]$.

Algorithm:
- Before starting the searching, insert all possible sums with pairs of elements into the hash table.
- For each element of the input array, insert into the hash table. Let us say the current element is $A[X]$.
- Check whether there exists a hash entry in the table with key: $K - A[X]$.
- If such element exists then scan the element pairs of $K - A[X]$ and return all possible pairs by including $A[X]$ also.
- If no such element exists (with $K - A[X]$ as key) then go to next element.

Time Complexity: Time for storing all possible pairs in Hash table + searching = $O(n^2) + O(n^2) \approx O(n^2)$.
Space Complexity: $O(n)$.

Problem-36   Given an array of n integers, the $3 - sum\ problem$ is to find three integers whose sum is closest to *zero*.

Solution: This is same as that of Problem-32 with K value is zero.

Problem-37   Let A be an array of n distinct integers. Suppose A has the following property: there exists an index $1 \le k \le n$ such that $A[1],...,A[k]$ is an increasing sequence and $A[k+1],...,A[n]$ is a decreasing sequence. Design and analyze an efficient algorithm for finding k.
Similar question: Let us assume that the given array is sorted but starts with negative numbers and ends with positive numbers [such functions are called monotonically increasing function]. In this array find the starting index of the positive numbers. Assume that we know the length of the input array. Design a $O(logn)$ algorithm.

Solution: Let us use a variant of the binary search.
```
int Search (int A[], int n, int first, int last) {
    int mid, first = 0, last = n-1;
    while(first <= last) {
        // if the current array has size 1
        if(first == last)
            return A[first];
        // if the current array has size 2
        else if(first == last-1)
            return max(A[first], A[last]);
        // if the current array has size 3 or more
        else {
            mid = first + (last-first)/2;
            if(A[mid-1] < A[mid] && A[mid] > A[mid+1])
                return A[mid];
            else if(A[mid-1] < A[mid] && A[mid] < A[mid+1])
                first = mid+1;
            else if(A[mid-1] > A[mid] && A[mid] > A[mid+1])
                last = mid-1;
            else    return INT_MIN ;
        } // end of else
    } // end of while
}
```

The recursion equation is $T(n) = 2T(n/2) + c$. Using master theorem, we get O($logn$).

Problem-38   If we don't know n, how do we solve the Problem-37?

Solution: Repeatedly compute $A[1], A[2], A[4], A[8], A[16]$, and so on until we find a value of n such that $A[n] > 0$.

Time Complexity: O($logn$), since we are moving at the rate of 2.

Refer *Introduction to Analysis of Algorithms* chapter for details on this.

Problem-39   Given an input array of size unknown with all $1's$ in the beginning and $0's$ in the end. Find the index in the array from where $0's$ start. Consider there are millions of $1's$ and $0's$ in the array. E.g. array contents 1111111.......1100000.........0000000.

Solution: This problem is almost similar to Problem-38. Check the bits at the rate of 2^K where $k = 0, 1, 2$ ....

Since we are moving at the rate of 2, the complexity is O($logn$).

Problem-40   Given a sorted array of n integers that has been rotated an unknown number of times, give a O($log\ n$) algorithm that finds an element in the array.
Example: Find 5 in array (15 16 19 20 25 1 3 4 5 7 10 14) **Output**: 8 (the index of 5 in the array)

Solution: Let us assume that the given array is $A[]$and use the solution of Problem-37 with extension. The function below *FindPivot* returns the k value (let us assume that this function return the index instead of value). Find the pivot point, divide the array into two sub-arrays and call binary search.

The main idea for finding pivot is – for a sorted (in increasing order) and pivoted array, pivot element is the only element for which next element to it is smaller than it. Using above criteria and binary search methodology we can get pivot element in O($logn$) time.

Algorithm:
1) Find out pivot point and divide the array in two sub-arrays.
2) Now call binary search for one of the two sub-arrays.
   a. if element is greater than first element then search in left subarray
   b. else search in right subarray
3) If element is found in selected sub-array then return index *else* return −1.

```
int FindPivot(int A[], int start, int finish) {
    if(finish - start == 0)
            return start;
    else if(start == finish - 1) {
            if(A[start] >= A[finish])
                    return start;
            else     return finish;
    }
    else {
            mid = start + (finish-start)/2;
            if(A[start] >= A[mid])
                    return FindPivot(A, start, mid);
            else     return FindPivot(A, mid, finish);
    }
}
int Search(int A[], int n, int x) {
    int pivot = FindPivot(A, 0, n-1);
    if(A[pivot] == x)
        return pivot;
    if(A[pivot] <= x)
        return BinarySearch(A, 0, pivot-1, x);
    else     return BinarySearch(A, pivot+1, n-1, x);
}
int BinarySearch(int A[], int low, int high, int x) {
    if(high >= low)    {
            int mid = low + (high - low)/2;
            if(x == A[mid])
                    return mid;
            if(x > A[mid])
                    return BinarySearch(A, (mid + 1), high, x);
            else     return BinarySearch(A, low, (mid -1), x);
    }
    return -1;       /*Return -1 if element is not found*/
}
```

Time complexity:O($logn$).

Problem-41   For Problem-40, can we solve in one scan?

Solution: Yes.

```
int BinarySearchRotated(int A[], int start, int finish, int data) {
    int mid;
    if(start > finish)
            return -1;
    mid = start + (finish - start) / 2;
    if(data == A[mid])
            return mid;
    else if(A[start] <= A[mid]) {        // start half is in sorted order.
            if(data >= A[start] && data < A[mid])
                    return BinarySearchRotated(A, start, mid - 1, data);
            else    return BinarySearchRotated(A, mid + 1, finish, data);
    }
    else {    // A[mid] <= A[finish], finish half is in sorted order.
            if(data > A[mid] && data <= A[finish])
                    return BinarySearchRotated(A, mid + 1, finish, data);
            else    return BinarySearchRotated(A, start, mid - 1, data);
    }
}
```

Time complexity:$O(logn)$.

Problem-42   **Bitonic search:** An array is *bitonic* if it is comprised of an increasing sequence of integers followed immediately by a decreasing sequence of integers. Given a bitonic array A of n distinct integers, describe how to determine whether a given integer is in the array in $O(logn)$ steps.

Solution: The solution is the same as that for Problem-37.

Problem-43   Yet, other way of framing Problem-37.
Let $A[]$ be an array that starts out increasing, reaches a maximum, and then decreases. Design an $O(logn)$ algorithm to find the index of the maximum value.

Problem-44   Give an $O(nlogn)$ algorithm for computing the median of a sequence of n integers.

Solution: Sort and return element at $\frac{n}{2}$.

Problem-45   Given two sorted lists of size m and n, find median of all elements in $O(log\ (m + n))$ time.

Solution: Refer *Divide and Conquer* chapter.

Problem-46   Give a sorted array A of n elements, possibly with duplicates, find the index of the first occurrence of a number in $O(logn)$ time.

Solution: To find the first occurrence of a number we need to check for the following condition. Return the position if any one of the following is true:

```
            mid == low && A[mid] == data  ||  A[mid] == data && A[mid-1] < data
```

```
int BinarySearchFirstOccurrence(int A[], int low, int high, int data) {
    int mid;
    if(high >= low) {
            mid = low + (high-low) / 2;
            if((mid == low && A[mid] == data) || (A[mid] == data && A[mid - 1] < data))
                    return mid;
            // Give preference to left half of the array
            else if(A[mid] >= data)
                    return BinarySearchFirstOccurrence (A, low, mid - 1, data);
            else    return BinarySearchFirstOccurrence (A, mid + 1, high, data);
    }
    return -1;
}
```

Time Complexity: $O(logn)$.

Problem-47   Given a sorted array A of n elements, possibly with duplicates. Find the index of the last occurrence of a number in $O(logn)$ time.

Solution: To find the last occurrence of a number we need to check for the following condition. Return the position if any one of the following is true:

```
            mid == high && A[mid] == data  ||  A[mid] == data && A[mid+1] > data
```

```
int BinarySearchLastOccurrence(int A[], int low, int high, int data) {
    int mid;
    if(high >= low) {
```

```
                mid = low + (high-low) / 2;
                if((mid == high && A[mid] == data) || (A[mid] == data && A[mid + 1] > data))
                        return mid;
                // Give preference to right half of the array
                else if(A[mid] <= data)
                        return BinarySearchLastOccurrence (A, mid + 1, high, data);
                else    return BinarySearchLastOccurrence (A, low, mod - 1, data);
        }
        return -1;
}
```

Time Complexity: $O(logn)$.

Problem-48 Given a sorted array of n elements, possibly with duplicates. Find the number of occurrences of a number.

Brute Force Solution: Do a linear search over the array and increment count as and when we find the element data in the array.

```
int LinearSearchCount(int A[], int n, int data) {
        int count = 0;
        for (int i = 0; i < n; i++)
                if(A[i] == data)
                        count++;
        return count;
}
```

Time Complexity: $O(n)$.

Problem-49 Can we improve the time complexity of Problem-48?

Solution: Yes. We can solve this by using one binary search call followed by another small scan.

Algorithm:
- Do a binary search for the *data* in the array. Let us assume its position is K.
- Now traverse towards left from K and count the number of occurrences of *data*. Let this count be *leftCount*.
- Similarly, traverse towards right and count the number of occurrences of *data*. Let this count be *rightCount*.
- Total number of occurrences = *leftCount* + 1 + *rightCount*

Time Complexity – $O(logn + S)$ where S is the number of occurrences of *data*.

Problem-50 Is there any alternative way of solving Problem-48?

Solution:

Algorithm:
- Find first occurrence of *data* and call its index as *firstOccurrence* (for algorithm refer Problem-46)
- Find last occurrence of *data* and call its index as *lastOccurrence* (for algorithm refer Problem-47)
- Return *lastOccurrence* − *firstOccurrence* + 1

Time Complexity = $O(logn + logn) = O(logn)$.

Problem-51 What is the next number in the sequence $1, 11, 21$ and why?

Solution: Read the given number loudly. This is just a fun problem.
        One One
        Two Ones
        One two, one one→ 1211
So answer is, the next number is the representation of previous number by reading it loudly.

Problem-52 Finding second smallest number efficiently.

Solution: We can construct a heap of the given elements using up just less than n comparisons (Refer *Priority Queues* chapter for algorithm). Then we find the second smallest using $logn$ comparisons for the GetMax() operation. Overall, we get $n + logn + constant$.

Problem-53 Is there any other solution for Problem-52?

Solution: Alternatively, split the n numbers into groups of 2, perform $n/2$ comparisons successively to find the largest using a tournament-like method. The first round will yield the maximum in $n − 1$ comparisons. The second round will be performed on the winners of the first round and the ones the maximum popped. This will yield $logn − 1$ comparisons for a total of $n + log n − 2$. The above solution is called *tournament problem*.

Problem-54 An element is a majority if it appears more than $n/2$ times. Give an algorithm takes an array of n element as argument and identifies a majority (if it exists).

Solution: The basic solution is to have two loops and keep track of maximum count for all different elements. If maximum count becomes greater than $n/2$ then break the loops and return the element having maximum count. If maximum count doesn't become more than $n/2$ then majority element doesn't exist.

Time Complexity: $O(n^2)$. Space Complexity: $O(1)$.

Problem-55   Can we improve Problem-54 time complexity to $O(nlogn)$?

Solution: Using binary search we can achieve this. Node of the Binary Search Tree (used in this approach) will be as follows.

```
struct TreeNode {
    int element;
    int count;
    struct TreeNode *left;
    struct TreeNode *right;
} BST;
```

Insert elements in BST one by one and if an element is already present then increment the count of the node. At any stage, if count of a node becomes more than $n/2$ then return. The method works well for the cases where $n/2 + 1$ occurrences of the majority element is present in the starting of the array, for example $\{1, 1, 1, 1, 1, 2, 3, \text{and } 4\}$.

Time Complexity: If a binary search tree is used then worst time complexity will be $O(n^2)$. If a balanced-binary-search tree is used then $O(nlogn)$. Space Complexity: $O(n)$.

Problem-56   Is there any other of achieving $O(nlogn)$ complexity for Problem-54?

Solution: Sort the input array and scan the sorted array to find the majority element.

Time Complexity: $O(nlogn)$. Space Complexity: $O(1)$.

Problem-57   Can we improve the complexity for Problem-54?

Solution: If an element occurs more than $n/2$ times in A then it must be the median of A. But, the reverse is not true, so once the median is found, we must check to see how many times it occurs in A. We can use linear selection which takes $O(n)$ time (for algorithm refer *Selection Algorithms* chapter).

```
int CheckMajority(int A[], in n) {
    1)  Use linear selection to find the median m of A.
    2)  Do one more pass through A and count the number of occurrences of m.
        a.  If m occurs more than n/2 times then return true;
        b.  Otherwise return false.
}
```

Problem-58   Is there any other way of solving Problem-54?

Solution: Since only one element is repeating, we can use simple scan of the input array by keeping track of count for the elements. If the count is 0 then we can assume that the element is coming first time otherwise that the resultant element.

```
int MajorityNum(int[] A, int n) {
    int majNum, count = 0, element = -1;
    for(int i = 0; i < n; i++) {
            // If the counter is 0 then set the current candidate to majority
            // num and set the counter to 1.
            if(count == 0) {
                    element = A[i];
                    count = 1;
            }
            else if(element == A[i]) {
                    // Increment counter If the counter is not 0 and
                    // element is same as current candidate.
                    count++;
            }
            else {  // Decrement counter If the counter is not 0
                //and element is different from current candidate.
                    count--;
            }
    }
    return element;
}
```

Time Complexity: $O(n)$. Space Complexity: $O(1)$.

Problem-59   Given an array of $2n$ elements of which n elements are same and the remaining n elements are all different. Find the majority element.

Solution: The repeated elements will occupy half the array. No matter what arrangement it is, only one of the below will be true,

- All duplicate elements will be at a relative distance of 2 from each other. Ex: n, 1, n, 100, n, 54, n ...
- At least two duplicate elements will be next to each other
  Ex: $n, n, 1, 100, n, 54, n, ...$
         $n, 1, n, n, n, 54, 100 ...$
         $1, 100, 54, n, n, n, n. ....$

In worst case, we will need two passes over the array,

- First Pass: compare $A[i]$ and $A[i + 1]$
- Second Pass: compare $A[i]$ and $A[i + 2]$

Something will match and that's your element. This will cost $O(n)$ in time and $O(1)$ in space.

Problem-60   Given an array with $2n + 1$ integer elements, n elements appear twice in arbitrary places in the array and a single integer appears only once somewhere inside. Find the lonely integer with $O(n)$ operations and $O(1)$ extra memory.

Solution: Except one element all other elements are repeated. We know that $A\ XOR\ A = 0$. Based on this if we XOR all the input elements then we get the remaining element.

```
int Solution(int* A) {
    int i, res;
    for (i = res = 0; i < 2n+1; i++)
        res = res ^ A[i];
    return res;
}
```

Time Complexity: $O(n)$. Space Complexity: $O(1)$.

Problem-61   **Throwing eggs from an n-story building:** Suppose we have an n story building and a number of eggs. Also assume that an egg breaks if it is thrown off floor F or higher, and will not break otherwise. Devise a strategy to determine the floor F, while breaking $O(logn)$ eggs.

Solution: Refer *Divide and Conquer* chapter.

Problem-62   **Local minimum of an array:** Given an array A of n distinct integers, design an $O(logn)$ algorithm to find a *local minimum*: an index i such that $A[i - 1] < A[i] < A[i + 1]$.

Solution: Check the middle value $A[n/2]$, and two neighbors $A[n/2 - 1]$ and $A[n/2 + 1]$. If $A[n/2]$ is local minimum, stop; otherwise search in half with smaller neighbor.

Problem-63   Give an $n \times n$ array of elements such that each row is in ascending order and each column is in ascending order, devise an $O(n)$ algorithm to determine if a given element x in the array. You may assume all elements in the $n \times n$ array are distinct.

Solution: Let us assume that the given matrix is $A[n][n]$. Start with the last row, first column [or first row - last column]. If the element we are searching for is greater than the element at $A[1][n]$, then the column 1 can be eliminated. If the search element is less than the element at $A[1][n]$, then the last row can be completely eliminated. Once the first column or the last row is eliminated, start over the process again with left-bottom end of the remaining array. In this algorithm, there would be maximum n elements that the search element would be compared with.

Time Complexity: $O(n)$. This is because we will traverse at most $2n$ points. Space Complexity: $O(1)$.

Problem-64   Given an $n \times n$ array a of n^2 numbers, give an $O(n)$ algorithm to find a pair of indices i and j such that $A[i][j] < A[i + 1][j], A[i][j] < A[i][j + 1], A[i][j] < A[i - 1][j]$, and $A[i][j] < A[i][j - 1]$.

Solution: This problem is same as Problem-63.

Problem-65   Given $n \times n$ matrix, and in each row all 1's are followed 0's. Find row with maximum number of 0's.

Solution: Start with first row, last column. If the element is 0 then move to the previous column in the same row and at the same time increase the counter to indicate the maximum number of 0's. If the element is 1 then move to next row in the same column. Repeat this process until we reach last row, first column.

Time Complexity: $O(2n) \approx O(n)$ (similar to Problem-63).

Problem-66   Given an input array of size unknown with all numbers in the beginning and special symbols in the end. Find the index in the array from where special symbols start.

Solution: Refer *Divide and Conquer* chapter.

Problem-67   **Separate Even and Odd numbers:** Given an array $A[ ]$, write a function that segregates even and odd numbers. The functions should put all even numbers first, and then odd numbers. **Example**: Input = $\{12, 34, 45, 9, 8, 90, 3\}$ Output = $\{12, 34, 90, 8, 9, 45, 3\}$

Note: In the output, order of numbers can be changed, i.e., in the above example 34 can come before 12 and 3 can come before 9.

Solution: The problem is very similar to *Separate 0's and 1's* (Problem-68) in an array, and both problems are variations of the famous *Dutch national flag problem.*

Algorithm: Logic is similar to Quick sort.
1) Initialize two index variables left and right: $left = 0$, $right = n - 1$
2) Keep incrementing left index until we see an odd number.
3) Keep decrementing right index until we see an even number.
4) If $left < right$ then swap $A[left]$ and $A[right]$

```
void DutchNationalFlag(int A[], int n) {
    /* Initialize left and right indexes */
    int left = 0, right = n-1;
    while(left < right) {
        /* Increment left index while we see 0 at left */
        while(A[left]%2 == 0 && left < right)
            left++;
        /* Decrement right index while we see 1 at right */
        while(A[right]%2 == 1 && left < right)
            right--;
        if(left < right) {
            /* Swap A[left] and A[right]*/
            swap(&A[left], &A[right]);
            left++;
            right--;
        }
    }
}
```

Time Complexity: $O(n)$.

Problem-68   The following is another way of structuring Problem-67, but with little difference.

Separate 0's and 1's in an array: We are given an array of 0's and 1's in random order. Separate 0's on left side and 1's on right side of the array. Traverse array only once.

Input array $= [0, 1, 0, 1, 0, 0, 1, 1, 1, 0]$ **Output array** $= [0, 0, 0, 0, 0, 1, 1, 1, 1, 1]$

Solution: Counting 0's or 1's
1. Count the number of $0's$. Let count be C.
2. Once we have count, put C 0's at the beginning and $1's$ at the remaining $n - C$ positions in array.

Time Complexity: $O(n)$. This solution scans the array two times.

Problem-69   Can we solve Problem-68 in one scan?

Solution: Yes. Use two indexes to traverse: Maintain two indexes. Initialize first index left as 0 and second index right as $n - 1$. Do following while $left < right$:
1) Keep incrementing index left while there are 0s at it
2) Keep decrementing index right while there are 1s at it
3) If left < right then exchange $A[left]$ and $A[right]$

```
/*Function to put all 0s on left and all 1s on right*/
void Separate0and1(int A[], int n) {
    /* Initialize left and right indexes */
    int left = 0, right = n-1;
    while(left < right) {
        /* Increment left index while we see 0 at left */
        while(A[left] == 0 && left < right)
            left++;
        /* Decrement right index while we see 1 at right */
        while(A[right] == 1 && left < right)
            right--;
        /* If left is smaller than right then there is a 1 at left
        and a 0 at right.  Swap A[left] and A[right]*/
        if(left < right) {
            A[left] = 0;
            A[right] = 1;
            left++;
            right--;
        }
    }
}
```

Time Complexity: $O(n)$. Space Complexity: $O(1)$.

Problem-70 **Sort an array of 0's, 1's and 2's [or R's, G's and B's]:** Given an array $A[]$ consisting 0's, 1's and 2's, give an algorithm for sorting $A[]$.The algorithm should put all 0's first, then all 1's and finally all the 2's at the end. **Example Input** = {0,1,1,0,1,2,1,2,0,0,0,1}, **Output** = {0, 0, 0, 0, 0, 1, 1, 1, 1, 1, 2, 2}

Solution:

```
void Sorting012sDutchFlagProblem(int A[],int n){
    int low=0,mid=0,high=n-1;
    while(mid <=high){
        switch(A[mid]){
            case 0:
                swap(A[low],A[mid]);
                low++;mid++;
                break;
            case 1:
                mid++;
                break;
            case 2:
                swap(A[mid],A[high]);
                high--;
                break;
        }
    }
}
```

Time Complexity: $O(n)$. Space Complexity: $O(1)$.

Problem-71 **Maximum difference between two elements:** Given an array $A[]$ of integers, find out the difference between any two elements such that larger element appears after the smaller number in $A[]$.
Examples: If array is $[2, 3, 10, 6, 4, 8, 1]$ then returned value should be 8 (Diff between 10 and 2). If array is $[7, 9, 5, 6, 3, 2]$ then returned value should be 2 (Difference between 7 and 9)

Solution: Refer *Divide and Conquer* chapter.

Problem-72 Given an array of 101 elements. Out of them 25 elements are repeated twice, 12 elements are repeated 4 times and one element is repeated 3 times. Find the element which repeated 3 times in O(1).

Solution: Before solving this problem let us consider the following *XOR* operation property: $a\ XOR\ a = 0$. That means, if we apply the *XOR* on same elements then the result is 0.

Algorithm:

* *XOR* all the elements of the given array and assume the result is A.
* After this operation, 2 occurrences of number which appeared 3 times becomes 0 and one occurrence remains the same.
* The 12 elements that are appearing 4 times become 0.
* The 25 elements that are appearing 2 times become 0.
* So just *XOR'ing* all the elements give the result.

Time Complexity: $O(n)$, because we are doing only one scan. Space Complexity: $O(1)$.

Problem-73 Given a number n, give an algorithm for finding the number of trailing zeros in $n!$.

Solution:

```
int NumberOfTrailingZerosInNumber(int n) {
    int i, count = 0;
    if(n < 0)  return -1;
    for (i = 5; n / i > 0; i *= 5)
            count += n / i;
    return count;
}
```

Time Complexity: $O(logn)$.

Problem-74 Given an array of $2n$ integers in the following format $a1\ a2\ a3\dots an\ b1\ b2\ b3\dots bn$. Shuffle the array to $a1\ b1\ a2\ b2\ a3\ b3\dots an\ bn$ without any extra memory.

Solution: A brute force solution involves two nested loops to rotate the elements in the second half of the array to the left. The first loop runs n times to cover all elements in the second half of the array. The second loop rotates the elements to the left. Note that the start index in the second loop depends on which element we are rotating and the end index depends on how many positions we need to move to the left.

```
void ShuffleArray() {
```

```
        int n = 4;
        int A[] = {1,3,5,7,2,4,6,8};
        for (int i = 0, q =1, k = n; i < n; i++, k++, q++) {
                for (int j = k; j > i + q; j--) {
                        int tmp = A[j-1];
                        A[j-1] = A[j];
                        A[j] = tmp;
                }
        }
        for (int i = 0; i  < 2*n; i++)
                printf("%d", A[i]);
}
```

Time Complexity: $O(n^2)$.

Problem-75   Can we improve Problem-74 solution?

Solution: Refer Divide and Concur chapter. A better solution of time complexity $O(nlogn)$ can be achieved using *Divide and Concur* technique. Let us take an example
  1. Start with the array: $a1\ a2\ a3\ a4\ b1\ b2\ b3\ b4$
  2. Split the array into two halves: $a1\ a2\ a3\ a4 : b1\ b2\ b3\ b4$
  3. Exchange elements around the center: exchange $a3\ a4$ with $b1\ b2$ you get: $a1\ a2\ b1\ b2\ a3\ a4\ b3\ b4$
  4. Split $a1\ a2\ b1\ b2$ into $a1\ a2 : b1\ b2$ then split $a3\ a4\ b3\ b4$ into $a3\ a4 : b3\ b4$
  5. Exchange elements around the center for each subarray you get: $a1\ b1\ a2\ b2$ and $a3\ b3\ a4\ b4$

Note that this solution only handles the case when $n = 2^i$ where $i = 0, 1, 2, 3$ etc. In our example $n = 2^2 = 4$ which makes it easy to recursively split the array into two halves. The basic idea behind swapping elements around the center before calling the recursive function is to produce smaller size problems. A solution with linear time complexity may be achieved if the elements are of specific nature. For example, if you can calculate the new position of the element using the value of the element itself. This is nothing but a hashing technique.

Problem-76   Given an Aay A[], find the maximum j – i such that A[j] > A[i]. For example, Input: {34, 8, 10, 3, 2, 80, 30, 33, 1} and Output: 6 (j = 7, i = 1).

Solution: Brute Force Approach: Run two loops. In the outer loop, pick elements one by one from left. In the inner loop, compare the picked element with the elements starting from right side. Stop the inner loop when you see an element greater than the picked element and keep updating the maximum j-i so far.

```
int maxIndexDiff(int A[], int n){
    int maxDiff = -1;
    int i, j;

    for (i = 0; i < n; ++i){
        for (j = n-1; j > i; --j){
            if(A[j] > A[i] && maxDiff < (j - i))
                maxDiff = j - i;
        }
    }
    return maxDiff;
}
```

Time Complexity: $O(n^2)$. Space Complexity: $O(1)$.

Problem-77   Can we improve the complexity of Problem-76?

Solution: To solve this problem, we need to get two optimum indexes of A[]: left index i and right index j. For an element A[i], we do not need to consider A[i] for left index if there is an element smaller than A[i] on left side of A[i]. Similarly, if there is a greater element on right side of A[j] then we do not need to consider this j for right index.

So we construct two auxiliary Aays LeftMins[] and RightMaxs[] such that LeftMins[i] holds the smallest element on left side of A[i] including A[i], and RightMaxs[j] holds the greatest element on right side of A[j] including A[j]. After constructing these two auxiliary arrays, we traverse both these arrays from left to right.

While traversing LeftMins[] and RightMaxs[] if we see that LeftMins[i] is greater than RightMaxs[j], then we must move ahead in LeftMins[] (or do i++) because all elements on left of LeftMins[i] are greater than or equal to LeftMins[i]. Otherwise we must move ahead in RightMaxs[j] to look for a greater $j - i$ value.

```
int maxIndexDiff(int A[], int n){
    int maxDiff;
    int i, j;
    int *LeftMins = (int *)malloc(sizeof(int)*n);
    int *RightMaxs = (int *)malloc(sizeof(int)*n);
    LeftMins[0] = A[0];
    for (i = 1; i < n; ++i)
        LeftMins[i] = min(A[i], LeftMins[i-1]);
```

```
    RightMaxs[n-1] = A[n-1];
    for (j = n-2; j >= 0; --j)
      RightMaxs[j] = max(A[j], RightMaxs[j+1]);

    i = 0, j = 0, maxDiff = -1;
    while (j < n && i < n){
      if (LeftMins[i] < RightMaxs[j]){
        maxDiff = max(maxDiff, j-i);
        j = j + 1;
      }
      else
        i = i+1;
    }
    return maxDiff;
}
```

Time Complexity: O(*n*). Space Complexity: O(*n*).

Problem-78   Given an array of elements, how do you check whether the list is pairwise sorted or not? A list is considered pairwise sorted if each successive pair of numbers is in non-decreasing order.

Answer:

```
int checkPairwiseSorted(int A[], int n) {
  if (n == 0 || n == 1)
    return 1;
  for (int i = 0; i < n - 1; i += 2){
    if (A[i] > A[i+1])
      return 0;
  }
  return 1;
}
```

Time Complexity: O(*n*). Space Complexity: O(1).

Problem-79   Given an array of *n* elements, how do you print the frequencies of elements without using extra space. Assume all elements are positive, editable and less than *n*.

Answer: Use negation technique.

```
void frequencyCounter(int A[],int n){
    int pos = 0;
    while(pos < n){
        int expectedPos = A[pos] - 1;
        if(A[pos] > 0 && A[expectedPos] > 0){
            swap(A[pos], A[expectedPos]);
            A[expectedPos] = -1;
        }
        else if(A[pos] > 0){
            A[expectedPos] --;
            A[pos ++] = 0;
        }
        else{
            pos ++;
        }
    }
    for(int i = 0; i < n; ++i){
        printf("%d frequency is %d\n", i + 1 ,abs(A[i]));
    }
}
int main(int argc, char* argv[]){
    int A[] = {10, 10, 9, 4, 7, 6, 5, 2, 3, 2, 1};
    frequencyCounter(A, sizeof(A)/ sizeof(A[0]));
    return 0;
}
```

Array should have numbers in the range [1, n].(where *n* is the size of the array). The if condition (A[pos] > 0 && A[expectedPos] > 0) means that both the numbers at indices *pos* and *expectedPos* are actual numbers in the array but not their frequencies. So we will swap them so that the number at the index *pos* will go to the position where it should have been if the numbers 1, 2, 3, ..., *n* are kept in 0, 1, 2, ..., *n* − 1 indices. In the above example input array, initially *pos* = 0, so 10 at index 0 will go to index 9 after swap. As this is the first occurrence of 10 make it to -1. Note that we are storing the frequencies as negative numbers to differentiate between actual numbers and frequencies.

The else if condition (A[pos] > 0) means A[pos] is a number and A[expectedPos] is its frequency without including the occurrence of A[pos]. So increment the frequency by 1 (that is decrement by 1 in terms of negative numbers). As we counted its occurrence we need to move to next *pos*, so *pos* + + but before moving to that next position we should make the frequency of the number *pos* + 1 which corresponds to index *pos* to be zero, since such number is not yet occurred.

The final else part means current index *pos* already has the frequency of the number *pos* + 1, so move to next *pos*, hence *pos* + +.

Time Complexity: O(n). Space Complexity: O(1).

Problem-80 Given an array containing the elements in the range 0. . n-1 but in random order, how do you sort the array with single loop.

Solution:

```cpp
#include <iostream>
using namespace std;
void singleLoopSort(int Ary[], int size){
    for(int i = 0; i < size; ){
        if( Ary[i] != i){
            int t = Ary[Ary[i]];
            Ary[Ary[i]] = Ary[i];
            Ary[i] = t;
            cout << Ary[i] << " " << Ary[Ary[i]] << endl;
        }
        else
            i++;
    }
}
int main(int argc, char* argv[]){
    int Ary[] = {3, 7, 2, 5, 1, 8, 4, 0, 9, 6};
    singleLoopSort(Ary, 10);
    for(int i = 0; i < 10; i ++){
        cout << Ary[i] << " ";
    }
    return 0;
}
```

Time Complexity: O(n^2). Space Complexity: O(1).

Chapter-18

SELECTION ALGORITHMS [MEDIANS]

18.1 What are Selection Algorithms?

Selection algorithm is an algorithm for finding the kth smallest/largest number in a list (also called as k^{th} order statistic). This includes, finding the minimum, maximum, and median elements. For finding k^{th} order statistic, there are multiple solutions which provide different complexities and in this chapter we will enumerate those possibilities.

18.2 Selection by Sorting

Selection problem can be converted to **sorting** problem. In this method, we first sort the input elements and then get the desired element. It is efficient if we want to perform many selections.

For example, let us say we want to get the minimum element. After sorting the input elements we can simply return the first element (assuming the array is sorted in ascending order). Now, if we want to find the second smallest element, we can simply return the second element from the sorted list. That means, for the second smallest element we are not performing the sorting again. Same is the case with subsequent queries too. Even if we want to get k^{th} smallest element, just one scan of sorted list is enough for finding the element (or we can return the kth-indexed value if the elements are in the array).

From the above discussion what we can say is, with the initial sorting we can answer any query in one scan, O(n). In general, this method requires O($nlogn$) time (for *sorting*), where n is the length of the input list. Suppose we are performing n queries then the average cost per operation is just $\frac{n\,logn}{n} \approx$O($logn$). This kind of analysis is called *amortized* analysis.

18.3 Partition-based Selection Algorithm

For algorithm check Problem-6. This algorithm is similar to Quick sort.

18.4 Linear Selection algorithm - Median of Medians algorithm

Worst-case performance	O(n)
Best case performance	O(n)
Worst case space complexity	O(1) auxiliary

Refer to Problem-11.

18.5 Finding the K Smallest Elements in Sorted Order

For algorithm check Problem-6. This algorithm is similar to Quick sort.

18.6 Problems on Selection Algorithms

Problem-1   Find the largest element in an array A of size n.
     Input: positive integer n, array of elements A indexed from 0 to $n - 1$.
     Output: variable large, whose value is the largest element in A.

Solution: Scan the complete array and return the largest element.

```
void FindLargestInArray(int n, const int A[]) {
    int large = A[0];
    for (int i = 1; i <= n-1; i++)
        if(A[i] > large)
            large = A[i];
    printf("Largest:%d", large);
}
```

Time Complexity - O(n). Space Complexity - O(1).

Note: Any deterministic algorithm that can find the largest of n keys by comparisons of keys takes at least $n - 1$ comparisons.

Problem-2   Find the smallest and largest elements in an array A of size n.

Input: positive integer n, array of elements A indexed from 1 to n.

Output: variables small and large, whose values are the smallest and largest elements in A.

Solution:

```
void FindSmallestAndLargestInArray (int A[], int n) {
    int small = A[0];
    int large =A[0];
    for (int i = 1; i <= n-1; i++)
        if(A[i] < small)
                small = A[i];
        else if(A[i] > large)
                large = A[i];
    printf("Smallest:%d, Largest:%d", small, large);
}
```

Time Complexity - O(n). Space Complexity - O(1). The worst-case number of comparisons is $2(n - 1)$.

Problem-3   Can we improve the previous algorithms?

Solution: Yes. We can do this by comparing in pairs.

```
// n is assumed to be even. Compare in pairs.
void FindWithPairComparison (int A[], int n) {
    int large = small = -1;
    for (int i = 0; i <= n - 1; i = i + 2) {          // Increment i by 2.
        if(A[i] < A[i + 1]) {
                if(A[i] < small)
                        small = A[i];
                if(A[i + 1] > large)
                        large = A[i + 1];
        }
        else {    if(A[i + 1] < small)
                        small = A[i + 1];
                if(A[i] > large)
                        large = A[i];
        }
    }
    printf("Smallest:%d, Largest:%d", small, large);
}
```

Time Complexity - O(n). Space Complexity - O(1).

Number of comparisons: $\begin{cases} \frac{3n}{2} - 2, if\ n\ is\ even \\ \frac{3n}{2} - \frac{3}{2}\ if\ n\ is\ odd \end{cases}$

Summary:

Straightforward comparison – $2(n - 1)$ comparisons
Compare for min only if comparison for max fails
Best case: increasing order – $n - 1$ comparisons
Worst case: decreasing order – $2(n - 1)$ comparisons
Average case: $3n/2 - 1$ comparisons

Note: For divide and conquer techniques refer to *Divide and Conquer* chapter.

Problem-4   Give an algorithm for finding the second largest element in the given input list of elements.

Solution: Brute Force Method

Algorithm:
- Find largest element: needs $n - 1$ comparisons
- Delete (discard) the largest element
- Again find largest element: needs $n - 2$ comparisons

Total number of comparisons: $n - 1 + n - 2 = 2n - 3$

Problem-5   Can we reduce the number of comparisons in Problem-4 solution?

Solution: The Tournament method: For simplicity, assume that the numbers are distinct and that n is a power of 2. We pair the keys and compare the pairs in rounds until only one round remains.

If the input has eight keys, there are four comparisons in the first round, two in the second, and one in the last. The winner of the last round is the largest key. The figure below shows the method. The tournament method directly applies only when n is a power of 2.

When this is not the case, we can add enough items to the end of the array to make the array size a power of 2. If the tree is complete then the maximum height of the tree is $logn$. If we construct the complete binary tree, we need $n-1$ comparisons to find the largest.

The second largest key has to be among the ones that were lost in a comparison with the largest one. That means, the second largest element should be one of the opponents of largest element. The number of keys that are lost to the largest key is the height of the tree, i.e. $logn$ [if the tree is a complete binary tree].

Then using the selection algorithm to find the largest among them take $logn - 1$ comparisons. Thus the total number of comparisons to find the largest and second largest keys is $n + logn - 2$.

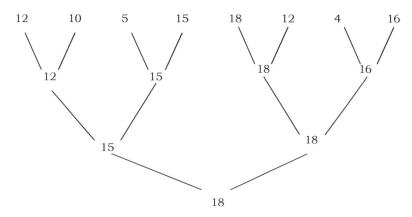

Problem-6   Find the k-smallest elements in an array S of n elements using partitioning method.

Solution: Brute Force Approach: Scan through the numbers k times to have the desired element. This method is the one used in bubble sort (and selection sort), every time we find out the smallest element in the whole sequence by comparing every element. In this method, the sequence has to be traversed k times. So the complexity is O($n \times k$).

Problem-7   Can we use sorting technique for solving Problem-6?

Solution: Yes. Sort and take first k elements.
   1.   Sort the numbers.
   2.   Pick the first k elements.

The complexity is very trivial. Sorting of n numbers is of O($nlogn$) and picking k elements is of O(k). The total complexity is O($nlogn + k$) $=$ O($nlogn$).

Problem-8   Can we use *tree sorting* technique for solving Problem-6?

Solution: Yes.
   a)   Insert all the elements to a binary search tree.
   b)   Do an InOrder traversal until and print k elements which will be the smallest ones. So, we have the k smallest elements.

The cost of creation of a binary search tree with n elements is O($nlogn$) and the traversal upto k elements is O(k). Hence the complexity is O($nlogn + k$) $=$ O($nlogn$).

Disadvantage: If the numbers are sorted in descending order, we will be getting a tree which will be skewed towards left. In that case, construction of the tree will be $0 + 1 + 2 + ... + (n - 1) = \frac{n(n-1)}{2}$ which is O(n^2). To escape from this, we can keep the tree balanced, so that the cost of constructing the tree will be only $nlogn$.

Problem-9   Can we improve *tree sorting* technique for solving Problem-6?

Solution: Yes. Use a smaller tree to give the same result.

   1.   Take the first k elements of the sequence to create a balanced tree of k nodes (this will cost $klogk$).
   2.   Take the remaining numbers one by one, and
        a)   If the number is larger than the largest element of the tree, return
        b)   If the number is smaller than the largest element of the tree, remove the largest element of the tree and add the new element. This step is to make sure that a smaller element replaces a larger element from the tree. And of course the cost of this operation is $logk$ since the tree is a balanced tree of k elements.

Once Step 2 is over, the balanced tree with k elements will have the smallest k elements. The only remaining task is to print out the largest element of the tree.

Time Complexity:
- For the first k elements, we make the tree. Hence the cost is $klogk$.
- For the rest $n - k$ elements, the complexity is O($logk$).

Step 2 has a complexity of $(n - k) logk$. The total cost is $klogk + (n - k) logk = nlogk$ which is O($nlogk$). This bound is actually better than the ones provided earlier.

Problem-10   Can we use partitioning technique for solving Problem-6?

Solution: Yes.

Algorithm
1. Choose a pivot from the array.
2. Partition the array so that: A[low...$pivotpoint - 1$] <= $pivotpoint$ <= A[$pivotpoint + 1..high$].
3. if k < $pivotpoint$ then it must be on the left of pivot, so do the same method recursively on the left part.
4. if k = $pivotpoint$ then it must be the pivot and print all the elements from low to $pivotpoint$.
5. if k > $pivotpoint$ then it must be on the right of pivot, so do the same method recursively on the right part.

The top-level call would be kthSmallest = Selection(1, n, k).

```
int Selection (int low, int high, int k) {
    int pivotpoint;
    if(low == high)
            return S[low];
    else {
            pivotpoint = Partition(low, high);
            if(k == pivotpoint)
                    return S[pivotpoint];   //we can print all the elements from low to pivotpoint.
            else if(k < pivotpoint)
                    return Selection (low, pivotpoint - 1, k);
            else     return Selection (pivotpoint + 1, high, k);
    }
}
void Partition (int low, int high) {
    int i, j, pivotitem;
    pivotitem = S[low];
    j = low;
    for (i = low + 1; i <= high; i++)
            if(S[i] < pivotitem) {
                    j++;
                    Swap S[i] and S[j];
            }
    pivotpoint = j;
    Swap S[low] and S[pivotpoint];
    return pivotpoint;
}
```

Time Complexity: O(n^2) in worst case as similar to Quicksort. Although the worst case is the same as that of Quicksort, this performs much better on the average [O($nlogk$) − Average case].

Problem-11   Find the kth-smallest element in an array S of n elements in best possible way.

Solution: This problem is similar to Problem-6 and all the solutions discussed for Problem-6 are valid for this problem. The only difference is that instead of printing all the k elements we print only the kth element. We can improve the solution by using *median of medians* algorithm.

Median is a special case of the selection algorithm. The algorithm Selection(A, k) to find the kth smallest element from set A of n elements is as follows:

Algorithm: *Selection*(A, k)

1. Partition A into $ceil\left(\frac{length(A)}{5}\right)$ groups, with each group having five items (last group may have fewer items).
2. Sort each group separately (e.g., insertion sort).
3. Find the median of each of the $\frac{n}{5}$ groups and store them in some array (let us say A').
4. Use *Selection* recursively to find the median of A' (median of medians). Let us asay the median of medians is m.
$$m = Selection(A', \frac{\frac{length(A)}{5}}{2});$$
5. Let q = # elements of A smaller than m;
6. If($k == q + 1$)

return m;

/* Partition with pivot */

7. Else partition A into X and Y

    a. X = {items smaller than m}

    b. Y = {items larger than m}

    /* Next,form a subproblem */

8. If($k < q + 1$)

    return Selection(X, k);

9. Else

    return Selection(Y, k – (q+1));

Before developing recurrence, let us consider the representation below of the input. In the figure each circle is an element and each column is grouped with 5 elements. The black circles indicate the median in each group of 5 elements. As discussed, sort each column using constant time insertion sort.

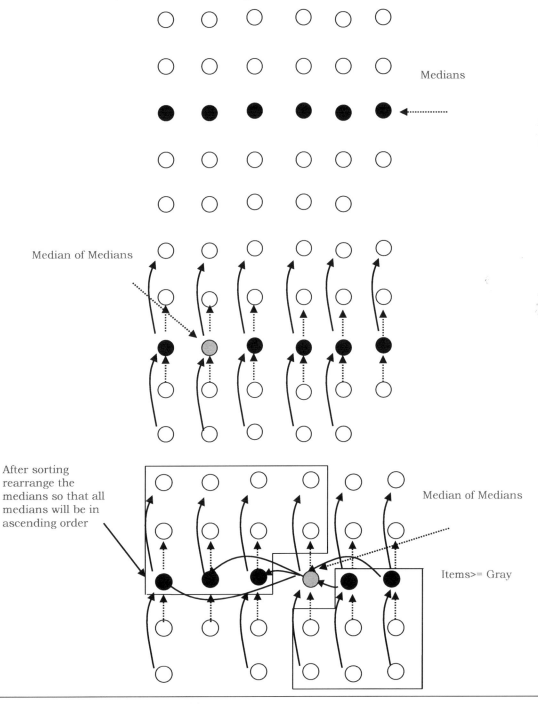

In the figure above the gray circled item is the median of medians (let us call this m). It can be seen that at least 1/2 of 5 element group medians $\leq m$. Also, these 1/2 of 5 element groups contribute 3 elements that are $\leq m$ except 2 groups [last group which may contain fewer than 5 elements and other group which contains m]. Similarly, at least 1/2 of 5 element groups contribute 3 elements that are $\geq m$ as shown above. 1/2 of 5 element groups contribute 3 elements except 2 groups gives: $3(\lceil \frac{1}{2}\lceil \frac{n}{5}\rceil \rceil - 2) \approx \frac{3n}{10} - 6$. The remaining are $n - \frac{3n}{10} - 6 \approx \frac{7n}{10} + 6$. Since $\frac{7n}{10} + 6$ is greater than $\frac{3n}{10} - 6$ we need to consider $\frac{7n}{10} + 6$ for worst.

Components in recurrence:

1. In our selection algorithm, we choose m, which is the median of medians, to be a pivot and partition A into two sets X and Y. We need to select the set which gives maximum size (to get the worst case).
2. The time in function *Selection* when called from procedure *partition*. The number of keys in the input to this call to *Selection* is $\frac{n}{5}$.
3. The number of comparisons required to partition the array. This number is $length(S)$, let us say n.

We have established the following recurrence: $T(n) = T\left(\frac{n}{5}\right) + \Theta(n) + Max\{T(X), T(Y)\}$

From the above discussion we have seen that, if we select median of medians m as pivot, the partition sizes are: $\frac{3n}{10} - 6$ and $\frac{7n}{10} + 6$. If we select the maximum of these, then we get:

$$
\begin{aligned}
T(n) &= T\left(\frac{n}{5}\right) + \Theta(n) + T\left(\frac{7n}{10} + 6\right) \\
&\approx T\left(\frac{n}{5}\right) + \Theta(n) + T\left(\frac{7n}{10}\right) + O(1) \\
&\leq c\frac{7n}{10} + c\frac{n}{5} + \Theta(n) + O(1)
\end{aligned}
$$
Finally, $T(n) = \Theta(n)$.

Problem-12 In Problem-11, we divided the input array into groups of 5 elements. The constant 5 play an important part in the analysis. Can we divide in groups of 3 which work in linear time?

Solution: In this case the modification causes the routine to take more than linear time. In the worst case, at least half the $\lceil \frac{n}{3}\rceil$ medians found in the grouping step are greater than the median of medians m, but two of those groups contribute less than two elements larger than m. So as an upper bound, the number of elements larger than pivotpoint is at least:

$$2(\lceil \frac{1}{2}\lceil \frac{n}{3}\rceil \rceil - 2) \geq \frac{n}{3} - 4$$

Likewise this is a lower bound. Thus up to $n - (\frac{n}{3} - 4) = \frac{2n}{3} + 4$ elements are fed into the recursive call to *Select*. The recursive step that finds the median of medians runs on a problem of size $\lceil \frac{n}{3}\rceil$, and consequently the time recurrence is:

$$T(n) = T(\lceil n/3\rceil) + T(2n/3 + 4) + \Theta(n)$$

Assuming that $T(n)$ is monotonically increasing, we may conclude that $T(\frac{2n}{3} + 4) \geq T(\frac{2n}{3}) \geq 2T(\frac{n}{3})$, and we can say upper bound for this as $T(n) \geq 3T(\frac{n}{3}) + \Theta(n)$, which is $O(nlogn)$. Therefore, we cannot select 3 as the group size.

Problem-13 Like in Problem-12, can we use groups of size 7?

Solution: Following a similar reasoning, we once more modify the routine, now to use groups of 7 instead of 5. In the worst case, at least half the $\lceil \frac{n}{7}\rceil$ medians found in the grouping step are greater than the median of medians m, but two of those groups contribute less than four elements larger than m. As an upper bound, the number of elements larger than pivotpoint is at least:

$$4(\lceil \frac{1}{2}\lceil \frac{n}{7}\rceil \rceil - 2) \geq \frac{2n}{7} - 8.$$

Likewise this is a lower bound. Thus up to $n - (\frac{2n}{7} - 8) = \frac{5n}{7} + 8$ elements are fed into the recursive call to Select. The recursive step that finds the median of medians runs on a problem of size $\lceil \frac{n}{7}\rceil$, and consequently the time recurrence is

$$
\begin{aligned}
T(n) &= T(\lceil \frac{n}{7}\rceil) + T(\frac{5n}{7} + 8) + O(n) \\
T(n) &\leq c\lceil \frac{n}{7}\rceil + c(\frac{5n}{7} + 8) + O(n) \\
&\leq c\frac{n}{7} + c\frac{5n}{7} + 8c + an, a \text{ is a constant} \\
&= cn - c\frac{n}{7} + an + 9c \\
&= (a + c)n - (c\frac{n}{7} - 9c).
\end{aligned}
$$

This is bounded above by $(a + c)n$ provided that $c\frac{n}{7} - 9c \geq 0$. $\therefore$ We can select 7 as the group size.

Problem-14 Given two arrays each containing n sorted elements, give an $O(logn)$-time algorithm to find the median of all $2n$ elements.

Otherway of framing the question: Let A and B be two sorted arrays of n elements each. We can easily find the kth smallest element in A in O(1) time by just outputting $A[k]$. Similarly, we can easily find the kth smallest element in B. Give an O($logk$) time algorithm to find the kth smallest element overall { *i.e.,* the kth smallest in the union of A and B.

Solution: The simple solution to this problem is to merge the two lists and then take the average of the middle two elements (note the union always contains an even number of values). But, the merge would be $\Theta(n)$, so that doesn't satisfy the problem statement.

To get $logn$ complexity, the general idea which we get is using binary search. Let *medianA* and *medianB* be the medians of the respective lists (which are easily found since both lists are sorted). If *medianA* == *medianB*, then that's the overall median of the union and we are done. Otherwise, the median of the union must be between *medianA* and *medianB*. Suppose that *medianA* < *medianB* (opposite case is entirely similar). Then we need to find the median of the union of the following two sets:

$$\{x \text{ in } A \mid x >= medianA\}\{x \text{ in } B \mid x <= medianB\}$$

We can do this recursively by resetting the "boundaries" of the two arrays. The algorithm tracks both arrays (which are sorted) using two indices. These indices are used to access and compare the median of both arrays to find where the overall median lies.

```
FindMedian(int A[], int alo , int ahi, int B[], int blo int bhi) {
    amid = alo + (ahi-alo)/2;
    amed = a[amid];
    bmid = blo + (bhi-blo)/2;
    bmed = b[bmid];
    if( ahi - alo + bhi - blo < 4) {
            Handle the boundary cases and solve it smaller problem in O(1) time.
            return;
    }
    else if(amed < bmed)
            FindMedian(A, amid, ahi, B, blo, bmid+1);
    else    FindMedian(A, alo, amid+1,B, bmid+1, bhi);
}
```

Time Complexity: O($logn$), since we are reducing the problem size by half every time.

Problem-15   **Find the k smallest elements in sorted order:** Given a set of n elements from a totally-ordered domain, find the k smallest elements, and list them in sorted order. Analyze the worst-case running time of the best implementation of the approach.

Solution: Sort the numbers, and list the k smallest.

$T(n)$ = Time complexity of sort + listing k smallest elements = $\Theta(nlogn) + \Theta(n) = \Theta(nlogn)$.

Problem-16   For Problem-15, if we follow the approach below then what is the complexity?

Solution: Using the priority queue data structure from heap sort, construct a min-heap over the set, and perform extract-min k times. Refer to *Priority Queues (Heaps)* chapter for more details.

Problem-17   For Problem-15, if we follow the approach below then what is the complexity?
    Find the kth-smallest element of the set, partition around this pivot element, and sort the k smallest elements.

Solution:
$$T(n) = Time\ complexity\ of\ kth - smallest\ + Finding\ pivot\ + Sorting\ prefix$$
$$= \Theta(n) + \Theta(n) + \Theta(klogk) = \Theta(n + klogk)$$
Since, $k \leq n$, this approach is bettern than Problem-15 and Problem-16 solutions.

Problem-18   Find k nearest neighbors to the median of n distinct numbers in O(n) time.

Solution: Let us assume that the array elements are sorted. Now find the median of n numbers and call its index as X (since array is sorted, median will be at $\frac{n}{2}$ location). All we need to do is to select k elements with the smallest absolute differences from the median moving from $X - 1$ to 0 and $X + 1$ to $n - 1$ when the median is at index m.

Time Complexity: Each step takes $\Theta(n)$ and the total time complexity of the algorithm is $\Theta(n)$.

Problem-19   Is there any other way of solving Problem-15?

Solution: Assume for simplicity that n is odd and k is even. If set A is in sorted order, the median is in position $n/2$ and the k numbers in A that are closest to the median are in positions $(n - k)/2$ through $(n + k)/2$.

We first use linear time selection to find the $(n - k)/2, n/2,$ and $(n + k)/2$ elements and then pass through the set A to find the numbers less than $(n + k)/2$ element, greater than the $(n - k)/2$ element, and not equal to the $n/2$ element. The algorithm takes O(n) time as we use linear time selection exactly three times and traverse the n numbers in A once.

Problem-20   Given (x, y) coordinates of n houses, where should you build a road parallel to x-axis to minimize construction cost of building driveways?

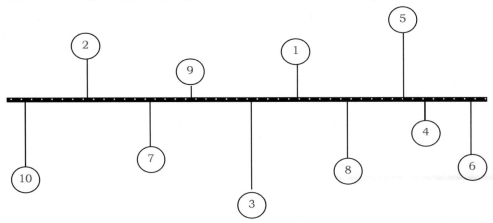

Solution: The road costs nothing to build. It is the driveways that cost money. Driveway cost is proportional to its distance to road. Obviously, they will be perpendicular. Solution is to put street at median of y coordinates.

Problem-21   Given a big file containing billions of numbers. Find maximum 10 numbers from that file.

Solution: Refer *Priority Queues* chapter.

Problem-22   Suppose there is a milk company. The company collects milk every day from all its agents. The agents are located at different places. To collect the milk, what is the best place to start so that the least amount of total distance is travelled?

Solution: Starting at median reduces total distance travelled because it is the place which is at the center to all remaining places.

Chapter-19

SYMBOL TABLES

19.1 Introduction

Since childhood, we all have used a dictionary, and many of us have a word processor (say, Microsoft Word), which comes with spell checker. The spell checker is also a dictionary but limited in scope. There are many real time examples for dictionaries and few of them are:

- Spelling checker
- The data dictionary found in database management applications
- Symbol tables generated by loaders, assemblers, and compilers
- Routing tables in networking components (DNS lookup)

In computer science, we generally use the term symbol table rather than dictionary, when referring to the ADT.

19.2 What are Symbol Tables?

We can define the *symbol table* as a data structure that associates a *value* with a *key*. It supports the following operations:

- Search whether a particular name is in the table
- Get the attributes of that name
- Modify the attributes of that name
- Insert a new name and its attributes
- Delete a name and its attributes

There are only three basic operations on symbol tables: searching, inserting, and deleting.

Example: DNS lookup. Let us assume that the key in this case is URL and value is an IP address.

- Insert URL with specified IP address
- Given URL, find corresponding IP address

Key[Website]	Value [IP Address]
www.abc.com	128.112.136.11
www.def.com	128.112.128.15
www.ghi.com	130.132.143.21
www.klm.com	128.103.060.55
www.CareerMonk.com	209.052.165.60

19.3 Symbol Table Implementations

Before implementing symbol tables, let us enumerate the possible implementations. Symbol tables can be implemented in many ways and some of them are listed below.

Unordered Array Implementation

With this method, just maintaining an array is enough. It needs O(n) time for searching, insertion and deletion in the worst case.

Ordered [Sorted] Array Implementation

In this we maintain a sorted array of keys and values.
- Store in sorted order by key
- keys[i] = i^{th} largest key
- values[i] = value associated with i^{th} largest key

Since the elements are sorted and stored in arrays, we can use simple binary search for finding an element. It takes O($log n$) time for searching and O(n) time for insertion and deletion in the worst case.

Unordered Linked List Implementation

Just maintaining a linked list with two data values is enough for this method. It needs $O(n)$ time for searching, insertion and deletion in the worst case.

Ordered Linked List Implementation

In this method, while inserting the keys, maintain the order of keys in the linked list. Even if the list is sorted, in the worst case it needs $O(n)$ time for searching, insertion and deletion.

Binary Search Trees Implementation

Refer *Trees* chapter. Advantages of this method are it does not need much code and fast search [$O(logn)$ on average].

Balanced Binary Search Trees Implementation

Refer *Trees* chapter. It is an extension of binary search trees implementation and takes $O(logn)$ in worst case for search, insert and delete operations.

Ternary Search Implementation

Refer *String Algorithms* chapter. This is one of the important methods used for implementing dictionaries.

Hashing Implementation

This method is important. For complete discussion refer to *Hashing* chapter.

19.4 Comparison of Symbol Table Implementations

Let us consider the following comparison table for all the implementations.

Implementation	Search	Insert	Delete
Unordered Array	n	n	n
Ordered Array (can be implemented with array binary search)	$logn$	n	n
Unordered List	n	n	n
Ordered List	n	n	n
Binary Search Trees ($O(logn)$ on average)	$logn$	$logn$	$logn$
Balanced Binary Search Trees ($O(logn)$ in worst case)	$logn$	$logn$	$logn$
Ternary Search (only change is in logarithms base)	$logn$	$logn$	$logn$
Hashing ($O(1)$ on average)	1	1	1

Notes:
- In the above table, n is the input size.
- Table indicates the possible implementations discussed in this book. But, there could be other implementations.

Chapter-20

HASHING

20.1 What is Hashing?

Hashing is a technique used for storing and retrieving information as fast as possible. It is used to perform optimal search and is useful in implementing symbol tables.

20.2 Why Hashing?

In *Trees* chapter we have seen that balanced binary search trees support operations such as *insert*, *delete* and *search* in O(*logn*) time. In applications if we need these operations in O(1), then hashing provides a way. Remember that worst case complexity of hashing is still O(*n*), but it gives O(1) on the average.

20.3 HashTable ADT

The common operations on hash table are:

- CreatHashTable: Creates a new hash table
- HashSearch: Searches the key in hash table
- HashInsert: Inserts a new key into hash table
- HashDelete: Deletes a key from hash table
- DeleteHashTable: Deletes the hash table

20.4 Understanding Hashing

In simple terms we can treat *array* as a hash table. For understanding the use of hash tables, let us consider the following example: Give an algorithm for printing the first repeated character if there are duplicated elements in it. Let us think about the possible solutions. The simple and brute force way of solving is: given a string, for each character check whether that character is repeated or not. Time complexity of this approach is O(n^2) with O(1) space complexity.

Now, let us find the better solution for this problem. Since our objective is to find the first repeated character, what if we remember the previous characters in some array?

We know that the number of possible characters is 256 (for simplicity assume *ASCII* characters only). Create an array of size 256 and initialize it with all zeros. For each of the input characters go to the corresponding position and increment its count. Since we are using arrays, it takes constant time for reaching any location. While scanning the input, if we get a character whose counter is already 1 then we can say that the character is the one which is repeating first time.

```
char FirstRepeatedChar ( char *str ) {
    int i, len=strlen(str);
    int count[256]; //additional array
    for(i=0; i<256; ++i)
        count[i] = 0;

    for(i=0; i<len; ++i) {
        if(count[str[i]]==1) {
            printf("%c", str[i]);
            break;
        }
        else count[str[i]]++;
    }

    if(i==len)
```

```
            printf("No Repeated Characters");
        return 0;
}
```

Why not Arrays?

In the previous problem, we have used an array of size 256 because we know the number of different possible characters [256] in advance. Now, let us consider a slight variant of the same problem. Suppose the given array has numbers instead of characters then how do we solve the problem?

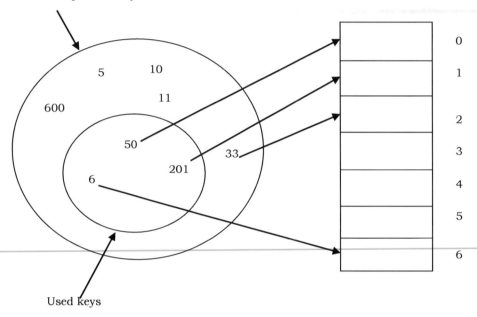

In this case the set of possible values is infinity (or at least very big). Creating a huge array and storing the counters is not possible. That means there are a set of universal keys and limited locations in the memory. If we want to solve this problem we need to somehow map all these possible keys to the possible memory locations.

From the above discussion and diagram it can be seen that we need a mapping of possible keys to one of the available locations. As a result using simple arrays is not the correct choice for solving the problems whose possible keys are very big. The process of mapping the keys to locations is called *hashing*.

Note: For now, do not worry about how the keys are mapped to locations. That depends on the function used for conversions. One such simple function is *key % table size*.

20.5 Components of Hashing

Hashing has four key components:

1) Hash Table
2) Hash Functions
3) Collisions
4) Collision Resolution Techniques

20.6 Hash Table

Hash table is a generalization of array. With an array, we store the element whose key is k at a position k of the array. That means, given a key k, we find the element whose key is k by just looking in the kth position of the array. This is called *direct addressing*.

Direct addressing is applicable when we can afford to allocate an array with one position for every possible key. Suppose we do not have enough space to allocate a location for each possible key then we need a mechanism to handle this case. Other way of defining the scenario is, if we have less locations and more possible keys then simple array implementation is not enough.

In these cases one option is to use hash tables. Hash table or hash map is a data structure that stores the keys and their associated values. Hash table uses a hash function to map keys to their associated values. General convention is that we use a hash table when the number of keys actually stored is small relative to the number of possible keys.

20.7 Hash Function

The hash function is used to transform the key into the index. Ideally, the hash function should map each possible key to a unique slot index, but it is difficult to achieve in practice.

How to Choose Hash Function?

The basic problems associated with the creation of hash tables are:

- An efficient hash function should be designed so that it distributes the index values of inserted objects uniformly across the table.
- An efficient collision resolution algorithm should be designed so that it computes an alternative index for a key whose hash index corresponds to a location previously inserted in the hash table.
- We must choose a hash function which can be calculated quickly, returns values within the range of locations in our table, and minimizes collisions.

Characteristics of Good Hash Functions

A good hash function should have the following characteristics:

- Minimize collision
- Be easy and quick to compute
- Distribute key values evenly in the hash table
- Use all the information provided in the key
- Have a high load factor for a given set of keys

20.8 Load Factor

The load factor of a non-empty hash table is the number of items stored in the table divided by the size of the table. This is the decision parameter used when we want to rehash *or* expand the existing hash table entries. This also helps us in determining the efficiency of the hashing function. That means, it tells whether the hash function is distributing the keys uniformly or not.

$$Load\ factor = \frac{Number\ of\ elements\ in\ hash\ table}{Hash\ Table\ size}$$

20.9 Collisions

Hash functions are used to map each key to different address space but practically it is not possible to create such a hash function and the problem is called *collision*. Collision is the condition where two records are stored in the same location.

20.10 Collision Resolution Techniques

The process of finding an alternate location is called *collision resolution*. Even though hash tables are having collision problem, they are more efficient in many cases comparative to all other data structures like search trees. There are a number of collision resolution techniques, and the most popular are open addressing and chaining.

- **Direct Chaining:** An array of linked list application
  - o Separate chaining
- **Open Addressing:** Array based implementation
  - o Linear probing (linear search)
  - o Quadratic probing (nonlinear search)
  - o Double hashing (use two hash functions)

20.11 Separate Chaining

Collision resolution by chaining combines linked representation with hash table. When two or more records hash to the same location, these records are constituted into a singly-linked list called a *chain*.

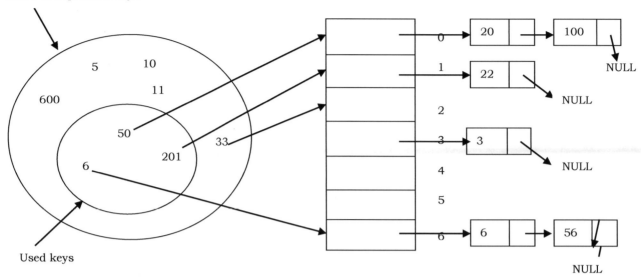

20.12 Open Addressing

In open addressing all keys are stored in the hash table itself. This approach is also known as *closed hashing*. This procedure is based on probing. A collision is resolved by probing.

Linear Probing

Interval between probes is fixed at 1. In linear probing, we search the hash table sequentially starting from the original hash location. If a location is occupied, we check the next location. We wrap around from the last table location to the first table location if necessary. The function for rehashing is the following:

$$rehash(key) = (n + 1)\% \ tablesize$$

One of the problems with linear probing is that table items tend to cluster together in the hash table. This means that table contains groups of consecutively occupied locations that are called *clustering*.

Clusters can get close to one another, and merge into a larger cluster. Thus, the one part of the table might be quite dense, even though another part has relatively few items. Clustering causes long probe searches and therefore decreases the overall efficiency.

The next location to be probed is determined by the step-size, where other step-sizes (than one) are possible. The step-size should be relatively prime to the table size, i.e. their greatest common divisor should be equal to 1. If we choose the table size to be a prime number, then any step-size is relatively prime to the table size. Clustering cannot be avoided by larger step-sizes.

Quadratic Probing

Interval between probes increases proportional to the hash value (the interval thus increasing linearly and the indices are described by a quadratic function). The problem of Clustering can be eliminated if we use quadratic probing method. In quadratic probing, we start from the original hash location i.

If a location is occupied, we check the locations $i + 1^2$, $i + 2^2$, $i + 3^2$, $i + 4^2$...
We wrap around from the last table location to the first table location if necessary.

The function for rehashing is the following:

$$rehash(key) = (n + k^2)\% \ tablesize$$

Example: Let us assume that the table size is **11 (0..10)**

Hash Function: $h(key) = key \bmod 11$

Insert keys:

$31 \bmod 11 = 9$

$19 \bmod 11 = 8$

$2 \bmod 11 = 2$

0	
1	
2	2
3	13
4	25
5	5
6	24
7	9
8	19
9	31
10	21

$13 \bmod 11 = 2 \rightarrow 2 + 12 = 3$

$25 \bmod 11 = 3 \rightarrow 3 + 12 = 4$

$24 \bmod 11 = 2 \rightarrow 2 + 12, 2 + 22 = 6$

$21 \bmod 11 = 10$

$9 \bmod 11 = 9 \rightarrow 9 + 1^2, \ 9 + 2^2 \bmod 11, \ 9 + 3^2 \bmod 11 = 7$

Even though clustering is avoided by quadratic probing, still there are chances of clustering. Clustering is caused by multiple search keys mapped to the same hash key. Thus, the probing sequence for such search keys is prolonged by repeated conflicts along the probing sequence. Both linear and quadratic probing use a probing sequence that is independent of the search key.

Double Hashing

Interval between probes is computed by another hash function. Double hashing reduces clustering in a better way. The increments for the probing sequence are computed by using a second hash function. The second hash function $h2$ should be:

$$h2(key) \neq 0 \text{ and } h2 \neq h1$$

We first probe the location $h1(key)$. If the location is occupied, we probe the location $h1(key) + h2(key)$, $h1(key) + 2 * h2(key)$, ...

Example:

Table size is 11 (0..10)
Hash Function: assume $h1(key) = key \bmod 11$ and
$\qquad h2(key) = 7 - (key \bmod 7)$

Insert keys:

$58 \bmod 11 = 3$
$14 \bmod 11 = 3 \rightarrow 3 + 7 = 10$
$91 \bmod 11 = 3 \rightarrow 3 + 7, 3 + 2 * 7 \bmod 11 = 6$
$25 \bmod 11 = 3 \rightarrow 3 + 3, 3 + 2 * 3 = 9$

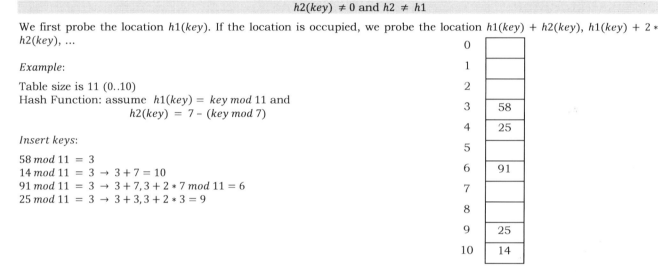

20.13 Comparison of Collision Resolution Techniques

Comparisons: Linear Probing vs. Double Hashing

The choice between linear probing and double hashing depends on the cost of computing the hash function and on the load factor [number of elements per slot] of the table. Both use few probes but double hashing take more time because it hashes to compare two hash functions for long keys.

Comparisons: Open Addressing vs. Separate Chaining

It is somewhat complicated because we have to account for the memory usage. Separate chaining uses extra memory for links. Open addressing needs extra memory implicitly within the table to terminate probe sequence. Open-addressed hash tables cannot be used if the data does not have unique keys. An alternative is to use separate chained hash tables.

Comparisons: Open Addressing methods

Linear Probing	Quadratic Probing	Double hashing
Fastest among three	Easiest to implement and deploy	Makes more efficient use of memory
Uses few probes	Uses extra memory for links and it does not probe all locations in the table	Use few probes but take more time
A problem occurs known as primary clustering	A problem occurs known as secondary clustering	More complicated to implement
Interval between probes is fixed - often at 1.	Interval between probes increases proportional to the hash value	Interval between probes is computed by another hash function

20.14 How Hashing Gets O(1) Complexity?

From the previous discussion, one doubts how hashing gets O(1) if multiple elements map to the same location?

The answer to this problem is simple. By using load factor we make sure that each block (for example linked list in separate chaining approach) on the average stores maximum number of elements less than *load factor*. Also, in practice this load factor is a constant (generally, 10 or 20). As a result, searching in 20 elements or 10 elements becomes constant.

If the average number of elements in a block is greater than load factor then we rehash the elements with bigger hash table size. One thing we should remember is that we consider average occupancy (total number of elements in the hash table divided by table size) while deciding the rehash. The access time of table depends on the load factor which in turn depends on the hash function. This is because hash function distributes the elements to hash table. For this reason, we say hash table gives O(1) complexity on the average. Also, we generally use hash tables in cases where searches are more than insertion and deletion operations.

20.15 Hashing Techniques

There are two types of hashing techniques: static hashing and dynamic hashing

Static Hashing

If the data is fixed then static hashing is useful. The set of keys is kept fixed and given in advance in static hashing. In static hashing the number of primary pages in the directory are kept fixed.

Dynamic Hashing

If data is not fixed static hashing can give bad performance and dynamic hashing is the alternative for such types of data. The set of keys can change dynamically in this.

20.16 Problems for which Hash Tables are not Suitable

- Problems for which data ordering is required.
- Problems having multidimensional data.
- Prefix searching especially if the keys are long and of variable-lengths.
- Problems that have dynamic data
- Problems in which the data does not have unique keys.

20.7 Bloom Filters

A Bloom filter is a probabilistic data structure which was designed to check whether an element is present in a set with memory and time efficiency. It tells us that the element either definitely is *not* in the set or may be in the set. The base data structure of a Bloom filter is a *Bit Vector*.

The algorithm was invented in 1970 by Burton Bloom and it relies on the use of a number of different hash functions.

How it works?

A Bloom filter starts off with a bit array initialized to zero. To store a data value we simply apply k different hash functions and treat the resulting k values as indices into the array and set each of the k array elements to 1. We repeat this for every element that we encounter.

Now suppose an element turns up and we want to know if we have seen it before. What we do is apply the k hash functions and look up the indicated array elements. If any of them are 0 we can be 100% sure that we have never encountered the element before - if we had the bit would have been set to 1. However even if all of them are one then we can't conclude that we have seen the element before because all of the bits could have been set by the k hash functions applied to multiple other elements. All we can conclude is that it is likely that we have encountered the element before.

Note that it is not possible to remove an element from a Bloom filter. The reason is simply that we can't unset a bit that appears to belong to an element because it might also be set by another element.

If the bit array is mostly empty i.e. set to zero and the k hash functions are independent of one another then the probability of a false positive (i.e. concluding that we have seen a data item when we actually haven't) is low. For example, if there are only k bits set we can conclude that the probability of a false positive is very close to zero as the only possibility of error is that we entered a data item that produced the same k hash values - which is unlikely as long as the has functions are independent.

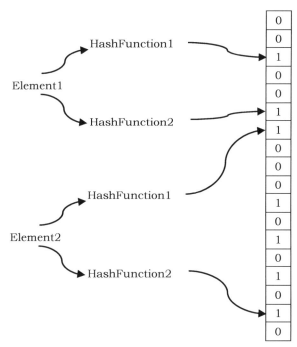

Now that the bits in the bit vector have been set for *Element*1 and *Element*2; we can query the bloom filter to tell us if something has been seen before.

The element is hashed but instead of setting the bits, this time a check is done and if the bits that would have been set are already set the bloom filter will return true that the element has been seen before.

As the bit array fills up the probability of a false positive slowly increases. Of course when the bit array is full every element queried is identified as having been seen before. So clearly we can trade space for accuracy as well as for time.

One-time removal of an element from a Bloom filter can be simulated by having a second Bloom filter that contains elements that have been removed. However, false positives in the second filter become false negatives in the composite filter, which may be undesirable. In this approach re-adding a previously removed item is not possible, as one would have to remove it from the *removed* filter.

Selecting hash functions

The requirement of designing k different independent hash functions can be prohibitive for large k. For a good hash function with a wide output, there should be little if any correlation between different bit-fields of such a hash, so this type of hash can be used to generate multiple *different* hash functions by slicing its output into multiple bit fields. Alternatively, one can pass k different initial values (such as 0, 1, ..., k - 1) to a hash function that takes an initial value; or add (or append) these values to the key. For larger m and/or k, independence among the hash functions can be relaxed with negligible increase in false positive rate.

Selecting size of bit vector

A Bloom filter with 1% error and an optimal value of k, in contrast, requires only about 9.6 bits per element — regardless of the size of the elements. This advantage comes partly from its compactness, inherited from arrays, and partly from its probabilistic nature. The 1% false-positive rate can be reduced by a factor of ten by adding only about 4.8 bits per element.

Space Advantages

While risking false positives, Bloom filters have a strong space advantage over other data structures for representing sets, such as self-balancing binary search trees, tries, hash tables, or simple arrays or linked lists of the entries. Most of these require storing at least the data items themselves, which can require anywhere from a small number of bits, for small integers, to an arbitrary number of bits, such as for strings (tries are an exception, since they can share storage between elements with equal prefixes). Linked structures incur an additional linear space overhead for pointers.

However, if the number of potential values is small and many of them can be in the set, the Bloom filter is easily surpassed by the deterministic bit array, which requires only one bit for each potential element.

Time Advantages

Bloom filters also have the unusual property that the time needed either to add items or to check whether an item is in the set is a fixed constant, $O(k)$, completely independent of the number of items already in the set. No other constant-space set data structure has this property, but the average access time of sparse hash tables can make them faster in practice than some Bloom filters. In a hardware implementation, however, the Bloom filter shines because its k lookups are independent and can be parallelized.

Implementation

Refer *Problems Section*.

20.18 Problems on Hashing

Problem-1   Implement separate chaining collision resolution technique and discuss time complexities of each function.

Solution: To create a hashtable of given size, say n, we allocate an array of n/L (whose value is usually between 5 and 20) pointers to list, initialized to NULL. To perform *Search/Insert/Delete* operations, we first compute the index of the table from the given key by using *hashfunction* and then do the corresponding operation in the linear list maintained at that location. To get uniform distribution of keys over a hashtable, maintain table size as prime number.

```
#define LOAD_FACTOR 20
struct ListNode {                          struct HashTableNode {
    int key;                                   int bcount;        //Number of elements in block
    int data;                                  struct ListNode *next;
    struct ListNode *next;                 };
};
                                           struct HashTable {
                                               int tsize;
                                               int count;         //Number of elements in table
                                               struct HashTableNode **Table;
                                           };

struct HashTable *CreatHashTable(int size) {
    struct HashTable *h;
    h = (struct HashTable *)malloc(sizeof(struct HashTable));
    if(!h) return NULL;
    h→tsize = size/ LOAD_FACTOR;
    h→count = 0;
    h→Table = (struct HashTableNode **) malloc( sizeof(struct HashTableNode *) * h→tsize);
    if(!h→Table) {
            printf("Memory Error");
            return NULL;
    }
    for(int i=0; i < h→tsize; i++) {
            h→Table[i]→next = NULL;
            h→Table[i]→bcount = 0;
    }
    return h;
}
int HashSearch(Struct HashTable *h, int data) {
    struct ListNode *temp;
    temp = h→Table[Hash(data, h→tsize)]→next;        //Assume Hash is a built-in function
    while(temp) {
            if(temp→data == data)
                    return 1;
            temp = temp→next;
    }
    return 0;
}
int HashInsert(Struct HashTable *h, int data) {
    int index;
    struct ListNode *temp, *newNode;
    if(HashSearch(h, data))
            return 0;
    index = Hash(data, h→tsize);                //Assume Hash is a built-in function
    temp = h→Table[index]→next;
    newNode = (struct ListNode *) malloc(sizeof(struct ListNode));
    if(!newNode) {
            printf("Out of Space"); return -1;
    }
    newNode→key = index;
    newNode→data = data;
    newNode→next = h→Table[index]→next;
    h→Table[index]→next = newNode;
    h→Table[index]→bcount++;
```

```
        h→count++;
        if(h→count / h→tsize  > LOAD_FACTOR)
                Rehash(h);
        return 1;
    }
    int HashDelete(Struct HashTable *h, int data) {
        int index;
        struct ListNode *temp, *prev;
        index = Hash(data, h→tsize);
        for(temp = h→Table[index]→next, prev = NULL; temp; prev = temp, temp = temp→next) {
                if(temp→data == data) {
                        if(prev != NULL)
                                prev→next = temp→next;
                        free(temp);
                        h→Table[index]→bcount--;
                        h→count--;
                        return 1;
                }
        }
        return 0;
    }
    void Rehash(Struct HashTable *h) {
        int oldsize, i, index;
        struct ListNode *p, * temp, *temp2;
        struct HashTableNode **oldTable;
        oldsize = h→tsize;
        oldTable = h→Table;
        h→tsize = h→tsize * 2;
        h→Table = (struct HashTableNode **) malloc(h→tsize * sizeof(struct HashTableNode *));
        if(!h→Table) {
                printf( "Allocation Failed");
                return;
        }
        for(i = 0; i < oldsize; i++) {
                for(temp = oldTable[i]→next; temp; temp = temp→next) {
                        index = Hash(temp→data, h→tsize);
                        temp2 = temp; temp = temp→next;
                        temp2→next = h→Table[index]→next;
                        h→Table[index]→next = temp2;
                }
        }
    }
```

CreatHashTable – O(n). HashSearch – O(1) average. HashInsert – O(1) average. HashDelete – O(1) average.

Problem-2   Given an array of characters, give an algorithm for removing the duplicates.

Solution: Start with the first character and check whether it appears in the remaining part of the string using simple linear search. If it repeats then bring the last character to that position and decrement the size of the string by one. Continue this process for each distinct character of the given string.

```
int elem(int *A, size_t n, int e){
   for (int i = 0; i < n; ++i)
     if (A[i] == e)
        return 1;
   return 0;
}

int RemoveDuplicates(int *A, int n){
   int m = 0;
   for (int i = 0; i < n; ++i)
     if (!elem(A, m, A[i]))
        A[m++] = A[i];
   return m;
}
```

Time Complexity: O(n^2). Space Complexity: O(1).

Problem-3   Can we find any other idea to solve this problem in better time than O(n^2)? Observe that order of characters in solutions do not matter.

Solution: Use sorting to bring the repeated characters together. Finally scan through the array to remove duplicates in consecutive positions.

```
int Compare(const void* a, const void *b) {
    return *(char*)a - *(char*)b;
}
void RemoveDuplicates(char s[]) {
    int last, current;
    QuickSort(s, strlen(s), sizeof(char), Compare);
    current = 0, last = 0;
    for(; s[current]; i++) {
            if(s[last] != s[current])
                    s[++last] = s[current];
    }
}
```

Time Complexity: $\Theta(nlogn)$. Space Complexity: $O(1)$.

Problem-4 Can we solve this problem in single pass over given array?

Solution: We can use hash table to check whether a character is repeating in the given string or not. If the current character is not available in hash table then insert it into hash table and keep that character in the given string also. If the current character exists in the hash table then skip that character.

```
void RemoveDuplicates(char s[]) {
    int src, dst;
    struct HastTable *h;
    h = CreatHashTable();
    current = last = 0;
    for(; s[current]; current++) {
            if( !HashSearch(h, s[current]))        {
                    s[last++] = s[current];
                    HashInsert(h, s[current]);
            }
    }
    s[last] = '\0';
}
```

Time Complexity: $\Theta(n)$ on average. Space Complexity: $O(n)$.

Problem-5 Given two arrays of unordered numbers, check whether both arrays have the same set of numbers?

Solution: Let us assume that two given arrays are A and B. A simple solution to the given problem is: for each element of A check whether that element is in B or not. A problem arises with this approach if there are duplicates. For example consider the following inputs:

$$A = \{2,5,6,8,10,2,2\}$$
$$B = \{2,5,5,8,10,5,6\}$$

The above algorithm gives the wrong result because for each element of A there is an element in B also. But if we look at the number of occurrences then they are not the same. This problem we can solve by moving the elements which are already compared to the end of list. That means, if we find an element in B, then we move that element to the end of B and in the next searching we will not find those elements. But the disadvantage of this is it needs extra swaps. Time Complexity of this approach is $O(n^2)$. Since for each element of A we have to scan B.

Problem-6 Can we improve the time complexity of Problem-5?

Solution: Yes. To improve the time complexity, let us assume that we have sorted both the lists. Since the sizes of both arrays are n, we need $O(n\log n)$ for sorting them. Now we just need to scan both the arrays with two pointers and see whether they point to the same element every time and keep moving the pointers until we reach the end of arrays.

Time Complexity of this approach is $O(n\log n)$. This is because we need $O(n\log n)$ for sorting the arrays. After sorting, we need $O(n)$ time for scanning but it is less compared to $O(n\log n)$.

Problem-7 Can we further improve the time complexity of Problem-5?

Solution: Yes, by using hash table. For this, consider the following algorithm.

Algorithm:
- Construct the hash table with array A elements as keys.
- While inserting the elements keep track of number frequency for each number. That means, if there are duplicates, then increment the counter of that corresponding key.
- After constructing the hash table for $A's$ elements, now scan the array B.
- For each occurrence of $B's$ elements reduce the corresponding counter values.
- At the end, check whether all counters are zero or not
- If all counters are zero then both arrays are same otherwise the arrays are different.

Time Complexity: O(n) for scanning the arrays. Space Complexity: O(n) for hash table.

Problem-8 Given a list of number pairs. If $pair(i, j)$ exist, and $pair(j, i)$ exist report all such pairs. For example, {{1,3},{2,6},{3,5},{7,4},{3,5},{8,7}} here, {3,5} and {5,3} are present. To report this pair, when you encounter {5,3}. We call such pairs as symmetric pairs. So, given an efficient algorithm for finding all such pairs.

Solution: By using hashing, we can solve this problem just in one scan and consider the following algorithm.

Algorithm:
- Read pairs of elements one by one and insert them into the hash table. For each pair, consider the first element as key and second element as value.
- While inserting the elements, check if the hashing of second element of the current pair is same as of first number of the current pair.
- If they are same then that indicates symmetric pair exits and output that pair.
- Otherwise, insert that element in to that. That means, use first number of current pair as key and second number as value and insert into the hash table.
- By the time we complete the scanning of all pairs, we output all the symmetric pairs.

Time Complexity: O(n) for scanning the arrays. Note that we are doing only scan of the input. Space Complexity: O(n) for hash table.

Problem-9 Given a singly linked list, check whether it has any loop in it or not.

Solution: Using Hash Tables
Algorithm:
- Traverse the linked list nodes one by one.
- Check if the nodes address is there in the hash table or not.
- If it is already there in the hash table then that indicates that we are visiting the node which was already visited. This is possible only if the given linked list has a loop in it.
- If the address of the node is not there in the hash table then insert that nodes address into the hash table.
- Continue this process until we reach end of the linked list *or* we find loop.

Time Complexity: O(n) for scanning the linked list. Note that we are doing only scan of the input. Space Complexity: O(n) for hash table.

Note: for efficient solution refer *Linked Lists* chapter.

Problem-10 Given an array of 101 elements. Out of them 50 elements are distinct, 24 elements are repeated 2 times and one element is repeated 3 times. Find the element which repeated 3 times in O(1).

Solution: Using Hash Tables
Algorithm:
- Scan the input array one by one.
- Check if the element is already there in the hash table or not.
- If it is already there in the hash table then increment its counter value [this indicates the number of occurrence of the element].
- If the element is not there in the hash table then insert that node into the hash table with counter value 1.
- Continue this process until we reach end of the array.

Time Complexity: O(n), because we are doing two scans. Space Complexity: O(n), for hash table.

Note: For efficient solution refer *Searching* chapter.

Problem-11 Given m sets of integers that have n elements in them. Give an algorithm to find an element which appeared in maximum number of sets?

Solution: Using Hash Tables
Algorithm:
- Scan the input sets one by one.
- For each element keep track of the counter. Counter indicates the frequency of the occurrences in all the sets.
- After completing scanning of all the sets, select the one which has the maximum counter value.

Time Complexity: O(mn), because we need to scan all the sets. Space Complexity: O(mn), for hash table. Because, in the worst case all the elements may be different.

Problem-12 Given two sets A and B, and a number K, Give an algorithm for finding whether there exists a pair of elements, one from A and one from B, that add up to K.

Solution: For simplicity, let us assume that the size of A is m and size of B is n.
Algorithm:
- Select the set which has minimum elements.
- For the selected set create a hash table. We can use both key and value as the same.
- Now scan the second array and check whether (K-*selected element)* exits in the hash table or not.
- If it exits then return the pair of elements.
- Otherwise continue until we reach end of the set.

Time Complexity: $O(Max(m,m))$, because we are doing two scans. Space Complexity: $O(Min(m,m))$, for hash table. We can select the small set for creating the hash table.

Problem-13 Give an algorithm to remove specified characters from a given string.

Solution: For simplicity, let us assume that the maximum number of different characters is 256. First we create an auxiliary array initialized to 0. Scan the characters to be removed and for each of those characters we set the value to 1, which indicates that we need to remove that character.

After initialization, scan the input string and for each of the characters, we check whether that character needs to be deleted or not. If the flag is set then we simply skip to the next character otherwise we keep the character in the input string. Continue this process until we reach the end of the input string. All these operations we can do in-place as given below.

```
void RemoveChars(char str[], char removeTheseChars[]) {
    int srcInd, destInd;
    int auxi[256]; //additional array
    for(srcInd =0; srcInd<256; srcIndex++)
            auxi[srcInd]=0;
    //set true for all characters to be removed
    srcIndex=0;
    while(remove[srcInd]) {
            auxi[removeTheseChars[srcInd]]=1;
            srcInd++;
    }
    //copy chars unless it must be removed
    srcInd=destInd=0;
    while(str[srcInd++]) {
            if(!auxi[str[srcInd]])
                    str[destInd++]=str[srcInd];
    }
}
```

Time Complexity = Time for scanning the characters to be removed + Time for scanning the input array
$$= O(n) + O(m) \approx O(n).$$

Where m is the length of the characters to be removed and n is the length of the input string. Space Complexity: $O(m)$, length of the characters to be removed. But since we are assuming the maximum number of different characters is 256, we can treat this as a constant. But we should keep in mind that when we are dealing with multi-byte characters the total number of different characters is much more than 256.

Problem-14 Give an algorithm for finding the first non-repeated character in a string. For example, the first non-repeated character in the string "*abzddab*" is '*z*'.

Solution: The solution to this problem is trivial. For each character in the given string, we can scan the remaining string if that character appears in it. If does not appears then we are done with the solution and return that character. If the character appears in the remaining string then go to the next character.

```
char FirstNonRepeatedChar( char *str ) {
    int i, j, repeated = 0;
    int len = strlen(str);
    for(i = 0; i < len; i++ )     {
            repeated = 0;
            for( j = 0; j < len; j++ )      {
                    if( i != j && str[i] == str[j] ) {
                            repeated = 1;
                            break;
                    }
            }
            if( repeated == 0 )        // Found the first non-repeated character
                    return str[i];
    }
    return '';
}
```

Time Complexity: $O(n^2)$, for two for loops. Space Complexity: $O(1)$.

Problem-15 Can we improve the time complexity of Problem-13?

Solution: Yes. By using hash tables we can reduce the time complexity. Create a hash table by reading all the characters in the input string and keeping count of the number of times each character appears. After creating the hash table, we can read the hash table entries to see which element has a count equal to 1. This approach takes $O(n)$ space but reduces the time complexity also to $O(n)$.

```
char FirstNonRepeatedCharUsinghash( char * str ) {
```

```
        int i, len=strlen(str);
        int count[256]; //additional array
        for(i=0;i<len;++i)
                count[i] = 0;
        for(i=0;i<len;++i)
                count[str[i]]++;
        for(i=0; i<len; ++i) {
                if(count[str[i]]==1) {
                        printf("%c",str[i]);
                        break;
                }
        }
        if(i==len) printf("No Non-repeated Characters");
        return 0;
}
```

Time Complexity: We have O(n) to create the hash table and another O(n) to read the entries of hash table. So the total time is O(n) + O(n) =O($2n$) $\approx$O(n).

Space Complexity: O(n) for keeping the count values.

Problem-16   Given a string, give an algorithm for finding the first repeating letter in a string?

Solution: The solution to this problem is almost similar to Problem-13 and Problem-15. The only difference is, instead of scanning the hash table twice we can give the answer in one scan itself. This is because while inserting into the hash table we can see whether that element already exists or not. If it already exits then we just need to return that character.

```
    char FirstRepeatedCharUsinghash( char * str ) {
        int i, len=strlen(str);
        int count[256]; //additional array
        for(i=0;i<len;++i)
                count[i] = 0;
        for(i=0; i<len; ++i) {
                if(count[str[i]]==1) {
                        printf("%s",str[i]);
                        break;
                }
                else count[str[i]]++;
        }
        if(i==len) printf("No Repeated Characters");
        return 0;
}
```

Time Complexity: We have O(n) for scanning and create the hash table. Note that we need only one scan for this problem. So the total time is O(n). Space Complexity: O(n) for keeping the count values.

Problem-17   Given an array of n numbers. Give an algorithm which displays all pairs whose sum is S.

Solution: This problem is similar to Problem-12. But instead of using two sets we use only one set.

Algorithm:
- Scan the elements of the input array one by one and create a hash table. We can use both key and value are same.
- After creating the hash table, again scan the input array and check whether ($S - selected\ element$) exits in the hash table or not.
- If it exits then return the pair of elements.
- Otherwise continue until we read all the elements of the array.

Time Complexity: We have O(n) to create the hash table and another O(n) to read the entries of hash table. So the total time is O(n) +O(n) =O($2n$) $\approx$O(n). Space Complexity: O(n) for keeping the count values.

Problem-18   Is there any other way of solving Problem-17?

Solution: Yes. The alternative solution to this problem involves sorting. First sort the input array. After sorting, use two pointers one at the starting and another at the ending. Each time add the values of both the indexes and see if their sum is equal to S. If they are equal then print that pair. Otherwise increase left pointer if the sum is less than S and decrease the right pointer if the sum is greater than S.

Time Complexity: Time for sorting + Time for scanning = O($nlogn$)+O(n)$\approx$O($nlogn$). Space Complexity: O(1).

Problem-19   We have a file with millions of lines of data. Only two lines are identical; the rest are all unique. Each line is so long that it may not even fit in memory. What is the most efficient solution for finding the identical lines?

Solution: Since complete line may not fit into the main memory, read the line partially and compute the hash from that partial line. Next, again read the next part of line and compute the hash. This time use the previous has also while computing the new hash value. Continue this process until we find the hash for complete line.

Do this for each line and store all the hash values in some file [or maintain some hash table of these hashes]. At any point if we get same hash value, then read the corresponding lines part by part and compare.

Note: Refer *Searching* chapter for related problems.

Problem-20 If h is the hashing function and is used to hash n keys in to a table of size s, where $n <= s$, the expected number of collisions involving a particular key X is :

(A) less than 1.   (B) less than n.   (C) less than s.   (D) less than $\frac{n}{2}$.

Solution: A.

Problem-21 Implement Bloom Filters

Solution:

```
typedef unsigned int (*hashFunctionPointer)(const char *);
struct Bloom{
    int bloomArraySize;
    unsigned char *bloomArray;
    int nHashFunctions;
    hashFunctionPointer *funcsArray;
};
#define SETBLOOMBIT(a, n) (a[n/CHAR_BIT] |= (1<<(n%CHAR_BIT)))
#define GETBLOOMBIT(a, n) (a[n/CHAR_BIT] & (1<<(n%CHAR_BIT)))
struct Bloom *createBloom(int size, int nHashFunctions, ...){
    struct Bloom *blm;
    va_list l;
    int n;
    if(!(blm=malloc(sizeof(struct Bloom))))
        return NULL;
    if(!(blm→bloomArray=calloc((size+CHAR_BIT-1)/CHAR_BIT, sizeof(char)))) {
        free(blm);
        return NULL;
    }
    if(!(blm→funcsArray=(hashFunctionPointer*)malloc(nHashFunctions*sizeof(hashFunctionPointer)))) {
        free(blm→bloomArray);
        free(blm);
        return NULL;
    }
    va_start(l, nHashFunctions);
    for(n=0; n<nHashFunctions; ++n) {
        blm→funcsArray[n]=va_arg(l, hashFunctionPointer);
    }
    va_end(l);
    blm→nHashFunctions=nHashFunctions;
    blm→bloomArraySize=size;
    return blm;
}
int deleteBloom(struct Bloom *blm){
    free(blm→bloomArray);
    free(blm→funcsArray);
    free(blm);
    return 0;
}
int addElementBloom(struct Bloom *blm, const char *s){
    int n;
    for(n=0; n<blm→nHashFunctions; ++n) {
        SETBLOOMBIT(blm→bloomArray, blm→funcsArray[n](s)%blm→bloomArraySize);
    }
    return 0;
}
int checkElementBloom(struct Bloom *blm, const char *s){
    int n;
```

```
        for(n=0; n<blm→nHashFunctions; ++n) {
            if(!(GETBLOOMBIT(blm→bloomArray, blm→funcsArray[n](s)%blm→bloomArraySize))) return 0;
        }
        return 1;
}
unsigned int shiftAddXORHash(const char *key){
    unsigned int h=0;
    while(*key) h^=(h<<5)+(h>>2)+(unsigned char)*key++;
    return h;
}
unsigned int XORHash(const char *key){
    unsigned int h=0;
    hash_t h=0;
    while(*key) h^=*key++;
    return h;
}
int test(){
    FILE *fp;
    char line[1024];
    char *p;
    struct Bloom *blm;
    if(!(blm=createBloom(1500000, 2, shiftAddXORHash, XORHash))) {
        fprintf(stderr, "ERROR: Could not create Bloom filter\n");
        return -1;
    }
    if(!(fp=fopen("path", "r"))) {
        fprintf(stderr, "ERROR: Could not open file %s\n", argv[1]);
        return -1;
    }
    while(fgets(line, 1024, fp)) {
        if((p=strchr(line, '\r'))) *p='\0';
        if((p=strchr(line, '\n'))) *p='\0';
        addElementBloom(blm, line);
    }
    fclose(fp);

    while(fgets(line, 1024, stdin)) {
        if((p=strchr(line, '\r'))) *p='\0';
        if((p=strchr(line, '\n'))) *p='\0';

        p=strtok(line, " \t,.;:\r\n?!-/()");
        while(p) {
            if(!checkBloom(blm, p)) {
                printf("No match for ford \"%s\"\n", p);
            }
            p=strtok(NULL, " \t,.;:\r\n?!-/()");
        }
    }
    deleteBloom(blm);
    return 1;
}
```

Chapter-21

STRING ALGORITHMS

21.1 Introduction

To understand the importance of string algorithms let us consider the case of entering the URL (Uniform Resource Locator) in any browser (say, Internet Explorer, Firefox, or Google Chrome). You will observe that after typing the prefix of the URL, a list of all possible URLs is displayed. That means, the browsers are doing some internal processing and giving us the list of matching URLs. This technique is sometimes called *auto – completion*.

Similarly, consider the case of entering the directory name in command line interface (in both *Windows* and *UNIX*). After typing the prefix of the directory name if we press *tab* button, then we get a list of all matched directory names available. This is another example of auto completion.

In order to support these kind of operations, we need a data structure which stores the string data efficiently. In this chapter, we will look at the data structures that are useful for implementing string algorithms.

We start our discussion with the basic problem of strings: given a string, how do we search a substring (pattern)? This is called *string matching* problem. After discussing various string matching algorithms, we will see different data structures for storing strings.

21.2 String Matching Algorithms

In this section, we concentrate on checking whether a pattern P is a substring of another string T (T stands for text) or not. Since we are trying to check a fixed string P, sometimes these algorithms are called *exact string matching* algorithms. To simplify our discussion let us assume that the length of given text T is n and the length of the pattern P which we are trying to match has the length m. That means, T has the characters from 0 to $n - 1$ ($T[0 \ldots n - 1]$) and P has the characters from 0 to $m - 1$ ($P[0 \ldots m - 1]$). This algorithm is implemented in $C + +$ as *strstr()*.

In the subsequent sections, we start with brute force method and gradually move towards better algorithms.

- Brute Force Method
- Robin-Karp String Matching Algorithm
- String Matching with Finite Automata
- KMP Algorithm
- Boyce-Moore Algorithm
- Suffix Trees

21.3 Brute Force Approach

In this method, for each possible position in the text T we check whether the pattern P matches or not. Since the length of T is n, we have $n - m + 1$ possible choices for comparisons. This is because we do not need to check last $m - 1$ locations of T as the pattern length is m. The following algorithm searches for the first occurrence of a pattern string P in a text string T.

Algorithm

```
int BruteForceStringMatch (int T[], int n,  int P[], int m) {
    for (int i  = 0; i <=n - m; i++) {
        int j  = 0;
        while (j < m && P[j] == T[i + j])
            j  = j + 1;
        if(j == m )
        return i;
    }
    return -1;
}
```

Time Complexity: $O((n - m + 1) \times m) \approx O(n \times m)$. Space Complexity: $O(1)$.

21.4 Robin-Karp String Matching Algorithm

In this method, we will use the hashing technique and instead of checking for each possible position in T, we check only if the hashing of P and hashing of m characters of T gives the same result.

Initially, apply hash function to first m characters of T and check whether this result and P's hashing result is same or not. If they are not same then go to the next character of T and again apply hash function to m characters (by starting at second character). If they are same then we compare those m characters of T with P.

Selecting Hash Function

At each step, since we are finding the hash of m characters of T, we need an efficient hash function. If the hash function takes O(m) complexity in every step then the total complexity is O($n \times m$). This is worse than brute force method because first we are applying the hash function and also comparing.

Our objective is to select a hash function which takes O(1) complexity for finding the hash of m characters of T every time. Then only we can reduce the total complexity of the algorithm.

If the hash function is not good (worst case), then the complexity of Robin-Karp algorithm complexity is O($(n - m + 1) \times m$) $\approx$ O($n \times m$). If we select a good hash function then the complexity of Robin-Karp algorithm complexity is O($m + n$). Now let us see how to select a hash function which can compute the hash of m characters of T at each step in O(1).

For simplicity, let's assume that the characters used in string T are only integers. That means, all characters in $T \in \{0, 1, 2, \ldots, 9\}$. Since all of them are integers, we can view a string of m consecutive characters as decimal numbers. For example, string "61815" corresponds to the number 61815.

With the above assumption, the pattern P is also a decimal value and let us assume that decimal value of P is p. For the given text $T[0..n-1]$, let $t(i)$ denote the decimal value of length$-m$ substring $T[i..i+m-1]$ for $i = 0, 1, \ldots, n-m-1$. So, $t(i) == p$ if and only if $T[i..i+m-1] == P[0..m-1]$.

We can compute p in O(m) time using Horner's Rule as:

$$p = P[m-1] + 10(P[m-2] + 10(P[m-3] + \ldots + 10\,(P[1] + 10\,P[0])\ldots))$$

Code for above assumption is:

```
value = 0;
for (int i = 0; i < m-1; i++) {
    value = value * 10;
    value = value + P[i];
}
```

We can compute all $t(i)$, for $i = 0, 1, \ldots, n-m-1$ values in a total of $O(n)$ time. The value of $t(0)$ can be similarly computed from $T[0..m-1]$ in O(m) time. To compute the remaining values $t(0), t(1), \ldots, t\,(n-m-1)$, understand that $t(i+1)$ can be computed from $t(i)$ in constant time.

$$t(i+1) = 10 * (t(i) - 10^{m-1} * T[i]) + T[i+m-1]$$

For example, if $T = $ "123456" and $m = 3$
$$t(0) = 123$$
$$t(1) = 10 * (123 - 100 * 1) + 4 = 234$$

Step by Step explanation

First : remove the first digit : $123 - 100 * 1 = 23$
Second: Multiply by 10 to shift it : $23 * 10 = 230$
Third : Add last digit : $230 + 4 = 234$

The algorithm runs by comparing, $t(i)$ with p. When $t(i) == p$, then we have found the substring P in T, starting from position i.

21.5 String Matching with Finite Automata

In this method we use the finite automata which is the concept of Theory of Computation (ToC). Before looking at the algorithm, first let us see the definition of finite automata.

Finite Automata: A finite automaton F is a 5-tuple $(Q, q_0, A, \sum, \delta)$, where

- Q is a finite set of states
- $q_0 \in Q$ is the start state
- $A \subseteq Q$ is a set of accepting states
- $\sum$ is a finite input alphabet
- δ is the transition function that gives the next state for a given current state and input

How does Finite Automata Work?

- The finite automaton F begins in state q_0
- Reads characters from Σ one at a time
- If F is in state q and reads input character a, F moves to state $\delta(q, a)$
- At the end if its state is in A, then we say, F accepted the input string read so far
- If the input string is not accepted is called rejected string

Example: Let us assume that $Q = \{0,1\}, q_0 = 0, A = \{1\}, \Sigma = \{a, b\}$. $\delta(q, a)$ as shown in the transition table/diagram. This accepts strings that end in an odd number of a's; e.g., *abbaaa* is accepted, *aa* is rejected.

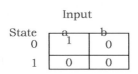

Transition Function/Table

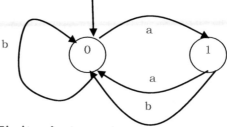

Important Notes for Constructing the Finite Automata

For building the automata, first we start with initial state. The FA will be in state k if k characters of the pattern have been matched. If the next text character is equal to pattern character c, we have matched $k + 1$ characters, and the FA enters state $k + 1$. If the next text character is not equal to pattern character, then the FA go to a state $0, 1, 2, \ldots,$ or k, depending on how many initial pattern characters match text characters ending with c.

Matching Algorithm

Now, let us concentrate on the matching algorithm.

- For a given pattern $P[0..m-1]$, first we need to build a finite automaton F
    - The state set is $Q = \{0, 1, 2, \ldots, m\}$
    - The start state is 0
    - The only accepting state is m
    - Time to build F can be large if Σ is large
- Scan the text string $T[0..n-1]$ to find all occurrences of the pattern $P[0..m-1]$
- String matching is efficient: $\Theta(n)$
    - Each character is examined exactly once
    - Constant time for each character
    - But the time to compute δ (transition function) is $O(m|\Sigma|)$. This is because δ has $O(m|\Sigma|)$ entries. If we assume $|\Sigma|$ is constant then the complexity becomes $O(m)$.

Algorithm:

```
//Input: Pattern string P[0..m-1], δ and F
//Goal: All valid shifts displayed
FiniteAutomataStringMatcher(int P[], int m, F, δ) {
    q = 0;
    for (int i = 0; i < m; i++)
        q = δ(q,T[i]);

    if(q == m)
        printf("Pattern occurs with shift: %d", i-m);
}
```

Time Complexity: $O(m)$.

21.6 KMP Algorithm

As before, let us assume that T is the string to be searched and P is the pattern to be matched. This algorithm was given by Knuth, Morris and Pratt. It takes $O(n)$ time complexity for searching a pattern. To get $O(n)$ time complexity, it avoids the comparisons with elements of T that were previously involved in comparison with some element of the pattern P.

The algorithm uses a table and in general we call it as *prefix function* or *prefix table* or *fail function* F. First we will see how to fill this table and later how to search for a pattern using this table. The prefix function, F for a pattern stores the knowledge about how the pattern matches against shifts of itself. This information can be used to avoid useless shifts of the pattern P. It means that, this table can be used for avoiding backtracking on the string T.

Prefix Table

```
int F[]; //assume F is a global array
void Prefix-Table(int P[], int m) {
    int i=1,j=0, F[0]=0;

    while(i<m) {
        if(P[i]==P[j]) {
            F[i]=j+1;
            i++;
            j++;
        }
        else if(j>0)
            j=F[j-1];
        else {
            F[i]=0;
            i++;
        }
    }
}
```

As an example, assume that $P = a\ b\ a\ b\ a\ c\ a$. For this pattern, les us follow the step-by-step instructions for filling the prefix table F. Initially: $m = length[P] = 7, F[0] = 0$ and $F[1] = 0$.

Step 1: $i = 1, j = 0, F[1] = 0$

	0	1	2	3	4	5	6
P	a	b	a	b	a	c	a
F	0	0					

Step 2: $i = 2, j = 0, F[2] = 1$

	0	1	2	3	4	5	6
P	a	b	a	b	a	c	a
F	0	0	1				

Step 3: $i = 3, j = 1, F[3] = 2$

	0	1	2	3	4	5	6
P	a	b	a	b	a	c	a
F	0	0	1	2			

Step 4: $i = 4, j = 2, F[4] = 3$

	0	1	2	3	4	5	6
P	a	b	a	b	a	c	a
F	0	0	1	2	3		

Step 5: $i = 5, j = 3, F[5] = 1$

	0	1	2	3	4	5	6
P	a	b	a	b	a	c	a
F	0	0	1	2	3	0	

Step 6: $i = 6, j = 1, F[6] = 1$

	0	1	2	3	4	5	6
P	a	b	a	b	a	c	a
F	0	0	1	2	3	0	1

At this step filling of prefix table is complete.

Matching Algorithm

The KMP algorithm takes pattern P, string T and prefix function F as input, finds a match of P in T.

```
int KMP(char T[], int n, int P[], int m) {
    int i=0,j=0;

    Prefix-Table(P,m);

    while(i<n) {
        if(T[i]==P[j]) {
            if(j==m-1)
                return i-j;
            else {
                i++;
                j++;
            }
        }
        else if(j>0)
            j=F[j-1];
```

```
        else
            i++;
    }
    return -1;
}
```

Time Complexity: $O(m + n)$, where m is the length of the pattern and n is the length of the text to be searched. Space Complexity: $O(m)$.

To understand the process let us go through an example. For our example, assume that $T = b\,a\,c\,b\,a\,b\,a\,b\,a\,b\,a\,c\,a\,c\,a$ & $P = a\,b\,a\,b\,a\,c\,a$. Since we have already filled the prefix table, let us use it and go to the matching algorithm. Initially: $n = size\ of\ T = 15$; $m = size\ of\ P = 7$.

Step 1: $i = 0$, $j = 0$, comparing $P[0]$ with $T[0]$. $P[0]$ does not match with $T[0]$. P will be shifted one position to the right.

T	b	a	c	b	a	b	a	b	a	b	a	c	a	c	a
P	a	b	a	b	a	c	a								

Step 2: $i = 1$, $j = 0$, comparing $P[0]$ with $T[1]$. $P[0]$ matches with $T[1]$. Since there is a match, P is not shifted.

T	b	a	c	b	a	b	a	b	a	b	a	c	a	c	a
P		a	b	a	b	a	c	a							

Step 3: $i = 2$, $j = 1$, comparing $P[1]$ with $T[2]$. $P[1]$ does not match with $T[2]$. Backtracking on P, comparing $P[0]$ and $T[2]$.

T	b	a	c	b	a	b	a	b	a	b	a	c	a	c	a
P		a	b	a	b	a	c	a							

Step 4: $i = 3$, $j = 0$, comparing $P[0]$ with $T[3]$. $P[0]$ does not match with $T[3]$.

T	b	a	c	b	a	b	a	b	a	b	a	c	a	c	a
P				a	b	a	b	a	c	a					

Step 5: $i = 4$, $j = 0$, comparing $P[0]$ with $T[4]$. $P[0]$ matches with $T[4]$.

T	b	a	C	b	a	b	a	b	a	b	a	c	a	c	A
P					a	b	a	b	a	c	a				

Step 6: $i = 5$, $j = 1$, comparing $P[1]$ with $T[5]$. $P[1]$ matches with $T[5]$.

T	b	a	c	b	a	b	a	b	a	b	a	c	a	c	a
P					a	b	a	b	a	c	a				

Step 7: $i = 6$, $j = 2$, comparing $P[2]$ with $T[6]$. $P[2]$ matches with $T[6]$.

T	b	a	c	b	a	b	a	b	a	b	a	c	a	c	a
P					a	b	a	b	a	c	a				

Step 8: $i = 7$, $j = 3$, comparing $P[3]$ with $T[7]$. $P[3]$ matches with $T[7]$.

T	b	a	c	b	a	b	a	b	a	b	a	c	a	c	a
P					a	b	a	b	a	c	a				

Step 9: $i = 8$, $j = 4$, comparing $P[4]$ with $T[8]$. $P[4]$ matches with $T[8]$.

T	b	a	c	b	a	b	a	b	a	b	a	c	a	c	a
P					a	b	a	b	a	c	a				

Step 10: $i = 9$, $j = 5$, comparing $P[5]$ with $T[9]$. $P[5]$ does not matches with $T[9]$. Backtracking on P, comparing $P[4]$ with $T[9]$ because after mismatch $j = F[4] = 3$.

T	b	a	c	b	a	b	a	b	a	b	a	c	a	c	a
P					a	b	a	b	a	c	a				

Comparing $P[3]$ with $T[9]$.

T	b	a	c	b	a	b	a	b	a	b	a	c	a	c	A
P							a	b	a	b	a	c	a		

Step 11: $i = 10$, $j = 4$, comparing $P[4]$ with $T[10]$. $P[4]$ matches with $T[10]$.

T	b	a	c	b	a	b	a	b	a	b	a		a	c	A
P						a	b	a	b	a		c	a		

Step 12: $i = 11$, $j = 5$, comparing $P[5]$ with $T[11]$. $P[5]$ matches with $T[11]$.

T	b	a	c	b	a	b	a	b	a	b	a	c		a	c	A
P						a	b	a	b	a	c		a			

Step 13: $i = 12$, $j = 6$, comparing $P[6]$ with $T[12]$. $P[6]$ matches with $T[12]$.

T	b	a	c	b	a	b	a	b	a	b	a	c	a		c	a
P						a	b	a	b	a	c	a				

Pattern P has been found to completely occur in string T. The total number of shifts that took place for the match to be found are: $i - m = 13 - 7 = 6$ shifts.

Notes:
- KMP performs the comparisons from left to right
- KMP algorithm needs a preprocessing (prefix function) which takes O(m) space and time complexity
- Searching takes in O($n + m$) time complexity (does not depend on alphabet size)

21.7 Boyce-Moore Algorithm

Like KMP algorithm, this also does some pre-processing and we call it *last function*. The algorithm scans the characters of the pattern from right to left beginning with the rightmost character. During the testing of a possible placement of pattern P in T, a mismatch is handled as follows:

Let us assume that the current character being matched is $T[i] = c$ and the corresponding pattern character is $P[j]$. If c is not contained anywhere in P, then shift the pattern P completely past $T[i]$. Otherwise, shift P until an occurrence of character c in P gets aligned with $T[i]$. This technique avoids needless comparisons by shifting pattern relative to text. The *last* function takes O($m + |\sum|$) time and actual search takes O(nm) time. Therefore the worst case running time of Boyer-Moore algorithm is O($nm + |\sum|$). This indicates that the worst-case running time is quadratic, in case of $n == m$, the same as the brute force algorithm.

- Boyer-Moore algorithm is very fast on large alphabet (relative to the length of the pattern).
- For small alphabet, Boyce-Moore is not preferable.
- For binary strings KMP algorithm is recommended.
- For the very shortest patterns, the brute force algorithm is better.

21.8 Data Structures for Storing Strings

If we have a set of strings (for example, all words in dictionary) and a word which we want to search in that set, in order to perform the search operation faster, we need an efficient way of storing the strings. To store sets of strings we can use any of the following data structures.

- Hashing Tables
- Binary Search Trees
- Tries
- Ternary Search Trees

21.9 Hash Tables for Strings

As seen in *Hashing* chapter, we can use hash tables for storing the integers or strings. In this case, the keys are nothing but the strings. The problem with hash table implementation is that, we lose the ordering information. Since, after applying the hash function, we do not know where it will map to. As a result some queries take more time. For example, to find all words starting with letter "K", then using hash table representation we need to scan the complete hash table. This is because the hash function takes the complete key, performs hash on it and we do not know the location of each word.

21.10 Binary Search Trees for Strings

In this representation, every node is used for sorting the strings alphabetically. This is possible because strings have a natural ordering: A comes before B, which comes before C, and so on. This is because words can be ordered and we can use a Binary Search Tree (BST) to store and retrieve them. For example, let us assume that we want to store the following strings using BSTs:

this is a career monk string

For the given string there are many ways of representing them in BST and one such possibility is shown in the tree below.

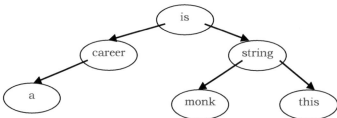

Issues with Binary Search Tree Representation

This method is good in terms of storage efficiency. But the disadvantage of this representation is that, at every node, the search operation performs the complete match of the given key with the node data and as a result the time complexity of search operation increases. So, from this we can say that BST representation of strings is good in terms of storage but not in terms of time.

21.11 Tries

Now, let us see the alternative representation which reduces the time complexity of search operation. The name *trie* is taken from the word re"trie".

What is a Trie?

A *trie* is a tree and each node in it contains the number of pointers equal to the number of characters of the alphabet. For example, if we assume that all the strings are formed with English alphabet characters "a" to "z" then each node of the trie contains 26 pointers. Suppose we want to store the strings "a", "all", "als" and "as", *trie* for these strings will look like:

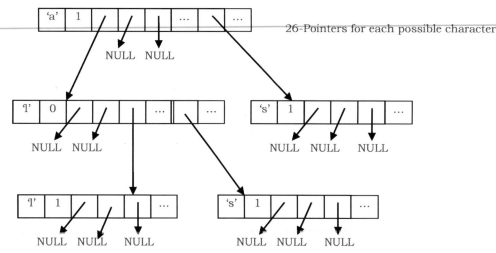

26-Pointers for each possible character

A trie data structure can be declared as:

```
struct TrieNode {
    char data;                    // Contains the current node character.
    int is_End_Of_String;         // Indicates whether the string formed from root to
                                  // current node is a string or not
    struct TrieNode *child[26];   // Pointers to other tri nodes
};
```

Why Tries?

The tries can insert and find strings in $O(L)$ time (where L represent the length of a single word). This is much faster than hash table and binary search tree representations.

Trie Declaration

Structure of the TrieNode had data (char), is_End_Of_String (boolean) and a collection of child nodes (Collection of TrieNode's). It has one more method called subNode(char). This method takes a character as argument and will return the child node of that character type if that is present. The basic element - TrieNode of a TRIE data structure looks like this:

```
struct TrieNode {
    char data;
    int is_End_Of_String;
    struct TrieNode *child[];
};
struct TrieNode *TrieNode subNode(struct TrieNode *root, char c){
    if(root! = NULL){
        for(int i=0; i < 26; i++){
            if(root.child[i]→data == c)
                return root.child[i];
        }
    }
    return NULL;
}
```

Now that we have defined our TrieNode, let's go ahead and look at the other operations of TRIE. Fortunately, the TRIE data structure is simple to implement since it has two major methods insert() and search(). Let's look at the elementary implementation of both these methods.

Inserting a String in Trie

To insert a string, we just need to start at the root node and follow the corresponding path (path from root indicates the prefix of the give string). Once we reach the NULL pointer, we just need to create a skew of tail nodes for the remaining characters of the given string.

```
void InsertInTrie(struct TrieNode *root, char *word) {
    if(!*word)
        return;
    if(!root) {
        struct TrieNode *newNode = (struct TrieNode *) malloc (sizeof(struct TrieNode *));
        newNode→data=*word;
        for(int i =0; i<26; i++)
            newNode→child[i]=NULL;
        if(!*(word+1))
            newNode→is_End_Of_String = 1;
        else
            newNode→child[*word] = InsertInTrie(newNode→child[*word], word+1);
        return newNode;
    }
    root→child[*word] = InsertInTrie(root→child[*word], word+1);
    return root;
}
```

Time Complexity: $O(L)$, where L is the length of the string to be inserted.

Note: For real dictionary implementation we may need few more checks such as checking whether the given string is already there in dictionary or not.

Searching a String in Trie

Same is the case with search operation: we just need to start at root and follow the pointers. The time complexity of search operation is equal to the length of the given string which we want to search.

```
int SearchInTrie(struct TrieNode *root, char *word) {
    if(!root)
        return -1;
    if(!*word) {
        if(root→ is_End_Of_String)
            return 1;
        else
            return -1;
    }
    if(root→data == *word)
```

```
                 return  SearchInTrie(root→child[*word], word+1);
        else
            return -1;
}
```

Time Complexity: O(L), where L is the length of the string to be searched.

Issues with Tries Representation

The main disadvantage of tries is that they need lot of memory for storing the strings. As we have seen above, for each node we have too many node pointers. In many cases, the occupancy of each node is less. The final conclusion regarding tries data structure is that they are faster but require huge memory for storing the strings.

Note: There are some improved tries representations called *trie compression techniques*. But, even with those techniques we can only reduce the memory at leaves but not at the internal nodes.

21.12 Ternary Search Trees

This representation was initially given by Jon Bentley and Sedgewick. A ternary search tree takes the advantages of binary search trees and tries. That means it combines the memory efficiency of BSTs and time efficiency of tries.

Ternary Search Trees Declaration

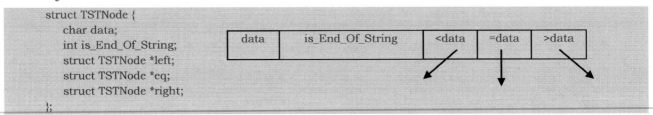

```
struct TSTNode {
    char data;
    int is_End_Of_String;
    struct TSTNode *left;
    struct TSTNode *eq;
    struct TSTNode *right;
};
```

| data | is_End_Of_String | <data | =data | >data |

Ternary Search Tree (TST) uses three pointers:

- The *left* pointer points to the TST containing all the strings which are alphabetically less than *data*.
- The *right* pointer points to the TST containing all the strings which are alphabetically greater than *data*.
- The *eq* pointer points to the TST containing all the strings which are alphabetically equal to *data*. That means, if we want to search for a string, and if the current character of input string and *data* of current node in TST are same then we need to proceed to the next character in the input string and search it in the subtree which is pointed by *eq*.

Inserting strings in Ternary Search Tree

For simplicity let us assume that we want to store the following words in TST (also assume the same order): *boats, boat, bat* and *bats*. Initially, let us start with *boats* string.

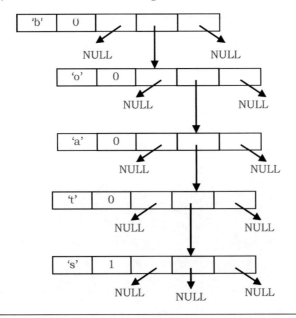

Now if we want to insert the string *boat*, then the TST becomes [the only change is setting the *is_End_Of_String* flag of "*t*" node to 1]:

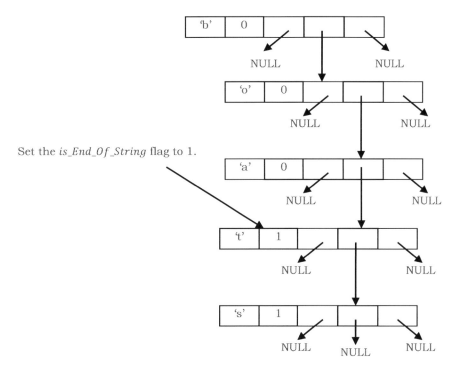

Set the *is_End_Of_String* flag to 1.

Now, let us insert the next string: *bat*

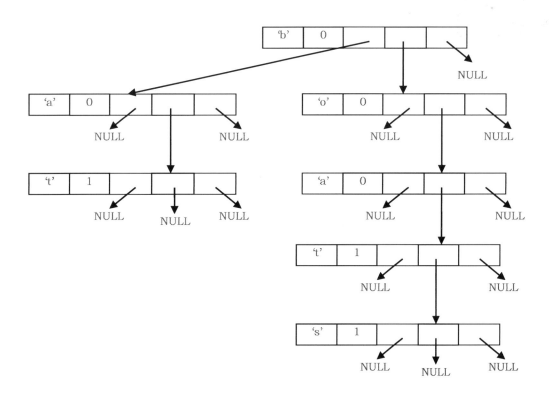

Now, let us insert the final word: *bats*.

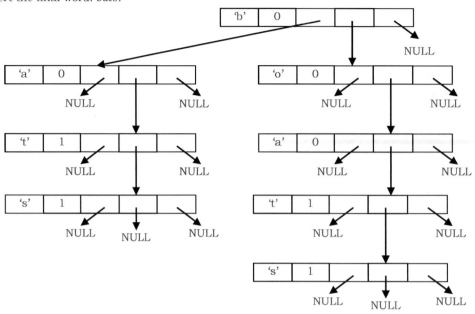

Based on these examples, we can write insertion algorithm as below. We will combine the insertion operation of BST and tries.

```
struct TSTNode *InsertInTST(struct TSTNode *root, char *word) {
    if(root == NULL) {
        root = (struct TSTNode *) malloc(sizeof(struct TSTNode));
        root→data = *word;
        root→is_End_Of_String = 1;
        root→left = root→eq = root→right = NULL;
    }
    if(*word < root→data)
        root→left = InsertInTST (root→left, word);
    else if(*word == root→data) {
        if(*(word+1))
            root→eq = InsertInTST (root→eq, word+1);
        else    root→is_End_Of_String = 1;
    }
    else    root→right = InsertInTST (root→right, word);
    return root;
}
```

Time Complexity: O(L), where L is the length of the string to be inserted.

Searching in Ternary Search Tree

If after inserting the words we want to search for them, then we have to follow the same rules as that of binary search. The only difference is, in case of match we should check for the remaining characters (in *eq* subtree) instead of return. Also, like BSTs we will see both recursive and non recursive versions of search method.

```
int SearchInTSTRecursive(struct TSTNode *root, char *word) {
    if(!root)
        return -1;
    if(*word < root→data)
        return SearchInTSTRecursive(root→left, word);
    else if(*word > root→data)
        return SearchInTSTRecursive(root→right, word);
    else {
        if(root→is_End_Of_String && *(word+1)==0)
        return 1;
        return SearchInTSTRecursive(root→eq, ++word);
    }
}
int SearchInTSTNon-Recursive(struct TSTNode *root, char *word) {
    while (root) {
```

```
            if(*word < root→data)
                root = root→left;
            else if(*word == root→data) {
                if(root→is_End_Of_String && *(word+1) == 0)
                    return 1;
                word++;
                root = root→eq;
            }
            else
                root = root→right;
        }
        return -1;
}
```

Time Complexity: O(L), where L is the length of the string to be searched.

Displaying All Words of Ternary Search Tree

Suppose we want to print all the strings of TST then we can use the following algorithm. If we want to print them in sorted order, we need to follow inorder traversal of TST.

```
    char word[1024];
    void DisplayAllWords(struct TSTNode *root) {
        if(!root)
            return;
        DisplayAllWords(root→left);
        word[i] = root→data;
        if(root→is_End_Of_String) {
            word[i] = '\0';
            printf("%c",word);
        }
        i++;
        DisplayAllWords(root→eq);
        i--;
        DisplayAllWords(root→right);
    }
```

Finding Length of Largest Word in TST

This is similar to finding height of the BST and can be found as:

```
    int MaxLengthOfLargestWordInTST(struct TSTNode *root) {
        if(!root)
            return 0;
        return Max(MaxLengthOfLargestWordInTST(root→left),
            MaxLengthOfLargestWordInTST(root→eq)+1,
            MaxLengthOfLargestWordInTST(root→right)));
    }
```

21.13 Comparing BSTs, Tries and TSTs

- Hash table and BST implementation stores complete string at each node. As a result they take more time for searching. But they are memory efficient.
- TSTs can grow and shrink dynamically but hash tables resize only based on load factor.
- TSTs allow partial search where as BSTs and hash tables do not support them.
- TSTs can display the words in sorted order but in hash tables we cannot get the sorted order.
- Tries perform search operations very fast but they take huge memory for storing the string.
- TST combines the advantages of BSTs and Tries. That means it combines the memory efficiency of BSTs and time efficiency of tries.

21.14 Suffix Trees

Suffix trees are an important data structure for strings. With suffix trees we can answer the queries very fast. But it needs some preprocessing and construction of suffix tree. Even though construction of suffix tree is complicated, it solves many other string-related problems in linear time.

Note: Suffix trees use a tree (suffix tree) for one string whereas, Hash tables, BSTs, Tires and TSTs store a set of strings. That means, suffix tree answers the queries related to one string.

Let us see the terminology we use for this representation.

Prefix and Suffix

For given a string $T = T_1 T_2 \dots T_n$, *prefix* of T is a string $T_1 \dots T_i$ where i can take values from 1 to n. For example, if $T = banana$, then the prefixes of T are: $b, ba, ban, bana, banan, banana$.

Similarly, for given a string $T = T_1 T_2 \dots T_n$, *suffix* of T is a string $T_i \dots T_n$ where i can take values from n to 1. For example, if $T = banana$, then the suffixes of T are: $a, na, ana, nana, anana, banana$.

Observation

From the above example, we can easily see that for a given a text T and a pattern P, the exact string matching problem can also be defined as:
- Find a suffix of T such that P is a prefix of this suffix   *or*
- Find a prefix of T such that P is a suffix of this prefix.

Example: Let the text to be searched be $T = accbkkbac$ and the pattern be $P = kkb$. For this example, P is a prefix of the suffix $kkbac$ and also a suffix of the prefix $accbkkb$.

What is a Suffix Tree?

In simple terms, the suffix tree for text T is a Trie-like data structure that represents the suffixes of T. The definition of suffix trees can be given as: A suffix tree for a n character string $T[1 \dots n]$ is a rooted tree with the following properties.

- Suffix tree will contain n leaves which are numbered from 1 to n
- Each internal node (except root) should have at least 2 children
- Each edge in tree is labeled by a nonempty substring of T
- No two edges out of a node (children edges) begins with the same character
- The paths from the root to the leaves represent all the suffixes of T

The Construction of Suffix Trees

Algorithm
1. Let S be the set of all suffixes of T. Append $ to each of the suffix.
2. Sort the suffixes in S based on their first character.
3. For each group S_c ($c \in \sum$):
   (i)   If S_c group has only one element, then create a leaf node.
   (ii)   Otherwise, find the longest common prefix of the suffixes in S_c group, create an internal node, and recursively continue with Step 2, S being the set of remaining suffixes from S_c after splitting off the longest common prefix.

For better understanding, let us go through an example. Let the given text be $T = tatat$. For this string, give a numbering to each of the suffixes.

Index	Suffix
1	$
2	t$
3	at$
4	tat$
5	atat$
6	tatat$

Now, sort the suffixes based on their initial characters.

Index	Suffix	
1	$	Group S_1 based on a
3	at$	Group S_2 based on a
5	atat$	
2	t$	
4	tat$	Group S_3 based on t
6	tatat$	

In the three groups the first group has only one element. So, as per the algorithm create a leaf node for it and the same is shown below.

Now, for S_2 and S_3 (as they are having more than one element), let us find the longest prefix in the group and the result is shown below.

Group	Indices for this group	Longest Prefix of Group Suffices
S_2	3, 5	at
S_3	2, 4, 6	t

For S_2 and S_3, create internal nodes and the edge contains the longest common prefix of those groups.

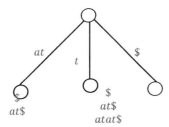

Now we have to remove the longest common prefix from S_2 and S_3 group elements.

Group	Indices for this group	Longest Prefix of Group Suffices	Resultant Suffixes
S_2	3, 5	at	$, at$
S_3	2, 4, 6	t	$, at$, atat$

Out next step is, solving S_2 and S_3 recursively. First let us take S_2. In this group, if we sort them based on their first character, it is easy to see that the first group contains only one element $ and the second group also contains only one element, at$. Since both groups have only one element, we can directly create leaf nodes for them.

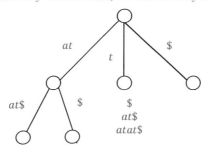

At this step, both S_1 and S_2 elements are done and the only remaining group is S_3. As similar to earlier steps, in S_3 group, if we sort them based on their first character, it is easy to see that there is only one element in first group and it is $. For S_3 remaining elements remove the longest common prefix.

Group	Indices for this group	Longest Prefix of Group Suffices	Resultant Suffixes
S_3	4, 6	at	$, at$

In the S_3 second group, there are two elements and among them one is $ and other is at$. We can directly add the leaf nodes for the first group element $. Let us add S_3 subtree as shown below.

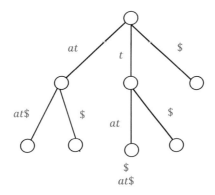

Now, S_3 contains two elements. If we sort them based on their first character, it is easy see that there are only two elements and among them one is $ and other is *at*$. We can directly add the leaf nodes for them. Let us add S_3 subtre as shown below.

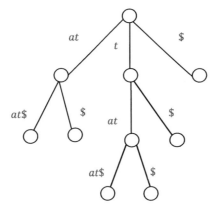

Since there are no more elements, this is the completion of construction of suffix tree for string $T = tatat$. The time-complexity of the construction of a suffix tree using the above algorithm is $O(n^2)$ where n is the length of the input string because there are n distinct suffixes. The longest has length n, the second longest has length $n - 1$ and so on.

Note:
- There are $O(n)$ algorithms for constructing suffix trees.
- To improve the complexity, we can use indices instead of string for branches.

Applications of Suffix Trees

All the problems below (not limited to these) on strings can be solved with suffix trees very efficiently (for algorithms refer *Problems* section).

- **Exact String Matching:** Given a text T and a pattern P, how do we check whether P appears in T or not?
- **Longest Repeated Substring:** Given a text T how do we find the substring of T which is the maximum repeated substring?
- **Longest Palindrome:** Given a text T how do we find the substring of T which is the longest palindrome of T?
- **Longest Common Substring:** Given two strings, how do we find the longest common substring?
- **Longest Common Prefix:** Given two strings $X[i \dots n]$ and $Y[j \dots m]$, how do we find the longest common prefix?
- How do we search for a regular expression in given text T?
- Given a text T and a pattern P, how do we find the first occurrence of P in T?

21.15 Problems on Strings

Problem-1   Given a paragraph of words, give an algorithm for finding the word which appears maximum number of times. If the paragraph is scrolled down(some words disappear from first frame, some words still appear and some are new words), give the maximum occurring word. Thus, it should be dynamic.

Solution: For this problem we can use combination of priority queues and tries. We start by creating a trie in which we insert a word as it appears and at every leaf of trie. Its node contains that word along with a pointer that points to the node in the heap [priority queue] which we also create. This heap contains nodes whose structure contains a *counter*. This is its frequency and also a pointer to that leaf of trie, which contain that word so that there is no need to store this word twice.

Whenever a new word comes we find it in trie, if it is already there then we increase the frequency of node in heap corresponding to that word and call it heapify. This is done so that at any point of time we can get the word of maximum frequency. While scrolling, when a word goes out of scope, we decrement the counter in Heap. If the new frequency is still greater than zero, heapify the heap to incorporate the modification. If new frequency is zero, delete the node from heap and delete it from trie.

Problem-2   Given two strings how can we find the longest common substring?

Solution: Let us assume that the given two strings are T_1 and T_2. The longest common substring of two strings, T_1 and T_2, can be found by building a generalized suffix tree for T_1 and T_2. That means, we need to build a single suffix tree for both the strings.

Each node is marked to indicate if it represents a suffix of T_1 or T_2 or both. This indicates that, we need to use different marker symbols for both the strings (for example, we can use $ for the first string and # for the second symbol). After constructing the common suffix tree, the deepest node marked for both T_1 and T_2 represents the longest common substring.

Alternative solution: We can build a suffix tree for the string $T_1\$T_2\#$. This is equivalent to building a common suffix tree for both the strings.

Time Complexity: $O(m + n)$, where m and n are the lengths of input strings T_1 and T_2.

Problem-3   **Longest Palindrome:** Given a text T how do we find substring of T which is the longest palindrome of T?

Solution: The longest palindrome of $T[1..n]$ can be found in $O(n)$ time. The algorithm is, first build a suffix tree for $T\$reverse(T)\#$ or build a generalized suffix tree for T and $reverse(T)$. After building the suffix tree, find the deepest node marked with both $ and #. Basically it means to find the longest common substring.

Problem-4   Given a string (word), give an algorithm for finding the next word in dictionary.

Solution: Let us assume that we are using Trie for storing the dictionary words. To find the next word in Tries we can follow a simple approach as shown below. Starting from the rightmost character, increment the characters one by one. Once we reach Z, move to next character on left side.

Whenever we increment, check if the word with the incremented character exists in dictionary or not. If it exists, then return the word, otherwise increment again. If we use TST, then we can find the inorder successor for the current word.

Problem-5   Give an algorithm for reversing a string.

Solution:

```
//If the str is editable
char *ReversingString(char str[]) {
    char temp, start, end;
    if(str == NULL || *str == '\0')
            return str;
    for (end = 0; str[end]; end++);

    end--;
    for (start = 0; start < end; start++, end--) {
            temp = str[start];
        str[start] = str[end];
        str[end] = temp;
    }
    return str;
}
```

Time Complexity: $O(n)$, where n is the length of the given string. Space Complexity: $O(n)$.

Problem-6   If the string is not editable, how do we create a string that is the reverse of given string?

Solution: If the string is not editable, then we need to create an array and return the pointer of that.

```
//If str is a const string (not editable)
char* ReversingString(char* str) {
    int start, end, len;
    char temp, *ptr=NULL;
    len=strlen(str);
    ptr=malloc(sizeof(char)*(len+1));
    ptr=strcpy(ptr,str);
    for (start=0, end=len-1; start<=end; start++, end--) {        //Swapping
        temp=ptr[start];
        ptr[start]=ptr[end];
        ptr[end]=temp;
    }
    return ptr;
}
```

Time Complexity: $O\left(\frac{n}{2}\right) \approx O(n)$, where n is the length of the given string. Space Complexity: $O(n)$.

Problem-7   Can we reverse the string without using any temporary variable?

Solution: Yes, we can use XOR logic for swapping the variables.

```
char* ReversingString(char *str) {
    int end= strlen(str)-1;
    int start = 0;
    while( start<end ) {
        str[start] ^= str[end];
        str[end]  ^= str[start];
        str[start] ^= str[end];
        ++start;
        --end;
    }
    return str;
```

```
}
```

Time Complexity: $O\left(\frac{n}{2}\right) \approx O(n)$, where n is the length of the given string. Space Complexity: $O(n)$.

Problem-8 Given a text and a pattern, give an algorithm for matching pattern in text. Assume ? (single character matcher) and * (multi character matcher) are the wild card characters.

Solution: Brute Force Method. For efficient method refer theory section.

```
int PatternMatching(char *text, char *pattern) {
    if(*pattern == 0)
        return 1;
    if(*text == 0)
        return *p == 0;
    if('?' == *pattern)
        return PatternMatching(text+1,pattern+1) || PatternMatching(text,pattern+1);
    if('*' == *pattern)
        return PatternMatching(text+1,pattern) || PatternMatching(text,pattern+1);
    if(*text == *pattern)
        return PatternMatching(text+1,pattern+1);
    return -1;
}
```

Time Complexity: $O(mn)$, where m is the length of the text and n is the length of the pattern.
Space Complexity: $O(1)$.

Problem-9 Give an algorithm for reversing words in a sentence.
Example: Input: "This is a Career Monk String", Output: "String Monk Career a is This"

Solution: Start from the beginning and keep on reversing the words. The below implementation assumes that ' ' (space) is the delimiter for words in given sentence.

```
void ReverseWordsInSentences(char *text) {
    int worsStart, wordEnd, length;
    length = strlen(text);
    ReversingString(text, 0, length-1);
    for(worsStart = wordEnd = 0; wordEnd < length; wordEnd ++) {
        if(text[wordEnd] != ' ') {
            worsStart = wordEnd;
            while (text[wordEnd] != ' ' && wordEnd < length)
                wordEnd ++;
            wordEnd--;
            //Found current word, reverse it now.
            ReverseWord(text, worsStart, wordEnd);
        }
    }
}
void ReversingString(char text[], int start, int end) {
    for (char temp; start < end; start++, end--) {
        temp = str[end];
        str[end] = str[start];
        strstart] = temp;
    }
}
```

Time Complexity: $O(2n) \approx O(n)$, where n is the length of the string. Space Complexity: $O(1)$.

Problem-10 **Permutations of a string [anagrams]:** Give an algorithm for printing all possible permutations of the characters in a string. Unlike combinations, two permutations are considered distinct if they contain the same characters, but in a different order. For simplicity assume that each occurrence of a repeated character is a distinct character. That is, if the input is "aaa", the output should be six repetitions of "aaa". The permutations may be output in any order.

Solution: The solution is got by generating n! strings each of length n, where n is the length of the input string.

```
void Permutations(int depth, char *permutation, int *used, char *original) {
    int length = strlen(original);
    if(depth == length) printf("%c",permutation);
    else {
        for (int i = 0; i < length; i++) {
            if(!used[i]) {
                used[i] = 1;
                permutation[depth] = original[i];
```

```
                         Permutations(depth + 1, permutation, used, original);
                         used[i] = 0;
                  }
            }
      }
}
```

Problem-11   **Combinations of a String:** Unlike permutations, two combinations are considered to be the same if they contain the same characters, but may be in a different order. Give an algorithm that prints all possible combinations of the characters in a string. For example, "*ac*" and "*ab*" are different combinations from the input string "*abc*", but "*ab*" is the same as "*ba*".

Solution: The solution is got by generating $n!/r!\,(n-r)!$ strings each of length between 1 and n where n is the length of the given input string.

Algorithm:

> For each of the input characters
>> a.   Put the current character in output string and print it.
>> b.   If there are any remaining characters, generate combinations with those remaining characters.

```
void Combinations(int depth, char *combination, int start, char *original) {
    int length = strlen(original);
    for (int i = start; i < length; i++) {
    combination[depth] = original[i];
    combination[depth +1] = '\0';
    printf("%c", combination);
    if(i < length -1)
        Combinations(depth + 1, combination, start + 1, original);
    }
}
```

Problem-12   Given a matrix with size $n \times n$ containing random integers. Give an algorithm which checks whether rows match with a column(s) or not. For example, If, i^{th} row matches with j^{th} column, and i^{th} row contains the elements - [2,6,5,8,9]. Then j^{th} column would also contain the elements - [2,6,5,8,9].

Solution: We can build a trie for the data in the columns (rows would also work). Then we can compare the rows with the trie. This would allow us to exit as soon as the beginning of a row does not match any column (backtracking). Also this would let us check a row against all columns in one pass.

If we do not want to waste memory for empty pointers then we can further improve the solution by constructing a suffix tree.

Problem-13   Write a method to replace all spaces in a string with '%20'. Assume string has sufficient space at end of string to hold additional characters.

Solution: Find the number of spaces. Then, starting from end (assuming string has enough space), replace the characters. Starting from end reduces the overwrites.

```
void encodeSpaceWithString(char* A){
    char *space = "%20";
    int stringLength = strlen(A);
    if(stringLength ==0){
       return;
    }
    int i, numberOfSpaces = 0;
    for(i = 0; i < stringLength; i++){
       if(A[i] == ' ' || A[i] == '\t'){
          numberOfSpaces ++;
       }
    }
    if(!numberOfSpaces)
       return;
    int newLength = len + numberOfSpaces * 2;
    A[newLength] = '\0';
    for(i = stringLength-1; i >= 0; i--){
       if(A[i] == ' ' || A[i] == '\t'){
          A[newLength--] = '0';
          A[newLength--] = '2';
          A[newLength--] = '%';
       }
       else{
          A[newLength--] = A[i];
```

}
}
}

Time Complexity: O(*n*). Space Complexity: O(1). Here, we do not have to worry on the space needed for extra characters. We have to see how much extra space is needed for filling that.

Problem-14 Given two long integers how do you add them?
For example: Number1=1234562787982380935327654326624764276464563534256354548S4
Number2=123456278798238093S327654326624764276464563534248758758756
Result=123456278798238093S3276S43266247642764645635342S634436746432

Solution:

```
#include <iostream>
#include <string>
#include <iomanip>
using namespace std;
string CalcLongNumsSum(string number1, string number2){
    string result;
    int carry(0);
    if (number1.empty() || number2.empty()){
        return number1 + number2;
    }
    reverse(number1.begin(), number1.end());
    reverse(number2.begin(), number2.end());
    int len = number1.size() > number2.size() ? number1.size() : number2.size();
    for (int i = 0; i < len; ++i){
        int d1 = (i < number1.size()) ? number1[i] - '0' : 0;
        int d2 = (i < number2.size()) ? number2[i] - '0' : 0;
        result.push_back((d1 + d2 + carry) % 10 + '0');
        carry = (carry + d1 + d2) / 10;
    }
    if (carry > 0){
        result.push_back(carry + '0');
    }
    reverse(result.begin(), result.end());
    return result;
}

void Testing(string number1, string number2){
    string result = CalcLongNumsSum(number1, number2);
    cout << string(1 + result.size() - number1.size(), ' ') << number1 << endl;
    cout << '+' << string(result.size() - number2.size(), ' ') << number2 << endl;
    cout << '=' << result << endl;
    cout << endl;
}
int main(){
    Testing("1234", "");
    Testing("1234", "99");
    Testing("1233434323432454521", "99872343237868642");
    return 0;
}
```

ALGORITHMS DESIGN TECHNIQUES

Chapter-22

22.1 Introduction

In the previous chapters, we have seen many algorithms for solving different kinds of problems. Before solving a new problem, the general tendency is to look for the similarity of current problem with other problems for which we have solutions. This helps us in getting the solution easily.

In this chapter, we will see different ways of classifying the algorithms and in subsequent chapters we will focus on a few of them (say, Greedy, Divide and Conquer and Dynamic Programming).

22.2 Classification

There are many ways of classifying algorithms and few of them are shown below:

- Implementation Method
- Design Method
- Other Classifications

22.3 Classification by Implementation Method

Recursion or Iteration

A *recursive* algorithm is one that calls itself repeatedly until a base condition is satisfied. It is a common method used in functional programming languages like $C, C++$, etc..

Iterative algorithms use constructs like loops and sometimes other data structures like stacks and queues to solve the problems.

Some problems are suited for recursive and other suited for iterative. For example, *Towers of Hanoi* problem can be easily understood in recursive implementation. Every recursive version has an iterative version, and vice versa.

Procedural or Declarative (Non-Procedural):

In *Declarative* programming languages, we say what we want without having to say how to do it. With *procedural* programming, we have to specify exact steps to get the result. For example, SQL is more declarative than procedural, because the queries don't specify steps to produce the result. Examples for procedural languages include: C, PHP, PERL, etc..

Serial or Parallel or Distributed

In general, while discussing the algorithms we assume that computers execute one instruction at a time. These are called *serial* algorithms.

Parallel algorithms take advantage of computer architectures to process several instructions at a time. They divide the problem into subproblems and serve them to several processors or threads. Iterative algorithms are generally parallelizable.

If the parallel algorithms are distributed on to different machines then we call such algorithms as *distributed* algorithms.

Deterministic or Non-Deterministic

Deterministic algorithms solve the problem with a predefined process whereas $non-deterministic$ algorithms guess the best solution at each step through the use of heuristics.

Exact or Approximate

As we have seen, for many problems we are not able to find the optimal solutions. That means, the algorithms for which we are able to find the optimal solutions are called *exact* algorithms. In computer science, if we do not have optimal solution, then we give approximation algorithms. Approximation algorithms are generally associated with NP-hard problems (refer *Complexity Classes* chapter for more details).

22.4 Classification by Design Method

Another way of classifying algorithms is by their design method.

Greedy Method

Greedy algorithms work in stages. In each stage, a decision is made that is good at that point, without bothering about the future consequences. Generally, this means that some *local best* is chosen. It assumes that local good selection makes the *global* optimal solution.

Divide and Conquer

The D & C strategy solves a problem by:

1) Divide: Breaking the problem into sub problems that are themselves smaller instances of the same type of problem.
2) Recursion: Recursively solving these sub problems.
3) Conquer: Appropriately combining their answers.

Examples: merge sort and binary search algorithms.

Dynamic Programming

Dynamic programming (DP) and memoization work together. The difference between DP and divide and conquer is that incase of the latter there is no dependency among the sub problems, whereas in DP there will be overlap of sub problems. By using memoization [maintaining a table for already solved sub problems], DP reduces the exponential complexity to polynomial complexity ($O(n^2)$, $O(n^3)$, etc.) for many problems.

The difference between dynamic programming and recursion is in memoization of recursive calls. When sub problems are independent and if there is no repetition, memoization does not help, hence dynamic programming is not a solution for all problems. By using memoization [maintaining a table of sub problems already solved], dynamic programming reduces the complexity from exponential to polynomial.

Linear Programming

In linear programming, there are inequalities in terms of inputs and *maximize* (or *minimize*) some linear function of the inputs. Many problems (example: maximum flow for directed graphs) can be discussed using linear programming.

Reduction [Transform and Conquer]

In this method we solve the difficult problem by transforming it into a known problem for which we have asymptotically optimal algorithms. In this method, the goal is to find a reducing algorithm whose complexity is not dominated by the resulting reduced algorithms. For example, selection algorithm for finding the median in a list involves first sorting the list and then finding out the middle element in the sorted list. These techniques are also called *transform and conquer*.

22.5 Other Classifications

Classification by Research Area

In computer science each field has its own problems and needs efficient algorithms. Examples: search algorithms, sorting algorithms, merge algorithms, numerical algorithms, graph algorithms, string algorithms, geometric algorithms, combinatorial algorithms, machine learning, cryptography, parallel algorithms, data compression algorithms and parsing techniques and more.

Classification by Complexity

In this classification, algorithms are classified by the time they take to find a solution based on their input size. Some algorithms take linear time complexity ($O(n)$) and others may take exponential time, and some never halt. Note that some problems may have multiple algorithms with different complexities.

Randomized Algorithms

Few algorithms make choices randomly. For some problems the fastest solutions must involve randomness. Example: Quick sort.

Branch and Bound Enumeration and Backtracking

These were used in Artificial Intelligence and we do not need to explore these fully. For backtracking method refer *Recusion and Backtracking* chapter.

Note: In the next few chapters we discuss these [greedy, divide and conquer and dynamic programming] design techniques. Importance is given to these techniques as the number of problems solved with these techniques is more as compared to others.

Chapter-23

GREEDY ALGORITHMS

23.1 Introduction

Let us start our discussion with simple theory which will give us an idea about the greedy technique. In the game of *Chess*, every time we make a decision about a move, we have to think about the future consequences as well. Whereas, in the game of *Tennis* (or *Volley Ball*), our action is based on current situation, which looks right at that moment, without bothering about the future consequences. This means that in some cases making a decision which looks right at that moment gives the best solution (*Greedy*) and for others it's not. Greedy technique is best suited for the second class of problems.

23.2 Greedy strategy

Greedy algorithms work in stages. In each stage, a decision is made that is good at that point, without bothering about the future. This means that some *local best* is chosen. It assumes local good selection makes global optimal solution.

23.3 Elements of Greedy Algorithms

The two basic properties of optimal greedy algorithms are:

1) Greedy choice property
2) Optimal substructure

Greedy choice property: This property says that globally optimal solution can be obtained by making a locally optimal solution (greedy). The choice made by a greedy algorithm may depend on earlier choices but not on future. It iteratively makes one greedy choice after another and reduces the given problem into a smaller one.

Optimal substructure: A problem exhibits optimal substructure if an optimal solution to the problem contains optimal solutions to the subproblems. That means we can solve subproblems and build up the solutions to solve larger problems.

23.4 Does Greedy Always Work?

Making locally optimal choices does not always work. Hence, greedy algorithms will not always give best solutions. We will see such examples in *Problems* section and in *Dynamic Programming* chapter.

23.5 Advantages and Disadvantages of Greedy Method

The main advantage of greedy method is that it is straightforward, easy to understand and easy to code. In greedy algorithms, once we make a decision, we do not have to spend time in re-examining already computed values.
Its main disadvantage is that for many problems there is no greedy algorithm. That means, in many cases there is no guarantee that making locally optimal improvements in a locally optimal solution gives the optimal global solution.

23.6 Greedy Applications

- Sorting: Selection sort, Topological sort
- Priority Queues: Heap sort
- Huffman coding compression algorithm
- Prim's and Kruskal's algorithms
- Shortest path in Weighted Graph [Dijkstra's]
- Coin change problem
- Fractional Knapsack problem
- Disjoint sets-UNION by size and UNION by height (or rank)
- Making change problem
- Job scheduling algorithm
- Greedy techniques can be used as approximation algorithm for complex problems

23.7 Understanding Greedy Technique

For better understanding let us go through an example. For more details, refer the topics of *Greedy* applications.

Huffman coding algorithm

Definition: Given a set of n characters from the alphabet A [each character c $\in$ A] and their associated frequency freq(c), find a binary code for each character c $\in$ A, such that $\sum_{c \in A}$ freq(c)|binarycode(c)| is minimum, where | binarycode(c)| represents the length of binary code of character c. That means sum of lengths of all character codes should be minimum [sum of each characters frequency multiplied by number of bits in the representation].

The basic idea behind Huffman coding algorithm is to use fewer bits for more frequently occurring characters. Huffman coding algorithm compresses the storage of data using variable length codes. We know that each character takes 8 bits for representation. But in general, we do not use all of them. Also, we use some characters more frequently than others. When reading a file, generally system reads 8 bits at a time to read a single character. But this coding scheme is inefficient. The reason for this is that some characters are more frequently used than other characters.

Let's say that the character *'e'* is used 10 times more frequently than the character *'q'*. It would then be advantageous for us to use a 7 bit code for e and a 9 bit code for q instead because that could reduce our overall message length.

On average, using Huffman coding on standard files can reduce them anywhere from 10% to 30% depending to the character frequencies. The idea behind the character coding is to give longer binary codes for less frequent characters and groups of characters. Also, the character coding is constructed in such a way that no two character codes are prefixes of each other. **Example:** Let's assume that after scanning a file we found the following character frequencies:

Character	Frequency
a	12
b	2
c	7
d	13
e	14
f	85

In this, create a binary tree for each character that also stores the frequency with which it occurs (as shown below).

The algorithm works as follows: Find the two binary trees in the list that store minimum frequencies at their nodes. Connect these two nodes at a newly created common node that will store no character but will store the sum of the frequencies of all the nodes connected below it. So our picture looks like follows:

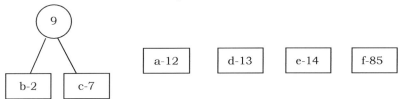

Repeat this process until only one tree is left:

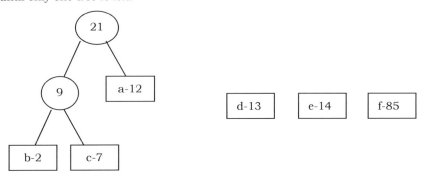

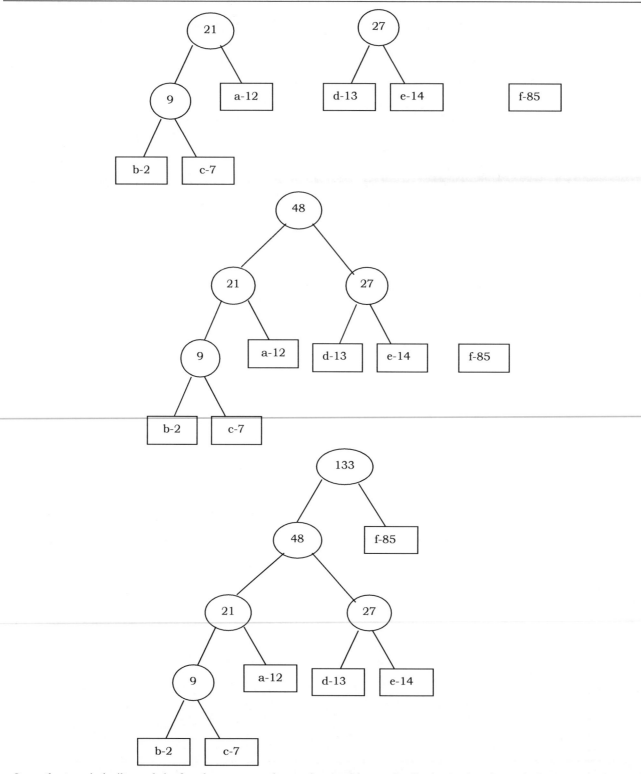

Once the tree is built, each leaf node corresponds to a letter with a code. To determine the code for a particular node, traverse from the root to the leaf node. For each move to the left, append a 0 to the code and for each move right append a 1. As a result for the above generated tree, we get the following codes:

Letter	Code
A	001
B	0000
C	0001
D	010
E	011
F	1

Calculating Bits Saved: Now, let us see how many bits that Huffman coding algorithm is saving. All we need to do for this calculation is see how many bits are originally used to store the data and subtract from that how many bits are used to store the data using the Huffman code.

In the above example, since we have six characters, let's assume each character is stored with a three bit code. Since there are 133 such characters (multiply total frequencies with 3), the total number of bits used is $3 * 133 = 399$. Using the Huffman coding frequencies we can calculate the new total number of bits used:

Letter	Code	Frequency	Total Bits
a	001	12	36
b	0000	2	8
c	0001	7	28
d	010	13	39
e	011	14	42
f	1	85	85
Total			238

Thus, we saved $399 - 238 = 161$ bits, or nearly 40% storage space.

```
HuffmanCodingAlgorithm(int A[], int n) {
    Initialize a priority queue, PQ, to contain the n elements in A;
    struct BinaryTreeNode *temp;
    for (i = 1; i<n; i++) {
        temp  = (struct *)malloc(sizeof(BinaryTreeNode));
        temp→left =  Delete-Min(PQ);
        temp→right =  Delete-Min(PQ);
        temp→data = temp→left→data + temp→right→data;
        Insert temp to PQ;
    }
    return PQ;
}
```

Time Complexity: $O(nlogn)$, since there will be *one* build_heap, $2n - 2$ delete_mins, and $n - 2$ inserts, on a priority queue that never has more than n elements. Refer *Priority Queues* chapter for details.

23.8 Problems on Greedy Algorithms

Problem-1 Given an array F with size n. Assume the array content $F[i]$ indicates the length of the ith file and we want to merge all these files into one single file. Check whether the following algorithm gives the best solution for this problem or not?
Algorithm: Merge the files contiguously. That means select the first two files and merge them. Then select the output of previous merge and merge with third file and keep going.
Note: Given two files A and B with sizes m and n, the complexity of merging is $O(m + n)$.

Solution: This algorithm will not produce the optimal solution. For counter example, let us consider the following file sizes array.

$$F = \{10,5,100,50,20,15\}$$

As per the above algorithm, we need to merge the first two files (10 and 5 size files) and as a result we get the following list of files. In the list below, 15 indicates the cost of merging two files with sizes 10 and 5.

$$\{15,100,50,20,15\}$$

Similarly, merging 15 with next file 100 produces: $\{115,50,20,15\}$. For the subsequent steps the list becomes,

$$\{165,20,15\}, \{185,15\}$$

Finally, $\{200\}$
The total cost of merging = Cost of all merging operations = $15 + 115 + 165 + 185 + 200 = 680$.

To see whether the above result is optimal or not, consider the order: $\{5, 10, 15, 20, 50, 100\}$. For this example, following the same approach, the total cost of merging $= 15 + 30 + 50 + 100 + 200 = 395$. So, the given algorithm is not giving the best (optimal) solution.

Problem-2 Similar to Problem-1, does the following algorithm gives optimal solution?
Algorithm: Merge the files in pairs. That means after the first step, the algorithm produces the $n/2$ intermediate files. For the next step, we need to consider these intermediate files and merge them in pairs and keep going.

Note: Sometimes this algorithm is called 2-way merging. Instead of two files at a time, if we merge K files at a time then we call it as K-way merging.

Solution: This algorithm will not produce the optimal solution and consider the previous example for counter example. As per the above algorithm, we need to merge the first pair of files (10 and 5 size files), second pair of files (100 and 50) and third pair of files (20 and 15). As a result we get the following list of files.

$$\{15, 150, 35\}$$

Similarly, merge the output in pairs and this step produces [in the below, the third element does not have pair element, so keep it same]:

$$\{165,35\}$$

Finally,

$$\{185\}$$

The total cost of merging = Cost of all merging operations = $15 + 150 + 35 + 165 + 185 = 550$. This is much more than 395 (of the previous problem). So, the given algorithm is not giving the best (optimal) solution.

Problem-3   In Problem-1, what is the best way to merge *all the files* into a single file?

Solution: Using greedy algorithm we can reduce the total time for merging the given files. Let us consider the following algorithm.

Algorithm
1. Store file sizes in a priority queue. The key of elements are file lengths.
2. Repeat the following until there is only one file:
   a. Extract two smallest elements X and Y.
   b. Merge X and Y and insert this new file in the priority queue.

Variant of same algorithm:
1. Sort the file sizes in ascending order.
2. Repeat the following until there is only one file:
   a. Take first two elements (smallest) X and Y.
   b. Merge X and Y and insert this new file in the sorted list.

To check the above algorithm, let us trace it with previous example. The given array is:

$$F = \{10,5,100,50,20,15\}$$

As per the above algorithm, sorting the list it becomes: $\{5, 10, 15, 20, 50, 100\}$. We need to merge the two smallest files (5 and 10 size files) and as a result we get the following list of files. In the list below, 15 indicates the cost of merging two files with sizes 10 and 5.

$$\{15,15,20,50,100\}$$

Similarly, merging two smallest elements (15 and 15) produces: $\{20,30,50,100\}$. For the subsequent steps the list becomes,

$$\{50,50,100\} \quad //merging\ 20\ and\ 30$$
$$\{100,100\} \quad //merging\ 20\ and\ 30$$

Finally,

$$\{200\}$$

The total cost of merging = Cost of all merging operations = $15 + 30 + 50 + 100 + 200 = 395$. So, this algorithm is producing the optimal solution for this merging problem.

Time Complexity: O($nlogn$) time using heaps to find best merging pattern plus the optimal cost of merging the files.

Problem-4   **Interval Scheduling Algorithm:** Given a set of n intervals $S = \{(start_i, end_i)|1 \le i \le n\}$. Let us assume that we want to find a maximum subset S' of S such that no pair of intervals in S' overlaps. Check whether the following algorithm works or not.

Algorithm:
while (S is not empty) {
    Select the interval I that overlaps the least number of other intervals.
    Add I to final solution set S'.
    Remove all intervals from S that overlap with I.
}

Solution: This algorithm does not solve the problem of finding a maximum subset of non-overlapping intervals. Consider the following intervals. The optimal solution is $\{M, O, N, K\}$. However, the interval that overlaps with the fewest others is C, and the given algorithm will select C first.

Problem-5   In Problem-4, if we select the interval that starts earliest (also not overlapping with already chosen intervals), does it gives optimal solution?

Solution: No. It will not give optimal solution. Let us consider the example below. It can be seen that optimal solution is 4 whereas the given algorithm gives 1.

Optimal Solution

←

Given Algorithm gives

←

Problem-6   In Problem-4, if we select the shortest interval (but is not overlapping the already chosen intervals), does it gives optimal solution?

Solution: This also will not give optimal solution. Let us consider the example below. It can be seen that optimal solution is 2 whereas the algorithm gives 1.

Optimal Solution

←

Current Alg. gives

←

Problem-7   For Problem-4, what is the optimal solution?

Solution: Now, let us concentrate on the optimal greedy solution.

Algorithm:

        Sort intervals according to the right-most ends [end times];
        for every consecutive interval {
            –   If the left-most end is after the right-most end of the last selected interval then we select this interval
            –   Otherwise we skip it and go to the next interval
        }

Time complexity = Time for sorting + Time for scanning = O(nlogn + n) = O(nlogn).

Problem-8   Consider the following problem.

Input: S = {(start$_i$, end$_i$)|1 ≤ i ≤ n} of intervals. The interval (start$_i$, end$_i$), we can treat as a request for a room for a class with time start$_i$ to time end$_i$.

Output: Find an assignment of classes to rooms that uses the fewest number of rooms.

Consider the following iterative algorithm. Assign as many classes as possible to the first room, then assign as many classes as possible to the second room, then assign as many classes as possible to the third room, etc. Does this algorithm give the best solution?

Note: In fact, this problem is similar to interval scheduling algorithm. The only difference is the application.

Solution: This algorithm does not solve the interval-coloring problem. Consider the following intervals:

	A		
B	C	D	
	E	F	G

Maximizing the number of classes in the first room results in having {B, C, F, G} in one room, and classes A, D, and E each in their own rooms, for a total of 4. The optimal solution is to put A in one room, { B, C, D } in another, and {E, F, G} in another, for a total of 3 rooms.

Problem-9   For Problem-8, consider the following algorithm. Process the classes in increasing order of start times. Assume that we are processing class C. If there is a room R such that R has been assigned to an earlier class, and C can be assigned to R without overlapping previously assigned classes, then assign C to R. Otherwise, put C in a new room. Does this algorithm solve the problem?

Solution: This algorithm solves the interval-coloring problem. Note that if the greedy algorithm creates a new room for the current class c_i, then because it examines classes in order of start times, c_i start point must intersect with the last class in all of the current rooms. Thus when greedy creates the last room, n, it is because the start time of the current class intersects with $n - 1$ other classes. But we know that for any single point in any class it can only intersect with at most s other class, it must then be that $n \leq S$. As s is a lower bound on the total number needed and greedy is feasible it is thus also optimal.

Note: For optimal solution refer Problem 7 and for code refer Problem-10.

Problem-10   Suppose we are given two arrays *Start*[1..*n*] and *Finish*[1..*n*] listing the start and finish times of each class. Our task is to choose the largest possible subset $X \in \{1, 2, ..., n\}$ so that for any pair $i, j \in X$, either *Start*[i] > *Finish*[j] or *Start*[j] > *Finish*[i]

Solution: Our aim is to finish the first class as early as possible, because that leaves us with the most remaining classes. We scan through the classes in order of finish time, whenever we encounter a class that doesn't conflict with latest class so far then take that class.

```
int LargestTasks(int Start[], int n,  int Finish []) {
    sort Finish[];
    rearrange Start[] to match;
    count = 1;
    X[count]  = 1;
    for (i = 2;  i<n;  i++) {
            if(Start[i] > Finish[X[count]])        {
                    count  = count + 1;
                    X[count] =  I;
            }
    }
    return X[1 .. count];
}
```

This algorithm clearly runs in O(*nlogn*) time due to sorting.

Problem-11   Consider the making change problem in country India. The input to this problem is an integer *M*. The output should be the minimum number of coins to make *M* rupees of change. In India, assume the available coins are 1, 5, 10, 20, 25, 50 rupees. Assume that we have an unlimited number of coins of each type.

For this problem, does the following algorithm produce optimal solution or not? Take as many coins as possible from the highest denominations. So for example, to make change for 234 rupees the greedy algorithms would take four 50 rupee coins, one 25 rupee coin, one 5 rupee coin, and four 1 rupee coins.

Solution: The greedy algorithm is not optimal for the problem of making change with the minimum number of coins when the denominations are 1, 5, 10, 20, 25, and 50. In order to make 40 rupees, the greedy algorithm would use three coins of 25, 10, and 5 rupees. The optimal solution is to use two 20-shilling coins.

Note: For optimal solution, refer *Dynamic Programming* chapter.

Problem-12   Let us assume that we are going for long drive between cities A and B. In preparation for our trip, we have downloaded a map that contains the distances in miles between all the petrol stations on our route. Assume that our cars tanks can hold petrol for *n* miles. Assume that the value *n* is given. Suppose we stop at every point, does it give the best solution?

Solution: Here the algorithm does not produce optimal solution. Obvious Reason: filling at each petrol station does not produce optimal solution.

Problem-13   For the problem Problem-12, stop if and only if you don't have enough petrol to make it to the next gas station, and if you stop, fill the tank up all the way. Prove or disprove that this algorithm correctly solves the problem.

Solution: The greedy approach works: We start our trip from *A* with a full tank. We check our map to determine the farthest petrol station on our route within *n* miles. Stop at that petrol station, fill up our tank and we check our map again to determine the farthest petrol station on our route within n miles from this stop. Repeat the process until we get to *B*.

Note: For code, refer *Dynamic Programming* chapter.

Problem-14   **Fractional Knapsack problem:** Given items $t_1, t_2, ..., t_n$ (items we might want to carry in our backpack) with associated weights $s_1, s_2, ..., s_n$ and benefit values $v_1, v_2, ..., v_n$, how can we maximize the total benefit considering that we are subject to an absolute weight limit *C*?

Solution:
Algorithm:
1)   Compute value per size density for each item $d_i = \frac{v_i}{s_i}$.
2)   Sort each item by their value density.
3)   Take as much as possible of the density item not already in the bag

Time Complexity: O(*n logn*) for sorting and O(*n*) for greedy selections.

Note: The items can be entered into a priority queue and retrieved one by one until either the bag is full or all items have been selected. This actually has a better runtime of O(*n* + *clogn*) where *c* is the number of items that actually get selected in the solution. There is a savings in runtime if $c = O(n)$, but otherwise there is no change in the complexity.

DIVIDE AND CONQUER ALGORITHMS

Chapter-24

24.1 Introduction

In *Greedy* chapter, we have seen that for many problems Greedy strategy failed to provide optimal solutions. Among those problems, there are some that can be easily solved by using *Divide and Conquer* (D & C) technique.

Divide and Conquer is an important algorithm design technique based on recursion. The *D & C* algorithm works by recursively breaking down a problem into two or more sub problems of the same type, until they become simple enough to be solved directly. The solutions to the sub problems are then combined to give a solution to the original problem.

24.2 What is Divide and Conquer Strategy?

The D & C strategy solves a problem by:

1) *Divide*: Breaking the problem into sub problems that are themselves smaller instances of the same type of problem.
2) *Recursion*: Recursively solving these sub problems.
3) *Conquer*: Appropriately combining their answers.

24.3 Does Divide and Conquer Always Work?

It's not possible to solve all the problems with Divide & Conquer technique. As per the definition of D & C the recursion solves the subproblems which are of same type. For all problems it is not possible to find the subproblems which are same size and D & C is not a choice for all problems.

24.4 Divide and Conquer Visualization

For better understanding, consider the following visualization. Assume that n is the size of original problem. As described above, we can see that the problem is divided into sub problems with each of size n/b (for some constant b). We solve the sub problems recursively and combine their solutions to get the solution for the original problem.

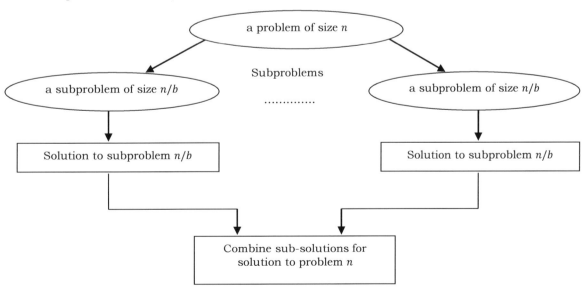

```
DivideAndConquer ( P ) {
    if( small ( P ) )
        // P is very small so that a solution is obvious
```

```
                return solution ( n );
                divide the problem P into k sub problems P1, P2, ..., Pk;
                return (
                    Combine (
                        DivideAndConquer ( P1 ),
                        DivideAndConquer ( P2 ),
                        ...
                        DivideAndConquer ( Pk )
                    )
                );
        }
```

24.5 Understanding Divide and Conquer

For clear understanding of $D \& C$, let us consider a story. There was an old man who was a rich farmer and had seven sons. He was afraid that when he died, his land and his possessions would be divided among his seven sons, and that they would quarrel with one another. He gathered them together and showed them seven sticks that he had tied together and told them that anyone who could break the bundle would inherit everything. They all tried, but no one could break the bundle. Then the old man untied the bundle and broke the sticks one by one. The brothers decided that they should stay together and work together and succeed together. The moral for problem solvers is different. If we can't solve the problem, divide it into parts, and solve one part at a time.

In earlier chapters we have already solved many problems based on D & C strategy: like Binary Search, Merge Sort, Quick Sort, etc.... Refer those topics to get an idea of how D & C works. Below are few other real-time problems which can easily be solved with D & C strategy. For all these problems we can find the subproblems which are similar to original problem.

1. Looking for a name in a phone book: We have a phone book with names in alphabetical order. Given a name, how do we find whether that name is there in the phone book or not?
2. Breaking a stone into dust: We want to convert a stone into dust (very small stones).
3. Finding the exit in a hotel: We are at the end of a very long hotel lobby with a long series of doors, with one door next to you. We are looking for the door that leads to the exit.
4. Finding our car in a parking lot.

24.6 Advantages of Divide and Conquer

Solving difficult problems: $D \& C$ is a powerful method for solving difficult problems. As an example, consider Tower of Hanoi problem. This requires breaking the problem into subproblems, solving the trivial cases and combining subproblems to solve the original problem. Dividing the problem into subproblems so that subproblems can be combined again is a major difficulty in designing a new algorithm. For many such problems D & C provides simple solution..

Parallelism: Since D & C allows us to solve the subproblems independently, they allow execution in multi-processor machines, especially shared-memory systems where the communication of data between processors does not need to be planned in advance, because different subproblems can be executed on different processors

Memory access: D & C algorithms naturally tend to make efficient use of memory caches. This is because once a subproblem is small, all its subproblems can be solved within the cache, without accessing the slower main memory.

24.7 Disadvantages of Divide and Conquer

One disadvantage of $D \& C$ approach is that recursion is slow. This is because of the overhead of the repeated subproblem calls. Also, $D \& C$ approach needs stack for storing the calls (the state at each point in the recursion). Actually this depends upon the implementation style. With large enough recursive base cases, the overhead of recursion can become negligible for many problems.

Another problem with D & C is that, for some problems, it may be more complicated than an iterative approach. For example, to add n numbers, a simple loop to add them up in sequence is much easier than a divide-and-conquer approach that breaks the set of numbers into two halves, adds them recursively, and then adds the sums.

24.8 Master Theorem

As stated above, in $D \& C$ method, we solve the sub problems recursively. All problems are generally defined in terms of recursive definitions. These recursive problems can easily be solved using Master theorem. For details on Master theorem refer *Introduction to Analysis of Algorithms* chapter. Just for the continuity, let us reconsider the Master theorem.

If the recurrence is of the form $T(n) = aT(\frac{n}{b}) + \Theta(n^k log^p n)$, where $a \geq 1$, $b > 1, k \geq 0$ and p is a real number, then the complexity can be directly given as:

1) If $a > b^k$, then $T(n) = \Theta(n^{log_b^a})$
2) If $a = b^k$
   a. If $p > -1$, then $T(n) = \Theta(n^{log_b^a} log^{p+1} n)$
   b. If $p = -1$, then $T(n) = \Theta(n^{log_b^a} log log n)$
   c. If $p < -1$, then $T(n) = \Theta(n^{log_b^a})$
3) If $a < b^k$
   a. If $p \geq 0$, then $T(n) = \Theta(n^k log^p n)$
   b. If $p < 0$, then $T(n) = O(n^k)$

24.9 Divide and Conquer Applications

- Binary Search
- Merge Sort
- Quick Sort
- Median Finding
- Min and Max Finding
- Matrix Multiplication
- Closest Pair problem

24.10 Problems on Divide and Conquer

Problem-1   Let us consider an algorithm A which solves problems by dividing them into five subproblems of half the size, recursively solving each subproblem, and then combining the solutions in linear time. What is the complexity of this algorithm?

Solution: Let us assume that the input size is n and $T(n)$ defines the solution to the given problem. As per the description, algorithm divides the problem into 5 sub problems with each of size $\frac{n}{2}$. So we need to solve $5T(\frac{n}{2})$ subproblems. After solving these sub problems the given array (linear time) is scanned to combine these solutions. The total recurrence algorithm for this problem can be given as:

$$T(n) = 5T\left(\frac{n}{2}\right) + O(n)$$

Using Master theorem (of D & C), we get the complexity as $O(n^{log_2^5}) \approx O(n^{2+}) \approx O(n^3)$

Problem-2   Similar to Problem-1, an algorithm B solves problems of size n by recursively solving two subproblems of size $n - 1$ and then combining the solutions in constant time. What is the complexity of this algorithm?

Solution: Let us assume that input size is n and $T(n)$ defines the solution to the given problem. As per the description of algorithm we divide the problem into 9 sub problems with each of size $\frac{n}{3}$. So we need to solve $9T(\frac{n}{3})$ sub problems. After solving the sub problems, the algorithm takes quadratic time to combine these solutions. The total recurrence algorithm for this problem can be given as:

$$T(n) = 2T(n - 1) + O(1)$$

Using Master theorem (of *Subtract and Conquer*), we get the complexity as $O\left(n^0 2^{\frac{n}{1}}\right) = O(2^n)$. (Refer *Introduction* chapter for more details).

Problem-3   Again similar to Problem-1, another algorithm C solves problems of size n by dividing them into nine subproblems of size $\frac{n}{3}$, recursively solving each subproblem, and then combining the solutions in $O(n^2)$ time. What is the complexity of this algorithm?

Solution: Let us assume that the input size is n and $T(n)$ defines the solution to the given problem. As per the description of algorithm we are dividing the problem in to 9 sub problems with each of size $\frac{n}{3}$. So we need to solve $9T(\frac{n}{3})$ subproblems. After solving the subproblems, the algorithm is taking quadratic time to combine these solutions. The total recurrence algorithm for this problem can be given as:

$$T(n) = 9T\left(\frac{n}{3}\right) + O(n^2)$$

Using D & C Master theorem, we get the complexity as $O(n^2 log n)$.

Problem-4   Write a recurrence and solve it.
```
void function(n) {
    if(n > 1) {
        printf(("*");
        function(n/2);
```

$$\text{function}\left(\tfrac{n}{2}\right);$$

```
        }
    }
```

Solution: Let us assume that the input size is n and $T(n)$ defines the solution to the given problem. As per the given code after printing the character, and dividing the problem in to 2 subproblems with each of size $\frac{n}{2}$ and solving them. So we need to solve $2T(\frac{n}{2})$ subproblems.

After solving these subproblems, the algorithm is not doing anything for combining the solutions. The total recurrence algorithm for this problem can be given as:

$$T(n) = 2T\left(\frac{n}{2}\right) + O(1)$$

Using Master theorem (of D & C), we get the complexity as $O(n^{\log_2^2}) \approx O(n^1) = O(n)$.

Problem-5   Given an array, give an algorithm for finding the maximum and minimum.

Solution: Refer *Selection Algorithms* chapter.

Problem-6   Discuss Binary Search and its complexity.

Solution: Refer *Searching* chapter for discussion on Binary Search.

Analysis: Let us assume that input size is n and $T(n)$ defines the solution to the given problem. The elements are in sorted order. In binary search we take the middle element and check whether the element to be searched is equal to that element or not. If it is equal then we return that element.

If the element to be searched is greater than the middle element then we consider the left sub-array for finding the element and discard the right sub-array. Similarly, if the element to be searched is less than the middle element then we consider the right sub-array for finding the element and discard the left sub-array.

What this means is, in both the cases we are discarding half of the sub-array and considering the remaining half only. Also, at every iteration we are dividing the elements into two equal halves.

As per the above discussion every time we divide the problem into 2 sub problems with each of size $\frac{n}{2}$ and solve one $T(\frac{n}{2})$ sub problem. The total recurrence algorithm for this problem can be given as:

$$T(n) = T\left(\frac{n}{2}\right) + O(1)$$

Using Master theorem (of D & C), we get the complexity as $O(\log n)$.

Problem-7   Consider the modified version of binary search. Let us assume that the array is divided into 3 equal parts (ternary search) instead of two equal parts. Write the recurrence for this ternary search and find its complexity.

Solution: From the discussion on Problem-5, binary search has the recurrence relation: $T(n) = T\left(\frac{n}{2}\right) + O(1)$. Similar to Problem-5 discussion, instead of 2 in the recurrence relation we use "3". That indicates that we are dividing the array into 3 sub-arrays with equal size and considering only one of them. So, the recurrence for the ternary search can be given as:

$$T(n) = T\left(\frac{n}{3}\right) + O(1)$$

Using Master theorem (of *D & C*), we get the complexity as $O(\log_3^n) \approx O(\log n)$ (we don't have to worry about the base of $\log$ as they are constants).

Problem-8   In Problem-5, what if we divide the array into two sets of sizes approximately one-third and two-thirds.

Solution: We now consider a slightly modified version of ternary search in which only one comparison is made which creates two partitions, one of roughly $\frac{n}{3}$ elements and the other of $\frac{2n}{3}$. Here the worst case comes when the recursive call is on the larger $\frac{2n}{3}$ element part. So the recurrence corresponding to this worst case is:

$$T(n) = T\left(\frac{2n}{3}\right) + O(1)$$

Using Master theorem (of D & C), we get the complexity as $O(\log n)$. It is interesting to note that we will get the same results for general k-ary search (as long as k is a fixed constant which does not depend on n) as n approaches infinity.

Problem-9   Discuss Merge Sort and its complexity.

Solution: Refer *Sorting* chapter for discussion on Merge Sort. In Merge Sort, if the number of elements are greater than 1 then divide them into two equal subsets, the algorithm is recursively invoked on the subsets, and the returned sorted subsets are merged to provide a sorted list of the original set. The recurrence equation of the Merge Sort algorithm is:

$$T(n) = \begin{cases} 2T\left(\frac{n}{2}\right) + O(n), & \text{if } n > 1 \\ 0 & , \text{if } n = 1 \end{cases}$$

If we solve this recurrence using D & C Master theorem gives O($n\log n$) complexity.

Problem-10   Discuss Quick Sort and its complexity.

Solution: Refer *Sorting* chapter for discussion on Quick Sort. For Quick Sort we have different complexities for best case and worst case.

Best Case: In *Quick Sort,* if the number of elements is greater than 1 then they are divided into two equal subsets, and the algorithm is recursively invoked on the subsets. After solving the sub problems we don't need to combine them. This is because in *Quick Sort* they are already in sorted order. But, we need to scan the complete elements to partition the elements. The recurrence equation of *Quick Sort* best case is

$$T(n) = \begin{cases} 2T\left(\frac{n}{2}\right) + O(n), if \ n > 1 \\ 0 \quad\quad\quad\quad , if \ n = 1 \end{cases}$$

If we solve this recurrence using Master theorem of D & C gives O($nlogn$) complexity.

Worst Case: In the worst case, Quick Sort divides the input elements into two sets and one of them contains only one element. That means other set has $n - 1$ elements to be sorted. Let us assume that the input size is n and $T(n)$ defines the solution to the given problem. So we need to solve $T(n-1)$, $T(1)$ subproblems. But to divide the input into two sets Quick Sort needs one scan of the input elements (this takes O(n)).

After solving these sub problems the algorithm takes only a constant time to combine these solutions. The total recurrence algorithm for this problem can be given as:$T(n) = T(n-1) + O(1) + O(n)$.

This is clearly a summation recurrence equation. So, $T(n) = \frac{n(n+1)}{2} = O(n^2)$.

Note: For the average case analysis, refer *Sorting* chapter.

Problem-11   Given an infinite array in which the first n cells contain integers in sorted order and the rest of the cells are filled with some special symbol (say, $). Assume we do not know the n value. Give an algorithm that takes an integer K as input and finds a position in the array containing K, if such a position exists, in O($logn$) time.

Solution: Since we need an O($logn$) algorithm, we should not search for all the elements of the given list (which gives O(n) complexity). To get O($logn$) complexity one possibility is to use binary search. But in the given scenario we cannot use binary search as we do not know the end of list. Our first problem is to find the end of the list. To do that, we can start at first element and keep searching with doubled index. That means we first search at index 1 then, 2,4,8 ...

```
int FindInInfiniteSeries(int A[])  {
    int mid, l = r = 1;
    while( A[r] != '$') {
        l = r;
        r = r × 2;
    }
    while( r - 1 > 1 ) {
        mid = (r - 1)/2 + l;
        if( A[mid] == '$')
                r = mid;
        else      l = mid;
    }
}
```

It is clear that, once we identified a possible interval A[$i,...,2i$] in which K might be, its length is at most n (since we have only n numbers in the array A), so searching for K using binary search takes O($logn$) time.

Problem-12   Given a sorted array of non-repeated integers A[1..n], check whether there is an index i for which A[i] = i. Give a divide-and-conquer algorithm that runs in time O($logn$).

Solution: We can't use binary search on the array as it is. If we want to keep the O($logn$) property of the solution we have to implement our own binary search. If we modify the array (in place or in a copy) and subtract i from A[i], we can then use binary search. The complexity for doing so is O(n).

Problem-13   We are given two sorted lists of size n. Give an algorithm for finding the median element in the union of the two lists.

Solution: We use the Merge Sort process. Use *merge* procedure of merge sort (refer *Sorting* chapter). Keep track of count while comparing elements of two arrays. If count becomes n (since there are 2n elements), we have reached the median. Take the average of the elements at indexes $n - 1$ and n in the merged array.

Time Complexity: O(n).

Problem-14   Can we give algorithm if the sizes of two lists are not same?

Solution: The solution is similar to previous problem. Let us assume that the lengths of two lists are m and n. In this case we need to stop when counter reaches ($m + n$)/2.

Time Complexity: O(($m + n$)/2).

Problem-15   Can we improve the time complexity of Problem-13 to O($logn$)?

Solution: Yes, using D & C approach. Let us assume that the given two lists are $L1$ and $L2$.

Algorithm:

1. Find the medians of the given sorted input arrays $L1[]$ and $L2[]$. Assume that those medians are $m1$ and $m2$.
2. If $m1$ and $m2$ are equal then return $m1$ (or $m2$).
3. If $m1$ is greater than $m2$, then the final median will be below two sub arrays.
4. From first element of $L1$ to $m1$.
5. From $m2$ to last element of $L2$.
6. If $m2$ is greater than $m1$, then median is present in one of the two sub arrays below.
7. From $m1$ to last element of $L1$.
8. From first element of $L2$ to $m2$.
9. Repeat the above process until size of both the sub arrays becomes 2.
10. If size of the two arrays is 2 then use the formula below to get the median.
11. Median $= (max(L1[0], L2[0]) + min(L1[1], L2[1])/2$

Time Complexity: $O(logn)$. Since we are considering only half of the input and throwing the remaining half.

Problem-16 Given an input array A. Let us assume that there can be duplicates in the list. Now search for an element in the list in such a way that we get the highest index if there are duplicates.

Solution: Refer *Searching* chapter.

Problem-17 Discuss Strassen's Matrix Multiplication Algorithm using Divide and Conquer. That means, given two $n \times n$ matrices, A and B, compute the $n \times n$ matrix $C = A \times B$, where the elements of C are given by

$$C_{i,j} = \sum_{k=0}^{n-1} A_{i,k} B_{k,j}$$

Solution: Before Strassen's algorithm, first let us see the basic divide and conquer algorithm. The general approach we follow for solving this problem is given below. To determine, $C[i,j]$ we need to multiply the ith row of A with j^{th} column of B.

```
// Initialize C.
for i = 1 to n
  for j = 1 to n
    for k = 1 to n
      C[i, j] += A[i, k] * B[k, j];
```

The matrix multiplication problem can be solved with D & C technique. To implement a D & C algorithm we need to break the given problem into several subproblems that are similar to the original one. In this instance we view each of the $n \times n$ matrices as a 2×2 matrix, the elements of which are $\frac{n}{2} \times \frac{n}{2}$ submatrices. So, the original matrix multiplication, $C = A \times B$ can be written as:

$$\begin{bmatrix} C_{1,1} & C_{1,2} \\ C_{2,1} & C_{2,2} \end{bmatrix} = \begin{bmatrix} A_{1,1} & A_{1,2} \\ A_{2,1} & A_{2,2} \end{bmatrix} \times \begin{bmatrix} B_{1,1} & B_{1,2} \\ B_{2,1} & B_{2,2} \end{bmatrix}$$

where each $A_{i,j}$, $B_{i,j}$, and $C_{i,j}$ is a $\frac{n}{2} \times \frac{n}{2}$ matrix.

From the given definition o f $C_{i,j}$, we get that the result sub matrices can be computed as follows:

$$C_{1,1} = A_{1,1} \times B_{1,1} + A_{1,2} \times B_{2,1}$$
$$C_{1,2} = A_{1,1} \times B_{1,2} + A_{1,2} \times B_{2,2}$$
$$C_{2,1} = A_{2,1} \times B_{1,1} + A_{2,2} \times B_{2,1}$$
$$C_{2,2} = A_{2,1} \times B_{1,2} + A_{2,2} \times B_{2,2}$$

Here the symbols + and × are taken to mean addition and multiplication (respectively) of $\frac{n}{2} \times \frac{n}{2}$ matrices.

In order to compute the original $n \times n$ matrix multiplication we must compute eight $\frac{n}{2} \times \frac{n}{2}$ matrix products (*divide*) followed by four $\frac{n}{2} \times \frac{n}{2}$ matrix sums (*conquer*). Since matrix addition is an $O(n^2)$ operation, the total running time for the multiplication operation is given by the recurrence:

$$T(n) = \begin{cases} O(1) & , for\ n = 1 \\ 8T\left(\frac{n}{2}\right) + O(n^2) & , for\ n > 1 \end{cases}$$

Using master theorem, we get, $T(n) = O(n^3)$.

Fortunately, it turns out that one of the eight matrix multiplications is redundant (found by Strassen). Consider the following series of seven $\frac{n}{2} \times \frac{n}{2}$ matrices:

$$M_0 = \left(A_{1,1} + A_{2,2}\right) \times \left(B_{1,1} + B_{2,2}\right)$$
$$M_1 = \left(A_{1,2} - A_{2,2}\right) \times \left(B_{2,1} + B_{2,2}\right)$$
$$M_2 = \left(A_{1,1} - A_{2,1}\right) \times \left(B_{1,1} + B_{1,2}\right)$$

$$M_3 = (A_{1,1} + A_{1,2}) \times B_{2,2}$$
$$M_4 = A_{1,1} \times (B_{1,2} - B_{2,2})$$
$$M_5 = A_{2,2} \times (B_{2,1} - B_{1,1})$$
$$M_6 = (A_{21} + A_{2,2}) \times B_{1,1}$$

Each equation above has only one multiplication. Ten additions and seven multiplications are required to compute M_0 through M_6. Given M_0 through M_6, we can compute the elements of the product matrix C as follows:

$$C_{1,1} = M_0 + M_1 - M_3 + M_5$$
$$C_{1,2} = M_3 + M_4$$
$$C_{2,1} = M_5 + M_6$$
$$C_{2,2} = M_0 - M_2 + M_4 - M_6$$

This approach requires seven $\frac{n}{2} \times \frac{n}{2}$ matrix multiplications and $18 \ \frac{n}{2} \times \frac{n}{2}$ additions. Therefore, the worst-case running time is given by the following recurrence:

$$T(n) = \begin{cases} O(1) & , for \ n = 1 \\ 7T\left(\frac{n}{2}\right) + O(n^2) & , for \ n = 1 \end{cases}$$

Using master theorem, we get, $T(n) = O\left(n^{\log_2^7}\right) = O(n^{2.81})$.

Problem-18 **Stock Pricing Problem:** Consider the stock price of *CareerMonk.com* in n consecutive days. That means the input consists of an array with stock prices of the company. We know that stock price will not be the same on all the days. In the input stock prices there may be dates where the stock is high when we can sell the current holdings and there may be days when we can buy the stock. Now our problem is to find the day on which we can buy the stock and the day on which we can sell the stock so that we can make maximum profit.

Solution: As given in problem let us assume that the input is an array with stock prices [integers]. Let us say the given array is $A[1],...,A[n]$. From this array we have to find two days [one for buy and one for sell] in such a way that we can make maximum profit. Also, another point to make is that buy date should be before sell date. One simple approach is to look at all possible buy and sell dates.

```
void StockStrategy(int A[], int n, int *buyDateIndex, int *sellDateIndex) {
        int j, profit=0;
        *buyDateIndex =0; *sellDateIndex =0;
        //indicates buy date
        for (int i  = 1; i < n; i++)
                //indicates sell date
                for( j  = i; j < n;  j++)
                        if(A[j] - A[i] > profit)              {
                                profit = A[j] - A[i];
                                *buyDateIndex = i;
                                *sellDateIndex = j;
                        }
}
```

The two nested loops takes $n(n + 1)/2$ computations, so this takes time $\Theta(n^2)$.

Problem-19 For Problem-18, can we improve the time complexity?

Solution: Yes, by opting for the Divide-and-Conquer $\Theta(nlogn)$ solution. Divide the input list into two parts and recursively find the solution in both the parts. Here, we get three cases:

* *buyDateIndex* and *sellDateIndex* both are in the earlier time period.
* *buyDateIndex* and *sellDateIndex* both are in the later time period.
* *buyDateIndex* is in the earlier part and *sellDateIndex* is in the later part of the time period.

The first two cases can be solved with recursion. The third case needs care. This is because *buyDateIndex* is one side and *sellDateIndex* is on other side. In this case we need to find the minimum and maximum prices in the two sub-parts and this we can solve in linear-time.

```
void StockStrategy(int A[], int left, int right) {
        //Declare the necessary variables;
        if(left + 1 = right)
                return (0, left, left);

        mid   = left + (right - left) / 2;

        (profitLeft, buyDateIndexLeft, sellDateIndexLeft) =  StockStrategy(A, left, mid);
        (profitRight, buyDateIndexRight, sellDateIndexRight)  = StockStrategy(A, mid, right);
        minLeft  = Min(A, left, mid);

        maxRight  = Max(A, mid, right);
        profit  = A[maxRight] - A[minLeft];
```

```
        if(profitLeft > max{profitRight, profit})
                return (profitLeft, buyDateIndexLeft, sellDateIndexLeft);
        else if(profitRight > max{profitLeft, profit})
                return (profitRight, buyDateIndexRight, sellDateIndexRight);
        else    return (profit, minLeft, maxRight);
}
```

Algorithm *StockStrategy* is used recursively on two problems of half the size of the input, and in addition $\Theta(n)$ time is spent searching for the maximum and minimum prices. So the time complexity is characterized by the recurrence $T(n) = 2T(n/2) + \Theta(n)$ and by the Master theorem we get O(nlogn).

Problem-20   We are testing "unbreakable" laptops and our goal is to find out how unbreakable they really are. In particular, we work in an n-story building and want to find out the lowest floor from which we can drop the laptop without breaking it (call this "the ceiling"). Suppose we are given two laptops and want to find the highest ceiling possible. Give an algorithm that minimizes the number of tries we need to make $f(n)$ (hopefully, $f(n)$ is sub-linear, as a linear $f(n)$ yields a trivial solution).

Solution: For the given problem, we cannot use binary search as we cannot divide the problem and solve it recursively. Let us take some example for understanding the scenario. Let us say 14 is the answer. That means we need 14 drops for finding the answer. First we drop from height 14, if it breaks we try all floors from 1 to 13. If it doesn't break then we are left 13 drops, so we will drop it from $14 + 13 + 1 = 28^{th}$ floor. The reason being if it breaks at 28th floor we can try all the floors from 15 to 27 in 12 drops (total of 14 drops). Now if it did not break then we are left with 11 drops and we can try to figure out the floor in 14 drops.

From the above example, it can be seen that we first tried with a gap of 14 floors, and then followed by 13 floors, then 12 and so on. So if the answer is k then we are trying the intervals at $k, k-1, k-2 \ldots 1$. Given number of floors is n, we have to relate these two. Since the maximum floor from which we can try is n, the total skips should be less than n. This gives:

$$k + (k-1) + (k-2) + \cdots + 1 \le n$$
$$\frac{k(k+1)}{2} \le n$$
$$k \le \sqrt{n}$$

Complexity of this process is O($\sqrt{n}$).

Problem-21   Given n numbers, check if any two are equal.

Solution: Refer *Searching* chapter.

Problem-22   Give an algorithm to find out if an integer is a square? E.g. 16 is, 15 isn't.

Solution: Initially let us say $i = 2$. Compute the value $i \times i$ and see if it is equal to the given number. If it is equal then we are done otherwise increment the i vlaue. Continue this process until we reach $i \times i$ greater than or equal to the given number.

Time Complexity: O($\sqrt{n}$). Space Complexity: O(1).

Problem-23   Given an array of $2n$ integers in the following format $a1\ a2\ a3 \ldots an\ b1\ b2\ b3 \ldots bn$. Shuffle the array to $a1\ b1\ a2\ b2\ a3\ b3 \ldots an\ bn$ without any extra memory.

Solution: Let us take an example (for brute force solution refer *Searching* chapter)

1) Start with the array: $a1\ a2\ a3\ a4\ b1\ b2\ b3\ b4$
2) Split the array into two halves: $a1\ a2\ a3\ a4 : b1\ b2\ b3\ b4$
3) Exchange elements around the center: exchange $a3\ a4$ with $b1\ b2$ you get: $a1\ a2\ b1\ b2\ a3\ a4\ b3\ b4$
4) Split $a1\ a2\ b1\ b2$ into $a1\ a2 : b1\ b2$ then split $a3\ a4\ b3\ b4$ into $a3\ a4 : b3\ b4$
5) Exchange elements around the center for each subarray you get: $a1\ b1\ a2\ b2$ and $a3\ b3\ a4\ b4$

Please note that this solution only handles the case when $n = 2^i$ where $i = 0, 1, 2, 3$ etc. In our example $n = 2^2 = 4$ which makes it easy to recursively split the array into two halves. The basic idea behind swapping elements around the center before calling the recursive function is to produce smaller size problems. A solution with linear time complexity may be achieved if the elements are of specific nature. For example you can calculate the new position of the element using the value of the element itself. This is a hashing technique.

```
    void ShuffleArray(int A[], int l, int r) {
        //Array center
        int c = l + (r-l)/2, q = 1 + l + (c-l)/2;
        if(l == r) //Base case when the array has only one element
                return;
        for (int k = 1, i = q; i <= c; i++, k++) {
                //Swap elements around the center
                int tmp = A[i];    A[i] = A[c + k];    A[c + k] = tmp;
        }
```

```
    ShuffleArray(A, l, c);              //Recursively call the function on the left and right
    ShuffleArray(A, c + 1, r); );       //Recursively call the function on the right
}
```

Time Complexity: O($nlogn$).

Problem-24 **Nuts and Bolts Problem:** Given a set of n nuts of different sizes and n bolts such that there is a one-to-one correspondence between the nuts and the bolts, find for each nut its corresponding bolt. Assume that we can only compare nuts to bolts (cannot compare nuts to nuts and bolts to bolts).

Solution: Refer *Sorting* chapter.

Problem-25 **Maximum Value Contiguous Subsequence:** Given a sequence of n numbers $A(1)...A(n)$, give an algorithm for finding a contiguous subsequence $A(i)...A(j)$ for which the sum of elements in the subsequence is maximum. **Example**: {-2, **11, -4, 13**, -5, 2} → 20 and {1, -3, **4, -2, -1, 6**} → 7.

Solution: Divide this input into two halves. The maximum contiguous subsequence sum can occur in one of 3 ways:

- Case 1: It can be completely in the first half
- Case 2: It can be completely in the second half
- Case 3: It begins in the first half and ends in the second half

We begin by looking at case 3. To avoid the nested loop that results from considering all $n/2$ starting points and $n/2$ ending points independently. Replace two nested loops by two consecutive loops. The consecutive loops, each of size $n/2$ combine to require only linear work. Any contiguous subsequence that begins in the first half and ends in the second half must include both the last element of the first half and first element of the second half. What we can do in cases 1 and 2 is apply the same strategy of dividing into more halves. In summary, we do the following:

1) Recursively compute the maximum contiguous subsequence that resides entirely in the first half.
2) Recursively compute the maximum contiguous subsequence that resides entirely in the second half.
3) Compute, via two consecutive loops, the maximum contiguous subsequence sum that begins in the first half but ends in the second half.
4) Choose the largest of the three sums.

```
int MaxSumRec(int A[], int left, int right) {
    int MaxLeftBorderSum = 0, MaxRightBorderSum = 0;
    int LeftBorderSum = 0, RightBorderSum = 0;
    int mid = left + (right - left) / 2;

    if(left == right) // Base Case
        return A[left] > 0 ? A[left] : 0;

    int MaxLeftSum = MaxSumRec(A, left, mid);
    int MaxRightSum = MaxSumRec(A, mid + 1, right);

    for (int i = mid; i >= left; i--) {
        LeftBorderSum += A[i];
        if(LeftBorderSum > MaxLeftBorderSum)
            MaxLeftBorderSum = LeftBorderSum;
    }

    for (int j = mid + 1; j <= right; j++) {
        RightBorderSum += A[j];
        if(RightBorderSum > MaxRightBorderSum)
            MaxRightBorderSum = RightBorderSum;
    }
    return Max(MaxLeftSum, MaxRightSum,MaxLeftBorderSum + MaxRightBorderSum);
}

int MaxSubsequenceSum(int A, int n) {
    return n > 0 ? MaxSumRec(A, 0, n - 1) : 0;
}
```

The base case cost is 1. The program performs two recursive calls plus the linear work involved in computing the maximum sum for case 3. The recurrence relation is:

$$T(1) = 1$$
$$T(n) = 2T(n/2) + n$$

Using $D \& C$ Master theorem, we get the time complexity as $T(n) =$ O($nlogn$).

Note: For efficient solution refer *Dynamic Programming* chapter.

Problem-26 **Closest-Pair of Points:** Given a set of n points $S = \{p_1, p_2, p_3, ..., p_n\}$, where $p_i = (x_i, y_i)$. Find the pair of points having smallest distance among all pairs (assume that all points are in one dimension).

Solution: Let us assume that we have sorted the points. Since the points are in one dimension, all the points are in a line after we sort them (either on X-axis or Y-axis). The complexity of sorting is O($nlogn$). After sorting we can go through them to find the consecutive points with least difference. So the problem in one dimension is solved in $O(nlogn)$ time which is mainly dominated by sorting time.

Time Complexity: $O(nlogn)$.

Problem-27   For the Problem-26, how do we solve if the points are in two dimensional space?

Solution: Before going to algorithm, let us consider the following mathematical equation:

$$distance(p_1, p_2) = \sqrt{(x_1 - x_2)^2 - (y_1 - y_2)^2}$$

The above equation calculates the distance between two points $p_1 = (x_1, y_1)$ and $p_2 = (x_2, y_2)$.

Brute Force Solution:

- Calculate the distances between all the pairs of points. From n points there are n_{c_2} ways of selecting 2 points. $(n_{c_2} = O(n^2))$.
- After finding distances for all n^2 possibilities, we select the one which is giving the minimum distance and this takes $O(n^2)$.

The overall time complexity is $O(n^2)$.

Problem-28   Give $O(nlogn)$ solution for *closest pair* problem (Problem-27)?

Solution: To find $O(nlogn)$ solution, we can use the $D \& C$ technique. Before starting the divide-and-conquer process let us assume that the points are sorted by increasing x-coordinate. Divide the points into two equal halves based on median of x- coordinates. That means problem is divided into that of finding the closest pair in each of the two halves. For simplicity let us consider the following algorithm to understand the process.

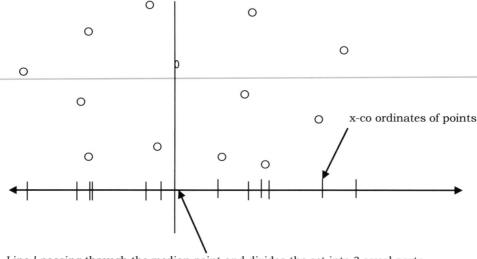

Line l passing through the median point and divides the set into 2 equal parts

Algorithm:

- Sort the given points in S (given set of points) based on their x −coordinates. Partition S into two subsets, S_1 and S_2, about the line l through median of S. This step is the *Divide* part of the $D \& C$ technique.
- Find the closest-pairs in S_1 and S_2 and call them L and R recursively.
- Now, steps-4 to 8 form the Combining component of the $D \& C$ technique.
- Let us assume that $\delta = min(L, R)$.
- Eliminate points that are farther than δ apart from l.
- Consider the remaining points and sort based on their y-coordinates.
- Scan the remaining points in the y order and compute the distances of each point to all its neighbors that are distanced no more than $2 \times \delta$ (that's the reason for sorting according to y).
- If any of these distances is less than δ then update δ.

Combining the results in linear time

Let $\delta = min(L, R)$, where L is the solution to first sub problem and R is the solution to second sub problem. The possible candidates for closest-pair, which are across the dividing line, are those which are less than δ distance from the line. So we need only the points which are inside the $2 \times \delta$ area across the dividing line as shown in the figure. Now, to check all points within distance δ from the line consider the following figure.

From the above diagram we can see that maximum of 12 points can be placed inside the square with a distance not less than δ. That means, we need to check only the distances which are within 11 positions in sorted list. This is similar to above one, but with the difference that in the above combining of subproblems, there are no vertical bounds. So we can apply the 12-point box tactic over all the possible boxes in the $2 \times \delta$ area with dividing line as middle line. As there can be a maximum of n such boxes in the area, the total time for finding the closest pair in the corridor is $O(n)$.

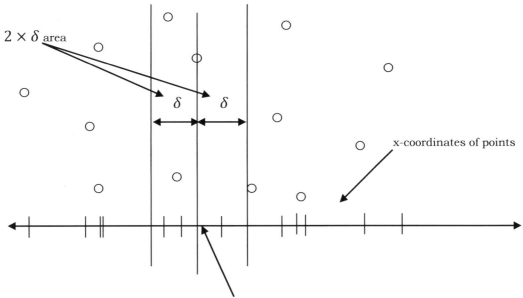

Line l passing through the median point and divides the set into 2 equal parts

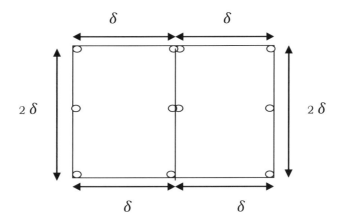

Analysis:

- Step-1 and Step-2 take $O(nlogn)$ for sorting and recursively finding the minimum.
- Step-4 takes $O(1)$.
- Step-5 takes $O(n)$ for scanning and eliminating.
- Step-6 takes $O(nlogn)$ for sorting.
- Step-7 takes $O(n)$ for scanning.

The total complexity, $T(n) = O(nlogn) + O(1) + O(n) + O(n) + O(n) \approx O(nlogn)$.

To calculate k^n, give algorithm and discuss its complexity.

Solution: The naive algorithm to compute k^n is: start with 1 and multiply by k until reaching k^n. For this approach; there are $n - 1$ multiplications and each takes constant time giving a $\Theta(n)$ algorithm.

But there is a faster way to compute k^n. For example,

$$9^{24} = (9^{12})^2 = ((9^6)^2)^2 = (((9^3)^2)^2)^2 = (((9^2 \cdot 9)^2)^2)^2$$

Note that taking square of a number needs only one multiplication; this way, to compute 9^{24} we need only 5 multiplications instead of 23.

```
int Exponential(int k, int n) {
    if (k == 0)
        return 1;
    else{
        if (n%2 == 1){
```

```
            a = Exponential(k, n-1);
            return a*k;
        }
        else{
            a= Exponential(k, n/2);
            return a*a;
        }
    }
}
```

Let T(n) be the number of multiplications required to compute k^n. For simplicity, assume $k = 2^i$ for some $i \geq 1$.

$$T(n) = T(\tfrac{n}{2}) + 1$$

Using master theorem we get T(n) = O($log n$).

Chapter-25

DYNAMIC PROGRAMMING

25.1 Introduction

In this chapter we will try to solve the problems for which we failed to get the optimal solutions using other techniques (say, *Divide & Conquer* and *Greedy* methods). Dynamic Programming (DP) is a simple technique but it can be difficult to master. One easy way to identify and solve DP problems is by solving as many problems as possible. The term *Programming* is not related to coding but it is from literature, and means filling tables (similar to *Linear Programming*).

25.2 What is Dynamic Programming Strategy?

Dynamic programming and memoization work together. The main difference between dynamic programming and divide and conquer is that in-case of the latter, sub problems are independent, whereas in DP there can be an overlap of sub problems. By using memoization [maintaining a table of sub problems already solved], dynamic programming reduces the exponential complexity to polynomial complexity ($O(n^2)$, $O(n^3)$, etc.) for many problems.

The major components of DP are:

- Recursion: Solves sub problems recursively.
- Memoization: Stores already computed values in table (*Memoization* means caching).

Dynamic Programming = Recursion + Memoization

25.3 Properties of Dynamic Programming Strategy

The two dynamic programming properties which can tell whether it can solve the given problem or not are:

- *Optimal substructure*: an optimal solution to a problem contains optimal solutions to sub problems.
- *Overlapping sub problems*: a recursive solution contains a small number of distinct sub problems repeated many times.

25.4 Can Dynamic Programming Solve All Problems?

Like Greedy and Divide and Conquer techniques, DP cannot solve every problem. There are problems which cannot be solved by any algorithmic technique [Greedy, Divide and Conquer and Dynamic Programming].

The difference between Dynamic Programming and straightforward recursion is in memoization of recursive calls. If the sub problems are independent and there is no repetition then memoization does not help, so dynamic programming is not a solution for all problems.

25.5 Dynamic Programming Approaches

Basically there are two approaches for solving DP problems:

- Bottom-up dynamic programming
- Top-down dynamic programming

Bottom-up Dynamic Programming

In this method, we evaluate the function starting with smallest possible input argument value and then we step through possible values, slowly increasing input argument value. While computing the values we store all computed values in a table (memory). As larger arguments are evaluated, pre-computed values for smaller arguments can be used.

Top-down Dynamic Programming

In this method, the problem is broken into sub problems; each of these sub problems solved; and the solutions remembered, in case they need to be solved. Also, we save each computed value as final action of recursive function and as the first action we check if pre-computed value exists.

Bottom-up versus Top-down Programming

In bottom-up programming, programmer has to select values to calculate and decide order of calculation. In this case, all sub problems that might be needed are solved in advance and then used to build up solutions to larger problems. In top-down programming, recursive structure of original code is preserved, but unnecessary recalculation is avoided. The problem is broken into sub problems, these sub problems are solved and the solutions remembered, in case they need to be solved again.

Note: Some problems can be solved with both the techniques and we will see such examples in next section.

25.6 Examples of Dynamic Programming Algorithms

- Many string algorithms including longest common subsequence, longest increasing subsequence, longest common substring, edit distance.
- Algorithms on graphs can be solved efficiently: Bellman-Ford algorithm for finding the shortest distance in a graph, Floyd's All-Pairs shortest path algorithm etc...
- Chain matrix multiplication
- Subset Sum
- 0/1 Knapsack
- Travelling salesman problem and many more

25.7 Understanding Dynamic Programming

Before going to problems, let us understand how DP works through examples.

Fibonacci Series

In Fibonacci series, the current number is the sum of previous two numbers. The Fibonacci series is defined as follows:

$$
\begin{aligned}
Fib(n) &= 0, && for\ n = 0 \\
&= 1, && for\ n = 1 \\
&= Fib(n-1) + Fib(n-2), && for\ n > 1
\end{aligned}
$$

The recursive implementation can be given as:

```
int RecursiveFibonacci(int n) {
    if(n == 0)
        return 0;
    if(n == 1)
        return 1;
    return RecursiveFibonacci(n -1) + RecursiveFibonacci(n -2);
}
```

Solving the above recurrence gives,

$$T(n) = T(n-1) + T(n-2) + 1 \approx \left(\frac{1+\sqrt{5}}{2}\right)^n \approx 2^n = O(2^n)$$

Note: For proof, refer *Introduction* chapter.

How does Memoization help?

Calling $fib(5)$ produces a call tree that calls the function on the same value many times:

$fib(5)$
$fib(4) + fib(3)$
$(fib(3) + fib(2)) + (fib(2) + fib(1))$
$((fib(2) + fib(1)) + (fib(1) + fib(0))) + ((fib(1) + fib(0)) + fib(1))$
$(((fib(1) + fib(0)) + fib(1)) + (fib(1) + fib(0))) + ((fib(1) + fib(0)) + fib(1))$

In the above example, $fib(2)$ was calculated three times (overlapping of subproblems). If n is big then many more values of fib (sub problems) are recalculated, which leads to an exponential time algorithm. Instead of solving the same sub problems again and again we can store the previous calculated values and reduce the complexity.

Memorization works like this: Start with a recursive function and add a table that maps the functions parameter values to the results computed by the function. Then if this function is called twice with the same parameters, we simply look up the answer in the table.

Improving: Now, we see how DP reduces this problem complexity from exponential to polynomial. As discussed earlier, there are two ways of doing this. One approach is bottom-up: these methods starts with lower values of input and keep building the solutions for higher values.

```
int fib[n];
int fib(int n) {
    // Check for base cases
```

```
    if(n == 0 || n == 1) return 1;
    fib[0] = 1;
    fib[1] = 1;
    for (int i = 2; i < n; i++)
        fib[i] = fib[i - 1] + fib[i - 2];
    return fib[n - 1];
}
```

Other approach is top-down. In this method, we preserve the recursive calls and use the values if they are already computed. The implementation for this is given as:

```
int fib[n];
    int fibonacci( int n ) {
    if(n == 1)
        return 1;
    if(n == 2)
        return 1;
    if( fib[n] != 0)
        return fib[n] ;
    return fib[n] = fibonacci(n-1) + fibonacci(n -2) ;
}
```

Note: For all problems, it may not be possible to find both top-down and bottom-up programming solutions.

Both the versions of Fibonacci series implementations clearly reduce the problem complexity to $O(n)$. This is because if a value is already computed then we are not calling the subproblems again. Instead, we are directly taking its value from table.

Time Complexity: $O(n)$. Space Complexity: $O(n)$, for table.

Further Improving: One more observation from the Fibonacci series is: The current value is the sum of previous two calculations only. This indicates that we don't have to store all the previous values. Instead if we store just the last two values, we can calculate the current value. Implementation for this is given below:

```
int fibonacci(int n) {
    int a = 0, b = 1, sum, i;
    for (i=0;i < n;i++) {
        sum = a + b;
        a = b;
        b = sum;
    }
    return sum;
}
```

Time Complexity: $O(n)$. Space Complexity: $O(1)$.

Note: This method may not be applicable (available) for all problems.

Observations: While solving the problems using DP, try to figure out the following:
- See how problems are defined in terms of subproblems recursively.
- See if we can use some table [memoization] to avoid the repeated calculations.

Factorial of a Number

As another example consider the factorial problem: $n!$ is the product of all integers between n and 1. Definition of recursive factorial can be given as:
$$n! = n * (n-1)!$$
$$1! = 1$$
$$0! = 1$$
This definition can easily be converted to implementation. Here the problem is finding the value of $n!$, and sub problem is finding the value of $(n-l)!$. In the recursive case, when n is greater than 1, function calls itself to find the value of $(n-l)!$ and multiplies that with n. In the base case, when n is 0 or 1, the function simply returns 1.

```
int fact(int n) {
    if(n == 1)
        return 1;
    else if(n == 0)
        return 1;
    else    // recursive case: multiply n by (n -1) factorial
        return n *fact(n -1);
}
```

The recurrence for the above implementation can be given as: $T(n) = n \times T(n-1) \approx O(n)$
Time Complexity: $O(n)$. Space Complexity: $O(n)$, recursive calls need a stack of size n.

In the above recurrence relation and implementation, for any n value, there are no repetitive calculations (*no overlapping of sub problems*) and the factorial function is not getting any benefits with dynamic programming. Now, let us say we want to compute a series of $m!$ for some arbitrary value m. Using the above algorithm, for each such call we can compute it in $O(m)$. For example, to find both $n!$ and $m!$ we can use the above approach, wherein the total complexity for finding $n!$ and $m!$ is $O(m + n)$.

Time Complexity: $O(n + m)$. Space Complexity: $O(max(m, n))$, recursive calls need a stack of size equal to the maximum of m and n.

Improving: Now let us see how DP reduces the complexity. From the above recursive definition it can be seen that $fact(n)$ is calculated from $fact(n - 1)$ and n and nothing else. Instead of calling $fact(n)$ every time, we can store the previous calculated values in a table and use these values to calculate a new value. This implementation can be given as:

```
int facto[n];
int fact(int n) {
    if(n == 1)
            return 1;
    else if(n == 0)
            return 1;
    //Already calculated case
    else if(facto[n]!=0)
            return facto[n];
    else     // recursive case: multiply n by (n -1) factorial
        return facto[n]= n *fact(n -1);
}
```

For simplicity, let us assume that we have already calculated $n!$ and want to find $m!$. For finding $m!$, we just need to see the table and use the existing entries if they are already computed. If $m < n$ then we do not have to recalculate $m!$. If $m > n$ then we can use $n!$ and call the factorial on remaining numbers only.

The above implementation clearly reduces the complexity to $O(max(m, n))$. This is because if the $fact(n)$ is already there then we are not recalculating the value again. If we fill these newly computed values then the subsequent calls further reduces the complexity.

Time Complexity: $O(max(m, n))$. Space Complexity: $O(max(m, n))$ for table.

Longest Common Subsequence

Given two strings: string X of length m $[X(1..m)]$, and string Y of length n $[Y(1..n)]$, find longest common subsequence: the longest sequence of characters that appear left-to-right (but not necessarily in a contiguous block) in both strings. For example, if X = "ABCBDAB" and Y = "BDCABA", the $LCS(X, Y)$ = {"BCBA", "BDAB", "BCAB"}. We can see there are several optimal solutions.

Brute Force Approach: One simple idea is to check every subsequence of $X[1..m]$ (m is the length of sequence X) to see if it is also a subsequence of $Y[1..n]$ (n is the length of sequence Y). Checking takes $O(n)$ time, and there are 2^m subsequences of X. The running time thus is exponential $O(n.2^m)$ and is not good for large sequences.

Recursive Solution: Before going to DP solution, let us form the recursive solution for this and later we can add memoization to reduce the complexity. Let's start with some simple observations about the LCS problem. If we have two strings, say "ABCBDAB" and "BDCABA", if we draw lines from the letters in the first string to the corresponding letters in the second, no two lines cross:

```
A  B   C   B D A B
|      |   |     |
B D C A B    A
```

From the above observation, we can see that current characters of X and Y may or may not match. That means, suppose that the two first characters differ. Then it is not possible for both of them to be part of a common subsequence - one or the other (or maybe both) will have to be removed. Finally, observe that once we have decided what to do with the first characters of the strings, the remaining sub problem is again a *LCS* problem, on two shorter strings. Therefore we can solve it recursively.

Solution to *LCS* should find two sequences in X and Y and let us say the starting index of sequence in X is i and starting index of sequence in Y is j. Also, assume that $X[i...m]$ is a substring of X starting at character i and going until the end of X and $Y[j...n]$ is a substring of Y starting at character j and going until the end of Y.

Based on the above discussion, here we get the possibilities as described below:

1) If $X[i]$ == $Y[j]$: $1 + LCS(i + 1, j + 1)$
2) If $X[i] \neq Y[j]$: $LCS(i, j + 1)$ // skipping j^{th} character of Y
3) If $X[i] \neq Y[j]$: $LCS(i + 1, j)$ // skipping i^{th} character of X

In the first case, if $X[i]$ is equal to $Y[j]$, we get a matching pair and can count it towards the total length of the *LCS*. Otherwise, we need to skip either i^{th} character of X or j^{th} character of Y and find the longest common subsequence. Now, $LCS(i, j)$ can be defined as:

$$LCS(i, j) = \begin{cases} 0, & if\ i = m\ or\ j = n \\ Max\{LCS(i, j+1), LCS(i+1, j)\}, & if\ X[i] \neq Y[j] \\ 1 + LCS[i+1, j+1], & if\ X[i] == Y[j] \end{cases}$$

LCS has many applications. In web searching, if we find the smallest number of changes that are needed to change one word into another. A *change* here is an insertion, deletion or replacement of a single character.

```
//Initial Call: LCSLength(X, 0, m-1, Y, 0, n-1);
int LCSLength( int X[], int i, int m, int Y[], int j, int n) {
    if (i == m || j == n)
        return 0;
    else
        if (X[i] == Y[j]) return 1 + LCSLength(X, i+1, m, Y, j+1, n);
        else return max( LCSLength(X, i+1, m, Y, j, n),  LCSLength(X, i, m, Y, j+1, n));
}
```

This is a correct solution but it is very time consuming. For example, if the two strings have no matching characters, so the last line always gets executed which give (if $m == n$) are close to O(2^n).

DP Solution: Adding Memoization: The problem with the recursive solution is that the same subproblems get called many different times. A subproblem consists of a call to *LCSLength*, with the arguments being two suffixes of X and Y, so there are exactly $(i + 1)(j + 1)$ possible subproblems (a relatively small number). If there are nearly 2^n recursive calls, some of these subproblems must be being solved over and over.

The DP solution is to check whenever we want to solve a sub problem, whether we've already done it before. So we look up the solution instead of solving it again. Implemented in the most direct way, we just add some code to our recursive solution. To do this, look up the code. This can be given as:

```
int LCS[1024][1024];
int LCSLength( int X[], int m, int Y[], int n ) {
    // base cases
    for( int i = 0; i <= m; i++ )
        LCS[i][n] = 0;
    for( int j = 0; j <= n; j++ )
        LCS[m][j] = 0;
    for( int i = m – 1; i >= 0; i-- ) {
        for( int j = n – 1; j >= 0; j-- ) {
            LCS[i][j] = LCS[i + 1][j + 1]; // matching X[i] to Y[j]

                if( X[i] == Y[j] )
                        LCS[i][j]++; // we get a matching pair

                // the other two cases – inserting a gap
                if(LCS[i][j + 1] > LCS[i][j] )
                        LCS[i][j] = LCS[i][j + 1];
                if(LCS[i + 1][j] > LCS[i][j] )
                        LCS[i][j] = LCS[i + 1][j];
        }
    }
    return LCS[0][0];
}
```

First, take care of the base cases. We have created *LCS* table with one row and one column larger than the lengths of the two strings. Then run the iterative DP loops to fill each cell in the table. This is like doing recursion backwards, or bottom up.

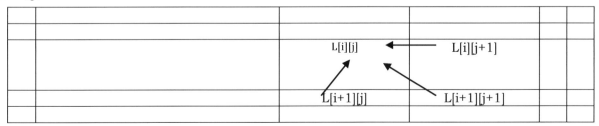

The value of $LCS[i][j]$ depends on 3 other values ($LCS[i + 1][j + 1]$, $LCS[i][j + 1]$ and $LCS[i + 1][j]$), all of which have larger values of i or j. They go through the table in the order of decreasing i and j values. This will guarantee that when we need to fill in the value of $LCS[i][j]$, we already know the values of all of the cells on which it depends.

Time Complexity: $O(mn)$, since i takes values from 1 to m and and j takes values from 1 to n. Space Complexity: $O(mn)$.

Note: In the above discussion, we have assumed $LCS(i,j)$ is the length of the LCS with $X[i ... m]$ and $Y[j ... n]$. We can solve the problem by changing the definition as $LCS(i,j)$ is the length of the LCS with $X[1 ... i]$ and $Y[1 ... j]$.

Printing the subsequence: Above algorithm can find the length of the longest common subsequence but cannot give the actual longest subsequence. To get the sequence, we trace it through the table. Start at cell $(0,0)$. We know that the value of $LCS[0][0]$ was the maximum of 3 values of the neighboring cells. So we simply recompute $LCS[0][0]$ and note which cell gave the maximum value. Then we move to that cell (it will be one of $(1,1)$, $(0,1)$ or $(1,0)$) and repeat this until we hit the boundary of the table. Every time we pass through a cell (i,j) where $X[i] == Y[j]$, we have a matching pair and print $X[i]$. At the end, we will have printed the longest common subsequence in $O(mn)$ time.

An alternative way of getting path is to keep a separate table, for each cell. This will tell us which direction we came from when computing the value of that cell. At the end, we again start at cell $(0,0)$ and follow these directions until the opposite corner of the table.

From the above examples, I hope you understood the idea behind DP. Now let us see more problems which can be easily solved using DP technique.

Note: As we have seen above, in DP the main component is recursion. If we know the recurrence then converting that to code is a minimal task. For the problems below, we concentrate on getting recurrence.

25.8 Problems on Dynamic Programming

Problem-1 Convert the following recurrence to code.

$$T(0) = T(1) = 2$$

$$T(n) = \sum_{i=1}^{n-1} 2 \times T(i) \times T(i-1), \text{for n} > 1$$

Solution: The code for the given recursive formula can be given as:

```
int f(int n) {
    int sum = 0;
    if(n==0 || n==1) //Base Case
        return 2;
    //recursive case
    for(int i=1; i < n;i++)
        sum += 2 * T(i) * T(i-1);
    return sum;
}
```

Problem-2 Can we improve the solution to Problem-1 using memoization of DP?

Solution: Yes. Before finding a solution, let us see how the values are calculated.

$$T(0) = T(1) = 2$$
$$T(2) = 2 * T(1) * T(0)$$
$$T(3) = 2 * T(1) * T(0) + 2 * T(2) * T(1)$$
$$T(4) = 2 * T(1) * T(0) + 2 * T(2) * T(1) + 2 * T(3) * T(2)$$

From the above calculations it is clear that, there are lots of repeated calculations with the same input values. Let us use table for avoiding these repeated calculations and the implementation can be given as:

```
int f(int n) {
    T[0] = T[1] = 2;
    for(int i=2; i <= n; i++) {
        T[i] = 0;
        for (int j=1; j < i; j++)
            T[i] +=2 * T[j] * T[j-1];
    }
    return T[n];
}
```

Time Complexity: $O(n^2)$, two *for* loops. Space Complexity: $O(n)$, for table.

Problem-3 Can we further improve the complexity of Problem-2?

Solution: Yes, since all sub problem calculations are dependent only on previous calculations, code can be modified as:

```
int f(int n) {
    T[0] = T[1] = 2;
    T[2] = 2 * T[0] * T[1];
```

```
        for(int i=3; i <= n; i++)
            T[i]=T[i-1] + 2 * T[i-1] * T[i-2];
        return T[n];
}
```

Time Complexity: $O(n)$, since only one *for* loop. Space Complexity: $O(n)$.

Problem-4   **Maximum Value Contiguous Subsequence:** Given an array of n numbers, give an algorithm for finding a contiguous subsequence $A(i)...A(j)$ for which the sum of elements is maximum.
   Example: $\{-2, 11, -4, 13, -5, 2\} \rightarrow 20$ and $\{1, -3, 4, -2, -1, 6\} \rightarrow 7$

Solution: Input: Array $A(1) ... A(n)$ of n numbers.
Goal: If there are no negative numbers then the solution is just the sum of all elements in the given array. If negative numbers are there, then our aim is to maximize the sum [there can be negative number in the contiguous sum].

One simple and brute force approach is to see all possible sums and select the one which has maximum value.

```
int MaxContigousSum(int A[], in n) {
    int maxSum = 0;
    for(int i = 0; i < n; i++)                  // for each possible start point
            for(int j = i; j < n; j++)    {      // for each possible end point
                    int currentSum = 0;
                    for(int k = i; k <= j; k++)
                            currentSum += A[k];
                    if(currentSum > maxSum)
                            maxSum = currentSum;

            }
    }
    return maxSum;
}
```

Time Complexity: $O(n^3)$. Space Complexity: $O(1)$.

Problem-5   Can we improve the complexity of Problem-4?

Solution: Yes. One important observation is that, if we have already calculated the sum for the subsequence $i, ..., j - 1$, then we need only one more addition to get the sum for the subsequence $i, ..., j$. But, the Problem-4 algorithm ignores this information. If we use this fact, we can get an improved algorithm with the running time $O(n^2)$.

```
int MaxContigousSum(int A[], int n) {
    int maxSum = 0;
    for( int i = 0; i < n;  i++) {
            int currentSum = 0;
            for( int j = i; j < n; j++)     {
                    currentSum += a[j];
                    if(currentSum > maxSum)
                            maxSum = currentSum;

            }
    }
    return maxSum;
}
```

Time Complexity: $O(n^2)$. Space Complexity: $O(1)$.

Problem-6   Can we solve Problem-4 using Dynamic Programming?

Solution: Yes. For simplicity, let us say, $M(i)$ indicates maximum sum over all windows ending at i.

Given Array, A: recursive formula considers the case of selecting i^{th} element

$A[i]$

To find maximum sum we have to do one of the following and select maximum among them.

   • Either extend the old sum by adding $A[i]$
   • or start new window starting with one element $A[i]$

$$M(i) = Max\begin{cases} M(i-1) + A[i] \\ 0 \end{cases}$$

Where, $M(i - 1) + A[i]$ indicates the case of extending the previous sum by adding $A[i]$ and 0 indicates the new window starting at $A[i]$.

```
    int MaxContigousSum(int A[], int n) {
```

```
        int M[n] = 0, maxSum = 0;
        if(A[0] > 0)
            M[0] = A[0];
        else M[0] = 0;
        for( int i = 1; i < n;  i++) {
                if( M[i-1] + A[i] > 0)
                        M[i] = M[i-1] + A[i];
                else      M[i] = 0;
        }
        for( int i = 0; i < n;  i++)
                if(M[i] > maxSum)
                        maxSum = M[i];
        return maxSum;
}
```

Time Complexity: O(n). Space Complexity: O(n), for table.

Problem-7   Is there any other way of solving Problem-4?

Solution: Yes. We can solve this problem without DP too (without memory). The algorithm is little tricky. One simple way is to look for all positive contiguous segments of the array (*sumEndingHere*) and keep track of maximum sum contiguous segment among all positive segments (*sumSoFar*). Each time we get a positive sum compare it with *sumSoFar* and update *sumSoFar* if it is greater than *sumSoFar*. Let us consider the following code for the above observation.

```
int MaxContigousSum(int A[], int n) {
    int sumSoFar = 0, sumEndingHere = 0;

    for(int i = 0; i < n; i++)    {
            sumEndingHere = sumEndingHere + A[i];
            if(sumEndingHere < 0) {
                    sumEndingHere = 0;
                    continue;
            }
            if(sumSoFar < sumEndingHere)
                    sumSoFar = sumEndingHere;
    }
    return sumSoFar;
}
```

Note: Algorithm doesn't work if the input contains all negative numbers. It returns 0 if all numbers are negative. For overcoming this we can add an extra check before actual implementation. The phase will look if all numbers are negative, if they are it will return maximum of them (or smallest in terms of absolute value).

Time Complexity: O(n), because we are doing only one scan. Space Complexity: O(1), for table.

Problem-8   In Problem-7 solution, we have assumed that $M(i)$ indicates maximum sum over all windows ending at i. Can we assume $M(i)$ indicates maximum sum over all windows starting at i and ending at n?

Solution: Yes. For simplicity, let us say, $M(i)$ indicates maximum sum over all windows starting at i.

Given Array, A: recursive formula considers the case of selecting i^{th} element

$A[i]$

To find maximum window we have to do one of the following and select maximum among them.

- Either extend the old sum by adding $A[i]$
- or start new window starting with one element A[i]

$$M(i) = Max \begin{cases} M(i+1) + A[i], & if \ M(i+1) + A[i] > 0 \\ 0 & , & if \ M(i+1) + A[i] <= 0 \end{cases}$$

Where, $M(i+1) + A[i]$ indicates the case of extending the previous sum by adding $A[i]$ and 0 indicates the new window starting at $A[i]$.

Time Complexity: O(n). Space Complexity: O(n), for table.

Note: For O($nlogn$) solution refer *Divide and Conquer* chapter.

Problem-9   Given a sequence of n numbers $A(1)...A(n)$, give an algorithm for finding a contiguous subsequence $A(i)...A(j)$ for which the sum of elements in the subsequence is maximum. Here the condition is we should not select *two* contiguous numbers.

Solution:

Given Array, A: recursive formula considers the case of selecting i^{th} element

Let us see how DP solves this problem. Assume that $M(i)$ represents the maximum sum from 1 to i numbers without selecting two contiguous numbers. While computing $M(i)$, the decision we have to make is, whether to select i^{th} element or not. This gives us two possibilities and based on this we can write the recursive formula as:

$$M(i) = \begin{cases} Max\{A[i] + M(i-2), M(i-1)\}, if\ i > 2 \\ A[1], & if\ i = 1 \\ Max\{A[1], A[2]\}, & if\ i = 2 \end{cases}$$

- The first case indicates whether we are selecting the ith element or not. If we don't select the ith element then we have to maximize the sum using the elements 1 to $i - 1$. If i^{th} element is selected then we should not select $i - 1^{th}$ element and need to maximize the sum using 1 to $i - 2$ elements.
- In the above representation, the last two cases indicate the base cases.

```
int maxSumWithNoTwoContinuousNumbers(int A[], int n) {
    int M[n+1];
    M[0]=A[0];
    M[1]=(A[0]>A[1]?A[0]:A[i]);
    for(i=2; i<n; i++)
        M[i]= (M[i-1]>M[i-2]+A[i]? M[i-1]: M[i-2]+A[i]);
    return M[n-1];
}
```

Time Complexity: O(n). Space Complexity: O(n).

Problem-10   In Problem-9, we assumed that $M(i)$ represents the maximum sum from 1 to i numbers without selecting two contiguous numbers. Can we solve the same problem by changing the definition as: $M(i)$ represents the maximum sum from i to n numbers without selecting two contiguous numbers?

Solution: Yes. Let us assume that $M(i)$ represents the maximum sum from i to n numbers without selecting two contiguous numbers.

As similar to Problem-9 solution, we can write the recursive formula as:

$$M(i) = \begin{cases} Max\{A[i] + M(i+2), M(i+1)\}, if\ i > 2 \\ A[1], & if\ i = 1 \\ Max\{A[1], A[2]\}, & if\ i = 2 \end{cases}$$

- The first case indicates whether we are selecting the ith element or not. If we don't select the ith element then we have to maximize the sum using the elements $i + 1$ to n. If i^{th} element is selected then we should not select $i + 1^{th}$ element need to maximize the sum using $i + 2$ to n elements.
- In the above representation, the last two cases indicate the base cases.

Time Complexity: O(n). Space Complexity: O(n).

Problem-11   Given a sequence of n numbers $A(1) \dots A(n)$, give an algorithm for finding a contiguous subsequence $A(i) \dots A(j)$ for which the sum of elements in the subsequence is maximum. Here the condition is we should not select *three* continuous numbers.

Solution: Input: Array $A(1) \dots A(n)$ of n numbers.

Assume that $M(i)$ represents the maximum sum from 1 to i numbers without selecting three contiguous numbers. While computing $M(i)$, the decision we have to make is, whether to select i^{th} element or not. This gives us the following possibilities:

$$M(i) = Max \begin{cases} A[i] + A[i-1] + M(i-3) \\ A[i] + M(i-2) \\ M(i-1) \end{cases}$$

Given Array, A: recursive formula considers the case of selecting i^{th} element

		.....	.....	.....	?	

A[i-3]   A[i-2]   A[i-1]   A[i]

- In the given problem the restriction is not to select three continuous numbers, but we can select two elements continuously and skip the third one. That is what the first case says in the above recursive formula. That means we are skipping $A[i-2]$.
- The other possibility is, selecting i^{th} element and skipping second $i-1^{th}$ element. This is the second case (skipping $A[i-1]$).
- The third term defines the case of not selecting i^{th} element and as a result we should solve the problem with $i-1$ elements.

Time Complexity: O(n). Space Complexity: O(n).

Problem-12   In Problem-11, we assumed that $M(i)$ represents the maximum sum from 1 to i numbers without selecting three contiguous numbers. Can we solve the same problem by changing the definition as: $M(i)$ represents the maximum sum from i to n numbers without selecting three contiguous numbers?

Solution: Yes. The reasoning is very much similar. Let us see how DP solves this problem. Assume that $M(i)$ represents the maximum sum from i to n numbers without selecting three contiguous numbers.

While computing $M(i)$, the decision we have to make is, whether to select i^{th} element or not. This gives us the following possibilities:

$$M(i) = Max \begin{cases} A[i] + A[i+1] + M(i+3) \\ A[i] + M(i+2) \\ M(i+1) \end{cases}$$

Given Array, A: recursive formula considers the case of selecting i^{th} element

		?	.....	.....	.....	

A[i]   A[i+1]   A[i+2]   A[i+3]

- In the given problem the restriction is not to select three continuous numbers, but we can select two elements continuously and skip the third one. That is what the first case says in the above recursive formula. That means we are skipping $A[i+2]$.
- The other possibility is, selecting i^{th} element and skipping second $i-1^{th}$ element. This is the second case (skipping $A[i+1]$).
- And the third case is not selecting i^{th} element and as a result we should solve the problem with $i+1$ elements.

Time Complexity: O(n). Space Complexity: O(n).

Problem-13   **Catalan Numbers:** How many binary search trees are there with n vertices?

Solution:

Number of nodes, n	Number of Trees
1	
2	
3	

Binary Search Tree (BST) is a tree where the left subtree elements are less than root element and right subtree elements are greater than root element. This property should be satisfied at every node in the tree. The number of BSTs with n nodes is called *Catalan Number* and is denoted by C_n. For example, there are 2 BSTs with 2 nodes (2 choices for the root) and 5 BSTs with 3 nodes.

Let us assume that the nodes of the tree are numbered from 1 to n. Among the nodes, we have to select some node as root and divide the nodes which are less than root node into left sub tree and elements greater than root node into right sub tree. Since we have already numbered the vertices, let us assume that the root element we selected is i^{th} element.

If we select i^{th} element as root then we get $i-1$ elements on left sub-tree and $n-i$ elements on right sub tree. Since C_n is the Catalan number for n elements, C_{i-1} represents the Catalan number for left sub tree elements ($i-1$ elements) and C_{n-i} represents the Catalan number for right sub tree elements. The two sub trees are independent of each other, so we simply multiply the two numbers. That means, the Catalan number for a fixed i value is $C_{i-1} \times C_{n-i}$.

Since there are n nodes, for i we will get n choices. The total Catalan number with n nodes can be given as:

$$C_n = \sum_{i=1}^{n} C_{i-1} \times C_{n-i}$$

```
int CatalanNumber( int n ) {
    if( n == 0 )
        return 1;
    int count = 0;
    for( int i = 1; i <= n; i++ )
            count += CatalanNumber (i -1) * CatalanNumber (n -i);
    return count;
}
```

Time Complexity: $O(4^n)$. For proof, refer *Introduction* chapter.

Problem-14   Can we improve the time complexity of Problem-13 using DP?

Solution: The recursive call, C_n depends only on the numbers C_0 to C_{n-1} and for any value of i, there are lot of recalculations. We will keep a table of previously computed values of C_i. If the function *CatalanNumber*() is called with parameter i, and if it is already computed before then we can simply avoid recalculating the same subproblem.

```
int Table[1024];
int CatalanNumber( int n ) {
    if( Table[n] ) != 1 ) return Table[n];
    Table[n] = 0;
    for( int i = 1; i <= n; i++ )
            Table[n] += CatalanNumber( i -1) * CatalanNumber(n -i);
    return Table[n];
}
```

The time complexity of this implementation $O(n^2)$, because to compute *CatalanNumber*(n), we need to compute all of the *CatalanNumber*(i) values between 0 and $n-1$, and each one will be computed exactly once, in linear time.

In mathematics, Catalan Number can be represented by direct equation as: $\frac{(2n)!}{n!(n+1)!}$.

Problem-15   **Matrix Product Parenthesizations:** Given a series of matrices: $A_1 \times A_2 \times A_3 \times \ldots \times A_n$ with their dimensions, what is the best way to parenthesize them so that it produces the minimum number of total multiplications. Assume that we are using standard matrix and not Strassen's matrix multiplication algorithm.

Solution: Input: Sequence of matrices $A_1 \times A_2 \times A_3 \times \ldots \times A_n$, where A_i is a $P_{i-1} \times P_i$. The dimensions are given in an array P.
Goal: Parenthesize the given matrices in such a way that it produces optimal number of multiplications needed to compute $A_1 \times A_2 \times A_3 \times \ldots \times A_n$.

For matrix multiplication problem, there are many possibilities. This is because matrix multiplication is associative. It does not matter how we parenthesize the product, the result will be the same. As an example, for four matrices A, B, C, and D, the possibilities could be:

$$(ABC)D = (AB)(CD) = A(BCD) = A(BC)D = ..$$

Multiplying $(p \times q)$ matrix with $(q \times r)$ matrix requires pqr multiplications. Each of the above possibility produces different number of products during multiplication. To select the best one, we can go through each possible parenthesizations (brute force), but this requires $O(2^n)$ time and is very slow. Now let us use DP to improve this time complexity. Assume that, $M[i,j]$ represents the least number of multiplications needed to multiply $A_i \cdots A_j$.

$$M[i,j] = \begin{cases} 0 & , if\ i = j \\ Min\{M[i,k] + M[k+1,j] + P_{i-1}P_kP_j\}, if\ i < j \end{cases}$$

The above recursive formula says that we have to find point k such that it produces the minimum number of multiplications. After computing all possible values for k, we have to select the k value which gives minimum value. We can use one more table (say, $S[i,j]$) to reconstruct the optimal parenthesizations. Compute the $M[i,j]$ and $S[i,j]$ in a bottom-up fashion.

```
/* P is the sizes of the matrices, Matrix i has the dimension P[i-1] x P[i].
M[i,j] is the best cost of multiplying matrices i through j
S[i,j] saves the multiplication point and we use this for back tracing */
void MatrixChainOrder(int P[], int length) {
    int n = length - 1, M[n][n], S[n][n];

    for (int i = 1; i <= n; i++)
        M[i][i] = 0;

    // Fills in matrix by diagonals
    for (int l=2; l<= n; l++)    {        // l is chain length
        for (int i=1; i<= n -l+1; i++) {
            int j = i+l-1;
            M[i][j] = MAX_VALUE;
            // Try all possible division points i..k and k..j
            for (int k=i; k<=j-1; k++) {
                int thisCost = M[i][k] + M[k+1][j] + P[i-1]*P[k]*P[j];
                if(thisCost < M[i][j]) {
                    M[i][j] = thisCost;
                    S[i][j] = k;
                }
            }
        }
    }
}
```

How many sub problems are there? In the above formula, i can range from $1\ to\ n$ and j can range from $1\ to\ n$. So there are a total of n^2 subproblems and also, we are doing $n-1$ such operations [since the total number of operations we need for $A_1 \times A_2 \times A_3 \times \ldots \times A_n$ are $n-1$]. So the time complexity is $O(n^3)$. Space Complexity: $O(n^2)$.

Problem-16   For the Problem-15, can we use greedy method?

Solution: *Greedy* method is not an optimal way of solving this problem. Let us go through some counter example for this. As we have seen already, *greedy* method makes the decision which is good locally and it does not consider the future optimal solutions. In this case, if we use *greedy* then we always do the cheapest multiplication first. Sometimes, it returns a parenthesization that is not optimal.

Example: Consider $A_1 \times A_2 \times A_3$ with dimentions 3×100, 100×2 and 2×2. Based on *greedy* we parenthesize them as: $A_1 \times (A_2 \times A_3)$ with $100 \cdot 2 \cdot 2 + 3 \cdot 100 \cdot 2 = 1000$ multiplications. But the optimal solution to this problem is: $(A_1 \times A_2) \times A_3$ with $3 \cdot 100 \cdot 2 + 3 \cdot 2 \cdot 2 = 612$ multiplications. $\therefore$ we cannot use *greedy* for solving this problem.

Problem-17   **Integer Knapsack Problem [Duplicate Items Permitted]:** Given n types of items, where the ith item type has an integer size s_i and a value v_i. We need to fill a knapsack of total capacity C with items of maximum value. We can add multiple items of the same type to the knapsack.
      Note: For Fractional Knapsack problem refer *Greedy Algorithms* chapter.

Solution: Input: n types of items where i^{th} type item has the size s_i and value v_i. Also, assume infinite number of items for each item type.
Goal: Fill the knapsack with capacity C by using n types of items and with maximum value.

One important note is that it's not compulsory to fill the knapsack completely. That means, filling the knapsack completely [of size C] if we get a value V and without filling the knapsack completely [let us say $C-1$] with value U and if V < U then we consider the second one. In this case, we are basically filling the knapsack of size $C-1$. If we get the same situation for $C-1$ also then we try to fill the knapsack with $C-2$ size and get the maximum value.

Let us say M(j) denote the maximum value we can pack into a j size knapsack. We can express M(j) recursively in terms of solutions to sub problems as follows:

$$M(j) = \begin{cases} max\{M(j-1), max_{i=1\ to\ n}\big(M(j-s_i)\big) + v_i\}, & if\ j \geq 1 \\ 0, & if\ j \leq 0 \end{cases}$$

For this problem the decision depends on whether we select a particular i^{th} item or not for a knapsack of size j.

*   If we select i^{th} item then we add its value v_i to optimal solution and decrease the size of the knapsack to be solved to $j - s_i$.
*   If we do not select the item then check whether we can get better solution for the knapsack of size $j - 1$.

The value of $M(C)$ will contain the value of the optimal solution. We can find the list of items in the optimal solution by maintaining and following "back pointers".

Time Complexity: Finding each $M(j)$ value will require $\Theta(n)$ time, and we need to sequentially compute C such values. Therefore, total running time is $\Theta(nC)$. Space Complexity: $\Theta(C)$.

Problem-18 **0-1 Knapsack Problem:** For Problem-17, how do we solve if the items are not duplicated (not having infinite number of items for each type and each item is allowed to use for 0 or 1 time)?

Real-time example: Suppose we are going by flight, we know that there is a limitation on the luggage weight. Also, the items which we are carrying can be of different types (like laptops, etc.). In this case, our objective is to select the items with maximum value. That means, we need to tell the customs officer to select the items which have more weight and less value (profit).

Solution: Input is a set of n items with sizes s_i and values v_i and a Knapsack of size C which we need to fill with subset of items from the given set. Let us try to find the recursive formula for this problem using DP. Let $M(i,j)$ represent the optimal value we can get for filling up a knapsack of size j with items $1 \dots i$. The recursive formula can be given as:

$$M(i,j) = Max\{M(i-1,j), M(i-1,j-s_i) + v_i\}$$

i^{th} item is not used i^{th} item is used

Time Complexity: O(nC), since there are nC subproblems to be solved and each of them takes O(1) to compute. Space Complexity: O(nC), where as Integer Knapsack takes only O(C).

Now let us consider the following diagram which helps us in reconstructing the optimal solution and also gives further understanding. Size of below matrix is M.

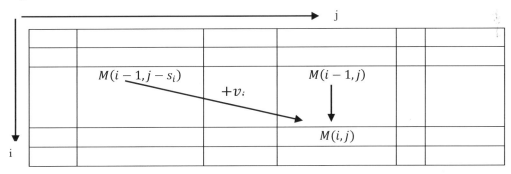

Since i take values from $1 \dots n$ and j takes values from $1 \dots C$, there are a total of nC subproblems. Now let us see what the above formula says:

- $M(i-1,j)$: Indicates the case of not selecting i^{th} item. In this case, since we are not adding any size to knapsack we have to use the same knapsack size for subproblems but excluding i^{th} item. The remaining items are $i-1$.
- $M(i-1,j-s_i) + v_i$ Indicates the case where we have selected the ith item. If we add the ith item then we have to reduce the subproblem knapsack size to $j - s_i$ and at the same time we need to add the value v_i to optimal solution. The remaining items are $i-1$.

Now, after finding all $M(i,j)$ values the optimal objective value can be obtained as: $Max_j\{M(n,j)\}$
This is because we do not know what amount of capacity gives the best solution.

Inorder to compute some value $M(i,j)$, we take the maximum of $M(i-1,j)$ and $M(i-1,j-s_i) + v_i$. These two values ($M(i,j)$ and $M(i-1,j-s_i)$) appears in previous row and also in some previous column. So, $M(i,j)$ can be computed just by looking at two values in the previous row in the table.

Problem-19 **Making Change:** Given n types of coin denominations of values $v_1 < v_2 < \dots < v_n$ (integers). Assume $v_1 = 1$, so that we can always make change for any amount of money C. Give an algorithm which makes change for an amount of money C with as few coins as possible.

Solution: This problem is identical to the Integer Knapsack problem. In our problem, we have coin denominations, each of value v_i. We can construct an instance of a Knapsack problem for each item has a size s_i, which is equal to the value of v_i coin denomination. In the Knapsack we can give value of every item as -1. Now, it is easy to understand an optimal way to make money C with fewest coins is completely equivalent to the optimal way to fill the Knapsack of size C. This is because since every value has a value of -1, and the Knapsack algorithm uses as few items as possible which correspond to as few coins as possible.

Let us try formulating the recurrence. Let $M(j)$ indicates the minimum number of coins required to make a change for the amount of money equal to j.

$$M(j) = Min_i\{M(j-v_i)\} + 1$$

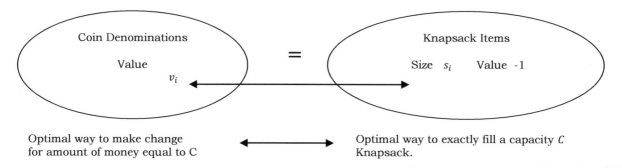

Optimal way to make change for amount of money equal to C

Optimal way to exactly fill a capacity C Knapsack.

What this says is, if coin denomination i was the last denomination coin added to solution, then the optimal way to finish the solution with that one is to optimally make change for the amount of money $j - v_i$ and then add one extra coin of value v_i.

```
int Table[128] ; //Initialization
int MakingChange(int n) {
    if(n < 0) return -1;
    if(n == 0) return 0;
    if(Table[n] != -1)
            return Table[n];
    int ans = -1;
    for ( int i = 0 ; i < num_denomination ; ++i )
            ans = Min( ans , MakingChange(n - denominations [ i ] ) ) ;

    return Table[ n ] = ans + 1 ;
}
```

Time Complexity: $O(nC)$. Since we are solving C sub problems and each of them requires minimization of n terms. Space Complexity: $O(nC)$.

Problem-20 **Longest Increasing Subsequence:** Given a sequence of n numbers A_1 . . .A_n, determine a subsequence (not necessarily contiguous) of maximum length in which the values in the subsequence form a strictly increasing sequence.

Solution:

Input: Sequence of n numbers A_1 . . .A_n.

Goal: To find subsequence that is just a subset of elements and it does not happen to be contiguous. But the elements in the subsequence should form strictly increasing sequence and at the same time the subsequence contains as many elements as possible.

For example, if the sequence is $(5,6,2,3,4,1,9,9,8,9,5)$, then $(5,6), (3,5), (1,8,9)$ are all increasing sub-sequences. The longest one of them is $(2, 3, 4, 8, 9)$, and we want an algorithm for finding it.

First, let us concentrate on the algorithm for finding the longest subsequence. Later, we can try printing the sequence itself by tracing the table. Our first step is finding the recursive formula. First, let us create the base conditions. If there is only one element in the input sequence then we don't have to solve the problem and just need to return that element. For any sequence we can start with the first element ($A[1]$). Since we know the first number in the LIS, let's find the second number ($A[2]$). If $A[2]$ is larger than $A[1]$ then include $A[2]$ also. Otherwise, we are done – the LIS is the one element sequence ($A[1]$).

Now, let us generalize the discussion and decide about i^{th} element. Let $L(i)$ represent the optimal subsequence which is starting at position $A[1]$ and ending at $A[i]$. The optimal way to obtain a strictly increasing subsequence ending at position i is to extend some subsequence starting at some earlier position j. For this the recursive formula can written as:

$$L(i) = Max_{j<i \text{ and } A[j]<A[i]}\{L(j)\} + 1$$

The above recurrence says that we have to select some earlier position j which gives the maximum sequence. The 1 in the recursive formula indicates the addition of ith element.

```
1     .......              j         ...........              i
```


Now after finding maximum sequence for all positions we have to select the one among all positions which gives the maximum sequence and it is defined as:

$$Max_i\{L(i)\}$$

```
int LISTable [1024];
int LongestIncreasingSequence( int A[], int n ) {
```

```
    int i, j, max = 0;
    for ( i = 0; i < n; i++ )
            LISTable[i] = 1;
    for ( i = 0; i< n; i++ ) {
            for ( j = 0; j < i; j++ ) {
                    if( A[i] > A[j] && LISTable[i] < LISTable[j] + 1 )
                            LISTable[i] = LISTable[j] + 1;
            }
    }
    for ( i = 0; i < n; i++) {
            if( max < LISTable[i] )
                    max = LISTable[i];
    }
    return max;
}
```

Time Complexity: $O(n^2)$, since two *for* loops. Space Complexity: $O(n)$, for table.

Problem-21 **Longest Increasing Subsequence:** In Problem-20, we assumed that $L(i)$ represents the optimal subsequence which is starting at position $A[1]$ and ending at $A[i]$. Now, let us change the definition of $L(i)$ as: $L(i)$ represents the optimal subsequence which is starting at position $A[i]$ and ending at $A[n]$. With this approach can we solve the problem?

Solution: Yes.

$$i \qquad\qquad . \qquad\qquad j \quad ..... \quad n$$

Let $L(i)$ represent the optimal subsequence which is starting at position $A[i]$ and ending at $A[n]$. The optimal way to obtain a strictly increasing subsequence starting at position i is going to be to extend some subsequence starting at some later position j. For this the recursive formula can be written as:

$$L(i) = Max_{i<j \text{ and } A[i]<A[j]}\{L(j)\} + 1$$

We have to select some later position j which gives the maximum sequence. The 1 in the recursive formula is the addition of ith element. After finding maximum sequence for all positions select the one among all positions which gives the maximum sequence and it is defined as:

$$Max_i\{L(i)\}$$

```
int LISTable [1024];
int LongestIncreasingSequence( int A[], int n ) {
    int i, j, max = 0;
    for ( i = 0; i < n; i++ )
            LISTable[i] = 1;
    for(i = n - 1; i >= 0; i++) {
            // try picking a larger second element
            for( j = i + 1; j < n; j++ )    {
                    if( A[i] < A[j] && LISTable [i] < LISTable [j] + 1)
                            LISTable[i] = LISTable[j] + 1;
            }
    }
    for ( i = 0; i < n; i++ ) {
            if( max < LISTable[i] )
                    max = LISTable[i];
    }
    return max;
}
```

Time Complexity: $O(n^2)$, since two nested *for* loops. Space Complexity: $O(n)$, for table.

Problem-22 Is there an alternative way of solving Problem-20?

Solution: **Yes**. The other method is to sort the given sequence and save it into another array and then take out the "Longest Common Subsequence" (LCS) of the two arrays. This method has a complexity of $O(n^2)$. For LCS problem refer *theory section* of this chapter.

Problem-23 **Box Stacking:** Assume that we are given a set of n rectangular $3-D$ boxes. The dimensions of ith box are height h_i, width w_i and depth d_i. Now we want to create a stack of boxes which is as tall as possible, but we can only stack a box on top of another box if the dimensions of the $2-D$ base of the lower box are each strictly larger than those of the $2-D$ base of the higher box. We can rotate a box so that any side functions as its base. It is possible to use multiple instances of the same type of box.

Solution: Box stacking problem can be reduced to LIS.

Input: n boxes where i^{th} with height h_i, width w_i and depth d_i. For all n boxes we have to consider all the orientations with respect to rotation. That is, if we have, in the original set a box with dimensions $1 \times 2 \times 3$. Then we consider 3 boxes,

$$1 \times 2 \times 3 \Longrightarrow \begin{cases} 1 \times (2 \times 3), \textit{with height } 1, \textit{base } 2 \textit{ and width } 3 \\ 2 \times (1 \times 3), \textit{with height } 2, \textit{base } 1 \textit{ and width } 3 \\ 3 \times (1 \times 2), \textit{with height } 3, \textit{base } 1 \textit{ and width } 2 \end{cases}$$

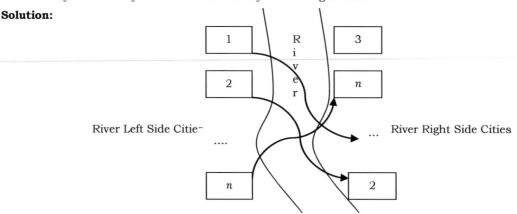

Decreasing base area

This simplification allows us to forget about the rotations of the boxes and we just focus on stacking of n boxes with each height as h_i and a base area of $(w_i \times d_i)$. Also assume that $w_i \le d_i$. Now what we do is, make a stack of boxes that is as tall as possible and has maximum height. We allow a box i on top of box j only if box i is smaller than box j in both the dimensions. That means, if $w_i < w_j$ && $d_i < d_j$. Now let us solve this using DP. First select the boxes in the order of decreasing base area.

Now, let us say $H(j)$ represents the tallest stack of boxes with box j on top. This is very similar to LIS problem because stack of n boxes with ending box j is equal to finding a subsequence with first j boxes due to the sorting by decreasing base area. The order of the boxes on the stack is going to be equal to order of the sequence.

Now we can write $H(j)$ recursively. In order to form a stack which ends on box j, we need to extend some previous stack which is ending at i. That means, we need to put j box on top of stack [i box is the current top of stack]. To put j box on top of stack we should satisfy the condition $w_i > w_j$ and $d_i > d_j$ [these ensures the low level box has more base than boxes above it]. Based on this logic, we can write the recursive formula as:

$$H(j) = Max_{i<j\ and\ w_i>w_j\ and\ d_i>d_j} \{H(i)\} + h_i$$

As similar to LIS problem, at the end we have to select the best j over all potential values. This is because we are not sure which box might end up on top.

$$Max_j\{H(j)\}$$

Time Complexity: $O(n^2)$.

Problem-24 **Building Bridges in India:** Consider a very long, straight river which moves from north to south. Assume there are n cities on both sides of the river: n cities on left of the river and n cities on the right of the river. Also, assume that these cities are numbered from 1 to n but the order is not known. Now we want to connect as many left-right pairs of cities as possible with bridges such that no two bridges cross. When connecting cities, we can only connect city i on the left side to city i on the right side.

Solution:

Input: Two pairs of sets with each numbered from 1 to n.
Goal: Construct as many bridges as possible without any crosses between left side cities to right side cities of the river.

To understand better let us consider the diagram below. In the diagram it can be seen that there are n cities on left side of river and n cities on right side of river. Also, note that we are connecting the cities which have the same number [requirement in problem]. Our goal is to map maximum cities on left side of river to the cities on the right side of the river without any cross edges. Just to make it simple, let us sort the cities on one side of the river.

If we observe carefully, since the cities on left side are already sorted, the problem can be simplified to finding the maximum increasing sequence. That means we have to use LIS solution for finding the maximum in increasing sequence on the right side cities of the river.

Time Complexity: $O(n^2)$, (same as LIS).

Problem-25   **Subset Sum:** Given a sequence of n positive numbers $A_1 \ldots A_n$, give an algorithm which checks whether there exists a subset of A whose sum of all numbers is T?

Solution: This is a variation of the Knapsack problem. As an example, consider the following array:

$$A = [3, 2, 4, 19, 3, 7, 13, 10, 6, 11]$$

Suppose we want to check whether there is any subset whose sum is 17. The answer is yes, because the sum of $4 + 13 = 17$ and therefore $\{4, 13\}$ is such a subset.

Let us try solving this problem using DP. We will define $n \times T$ matrix, where n is the number of elements in our input array and T is the sum we want to check.

Let, $M[i, j] = 1$ if it is possible to find a subset of the numbers 1 through i that produce sum j and $M[i, j] = 0$ otherwise.

$$M[i, j] = Max(M[i - 1, j], M[i - 1, j - A_i])$$

According to the above recursive formula similar to Knapsack problem, we check if we can get the sum j by not including the element i in our subset, and we check if we can get the sum j by including i by checking if the sum $j - A_i$ exists without the ith element. This is identical to Knapsack, except that we are storing a 0/1's instead of values. In the below implementation we can use binary OR operation to get the maximum among $M[i - 1, j]$ and $M[i - 1, j - A_i]$.

```
int SubsetSum( int A[], int n, int  T ) {
    int i, j, M[n+1][T +1];
    M[0][0]=0;
    for (i=1; i<= T; i++)
        M[0][i]= 0;
    for (i=1; i<=n; i++) {
        for (j = 0; j<= T; j++) {
            M[i][j] = M[i-1][j] || M[i-1][j - A[i]];
        }
    }
    return M[n][T];
}
```

How many subproblems are there? In the above formula, i can range from $1\ to\ n$ and j can range from $1\ to\ T$. There are a total of nT subproblems and each one takes $O(1)$. So the time complexity is $O(nT)$ and this is not polynomial as the running time depends on two variables [n and T], and we can see that they are exponential function of the other. Space Complexity: $O(nT)$.

Problem-26   Given a set of n integers and sum of all numbers is at most K. Find the subset of these n elements whose sum is exactly half of the total sum of n numbers.

Solution: Assume that the numbers are $A_1 \ldots A_n$. Let us use DP to solve this problem. We will create a boolean array T with size equal to $K + 1$. Assume that $T[x]$ is 1 if there exists a subset of given n elements whose sum is x. That means, after the algorithm finishes, $T[K]$ will be 1 if and only if there is a subset of the numbers that has sum K. Once we have that value then we just need to return $T[K/2]$. If it is 1, then there is a subset that adds up to half the total sum.

Initially we set all values of T to 0. Then we set $T[0]$ to 1. This is because we can always build 0 by taking an empty set. If we have no numbers in A, then we are done! Otherwise, we pick the first number, $A[0]$. We can either throw it away or take it into our subset. This means that the new $T[]$ should have $T[0]$ and $T[A[0]]$ set to 1. This creates the base case. We continue by taking the next element of A.

Suppose that we have already taken care of the first $i - 1$ elements of A. Now we take A[i] and look at our table T[]. After processing i − 1 elements, the array T has a 1 in every location that corresponds to a sum that we can make from the numbers we have already processed. Now we add the new number, A[i]. What should the table look like? First of all, we can simply ignore A[i]. That means, no one should disappear from T[] – we can still make all those sums.

Now consider some location of T[j] that has a 1 in it. It corresponds to some subset of the previous numbers that add up to j. If we add A[i] to that subset, we will get a new subset with total sum j + A[i]. So we should set T[j + A[i]] to 1 as well. That's all. Based on above discussion, we can write the algorithm as:

```
bool T[10240];
bool SubsetHalfSum( int  A[], int n ) {
    int K = 0;
    for( int i = 0; i < n; i++ )
        K += A[i];
    T[0] = 1; // initialize the table
    for( int i = 1; i <= K; i++ )
```

```
        T[i] = 0;
    // process the numbers one by one
    for( int i = 0; i < n; i++ ) {
        for( int j = K - A[i]; j >= 0; j--)        {
            if( T[j] )
                T[j + A[i]] = 1;
        }
    }
    return T[K / 2];
}
```

In the above code, j loop moves from right to left. This reduces the double counting problem. That means, if we move from left to right, then we may do the repeated calculations.

Time Complexity: $O(nK)$, for the two *for* loops. Space Complexity: $O(K)$, for the boolean table T.

Problem-27   Can we improve the performance of Problem-26?

Solution: Yes. In the above code what we are doing is, the inner j loop is starting from K and moving left. That means, it is unnecessarily scanning the whole table every time.

What we actually want is to find all the 1 entries. At the beginning, only the 0th entry is 1. If we keep the location of the rightmost 1 entry in a variable, we can always start at that spot and go left instead of starting at the right end of the table.

To take full advantage of this, we can sort $A[]$ first. That way, the rightmost 1 entry will move to the right as slowly as possible. Finally, we don't really care about what happens in the right half of the table (after $T[K/2]$) because if $T[x]$ is 1, then $T[Kx]$ must also be 1 eventually – it corresponds to the complement of the subset that gave us x. The code based on above discussion is given below.

```
int T[10240];
int SubsetHalfSumEfficient( int  A[], int n ) {
    int K = 0;
    for( int i = 0; i < n; i++ )
            K += A[i];
    Sort(A,n));
    T[0] = 1; // initialize the table
    for( int i = 1; i <= sum; i++ )
            T[i] = 0;
    int R = 0; // rightmost 1 entry
    for( int i = 0; i < n; i++)    {        // process the numbers one by one
        for( int j = R; j >= 0; j--) {
            if( T[j] )
                T[j + A[i]] = 1;
            R = min(K / 2, R + C[i] );
        }
    }
    return T[K / 2];
}
```

After the improvements, the time complexity is still $O(nK)$, but we have removed some useless steps.

Problem-28   Partition problem is to determine whether a given set can be partitioned into two subsets such that the sum of elements in both subsets is same [same as previous problem but different way of asking]. For example, if A[] = {1, 5, 11, 5}, the array can be partitioned as {1, 5, 5} and {11}. Similarly, if A[] = {1, 5, 3}, the array cannot be partitioned into equal sum sets.

Solution: Let us try solving this problem in other way. Following are the two main steps to solve this problem:

- Calculate sum of the array. If sum is odd, there cannot be two subsets with equal sum, so return false.
- If sum of array elements is even, calculate $sum/2$ and find a subset of array with sum equal to $sum/2$.

The first step is simple. The second step is crucial, it can be solved either using recursion or Dynamic Programming.

Recursive Solution: Following is the recursive property of the second step mentioned above. Let subsetSum(A, n, sum/2) be the function that returns true if there is a subset of A[0..n-1] with sum equal to $sum/2$. The isSubsetSum problem can be divided into two sub problems

- isSubsetSum() without considering last element (reducing n to n-1)
- isSubsetSum considering the last element (reducing sum/2 by A[n-1] and n to n-1)

If any of the above sub problems return true, then return true.

$$subsetSum\,(A, n, sum/2) = isSubsetSum\,(A, n-1, sum/2) \,||\, subsetSum\,(A, n-1, sum/2 - A[n-1])$$

// A utility function that returns true if there is a subset of A[] with sum equal to given sum

```
bool subsetSum (int A[], int n, int sum){
  // Base Cases
  if (sum == 0)
    return true;

  if (n == 0 && sum != 0)
    return false;

  // If last element is greater than sum, then ignore it
  if (A[n-1] > sum)
    return subsetSum (A, n-1, sum);

  return subsetSum (A, n-1, sum) || subsetSum (A, n-1, sum-A[n-1]);
}

// Returns true if A[] can be partitioned in two subsets of equal sum, otherwise false
bool findPartition (int A[], int n){
  // calculate sum of the elements in Array
  int sum = 0;
  for (int i = 0; i < n; i++)
    sum += A[i];

  // If sum is odd, there cannot be two subsets with equal sum
  if (sum%2 != 0)
    return false;

  // Find if there is subset with sum equal to half of total sum
  return subsetSum (A, n, sum/2);
}
```

Time Complexity: $O(2^n)$ In worst case, this solution tries two possibilities (whether to include or exclude) for every element.

Dynamic Programming Solution: The problem can be solved using dynamic programming when the sum of the elements is not too big. We can create a 2D array $part[][]$ of size $(sum/2)*(n+1)$. And we can construct the solution in bottom up manner such that every filled entry has following property

$$part[i][j] = true \ if \ a \ subset \ of \ \{A[0], A[1], ..A[j-1]\} \ has \ sum \ equal \ to \ sum/2, otherwise \ false$$

```
// Returns true if A[] can be partitioned in two subsets of equal sum, otherwise false
bool findPartition (int A[], int n){
  int sum = 0;
  int i, j;
  // Calculate sum of all elements
  for (i = 0; i < n; i++)
    sum += A[i];

  if (sum%2 != 0)
    return false;

  bool part[sum/2+1][n+1];
  // initialize top row as true
  for (i = 0; i <= n; i++)
    part[0][i] = true;
  // initialize leftmost column, except part[0][0], as 0
  for (i = 1; i <= sum/2; i++)
    part[i][0] = false;

  // Fill the partition table in bottom up manner
  for (i = 1; i <= sum/2; i++) {
    for (j = 1; j <= n; j++) {
      part[i][j] = part[i][j-1];
      if (i >= A[j-1])
        part[i][j] = part[i][j] || part[i - A[j-1]][j-1];
    }
  }
  return part[sum/2][n];
}
```

Time Complexity: $O(sum \times n)$. Space Complexity: $O(sum \times n)$. Please note that this solution will not be feasible for arrays with big sum.

Problem-29   Counting Boolean Parenthesizations: Let us assume that we are given a boolean expression consisting of symbols $'true', 'false', 'and', 'or',$ and $'xor'$. Find the number of ways to parenthesize the expressions such that it will evaluate to *true*. For example, there is only 1 way to parenthesize $'true \ and \ false \ xor \ true'$ such that it evaluates to *true*.

Solution: Let the number of symbols be n and between symbols there are boolean operators like and, or, xor, etc. For example, $n = 4$, T or F and T xor F.

Our goal is to count the numbers of ways to parenthesize the expression with boolean operators so that it evaluates to *true*. In the above case, if we use like T or $((F$ and $T)$ xor $F)$ then it evaluates to true.

$$T \ or(\ (F \ and \ T)xor \ F) = True$$

Now let us see how DP solves this problem. Let, $T(i, j)$ represent the number of ways to parenthesize the sub expression with symbols $i \dots j$ [symbols means only T and F and not the operators] with boolean operators so that it evaluates to *true*. Also, i and j takes the values from 1 to n. For example, in the above case, $T(2, 4) = 0$ because there is no way to parenthesize the expression F and T xor F to make it *true*.

Just for simplicity and similarity, let $F(i, j)$ represent the numbers of ways to parenthesize the sub expression with symbols $i \dots j$ with boolean operators so that it evaluates to *false*. The base cases are $T(i, i)$ and $F(i, i)$.

Now we are going to compute $T(i, i + 1)$ and $F(i, i + 1)$ for all values of i. Similarly, $T(i, i + 2)$ and $F(i, i + 2)$ for all values of i and so on. Now let's generalize the solution.

$$T(i, j) = \sum_{k=i}^{j-1} \begin{cases} T(i, k)T(k + 1, j), & for\ "and" \\ Total(i, k)Total(k + 1, j) - F(i, k)F(k + 1, j), & for\ "or" \\ T(i, k)F(k + 1, j) + F(i, k)T(k + 1, j), & for\ "xor" \end{cases}$$

Where, $Total(i, k) = T(i, k) + F(i, k)$.

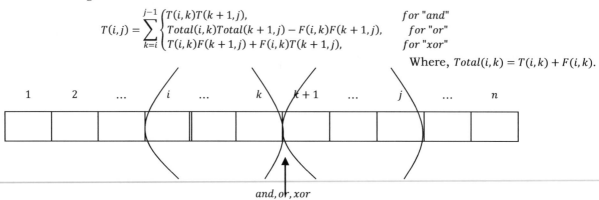

$$and, or, xor$$

What this above recursive formula says is, $T(i, j)$ indicates the number of ways to parenthesize the expression. Let us assume that we have some sub problems which are ending at k. Then the total number of ways to parenthesize from i to j is the sum of counts of parenthesizing from i to k and from $k + 1$ to j. To parenthesize between k and $k + 1$ there are three ways: "and", "or" and "xor".

1. If we use "and" between k and $k + 1$ then the final expression becomes *true* only when both are *true*. If both are *true* then we can include them to get the final count.
2. If we use "or", then if at least one of them is *true* then the result becomes *true*. Instead of including all the three possibilities for "or", we are giving one alternative where we are subtracting the "false" cases from total possibilities.
3. Same is the case with "xor". Conversation is as in above two cases.

After finding all the values we have to select the value of k which produces the maximum count and for k there are i to $j - 1$ possibilities.

How many subproblems are there? In the above formula, i can range from 1 to n and j can range from 1 to n. So there are a total of n^2 subproblems and also, we are doing summation for all such values. So the time complexity is $O(n^3)$.

Problem-30 **Optimal Binary Search Trees:** Given a set of n (sorted) keys $A[1..n]$, build the best binary search tree for the elements of A. Also assume that, each element is associated with *frequency* which indicates the number of times that particular item is searched in the binary search trees. That means, we need to construct a binary search tree so that the total search time will be reduced.

Solution: Before solving the problem let us understand the problem with an example. Let us assume that the given array is $A = [3, 12, 21, 32, 35]$. There are many ways to represent these elements two of which are listed below.

Of the two, which representation is better? The search time for an element depends on the depth of the node. The average number of comparisons for the first tree is: $\frac{1+2+2+3+3}{5} = \frac{11}{5}$ and for the second tree, the average number of comparisons is: $\frac{1+2+3+3+4}{5} = \frac{13}{5}$. Of the two, the first tree gives better results.

If frequencies are not given and if we want to search all elements then the above simple calculation is enough for deciding the best tree. If the frequencies are given then the selection depends on the frequencies of the elements and also the depth of the elements. For simplicity let us assume that, the given array is A and the corresponding frequencies are in array F. $F[i]$ indicates the frequency of ith element $A[i]$. With this, the total search time S(root) of the tree with *root* can be defined as:

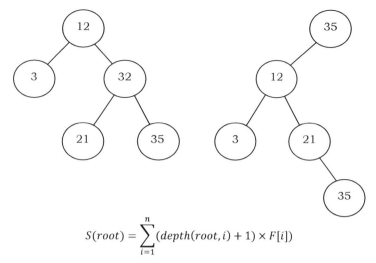

$$S(root) = \sum_{i=1}^{n}(depth(root,i)+1) \times F[i])$$

In the above expression, $depth(root,i)+1$ indicates the number of comparisons for searching the ith element. Since we are trying to create binary search tree, the left subtree elements are less than root element and right subtree elements are greater than root element. If we separate the left subtree time and right subtree time then the above expression can be written as:

$$S(root) = \sum_{i=1}^{r-1}(depth(root,i)+1) \times F[i]) + \sum_{i=1}^{n}F[i] + \sum_{i=r+1}^{n}(depth(root,i)+1) \times F[i])$$

Where r indicates the position of the root element in the array.

If we replace the left subtree and right subtree times with their corresponding recursive calls then the expression becomes:

$$S(root) = S(root \to left) + S(root \to right) + + \sum_{i=1}^{n}F[i]$$

Binary Search Tree node declaration

Refer *Trees* chapter.

```
struct BinarySearchTreeNode *OptimalBST(int A[], int F[], int low, int high) {
    int r, minTime = 0;
    struct BinarySearchTreeNode *newNode=(struct BinarySearchTreeNode *)
                                malloc(sizeof(struct BinarySearchTreeNode));
    if(!newNode) {
        printf("Memory Error");
        return;
    }
    for (r =0, r <= n-1; r++)    {
        root→left =  OptimalBST(A, F, low, r-1);
        root→left =  OptimalBST(A, F, r+1, high)
        root→data = A[r];
        if(minTime > S(root)) minTime = S(root);
    }
    return minTime;
}
```

Problem-31   Edit Distance: Given two strings A of length m and B of length n, transform A into B with a minimum number of operations of the following types: delete a character from A, insert a character into A, or change some character in A into a new character. The minimal number of such operations required to transform A into B is called the *edit distance* between A and B.

Solution:

Input: Two text strings A of length m and B of length n.
Goal: Convert string A into B with minimal conversions.

Before going to solution, let us consider the possible operations for converting string A into B.

- If $m > n$, we need to remove some characters of A
- If $m == n$, we may need to convert some characters of A
- If $m < n$, we need to remove some characters from A

So the operations we need are insertion of a character, replacement of a character and deletion of character and their corresponding cost codes are defined below.

Costs of operations:

Insertion of a character	c_i
Replacement of a character	c_r
Deletion of character	c_d

Now let us concentrate on recursive formulation of the problem. Let, $T(i, j)$ represents the minimum cost required to transform first i characters of A to first j characters of B. That means, $A[1...i]$ to $B[1...j]$.

$$T(i,j) = min \begin{cases} c_d + T(i-1,j) \\ T(i,j-1) + c_i \\ T(i-1,j-1), & if\ A[i] == B[j] \\ T(i-1,j-1) + c_r & if\ A[i] \neq B[j] \end{cases}$$

Based on above discussion we have the following cases.

- If we delete i^{th} character from A, then we have to convert remaining $i-1$ characters of A to j characters of B
- If we insert i^{th} character in A, then convert these i characters of A to $j-1$ characters of B
- If $A[i] == B[j]$, then we have to convert remaining $i-1$ characters of A to $j-1$ characters of B
- If $A[i] \neq B[j]$, then we have to replace i^{th} character of A to j^{th} character of B and convert remaining $i-1$ characters of A to $j-1$ characters of B

After calculating all the possibilities we have to select the one which gives the lowest cost.

How many subproblems are there? In the above formula, i can range from $1\ to\ m$ and j can range from $1\ to\ n$. This gives mn subproblems and each one take O(1) and the time complexity is O(mn). Space Complexity: O(mn) where m is number of rows and n is number of columns in the given matrix.

Problem-32   **All Pairs Shortest Path Problem: Floyd's Algorithm:** Given a weighted directed graph $G = (V, E)$, where $V = \{1, 2, ..., n\}$. Find the shortest path between any pair of nodes in the graph. Assume the weights are represented in the matrix $C[V][V]$, where $C[i][j]$ indicates the weight (or cost) between the nodes i and j. Also, $C[i][j] = \infty$ or -1 if there is no path from node i to node j.

Solution: Let us try to find the DP solution (Floyd's algorithm) for this problem. The Floyd's algorithm for all pairs shortest path problem uses matrix $A[1..n][1..n]$ to compute the lengths of the shortest paths. Initially,

$$A[i,j] = C[i,j]\ if\ i \neq j$$
$$= 0 \qquad if\ i = j$$

From the definition, $C[i,j] = \infty$ if there is no path from i to j. The algorithm makes n passes over A. Let $A_0, A_1, ..., A_n$ be the values of A on the n passes, with A_0 being the initial value.

Just after the $k-1^{th}$ iteration, $A_{k-1}[i,j]$ = smallest length of any path from vertex i to vertex j that does not pass through the vertices $\{k+1, k+2, ... n\}$. That means, it passes through the vertices possibly through $\{1, 2, 3, ..., k-1\}$.

In each iteration, the value $A[i][j]$ is updated with minimum of $A_{k-1}[i,j]$ and $A_{k-1}[i,k] + A_{k-1}[k,j]$.

$$A[i,j] = min \begin{cases} A_{k-1}[i,j] \\ A_{k-1}[i,k] + A_{k-1}[k,j] \end{cases}$$

The kth pass explores whether the vertex k lies on an optimal path from i to j, for all i, j. The same is shown in the diagram below.

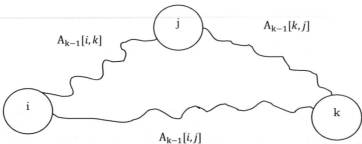

```
void Floyd(int C[][], int A[][], int n) {
    int i, j, k;
    for(i = 0, i <= n - 1;i + +)
        for(j = 0; j <= n - 1, j + +)
            A[i][j] = C[i][j];
    for(i = 0;i <= n - 1;i + +)
        A[i][i] = 0;
    for(k = 0;k <= n - 1;k + +) {
        for(i = 0;i <= n - 1;i + +) {
            for(j = 0;j <= n - 1, j + +)
                if(A[i][k] + A[k][j] < A[i][j])
                    A[i][j] = A[i][k] + A[k][j];
```

```
            }
        }
    }
```

Time Complexity: $O(n^3)$.

Problem-33   **Optimal Strategy for a Game:** Consider a row of n coins of values $v_1 \ldots v_n$, where n is even [since it's a two player game]. We play this game with the opponent. In each turn, a player selects either the first or last coin from the row, removes it from the row permanently, and receives the value of the coin. Determine the maximum possible amount of money we can definitely win if we move first.

Solution:

Input: A row of n coins $v_1 \ldots v_n$ which are kept on some table.

Goal: Maximize the sum of values selected during the game. If we start the game, then we should win the game. That means, we have to maximize the total values selected. One important note, we should not bother about the opponents moves.

Let us solve the problem using our DP technique. In each turn either we *or* our opponent selects the coin only from ends of the row. Let us define the subproblems as:

$V(i, j)$: denotes the maximum possible value we can definitely win if it is our turn and the only coins remaining are $v_i \ldots v_j$.

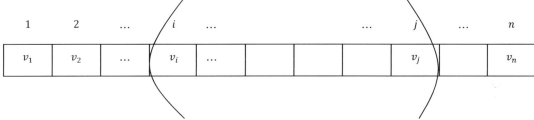

Base Cases: $V(i, i), V(i, i + 1)$ for all values of i.

From these value, we can compute $V(i, i + 2), V(i, i + 3)$ and so on. Now let us define $V(i, j)$ for each sub problem as:

$$V(i,j) = Max\left\{Min\begin{cases} V(i+1, j-1) \\ V(i+2, j) \end{cases} + v_i, Min\begin{cases} V(i, j-2) \\ V(i+1, j-1) \end{cases} + v_j\right\}$$

In the recursive call we have to focus on i^{th} coin to j^{th} coin ($v_i \ldots v_j$). Since it is our turn to pick the coin, we have two possibilities: either we can pick v_i or v_j. The first term indicates the case if we select i^{th} coin (v_i) and second term indicates the case of selecting j^{th} coin (v_j). The outer *Max* indicates that we have to select the coin which gives maximum value. Now let us focus on the terms:

- Selecting i^{th} coin: If we select the ith coin then remaining range is from $i + 1\ to\ j$. Since we selected i^{th} coin we get the value v_i for that. From the remaining range $i + 1\ to\ j$, the opponents can select either $i + 1^{th}$ coin or j^{th} coin. But the opoonents selection should be minimized as much as possible [the *Min* term]. Same is described in below figure.

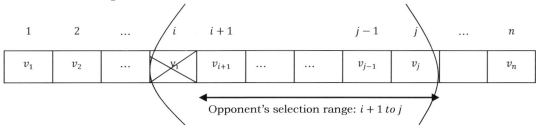

- Selecting j^{th} coin: Here also the argument is same as above. If we select the jth coin then remaining range is from $i\ to\ j - 1$. Since we selected j^{th} coin we get the value v_j for that. From the remaining range $i\ to\ j - 1$, the ooponent can select either i^{th} coin or $j - 1^{th}$ coin. But the opoonents selection should be minimized as much as possible [the *Min* term].

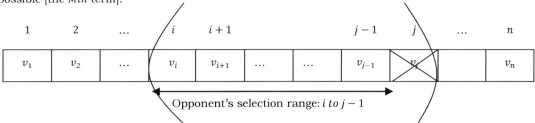

How many subproblems are there? In the above formula, i can range from $1\ to\ n$ and j can range from $1\ to\ n$. There are a total of n^2 subproblems and each takes $O(1)$ and the total time complexity is $O(n^2)$.

Problem-34 **Tiling:** Assume that we use dominoes measuring 2×1 to tile an infinite strip of height 2. How many ways can one tile a $2 \times n$ strip of square cells with 1×2 dominoes?

Solution:

Notice that we can put tiles either vertically or horizontally. For putting vertical tiles, we need a gap of at least 2×2. For putting horizontal tiles, we need a gap of 2×1. In this manner, this problem reduces to find the number of ways to partition n using the numbers 1 and 2 with order considered relevant [1]. For example: $11 = 1 + 2 + 2 + 1 + 2 + 2 + 1$. If we have to find such arrangements for 12, we can either place a 1 at the end or can add 2 in the arrangements possible with 10. Similarly, let us say we have F_n possible arrangements for n. Then for $(n + 1)$, we can either place just 1 in the end *or* we can find possible arrangements for $(n - 1)$ and put a 2 in the end. Going by above theory:

$$F_{n+1} = F_n + F_{n-1}$$

Let's verify above theory for our original problem:

- In how many ways, can we fill a 2×1, strip: $1 \rightarrow$ Only one vertical tile.
- In how many ways, can we fill a 2×2, strip: $2 \rightarrow$ Either 2 horizontal or 2 vertical tiles.
- In how many ways, can we fill a 2×3, strip: $3 \rightarrow$ Either put a vertical tile in 2 solutions possible for 2×2 strip or put 2 horizontal tiles in only solution possible for 2×1 strip. $(2 + 1 = 3)$.
- Similarly in how many ways, can we fill a $2 \times n$, strip: Either put a vertical tile in solutions possible for $2 X (n - 1)$ strip or put 2 horizontal tiles in solution possible for $2 \times (n - 2)$ strip. $(F_{n-1} + F_{n-2})$.

- That's how, we verified that our final solution: $F_n = F_{n-1} + F_{n-2}$ with $F_1 = 1$ and $F_2 = 2$.

Problem-35 **Longest Palindrome Subsequence:** A sequence is a palindrome if it reads the same whether we read it left to right or right to left. For example A, C, G, G, G, G, C, A. Given a sequence of length n devise an algorithm to output length of the longest palindrome subsequence. For example, the string, $A, G, C, T, C, B, M, A, A, C, T, G, G, A, M$ has many palindromes as subsequences, for instance: $A, G, T, C, M, C, T, G, A$ has length 9.

Solution: Let us use DP to solve this problem. If we look at the sub-string A[i,..,j] of the string A, then we can find a palindrome of length at least 2 if A[i] == A[j]. If they are not same then we have to find the maximum length palindrome in subsequences A[i + 1,...,j] and A[i,...,j − 1].

Also every character $A[i]$ is a palindrome of length 1. Therefore base cases are given by $A[i,i] = 1$. Let us define the maximum length palindrome for the substring A[i,...,j] as L(i, j).

$$L(i,j) = \begin{cases} L(i + 1, j - 1) + 2, & if\ A[i] == A[j] \\ Max\{L(i + 1, j), L(i, j - 1)\}, & otherwise \end{cases}$$
$$L(i, i) = 1\ for\ all\ i = 1\ to\ n$$

```
int LongestPalindromeSubsequence(int A[], int n) {
    int max = 1;
    int i,k, L[n][ n];
    for (i = 1; i<= n -1; i++) {
        L[i][i] =1;
        if(A[i]==A[i+1]) {
            L[i][i + 1] = 1;
            max = 2;
        }
        else   L[i][i + 1] = 0;
    }
    for (k=3;k<= n;k++) {
            for (i = 1;i <= n-k +1; i++) {
                j = i + k - 1;
                if(A[i] == A[j])     {
                    L[i, j] = 2 + L[i + 1][j - 1];
                    max = k;
                }
                else     L[i, j] = max(L[i + 1][j - 1], L[i][j - 1]);
            }
    }
    return max;
}
```

Time Complexity: First for loop takes $O(n)$ time while the second for loop takes $O(n - k)$ which is also $O(n)$. Therefore, the total running time of the algorithm is given by $O(n^2)$.

Problem-36   **Longest Palindrome Substring:** Given a string A, we need to find the longest sub-string of A such that the reverse of it is exactly the same.

Solution: The basic difference between longest palindrome substring and longest palindrome subsequence is that, in case of longest palindrome substring the output string should be the contiguous characters which gives the maximum palindrome and in case of longest palindrome subsequence the output is the sequence of characters where the characters might not be in contiguous but they should be in increasing sequence with respect to their positions in the given string.

Brute-force solution exhaustively checks all $n\,(n + 1)\,/\,2$ possible substrings of the given n-length string, tests each one if it's a palindrome, and keeps track of the longest one seen so far. This has worst-case complexity $O(n^3)$, but we can easily do better by realizing that a palindrome is centered on either a letter (for odd-length palindromes) or a space between letters (for even-length palindromes). Therefore we can examine all $n + 1$ possible centers and find the longest palindrome for that center, keeping track of the overall longest palindrome. This has worst-case complexity $O(n^2)$.

Let us use DP to solve this problem. It is worth noting that there are no more than $O(n^2)$ substrings in a string of length n (while there are exactly 2^n subsequences). Therefore, we could scan each substring, check for palindrome and update the length of the longest palindrome substring discovered so far. Since the palindrome test takes time linear in the length of the substring, this idea takes $O(n^3)$ algorithm. We can use DP to improve this. For $1 \le i \le j \le n$, define

$$L(i,j) = \begin{cases} 1, & \text{if } A[i] \dots . A[j] \text{ is a palindrome substring,} \\ 0, & \text{otherwise} \end{cases}$$
$$L[i,i] = 1,$$
$$L[i,j] = L[i, i + 1]\,, \text{if } A[i] == A[i + 1], \text{for } 1 \le i \le j \le n - 1.$$

Also, for string of length at least 3,
$$L[i,j] = (L[i + 1, j - 1] \text{ and } A[i] = A[j])\,.$$

Note that in order to obtain a well-defined recurrence, we need to explicitly initialize two distinct diagonals of the boolean array $L[i,j]$, since the recurrence for entry $[i,j]$ uses the value $[i - 1, j - 1]$, which is two diagonals away from $[i,j]$ (that means, for a substring of length k, we need to know the status of a substring of length $k - 2$).

```
int LongestPalindromeSubstring(int A[], int n) {
    int max = 1;
    int i,k, L[n][n];
    for (i = 1; i<=n-1; i++) {
        L[i][i] =1;
        if(A[i]==A[i+1]) {
            L[i][i + 1]  = 1;
            max = 2;
        }
        else  L[i][i + 1]  = 0;
    }
    for (k=3;k<=n;k++) {
        for (i = 1;i <= n-k +1; i++) {
            j = i + k - 1;
            if(A[i] == A[j] && L[i + 1][j - 1]) {
                L[i][j] =  1;
                max = k;
            }
            else     L[i][j]  = 0;
        }
    }
    return max;
}
```

Time Complexity: First for loop takes $O(n)$ time while the second for loop takes $O(n - k)$ which is also $O(n)$. Therefore the total running time of the algorithm is given by $O(n^2)$.

Problem-37   Given two strings S and T, give an algorithm to find the number of times S appears in T. It's not compulsory that all characters of S should appear contiguous to T. For example, if $S = ab$ and $T = abadcb$ then the solution is 4, because ab is appearing 4 times in $abadcb$.

Solution: Assume, $L(i,j)$ represents the count of how many times i characters of S appears in j characters of T.

$$L(i,j) = Max \begin{cases} 0, & \text{if } j = 0 \\ 1, & \text{if } i = 0 \\ L(i - 1, j - 1) + L(i, j - 1), & \text{if } S[i] == T[j] \\ L(i - 1, j), & \text{if } S[i] \ne T[j] \end{cases}$$

If we concentrate on the components of the above recursive formula,

- If $j = 0$, then since T is empty the count becomes 0.
- If $i = 0$, then we can treat empty string S also appearing in T and we can give the count as 1.
- If S[i] == T[j], means i^{th} character of S and j^{th} character of T are same. In this case we have to check the subproblems with $i - 1$ characters of S and $j - 1$ characters of T and also we have to count the result of i characters of S with $j - 1$ characters of T. This is because even all i characters of S might be appearing in $j - 1$ characters of T.
- If S[i] $\neq$ T[j], then we have to get the result of subproblem with $i - 1$ characters of S and j characters of T.

After computing all the values, we have to select the one which gives maximum count.

How many subproblems are there? In the above formula, i can range from $1\ to\ m$ and j can range from $1\ to\ n$. There are a total of mn subproblems and and each one takes O(1). Time Complexity is O(mn).
Space Complexity: O(mn) where m is number of rows and n is number of columns in the given matrix.

Problem-38 Given a matrix with n rows and m columns ($n \times m$). In each cell there are a number of apples. We start from the upper-left corner of the matrix. We can go down or right one cell. Finally, we need to arrive to the bottom-right corner. Find the maximum number of apples that we can collect. When we pass through a cell - we collect all the apples left there.

Solution: Let us assume that the given matrix is $A[n][m]$. The first thing that must be observed is that there are at most 2 ways we can come to a cell - from the left (if it's not situated on the first column) and from the top (if it's not situated on the most upper row).

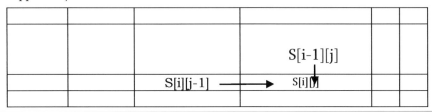

To find the best solution for that cell, we have to have already found the best solutions for all of the cells from which we can arrive to the current cell. From above, a recurrent relation can be easily obtained as:

$$S(i,j) = \left\{ A[i][j] + Max \begin{cases} S(i, j-1), & if\ j > 0 \\ S(i-1, j), & if\ i > 0 \end{cases} \right\}$$

$S(i,j)$ must be calculated by going first from left to right in each row and process the rows from top to bottom, or by going first from top to bottom in each column and process the columns from left to right.

```
int FindApplesCount(int A[][], int n, int m) {
    int S[n][m];
    for( int i = 1;i<=n;i++) {
        for(int j = 1;i<=m;j++) {
            S[i][j] = A[i][j];
            if(j>0 && S[i][j] < S[i][j] + S[i][j-1])
                S[i][j] += S[i][j-1];
            if(i>0 && S[i][j] < S[i][j] + S[i-1][j])
                S[i][j] +=S[i-1][j];
        }
    }
    return S[n][m];
}
```

How many such subproblems are there? In the above formula, i can range from $1\ to\ n$ and j can range from $1\ to\ m$. There are a total of nm subproblems and each one takes O(1). Time Complexity is O(nm). Space Complexity: O(nm), where m is number of rows and n is number of columns in the given matrix.

Problem-39 Similar to Problem-38, assume that, we can go down, right one cell or even in diagonal direction. We need to arrive at the bottom-right corner. Give DP solution to find the maximum number of apples we can collect.

Solution: Yes. The discussion is very similar to Problem-38. Let us assume that the given matrix is A[n][m]. The first thing that must be observed is that there are at most 3 ways we can come to a cell - from the left, from the top (if it's not situated on the uppermost row) or from top diagonal. To find the best solution for that cell, we have to have already found the best solutions for all of the cells from which we can arrive to the current cell. From above, a recurrent relation can be easily obtained:

$$S(i,j) = \left\{ A[i][j] + Max \begin{cases} S(i, j-1), & if\ j > 0 \\ S(i-1, j), & if\ i > 0 \\ S(i-1, j-1), & if\ i > 0\ and\ j > 0 \end{cases} \right\}$$

$S(i,j)$ must be calculated by going first from left to right in each row and process the rows from top to bottom, or by going first from top to bottom in each column and process the columns from left to right.

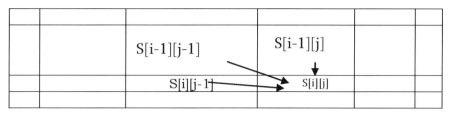

How many such subproblems are there? In the above formula, i can range from $1 \text{ } to \text{ } n$ and j can range from $1 \text{ } to \text{ } m$. There are a total of nm subproblems and each one takes O(1). Time complexity is O(nm).

Space Complexity: O(nm) where m is number of rows and n is number of columns in the given matrix.

Problem-40 **Maximum size square sub-matrix with all 1's:** Given a matrix with 0's and 1's, give an algorithm for finding the maximum size square sub-matrix with all 1s. For example, consider the binary matrix below.

$$0 \text{ } 1 \text{ } 1 \text{ } 0 \text{ } 1$$
$$1 \text{ } 1 \text{ } 0 \text{ } 1 \text{ } 0$$
$$0 \text{ } 1 \text{ } 1 \text{ } 1 \text{ } 0$$
$$1 \text{ } 1 \text{ } 1 \text{ } 1 \text{ } 0$$
$$1 \text{ } 1 \text{ } 1 \text{ } 1 \text{ } 1$$
$$0 \text{ } 0 \text{ } 0 \text{ } 0 \text{ } 0$$

The maximum square sub-matrix with all set bits is

$$1 \text{ } 1 \text{ } 1$$
$$1 \text{ } 1 \text{ } 1$$
$$1 \text{ } 1 \text{ } 1$$

Solution: Let us try solving this problem using DP. Let the given binary matrix be $B[m][m]$. The idea of the algorithm is to construct a temporary matrix $L[\ ][\ ]$ in which each entry $L[i][j]$ represents size of the square sub-matrix with all $1's$ including $B[i][j]$ and $B[i][j]$ is the rightmost and bottom-most entry in sub-matrix.

Algorithm:
- Construct a sum matrix $L[m][n]$ for the given matrix $B[m][n]$.
  - Copy first row and first columns as it is from $B[\ ][\ ]$ to $L[\ ][\ ]$.
  - For other entries, use following expressions to construct $L[\ ][\ ]$
    if($B[i][j]$)
    $$L[i][j] = min(L[i][j-1], L[i-1][j], L[i-1][j-1]) + 1;$$
    else $L[i][j] = 0;$
- Find the maximum entry in $L[m][n]$.
- Using the value and coordinates of maximum entry in $L[i]$, print sub-matrix of $B[\ ][\ ]$.

```
void MatrixSubSquareWithAllOnes(int B[][], int m, int n) {
    int i, j, L[m][n], max_of_s, max_i, max_j;
    // Setting first column of L[][]
    for(i = 0; i < m; i++)
        L[i][0] = B[i][0];
    // Setting first row of L[][]
    for(j = 0; j < n; j++)
        L[0][j] = B[0][j];
    // Construct other entries of L[][]
    for(i = 1; i < m; i++) {
        for(j = 1; j < n; j++) {
            if(B[i][j] == 1)
                L[i][j] = min(L[i][j-1], L[i-1][j], L[i-1][j-1]) + 1;
            else    L[i][j] = 0;
        }
    }
    max_of_s = L[0][0]; max_i = 0; max_j = 0;
    for(i = 0; i < m i++) {
        for(j = 0; j < n; j++) {
            if(L[i][j] > max_of_s) {
                max_of_s = L[i][j];
                max_i = i;
                max_j = j;
            }
        }
    }
    printf("Maximum sub-matrix");
    for(i = max_i; i > max_i - max_of_s; i--) {
        for(j = max_j; j > max_j - max_of_s; j--)
            printf("%d",B[i][j]);
```

```
        }
    }
```

How many subproblems are there? In the above formula, i can range from $1\ to\ n$ and j can range from $1\ to\ m$. There are a total of nm subproblems and each one takes $O(1)$. Time complexity is $O(nm)$. Space Complexity: $O(nm)$ where n is number of rows and m is number of columns in the given matrix.

Problem-41 **Maximum size sub-matrix with all 1's:** Given a matrix with 0's and 1's, give an algorithm for finding the maximum size sub-matrix with all 1s. For example, consider the binary matrix below.

1	1	0	0	1	0
0	1	1	1	1	1
1	1	1	1	1	0
0	0	1	1	0	0

The maximum sub-matrix with all set bits is

1	1	1	1
1	1	1	1

Solution: If we draw a histogram of all $1's$ cells in above rows for a particular row, then maximum all $1's$ sub-matrix ending in that row will be equal to maximum area rectangle in that histogram. Below is an example for 3rd row in above discussed matrix [1]:

1	1	0	0	1	0
0	1	1	1	1	1
1	1	1	1	1	0
0	0	1	1	0	0

If we calculate this area for all the rows, maximum area will be our answer. We can extend our solution very easily to find start and end co-ordinates. For this, we need to generate an auxiliary matrix $S[][]$ where each element represents the number of 1s above and including it, up until the first 0. $S[][]$ for above matrix will be as shown below:

```
1 1 0 0 1 0
0 2 1 1 2 1
1 3 2 2 3 0
0 0 3 3 0 0
```

Now we can simply call our maximum rectangle in histogram on every row in $S[][]$ and update the maximum area every time. Also we don't need any extra space for saving S. We can update original matrix (A) to S and after calculation, we can convert S back to A.

```
#define ROW 10
#define COL 10
int find_max_matrix(int A[ROW][COL]) {
    int max, cur_max = 0;
    //Calculate Auxilary matrix
    for (int i=1; i<ROW; i++)
        for(int j=0; j<COL; j++) {
            if(A[i][j] == 1)
                A[i][j] = A[i-1][j] + 1;
        }
    //Calculate maximum area in S for each row
    for (int i=0; i<ROW; i++) {
        max = MaxRectangleArea(A[i], COL);              //Refer Stacks Chapter
        if(max > cur_max)
            cur_max = max;
    }
    //Regenerate Oriignal matrix
    for (int i=ROW-1; i>0; i--)
        for(int j=0; j<COL; j++) {
            if(A[i][j])
                A[i][j] = A[i][j] - A[i-1][j];
        }
    return cur_max;
}
```

Problem-42 **Maximum sum sub-matrix:** Given an $n \times n$ matrix M of positive and negative integers, give an algorithm to find the sub-matrix with the largest possible sum.

Solution: Let $Aux[r,c]$ represent the sum of rectangular subarray of M with one corner at entry $[1,1]$ and the other at $[r,c]$. Since there are n^2, such possibilities, we can them in $O(n^2)$ time. After computing all possible sums, the sum of any rectangular subarray of M can be computed in constant time. This gives an $O(n^4)$ algorithm, we simply guess the lower-left and the upper-right corner of the rectangular subarray and use the Aux table to compute its sum.

Problem-43 Can we improve the complexity of Problem-42?

Solution: We can use Problem-4 solution with little variation. As we have seen that the maximum sum array of a $1-D$ array algorithm scans the array one entry at a time and keeps a running total of the entries. At any point, if this total becomes negative then set it to 0. This algorithm is called *Kadane's* algorithm. We use this as an auxiliary function to solve the two dimensional problem in the following way [1].

```
public void FindMaximumSubMatrix(int[][] A, int n){
    //computing the vertical prefix sum for columns
    int[][] M = new int[n][n];
    for (int i = 0; i < n; i++) {
        for (int j = 0; j < n; j++) {
            if (j == 0)
                M[j][i] = A[j][i];
            else
                M[j][i] = A[j][i] + M[j - 1][i];
        }
    }
    int maxSoFar = 0;
    int min , subMatrix;
    //iterate over the possible combinations applying Kadane's Alg.
    for (int i = 0; i < n; i++) {
        for (int j = i; j < n; j++) {
            min = 0;
            subMatrix = 0;
            for (int k = 0; k < n; k++) {
                if (i == 0)
                    subMatrix += M[j][k];
                else    subMatrix += M[j][k] - M[i - 1 ][k];
                if(subMatrix < min)
                    min = subMatrix;
                if((subMatrix - min) > maxSoFar)
                    maxSoFar = subMatrix - min;
            }
        }
    }
}
```

Time Complexity: $O(n^3)$.

Problem-44   Given a number n, find the minimum number of squares required to sum a given number n.
Examples: min[1] = 1 = 1^2, min[2] = 2 = $1^2 + 1^2$, min[4] = 1 = 2^2, min[13] = 2 = $3^2 + 2^2$.

Solution: This problem can be reduced to coin change problem. The denominations are 1 to $\sqrt{n}$. Now, we just need to make change for n with minimum number of denominations.

Problem-45   **Finding Optimal Number Of Jumps To Reach Last Element:** Given an array, start from the first element and reach the last by jumping. The jump length can be at most the value at the current position in the array. Optimum result is when you reach the goal in minimum number of jumps.
   Example: Given array A = {2,3,1,1,4}. Possible ways to reach the end (index list) are:
   a)   0,2,3,4 (jump 2 to index 2, and then jump 1 to index 3 and then jump 1 to index 4)
   b)   0,1,4 (jump 1 to index 1, and then jump 3 to index 4)
   Since second solution has only 2 jumps it is the optimum result.

Solution: This problem is a classic example of Dynamic Programming. Though we can solve this by brute-force it will be complex. We can use LIS problem approach for solving this. As soon as we traverse the array, we should find the minimum number of jumps for reaching that position (index) and update our result array. Once we reach the end, we have the optimum solution at last index in result array.

How can we find optimum number of jump for every position (index)? For first index, optimum number of jumps will be zero. Please note that if value at first index is zero, we can't jump to any element and return infinite. For $n + 1^{th}$ element, initialize result[$n + 1$] as infinite. Then we should go through a loop from $0 \dots n$, and at every index i, we should see if we are able to jump to $n + 1$ from i or not. If possible then see if total number of jump (result[i] $+ 1$) is less than result[$n + 1$], then update result[$n + 1$] else just continue to next index.

```
//Define MAX 1 less so that adding 1 doesn't make it 0
#define MAX 0xFFFFFFFE;
unsigned int jump(int *array, int n) {
    unsigned answer, int *result = new unsigned int[n];
    int i, j;
    //Boundry conditions
    if(n==0 || array[0] == 0)   return MAX;
    result[0] = 0;  //no need to jump at first element
    for (i = 1; i < n; i++) {
```

```
                result[i] = MAX; //Initialization of result[i]
                for (j = 0; j < i; j++) {
                        //check if jump is possible from j to is
                        if(array[j] >= (i-j)) {
                                //check if better solution available
                                if((result[j] + 1) < result[i])
                                        result[i] = result[j] + 1;     //updating result[i]
                        }
                }
        }
        answer = result[n-1];           //return result[n-1]
        delete[] result;
        return answer;
}
```

Above code will return optimum number of jumps. To find the jump indexes as well, we can very easily modify the code as per requirement.

Time Complexity: Since we are running 2 loops here and iterating from 0 to i in every loop then total time takes will be $1 + 2 + 3 + 4 + ... + n - 1$. So time efficiency $O(n) = O(n * (n - 1)/2) = O(n^2)$.

Space Complexity: $O(n)$ space for result array.

Problem-46   Explain what would happen if a dynamic programming algorithm is designed to solve a problem that does not have overlapping sub-problems.

Solution: It will be just a waste of memory, because the answers of sub-problems will never be used again. And the running time will be the same as using Divide & Conquer algorithm.

Problem-47   Christmas is approaching. You're helping Santa Clauses to distribute gifts to children. For ease of delivery, you are asked to divide n gifts into two groups such that the weight difference of these two groups is minimized. The weight of each gift is a positive integer. Please design an algorithm to find an optimal division minimizing the value difference. The algorithm should find the minimal weight difference as well as the groupings in $O(nS)$ time, where S is the total weight of these n gifts. Briefly justify the correctness of your algorithm.

Solution: This problem can be converted into making one set as close to $\frac{S}{2}$ as possible. We consider an equivelant problem of making one set as close to W=$\lfloor \frac{S}{2} \rfloor$ as possible. Define FD(i, w) to be the minimal gap between the weight of the bag and W when using the first i gifts only. WLOG, we can assume the weight of the bag is always less than or equal to W. Then fill the DP table for $0 \le i \le n$ and $0 \le w \le W$ in which F(0, w) = W for all w, and

$$FD(i, w) = min\{FD(i - 1, w - w_i) - w_i, FD(i - 1, w)\} \; if \; \{FD(i - 1, w - w_i) \ge w_i\}$$
$$= FD(i - 1, w) \; otherwise$$

This takes $O(nS)$ time. $FD(n, W)$ is the minimum gap. Finally, to reconstruct the answer, we backtrack from (n, W). During backtracking, if $FD(i, j) = FD(i - 1, j)$ then i is not selected in the bag and we move to F$(i - 1, j)$. Otherwise, i is selected and we move to F$(i - 1, j - w_i)$.

Chapter-26

MISCELLANEOUS CONCEPTS

26.1 Introduction

In this chapter we will cover the topics which are useful for interviews and exams.

26.2 Hacks on Bitwise Programming

In C and $C++$ we can work with bits effectively. First let us see the definitions of each bit operation and then move onto different techniques for solving the problems. Basically, there are six operators that C and $C++$ support for bit manipulation:

Symbol	Operation
&	Bitwise AND
|	Bitwise OR
^	Bitwise Exclusive-OR
«	Bitwise left shift
»	Bitwise right shift
~	Bitwise complement

26.2.1 Bitwise AND

The bitwise AND tests two binary numbers and returns bit values of 1 for positions where both numbers had a one, and bit values of 0 where both numbers did not have one:

```
      01001011
&     00010101
      ----------
      00000001
```

26.2.2 Bitwise OR

The bitwise OR tests two binary numbers and returns bit values of 1 for positions where either bit or both bits are one, the result of 0 only happens when both bits are 0:

```
      01001011
|     00010101
      ----------
      01011111
```

26.2.3 Bitwise Exclusive-OR

The bitwise Exclusive-OR tests two binary numbers and returns bit values of 1 for positions where both bits are different, if they are the same then the result is 0:

```
      01001011
^     00010101
      ----------
      01011110
```

26.2.4 Bitwise Left Shift

The bitwise left shift moves all bits in the number to the left and fills vacated bit positions with 0.

```
          01001011
<< 2
          --------
          00101100
```

26.2.5 Bitwise Right Shift

The bitwise right shift moves all bits in the number to the right.

$$01001011$$
$$\gg 2$$
$$\text{--------}$$
$$??010010$$

Note the use of ? for the fill bits. Where the left shift filled the vacated positions with 0, a right shift will do the same only when the value is unsigned. If the value is signed then a right shift will fill the vacated bit positions with the sign bit or 0, which is implementation-defined. So the best option is to never right shift signed values.

26.2.6 Bitwise Complement

The bitwise complement inverts the bits in a single binary number.

$$01001011$$
$$\sim$$
$$\text{--------}$$
$$10110100$$

26.2.7 Checking whether K-th bit is set or not

Let us assume that the given number is n. Then for checking the Kth bit we can use the expression: $n \,\&\, (1 \ll K - 1)$. If the expression is true then we can say the Kth bit is set (that means, set to 1).

Example:
$$n = 01001011 \text{ and } K = 4$$

$1 \ll K - 1$	00001000
$n \,\&\, (1 \ll K - 1)$	00001000

26.2.8 Setting K-th bit

For a given number n, to set the Kth bit we can use the expression: $n \mid 1 \ll (K - 1)$

Example:
$$n = 01001011 \text{ and } K = 3$$

$1 \ll K - 1$	00000100
$n \mid (1 \ll K - 1)$	01001111

26.2.9 Clearing K-th bit

To clear K^{th} bit of a given number n, we can use the expression: $n \,\&\, \sim(1 \ll K - 1)$

Example:
$$n = 01001011 \text{ and } K = 4$$

$1 \ll K - 1$	00001000
$\sim(1 \ll K - 1)$	11110111
$n \,\&\, \sim(1 \ll K - 1)$	01000011

26.2.10 Toggling K-th bit

For a given number n, for toggling the Kth bit we can use the expression: $n \,\wedge\, (1 \ll K - 1)$

Example:
$$n = 01001011 \text{ and } K = 3$$

$1 \ll K - 1$	00000100
$n \,\wedge\, (1 \ll K - 1)$	01001111

26.2.11 Toggling Rightmost One bit

For a given number n, for toggling rightmost one bit we can use the expression: $n \,\&\, n - 1$

Example:
n		= 01001011
$n - 1$		01001010
$n \,\&\, n - 1$		01001010

26.2.12 Isolating Rightmost One bit

For a given number n, for isolating rightmost one bit we can use the expression: $n \,\&\, -n$

Example:
n	= 01001011
$-n$	10110101
$n \,\&\, -n$	00000001

Note: For computing $-n$, use two's complement representation. That means, toggle all bits and add 1.

26.2.13 Isolating Rightmost Zero bit

For a given number n, for isolating rightmost zero bit we can use the expression: $\sim n \, \& \, n + 1$

Example:

$$
\begin{aligned}
n &= \quad 01001011 \\
\sim n &\quad\quad 10110100 \\
n + 1 &\quad\quad 01001100 \\
\sim n \, \& \, n + 1 &\quad\quad 00000100
\end{aligned}
$$

26.2.14 Checking Whether Number is Power of 2 or not

Given number n, to check whether the number is in 2^n form for not, we can use the expression: $if(n \, \& \, n - 1 == 0)$

Example:

$$
\begin{aligned}
n &= \quad\quad\quad 01001011 \\
n - 1 &\quad\quad\quad\quad 01001010 \\
n \, \& \, n - 1 &\quad\quad\quad\quad 01001010 \\
if(n \, \& \, n - 1 == 0) &\quad\quad\quad\quad\quad 0
\end{aligned}
$$

26.2.15 Multiplying Number by Power of 2

For a given number n, to multiply the number with 2^K we can use the expression: $n \ll K$

Example:

$$
\begin{aligned}
n &= \; 00001011 \text{ and } K = 2 \\
n \ll K &\quad 00101100
\end{aligned}
$$

26.2.16 Dividing Number by Power of 2

For a given number n, to divide the number with 2^K we can use the expression: $n \gg K$

Example:

$$
\begin{aligned}
n &= \; 00001011 \text{ and } K = 2 \\
n \gg K &\quad 00010010
\end{aligned}
$$

26.2.17 Finding Modulo of a Given Number

For a given number n, to find the %8 we can use the expression: $n \, \& \, 0x7$. Similarly, to find %32, use the expression: $n \, \& \, 0x1F$

Note: Similarly, we can find modulo value of any number.

26.2.18 Reversing the Binary Number

For a given number n, to reverse the bits (reverse (mirror) of binary number)we can use the following code snippet:

```
unsigned int n, nReverse = n;
int s = sizeof(n);
for (; n; n >>= 1) {
    nReverse <<= 1;
    nReverse |= n & 1;
    s--;
}
nReverse <<= s;
```

Time Complexity: This requires one iteration per bit and the number of iterations depends on the size of the number.

26.2.19 Counting Number of One's in number

For a given number n, to count the number of $1's$ in its binary representation we can use any of the following methods.

Method1: Process bit by bit

```
unsigned int n;
unsigned int count=0;
while(n) {
    count += n & 1;
    n >>= 1;
}
```

Time Complexity: This approach requires one iteration per bit and the number of iterations depends on system.

Method2: Using modulo approach

```
unsigned int n;
unsigned int count=0;
while(n) {
    if(n%2 ==1) count++;
```

```
        n = n/2;
    }
```

Time Complexity: This requires one iteration per bit and the number of iterations depends on system.

Method3: Using toggling approach: $n \& n - 1$

```
    unsigned int n;
    unsigned int count=0;
    while(n) {
        count++;
        n &= n - 1;
    }
```

Time Complexity: The number of iterations depends on the number of 1 bits in the number.

Method4: Using preprocessing idea. In this method, we process the bits in groups. For example if we process them in groups of 4 bits at a time, we create a table which indicates the number of one's for each of those possibilities (as shown below).

0000→0	0100→1	1000→1	1100→2
0001→1	0101→2	1001→2	1101→3
0010→1	0110→2	1010→2	1110→3
0011→2	0111→3	1011→3	1111→4

The following code to count the number of 1s in the number with this approach:

```
    int Table = {0,1,1,2,1,2,2,3,1,2,2,3,2,3,3,4};
    int count = 0;
    for(; n; n >>= 4)
        count = count + Table[n & 0xF];
    return count;
```

Time Complexity: This approach requires one iteration per 4 bits and the number of iterations depends on system.

26.2.20 Creating Mask for Trailing Zero's

For a given number n, to create a mask for trailing zeros, we can use the expression: $(n \& - n) - 1$

Example:

$$
\begin{aligned}
n &= \quad 01001011 \\
-n &\quad\quad 10110101 \\
n \& - n &\quad\quad 00000001 \\
(n \& - n) - 1 &\quad\quad 00000000
\end{aligned}
$$

Note: In the above case we are getting the mask as all zeros because there are no trailing zeros.

26.2.21 Swap all odd and even bits

Example: $n = \quad 01001011$

$$
\begin{aligned}
\text{Find even bits of given number (evenN)} &= n \& 0xAA \quad 00001010 \\
\text{Find odd bits of given number (oddN)} &= n \& 0x55 \quad 01000001 \\
evenN &>>= 1 \quad 00000101 \\
oddN &<<= 1 \quad 10000010 \\
\text{Final Expresion: evenN} &\mid oddN \quad 10000111
\end{aligned}
$$

26.2.22 Performing Average without Division

Is there a bit-twiddling algorithm to replace $mid = (low + high) / 2$ (used in Binary Search and Merge Sort) with something much faster?

We can use $mid = (low + high) >> 1$. Note that using $(low + high) / 2$" for midpoint calculations won't work correctly when integer overflow becomes an issue. We can use bit shifting and also overcome a possible overflow issue: $low + ((high - low)/ 2)$ and the bit shifting operation for this is $low + ((high - low) >> 1)$.

26.3 Other Programming Questions

Question-1   Give an algorithm for printing the matrix elements in spiral order.

Answer: Non-recursive solution involves directions right, left, up, down, and dealing their corresponding indices. Once the first row is printed, direction changes (from right) to down, the row is discarded by incrementing the upper limit. Once the last column is printed, direction changes to left, the column is discarded by decrementing the right hand limit.

```
void Spiral(int **A, int n) {
    int rowStart=0, columnStart=0;
```

```
    int rowEnd=n-1, columnEnd=n-1;
    while(rowStart<=rowEnd && columnStart<=columnEnd) {
        int i=rowStart, j=columnStart;
        for(j=columnStart; j<=columnEnd; j++) printf("%d ",A[i][j]);
        for(i=rowStart+1, j--; i<=rowEnd; i++) printf("%d ",A[i][j]);
        for(j=columnEnd-1, i--; j>=columnStart; j--) printf("%d ",A[i][j]);
        for(i=rowEnd-1, j++; i>=rowStart+1; i--) printf("%d ",A[i][j]);
        rowStart++; columnStart++; rowEnd--; columnEnd--;
    }
}
```

Time Complexity: $O(n^2)$. Space Complexity: $O(1)$.

Question-2   Give an algorithm for shuffling a deck of cards.

Answer: Assume that we want to shuffle an array of 52 cards, from 0 to 51 with no repeats, such as we might want for a deck of cards. First fill the array with the values in order, then go through the array and exchange each element with a randomly chosen element in the range from itself to the end. It's possible that an element will swap with itself, but there is no problem with that.

```
void Shuffle(int cards[], int n){
        srand(time(0));                         // initialize seed randomly
        for (int i=0; i<n; i++)
                cards[i] = i;                    // filling the array with card number
        for (int i=0; i<n; i++) {
                int r = i + (rand() % (52-i));   // Random remaining position.
                int temp = cards[i]; cards[i] = cards[r]; cards[r] = temp;
        }
        printf("Shuffled Cards:" );
        for (int i=0; i<n; i++)
                printf("%d", cards[i]);
}
```

Time Complexity: $O(n)$. Space Complexity: $O(1)$.

Question-3   Reversal algorithm for array rotation: Write a function rotate(A[], d, n) that rotates A[] of size n by d elements. For example, the array $1,2,3,4,5,6,7$ becomes $3,4,5,6,7,1,2$ after 2 rotations.

Answer: Consider the following algorithm.

Algorithm:

```
    rotate(Array[], d, n)
    reverse(Array[], 1, d) ;
    reverse(Array[], d + 1, n);
    reverse(Array[], l, n);
```

Let AB be the two parts of the input Array where A = Array[0..d-1] and B = Array[d..n-1]. The idea of the algorithm is:

```
    Reverse A to get ArB. /* Ar is reverse of A */
    Reverse B to get ArBr. /* Br is reverse of B */
    Reverse all to get (ArBr) r = BA.
    For example, if Array[] = [1, 2, 3, 4, 5, 6, 7], d =2 and n = 7 then, A = [1, 2] and B = [3, 4, 5, 6, 7]
    Reverse A, we get ArB = [2, 1, 3, 4, 5, 6, 7], Reverse B, we get ArBr = [2, 1, 7, 6, 5, 4, 3]
    Reverse all, we get (ArBr)r = [3, 4, 5, 6, 7, 1, 2]
```

Implementation:

```
/* Function to left rotate Array[] of size n by d */
void leftRotate(int Array[], int d, int n) {
  rvereseArray(Array, 0, d-1);
  rvereseArray(Array, d, n-1);
  rvereseArray(Array, 0, n-1);
}
void printArray(int Array[], int size){
  for(int i = 0; i < size; i++)
    printf("%d ", Array[i]);
  printf("%\n ");
}
/*Function to reverse Array[] from index start to end*/
void rvereseArray(int Array[], int start, int end) {
  int i;
  int temp;
  while(start < end){
    temp = Array[start];
```

```
    Array[start] = Array[end];
    Array[end] = temp;
    start++;
    end--;
  }
}
```

Question-4   Suppose you are given an array s[1...n] and a procedure reverse (s,i,j) which reverses the order of elements in between positions i and j (both inclusive). What does the following sequence
do, where 1 < k <= n:

```
        reverse (s, 1, k);
        reverse (s, k + 1, n);
        reverse (s, 1, n);
```

(a) Rotates s left by k positions (b) Leaves s unchanged (c) Reverses all elements of s (d) None of the above

Answer: (b). Effect of the above 3 reversals for any *k* is equivalent to left rotation of the array of size *n* by *k* [refer Question-3].

Question-5   Given a string that has set of words and spaces, write a program to move the spaces to *front* of string, you need to traverse the array only once and need to adjust the string in place.
     Input = "move these spaces to beginning"   *Output* ="   movethesepacestobeginning"

Answer: Maintain two indices *i* and *j*; traverse from end to beginning. If the current index contains char, swap chars in index *i* with index *j*. This will move all the spaces to beginning of the array.

```
void mySwap(char A[],int i,int j){              void main(int argc, char * argv[]){
    char temp=A[i];                                 char sparr[]="move these spaces to beginning";
    A[i]=A[j];                                      printf("Value of A is: %s\n", sparr);
    A[j]=temp;                                      moveSpacesToBegin(sparr);
}                                                   printf("Value of A is: %s", sparr);
void moveSpacesToBegin(char A[]){               }
    int i=strlen(A)-1;
    int j=i;
    for(; j>=0; j--){
        if(!isspace(A[j]))
            mySwap(A,i--,j);
    }
}
```

Time Complexity: O(*n*) where *n* is the number of characters in input array. Space Complexity: O(1).

Question-6   For the Question-5, can we improve the complexity?

Answer: We can avoid swap operation with a simple counter. But, it does not reduce the overall complexity.

```
void moveSpacesToBegin(char A[]){               int testCode(){
    int n=strlen(A)-1,count=n;                      char sparr[]="move these spaces to beginning";
    int i=n;                                        printf("Value of A is: %s\n", sparr);
    for(;i>=0;i--){                                 moveSpacesToBegin(sparr);
        if(A[i]!=' ')                               printf("Value of A is: %s", sparr);
            A[count--]=A[i];                    }
    }
    while(count>=0)
        A[count--]=' ';
}
```

Time Complexity: O(*n*), where *n* is the number of characters in input array. Space Complexity: O(1).

Question-7   Given a string that has set of words and spaces, write a program to move the spaces to *end* of string, you need to traverse the array only once and need to adjust the string in place.
     Input = "move these spaces to end" *Output* ="movethesepacestoend   "

Answer: Traverse the array from left to right. While traversing, maintain a counter for non-space elements in array. For every non-space character A[*i*], put the element at A[*count*] and increment *count*. After complete traversal, all non-space elements have already been shifted to front end and *count* is set as index of first 0. Now, all we need to do is that run a loop which fills all elements with spaces from *count* till end of the array.

```
void moveSpacesToEnd(char A[]){                 void testCode(int argc, char * argv[]){
    // Count of non-space elements                  char sparr[]="move these spaces to end";
    int count = 0;                                  printf("Value of A is: %s\n", sparr);
    int n =strlen(A)-1;                             moveSpacesToEnd(sparr);
    int i =0;                                       printf("Value of A is: %s", sparr);
    for (; i <= n; i++)                         }
        if (!isspace(A[i]))
            A[count++] = A[i];
```

```
        while (count <= n)
            A[++count] = ' ';
    }
```

Time Complexity: O(n) where n is number of characters in input array. Space Complexity: O(1).

Question-8   Moving Zeros to end: Given an array of n integers, move all the zeros of a given array to the end of the array. For example, if the given arrays is {1, 9, 8, 4, 0, 0, 2, 7, 0, 6, 0}, it should be changed to {1, 9, 8, 4, 2, 7, 6, 0, 0, 0, 0}. The order of all other elements should be same.

Answer:: Maintain two variables *i* and *j*; and initialize with 0. For each of the array element A[i], if A[i] non-zero element, then replace the element A[j] with element A[i]. Variable *i* will always be incremented till n - 1 but we will increment *j* only when the element pointed by *i* is non-zero.

```
void moveZerosToEnd(int A[], int size){          int testCode(){
    int i=0,j=0;                                     int A[ ] = {1,9,8,4,0,0,2,7,0,6,0};
    while (i <= size - 1){                           int i;
        if (A[i] != 0){                              int size = sizeof(A) / sizeof(A[0]);
            A[j++] = A[i];                           moveZerosToEnd(A, size);
        }                                            for (i = 0; i <= size - 1; i++)
        i++;                                             printf("%d ", A[i]);
    }                                                return 0;
    while (j <= size - 1)                         }
        A[j++] = 0;
}
```

Time Complexity: O(n). Space Complexity: O(1).

Question-9   For the Question-8, can we improve the complexity?

Answer: Using simple swap technique we can avoid the unnecessary second *while* loop from the above code.

```
void mySwap(int A[],int i,int j){
    int temp=A[i];
    A[i]=A[j];
    A[j]=temp;
}
void moveZerosToEnd(int A[], int len){
    int i, j;
    for(i=0,j=0; i<len; i++)    {
        if (A[i] !=0)
            mySwap(A,j++,i);
    }
}
```

Time Complexity: O(n). Space Complexity: O(1).

Question-10   *Variant* of Question-8 and Question-9: Given an array containing negative and positive numbers; give an algorithm for separating positive and negative numbers in it. Also, maintain the relative order of positive and negative numbers. Input: -5, 3, 2, -1, 4, -8 Output: -5 -1 -8 3 4 2

Answer: In the *moveZerosToEnd* function, just replace the condition A[i] ! =0 with A[i] < 0.

Question-11   Given an N X N matrix, rotate it bye 90 degrees in place.

Sample Input

1	2	3	4
9	8	5	6
6	5	3	7
9	3	6	8

Sample Output:

9	6	9	1
3	5	8	2
6	3	5	3
8	3	6	4

Answer: The key is to solve this problem in *layers* from outer ones to inner ones as follows. In our example we have two layers:

Outer Layer

1	2	3	4
9			6
6			7
9	3	6	8

Inner Layer:

	5	8	
	3	5	

The idea is to do a *four − way* swap variable, we need to move the values from top -> right, right -> bottom, bottom -> left and left -> top, can we do it by using only one extra variable? Yes, we can.

At each layer we are going to loop through the elements and swap them as follows:

1.   Save the ith element in the top array in a temporary variable (in our example the top array is [1 2 3 4]).
2.   Move the ith element from left to top.
3.   Move the ith element from bottom to left.

4. Move the ith element from right to bottom.
5. Save the value of our temporary variable in the ith position in the right array.

```
void rotateMatrixBy90Degrees(int **matrix, int size){
    for(int layer = 0; layer < size / 2; layer ++){
        for(int i = layer; i < size - layer - 1; i ++){
            int t = matrix[level][i];
            matrix[layer][i] = matrix[i][size - 1 - layer];
            matrix[i][size - 1 - layer] = matrix[size - 1 - layer][size - 1 - i];
            matrix[size - 1 - layer][size - 1 - i] = matrix[size - 1 - i][ layer];
            matrix[size - 1 - i][ layer] = t;
        }
    }
}
```

Question-12   Create a matrix of size $m \times n$ (m rows and n columns) in which every element is either 1 or 0. The 1s and 0s must be filled alternatively, the matrix should have outermost rectangle of 1s, then a rectangle of 0s, then a rectangle of 1s, and so on. Sample Input: m = 6, n = 7, Output: Following matrix

1	1	1	1	1	1	1
1	0	0	0	0	0	1
1	0	1	1	1	0	1
1	0	1	1	1	0	1
1	0	0	0	0	0	1
1	1	1	1	1	1	1

Answer: The key of this solution is similar to Question-1, but instead of printing the data just insert the symbols. Also, we need to keep track of current symbol being used for alternative insert.

```
void FillMatrix(int **A, int m, int n) {
    int rowStart=0, columnStart=0, rowEnd=n-1, columnEnd=n-1;
    int currentSymbol = 1;
    while(rowStart<=rowEnd && columnStart<=columnEnd) {
        int i=rowStart, j=columnStart;
        for(j=columnStart; j<=columnEnd; j++) printf("%d ", currentSymbol);
        for(i=rowStart+1, j--; i<=rowEnd; i++) printf("%d ", currentSymbol);
        for(j=columnEnd-1, i--; j>=columnStart; j--) printf("%d ", currentSymbol);
        for(i=rowEnd-1, j++; i>=rowStart+1; i--) printf("%d ", currentSymbol);
        currentSymbol = 1- currentSymbol;
        rowStart++; columnStart++; rowEnd--; columnEnd--;
    }
}
```

Time Complexity: $O(n^2)$. Space Complexity: $O(1)$.

Question-13   Given a number n, find the smallest number p such that if we multiply all digits of p, we get n. The result p should have minimum two digits.

Examples:	
Input: n = 36, Output: p = 49	4*9 = 36 and 49 is the smallest such number
Input: n = 100, Output: p = 455	4*5*5 = 100 and 455 is the smallest such number
Input: n = 1, Output:p = 11	1*1 = 1
Input: n = 13, Output: Not Possible	

Answer:

```
// prints the smallest number whose digits multiply to n
void findSmallest(int n){
    int i, j=0;
    int OutPut[MAX]; // To sore digits of OutPut in reverse order
    if (n < 10){        // Case 1: If number is smaller than 10
        printf("%d", n+10);
        return;
    }
    // Case 2: Start with 9 and try every possible digit
    for (i=9; i>1; i--){
        // If current digit divides n, then store all occurrences of current digit in OutPut
        while (n%i == 0){
            n = n/i;
            OutPut[j] = i;
            j++;
        }
    }
```

```
    }
    // If n could not be broken in form of digits (prime factors of n are greater than 9)
    if (n > 10){
        printf("Not possible");
        return;
    }
    for (i=j-1; i>=0; i--)
        printf("%d", OutPut[i]);
}
```

Chapter-27

NON-TECHNICAL HELP

27.1 Tips

- Arrive 5-10 minutes before the interview. Never arrive too late or too early. If you are running late due to some unavoidable situation, call ahead and make sure that the interviewers know your situation. Also, be apologetic for arriving late due to unfortunate situation.
- *First impressions* are everything: Firm handshake, maintain eye contact, smile, watch your body language, be pleasant, dress neatly and know the names of your interviewers and thank them by their names for the opportunity.
- Try, *not* to show that you are *nervous*. Every body is nervous for interviews but try not to show it. [Hint: Just think that even if you do not get the job, it is a good learning experience and you would do better in your next interview and appreciate yourself for getting this far. You can always learn from your mistakes and do better at your next interview.]
- It is good to be confident but *do not* make up your answer or try to *bluff*. If you put something in your resume then better be prepared to back it up. Be honest to answer technical questions because you are not expected to remember everything (for example, you might know a few design patterns but not all of them etc.). If you have not used a design pattern in question, request the interviewer, if you could describe a different design pattern. Also, try to provide brief answers, which means not too long and not too short like yes or no. Give examples of times you performed that particular task. If you would like to expand on your answer, ask the interviewer if you could elaborate or go on. It is okay to verify your answers every now and then but avoid verifying or validating your answers too often because the interviewer might think that you lack self-confidence or you cannot work independently. But if you do not know the answer to a particular question and keen to know the answer, you could politely request for an answer but should not request for answers too often. If you think you could find the answer(s) readily on the internet then try to remember the question and find the answer(s) soon after your interview.
- You should also *ask questions* to make an impression on the interviewer. Write out specific questions you want to ask and then look for opportunities to ask them during the interview. Many interviewers end with a request to the applicant as to whether they have anything they wish to add. This is an opportunity for you to end on a positive note by making succinct statements about why you are the best person for the job.
- Try to be yourself. Have a good sense of humor, a smile and a positive outlook. Be friendly but you should not tell the sagas of your personal life. If you cross your boundaries then the interviewer might feel that your personal life will interfere with your work.
- *Be confident.* I have addressed many of the popular technical questions in this book and it should improve your confidence. If you come across a question relating to a new piece of technology you have no experience, then you can mention that you have a very basic understanding and demonstrate that you are a quick learner by reflecting back on your past job where you had to quickly learn a new piece of a technology or a framework. Also, you can mention that you keep a good rapport with a network of talented *Java/J2EE* developers or mentors to discuss any design alternatives or work a rounds to a pressing problem.
- Unless asked, do *not talk about money*. Leave this topic until the interviewer brings it up or you can negotiate this with your agent once you have been offered the position. At the interview you should try to sell or promote your technical skills, business skills, ability to adapt to changes, and interpersonal skills. Prior to the interview find out what skills are required by thoroughly reading the job description or talking to your agent for the specific job and be prepared to promote those skills (Sometimes you would be asked why you are the best person for the job?). You should come across as you are more keen on technical challenges, learning a new piece of technology, improving your business skills etc. as opposed to coming across as you are only interested in money.
- Speak *clearly, firmly* and with *confidence* but should not be aggressive and egoistical. You should act interested in the company and the job and make all comments in a positive manner. Should not speak negatively about past colleagues or employers. Should not excuse yourself halfway through the interview, even if you have to use the bathroom. Should not ask for refreshments or coffee but accept it if offered.
- At the end of the interview, thank the interviewers by their names for their time with a *firm handshake*, maintain eye contact and ask them about the next steps if not already mentioned to know where you are at the process and show that you are interested.
- Try to find out the needs of the project in which you will be working and the needs of the people within the project.

- 80% of the interview questions are based on your *own resume*.
- Where possible briefly demonstrate how you applied your skills/knowledge in the key areas [design concepts, transactional issues, performance issues, memory leaks etc.], business skills, and interpersonal skills as described in this book. Find the right time to raise questions and answer those questions to show your strength.
- Be honest to answer technical questions, you are not expected to remember everything (for example you might know a few design patterns but not all of them etc.). If you have not used a design pattern in question, request the interviewer, if you could describe a different design pattern.
- Do not be critical, focus on what you can do. Also try to be humorous to show your smartness.
- Do not act superior.

27.2 Sample Non-Technical Questions

Question-1   Why are you leaving your current position?

Sample Answer: Do not criticize your previous employer or co-workers or sound too opportunistic. It is fine to mention a major problem like a buyout, budget constraints or merger. You may also say that your chance to make a contribution is very low due to companywide changes or looking for a more challenging senior or designer role.

Question-2   What do you like and/or dislike most about your current and/or last position?

Sample Answer: The interviewer is trying to find the compatibility with the open position. So, do not say anything like:
- You dislike overtime.
- You dislike management or co-workers etc.

It is safe to say:
- You like challenges.
- Opportunity to grow into design, architecture, performance tuning etc.
- Opportunity to learn and/or mentor junior developers..
- You dislike frustrating situations like identifying a memory leak problem or a complex transactional or a concurrency issue. You want to get on top of it as soon as possible.

Question-3   How do you handle pressure? Do you like or dislike these situations?

Sample Answer: These questions could mean that the open position is pressure-packed and may be out of control. Know what you are getting into. If you do perform well under stress then give a descriptive example. High achievers tend to perform well in pressure situations.

Question-4   What are your strengths and weaknesses?

Sample Answer:

Strengths:
- Taking initiatives and being pro-active: You can illustrate how you took initiative to fix a transactional issue, a performance problem or a memory leak problem.
- Design skills: You can illustrate how you designed a particular application using OO concepts.
- Problem solving skills: Explain how you will break a complex problem into more manageable sub-sections and then apply brain storming and analytical skills to solve the complex problem. Illustrate how you went about identifying a scalability issue or a memory leak problem.
- Communication skills: Illustrate that you can communicate effectively with all the team members, business analysts, users, testers, stake holders etc.
- Ability to work in a team environment as well as independently: Illustrate that you are technically sound to work independently as well as have the interpersonal skills to fit into any team environment.
- Hardworking, honest, and conscientious etc. are the adjectives to describe you.

Weaknesses: Select a trait and come up with a solution to overcome your weakness. Stay away from personal qualities and concentrate more on professional traits for example:
- I pride myself on being an attention to detail guy but sometimes miss small details. So I am working on applying the 80/20 principle to manage time and details. Spend 80% of my effort and time on 20% of the tasks, which are critical and important to the task at hand.
- Some times when there is a technical issue or a problem I tend to work continuously until I fix it without having a break. But what I have noticed and am trying to practice is that taking a break away from the problem and thinking outside the square will assist you in identifying the root cause of the problem sooner.

Question-5   What are your career goals? Where do you see yourself in 5-10 years?

Sample Answer: Be realistic. For example:
- Next 2-3 years to become a senior developer or a team lead.
- Next 3-5 years to become a solution designer or an architect.

Question-6   Give me an example of a time when you set a goal and were able to achieve it? Give me an example of a time you showed initiative and took the lead? Tell me about a difficult decision you made in the last year? Give me an example of a time you motivated others? Tell me about a most complex project you were involved in?

Sample Answer: This is a behavioral testing question.

Situation: When you were working for the *CareerMonk* Corporation, the overnight batch process called the "Data Packager" was developed for a large fast food chain which has over 100 stores. This overnight batch process is responsible for performing a very database intensive search and compute changes like cost of ingredients, selling price, new menu item etc. made in various retail stores and package those changes into XML files and send those XML data to the respective stores where they get uploaded into their point of sale registers to reflect the changes. This batch process had been used for the past two years, but since then the number of stores had increased and so did the size of the data in the database. The batch process, which used to take 6-8 hours to complete, had increased to 14-16 hours, which obviously started to adversely affect the daily operations of these stores. The management assigned you with the task of improving the performance of the batch process to 5-6 hours (i.e. suppose to be an overnight process).

Action: After having analyzed the existing design and code for the "Data Packager", you had to take the difficult decision to let the management know that this batch process needed to be re-designed and re-written as opposed to modifying the existing code, since it was poorly designed. It is hard to extend, maintain (i.e. making a change in one place can break the code somewhere else and so on) and had no object reuse through caching (makes too many unnecessary network trips to the database) etc. The management was not too impressed with this approach and concerned about the time required to rewrite this batch process since the management had promised the retail stores to provide a solution within 8-12 weeks. You took the initiative and used your persuasive skills to convince the management that you would be able to provide a re-designed and re-written solution within the 8-12 weeks with the assistance of 2-3 additional developers and two testers.

You were entrusted with the task to rewrite the batch process and you set your goal to complete the task in 8 weeks. You decided to build the software iteratively by building individual vertical slices as opposed to the big bang waterfall. You redesigned and wrote the code for a typical use case from end to end (i.e. full vertical slice) within 2 weeks and subsequently carried out functional and integration testing to iron out any unforeseen errors or issues. Once the first iteration is stable, you effectively communicated the architecture to the management and to your fellow developers. Motivated and mentored your fellow developers to build the other iterations, based on the first iteration. At the end of iteration, it was tested by the testers, while the developers moved on to the next iteration.

Results: After having enthusiastically worked to your plan with hard work, dedication and teamwork, you were able to have the 90% of the functionality completed in 9 weeks and spent the next 3 weeks fixing bugs, tuning performance and coding rest of the functionality. The fully functional data packager was completed in 12 weeks and took only 3-4 hours to package *XML* data for all the stores. The team was under pressure at times but you made them believe that it is more of a challenge as opposed to think of it as a stressful situation. The newly designed data packager was also easier to maintain and extend. The management was impressed with the outcome and rewarded the team with an outstanding achievement award. The performance of the newly developed data packager was further improved by 20% by tuning the database (i.e. partitioning the tables, indexing etc.).

Question-7   Describe a time when you were faced with a stressful situation that demonstrated your coping skills? Give me an example of a time when you used your fact finding skills to solve a problem? Describe a time when you applied your analytical and/or problem solving skills?

Sample Answer: This is also a behavioral testing question.

Situation: When you were working for the Life insurance corporation, you were responsible for the migration of an online insurance application (i.e. external website) to a newer version of application server (i.e. the current version is no longer supported by the vendor). The migration happened smoothly and after a couple of days of going live, you started to experience "OutOfMemoryError", which forced you to restart the application server every day. This raised a red alert and the immediate and the senior management were very concerned and consequently constantly calling for meetings and updates on the progress of identifying the root cause of this issue. This has created a stressful situation.

Action: You were able to have a positive outlook by believing that this is more of a challenge as opposed to think of it as a stressful situation. You needed to be composed to get your analytical and problem solving skills to get to work. You spent some time finding facts relating to "OutOfMemoryError". You were tempted to increase the heap space as suggested by fellow developers but the profiling and monitoring did not indicate that was the case. The memory usage drastically increased during and after certain user operations like generating PDF reports. The generation of reports used some third party libraries, which dynamically generated classes from your templates. So you decided to increase the area of the memory known as the "perm", which sits next to the heap. This "perm" space is consumed when the classes are dynamically generated from templates during the report generation.

```
java -XX:PermSize=256M -XX:MaxPermSize=256M
```

Results: After you have increased the "perm" size, the "OutOfMemoryError" has disappeared. You kept monitoring it for a week and everything worked well. The management was impressed with your problem solving, fact finding and analytical skills, which had contributed to the identification of the not so prevalent root cause and the effective communication with the other teams like infrastructure, production support, senior management, etc. The management also identified your ability to cope under stress and offered you a promotion to lead a small team of 4 developers.

Question-8   Describe a time when you had to work with others in the organization to accomplish the organizational goals? Describe a situation where others you worked on a project disagreed with your ideas, and what did you do? Describe a situation in which you had to collect information by asking many questions of several people? What has been your experience in giving presentations to small or large groups? How do you show considerations for others?

Sample Answer: This is also a behavioral testing question.

Situation: You were working for *CareerMonk* Pvt. Ltd financial services organization. You were part of a development team responsible for enhancing an existing online web application, which enables investors and advisors view and manage their financial portfolios. The websites of the financial services organizations are periodically surveyed and rated by an independent organization for their ease of use, navigability, content, search functionality etc. Your organization was ranked 21st among 23 websites reviewed. Your chief information officer was very disappointed with this poor rating and wanted the business analysts, business owners (i.e. within the organization) and the technical staff to improve on the ratings before the next ratings, which would be done in 3 months.

Action: The business analysts and the business owners quickly got into work and came up with a requirements list of 35 items in consultation with the external business users such as advisors, investors etc. You were assigned the task of working with the business analysts, business owners (i.e. internal), and project managers to provide a technical input in terms of feasibility study, time estimates, impact analysis etc. The business owners had a preconceived notion of how they would like things done. You had to analyze the outcome from both the business owners' perspective and technology perspective. There were times you had to use your persuasive skills to convince the business owners and analysts to take an alternative approach, which would provide a more robust solution. You managed to convince the business owners and analysts by providing visual mock-up screen shots of your proposed solution, presentation skills, ability to communicate without any technical jargons, and listening carefully to business needs and discussing your ideas with your fellow developers (i.e. being a good listener, respecting others' views and having the right attitude even if you know that you are right). You also strongly believe that good technical skills must be complemented with good interpersonal skills and the right attitude. After 2-3 weeks of constant interaction with the business owners, analysts and fellow developers, you had helped the business users to finalize the list of requirements. You also took the initiative to apply the agile development methodology to improve communication and cooperation between business owners and the developers.

Results: You and your fellow developers were not only able to effectively communicate and collaborate with the business users and analysts but also provided progressive feedback to each other due to iterative approach. The team work and hard work had resulted in a much improved

Question-9   What past accomplishments gave you satisfaction? What makes you want to work hard?

Sample Answer:

- Material rewards such as salary, perks, benefits etc. naturally come into play but focus on your achievements or accomplishments than on rewards.
- Explain how you took pride in fixing a complex performance issue or a concurrency issue. You could substantiate your answer with a past experience. For example while you were working for Bips telecom, you pro-actively identified a performance issue due to database connection resource leak. You subsequently took the initiative to notify your team leader and volunteered to fix it by adding finally {} blocks to close the resources.
- If you are being interviewed for a position, which requires your design skills then you could explain that in your previous job with an insurance company you had to design and develop a sub-system, which gave you complete satisfaction. You were responsible for designing the data model using entity relationship diagrams (E-R diagrams) and the software model using the component diagrams, class diagrams, sequence diagrams etc.
- If you are being interviewed for a position where you have to learn new pieces of technology/framework then you can explain with examples from your past experience where you were not only motivated to acquire new skills/knowledge but also proved that you are a quick and a pro-active learner.
- If the job you are being interviewed for requires production support from time to time, then you could explain that it gives you satisfaction because you would like to interact with the business users and/or customers to develop your business and communication skills by getting an opportunity to understand a system from the users perspective and also gives you an opportunity to sharpen your technical and problem solving skills. If you are a type of person who enjoys more development work then you can be honest about it and indicate that you would like to have a balance between development work and support work, where you can develop different aspects of your skills/knowledge. You could also reflect an experience from a past job, where each developer was assigned a weekly roster to provide support.
- You could say that, you generally would like to work hard but would like to work even harder when there are challenges.

References

[1] Akash. Programming Interviews. http://tech-queries.blogspot.com.

[2] Alfred V.Aho,J. E. (1983). Data Structures and Algorithms. Addison-Wesley.

[3] Alfred V.Aho, J. E. (1974). The Design and Analysis of Computer Algorithms. Addison-Wesley.

[4] Algorithms.Retrieved from http://www.cs.princeton.edu/algs4/home

[5] Anderson., S. E. Bit Twiddling Hacks. Retrieved 2010, from Bit Twiddling Hacks: http://www-graphics.stanford.edu /~seander/ bithacks.html

[6] Bentley, J. AT&T Bell Laboratories. Retrieved from AT&T Bell Laboratories.

[7] Database, P.Problem Database. Retrieved 2010, from Problem Database: datastructures.net

[8] Drozdek, A. (1996). Data Structures and Algorithms in $C++$.

[9] Ellis Horowitz, S. S. Fundamentals of Data Structures.

[10] James F. Korsh, L. J. Data Structures, Algorithms and Program Style Using C.

[11] John Mongan, N. S. (2002). Programming Interviews Exposed. . Wiley-India. .

[12] Kalid. P, NP, and NP-Complete. Retrieved from P, NP, and NP-Complete.: http://www.cs.princeton.edu/~kazad

[13] Knuth., D. E. (1973). Fundamental Algorithms, volume 1 of The Art of Computer Programming. Addison-Wesley.

[14] Knuth., D. E. (1981). Seminumerical Algorithms, volume 2 of The Art of Computer Programming. Addison-Wesley.

[15] Knuth., D. E. (1973). Sorting and Searching, volume 3 of The Art of Computer Programming. Addison-Wesley.

[16] Leon., J. S. Computer Algorithms. http://www.math.uic.edu/~leon/cs-mcs401-s08.

[17] OCF. Algorithms. Retrieved 2010, from Algorithms: http://www.ocf.berkeley.edu

[18] Parlante., N. Binary Trees. Retrieved 2010, from cslibrary.stanford.edu: cslibrary.stanford.edu

[19] Pryor, M. Tech Interview. Retrieved 2010, from Tech Interview: http://techinterview.org

[20] S. Dasgupta, C. P. Algorithms http://www.cs.berkeley.edu/~vazirani.

[21] Sedgewick., R. (1988). Algorithms. Addison-Wesley.

[22] Sells, C. (2010). Interviewing at Microsoft. Retrieved 2010, from Interviewing at Microsoft: http://www.sellsbrothers.com/fun/msiview

[23] Shene, C.-K. Linked Lists Merge Sort implementation. Retrieved 2010, from Linked Lists Merge Sort implementation: http://www.cs.mtu.edu/~shene

[24] Sinha, P. Linux Journal. Retrieved 2010, from http://www.linuxjournal.com/article/6828.

[25] T. H. Cormen, C. E. (1997). Introduction to Algorithms. Cambridge: The MIT press.

[26] Tsiombikas, J. Pointers Explained. http://nuclear.sdf-eu.org.

[27] Warren., H. S. (2003). Hackers Delight. Addison-Wesley.

[28] Weiss., M. A. (1992). Data Structures and Algorithm Analysis in C.

[29] wikipedia, T. F. The Free wikipedia. Retrieved from The Free wikipedia: en.wikipedia.org

[30] Zhang., C. programheaven. Retrieved 2010, programheaven.blogspot.com

[31] Technical Questions. www.ihas1337code.com